Interpretation of Cultural and Natural Resources

DOUGLAS M. KNUDSON

Department of Forestry and Natural Resources, Purdue University

TED T. CABLE

Department of Horticulture, Forestry and Recreation Resources, Kansas State University

LARRY BECK

Department of Recreation, Parks and Tourism, San Diego State University

Interpretation of Cultural and Natural Resources

Douglas M. Knudson
Department of Forestry and Natural Resources
Purdue University

Ted T. Cable
Department of Horticulture, Forestry and Recreation Resources
Kansas State University

Larry Beck
Department of Recreation, Parks and Tourism
San Diego State University

 Venture Publishing, Inc.
1999 Cato Avenue, State College, PA 16801

Production Manager: Richard Yocum
Design, Layout, and Graphics: Naomi Q. Gallagher
Manuscript Editing: Michele L. Barbin
Cover Design and Illustration: Sandra Sikorski
Printing and Binding: Jostens, Inc.

Photo Credits: TTC = Ted Cable; LB = Larry Beck; NPS = National Park Service; portraits of Susan Strauss, Lee Stetson, and Rich Pawling courtesy of the
subjects; all others that are unmarked = D. M. Knudson

Library of Congress Catalogue Card Number 94-61596
ISBN 0-910251-70-3

DEDICATED TO OUR WIVES

JUDY
DIANE
ANDREA

Contents

CHAPTER 4
VALUES OF INTERPRETATION FOR MANAGEMENT

CHAPTER 5
THE CLIENTS

SECTION III: HOW TO INTERPRET
CHAPTER 6
TRADITIONS, PRINCIPLES AND CHALLENGES

CHAPTER 7
FOUNDATIONS: HOW PEOPLE LEARN

CHAPTER 8
INTERPRETING TO THE MASSES

CHAPTER 9
THE PRINTED WORD

CHAPTER 10
EXHIBITS AND MUSEUMS

CHAPTER 11
SELF-GUIDING, NONPERSONAL INTERPRETATION

CHAPTER 12
PERFORMANCE INTERPRETATION

CHAPTER 13
HISTORICAL INTERPRETATION

CHAPTER 14
ARTS IN INTERPRETATION

SECTION IV: HOW TO MANAGE INTERPRETATION
CHAPTER 15
INTERPRETIVE PLANNING

CHAPTER 16
THE BUSINESS OF INTERPRETATION

CHAPTER 17
MAKING IT PAY

CHAPTER 18
PERSONNEL AND TRAINING

CHAPTER 19
EVALUATION

CHAPTER 20
LEGACY AND GROWTH OF A PROFESSION

APPENDIX A

FOREWORD

James M. Ridenour
Director, Eppley Institute, Indiana University
Former Director, National Park Service and
Indiana Department of Natural Resources

The term interpreter is often confusing to the general public. In my own book, *The National Parks Compromised,* the editor wanted to change the term from interpretive ranger to educational ranger because she didn't understand the use of the term. This confusion has been around for many years, but those associated with the profession have doggedly stayed with interpretation as the name of this field of study.

The significance of the interpretive profession may be demonstrated in this anecdote told by a friend, Ann Gati. When visiting Canyon de Chelly, Ann was chagrined to see her friend returning from a walk with a shard—a broken piece of pottery. Having studied ancient people's cultures, Ann was sensitive to the Native American traditions and scolded the friend for picking up the pottery. The response was, "Surely it will be in good hands. I am an artist and will value it. What is wrong with my taking it since I will value it?" Ann countered with the question, "Would you feel justified in going into someone's home and taking a spoon that had belonged to her grandmother just because you value it?"

Later in the day, a Navajo interpreter engaged Ann and the friend in a discussion of Native American spiritual beliefs. The friend was so taken with the new perspective that she asked if she should return the shard. The ranger responded, "No, leave it with me and I will cleanse it and pray over it before returning it to the earth. You may pray that the spirits return to it."

The philosophy and methodology of interpretation were presented in 1920 by Enos Mills, in his book *Adventures of a Nature Guide.* In 1957, Freeman Tilden further elaborated the concepts in a long-admired little book entitled *Interpreting Our Heritage.* The National Park Service's annual award (named after Tilden) recognizes the agency's top interpreters. The winners of this award are always very bright, creative people who understand the importance of interpretation and have sharply honed their skills to do the best job possible.

As Director of the National Park Service and the Indiana Department of Natural Resources, I always stressed that all employees and volunteers can and should take a role in interpretation. Sometimes the only employee a visitor might encounter may be the maintenance person working on a broken water line. That maintenance person needs to have enough exposure to the field of interpretation to satisfy the needs of the visitor or make the proper referral to the interpretive staff. That is why staff training sessions are so important.

Interpretive specialists should work directly with the public as well as train other staff to do so. As our society becomes older and more urban, the work of the interpreter gains importance. A citizenry that ignores or forgets its history and cultural roots will surely suffer the consequences. If we want to understand the violent events going on in other parts of the world, we need to understand what went on in our own country. For example, at the U.S. Civil War battle site at Antietam, volunteers burn 22,000 candles throughout the fields of the park during special ceremonies to help visitors comprehend one day's casualties. Compare that to the 57,000 deaths that the U.S. suffered in Viet Nam over many years. Effective interpretation puts these events in perspective.

Further, a technological people who ignore the natural processes and resources that support their civilization will likely make political and personal decisions that damage the environment. Regional, state, and national parks offer excellent types of classrooms. For example, inner-city school children from Dade County, Florida, visit the Everglades National park each year for interpretive tours and overnight camping. Without interpretation, these children, who rarely leave the city, would likely view the experience as a trip to the "swamp" and nothing more. Because of this educational program pioneered by interpretive ranger Sandy Dayhoff, children arrive anticipating what they will see and hear. They are coached in the ecological lessons of the Everglades—the wetlands upon which all life in South Florida depends. As Marjory Stoneman Douglas admonished in her book, *The Everglades: River of Grass,* "The future of South Florida, as for all once-beautiful and despoiled areas of our country, lies in aroused and informed public opinion and citizen action."

The private sector in this country knows that interpretation is important and they put big dollars behind this belief—some of it in the form of advertising, some of it in environmental education, some of it in private sector interpretation. Political leaders and the media engage in interpretation of one form or another. A new term has been coined in recent years—spin doctors. Spin doctors interpret, but are living proof that people should examine the motives of an interpreter as they listen to messages.

With the increasing number of enhanced forms of communication it has become increasingly important that our museum, camp, private and public land interpreters understand that they are in competition for people's time and attention. Television, the movies, the shopping malls, and a variety of new communications devices entice the potential consumer of cultural or natural interpretation. To become an effective interpreter requires considerable preparation, practice, skill, and innovation. Today's interpretive specialists must be professional. They must know the subject. They must understand the audience. They must master many forms of presentation.

Students preparing for the profession will find the principles and practices of interpretation in this book. It brings together the old traditions and principles of interpretation, and explain how and where the profession developed. It also compiles the recent research results and theoretical bases that underlie effective interpretive practice.

Practicing interpreters will find new ideas and strategies for improving their effectiveness. As the practice of interpretation grows more sophisticated, continual updating and self-education become important to experienced professionals.

Administrators who manage interpreters in their camps, parks, forests, industries, and museums will confirm the importance of interpretation as an integral part of management philosophy, resource protection, and service to the public.

As interpretation grows in importance to society, the interpreters must continue to study how to more effectively reach the members of the society, and to help new generations to better understand and protect our cultural and natural legacy. Reading this book is a wise investment of time. It directs and encourages interpreters to pursue professional improvement along the way.

PREFACE

This book concerns the principles, philosophies, and practices that are the essence of the rapidly growing profession of interpretation. The ideas and facts can help equip you with the knowledge and abilities to work as an interpreter. It aims at university students seeking a career in historical or nature interpretation. It aims at people already working in the field who want current information. It aims at docents and other volunteers who find themselves aiding or developing interpretative programs and wanting to know more about the tasks confronting them.

Perhaps you already have an interpretive job, but wish to expand some of your background and philosophy. Maybe your education left you a little short on some aspects of interpretation. Maybe you're a wildlife biologist or history major who seeks to expand your job potential. You may develop a better grasp on this professional field of interpretation through this book. You can also use the references cited for specific information on some of the interpretive skills. Above all, you will need to apply these ideas. Practice, investigate, and accept constructive criticism constantly.

SOME KEY QUESTIONS

Information that you can ponder and could use in your career as an interpreter, administrator or scientist arise from the answers to the questions listed below. The chapters that follow address these, based on research, opinions, philosophy and facts. As you read, you may want to ponder answers that are specific to a particular organization.

- Why do we spend billions of dollars each year to talk, demonstrate and exhibit to people? Is it worth it? Who pays?
- Some interpretation makes money directly. Should most or all interpretive services do the same?
- Is interpretation a frill that is "nice if there's enough money," or a key element of resource management strategy and a component of a civilized cultural community?
- What is an ideal interpretive approach or mix of media?
- Whom are interpreters trying to reach? What are they doing to people's minds?
- Who should do the interpretive front-line work? Volunteers, seasonal employees, or experienced permanent interpreters who know the museum or park intimately? Why?
- How should we measure productivity? How can we render accounts and justify future financing?
- What are the ethics of interpretation?
- How do we relate to resource management practices, agency goals, museum purposes, and company policy? Are we promoters?
- What's a naturalist's opportunity to measure and study the resources? Is resource monitoring really part of the job?
- How should we handle controversial or political topics? Do we stick to basic history, art, and ecological facts or do we apply some of our values to promote certain actions? When and how?

A YOUNG, EMERGING PROFESSION: AN ANCIENT TRADITION

Interpretation is a mystery word to some. It is referred to here, in general as the "transla-tion" of historic, cultural and natural phenomena so that the audience (e.g., visitors, partici-pants, anyone you reach) can better understand and enjoy them. The interpreter is one who transforms bare facts about the natural and cultural environment into stories and experiences that stimulate understanding and wisdom.

The tradition of and need for interpretation may be as old as human life, as the follow-ing slightly modified history by Charles Sharp (1969) suggests:

> Interpretation has been with us for a long time. You might say that our troubles started because we didn't have effective interpretation in the first park – Eden International Wildlife Sanctuary.

> Top Management had told Adam and Eve not to eat any fruit from the Tree of Knowledge, but they did not understand why. The Serpent induced Eve to harvest some of the Park attractions without due regard for protection of Park resources. Eve realized that she had broken all the regs in Title I and did not want to take the rap alone.

> With the sudden education of Adam, the basic principles of the Great Park Dilemma were evolved. Adam and Eve had started the battle between preservation versus nonconforming consumptive use of the resources.

> Communications with Top Management were swift in those days; decisions were even swifter. HE threw them out and closed the Park.

We usually associate interpretation with leisure-time pursuits in our cultural, educa-tional and outdoor recreation systems. We commonly practice this profession on properties used during leisure time, such as museums, parks, forests, wildlife refuges, nature preserves, historic sites, and historic buildings. Interpretive principles are applied in camps, environ-mental education programming, and in the expositions offered in museum exhibits and talks, on factory tours, in engineering works, sometimes even Congressional hearings. In-terpreters also use the mass media: radio, television and videotapes, film, newspapers and magazines. Increasingly, effective computer-based interpretation shows up in nature cen-ters and museums.

Interpretation's numerous media vary from personal, individual guiding services to world-wide broadcasts, from ten-minute patio talks to long books. The principles used aren't exclusive to interpreters of history or nature. They are used by teachers, news and sports broadcasters, entertainers, writers, and many others who communicate. The focus in this book on history-culture-nature utilizes many principles from the diverse fields of com-munications.

Communities, states and nations spend significant resources for interpretive services. This highly technical area requires personnel who have strong academic backgrounds in cultural and natural resources. In addition, interpreters must possess exceptional abilities in various communications media, in practical psychology, and program administration. The best interpreters possess some sort of star quality—an ability to use creative imagination in helping people understand and enjoy their cultural and natural environments. They see things with new perceptions, cutting to the core, finding the life stories, discovering the scientific details and turning them into fascinating presentations for other people. These people possess the rare talent—often acquired—of perceiving and then translating for the rest of us. Interpreters are the storytellers who transmit the essence and meaning of culture and nature to society.

Interpretation often serves as the key to appropriate visitor appreciation and enjoyment of a natural or cultural resource area. Interpreters are often the only agency or company personnel that visitors encounter. Thus, it functions as the major public-contact service of many land holding agencies of local, state and federal governments, private industries, most museums, and many tourist-based regions and enterprises.

Interpretation involves close and often intensive interaction with the public; interpretation is a principal way that the agency message and image is presented.

Interpretation is usually labor intensive, requiring substantial operating funds for highly talented, educated staff. On the other hand, it also often uses high capital investments in buildings, exhibits, signs, trails and transportation.

One can define the job by its basics: communicating the significance of places and events and revealing hidden meaning.

SOME THOUGHTS ON YOUR FUTURE IN INTERPRETATION

Interpretation offers one of the most demanding, dynamic, and exciting fields of work anywhere. This field employs (and requires) some of the most brilliant, creative, and openly sharing professionals of any endeavor.

To be an effective interpreter, you need to have a command of your technical field, communications, human relations, learning psychology, and of sensitivity toward people who are in recreational settings. You will benefit if you have some artistic sense, even skill—design, photography, music, and drama all play a role in our work. You have to keep up on scientific research and translate it to the public—a job that most scientists cannot do well.

You will have opportunities to work in the mass media, and to work face-to-face with children, families, and elderly visitors. You will also transmit your ideas by various mechanical and graphic means, through exhibits, models, booklets, signs, audio tapes and videotapes, computers, Geographic Information Systems, radio, TV, interactive CD-video, virtual reality, and the old standby slides and films (often via multi-media presentations). For environmental interpreters, science-based woodcraft and skill in telling true stories about the outdoors are basics. For the various cultural interpreters, command of their subject matter likewise is fundamental.

In other words, interpretation will challenge you, but it should not limit you. Your creativity keeps your opportunities open. Some interpreters' imaginations run rampant. You'll never run out of subject matter nor new ways of presenting it, unless you let yourself lose the excitement.

Many interpreters work in large museums, zoos, aquaria, and commercial attractions, serving hundreds of paying visitors every day by offering worthwhile information in an exciting, provocative way. Some people work out in the woods at trailside museums, camps or resorts, leading hikes and answering questions. Still others run raptor rehabilitation centers, helping visitors to get close-up, first-hand views of birds while learning their value within the ecosystem. Many interpreters get into the history, geology, or biology of a place deeply enough to represent it through first-hand role-playing, which takes visitors into the character of the place, even if they must imagine it many centuries ago or if it is a molecule so tiny that we can get into it only by enhanced imaginations or high-tech imagery.

You can work in all of these media, in all these environments, in all these ways and many others that have yet to be developed. Yet, the basis of it all is you, communicating attitudes, information, and opportunities by creating experiences for people so they are stimulated to better see and interpret the world around them. The interpreter must be highly intelligent, very well informed about all the resources of an area, and alertly responsive to the needs of the individuals being served.

We walk on the cutting edge of the emerging profession of interpretation. The U.S. is the clear leader in this field, followed very closely by Canada. The United Kingdom, Israel, and several European countries do a nice job too. Most Latin American countries have made major strides. Several museums and archæological districts in Brazil, Mexico and the Dominican Republic show the results of superior skills and imagination. Latin American national parks are advancing rapidly, some with the cooperation of the Peace Corps, the U.N.'s Food and Agricultural Organization, and other groups. Indonesia, India, Japan and several other countries also have developed fine private and public interpretive efforts, moving as quickly as funding allows toward an integrated program.

The advice of the World Wildlife Fund, the International Union for the Conservation of Nature, and the World Bank has advanced interpretive skills and facilities in many nations. Kenya has long promoted tourism through its guiding (safari) system that has substituted photography and nature study for hunting. Ghana appears to be on the verge of a major move into historical and natural interpretation. Many other places offer superb interpretation. But many international frontiers exist where the practice of this important recreational/ educational activity needs stimulus.

Within the United States and Canada, the opportunities abound. Civic, commercial, and public agencies increasingly take interpretation seriously, as a key part of the leisure services and community culture systems.

The tourism industry has awakened to the dollar value of interpretation. So have many museums, where managers no longer relegate education/interpretation programs to a secondary role (Able, 1991). Rather, they are led by a curator of interpretation or curator of education. Thousands of museums aim to better serve visitors who want to learn and experience something new. They make interpreters and educators as important as the details of the collections behind the scenes.

Many of America's 1,000 counties with park districts also seek to expand their interpretive efforts (and there are 2,000 counties still waiting for park districts). Right now, a few federal agencies seek to increase interpretation efforts, most notably the Bureau of Land Management, The Fish and Wildlife Service, and The Corps of Engineers.

The future seems bright. You are one of relatively few people who will carefully study a book on interpretation. Maybe it will help you to encourage some administrators, or new recruits in the field, as well as politicians and benefactors who'll help pay for stronger interpretation. This book and formal study can help give you confidence, experience, and a solid foundation for proceeding assertively.

A BRIEF PREVIEW OF THE SUBJECT

Sharpe (1982) defined interpretation as a service, a communication link that inspires, explains, and entertains. It helps people develop greater sensitivity to their surroundings. It is developmental, informational, and directional. The interpreter is a guide to the natural, historical and/or cultural environment.

The interpreter usually explains resources to people. What are the resources? They include the broad categories of human history and prehistory, geologic processes, animals, plants, ecological communities, social communities, engineering phenomena, and manufacturing processes, among other things. Interpreters work in all types of organizations and many different environments.

Objectives

In the recreational context, the interpreter seeks to increase the truly re-creational productivity of resources by leading participants to enriched experiences and appropriate, sensitive use of the resources.

Interpretation communicates information and perception about a park, forest, structure, battlefield, or an entire region's distinctive features and influences. It helps visitors understand and appreciate the special natural and cultural resources, how these have influenced the way the region has evolved, and how its protection or disappearance will affect the area's future. The individual should thus enjoy a richer life through enhanced perception of landscapes and historical artifacts.

Most importantly, interpretation provokes individual interest in continuing the process on one's own. The visitor should leave an interpretive encounter as a person ready to look closer, perceive better and learn more. Some advice from long ago defines this goal:

Do not try to satisfy your vanity by teaching a great many things. Awaken people's curiosity. It is enough to open minds; do not overload them. Put there just a spark. If there is some good flammable stuff, it will catch fire."

—Anatole France (in Jubenville, 1976)

Interpretation as Smart Management

Managers want to achieve their goals. "The principal function of administration of recreational areas is to improve the quality of public use" (Leopold, 1966). Interpretation helps do that.

National Park Service top executives have often said that interpretation is the most economical method of visitor management. It is cheaper to guide people than to arrest or correct them. It costs less to prevent damage by promoting understanding than to repair it. The interpretive program also seeks to help the public understand the reasons behind management policies and decisions.

The interpreter is the ambassador of the museum or the agency. In practice, all employees should be ambassador's aides. The interpreter can spread the responsibility by training these individuals, making sure they are well acquainted with the program, even with the natural resources of the property.

Professional Preparation and Practice

Few people, if any, have all the attributes and skills listed above. Which way should the profession go in hiring—good communicators or good scientists/historians? Risk (1982) correctly claimed that a natural science degree does not make an interpretive naturalist: "If anything, there may be a negative correlation" between a person with a degree in natural sciences and the ability to communicate. He apparently overstated for emphasis that "communication skill is of paramount importance."

If taken too seriously, this philosophy can endanger interpretive quality. Excellent communicators inhabiting some of the national parks know little or nothing of the subject matter. They do half the job well, performing for the visitors within their range of information. A policy of hiring actors and public speakers—or nice people—without historical or natural history training could leave the discerning public dissatisfied. If the goal is to impress only superficially, then the smoothest talker with the best chin, cheekbones and smile may represent the company or agency best (after all, we choose some elected officials for these qualities).

On the other hand, if an interpretive center or museum seeks to do the whole job—including research, monitoring, writing, answering and posing questions intelligently, building a variety of lifetime skills among the clients, planning, and training—its directors may best seek employees with good communications skills plus strong academic background in the subject matter plus high intelligence plus an engaging personality plus a sense of the artistic plus a sense of humor plus a sense of responsibility.

Your attitude as an interpreter is vital. The Greek root of "to educate" is "to draw out." To draw out enthusiasm, approach your interpretive task with a feeling of deep inspiration. Tilden (1967) called it love—love of the place, love of the processes, love of the people who come to you. By knowing the subject of interpretation very, very well, you can automatically love it. Your enthusiasm for it should mount as your knowledge deepens and as your commitment to interpret it grows. Your enthusiasm and inspiration will draw out the visitors so they can immerse themselves in the subject with you.

Literature Cited

Able, E. H., Jr. (1991). Nurturing the mind and the spirit is a museum mission. *Museum News* 70(3):104.

Jubenville, A. (1976). *Outdoor recreation planning*. Philadelphia, PA: W. B. Saunders Co.

Leopold, A. (1966). *A Sand county almanac: With other essays on conservation from Round River*. NY: Oxford University Press.

Risk, P. (1982). Educating for interpreter excellence. In G. W. Sharpe, *Interpreting the environment (2nd ed.)*, New York, NY: Wiley.

Sharp, C. C. (1969). The manager, interpretation's best friend. *Rocky Mountain-High Plains Parks and Recreation Journal*, 4(1):19-22.

Sharpe, G. W. (1982). *Interpreting the environment (2nd ed.)*. New York, NY: Wiley.

Tilden, F. (1967). *Interpreting our heritage (rev. ed)*. Chapel Hill, NC: University North Carolina Press.

What Is It and Who Does It?

Interpretation . . . is the most challenging and provocative area of growth in our field today. Its potential for good to our society sparks the imagination. Its value as a tool in our constant striving to build a better, more meaningful life for America has hardly been tapped.
—*Wilcox, 1969*

People who visit museums, parks, forests, wildlife refuges, camps, and similar areas want interpretation; they say so when asked (Walsh, 1991). Many ask for it when they don't find it. The next two chapters present the profession of interpretation in terms of what it does, of what it consists, and where interpreters practice.

The first chapter presents many of the definitions and terms used among interpreters. Then it defines the scope, history and philosophy of the practice of this profession. Chapter 2 focuses on providers of interpretive services, from the numerous private organizations to the thousands of public and quasi-public agencies. Several outstanding organizations appear in examples. A sampling of interpretive agencies is represented in several categories of lists.

Effective interpretation programs do more than serve museums, camp, and park visitors who come to the sites; they also take the resources to people through direct programming and the full use of communication media. The interpreter unites people with their resources and culture. In marketing terms, the interpreter serves an organization or museum as:

- the medium that "delivers" natural and cultural resources to the market—the citizens;
- the marketer who assures customer satisfaction;
- the communicator of resource values and agency policies; and
- the listener who hears the feedback of consumer wants and needs and translates them into even better interpretive programs.

Interpretation is important to our society as a way of acquainting the population with its life support system—the environment. It also acquaints the people with their heritage—usually on the sites where history happened and culture developed. For many people, participation in interpretative events is the only history and environmental study to which they are exposed.

The mission of interpretation consists of developing an informed and experienced citizenry in our natural and cultural heritage—no small or mean task. Brandt (1990) wrote of the idea in relation to students: "Success for all our students is now more than a romantic ideal; it is a political and economic necessity."

The challenge faced by interpreters certainly cannot be taken lightly or considered as marginally important to society. A healthy, informed, well-oriented citizenry depends upon effective interpretation.

Museum of Appalachia, a private recreation of a rural Tennessee village, interprets the 1800s lifestyle.

Literature Cited

Brandt, R. (1990). Secrets of success. *Educational Leadership, 48*(1):3.

Walsh, E. (Ed.). (1991). *Insights: Museums, visitors, attitudes, expectations; A focus group experiment.* Los Angeles, CA: J. Paul Getty Trust. 180 pp.

Wilcox, A. T. (1969). Professional preparation for interpretive services. *Rocky Mountain-High Plains Parks and Recreation Journal, 4*(1):11-14.

What is Interpretation?

Interpretation, as it has evolved in our profession, means the complex of media and personnel that tells the story of a park or recreation area. Interpreters are specialists who tell the story with films, lectures, tours, publications, exhibits, and so on. The "story" of an area usually means the history of an event, a person, or a natural phenomenon.

—Brown, 1971

Definitions

Simply and loosely described, interpreters serve as translators of the natural and cultural environment, helping their clients to better understand and enjoy museums, camps, and natural resource areas and therefore better understand their home environment. Yorke Edwards (1979) wrote:

> The job of interpretation is to open the minds of people so they can receive—on the world's best receiver, the human brain—the interesting signals that the world is constantly sending. And the messages sent, when added up, tell what the world is all about.

DICTIONARY DEFINITIONS

interpret:
   v.t. 1. to set forth the meaning of; explain; explicate; elucidate.
          3. to bring out the meaning of by performance or execution.
          5. to translate
   v.i. 8. to explain something; give an explanation

interpretation n.	interpreter n.
interpretative adj.	interpretive adj.
interpretatively adv.	interpretively adv.

PROFESSIONAL DEFINITIONS

The term interpretation refers to a function—long practiced in historical and natural resource areas. The following formal definitions describe several angles of this diverse field.

The American Association of Museums defines interpretation as "a planned effort to create for the visitor an understanding of the history and significance of events, people, and objects with which the site is associated" (Alderson and Low, 1985).

Makruski (1978), after an academic review of key concepts and philosophies, defined interpretation as:

> ✳ a kind of educational enterprise where the concern is that which is interesting to the visitor, or that which can be made interesting to the visitor, not that which someone else thinks the visitor ought to know, regardless of how interesting it is.✳

"Interpretation is both a program and an activity. The program establishes a set of objectives for the things we want our visitors to understand; the activity has to do with the skills and techniques by which the understanding is created" (Alderson and Low, 1985).

A widely-adopted definition came from Tilden (1967): "an educational activity which aims to reveal meanings and relationships through the use of original objects, by firsthand experience, and by illustrative media, rather than simply to communicate factual information." Tilden expected each interpreter to have other equally valid definitions. He emphasized his distaste at having to confine the word within a specific definition. "The true interpreter will not rest at any dictionary definition," he wrote. Then he offered another definition: "Interpretation is the revelation of a larger truth that lies behind any statement of fact." The interpreter "goes beyond the apparent to the real, beyond a part to a whole, beyond a truth to a more important truth" (Tilden, 1967).

✳These definitions suggest that interpretation is more than instruction in facts, something other than traditional education or training. It passes on the meaning of something and develops a deeper understanding. ✳

To emphasize that point, one can distinguish between interpretation and information. ✳Interpretation conveys the meaning of something through exposition or explanation. Information is the knowledge derived from study, experience or instruction. "It is information that is so often given to a visitor; it is interpretation that should have been accomplished.✳ Good interpretation uses all sorts of information" (Grater, 1976). Interpretation uses information as raw material (Tilden, 1967), then works it and presents it in ways that entice, interest, and make clear what the information means to people. "How well the visitor can understand the important meanings and relationships of our site depends on the program and the activity that together make up the interpretation" (Alderson and Low, 1985).

Overall, interpretation is how people communicate the significance of cultural and natural resources. It instills understanding and appreciation. It helps develop a strong sense of place. It presents an array of informed choices on how to experience the resources (Paskowsky, 1991). Historical interpreter Charles Sharp (1969) simply called it "that distillation of service, teaching, and enlightenment which we call interpretation."

RELATED TERMINOLOGY

Interpreters work in numerous situations and have many names. One estimate suggested that more than thirty organizational titles identify people who perform interpretation (Patterson and Follows, 1992). At least this many titles appear in the 1994 membership directory of the National Association for Interpretation. Curiously, "interpreter" was not a federal job series name until 1994, although thousands of federal employees interpret.

Interpretation saw only occasional use in the early years. Over time, the terms have changed, although the functions are quite similar. In the western national parks, they were called lecturers in the 1920s; most of them were scientists in universities during the winter. Yet, the work done at Palisades Interstate Park in New York came under the aegis of the public education department of the American Museum of Natural History starting in 1920 (Carr, 1933). Enos Mills (1920) used the term "nature guiding" to describe his work in the Rockies; this title also received wide acceptance in the 1920s. Mills later was one of the first to use the term "interpret" to describe nature guiding activities (Makruski, 1978).

As the Indiana State Parks began interpretive work in the late 1920s, they hired *nature guides;* less than ten years later, they called them *naturalists*, still a popular designation among private, local and state organizations. Now the terms *interpreter* and *naturalist* have become virtual synonyms in the Indiana Department of Natural Resources.

Stephen T. Mather, first director of the National Park Service (NPS), discussed interpretation as the process, and nature guides and museums as the media in 1930 (Makruski, 1978). However, in the 1930s, education came back as a parallel term to interpretation with the establishment of the NPS Bureau of Research and Education (Bryant and Atwood 1932). Russell (1947) of the NPS, starting in 1932, regularly wrote of the process of interpretation. Nature guide declined in use by the late 1930s.

Interpretation was the term used increasingly in the late 1930s, as **naturalists** and **historians** worked together in the NPS, the term expanded to include historic sites. By 1957, when Tilden first wrote his book, *Interpreting Our Heritage,* the dominant term was *interpretation,* which included those who explain history, art, archæology, and nature. The *Association of Interpretive Naturalists,* founded in 1961, and the *Western Interpreters Association,* established at about the same time, gave the name professional recognition. These two groups combined in 1987 as the *National Association for Interpretation,* thus perpetuating the use of the term. The Canadian professional association had long used the term in its name, *Interpretation Canada.*

Museums use the terms education curator, director of public programs, interpreter, educator, and docent (teacher). In the 1960s, the NPS educators, naturalists and historians officially became rangers via the Civil Service.

The USDA Forest Service called its program Visitor Information Services (VIS) in the 1960s to the mid-1980s, when the name changed to Interpretive Services.

Some bureaucratic preference to calling interpreters by name still exists. The Fish and Wildlife Service and Bureau of Land Management call their interpretive personnel "outdoor recreation planners," as well as rangers, biologists, and several other names. The Smithsonian Institution refers to its interpreters as public education personnel. Given all the variety in names, this book will refer to them as interpreters because their job requires that they interpret.

Purposes and Values of Interpretation

The *raison d'etre* of interpretation is to help other people gain a sense of place, to respond to the beauty of their environment, the significance of their history and their cultural surroundings.

Interpreters seek to produce enrichment of experience. They add value to leisure time and activity. Richer experiences in the outdoors may be ends in themselves. Any interpreter may aspire to helping provide what Maslow (1962) called *peak experiences*. These highly satisfying, usually joyful events often come from feeling at one with nature or from seeming to be transported back in history as if a participant in a different time. John Muir's ability to write clearly about his peak experiences in rhapsodic and poetic language described his exultation in natural surroundings:

> These beautiful days must enrich all my life.
> They do not exist as mere pictures . . . but
> they saturate themselves into every part
> of the body and live always.

Interpreters certainly add more than fun or rapture, although deeper, more enjoyable recreation is almost always a goal of interpretive work. Other goals exist, along with or as an extension of recreational experience. Perhaps the primary ulterior motive of agencies and individual interpreters is to lead people to greater concern and intelligent action to sustain the natural and cultural environment in which people live. In this regard, interpreters seek to enrich the mind of each visitor. This may take the form of helping visitors better understand the public or private "company" that manages the resources. This involves explaining goals, techniques, and results of the work of the company or agency, so visitors understand what they see going on around them. Although most interpreters rebel at the thought, a few agencies seek to use interpretation as a propaganda tool.

Interpreters do their jobs of enrichment and education by cultivating people's minds. They plant new ideas and, sometimes, refute old ones. They help transport imaginations to the past, to re-plan battles, to resolve technological problems, even to walk in young Abe Lincoln's footsteps. They lead clients to see many species of life (e.g., mushrooms, mosses, lichens, horsetails) where they only perceived one kind of "lower" plant life before.

Interpreters can do their work through many sensory techniques. To affect the whole person, they involve all the senses to help get the messages across—touch, smell, hearing, seeing, even taste—to perceive the past and the present. Scents in a restored old-time pharmacy help visitors identify medicinal plants. Canada's provincial park interpreters guide people to special valleys, bays and streams, and show them things they had looked at but never truly perceived.

They also use the sense of movement and kinetic skills. At a beach on a lake, the interpreter wades in the water with families and helps them net several dozen insects from the bottom, which before had only been sand and water to the visitor (Figure 1.1). At Chicago's Field Museum, floor interpreters help kids print their names in hieroglyphics, producing a souvenir to take home and provoking greater interest in the meanings of the Egyptian exhibit. Some ask visitors to do things that they might not have imagined doing; a young female naturalist somehow coaxes a group of dignified, older women to lie flat on

FIGURE 1.1
Forest Service Interpreter Angela Cannon interprets the life of lakes and ponds in northern Wisconsin by directly involving visitors.

the ground to examine the forest floor and count insects or seeds. In the early 1900s, Enos Mills "sold" the idea of Rocky Mountain National Park by guiding and coaxing visitors to the top of Long's Peak and other mountain redoubts, showing them the life and geology of the place as they puffed and perspired.

A family may come to a park or forest to fish or camp. There they encounter a friendly, eager person who offers a hike or campfire program, a brochure or exhibit. A well-prepared message or activity combined with a receptive visitor may result in clients seeing their campground, the lake and surrounding woods in a new light. Or, people visit an old house or capitol building or factory with little more than mild curiosity; they leave it with a new world open to them, having shared physically, emotionally, and intellectually in the story of the place and its significance to their lives (Figure 1.2, page 8).

Because interpretation is offered in recreation places, the visitors seek enjoyable, recreational types of interpretation. Some (e.g., Hultsman, Cottrell, and Hultsman, 1987) said that interpretation often turns out too serious (dull); therefore, perhaps we should sideline interpreters until they can prove that they can make interpretation more fun. Meanwhile, these critics suggested using recreation experts to provide the programming in recreation areas. The argument seems too strong, perhaps over-emphasizing entertainment, but it seems to take this kind of jolt to wake up some interpreters. The experience at Land Between the Lakes, where a traditional fishing crowd seemed to resist "nature study," helped form the thinking of the reporters cited above.

THE PRODUCT

The product of interpretive efforts reveals itself in the visitor's skill and understanding—ultimately in how well the visitors become able to interpret what they find. In other words, the professional interpreter aims to eventually turn clients into skilled amateur interpreters. How well the visitor understands the important meanings and relationships of the site as a result of the entire interpretive effort—exhibits, signs, talks, walks, brochures, audiovisual materials, and other presentations—becomes the final product.

FIGURE 1.2
Interpreting the marble industry, its processes, products, and history, helps visitors make connections to the many structures made of marble.

The interpreter achieves a basic goal when a visitor understands the reasons that the site is important to the community, state, nation, world, and most of all to the individual visitor (Alderson and Low, 1985).

Forest Service Interpretive Services defines its processes as orientation, information and interpretation. Specifically, forest service interpreters seek to:

1. **Orient** visitors to basic services information including safety hazards, food, shelter, gas, i.e., helping meet safety and physical needs. Although not interpretation itself, orientation is an essential prerequisite to receptivity to interpretive programs.

2. **Inform** about forest recreation opportunities, management activities, agency responsibilities, cultural and natural history. Site-specific questions open up opportunities to provide suggestions and to build a base for interpretation. Information may answer questions about what to do, the size of the forest, the location of trails, the kinds of flora or fauna, or why foresters are setting a brush fire.

3. Once the orientation and information needs are met, visitors are ready to become involved in natural and cultural resources **interpretation**. The messages aim to inspire them to care for their forests, understand management, and become involved in decisions.

Interpret by taking information beyond simple disjointed answers, showing relationships between resources and humans, telling a complete story of several themes. The activity builds on themes related to the history and nature of a particular forest; e.g., for the Hiawatha National Forest, these include the Hiawatha legend; early settlement; logging and forestry; the northwoods and waters (Pulsipher and Parker, 1980).

ADDING VALUE TO RECREATION MANAGEMENT

National Park Service top executives have long said that interpretation serves as the most economical method of visitor management. It is cheaper to guide people than to arrest or deter them. It is cheaper to prevent damage by information and appreciation than to repair damages. The use of interpretation as part of the management team that enriches visitor experience and explains management goals can, of course, be distorted (that doesn't make it any less valid as a concept). One park scientist (quoted by Chase, 1987) said that sometimes it seemed that "interpreters exist only to apologize for Park Service mistakes."

Ideally, the interpreter serves as part of the management team comprised of professionally and scientifically or historically trained persons. The key strengths the interpreters should offer the team include their knowledge of the cultural and ecological components of the resources, and their skills in communicating the information to visitors, administrators, and the general public.

Ideal of Interpretation

A guide's "chief aim was to arouse a permanent interest in nature's ways, and this by illuminating big principles."
—Mills, 1920

Tour guides' enthusiasm, skillfulness, desire, and willingness to share information can help visitors, young and old, make connections between their own lives and valued artifacts, art objects, and history as represented by museum collections.
—Grinder and McCoy, 1985

The ideal interpreter gets the messages across effectively to the greatest number of people who will voluntarily receive them. Messages are not confined only to those people who visit the museum or resource. Interpretation may be offered to visitors in front of TV sets, in cars, or other mechanical transport, although personal effort and physical experience often provide the most memorable and valuable learning experiences.

Providing many kinds of media is part of the ideal (Figure 1.3, page 10). Seek to reach people in various ways, including those who do not get to the museum or forest. Some will only read signs; others will seek out brochures, movies, slide shows, or other entertaining but informative programs; others will want tours or hikes, laboratory study and personal attention; still others may want only a few minutes in a visitor center to check the map, or one corner of a museum to check on a few key facts.

Do not ignore the picnickers because of an assumption that they're not interested in anything but a family reunion. Reach out unobtrusively with a few key interpretive signs, a short self-guided walk near the picnic area, a brochure in the picnic shelter about the significance of the place, or a portable exhibit box set up nearby with a roving interpreter available to talk informally with those who stop by. Seldom do interpreters even enter picnic areas, even though the majority of visitors to some parks come for picnicking.

⚹ Ideally, interpretation makes the apparently commonplace into someplace special. With time and patience the mulberry leaf becomes a silk gown. ⚹
——Chinese Proverb

Ideally, interpretation opens minds to wonder and new ways of perceiving the world, beyond the mechanical.

⚹ Any fool can count the number of seeds in an apple. Only God can count the number of apples in a seed. ⚹
——Anonymous

FIGURE 1.3
Many kinds of nonpersonal media get messages across effectively at a low cost per visitor contact. (NPS, Fred R. Bell)

Interpretation as Part of Recreation

Recreation consists of more than nonwork. Play goes beyond mere games. In leisure, people recognized the exuberance and importance of life itself. In our outdoor recreation time we can exult in the joy of fresh contact with the Creation—with the natural and cultural richness that surrounds us. We can play, jump and run with colt-like freedom. We can also seek to release and expand our minds in joy.

In our leisure we seek beautiful places. We search out inspirational history. We go for music, outdoor drama, games, and adventure. We yearn to enjoy the outdoors, to survive in environments different from home. People enjoy outdoor recreation in many ways—such as walking, swimming, technical rock climbing, and volunteering for archæological digs.

Interpreters' first concern should seek to enrich these recreational experiences. That means to help recreating visitors have more fun, a richer pleasure, and a deeper joy. Surprisingly, that can be done with rather serious subjects, but not necessarily with a somber approach. The greatest joy comes from tough achievements, finding oneself in tune with the Creation, and tuning into one's own history.

Interpreters seek to fill recreational experiences with that extra element of heightened appreciation, deeper understanding, new ways of seeing the world (Figure 1.4). George Hartzog (1974), former Director of the National Park Service, noted that:

> We who have spent our lives working in and for the parks should not expect other people to possess an instinctive knowledge of park values. . . . A sensitive enjoyment and understanding of national parks does not come naturally to most persons. The majority require assistance, educational and interpretive programs, and the opportunity for frequent visits.

Interpreters educate. Interpreters entertain. Interpreters exhibit. Interpreters inform. But most of all, interpreters enrich recreational experiences.

FIGURE 1.4
Archæologists on federal forests and parks interpret their findings to curious visitors and volunteer amateurs.

WHO IS COMING?

The recreational perspective deserves emphasis because that is where the interpretive audience is. People come to interpreters as part of a recreational experience. Many come with trepidation—*this could be pretty dull, but it is good for the kids*. Many show up at the visitor center to get information—*how do we find the neat places in this wildlife refuge?* Some come to the campfire program to fill the time between dishes and bedtime—*there is nothing else to do out here; let's go see what the ranger says*. Some come from a long tradition—*we always go to the nature programs*. All go on their leisure time in a recreational mode, hoping for more than a dry imitation of a schoolmarm teaching her lessons to children.

Know the visitor! The first and most important thing to know is that the visitor is in or approaching a recreational mode of thinking—not in a working mode nor in an educational mode. Even school kids that come on a bus with the teacher think that they're out of school.

Interpretation is a recreational activity. If interpreters do the recreational job well, they can usually achieve the other goals of interpretation, such as educating the visitors about how to live in the world lightly, deepening their sense of historical and cultural legacy, helping them feel more at home in the natural environment, provoking their interest and skill in seeing and comprehending the world around them, as well as self-serving goals such as reducing management and maintenance problems, promoting the agency's image, and understanding resource management decisions.

The rest of this book deals with how interpreters go about enriching recreational experiences through interpretation. It is fun for visitors, but serious business for the interpreter. They will have limited time with most visitors. Yet, they will seek to impress upon visitors the exceptional values and worth of the place they are interpreting. The interpreter seeks to relate that place to the visitors' lives, so their few moments, hours, or days with an interpreter will make a profound impression on the way that they probe into history and the environment. The interpreter seeks to make them more careful in their use of resources, in their respect for cultural heritage, and in their relationships with other peoples. In other words, interpreters add greater joy and pleasure to the visitor's skills for existing on this planet, by example and by their greater sense of kinship with the earth and its inhabitants.

Why Interpret?
Philosophy of Interpretation

Is interpretation just nice? Is it essential? Is it astute management and public relations? People have interpretive philosophies that relate to all of these opinions.

The authors of this book believe that interpretation, properly carried out, serves as an indispensable tool to achieve successful, intelligent cultural and natural resource stewardship. Interpretation lifts recreation beyond mundane fun to intelligent use of leisure time, and from appreciation to understanding of the cultural and natural environment. It also represents good business sense by the public and private agencies and institutions that have an opportunity to use interpreters. Their success and public support may be directly or indirectly related to effective interpretation. The missions of most museums, public land agencies, and some private enterprises directly relate to educational benefits of interpretation.

Rennie (1980) listed six objectives for interpretation, adapted here to both cultural and natural resources:

1. To increase the visitor's understanding, awareness, and appreciation of nature, of heritage, and of site resources;
2. To communicate messages relating to nature and culture, including natural and historical processes, ecological relationships, and human roles in the environment;
3. To involve people in nature and history through firsthand (personal) experience with the natural and cultural environment;
4. To affect the behavior and attitudes of the public concerning the wise use of natural resources, the preservation of cultural and natural heritage, and the respect and concern for the natural and cultural environment;
5. To provide an enjoyable and meaningful experience; and,
6. To increase public understanding and support for an agency's role, its management objectives, and its policies.

There are numerous horror stories in every country about lack of perception of special values. One that is historically relevant today goes back to the 1490s and then to the days of the dictatorship of Rafael Trujillo in the Dominican Republic. On the north coast is a spot where Columbus first landed in that country. There, in early 1493, he built what is believed to be the first European community in the new world. In his second voyage, he returned to the place with lime and bricks to reinforce the village, including a house for himself on a scenic rock outcrop. The village was occupied for many years; excavated burials and partial walls remained into the mid-twentieth century. Then, for a celebration of 450 years of the Great Commander, Mr. Trujillo decided to make "improvements" on this rather remote site. He sent in equipment and men to level the site and to make it look "neat." No interpretation existed before the leveling. The citizenry had no power to object, even if they had the information of this patrimony; circumstances produced a major archæological setback. Today, in the open and better-informed Dominican society, Dominicans interpret this unique spot by using the foundations of the buildings and the limited but spectacular archæological evidence recently uncovered.

Interpretation may help prevent other tragic events by building public support and understanding about the resources. Certainly, interpretation of the Grand Canyon prevented its damming on several occasions. Public support of natural and cultural wonders has developed over many decades of promotion and interpretation by public and private groups (Figure 1.5, page 14).

Through our museums, forests, parks and other natural resource areas arise opportunities to inform and educate the very people who can benefit from the resources. Interpretation can help these people feel a sense of connection to the resources. They can learn of the special values of these resources.

Frank Bracken, Deputy Secretary of the Interior, charged the National Park Service, in a 1991 speech at the Vail Symposium (unpublished), to develop an outreach program that teaches cultural, historical, and environmental education in parks. He recalled one of Abraham Lincoln's sentiments, that a nation with little regard for its past has little hope for its future.

The heritage of any nation lies in its natural resources, its special historic sites, and its cultural collections. The vigor and strength of its future arise from its people's healthy attachment to their roots.

FIGURE 1.5
Interpretation opens the book of history and nature so people can read inner secrets.

Literature Cited

Alderson, W. T. and Low, S. P. (1985). *Interpretation of historic sites (2nd ed.).* Nashville, TN: American Association for State and Local History.

Brown, W. E. (1971). *Islands of hope.* Arlington, VA: National Recreation and Park Association.

Bryant, H. C. and Atwood, W. W. Jr. (1932). *Research and education in the national parks.* Washington, DC: National Park Service.

Carr, W. H. (1933). *Blazing nature's trail (2nd ed.).* New York, NY: American Museum of Natural History, School Service Series No. 3.

Chase, A. (1987). *Playing God in Yellowstone.* San Diego, CA: Harcourt Brace Jovanovich, Inc.

Edwards, Y. (1979). *The land speaks: Organizing and running an interpretation system.* Toronto, ON: The National and Provincial Parks Association of Canada.

Grater, R. K. (1976). *The interpreter's handbook: Methods, skills, and techniques.* Globe, AZ: Southwest Parks and Monuments Association.

Grinder, A. L. and McCoy E. S. (1985). *The good guide: A source-book for interpreters, docents and tour guides.* Scottsdale, AZ: Ironwood Press.

Hartzog, G. (1974). Management considerations for optimum development and protection of national park resources. In *Proceedings, Second World Conference on National Parks,* 1972. Morges, Switzerland: IUCN.

Hultsman, J., Cottrell, R. L. and Hultsman, W. Z. (1987). *Planning parks for people.* State College, PA: Venture Publishing, Inc.

Makruski, E. (1978). "A conceptual analysis of 'environmental interpretation.'" Ph.D. dissertation, Ohio State University. Ann Arbor, MI: University Microfilms.

Maslow, A. (1962). Lessons from the peak experiences. *Journal of Humanistic Psychology,* 2(1):9-18.

Mills, E. A. (1920). *The adventures of a nature guide.* Garden City, NY: Doubleday, Page & Co.

Paskowsky, M. (Ed.). (1991). *Santa Fe National Historic Trail: Interpretive prospectus.* Harpers Ferry, WV: National Park Service.

Patterson, D. and Follows, D. (1992). What is an interpreter? *Legacy,* 3(6):32-33.

Pulsipher, G. L. and Parker, T. C. (1980). Integrating interpretation into land management planning: a Forest Service case study. In *Proceedings, National Workshop, Association of Interpretive Naturalists,* Cape Cod, CT.

Rennie, F. (1980). "Interpretive evaluation: An applied methodology for self-guided trails." Guelph, Ontario: M.Sc. thesis, University of Guelph.

Risk, P. (1982). Educating for interpreter excellence. In G. W. Sharpe, *Interpreting the Environment* (2nd ed.), New York, NY: John Wiley & Sons, Inc.

Russell, C. P. (1947). *One hundred years in Yosemite: The romantic story of early human affairs in the central Sierra Nevada.* London, England: Oxford University Press.

Sharp, C. C. (1969). The manager, interpretation's best friend. *Rocky Mountain-High Plains Parks and Recreation Journal,* 4(1):19-22.

Tilden, F. (1967). *Interpreting our heritage (rev. ed.).* Chapel Hill, NC: University of North Carolina Press.

Who Offers
Interpretation?

This chapter presents the broad array of organizations that provide interpretive services. It includes examples of facilities and modes used to present interpretive information. Two central messages should come through:

1. Professional interpreters work in various types of facilities, e.g., zoos, museums, historic structures, restored villages, farms, factories, utilities, theme parks, camps, resorts, caves, parks, forests, refuges, preserves, and schools.

2. Interpreters work for organizations at many levels of "ownership" or jurisdictions, including private, quasi-public, industrial, city, county, provincial/state, and federal.

One stereotype of an interpreter suggests a person wearing a uniform in a National Park or National Forest. Many interpreters, however, work privately, leading tours, consulting, writing, speaking, recording, or providing planning, training, and evaluation services and products to other interpreters. Thousands more work for county and city parks and museums, camps and companies (Box 2.1, page 18). Some interpreters work only in the summers, as seasonal naturalists or historians. In the off-seasons they teach, are homemakers, go to school, or work at other jobs. Most interpreters work for pay, but a large number of volunteers supply support (Figure 2.1). In some cases, volunteers alone keep visitor centers open.

FIGURE 2.1
A desert museum volunteer docent interprets a kestrel to visitors.

Selected Types of Interpretive Facilities

In contrast with the later data on the "ownership" of the resources, the following discussion deals with some major types of interpretive facilities where interpreters work, e.g., museums of all levels of ownership, interpretive villages and farms, zoos and aquaria, and camps. Other types of facilities, e.g., visitor centers, forests, parks, refuges, and reservoirs are discussed under the various levels of "ownership," and in future chapters.

BOX 2.1: DIVERSE ORGANIZATIONS EMPLOY INTERPRETERS

Abbeydale Industrial Hamlet, England	Minnesota Zoo, Apple Valley
Adirondack Museum, Blue Mtn. Lake, NY	Missouri Dept. of Natural Resources
Adirondack Park Agency, NY	National Audubon Society, U.S.
Alaska Museum of History and Art, Anchorage	National Museum of Natural Science, Ottawa
Alberta Provincial Museum, Canada	Atwater Kent Museum, Philadelphia, PA
Navajo Nation Museum, Window Rock, AZ	Baraboo Circus World Museum, WI
Black Creek Pioneer Village, Maple, Ont.	Oregon Coast Aquarium, Newport, OR
Brisbane Forest Park, Queensland, Australia	Ozark Folk Center, Mountain View, AR
Brookfield Zoo, Chicago, IL	Parks Canada, Ottawa
Bunratty Castle Folk Park, Co. Clare, Ireland	Peabody Museum, Yale U., New Haven, CT
Bureau of Land Management, western U.S.	Pennsylvania Power and Light Co, Turbotville, PA
Callaway Gardens, Pine Mountain, GA	City of Gastonia Museum, NC
Riverbank Zoo, Columbia, SC	Cleveland Museum of Art, OH
Sanborn Camps, Florissant, CO	Colonial Williamsburg Foundation, VA
Schlitz Audubon Center, Milwaukee, WI	Countryside Commission, U.K.
Scottish Natural Heritage, Scotland	Dothan Landmarks Foundation, Inc., AL
Sea World Education Department, Orlando, FL	Holden Arboretum, Mentor, OH
Kalamazoo Nature Center, Inc., MI	Sitnasuak Native Corp., Nome, AK
Living History Centre, Novato, CA	Stuhr Museum, Grand Island, NE
Lutherans Outdoors in SD, Custer, SD	The Farmers' Museum, Cooperstown, NY
The National Trust, U.K.	Tucson Unified School District, AZ
U.S. Army Corps of Engineers	Walt Disney World Co., Lake Buena Vista, FL
Wesselman Woods Nature Center, Evansville, IN	YMCA Outdoor Centers and Camps, U.S.

MUSEUMS

More than 7,000 museums in the U.S. and Canada appear in the list of the American Association of Museums (AAM); 700 are accredited by AAM. (In addition, the visitor centers of many state/provincial parks, BLM, and Forest Service areas, most nature centers, and many small local museums do not appear in the total.) Many military bases also have museums and collections of war material (Figure 2.2).

Education programs (interpretation) and interpretive exhibits are integral to virtually all museums. The most common interpretive methods used are exhibits, school education programs, docent-guided tours and public programs. Some museums go far beyond this. Two small museums and a list of larger operations follow.

FIGURE 2.2
Military bases often interpret their own histories through the equipment they've used over the years, such as Offatt AFB. (TTC)

The **Pratt Museum** opened in 1968 under the ægis of the Homer, Alaska, Society of Natural History. Its outstanding facilities and exhibits serve this small community and the tourism industry very well. The museum offers seven areas: (1) a botanical garden of Alaskan plants arranged by ecological communities (Figure 2.3), (2) art exhibition area, (3) history and early lifestyle displays, (4) fauna of ocean and land exhibits plus a Marine Mammal Information Center, (5) "Darkened Waters" oil spill exhibit (the museum made a twin that travels the U.S. and Canada), (6) store, and (7) reference library. This little "super-museum" also supports archæological research and an active educational program for schools and special groups. Members produce two interpretive quilts per year, adding to the warmth of the exhibit area.

FIGURE 2.3
The Pratt Museum in Homer, Alaska, interprets a small botanical garden of native species outside the building plus local art, animals, historical lifestyles, and current issues inside.

The **Ute Indian Museum,** Montrose, Colorado, was founded in 1956 by the Colorado Historical Society. This small museum focuses on ethnology of the Ute Indians. On the site of Chief Ouray's 400-acre farm it features artifacts and archæology, Ute pottery, costumes, paintings, and history. The interpretation is traditional museum-style with exhibits carrying the load.

A few other accredited museums with high standards and various purposes appear in Box 2.2. These include museums featuring natural history, children's features, specialized history, art, and anthropology. Some museums are eclectic (e.g., the Shelburne Museum); other more specialized museums interpret individual collections of automobiles, sculpture, a sporting event (e.g., the Iditarod Race, the Indianapolis 500), or the history of a sport, a business, or a community.

BOX 2.2: OUTSTANDING ACCREDITED U.S. MUSEUMS

Arizona-Sonora Desert Museum, Tucson, AZ
Bishop Museum, Honolulu, HI
Brandywine River Museum, Chadds Ford, PA
Carnegie Museum of Natural History, Pittsburgh, PA
Children's Museum, Indianapolis, IN
Coyote Point Museum for Environmental Education, San Mateo, CA (Figure 2.4)
Cumberland Science Museum, Nashville, TN
Desert Botanical Garden, Phoenix, AZ
Fairchild Tropical Garden, Miami, FL
Field Museum of Natural History, Chicago, IL (Figure 2.5)
Indianapolis Museum of Art, IN
Museum of the Great Plains, Lawton, OK
Mystic Seaport Museum, CT
Nature Center for Environmental Activities, Westport, CT
Portland Art Museum, OR
Shelburne Museum, VT (Figure 2.6)
State Historical Society of North Dakota, Bismarck, ND

INTERPRETIVE VILLAGES AND FARMS

Many restored or recreated villages and farms exist to interpret the past. At least a few suggest how people may live in the future.

Definitions of living history farms range from (1) an operation with a garden, a few modern breeds of animals, and a farmstead tended by an interpreter or two in period dress to (2) a facility recreating as many aspects of agricultural life as faithfully as possible, including using period crop varieties, historic livestock breeds, cultivating with historic methods, artifacts appropriate to the era and area, and a large staff of interpreters representing the range of agricultural life.

A survey of living history farms (Percy, 1981) revealed that 200 farms were worth $450 million in actual investment. Most of these farms have a stated goal of self-sufficiency, but gate and shop receipts often do not cover the operating costs. With an average of 50,000 visitors per year, the average operating cost per visitor was about 12 percent less than the average expenditure by a visitor. They generally raise funds through memberships, endowments, and foundation support.

FIGURE 2.4
A Coyote Point Museum interpreter (San Mateo County Parks) starts the visit with a snake on the entry porch.

FIGURE 2.5
Acres of floor space in the Field Museum of Natural History in Chicago interpret a wide diversity of subjects.

FIGURE 2.6
A two-story round barn, one of 37 buildings, serves as the entry portal of the private Shelburne Museum, a fascinating collection of collections.

The goal of a living history farm is to portray the agricultural life of a historic period. Yet, many visitors see little if any farming activities. Instead, they see crafts demonstrations, cooking, and historic buildings. Most of the farms sit on the edges of re-created villages.

Morwellham Quay, lies north of Plymouth, Devon, England. This private commercial outdoor museum offers wagon rides, a trip into a copper mine, dozens of old buildings, wharves, ships, barnyards, period clothing for visitor dress-up, costumed interpreters plus refreshments and food (Figure 2.7).

FIGURE 2.7
Morwellham Quay interprets a privately restored 19th Century river port, its mines, and farming in Devon, England.

At **Plimoth Plantation**, near Plymouth, Massachusetts, first-person interpreters converse with visitors as if they had just dropped in on the 1620 or 1630s Pilgrim settlement, located up the gentle valley from the Mayflower (owned by the same private company).

The **Greenfield Village and Henry Ford Museum**, Dearborn, Michigan, claims to be the nation's largest indoor-outdoor museum complex. Its 240 acres contain 100 historic structures. A 14-acre indoor museum features vehicles and relics of the industrial revolution. Started in 1929 by Henry Ford and now run through the University of Michigan, the grounds feature buildings from the 17th to the 19th centuries plus several trains. Some visitors claim to have spent an entire week at the facility without seeing it all.

At **Pioneer Arizona**, near Phoenix, a private, nonprofit corporation operates a 550-acre ranch to bring history alive. The feature is an 1860 ranch with its animals and cowboys as they settled the Southwest. The ranch house stands on the outskirts of a reconstructed settlement, with shops, church, saloon, miner's camp, stagecoach stop, and a few homes. Visitors mingle in the shade of the barn to watch horseshoeing, leather tanning, and old-fashioned home economics.

Parker Ranch, Waimea, Hawaii, runs cattle, tourism and a real estate office. For an entry fee ($16.50 in 1990), a visitor can learn the story of John Palmer Parker jumping ship 140 years ago and building a legacy on the ash and lava of Mauna Kea's slopes. A visitor center offers a high-quality audiovisual program. Then come tours of the original homestead, the stables, the mansion, and working fields.

Zoos and Aquaria

Zoological gardens are one of the most ancient of outdoor educational facilities. Before 1000 BC, China's Empress Tanki built a marble house of deer and Wen Wang established a 1,500 acre "Garden of Intelligence" (Ling-Yu) filled with animals. King Solomon, King Nebuchadrezzar, and Alexander the Great all were zoo-keepers. A 1519 zoo in Mexico employed 300 keepers. European cities revived zoo-keeping in the mid 1700s. One of the most innovative zoos emerged in 1828 with the Zoological Society of London which continues to lead in caring for and interpreting animals.

Zoo and aquarium objectives feature study and research on animals, public education, and preservation and breeding of endangered species. Many zoos and aquaria offer guided tours, educational programs (Box 2.3, page 24), educational labels, and tape-recorded talking signs. Owners and operators are usually municipal and/or private associations. Many others owned by individuals or companies offer interpretation and viewing to paying customers.

Approximately 1,500 live animal collections hold USDA licenses, 700 of which can be defined as zoos. Of these, 160 are accredited by the American Zoo and Aquarium Association, Oglebay Park, Wheeling, WV.* Virtually all of the accredited zoos and many of the others offer interpretation or education programs.

---

* (personal communication, AAZPA/AZAA)

BOX 2.3: SEA WORLD OF FLORIDA

The Education Department of this commercial enterprise "provides programs that introduce individuals to animals and their diverse environments in an effort to foster a lasting conservation ethic." The 1992 activity menu included 55 different program offerings plus 22 miscellaneous activities. Total program attendance for 1992 amounted to:

	Attendance
Instructional Programs	68,189
Guided Tours	62,644
Total	**130,833**

In addition, exhibit interpreters reached virtually all the 4,000,000 visitors who paid their way into the Sea World exhibits. Each interpreter (narrator) offered a 2-5 minute presentation at each of the ten major exhibits.

The company reached out to many schools. One effort produced new satellite TV programs. *All About Penguins* reached 400 schools, while *All About Manatees* went to 800 schools (about 1,000,000 viewers). Eight 50-minute interactive programs went national in 1993, along with others on whales and sharks. Sea World of Florida also produced a newspaper insert, *Mysteries of the Sea*, distributed through schools in three counties.

On site, the department offered special tours in Spanish for 1,200 guests. It put on a 3-hour open house for nearly 2,000 teachers. Its Camp Sea World School Program brought in 1,822 participants at three different age levels. Three college courses at a local community college and an annual symposium on Marine Mammals added a scholarly dimension to the staff's functions. The programming, summarized in broad groups:

School and Youth	40	activities
Teacher Programs	3	
Adult Programs	4	
Family Programs	3	
Publications	5	new
Miscellaneous	22	

The numerous curriculum and information booklets and teacher's guides available get reviewed by a curriculum Advisory Committee of teachers and administrators from local schools. A Sea World staff of 70, many with advanced degrees in natural history, runs this complex and productive private interpretation program.

Source: Sea World of Florida (1992)

The **Zoological Society of San Diego**, famous for its zoo and wild animal park, allows visitors to see animals without bars. The use of large paddocks at the Wild Animal Park, with travel by monorail through the habitat settings, helped set the trend for many other new zoos, including a strong interpretive and educational component. A 1994 innovation, "Night Time at the Zoo," boosted visitation during night hours when many animals are more active.

The **Indianapolis Zoo** operates an environmental education program and a large interpretive program. However, when a new chief executive officer of the zoo, Jeffrey Bonner, came on board in 1993, he told reporters that it should become more of an instructional center. He said that the animal and habitat exhibits were state-of-the-art, but more interpretation was needed.

On a smaller scale, the **Alaska Zoo,** in Anchorage, provides excellent interpretive signs and exhibits. As is typical of most zoos, exotic fauna provides a broad view of the world for visitors. The Alaska Zoo, however, gives major emphasis to Alaskan species.

CAMPS

At least 8,500 camps operate in the U.S., offering outdoor opportunities to youth and adults through private businesses, religious groups, municipal governments, and quasi-public agencies and organizations (e.g., YMCAs, Scouts, Salvation Army). About 5,500 of these are resident camps and 3,000 are day camps. The American Camping Association had 2,200 accredited in 1992, of which 1,320 were resident camps.[†]

Formal environmental education programs comprise an important part of 1,250 of the resident camps, with most others offering some kind of nature or history types of activities. Around the U.S., many YMCA camps, some church camps and a few Boy Scout camps have adopted environmental education as a major activity in the spring and fall seasons. Thus, they extend their incomes and staff productivity. Private summer camps near urban areas also provide environmental education opportunities during the "shoulder" seasons.

Various public agency and private organization camps emphasize conservation. Their goals usually aim: (1) to instill understanding, respect, and value for natural resources, (2) to train youth in recreational skills and ethics, (3) to introduce resource management and safety, and (4) to offer group recreation in outdoor settings. Among many sponsors, the National Wildlife Federation and the National Audubon Society provide adult and youth nature seminars in outdoor settings.

Among several state agencies sponsoring educational camps, the Vermont Fish and Wildlife Department offers one-week sessions of the Green Mountain Conservation Camps through a 9-week summer season. They focus on youth 12-14 years of age, featuring outdoor skills, life sports, and resource management. The New York Department of Environmental Conservation maintains three camps for summer environmental education. One is Camp Colby, where kids work with college-age counselors on 12 two-hour environmental education programs, alternated with sports and other physical activities. Several states (e.g., Wisconsin and Vermont) sponsor state Youth Conservation Corps camps. Youths 16-21 can qualify to work for pay, education, job skill development, and environmental service experience. They work on trails, environmental rehabilitation, signs, and rustic construction in national and state forests and state parks, as well as in some urban centers. All participants receive training in conservation, first aid, leadership skills, tool use, communications, and working as a team.

Other types of facilities, under several classes of ownership, include parks, industries, wildlife refuges, public and private forests, caves, resorts, and touring companies, are discussed in the following section.

[†] (personal communication, Gary Abell, American Camping Association)

Owners of Interpretive Facilities

WHERE INTERPRETERS WORK—ONE GENERAL VIEW

Study of the membership list of the National Association for Interpretation (NAI) gives an idea of where professional interpreters work. This professional society includes mostly U.S. members, the majority of whom specialize in natural history. A systematic sample of the list of 2,100 members selected a total of 134 active U.S. interpreters.** Table 2.1 indicates the employers of these 134 interpreters.

TABLE 2.1 U.S. INTERPRETERS IN NAI BY SECTOR OF EMPLOYERS

Type of Employer	Percent of total
Local Governments	32.1
Federal Agencies	31.3
Private	17.2
State Governments	9.7
University	9.7
Total (n=134)	100.0

Source: Sample of National Association for Interpretation Membership Directory, 1991

Governmental agencies employed nearly three-fourths of the interpreters sampled. Cities and counties accounted for about one-third, nearly all through park and recreation agencies. Five federal agencies combined for just under one-third of the membership of the professional society. Private employers employed about one NAI member in six. State-owned properties (mostly parks and museums) employed one in ten. University faculty and graduate assistants comprised the final ten percent of the membership. All but two of the members sampled held year-round jobs; few seasonals join NAI.

County park agencies led all other agencies, with nearly one-fifth of the NAI membership (Table 2.2 identifies the members by types of agencies). Municipal agencies employed the same percentage as National Park Service interpreters. The Bureau of Land Management had the fewest members but its numbers are growing rapidly as the agency expands its interpretive commitment and facilities.

** The sampling process also indicated that six percent of the membership was foreign—from Canada, Australia, India, Sweden, Taiwan, and England. Another three percent of the members worked in noninterpretive jobs. These foreign or nonactive interpreters were not included in the tables.

TABLE 2.2 LEVELS OF AGENCIES REPRESENTED IN U.S. MEMBERSHIP IN NAI

Jurisdiction of Agency	Percent of members
County/Multi-County	19.4
City/Town	12.7
National Park Service	12.7
State agencies	9.7
University faculty, graduate students	9.7
USDA Forest Service	9.0
Self-employed or private business	9.0
Private organization or foundation	8.2
US Army Corps of Engineers	4.5
US Fish & Wildlife Service	3.7
US Bureau of Land Management	1.5
Total (n=134)	100.0

Source: Sample of National Association for Interpretation Membership Directory, 1991

This list underrepresents several types of facilities where interpretation is practiced. For example, public and private zoos, museums, and camps employ interpreters/educators in rapidly growing numbers. The NAI has just begun to make an effort to reach these people, as well as cultural/historical interpreters. Likewise, private commercial interpreters are probably underrepresented. Unfortunately, the membership rolls of groups such as the American Camping Association and the American Association of Museums do not make it easy to separate out the interpreters from other classifications.

The following list of organizations that employ interpreters (Table 2.3, page 28) indicates the variety of resources and methods used in helping the visiting public to understand the character of many places in North America.

Private Sector Interpretation

INDUSTRIAL

The forest products industries may hold the lead among many industries that provide tours and explanations of their processes and products and environmental education. They have offered interpretive and educational materials for more than 50 years. Currently, the American Forest Foundation offers Project Learning Tree and Project Wild environmental education programs, along with many other sponsors. The American Forest Foundation is an off-shoot of the American Forest and Paper Association (AFPA). Project Learning Tree started in 1973, after several years of preparation by educators and biologists and pretesting in the classroom. Project Wild followed, built on the same foundations. In both cases, the sponsors insisted that the environmental education materials should not reflect an industry point of view but rather teach how to make decisions based on facts about the environment.

Project Learning Tree workshops and activity books reached more than 350,000 teachers by the beginning of 1993.

The American Forest Foundation also sponsors the Tree Farm Program, including tours of Tree Farms for teachers. These popular educational tours help inform teachers about the biological aspects of tree farming, from planting to harvesting and regeneration (Hutcherson, 1993).

TABLE 2.3 ORGANIZATIONS THAT PROVIDE INTERPRETIVE SERVICES

Government agencies
  Federal *(6 major U.S. agencies plus museums, tours, etc., in others)*
  State and Provincial *(3-7 agencies per state/province)*
  County and Township *(usually Park and Recreation agencies)*
  Municipal *(usually Park and Recreation agencies, museums and schools)*
  Tribal lands and centers *(museums, churches, cultural demonstrations)*

Private sector interpretation
  Industry: *Company plant tours, industry museums, forest parks and nature centers, entertainment/educational mass media, trade associations*
  Commercial firms: *Tourism/ecotourism package companies (often travel/transport), museums, exhibitions, resorts, camps, caves*
  Individuals: *Guides, program speakers, writers, performing and graphic artists*
  Nonprofit organizations: *Art societies, museums, zoos, botanical gardens, arboreta, historical societies, nature centers and sponsoring associations, camps, conservation groups.*

An industry consortium with Forest Service and city cooperation operates the **Trees for Tomorrow Natural Resource Education Center**, Eagle River, Wisconsin. Their cozy residential campus of outdoor learning has multiple nature trails, a river, forests, silvicultural samples, a library, classrooms, and dormitories. A bus opens the whole North Woods as a field station, with frequent visits to two national forests and several county forests. Fifty years of teaching conservation methods and ethics in a practical way allows visitors to see how the North Woods supplied wood products, wildlife, recreation, water protection and still kept the forest producing trees for the future. Clients include school groups, graduate-level teacher workshops, cross-country ski learning-tours, elderhostels, and field science challenge courses for gifted children, among others.

The **Corning Museum of Glass**, Corning, New York, demonstrates the highest quality of museology and interpretation. Virtually every visitor reports that this is one of the best exhibits of any kind that they have ever seen. It shows off some of the most beautiful glassware anywhere, as well as the process of turning common materials into glittering, useful, even precious, vessels and decorations. Principles of interpretive exhibitry live in this factory display and tour. Founded in 1951, the museum hosts 450,000 paying visitors per year. The nonprofit educational institution offers self-guided and guided tours, lectures, films, gallery talks, organized educational programs, seminars, and a wide variety of research on the history and technology of glass. The associated Corning Glass Center offers animated exhibits on the manufacturing and use of glass, audiovisual presentations, festivals, recitals, concerts, films, dramas, summer theater, conferences, and meetings.

The **Vermont Marble Company** provides an example of a company interpreting its product as a symbol of the state—for a charge. "The world's largest marble museum" has attracted tourists for over 50 years. The exhibit area employs a full-time sculptor who demonstrates carving and polishing techniques. The exhibit allows visitors to see some of the production floor. It also interprets through a film about how marble is formed, quarried, blocked, finished, and how the company does its work. It includes a Hall of Presidents, with relief carvings of all past presidents carved from pure statuary white marble.

Nearby, a farm store/forest enterprise interprets how to make maple syrup and sugar. **Dakin Farm**, a retail and mail order business selling Vermont products has an interpretive slide show and sugar house exhibit year-round. During four weeks of sugar making, it produces "Sugar on Snow," a home-grown festival. Over 10,000 participants come to learn at no charge.

Other well-known interpretive exhibits in industries are the Hershey Chocolate tours, several power generating facilities (e. g., nuclear, hydroelectric), most breweries, tobacco companies such as the state-of-the art museum and tour of the Philip Morris Company. Geevor Tin Mines in Pendeen, Cornwall, England, operates a tourist facility at its working mine. Three guided tours, including one underground, plus a video show of mine operations and a Cornish Mining Museum combine to make a rich interpretive experience in a rather bleak, fascinating landscape.

PRIVATE COMMERCIAL INTERPRETERS

Sea World of Florida/Busch Gardens offers numerous educational programs and publications, in addition to the daily interpretation to the visiting public at these large sea animal and terrestrial wildlife exhibits. Sea World of Florida began a TV satellite programming network with a series of programs on Marine Life (Erickson, 1992). Sea World, a subsidiary of Anheuser Busch offers several dozen other programs plus day-to-day exhibit interpretation, through an Education Department staffed by 70 people.

Callaway Gardens in Pine Mountain Georgia, supports an Education Department to operate a major interpretive enterprise. Its naturalists and horticulturists are professional members of the National Association for Interpretation. They offer many tours, seminars and educational publications at this huge botanical garden and forest resort.

Whale watch ships out of Provincetown, Massachusetts, and other locations carry interpreters who describe the actions, ecology, physiological processes, and migration of whales that are sighted. The commentaries may last 2 hours or more, including orientation, approach, long sighting events, and comments during part of the return trip. Similarly, private tour boats operate out of Seward and Homer, Alaska, cruising close to islands and up fjords to interpret wildlife, glaciers, and landforms.

Atlantis Submarines, Kona Coast, Hawaii, operates as a private firm. This underwater experience off the coast of the big island takes four dozen visitors down into the ocean to depths of 40-60 feet. Interpreters explain the coast, the volcanoes and the sea life during the 45-minute ride, at the rate of about $1.50 per minute per person.

Resort naturalists go back to the origins of the modern environmental interpretation business, when individual experts offered their services to resorts and individuals. Naturalists and historians still work at resorts. Forest Service/private sector partnerships operate resort naturalist programs in Minnesota, Arizona, and several other spots. The Forest Service (with help from the Audubon Society) provides recruiting, training, and uniforms. The resorts provide housing, food, salary, and the audiences. The interpreter offers activities that allow families to learn about the woods and lakes, understand safety, routing, and policies. Many resorts employ their own interpreters and guides, sometimes as a free service, sometimes as a client-paid option.

Free-lance interpreters offer services in many ways. White Fawn (Bessie Evans), a native American woman of Farmland and Vincennes, Indiana, promotes understanding and respect for Native Americans (Figure 2.8). One of many private American Indian interpreters, she travels a four state region, talking to church, school,

FIGURE 2.8   *White Fawn takes her cultural insight to schools and organizations in the Midwest.*

civic, and cultural groups, showing them artifacts, symbols, and modern crafts. She emphasizes the old ways of living with a healthful environment and the perception of the Creation as many interconnecting circles (Snyder, 1992). She made no charge until recently; with the charge came heavily increased requests.

In Tucson, Arizona, hotels and tourist information centers, "The Nature Guide" advertises guided hiking nature tours for 3-hour, 6-hour, and 2-day tour packages, custom adapted to party interests. Ecological, cultural, and taxonomic interpretation occurs during the hikes into the deserts and the mountain forests.

A Tucson astronomer offers guided astronomical tours called "Celestial Safari." The four to five hour tour includes transportation, star maps, information, gourmet picnic dinner, and refreshments. A company called Sabino Canyon Tours, Inc., provides narrated shuttlebus rides along a twisting road up into the canyon, on a special use permit with the Forest Service (Figure 2.9).

Richard N. Pawling, a university instructor in Pennsylvania, works part of the year as "History Alive!" This company interprets the history of laborers of the past two centuries.

He does "first person" living history performances, taking on the roles and persona of a canal boat captain, a coal miner, a blacksmith, and five other characters. He puts on workshops for archæologists, interpreters, teachers, historical societies, and industries.

✗ Alaska is a hot-bed of commercial interpretation in many forms: driver-guides, ship lecturers, railroad narrators, Native village interpreters, museum interpreters, cultural dance and crafts groups, river guides, flightseeing narrators, step-on guides, nature-guide led horseback trips, group escorts, visitor information service personnel, and resort-based naturalists.✗

Perhaps in no place as much as in Alaska do government and private interpreters combine their efforts so intimately. Call it ecotourism, heritage interpretation, or resource interpretation (Follows, 1992), it is a value-added product. From Gray Line Tours to individual resort owners, business seems brisk. Private, Forest Service, and National Park Service guides get on ships and ferrys, buses and trains to interpret the land and sea resources of coastal Alaska. In its first two years (1987 and 1988), the train between Whittier and Anchorage interpreted Turnagain Arm to 120,000 visitors in six programs per week (Follows, 1988). Interpretation links the travel-tourism industry with resource management agencies, museums, and cultural groups.

Private interpretive guides demonstrate that the public puts high value on their service. Clients pay for interpretive services, sometimes at quite a premium over what elected public bodies are willing to appropriate for similar services by public agencies. Guides step onto motor coaches from Canada and the lower 48 states to interpret Alaska; they make an hourly salary five times that of their government counterparts. Driver-Guides for the commercial wildlife tours in Denali National Park earn double the salary of NPS interpreters and, by at least one estimate, perform at a higher level of competence (Follows, 1992). More than one Alaskan resort/fishing camp/trip outfitter promotes their value to the consumer by noting the natural resources or historical background of the owner-operators who provide expert instruction and interpretation.

Outfitters Curt and Evelyn Farmer, of New Mexico, lead five-day hikes into the Pecos Wilderness. Llamas carry the goodies and tents. A naturalist on each trip explains history and the Native American heritage as well as aids in wildlife and wildflower

FIGURE 2.9
Private interpreters in Tucson, AZ, advertise their services in resorts and other tourist facilities.

identification. For $700 to $800 a week, Cameras, Horses, and Trails provides food, tents, and horses on the Beartooth Plateau or the Bighorn Range of northern Wyoming. The owner, Brad Cicci, helps spot wildlife, fish, and wildflowers. Dozens of similar outfitters serve mountainous areas of the U.S., Canada, and Australia, some as part of resort or dude ranches and some for hunting and fishing trips.

PRIVATE NONPROFIT

Numerous groups operate private institutions that serve the public interest and therefore are tax-exempt. YMCAs and their environmental education camps, scouts, Campfire, churches, historical societies, Audubon Societies, and many others offer diverse interpretive/educational programs and facilities (Figure 2.10 and 2.11). Just a few outstanding examples follow (also see Box 2.4).

BOX 2.4: KALAMAZOO NATURE CENTER

On the north side of Kalamazoo, Michigan, a private, nonprofit nature center offers a variety of interpretive events. The name Nature Center here covers a broad range of projects, the result of the fertile imagination of founder Dr. H. Lewis Batts and his staff. They work on energy efficiency throughout Kalamazoo. It provides environmental education for thousands of school children each year. It hosts tens of thousands of casual visitors who come to see the exhibits, the sun-rain room, the glen-view room, the book and gift store, the raptor center, or to walk the self-guiding trails.

The staff monitors groundwater quality throughout south central Michigan. The staff at the restored working homestead (Figure 2.12, page 35) offers clinics on animal-powered farming. Projects developed by board members include a farm animal area, a butterfly/hummingbird garden, a living herb and medicinal plant collection, and an elaborate sundial. The staff of about 10 permanent naturalists and educators conduct programs on the large property and throughout the community. They apply for grants and develop new project ideas to keep this vibrant, private facility in the vanguard of community nature centers.

The Nature Center for Environmental Activities, Inc., in Westport, Connecticut, started out as a youth museum in 1958. Its emphasis on natural history helped it expand as an outdoor education center and large natural history museum. The staff of five and trustees who operate the nonprofit corporation raise $850,000 per year for operations, partly from a grant by the City of Westport ($60,000), fees, services, and the gift shop (about 50 percent) and from donations and grants.

Colorado Outdoor Education Center, Sanborn Camps, Florissant, Colorado, a 6,000-acre property tucked behind Pikes Peak, offers a variety of adult and youth camping with a strong twist of environmental education. Three camp/conference centers operate with different groups, from youth to corporate and professional meetings. High ropes challenge courses, horseback riding, hiking, nature centers, heavy emphasis on ecological thinking makes this family-operated camp a national model. Summer employees are chosen with an eye toward their natural history skills and sensitivity to the environment.

The Carmel Mission interprets church history and the early influence of Fra Junipero Serra on California history.

Chewonki Foundation in Maine has run summer camp programs since 1915. The nonprofit institution also offers six-day introductory paddling trips on the Penobscot River. They emphasize environmental education and outdoor skills, as well as cooperation in cooking and other camp chores, at $525 per person for the privilege.

Morton Arboretum, Lisle, Illinois, operates from a nonprofit scientific foundation endowed by Joy Morton of salt fame. Its 1,500 acres contain 4,800 species of trees and shrubs, including areas of natural forests. A strong commitment to interpretation involves many publications, self-guiding trails, a visitor center, guided walks, and special events. Visitors may check out books from the horticultural library. A reading garden includes plants that relate to the history of botany. A plant clinic offers identification help and advises on selecting plants for homes. Field trips and classes for adults and families go on all year. Schools use the teaching facilities.

FIGURE 2.11
A Kenai, Alaska, native interprets the traditions and continuing influence of the Russian Orthodox church on Alaskan society.

These provide only a few samples of the many private organizations offering interpretation. Some of the others have names made famous from their products or services, such as Honeywell and National Audubon Society (Box 2.5). Most offer facilities supported by families or groups little-known outside their local area, such as the Evanston Environmental Association and the Clegg Botanical Garden. The huge private initiative and support of interpretation gets relatively little publicity within the profession, but it contributes considerably to the total interpretive supply available to consumers.

BOX 2.5: COMMUNITY NATURE CENTERS

A local park department or historical society may have a modest little nature center and historical museum, or there may be several centers in any county that are major attractions in themselves. Growth in the number of community nature centers has brought self-guiding trails, interactive visitor centers, as well as strong-guided educational programs to more of the public.

In the 1950s, the National Audubon Society set up several model nature centers and farms that still operate: Greenwich and Stamford, CT, El Monte, CA, and later, Aullwood center and farm near Dayton, OH. By 1961, with E. A. Matthiessen and Laurance S. Rockefeller joining in, the Nature Centers Planning Division set out to promote and provide ideas for community nature centers. The office extended its publications, planning assistance and guidance throughout the U.S. and Canada. Nature centers appeared in the Bahamas, Trinidad, Panama, England and Norway (Shomon, 1990). The goal of 1,000 nature centers by 1990 and 2,000 by the year 2000 seems attainable. By 1990, the number in America had reached 1,200, with a total capital investment exceeding $1.4 billion (Shomon, 1990). In addition to the centers listed above, the Schlitz Audubon Center near Milwaukee, WI, plus others in eight states serve as models for cities, counties, state Audubon Societies, and other private groups.

The physical concept of a community nature center involved at least 50 acres (average now exceeds 100 acres) with a planned interpretive building, well laid-out interpreted trails, facilities and devices, and a staff of well-trained administrators and teacher-naturalists. A community nature center can use a wide variety of thematic trails, as well as some special opportunities, installed for short periods. Aullwood Audubon Center features a series of loops with names such as Wet Woods Trail, Fox Meadow Trail, Ridge Trail, Wildflower Trail, Prairie Lane, Discovery Trail, Hawthorne Hill Trail, and Honey Bee Meadow.

Although the Nature Centers Planning Division exists no more, the work and assistance of the National Audubon Society gave much impetus to community nature centers. Shomon (1990), recalling his many years of encouraging these islands of green that formed land for learning, called it "one of the least heralded yet most successful developments of the American environmental movement."

FIGURE 2.12
*Historic homes open windows on the past, such as at the Delano Homestead,
Kalamazoo Nature Center.*

Local Governments

Local governments provide interpretive facilities that serve a large clientele, any of which make return visits. Among the thousands of U.S. local governments the designations include town, township, municipality, city, county, parish, and borough governments, as well as special park districts, historic districts, and school districts. A sampling of some of these follows to give a sense of their nature.

CITY AND TOWNSHIP PARKS

Increasing development of urban interpretation and city park/museum/zoo education departments provides new opportunities in municipal governments.

Seattle City Parks employ several interpreters permanently to run their Discovery Park interpretive center and trails, to offer environmental education at Camp Long, and to interpret animals at the Woodland Park Zoo. New major investments in Discovery Park interpretive center facilities add to the commitment of the city for an outstanding interpretive program.

The **Mississippi Agriculture and Forestry Museum** in Jackson, MS demonstrates city-state collaboration. The indoor-outdoor museum traces the history of Mississippi's two most important industries inside the 40,000 square foot exhibit center where dynamic exhibits tell the story of Mississippi's farmers and lumbermen. The Fortenberry-Parkman Farm restoration and the crossroads town offer living historical examples of life during the 1920s. Costumed interpreters go about their daily tasks while craftsmen and shopkeepers carry on their trades.

COUNTY PARKS

Most counties in the U.S. and virtually all the British counties (somewhat parallel to U.S. states) offer interpretation in one form or another. In the U.S., most counties support interpretation through a museum, which may involve joint public-private funding. More than 1,000 of the nation's 3,000 counties (parishes and boroughs in some states) have park and recreation departments; most of these offer interpretive services, museums, or nature centers (Figure 2.13).

Johnson County, Kansas, offers one of the most complete interpretive programs of any parks and recreation agency. Its ranger-interpreters combine law enforcement and interpretation. They work at several nature centers and in parks throughout the county, offering hundreds of programs per year in the parks and in schools.

Carroll County, Maryland, features three park complexes, each with a strong interpretive theme. At the center, a farm park provides costumed interpretation that revives the agrarian tradition of the county. To the North, a youth camp and new nature center focus on woodland skills and environmental education. The southern part of the county has a large nature center emphasizing aquatic and terrestrial ecology.

Atlantic County, New Jersey, Division of Parks and Recreation, operates the new Warren E. Fox Nature Center (Figure 2.14), many nature trails, a zoo, herb gardens, old factory

FIGURE 2.13
Sheep shearing by experts aid a farm days special event of Montgomery County Parks Department, MD.

ruins, and a veterans' cemetery. Special programs include artists in the park, an American Indian fashion show at a reservation, trips to museums and forests in other states, and many events at the major county parks.

Several multi-county special park districts feature interpretation through large staffs and fine interpretive facilities. Three examples are California's **East Bay Regional Park District, Michigan's Huron-Clinton Metropolitan Park District,** and **Maryland's National Capital Parks and Planning Commission.** Their staffs of 10-25 full-time interpreters consistently win top professional awards and provide leadership in the development of the interpretive field.

County Cornwall, England, provides several recreational facilities through its county council. One is the County Demonstration Garden at Probus, winner of the Carnegie Award for Outstanding Interpretation of British Heritage. The facility interprets techniques and designs for gardening, one of England's favorite pastimes. About 30 model gardens, from formal patterns to a nature reserve, cover eight acres. Modern and traditional techniques for small and large gardens, designs, shrub, herb, and wildflower culture, a children's nature trail, bird studies, and beekeeping exhibits all await the visitor. Courses, lectures, demonstrations, photographic and crafts exhibits add interest and depth. Once a week, an artist in residence works and coaches aspiring artists at the garden. The staff offers guided tours. A horticultural advisor, with an office and lab in the center of the park, offers solutions to plant and soil problems.

FIGURE 2.14
A new nature center graces one of the Atlantic County parks in southern New Jersey.

State Governments

STATE PARKS, FORESTS, REFUGES, NATURE PRESERVES, AND RESERVOIRS

Virtually every U.S. state park system and Canadian Provincial Park offers interpretive services to visitors. The Canadians seem to have an edge in their consistently excellent publications, visitor centers, trails, and programming. Several U.S. states do a fine job of explaining the cultural and natural characteristics of their properties; others dedicate few resources to the effort. Some states that lease reservoir sites from the Corps of Engineers or Bureau of Reclamation offer outstanding interpretive programming. State forests, wildlife areas, and nature preserves often include interpretive efforts, but usually on a less intensive basis than in parks and reservoirs. **Ontario Provincial Parks** exemplify superb interpretation through written and self-guiding facilities as well as personal services such as guided walks and evening programs. In some of the most popular parks, elaborate visitor centers and energetic outreach programs help multiply the interpretive effectiveness. This park system started the first officially organized programs of interpretation in Canada in the 1940s (Foley and Keith, 1979).

West Virginia State Parks offer "Nature and Recreation Programs" during three summer months at 18 parks, as well as year-round interpreters at four (McHenry, 1992). The goal, typical of most U.S. state park systems, aims to stimulate appreciation and awareness of the environment and to motivate involvement in the conservation of natural resources.

New York State's Adirondack Park Agency (APA), Division of Interpretive Programs, operates two new visitor centers in the heart of the 6-million acre Adirondack State Park, representing a cautious hop forward. A 1970 governor's study commission recommended APA involvement in interpretation, partly to assist local economies. In 1984, Governor Cuomo personally urged progress, finally achieved with the 1989 and 1990 dedications of the Visitor Interpretive Centers (Figure 2.15).

FIGURE 2.15
In large buildings with exhibits and auditoriums, two Adirondack Park Agency visitor centers which are surrounded by self-guiding trails produce intense programming for thousands of visitors.

The staff of nine, assisted by up to 100 volunteers, has two main interpretive purposes: (1) to influence the traveler in understanding the park's diverse resources and opportunities, and (2) to provide environmental education to schools and teachers. Collaborators include Paul Smiths College, St. Lawrence College, SUNY/Syracuse University, the nonprofit Adirondack Discovery organization (a superb volunteer interpretive lecture service itself), and the private Adirondack Museum. A private support group formed in 1989 as the Adirondack Park Institute, Inc. Its 1,000 members raised seed money allowing the interpreters to publish a Newsletter, to broadcast a radio program called Adirondack Field Notes, and to put on environmental education workshops. Visitor and teacher workshops, with a 25-volunteer steering committee, involved 10,000 participants in 1991.

Indiana's Department of Natural Resources offers year-round professional interpretation through its Divisions of State Parks, Reservoirs, Forestry, and Historic Preservation, as well as the State Museum. Several other divisions (Fish & Wildlife, Nature Preserves, Geological Survey) also support environmental education and interpretation. Permanent interpreters operate year-round at ten parks, four reservoirs, four memorials and one forest. Summer-time personnel additions provide interpretation in every state park and reservoir. They promote "intelligent use of leisure time." Five to seven programs per day plus visitor centers and self-guiding trails provide a full menu. In the other seasons, the permanent interpreters provide daily programs, school programs and special weekend events that each draw hundreds of visitors as well as keep the nature center operating. They write for newspapers and magazines; some produce weekly radio shows. For over 15 years, the interpretive team prepared and broadcast a weekly half-hour television program. In addition, the interpreters help keep track of endangered species and conduct special resource studies.

A distinct type of state-sanctioned nonprofit enterprise, **South Carolina Educational Television** employs a Director of Science and Nature Programming. He or she holds a natural history degree and serves as host of SC-ETV's Nature-Scene, featuring the diverse habitats of South Carolina, geology, fossils, native plants and animals of the state and the Southeast region of the U.S.

Tribal Interpretation

Several Tribes and American Indian Nations within North America developed strong interpretive programs and facilities. Navajo interpreters work at several National Park Service sites as well as guide visitors to the Monument Valley in Arizona. They led the formation of the Council for American Indian Interpretation, a branch of the National Association for Interpretation. Other groups provide the public a glimpse of their culture and skills through collaborating with private and public interpretive centers by offering special programs and demonstrations at major recreation areas. Three samples of tribal interpretive facilities follow.

Lac du Flambeau Chippewa Cultural Center and Museum, Lac du Flambeau, Wisconsin, built a beautiful small museum that interprets the history and culture of this branch of the Ojibway peoples. It displays artifacts, clothing, record-size fish, and interactions with European culture. At the center is an exhibit of the traditional way of life in the four seasons. Visitors walk in a circle around the four seasons exhibit—a subtle, powerful, kinesthetic interpretation using architectural symbolism.

Tsa-La-Gi, Tahlequah, Oklahoma, is one of many Cherokee Nation interpretive sites. In this authentic replica of 1700s Cherokee village and life, people work and play games, speaking only in their language, as Cherokee guides lead visitors through the village. Nearby, the Trail of Tears outdoor drama recounts the 1838-39 forced march from Georgia and Tennessee to Oklahoma.

Eklutna Village Historical Park, north of Anchorage, Alaska, provides visitors explanations of how native customs blended with the early Russian Orthodox evangelization, surviving together yet today (Figure 2.16). Owned by the small remnant of an Athapaskan village, the exhibits and explanations bring visitors into contact with native peoples in a very positive manner.

FIGURE 2.16
Eklutna Village, AK, residents interpret their traditions and history in a community-owned museum.

Federal Agencies

In the United States, six federal land managing agencies have major interpretive responsibilities. In addition, the Smithsonian Institution and other museum-oriented organizations offer valuable interpretive services. NASA also maintains a set of centers that interpret the space program (Figure 2.17). The efforts and policies of the six land agencies described here demonstrate the long traditions of some and emerging growth of others. Box 2.6 summarizes the qualifications sought for an interpretive position with the Forest Service, at a step or two above entry level.

FIGURE 2.17
The National Aeronautics and Space Administration (NASA) interprets many sites, including the Wallops Island Flight Facility's history through its interactive visitor center in Virginia.

BOX 2.6: A FEDERAL JOB: SKILLS NEEDED

A recent federal job announcement for an interpretive specialist included the following criteria on which a candidate would be evaluated:
1. Knowledge of interpretive planning concepts and ability to apply those concepts in public information and education programs.
2. Knowledge of effective graphic and interpretive design and skill in applying that knowledge to exhibits and other materials.
3. Ability to plan and conduct informational tours, interpretive talks, and public and internal presentations.
4. Ability to work effectively with diverse publics.

The job calls for a person with a full academic year of graduate study in a university or superior academic achievement as an undergraduate. The announcement also indicates preference for candidates with backgrounds in marketing, communications, or public relations. Pay is at GS-7 or GS-9 level.

NATIONAL FORESTS

The days have ended when the forest may be viewed only as trees and trees viewed only as timber. The soil and the water, the grasses and the shrubs, the fish and the wildlife, and the beauty that is the forest must become integral parts of resource managers' thinking and actions.

—Hubert Humphrey, 1976

The 191 million acres of national forests never were just commodities. In fact, in the early 1890s, President Benjamin Harrison proclaimed the first forest reserve (now Shoshone and Teton National Forests, Wyoming) to assure habitat for wildlife and the second (White River National Forest, Colorado) for its recreational and scenic values. Among its many products and services, the Forest Service includes recreation as a major component of its output—the agency provides more visitor-days of recreation than any other single agency in the U.S. Interpretation, although up and down since 1960, has new vigor and hope since about 1990.

Forest Service interpretive goals emphasize that the visitor should:
1. have an enjoyable experience, and
2. develop awareness, understanding and responsibility.

Out of this, the agency may achieve its ulterior management motives, that the visitor then becomes more supportive of the Forest Service's work. Interpretive programs can at least give a stronger sense of the agency's various public service roles, its functions and philosophies. In complex, multiple-use agencies such as the U.S. and State forest services and the Bureau of Land Management, sophisticated and energetic interpretation seems almost indispensable to effective understanding of the agency.

Yet, oddly, the Forest Service has had a very spotty record of interpretive effort. Brief periods of enthusiastic backing have alternated with long periods of inconsistent or weak support of interpretation. District and Forest officials have often maintained interpretive staff only through creative funding and innovative naming of interpretive positions. The results reveal themselves in lack of consistent programming, little continuity in natural history records and materials for national forests, and a fairly dispirited attitude toward professional interpretation among permanent professional employees.

In the federal Forest Service (and in many state forestry agencies), a few thoughtful and persistent people wrote intelligently and kept the idea of the benefits alive, at least on paper. Without consistent support, however, they could not develop a cadre of dedicated persons and traditions to demonstrate the value of interpretation. The tradition of interpretation has suffered some ruptures when unsympathetic or uninformed administrators at the district, forest, or regional level moved in and reassigned duties so that interpretation was virtually dismantled except in the politically popular visitor centers.

A 1988 analysis described the up and down association with interpretation. Guided walks, tours, campfire programs, slide shows, and so on, have long been associated with national forest recreation areas. "By the late 1970s, changing social values, strained government budgets, and the shift of public attention to other concerns all contributed to reductions in interpretive programming" (Forest Service, 1988). Recently, it reemerged. In 1990 and 1991, Chief Robertson and President Bush made major statements supporting high quality interpretive services, along with other initiatives. Limited funds began reaching the field in 1991, with steady growth in interpretive personnel. Time will tell whether this becomes another small swell on a choppy sea or a long-lasting support of an essential function that can serve the agency and the public well.

Along with the recent resurgence of interpreters have come innovations in: fees, private sector interpretation on public forests, combined federal and commercial travel interpretation, volunteers supplementing federal employees, and cooperating associations.

1. **Fees.** Visitors have indicated a willingness to pay for interpretive services. Increasingly, they pay fees for many types of quality interpretive programs.

2. **Private sector partnerships.** The Forest Service works with private outfitters, resorts, and other recreational businesses to blend interpretation into their amenity packages. In northern Minnesota, for example, the Forest Service and the Audubon Society train naturalists who work and live at resorts during the summer season. This helps the Forest Service get its messages of appropriate wilderness use and backcountry safety to the visitors entering federal lands from resorts. It also provides richer experiences for resort visitors.

3. **Travel interpretation.** Since 1970, USDA Forest Service interpreters have boarded various kinds of tour boats to interpret the Chugach and Tongass National Forests. A staff of ten interpreters services the four large (500-passenger) Alaska State Ferries in Southeast Alaska waters. An interpreter boards in Juneau, for example, for a 4-day round trip through the waterways that connect the communities in the Tongass National Forest. The interpreter operates a floating visitor center, offering a full array of programs. Narrative talks describe islands, glaciers, sea life, and regional ecology. They intersperse whale watches, bald eagle counts, and cultural interpretation with children's programs. Evening offerings include slide and film presentations. The interpreter goes to the information desk in a ship's lobby to help visitors plan their on-land expeditions. The Forest Service pays the interpreters, while the State Ferry System provides food and lodging. Forest Service interpreters also staff

a Gray Line tour boat and a small commercial ferry on the waters of the Chugach National Forest, paid for by the boat companies as part of their use permit. Similar arrangements exist for trains and buses elsewhere in the U.S.

4. **Volunteers.** Volunteers and student interns have replaced or supplemented seasonal interpretive staff on many federal properties. The long tradition of local parks and historical sites using volunteer guides started to grow on federal forest lands as the agency cut back services and employees in the 1980s. Local "friends" groups offered to provide services; the Forest Service embraced the help under the name of "partnerships."

5. **Cooperating Associations.** Private associations at national forest areas sell interpretive books, maps, and materials without going through the cumbersome federal treasury accounts. In 1987, there were 39 interpretive associations working with national forests in the U.S. (Forest Service, 1988).

NATIONAL WILDLIFE REFUGES

The U.S. Fish and Wildlife Service (FWS) of the Department of the Interior manages 90 million acres of federal lands, 85 percent of which are in Alaska. About 450 National Wildlife Refuges conserve habitat for migratory birds and other animals. The 345 refuges now open for public recreation and interpretation host about 37 million visitors annually.

Interpretation and education comprise an integral part of the policy of the Fish and Wildlife Service. The 1980 Service Management Plan contains specific goal statements to support the overall mission. The Interpretation and Recreation Service goal aims: "To inform and educate the public on environmental issues affecting fish and wildlife resources and provide compatible recreation on Service lands" (U.S. Fish and Wildlife Service, 1980). That word compatible gives refuge administrators room to restrict or expand interpretation.

National operational policies in that plan include the following: "Through educational activities, the FWS shall advance and exemplify the principles and practices of conservation and sound management . . . for the public's natural, cultural and recreational needs" (U.S. Fish and Wildlife Service, 1980).

The agency works with outdoor classrooms, interprets to recreation visitors, and supplies educational assistance for schools. On most properties, the current guideline is to focus interpretation on the wildlife species of that property.

Recent hiring of "Outdoor Recreation Planners" for interpretive work has brought many new individuals into the refuges. Few were prepared for interpretive work but sought to learn through professional meetings of the National Association of Interpreters and other groups.

Recent Fish and Wildlife Service policy ". . . placed a very high priority on the interpretation of wildlife values . . . " (Keystone Policy Dialogue, 1991). Publications, signing, exhibits, and visitor centers comprise the main interpretive tools. Many refuges also have active environmental education programs, with teacher workshops and development of outdoor classrooms. By the early 1990s, about 70 people were assigned to interpretation, with at least ten of those in regional offices. Thus, the Congress and the Office of Management and Budget had provided only enough personnel funds to average one interpreter per six refuges. For the 345 refuges open to the public for recreational use, 60 field interpreters were available (Keystone Policy Dialogue, 1991), supplemented by seasonal help. Despite the low numbers, however, excellent interpretive centers and programs operate in selected refuges. On the other sites, the Service relies heavily on administrative or research personnel, nonpersonal interpretation, and the work of volunteers.

Contracts with private interpretive firms produce virtually all the folders, signs, and exhibits through the Division of Refuges. The Office of Training and Education works on environmental education curricula and teaching materials. Excellent materials produced for schools and youth groups in the 1970s were out of print by the mid-1980s; renewing these or similar materials is a current objective. In 1992, no educational outreach program existed service-wide, but it grew quickly from 1993 on. Most interpretive functions fall to employees with the titles Park Ranger, Environmental Education Specialist, Biological Technician, or Outdoor Recreation Planner. People with other job titles, such as Watchable Wildlife Coordinator, Volunteer Coordinator, and others, also do some interpretive work.

Interpretive subject matter includes ecosystem functions, habitat requirements for different species, interrelationships among species, resource management methods and reasons, and identification of the different birds and mammals; in some refuges, reptiles, amphibians, fish, and plants are also featured. The Service publishes some of its information as study reports, articles, plans, brochures and other documents sent to administrative, technical, and lay audiences.

The Fish and Wildlife Service opened a new Service Training Center near Harpers Ferry, West Virginia in 1995. This provided a new dimension to the agency's growing dedication to interpretation, providing time and resources for regular training of interpreters.

This agency should benefit tremendously from carefully conceived interpretation. Its financial support has traditionally come mostly from hunters and fishermen who pay taxes and license fees that are earmarked for Fishing and Wildlife Service activities. Perhaps this guaranteed income has contributed to a relatively low sense of urgency for providing interpretation for the rest of the public. Yet, growing urban-based antipathy toward hunting could suggest the wisdom of providing wildlife-based interpretive services to aid in public support. As general appropriations become more important to funding, memorable interpretive experiences could help boost support of the refuge idea.

Most National Wildlife Refuges need interpretation to help make them attractive to people. Many refuges offer unspectacular views, except to people who appreciate the complexity of flat and wet landscapes (or very dry in some cases). On many refuges, the nonfishing/nonhunting visitor comes on a summer or fall weekend to enjoy the refuge and finds relatively few services. The Service provides a driving tour with a brochure or signs along the way. In some of the larger refuges, visitor centers contain excellent displays of waterfowl, local mammals, and ecology.

Two explanations come from field people: (1) the refuge is for the wildlife, not recreation, and (2) hardly anyone comes anyway. The first attitude suggests a narrow view of "recreation" and public use as if they were incompatible with the wildlife mission. It ignores interpretation as a key form of recreation. It seems to ignore the importance of aiding public perception of wildlife habitat. It fails to attract visitors to develop their appreciative forms of recreation. Good personal interpretation would help the visitor see that these rather modest-looking places and their wild inhabitants have special values and characteristics. The visitor could leave feeling that this is one of the great places, because of a memorable

experience. This takes knowledgeable and skillful interpreters backed by generous administrators. Recent interpretive efforts have attracted many more visitors to refuges.

Although many refuges still operate interpretive services as if most visits occur during
"normal government" weekday working hours, except during hunting season, a few provide
outstanding services. One example, the Chincoteague National Wildlife Refuge in Virginia,
offers porch talks, guided hikes, audiovisual shows, many useful identification brochures,
self-guiding trails, auto tours, evening programs, and a fine exhibit center. The Kenai National Wildlife Refuge has a major interpretive center near Soldotna, Alaska, including a
rustic environmental education facility, self-guiding trails, and an information cabin near the
eastern portal of the refuge.

In Canada, the Canadian Wildlife Service (CWS) also has a charge to provide interpretation programs, which it has carried out with excellent environmental centers at a few key
locations across the country. The Canada Wildlife Act of 1973 authorized the Minister of
Environment to promote and encourage interpretation including establishing facilities. The
Minister may also enter into agreements with provinces or other organizations to conduct
interpretive programs. The objective of wildlife interpretation, according to CWS policy, is
"to encourage and to provide opportunities for the development of awareness, enjoyment,
understanding and appreciation of Canada's wildlife heritage and its environment" (Foley
and Keith, 1979).

NATIONAL PARKS

Throughout the world, national parks and interpretation go together almost automatically.
The U.S. model carries the tradition of a living museum, where people can learn about their
natural and cultural heritage from diverse interpretive media. Such diverse countries as
Costa Rica, Brazil, South Africa, Kenya, Taiwan, Indonesia, Russia, and New Zealand provide well-trained, technical, permanent interpreters in at least some of their national parks.

The **National Parks Authority of England** offers regular interpretation through the
Countryside Commission employees. Approved private guides, however, lead many of the summertime guided walks and tours. They charge a modest fee for one to two hours. The procedure
amounts to meeting the guide at a trail head at the scheduled time, paying the fee, and setting off
with a group on the walk, al-
most always superbly interpreted (Figure 2.18). Countryside Commission rangers
offer free evening programs,
slide shows, and reference
information at the offices and
community buildings in the
parks.

FIGURE 2.18
*Approved private interpreters
lead guided walks in British
National Parks for a modest fee
(about US$2.00/person).*

Parks Canada, following the leads of the Provincial Parks of Ontario (1940s) and British Columbia (1950s), officially entered the interpretive field in the early 1960s (Foley and Keith, 1979). The national parks policy on interpretation states: "Interpretive programs will be provided to encourage an understanding and enjoyment of the park's natural values and to develop an awareness of man's relationship to and dependence on the natural environment." This had its foundation in the National Parks Act of 1930: "The parks are hereby dedicated to the people of Canada for their benefit, education and enjoyment . . . "

The **U.S. National Park Service** (NPS) has included interpretation in its programming since 1920; previous to that, private guides, scientists, and individual park superintendents provided interpretive services. Recent policy (National Park Service, 1988) stated:

> The National Park Service will conduct interpretive programs in all parks to instill an understanding and appreciation of the value of parks and their resources; to develop public support for preserving park resources; to provide the information necessary to ensure the successful adaptation of visitors to park environments; and to encourage and facilitate appropriate, safe, minimum-impact use of park resources.

This internal policy statement described a strong focus on the agency and the resource, rather than on visitor experiences. In practice, however, most NPS interpreters reverse the priority; they serve the agency by serving the people. To accomplish the goals of support and help to the park (ulterior motives), you must enhance visitor enjoyment and enrichment—through understanding, awareness, orientation, and positive provocation. A more detailed summary of the nature of NPS programming appears in Box 2.7.

BOX 2.7: INTERPRETIVE PROGRAM POLICY

U.S. National Park Service policy defines a six-part balanced interpretive program (National Park Service, 1988):
1. Information and Orientation—easy access to information needed for a safe and enjoyable park experience.
2. Understanding and Appreciation—foster deeper understanding of resources and values of the park, its regional context, and the National Park system.
3. Protection—offer a variety of opportunities to interact safely with and enjoy park resources while protecting the resources from overuse, damage, vandalism, and theft.
4. Participation and Skill Development—aid and motivate recreational skill development where appropriate.
5. Dialogue—provide means for communication of thoughts and desires among the public, neighbors, and park managers.
6. Education—provide interested users and educational groups with information needed to develop a thorough understanding of a park's resources, its regional context and the entire National Park system's significance and values.

Practice

Each park builds its interpretive program around themes based on that park's legislative history, its resources, and the broader NPS management goals. Management policies (NPS, 1988) state that "Interpretation will be based on research about the history, science, and condition of the resources, and on research about the needs, expectations, and behavior of visitors."

NPS officials have long supported interpretation. Once called education, then education and research, now interpretation, the activity has received the plaudits of most directors, if not the wholehearted support of Congress and field superintendents. Recent directors Mott and Ridenour often referred to interpreters as the keys to success of the national parks. This echoed the sentiments of the first director, Stephen T. Mather, who started hiring interpreters in 1920 with his personal funds.

Interpretive methods in the NPS can be roughly grouped into five categories:
1. Personal services—a cornerstone, long a tradition, considered in policy as the "most effective means of stimulating visitor understanding and appreciation...."
2. Publications—books, leaflets, maps, brochures, trail guides.
3. Exhibits—in museums, signs, waysides.
4. Audiovisual presentations.
5. Outreach services—environmental education, heritage education, other community and national programming.

In Glacier Bay National Park, NPS interpreters board 1,500-passenger cruise liners for a day, providing narratives and responses to questions from the bridge plus distributing and selling documents and educational publications. The ship's entry to the bay requires a fee for a special use permit; this helps pay for the interpreters. Cruise advertising invariably mentions NPS interpreters as an attraction.

Shiloh National Military Park, Tennessee, includes a visitor center with exhibits, a 25-minute film, guided walks and talks, supplemented by a self-guiding auto tour of the battlefield. The tour map and outdoor displays help to provide orientation to the ground on which the 1862 action took place.

At Fort Davis National Historic Site, Texas, a continuing program of restoration has saved and restored one-half of the original fort structures. The visitor center and museum, open daily year-around, provide audio programs, a slide show, and self-guiding tours of the grounds and several buildings are provided year-around. Costumed interpreters highlight the summer seasons by conducting tours, presenting demonstrations of frontier military life, and offering roving interpretation. An extensive self-guiding trail system leads visitors through parts of the property.

San Antonio Missions National Historical Park staff does historical, archæological, and preservation studies of the early history of Texas. Exhibits, tours, cultural demonstrations, and the stones themselves tell the story of the past, while the churches in the missions continue to serve their parishes.

CORPS OF ENGINEERS PROJECTS

The U.S. Army Corps of Engineers (COE) got into the civil works business in 1936. Its first tasks were to improve navigation and reduce the flooding hazards on the Mississippi River and its tributaries. By 1944, the organization got into the recreation business on the many reservoirs it was building. Not until 1965, however, could the Corps claim recreation as a legitimate benefit in project calculations for Congress. Now, the Corps manages nearly 2,000 water resource projects (Figure 2.19). Its civilian interpretive personnel help in administering an extensive recreation and conservation program at nearly 450 lakes plus navigation sites and levees. As the world's largest provider of water-based recreation, the agency controls 4,400 recreation areas, hosting 640 million visitors per year on two percent of the federal estate. At most flood control reservoirs, the Corps or a cooperating state agency provides interpretation through visitor centers and frequent outdoor programs.

FIGURE 2.19
The Army Corps of Engineers interprets its huge research model of San Francisco Bay.

The COE defines the function as: "Interpretive services are those communication services provided to the project visitors and others, which support management objectives and goals, tell the Corps story, and/or reveal meanings of and relationships between man-made, natural, cultural and other project features." (U.S. Army Corps of Engineers, Regiment 1130-2-428). The Corps' basic interpretive objectives include (Marcy, 1985):

    a. orient the public to the project,
    b. enhance visitor understanding and enjoyment of the project,
    c. aid in achieving management objectives, and
    d. gain public support by explaining Corps activities.

This strong project focus probably arises from COE awareness of public opinion. As Marcy (1985) put it:

> Many times the Corps is highly regarded in geographical areas that have experienced destructive flooding prior to the construction of flood control projects. However, there may also be individuals and organizations who look with disfavor upon the Corps for perceived adverse effects from these projects. In either case, it is vitally important for the public to know what the Corps' functions are, and the methods it uses to achieve specific objectives.

Interpretive services include:
- working the information desk,
- roving interpretation on the various recreation sites around each lake,
- slide presentations,
- hikes,
- school group programs,
- talks on and off property,
- signs and exhibits,
- brochures and publications,
- special events and festivals,
- campfire programs,
- self-guiding trails.

The Corps of Engineers sees itself as a steward of resources. Darrell Lewis, as COE Chief of Natural Resources, called for greater effort in environmental education for the public—"it is vital." The COE can also help spread use to the various resources around reservoirs by better information services to their visitors. Water safety occupies interpreters as a major message of their work (Chenoweth and Lee, 1989). The agency seeks stronger professionalization of the interpreter and recreation ranger series.

The Bonneville Lock and Dam Project, Washington/Oregon, interprets to 600,000 visitors per year through two visitor centers, an auditorium, three fish ladders, two historical sites, and display ponds in a fish hatchery. Corps of Engineers direct-hire career interpreters do the job.

The Hiram M. Chittenden Lock and Dam, Seattle, Washington, likewise interprets fish migration, maritime transportation, and history. Here, contract interpreters supervise the elaborate exhibit center, fish ladder exhibits, and historic flower gardens. A California businessman won a recent bid, hired experienced interpreters, and oversaw training. The Corps assures respectable levels of pay and quality of the work.

In addition to these two sites, the agency is most famous for its complete interpretive programs at hundreds of reservoirs throughout much of the nation.

BUREAU OF LAND MANAGEMENT

The biggest federal landowner in the U.S. has millions of acres of desert, rangelands, tundra and taiga—not the "pretty" places of standard tourism. A 1976 law gave the Bureau of Land Management (BLM) a mandate to manage these lands permanently for multiple uses—including recreation. At the same time, growing use put pressures on the desert resource and particularly artifacts from previous cultures. Interpretation came into play as a key to stronger management. Several visitor centers at key locations offer information to people to encourage seeing the BLM properties as something besides wastelands.

This agency, usually identified with desert grasslands, features tidal pools, seabirds, seals, and whales at the BLM's Yaquina Head Outstanding Natural Area, Newport, Oregon. Looming over the Pacific, steep cliffs support an 1872 lighthouse. Personal interpretation programs and roving naturalists enrich the opportunities for visitors.

One of the finest interpretive facilities anywhere is the BLM's Anasazi Cultural Heritage Center, near Dolores, Colorado. This facility offers a superb up-to-date interpretive museum. The surrounding environment suggests that the Ancient Ones are still there. Located on the Dominguez-Escalante Trail, it has small Anasazi ruins just outside the stunning southwestern building. The site offers beautiful views of Mesa Verde and Sleeping Ute Mountain—part of a Ute Reservation. The nearby McPhee Reservoir attracts many visitors to the area. Its construction prompted much of the archæological work. In the museum, visitors may imagine themselves in various environments and cogitate about how people survived on this arid Colorado Plateau. After studying life-size dioramas and models of the distant past, one can check comprehension on several computer quiz games that reinforce principles, key concepts, and survival strategies.

TENNESSEE VALLEY AUTHORITY (TVA)

This seven-state federal agency modified rivers and created reservoirs. Its primary purpose was to promote economic development in poverty stricken rural areas by providing inexpensive electricity and barge shipping. It ended up in the outdoor recreation business, often by helping states and counties to develop and interpret their parks systems, as well as managing and interpreting TVA lands along the reservoirs.

TVA's biggest interpretive program, however, operates at Land Between the Lakes (LBL), a 170,000-acre recreation demonstration property in Western Kentucky and Tennessee. Here, interpretation and environmental education focus on visitors and residents of local communities. Attractions include Homeplace—1850, a 19th century living history farm; Woodlands Nature Center, where visitors can see live wildlife exhibits and learn about natural resources; and Empire Farm, which has domestic animals, an observation beehive, and activities such as sheep shearing and weaving. A large buffalo herd roams a 200-acre pasture in LBL. The staff also provides a variety of environmental education programs, recreation and interpretive services for campers at several large campgrounds, the central orientation/interpretive center, and a group camp. Upward mobility for interpreters exists in TVA; the current Administrator of the LBL project worked many years in environmental education at Land Between the Lakes.

Summary

Diversity characterizes the interpretive field. No agency nor type of interpretation has a corner on the market. Cultural and natural resources interpreters can use many of the same techniques and principles, even though they work in widely different environments. All seek to provide visitors opportunities to better enjoy and understand their surroundings—in both space and time.

The chapter should drive out any misconceptions that interpretation involves only a few national park people out talking with the bird watchers and history buffs, that interpretation has nothing to do with business and industry, or that interpretation is a new thing, fabricated out of recent environmental concerns.

Rather:

1. The profession involves tens of thousands of interpreters in virtually every community, paid by thousands of employers in North America.
2. It appears to be expanding rapidly.
3. It should seek to engage all citizens, from beginners to the experts, from children to adults.
4. Interpretation serves many industries and private philanthropists as well as being a major and growing private business in itself, while still serving a large public agency market.
5. Museums, parks, forests, and camps have hired interpreters through many decades. The educational and recreational functions of these organizations have grown with an urbanized population and increasing public demand including that for interpretive services.

Literature Cited

Chenoweth, D. and Lee, S. (1989). Corps training in recreation interpretation. *Recnotes* [US Army COE], R-89(1):5-7.

Erickson, D. M. (1992). Live via satellite. In *Proceedings, National Interpreters Workshop*, NAI. San Francisco Bay Area, CA.

Fish and Wildlife Service. (1980). *Service management plan.* Washington, DC: U.S. Deptartment of the Interior.

Foley, J. P. and Keith, J. A. (1979). Interpretation in Canadian national parks and related resources—To what end? In *Conference II, Canadian National Parks Today and Tomorrow.* Ontario, Canada: University of Waterloo.

Follows, D. (1992). Resource interpretation as value-added product. In *Proceedings, National Interpreters Workshop*, NAI. San Francisco Bay Area, CA.

Follows, D. S. (1988). Resource interpretation: The transfusion into Alaska's tourism industry. In *Proceedings, National Interpreters Workshop*, NAI. San Diego, CA.

Forest Service. (1988). *An analysis of the outdoor recreation and wilderness situation in the United States: 1989-2040* (draft). Washington, DC: U.S. Department of Agriculture.

Humphrey, H. (1976). Comments on the National Forest Management Act. *122 Congressional Record 5610* (March 5).

Hutcherson, A. (1993). Teaching teachers about the forest. *Tree Farmer*, (Winter, 1993):11.

Keystone Policy Dialogue. (1991). *Biological diversity on federal lands, final consensus report.* Keystone, CO: The Keystone Center.

Marcy, J. B. (1985). Multi-faceted interpretation. *Trends*, 22(4):32-36.

McHenry, K. (1992). *1991 summer nature and recreation program attendance report.* Charleston, WV: West Virginia State Parks, internal report.

National Park Service. (1988). *Management policies.* Washington, DC: U.S. Dept. of the Interior.

Percy, D. O. (1981). *Living historical farms: The working museums.* Accokeek, MD: Accokeek Foundation, Inc.

Sea World of Florida. (1992). *Education department 1992 year-end report.* Orlando, FL.

Shomon, J. J. (1990). Community nature centers: Their history, development, and impact on environmental awareness. In *Proceedings, National Interpreters Workshop*, NAI, Charleston, SC.

Snyder, G. (1992). White Fawn: Apache/Cherokee teaches respect for traditional ways. *Outdoor Indiana 57*(5):30-35.

The art of interpretation is a powerful means for revealing that the land can react with kindness or with disastrous retaliations, depending on how it is treated . . . Knowing this is to know wisdom and delight in living life, as a person, as a citizen, as a bit of Earth's life. People do not understand land automatically. They must be shown. And they must have come to be shown because the story and its telling are more attractive than anything else they might do at the time.

—Yorke Edwards, 1979

If you asked several interpreters why they chose to work in their profession, you would probably get several different answers. Most interpreters find fascination in cultural and natural history. They find delight in continuing their quest for knowledge in these subject areas. Most interpreters have a genuine affinity for interacting with people and sharing their knowledge. Most enjoy interpreting much more than they would doing anything else; they receive pay for what they love to do.

For some interpreters it started as a calling, a profession, a commitment; for others it was mere serendipity. Many seek to "make a difference" in society with dedication and zeal. So, interpretation may be more than a job or occupation; rather it becomes a way of life, marked by depth of knowledge, a sense of wonder, serenity, and fulfillment. According to Barry Lopez, this is a high calling that many in our society don't recognize (Beck, 1989).

Although most interpreters commit to their work, some find it difficult to articulate precisely why their agency devotes scarce resources to provide an interpretive service. Yet, they often find it critical to explain the purposes and benefits of their work to agency administrators, fund-appropriating bodies, and the visiting public. Failure to do so clearly and convincingly may result in limited support for interpretation.

Some interpretation advocates say simply that "interpretation is a good thing." Clearer articulation would describe for whom and for what it is beneficial. This allows the professional to develop programs with a purpose, to analyze their effectiveness, and to account for the resources spent to produce that interpretation.

The real aim of interpretation is to affect people positively. It's about getting people excited about observing and studying what's around them. It gives them basic information and direction. It provokes and equips them to better interpret for themselves. An interpreter and the local interpretive center can serve as a long-term reference and personal growth center, where repeat visitors can reinforce and stretch their grasp of what they are finding in their personal interpretation. Such a center also serves as a meeting place for people of common interests, a place where they can act as a community of citizens, sharing their insights and concerns, developing strategies for constructive action to better understand and improve their cultural and natural environment.

Three major types of benefits result from interpretation: benefits to the individuals who participate, benefits to society in general, and benefits to the agency or company providing the interpretive services. Most of these benefits are hard to measure directly, but they are very real and worth considerable investment.

When an interpreter is at work, the primary focus is on benefiting individuals. This leads to the social benefits of an informed society whose citizens are in tune with their cultural and natural environment (Chapter 3). The benefits to the agency (Chapter 4) can be regarded as fortunate but incidental outcomes or by-products of an effective service to the public. Thus, interpretation differs from sales, advertising or publicity, where the primary beneficiary is the agency/company.

Sophisticated but Poorly Informed Visitors

Historic sites once served as shrines to the leaders of the nation's early years or to the fighters in our few wars. Their stories were taught by schools and family oral traditions. Therefore, the people visiting the sites already knew the meaning of the place and the value of the person/people to society. Should anyone arrive uninformed, another visitor could easily fill in some of the details. As the nation ages and history grows more complex, visitors don't have the same background information. The shrines may not communicate adequately to convey the old meanings of many historic places. Nevertheless, the visitor is both more sophisticated and less well informed than in the past. The interpreter needs to gauge the amount of understanding and knowledge the average visitor brings to the site, then determine how much interpretation to offer and its character.

Environmentally, many citizens show their sophisticated global breadth but shallow local depth. Interpreters are needed to help deepen environmental knowledge that urbanization and industry have handicapped (Van Tighem, 1990):

> Today there are thousands of people who never leave the urban illusion, except enclosed within the protective skin of a car or airplane. There are grown adults who have never breathed real air. There are thousands and thousands of children who will never have to worry about being eaten by a carnivore or dying of hypothermia.
>
> What do you call someone who wants to see wolves eliminated from national parks because they kill things?
>
> ... the industrial revolution was successful in at least one regard: it has isolated mankind from that which makes mankind real—the biosphere that sustains us, and of which we are one element.
>
> What do you call someone who drives five blocks to the grocery store and then complains about the smog? What do you call the sort of person who believes they have a God-given right to own a Jacuzzi,™ or a motorized tricycle?

Our environmental handicaps arise from our incompleteness, our lack of understanding, our loss of contact with what we are and what supports us. Interpreters are needed to help complete us, to reduce our handicaps.

One more seldom-discussed reason to interpret is to develop local support for conservation or historic preservation. Interpreters persuade the local citizens about the special nature of the area. Interpreters develop and enlist the communites'protective feelings rather than fighting the citizen's desire to declassify the park, the wilderness, the public ownership, to close down the museum, or to try to discredit the private owners. Somehow, local audiences can be the toughest clients. Cantankerous and greedy neighbors exist virtually everywhere. Some seem to oppose virtually any project that isn't their own. In public policy, the neighbors often carry clout that far exceeds their proportion of votes. Malcontents may not be changed by interpretation (surely not by propaganda), but they may face a rising tide of informed community members who support the museum or property.

Hiram Chittenden, Army Corps of Engineers, designed the roads in Yellowstone. He wrote of the local hostility problem that still exists near that great park, even among some of the state and federal Congressional delegations (Chittenden, 1895):

> To most people it will seem impossible that there should be any one who would seek the mutilation or destruction of this important reservation. Unfortunately there are many such. No session of Congress for twenty years has been free from attempted legislation hostile to the Park. The schemes to convert it into an instrument of private greed have been many, and strange as it may seem, they are invariably put forward by those very communities to whom the Park is, and must ever remain, the chief glory of their section. It is lamentable proof of the dearth of patriotic spirit that always betrays itself whenever the interests of individuals and of the public come into collision. . . .
>
> It will not do, however, to assume that because these schemes have hitherto failed, they will always continue to fail. Since they have their origin in speculative ventures, they will be put forward so long as they offer the least pecuniary inducement.

Interpreters and managers are trustees, not owners, of our national, state, and local heritage. Why interpret? To protect the public and private investment in the resource or the artifact collection by making it useful. Interpretation adds value to a museum, park, forest, industry, camp, etc., by helping its customers enjoy it more, learn more about it, make it part of their own lives. Interpretation basically serves these enterprises by making them valuable to customers. More directly, interpretation also serves the customers by enriching their own understanding of their environment and culture and their own relationships to it. Interpretation also serves the owners or managing agencies by helping people understand the needs and processes of management and developing empathy with the organization through intelligent, nonpropagandistic explanations.

Voyageurs give Scouts a sense of the transportation of the past during an historical festival.

Literature Cited

Beck, L. (1989). Conversations with Barry Lopez: Musings on interpretation. *Journal of Interpretation 13(3)*:

Chittenden, H. M. (1895). *The Yellowstone National Park*. Norman, OK: Oklahoma University Press (1964 reprint).

Edwards, Y. (1979). The land speaks: Organizing and running an interpretation system. Toronto, ON: The National and Provincial Parks Association of Canada.

Van Tighem, K. (1990). Words, perception and subversion. *InterpScan 18(1)*:8-9.

Values to People and Society

One of the things about being human is learning to see beyond the ordinary.

—Anonymous

Everybody needs beauty as well as bread,
places to play in as well as pray in
where nature may heal and cheer and
give strength to beauty and soul alike.

—John Muir

Why do people choose to spend their leisure time visiting nature centers and museums, attending interpretive programs and going on history tours or nature walks? Apparently, they derive some satisfaction or pleasure from interpretation or they would not attend voluntarily. Apparently, society derives enough benefit to provide public and private funds for the work of curators, interpreters, educators, and their often impressive places of work. This chapter explores some of the benefits which interpretation can provide to individuals and society.

Many interpreters are "public servants" in the legal sense, in that their salaries come from local, state, or federal tax dollars. Many other interpreters work directly for pay-as-you-go clients. All interpreters can strive to truly act as servants of the public in the broadest sense, in principle and spirit (Tilden, 1967). They can practice their profession with the attitude and motivation to serve others and fully achieve the potential impact of interpretation.

Benefits to the Individual

An interpreter basically seeks to enrich the experience of each individual client. The interpreter (especially at the local level) may seek to help enrich a client throughout an entire lifetime through repeated participation in progressive interpretive programs. This vision suggests an interpreter-client relationship through a long period of years, complementing those specialists who interpret at once-in-a-lifetime attractions, seeing individual visitors on unique occasions.

The benefits received by individuals can be classified as educational, recreational, and inspirational.

EDUCATIONAL BENEFITS

Traditional definitions of interpretation focused on the educational aspects of the interpretive experience. For example, Tilden's (1967) formal definition of interpretation begins with the statement that interpretation is "an educational activity . . ."

The learning experience associated with interpretation received more study and documentation than any other type of benefit. During the 1970s and early 1980s, numerous studies measured learning from exhibits and interpretive programs (e.g., Lime, Anderson, and Mech, 1978; Gallup and Risk, 1981; Lee, 1981).

Many people attend interpretive programs or facilities because they find that acquiring knowledge is an enjoyable and enriching experience itself. By having more knowledge about the cultural or natural resources of an area, their visit (or their home territory) becomes more meaningful and enjoyable (Figure 3.1). For example, knowing the best places to see rare birds in a forest facilitates an enjoyable experience for a visiting bird watcher. Likewise, understanding unique geologic features could prompt a family to stop and look closely at what otherwise might have seemed to be "just rocks."

FIGURE 3.1
Interpretation helps people perceive the beauty in the commonplace. (NPS)

Interpreters with the Missouri Department of Conservation formally linked the educational goals of individual interpretive programs with the state-mandated public education competencies and learner outcomes. Teachers get a list of competencies addressed in state interpretive programs. Linking these programs with public school curricula can be a win-win situation for the school administrators, the teachers, the students and the interpreters.

RECREATIONAL BENEFITS

Although people find learning to be a positive experience, most don't spend their leisure time seeking to attend dry, technical lectures. In fact, some are repelled at the thought of attending interpretive programs just because they imagine (or remember) them as too focused on the dull educational approach that exercises the mind in unpleasant ways. (Hultsman, Cottrell, and Hultsman, 1987). This does not mean that providing a recreational experience should be taken lightly nor that its results are frivolous nor merely entertaining.

Most interpreters offer their programs at recreational areas for people using leisure time. A useful guideline is that all interpretation should be recreational. Tilden (1967) recognized this: " . . . we cannot forget that people are with us mainly seeking enjoyment, not instruction." Therefore, seek to produce interpretation that is fun—stimulating, pleasurable, compelling fun—that produces true happiness and satisfaction.

Twenty-three hundred years ago, in his book *Politics*, Aristotle linked the existence of the "state" with the purpose of securing happiness for its citizens. He stressed that leisure time is the resource of true citizenship, that individuals should be able to use leisure time well. Leisure is better than work and is its end, according to Aristotle.

In the Declaration of Independence of the United States of America, Thomas Jefferson included the "pursuit of happiness" as one of three inalienable rights. True happiness produces more than temporary giddiness or some level of passing materialistic satisfaction.

In a very real sense, interpreters who provide meaningful recreational experience help "manufacture" happiness. That is, they provide the opportunity and context for pleasurable experiences. They help make a visit to a nature preserve, an historic home, or a seashore a richer, more memorable event because of something that they help the visitor do better or comprehend more readily. They make the special significance of the place more evident, thus enriching the visit.

Pleasant experiences seem necessary to maintain a high quality of life. They decrease stress (Selye, 1975), increase self-reliance and self esteem (Dustin, McAvoy and Beck, 1986), and improve mental and physical health (Levitt, 1991; Paffenbarger, Hyde and Dow, 1991).

John Burroughs (1916), the early naturalist, wrote that:

> To absorb a thing is better than to learn it, and we absorb what we enjoy. I am not merely contented, like Wordsworth's poetry, to enjoy what others understand. I must understand also; but above all things, I must enjoy. How much of my enjoyment springs from my knowledge I do not know. The joy of knowing is very great; the delight of picking up the threads of meaning here and there, and following them through the maze of confusing facts, I know well. To enjoy understandingly, that, I fancy, is the great thing to be desired.

Burroughs' succinct goal to "enjoy understandingly" presents a balanced approach to education and recreation that could serve as both a personal goal for interpreters and for their audiences, regardless of the media used (Cable, 1992).

Most researchers find it hard to quantify recreational benefits, even more so than educational benefits. Hence, fewer studies have measured these benefits. However, some participant surveys have revealed responses that indicated pleasurable satisfaction.

Virtually everyone who participated in wolf howling expeditions (Lime et al., 1978), eagle watches (Maupin, Witter, and Basset, 1980), prairie days (Maupin, Basset, Catlin, and Witter, 1982), and family nature classes (Gennao, Sigford, and Heller, 1983) found the programs enjoyable. Keyes and Hammitt (1983) reported that interpretive signs along major trails improved the recreational experiences of hikers. Moscardo (1988) developed a model based on the concept of "mindfulness" (alertness, awareness of the nature of a museum or area). Through a series of correlational analyses, he could link this state of mind to characteristics of exhibits. It related positively to visitor satisfaction.

INSPIRATIONAL BENEFITS

Good interpretation is fun, but the best interpretation moves one beyond the recreational to inspirational experiences.

Discovering the beauty in the workmanship of a piece of antique furniture, in a special adaptation of an insect, or in a majestic panoramic view is neither strictly educational nor merely "fun." It stretches the mind to something more. The feelings generated by such interpretive experiences can move a person profoundly, almost indescribably, making them very difficult to measure. Indeed, one of the characteristics of optimal experiences can be described by the word ineffability, that is, the inability to fully articulate the meaning of the experience (Maslow, 1962).

Enos Mills (1920) emphasized the inspirational component of interpretation: "a nature guide . . . is not a teacher. At all times, however, he has been rightfully associated with information and some form of education. But nature guiding, as we see it, is more inspirational than informational."

In other words, the interpreter's mission goes beyond just cajoling visitors into superficial awareness of key facts. The strong interpretive program will propel the participants along toward richer living, born of more sensitivity and action favoring their cultural and natural heritage, past, present, and future. A strong program develops the interpretive capability of the participant. It trains people to interpret their surroundings for themselves, not just to look, listen, and laugh. It should produce people whose sensitivities are changed, who walk closer to and lighter on their cultural and natural environments.

Interpreters can inspire by enhancing people's ability to sense quality in their surroundings. "Our ability to perceive quality in nature begins, as in art, with the pretty. It expands through successive stages of the beautiful to values as yet uncaptured by language" (Leopold, 1966). An interpreter assists people as they move through these stages so that eventually the individual will not only perceive beauty in and be inspired by spectacular mountain scenery, but by tall-grass prairie and cattail marsh as well (Figure 3.2).

In other words, the professional interpreter's function goes beyond that of an actor or character reciting a memorized spiel to visitors passing by and offering little else. The interpreter with only one campfire talk—even two—put on twice per week may be effective at a major tourist attraction where visitors come once in a lifetime. But where visitors come back, repeating the same house tour, alligator or sled dog history talk every week may do less than inspire the participants. It will almost surely cause interpreter burn-out.

FIGURE 3.2
*Even "seaweed" provokes a
story from a skilled interpreter.
(NPS, Richard Frear)*

INTERPRETIVE GROWTH PROCESS

Where the interpreter has the luxury of repeat visitors, opportunities for a long-term visitor growth process lie awaiting. It may consist of a three-day program for campers or a twenty-year set of skills set up by the interpreter and local experts. For example, a local nature center or historical museum usually has life members who could seek interpretive benefits for ten years or more. A progressive curriculum of reading, events and skill lessons could enhance their pleasure and intrigue with their surroundings all through their membership. Within this framework, an interpreter can set major goals, then specific targets for each client. Thus, the interpreter becomes a professional guide and counselor to the life (or repeat) member, offering stepwise progression through a menu of scaled interpretive opportunities. The interpreter's job can become more than a series of talks, exhibits and newsletters. It involves helping clients become experts at subjects such as local history, pioneer gardening, practical skills and crafts (Figure 3.3), bird behavior, tree biology and structure, and ecosystem dynamics.

FIGURE 3.3
*Coopers develop their skills at
Cooperstown in a one-week workshop
at the Farmers Museum.*

STRIKING A BALANCE

Including recreational, educational, and inspirational facets of interpretation in a balanced way in every interpretive task offers one of the most difficult challenges facing interpreters. It's tough to incorporate a happy medium of both information and entertainment in interpretive presentations and exhibits. Unfortunately, in many places, interpreters fail in achieving more than one of the possible benefits. Commonly, a lack of balance shows up in talks which take the form of speeches or lectures, lacking a recreational or entertainment component (Hultsman, Cottrell, and Hultsman, 1987). At the other extreme, some presentations evoke laughter or involve games and other fun activities, but may contain little or no information to provide any kind of educational or inspirational experience. Beginning interpreters often find it difficult to achieve a balance of fun, participation, and provocative information that can enrich and inspire the visitors' experience.

Tilden (1967) noted the difference between just informing and interpreting: "information, as such, is not interpretation. Interpretation is revelation based upon information. They are entirely different things. However, all interpretation includes information. . . . Information is the raw material of interpretation."

INTERPRETING FOR INDIVIDUAL GROWTH

By exploring motivation theories, one can achieve a deeper understanding of why education and recreation are personally desired by many and why interpretation may be perceived as inspiration.

Many theories help to explain people's motivations in visiting museums, forests, and interpretive events. Abraham Maslow (1954) developed a widely understood theory that offers insights into these motivations. His theory suggested that people have a hierarchy of needs or drives. He began with basic needs—physiological needs such as air, food, water, sleep, and sex. Then, as people meet these survival needs, they move up to more sophisticated and socially oriented needs such as identifying with a group, being accepted and loved. After satisfying these needs of social belonging, a person may escalate to needs for esteem and self-actualization (Figure 3.4).

The basic physiological needs of survival tend to dominate a person's attention if unmet, according to Maslow. If you are starving, your drive for food may override your need for social approval or intellectual satisfaction, at least in action. That doesn't imply that a hungry person loses the other needs; it just suggests that satisfying acute hunger takes top priority. In fact, the starving artist stereotype suggests that artistic self-actualization may arise from a need to meet basic needs (self-preservation).

The simplest characterization of Maslow's concept is to break the levels into two groups:

Basic needs
- physiological requirements such as air, food, water, sleep, and sex
- safety needs
- security needs

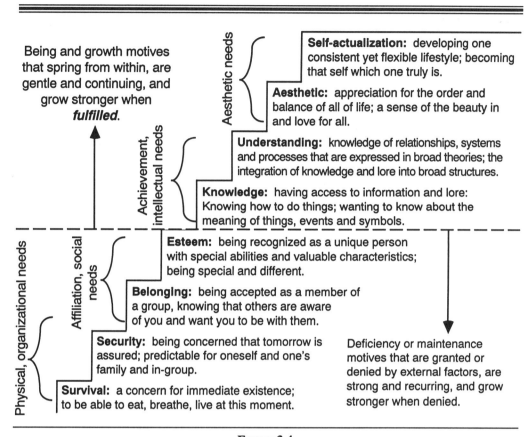

Being and growth motives that spring from within, are gentle and continuing, and grow stronger when *fulfilled*.

Aesthetic needs

Self-actualization: developing one consistent yet flexible lifestyle; becoming that self which one truly is.

Aesthetic: appreciation for the order and balance of all of life; a sense of the beauty in and love for all.

Achievement, intellectual needs

Understanding: knowledge of relationships, systems and processes that are expressed in broad theories; the integration of knowledge and lore into broad structures.

Knowledge: having access to information and lore: Knowing how to do things; wanting to know about the meaning of things, events and symbols.

Affiliation, social needs

Esteem: being recognized as a unique person with special abilities and valuable characteristics; being special and different.

Belonging: being accepted as a member of a group, knowing that others are aware of you and want you to be with them.

Physical, organizational needs

Security: being concerned that tomorrow is assured; predictable for oneself and one's family and in-group.

Survival: a concern for immediate existence; to be able to eat, breathe, live at this moment.

Deficiency or maintenance motives that are granted or denied by external factors, are strong and recurring, and grow stronger when denied.

FIGURE 3.4
Needs, actions, and incentives of human beings tend to scale upward. Usually lower level needs take precedence over higher level motives for activity (adapted from Maslow and others).

Growth needs
- love and belonging
- esteem
- self-actualization

Maslow (1954) identified humanly important self-actualization motives and referred to them as meta-needs. According to the theory, a person whose security needs are met but whose meta-needs are not met, falls into a syndrome of decay and experiences despair, apathy, and alienation.

Although Maslow thought the desire for self-actualization is the pinnacle of growth motivations and is universal in people, he thought it very difficult to attain because it was dependent on the lower needs being met. He said only about one person in ten is primarily motivated by self-actualization needs. Most are lower on the hierarchy, being preoccupied by trying to satisfy esteem, love, or security drives. Table 3.1 explains how interpreters can meet the needs of visitors regardless of their place in Maslow's theoretical framework.

TABLE 3.1 EXPANDED LEVELS OF VISITOR NEEDS AND HOW INTERPRETERS CAN MEET THEM

Levels of Need	How Interpreters Can Meet Visitor Needs
Self-actualization	Provide resources for independent exploration. Help visitors to develop interpretive materials from their own perspectives. Assist visitors to develop their own campfire programs.
Aesthetic	Offer seminars for reading and discussion with experts in diverse fields related to visitor interests. Lead guided walks to places of special or unusual interest. Bring in outside specialists for talks and visits (e.g., artists, scientists, top managers).
Understanding	Provide access to reports, plans, budgets, etc. Provide means for visitors to ask questions about policy, regulations, science, etc. Post questions and responses in convenient locations for all to see. Provide interpretive "exercises," "experiments," and other environmental education activities and tasks to allow visitors to perform specified tasks on their own time.
Knowledge	Provide access to data and diverse library resources. Provide times so interpreters can talk with visitors in an unstructured way. Arrange for visitors to see practical applications of principles, concepts, and ideas.
Esteem	Publicize a visitor's performance on bulletin boards, park newsletters, and campfire programs. Give visitors significant responsibilities on walks, at campfires, and slide shows.
Love and belonging	Call the visitor by name—ask for it and use it. Visit the campground and other park areas where people gather. Express your pleasure in working with visitors and with the individual.
Safety and security	Encourage and permit continued study in areas of visitor interest and ability. Publish park policies and follow them consistently. Act consistently, avoid punishment and sarcasm.
Physiological needs	Provide strong, consistent safety measures, making visitors aware of them. Have trained first-aid personnel and equipment in the area. Provide for health and sanitation.

Beck (1991) found that the characteristics of optimal experiences attained by wilderness recreationists at Canyonlands National Park coincided with those reported by social scientists, (e.g., Maslow, 1964; Csikszentmihalyi, 1975; Panzarella, 1980). Furthermore, interpretation can facilitate the realization of these powerful and enriching experiences (Beck, 1993). According to Csikszentmihalyi (1990), any small gain in promoting opportunities for optimal experiences "will make life more rich, more enjoyable, and more meaningful."

MEASURING INDIVIDUAL BENEFITS

In spite of the difficult task of providing experiences with multiple and simultaneous benefits, dedicated interpreters continue to aim for this lofty objective. Although quantifying successes remains difficult, the fact that people voluntarily come, often repeatedly, sometimes in great numbers, indicates that people find interpretive experiences to be valuable.

One way to quantify a value of the experiences is through economic valuation. Travel cost and contingent valuation techniques estimate the willingness to pay for a product or experience (Walsh, 1986). A contingent study at an interpretive center in Ontario, Canada found that visitors on the average were willing to pay $2.41 per person (about $5.00 in 1994 equivalent) to have access to self-guiding nature trails and an exhibit area (Cable, Knudson, and Stewart, 1984). Such economic analyses assess benefits of a wide array of public recreation resources. Some agencies require them to evaluate new projects and renovations. They have been underutilized in estimating the benefits of interpretive efforts.

Benefits to Society

In addition to benefits accruing to individuals from quality interpretation, collective benefits also accrue to society. Interpretation serves the public welfare. Benefits associated with recreation and interpretation include improved public health, family and community unity and stability, among others (Godbey, Grafe, and James, 1993). Even decreased crime rates and higher rehabilitation rates seem to correlate with the availability of recreational opportunities (Dustin, McAvoy, and Beck, 1982; White, 1991).

The California Legislature, among others, recognized that interpretation serves to improve social values (Department of Parks and Recreation, 1982). After an analysis of recreation needs, the legislature called for two nontraditional roles for interpretation: (1) helping visitors develop desired leisure skills and (2) increasing understanding of multicultural heritage. The recommendation suggested that leisure skills "development is needed for activities such as photography, camping, fishing, canoeing, and cross-country skiing. Such training should be presented to visitors as a way of increasing their enjoyment of park resources. Understanding of the environment and park values will be an important by-product of this effort." Likewise, "interpretation that further promotes awareness and understanding of California's rich multicultural heritage should be incorporated wherever possible. Beyond what is now being done to interpret California's cultural history, more linkages are needed to relate today's cultural diversity to past events. Each group's unique contributions should be recognized" (Department of Parks and Recreation, 1982).

In all nations, recent urbanization and immigration have separated many families from their roots. Many have left behind their cultural history and traditions as well as their attachment to the land. In the U.S. and Canada, for example, people changed from open country dwellers to city dwellers "more rapidly than any other people of the world" (Claxton, 1917). Until after the War Between the States (1861-1865), Americans were practically a pioneer people with no large cities. By World War I (1914-1917), about half the people lived under urban conditions in cities and towns. Today, over a dozen megalopoli contain most of our citizens and dominate the U.S. economy, mass communications, and political power. Yet, early in this century, many writers expressed concern for the disruption to personal and social psyche that has come with the benefits of urbanization. Claxton (1917) focused on our ruptured lifeline to nature and the need to interpret constructively:

> Out of the forests we came; they have been our home through all the ages. …Leisure will be dangerous to us unless we learn to use it wisely. We must learn to play simply and sanely, else leisure will mean for us only waste of time; and we shall waste ourselves with our time in harmful dissipation. We need seeds in the concrete jungle.

—White, 1991.

Specific values of interpretation to society include: (1) information for democratic decision-making, (2) identity with our land and culture, (3) awareness of global ecology, and (4) an ethical sense of our place in history and the present scheme of things.

1. Democracy requires an informed public.

Knowledge is vital in a democratic society, where the people make the fundamental decisions, either on policy or on the choice of those who shall make the policy. The founding fathers of the United States of America recognized the need for a well-informed public to sustain the governing principles of the new republic. They sponsored western exploration and interpretation of its results (e.g., Lewis and Clark), as well as many scientific inquiries and educational programs. The detailed knowledge about animals and plants that came from these trips became the common legacy of the nation. Thomas Jefferson sought to spread the benefits of natural history work beyond the scientific world to include the civic education of the nation's citizens. To this end, he sponsored public museums and libraries (Vogel, 1991).

The same has happened in British society. The regents have sponsored museums and public libraries to encourage an informed populace. In the British case, the emphasis was often on educating about the entire globe-circling empire and its many varieties of people, plants, animals, and ecological conditions. These (British and other) museum and their learned societies were associated directly with much of the remarkable scientific discovery and discourse through the past two centuries.

Gilbert Grosvenor, in a brief talk before the 75th anniversary celebration of the National Park Service, recalled that we are all neighbors on planet Earth. We face many critical issues of public policy and action. Yet, the average American voter doesn't know anything about the issues, alleged Mr. Grosvenor. In the next decade, citizens face tough decisions in the economy, in rejuvenating our inner cities and in supporting our critical parks and other outdoor recreation resources. It will be difficult unless voters are educated well enough to support our parks and other natural resource areas. "Today, they are not!" (Grosvenor, 1991). They must see that parks are connected to the rest of the world. Parks are show places where people can see why and where things happen in the natural world that supports humankind—if interpreters make sure that the parks educate us.

Educating the public doesn't have to happen only in schools. Parks, forests, and museums are also "classrooms." In fact, the National Park Service has 358 units that are classrooms, each able to teach something about our present and our past. Other federal agencies also offer interpretation in natural areas in hundreds of locations, from deserts to volcanic cones and glaciers. Likewise, there are over 1,000 state parks and well over 10,000 county parks where outdoor/historical learning may help us relate to our planet and the use of it.

Secretary of Education Lamar Alexander (1991) noted that education won't change by recipe, program, or formula. He recalled visiting an African community where each child was trained by the people in the village. An elder commented that it takes an entire village to educate one child. It seems sensible that all "villages" should include outdoor classrooms, where naturalists and historians help with educating the children—and the adults.

2. Identifying with our land and culture helps sustain a society.

Literary and artistic interpretation of the natural landscape played a major role in developing national identity in the United States and Canada. In the 1800s, hundreds of artists and writers expressed the land's natural beauty. The American landscape became a "wellspring of nationalism" (Vogel, 1991). What America lacked in comparison with Europe's rich human culture was made up for in wild grandeur and scenery (Nash, 1982). The features of the wild environment enriched the image of North America. The people accepted the notion that providence had specially blessed and endowed these nations and their peoples. The rugged character of wilderness, as interpreted in writing, lecturing, and art, became the special cultural identity, the uniquely American philosophy and painting styles, a form of a "cultural declaration of independence" (Vogel, 1991). Interpretation of this frontier culture and wild creatures by artists such as John James Audubon favorably impressed many famous and wealthy Europeans (Lindsey, 1985).

The citizens of any nation need to identify with the landscape, its natural and cultural resources. This helps them feel part of the nation and thereby promotes unity and a sense of belonging. National identity and pride grow from a sense of where one is, the special qualities of the immediate surroundings and the people inhabiting them. This healthy pride may prevent foolish actions that could destroy the special resources of a nation. It may help in our understanding the consequences of individual acts or community proposals. Children who grow up terrified of real and imagined things out in the unknown "woods" could someday destroy those unfamiliar haunts of perceived dangers. Likewise, if they never learn to enjoy the diversity of their fellow-citizens' customs, styles, and attitudes, they may be intolerant of those who are "different" and therefore perceive them as "dangerous."

A remarkable example exists in Indonesia's interpretation of its own cultural identity as a unique blending of many traditions. Every year, a week-long intensive course in religious and cultural diversity emphasizes the strength in the nation that comes from the collaboration of the different peoples of the five major religions. The interpreter-teachers are prominent members of the communities throughout the country. The participants are about 5-10 percent of the population each year, on a rotating basis. A more traditional form of interpretation in the "Mini-Indonesia" park near Jakarta features, in a beautiful setting, the customs, clothing, environment and architecture of the many different cultural components of the nation are featured in a beautiful setting (Figure 3.5). This elegant folk museum somehow unites the diversity in a most impressive, positive learning experience for Indonesians and visitors from abroad. Further, Indonesia's national parks and wildlife reserves, although still developing, conserve the natural elements of even densely populated Java and Bali, allowing people to learn of their natural heritage through a vigorous interpretation program.

FIGURE 3.5
Mini-Indonesia park near Jakarta interprets architectural and cultural diversity from some of Indonesia's 300 ethnic groups and 250 languages.

3. **Global ecological awareness is a third motive for interpretation.**
As we approach or surpass the Earth's capacity to sustain human population levels, we face many perplexing questions and must place high priority on the protection of ecological systems (Meadows, Meadows, & Randers, 1992). Now, the necessity is to interpret for sustainability as well as growth. As Edwards (1979) advocated for Canada: "The need is essentially an ecological awakening of a people in which interpretation plays a major role ... It must be a process of showing how to care for Canada to keep her productive."

The U.S. Environmental Protection Agency's Science Advisory Board identified four areas of greatest risk to the planet's future habitability (Reilly, 1991):

- Stratospheric ozone depletion.
- Global climate change.
- Species extinction and loss of biological diversity.
- Habitat alteration and destruction.

These risks demand that we see the world whole as interconnected and diverse, that we recognize our ability to alter fundamentally the planet's life support systems; that we accept our responsibility as stewards for the natural world.

Debate rages over these issues; many specious arguments arise and seem to stand, confusing the issues. For the people to get the facts and better understand these complex puzzles, interpretation can offer experience in the natural world to give them the practical framework to better perceive the problems and alternative solutions. If interpreters expect the people to act to save the quality of the earth, we must make the effort to (a) get them the facts, via well-informed people, and (b) give them opportunities for rich, enjoyable, and informative experiences in the outdoors. The historical perspective and demonstration of natural phenomena in an outdoor setting will get to at least some of the people.

4. Help people develop their ethical sense of place and role in the world.
To get people to care enough to change their lives, interpreters can offer them an understanding and appreciation of their place and role in the world, giving them facts and experience so they can shape their own values.

> One goal of environmental education is to get people to write alternate verses' for their lives, to care enough about how the world story is going that they want to make the story turn out 'right.'
> —Schuch, 1992

Perhaps the most fundamental need for interpretation arises from the philosophical or ethical need of "discovering the nature of nature, learning the story of our sources" (Rolston, 1988). Interpretation helps humans know our place in the scheme:
- of this creation,
- of human history and culture,
- of the niche in which each of us lives and moves.

In geological terms, "...we are still arriving, still figuring out where we dwell and what our roles here are" (Rolston, 1988).

As a people, we are, " . . . creating a new ethic (an epic) of place" (Rolston, 1988). We need stories of where we are, of what happened once upon a time and the meanings of these events for the present and future. We need to know the natural history and ecology of the many species that cohabit the planet with us, the rocks that support and shelter us, and the natural processes that control our destiny as a species. We need to recognize the intrinsic worth of fossils, artifacts, living plants, and animals, and other peoples, how they bring us value and how we, as the "wise overseers" of the planet, relate to them (Figure 3.6, page 70). We need to know the successes and failures of human history, the technology of how we convert and use our resources, and a sense of how we might improve.

Rolston (1988) summed up this objective: "Can we bring the sense of residence into focus? . . . We need an art of life to go with the science of natural history."

Long ago, Marcus Aurelius, in his Meditations 6:14, identified the need for finding the essential, the key values:

> Flux and change are forever renewing the fabric of the universe, just as the ceaseless sweep of time is forever renewing the face of the eternity. In such a running river, where there is no firm foothold, what is there for a man to value among all the many things that are racing past him?
> —Smith and Ehrenhard, 1991

FIGURE 3.6
A computer helps provoke curiosity about whales in the National Aquarium of Baltimore.

The interpreter seeks and points out the handholds and footholds that help people make their way through this complex, dynamic home of ours.

Summary

WHY INTERPRET?

1. To help people enjoy their lives more through perceptive outdoor recreation, to lift them beyond the basic levels of existence to heightened awareness and understanding of their environment.
2. To aid the development and sustainability of society, so people can live together more peaceably and more productively with other inhabitants of the planet.
3. To help people find footholds of values and truths, to provoke enthusiastic curiosity about our natural, historical and cultural environment.

Literature Cited

Alexander, L. (1991). Address to 75th Anniversary Symposium of National Park Service. Vail, Colorado: (unpublished).

Beck, L. (1991). Promoting opportunities for optimal experiences in nature. *Journal of Recreation and Leisure, 11*:76-83.

Beck, L. (1993). Optimal experiences in nature: Implications for interpreters. *Legacy, 4*(1):27-30.

Burroughs, J. (1916). *Under the apple trees.* New York, NY: William H. Wise & Co., Inc.

Cable, T. T., Knudson, D. M. and Stewart, D. J. (1984). The economic benefits to visitors of an interpretive facility. *Journal of Environmental Education, 15*(4):32-37.

Cable, T. T. (1992). To enjoy understandingly. *Legacy, 3*(2):8-9.

Claxton, P. P. (1917). Public schools and the national parks. In *Proceedings, National Parks Conference,* Jan. 2-6.

Csikszentmihalyi, M. (1975). *Beyond boredom and anxiety.* San Francisco, CA: Jossey-Bass.

Csikszentmihalyi, M. (1990). *Flow: The psychology of optimal experience.* New York, NY: Harper & Row, Publishers, Inc.

Department of Parks and Recreation. (1982). *Recreation needs in California: Report to the Legislature on the statewide recreation needs analysis.* Sacramento, CA: State of California—The Resources Agency.

Dustin, D., McAvoy, L. and Schultz, J. (1982). *Stewards of access: Custodians of choice.* Minneapolis, MN: Burgess Publishing Company.

Dustin, D., McAvoy, L. and Beck, L. (1986). Promoting recreationist self-sufficiency. *Journal of Park and Recreation Administration, 4*(4):43-52.

Edwards, Y. (1979). *The land speaks: Organizing and running an interpretation system.* Toronto, Canada: The National and Provincial Parks Association of Canada.

Gallup, T. P. and Risk, P. (1981). The use of cartoons in interpreting rules to campers. In *Proceedings, National Workshop,* AIN. Estes Park, CO.

Gennao, E., Sigford, A. and Heller, P. (1983). A course in winter ecology at a nature center for middle school children and their parents. *Journal of Environmental Education, 14*(4):23-25.

Godbey, G., Graefe, A. and James, S. (1993). Reality and perception: Where do we fit in? *Parks and Recreation, 28*(1):76-83, 110-111.

Grosvenor, G. (1991). Comments to 75th Anniversary Symposium of National Park Service. Vail, CO: (unpublished).

Hultsman, J., Cottrell, R. L., and Hultsman, W. Z. (1987). *Planning parks for people.* State College, PA: Venture Publishing, Inc.

Keyes, B. E. and Hammitt, W. E. (1983). Visitor reaction to interpretive signs on a destination-oriented forest trail. In *Proceedings, National Workshop,* AIN. West Layfette, IN: Purdue University.

Lee, T. R.. (1981). Beyond the quiz question. In *Proceedings, National Workshop,* AIN. Estes Park, CO.

Leopold, A. (1966). *A sand county almanac, with other essays on conservation from Round River.* New York, NY: Oxford University Press.

Levitt, L. (1991). Recreation for the mentally ill. In Driver, B., P. Brown, and G. Peterson. *Benefits of Leisure.* State College, PA: Venture Publishing, Inc.

Lime, D. W. Anderson, D. H., and Mech, L. D. (1978). Interpreting wildlife through guided expeditions. *Journal of Interpretation, 3*:10-16.

Lindsey, A. A. (1985). *The bicentennial of John James Audubon.* Bloomington, IN: Indiana University Press.

Maslow, A. (1954). *Motivation and personality.* New York, NY: Harper & Row Publishers, Inc.

Maslow, A. (1962). Lessons from the peak experiences. *Journal of Humanistic Psychology, 2*(1):9-18.

Maslow, A. (1964). *Religions, values, and peak experiences.* Columbus, OH: Ohio State University Press.

Maupin, G., Witter, D., and Bassett, B. (1980). Missouri eagle day programs. *Journal of Interpretation, 5*(1):3-9.

Maupin, G. T., Bassett, B., Catlin, D., and Witter, D. (1982). Missouri's prairie day: Methods and evaluation of an interpretive extravaganza. *Journal of Interpretation, 7*(2):31-39.

Meadows, D. H., Meadows, D. L., and Randers, J. (1992). *Beyond the limits.* Post Mills, VT: Chelsea Green Publishing Co.

Mills, E. A. (1920). *The adventures of a nature guide.* Garden City, NY: Doubleday, Page & Co.

Moscardo, G. M. (1988). Toward a cognitive model of visitor responses in interpretive centers. *Journal of Environmental Education, 20*(1):29-38.

Nash, R. (1982). *Wilderness and the American mind (3rd ed.).* New Haven, CT: Yale University Press.

Paffenbarger, R., Hyde, R., and Dow, A. (1991). Health benefits of physical activity. In Driver, B., P. Brown, and G. Peterson. *Benefits of Leisure.* State College, PA: Venture Publishing, Inc.

Panzarella, R. (1980). The phenomenology of aesthetic peak experiences. *Journal of Humanistic Psychology, 20*(1):69-85.

Reilly, W. K. (1991). Our national parks: Toward a new era of protection. Keynote speech, 75th Anniversary Symposium of the National Park Service. Vail, CO: (unpublished).

Rolston, H. III. (1988). *Environmental ethics.* Philadelphia, PA: Temple University Press.

Schuch, S. (1992). Reflections on doing "environmental songs" with kids. *Mason-Dixon By-Line* (NAI Region II Newsletter), *15*(3):1,4.

Selye, H. (1975). *Stress without distress.* Philadelphia, PA: J. B. Lippincott Company.

Smith, G. S. and Ehrenhard, J. E., (Eds). (1991). *Protecting the past.* Boca Raton, FL: CRC Press, Inc.

Tilden, F. (1967). *Interpreting our heritage (rev. ed).* Chapel Hill, NC: University of North Carolina Press.

Vogel, M. J. (1991). *Cultural connections: Museums and libraries of Philadelphia and the Delaware Valley.* Philadelphia, PA: Temple University Press.

Walsh, R. G. (1986). *Recreation economic decisions*: *Comparing benefits and costs.* State College, PA: Venture Publishing, Inc.

White, R. (1991). Planting seeds in a concrete jungle. In *Proceedings, National Interpreters Workshop*, NAI. Vail, CO.

Values of Interpretation for Management

Through interpretation, education; through education, appreciation; through appreciation, protection.

This slogan implies that interpretation plays a vital role in management of parks, forests, and refuges. The work of the interpreter goes far beyond entertainment and identifying the birds and flowers. Providing interpretation as recreational enrichment yields valuable by-product benefits to the resource management agencies and companies, as well as to private and public museums. Interpretation provokes people to know, appreciate, understand and eventually to love a place, a historic event, and/or a people. With a deep love comes a desire to nurture and maintain. Reilly (1991) observed that for the U.S. national parks:

> . . . education is vital, essential, if we are to enlist popular enthusiasm and support for protecting the parks. Through the national parks and other natural resource areas arise opportunities to inform and educate the very people who love the parks. Grass roots support is needed. It is based on people's sense of connection to the resources. Jacques Cousteau once observed, *'In the final analysis, people protect only what they love.'*

Interpreters provide the main proactive public contacts of a museum, land management agency or other organization. The visitors develop understanding and support for resources and their values primarily through interpretive events or contacts. Without interpretation of the resource management process, public support may occur only by accident or good luck.

An early prointerpretation policy came to National Park Service Director Stephen T. Mather in a May, 1918, letter from Secretary of the Interior Franklin K. Lane. It said: "The educational . . . use of the national parks should be encouraged in every practicable way." The policy included providing university and high school groups with special facilities for vacation studies. The general public could enjoy exhibits in park museums featuring mounted specimens of park flora and fauna. When Stephen Mather decided in 1919 to hire interpreters into the national parks the next year, he explained the action in terms of resource protection: to "counteract those persons who would selfishly destroy park values" (Weaver, 1982). Personal services started in 1920 in Yosemite and Yellowstone, under the direct sponsorship of the Director of the NPS (Mackintosh, 1992).

The Forest Service impetus for the Visitor Information Service came from a need to support policy. Recent growth in wildlife refuge interpretation responds to broadening public interest in nongame wildlife (Figure 4.1). Interpretation ensures that the public understands resource values, thereby building support that the managing agency or owner needs in order to function.

FIGURE 4.1

Explaining the agency on a U.S. Fish & Wildlife Service sign (TTC).

MANAGING FISH and WILDLIFE for PEOPLE

Administered by the U.S. Fish and Wildlife Service, the National Wildlife Refuge System manages and safeguards a network of lands and waters to produce fish and wildlife for people to enjoy. Over 400 National Wildlife Refuges provide protection and habitat for a variety of wildlife species.

National Wildlife Refuges are located in all parts of the country, and are open to public visitation. Hunting, fishing, wildlife observation, and photography are but a few of the activities that enable you to see and enjoy wildlife in a natural setting.

The interpreter often describes policy, the scientific evidence and reasoning that go into the major decision-making processes. Although the policy supported interpretation in these and many other agencies, the question of its efficacy still existed for some. Does interpretation pay back the investment made in it? Would the agency/organization better spend its money in some other way, e.g., newspaper advertising, TV programming, highway signs? Does interpretation really provide benefits in terms of aiding management?

Myth or Real Benefit?

Whenever one speaks of using interpretation as a management tool, he or she refers to modifying people's behavior in one way or another, sometimes to discourage littering or to encourage positive support of a museum or park fund drive or bond issue. Interpreters and most managers have confidence that interpretation provides a service many visitors seek, expect and appreciate. They "know" it produces positive public benefits, but they have a hard time pinning down how much or why.

At one time or another, many administrators and park professionals in academia have called on interpreters to provide better documentation of the management benefits they claimed. In fact, Hendee (1972a) published an article entitled "Challenging the Folklore of Environmental Education." He referred to the claimed benefits of interpretation as folklore and suggested that interpreters document these benefits with rigorous empirical research. Several questions were posed. Do these presumed benefits really exist? Other questions that arise include: Why is interpretation effective in some cases and not in others? Is it merely a matter of poor interpretive technique or good technique aimed at the wrong audience? How do experimental design and measurement problems affect evaluation of the outcomes of interpretive programs?

Examples of successful management have come from an atmosphere of public support created by interpretation. A Channel Island National Park decision to remove wild hogs from the park received public support after careful interpretation of the reasons and methods

(Spears, 1992). So did 1970s efforts at explaining the reasons for controlled burning in Yosemite. Although the press and politicians jumped into the 1988 Yellowstone fire events with both feet unshod, interpreters finally won much public understanding by explaining the basic facts underlying fire cycles and showing recuperative powers of the vegetation and soil. Sometimes management decisions have failed because interpretation did not fill the gap between the visitors and the managers, e.g., Olympic National Park's decision to remove mountain goats from the park.

Interpretation in Zambia's National Parks helped protect wildlife from poaching (Dillon, 1991). In Hawaii, interpretation lessened impacts of recreational use on coral reefs and improved visitor safety in Hanauma Bay (King and Tabata, 1992). Earlier (Clark, Burgess, and Hendee, 1972), littering behavior in a campground diminished markedly after trials of interpreting the consequences and costs through signs and brochures.

Many other individual cases proving the benefits of interpretation to management came from Sharpe and Gensler (1978). They indicated that interpretation had:

- decreased vandalism,
- decreased poaching of fish and wildlife,
- decreased other depreciative behavior, such as souvenir collecting and unauthorized motor bike use,
- increased compliance with park regulations,
- increased safety, and
- increased public support for policies and management practices.

This extensive collection of success stories illustrated that interpretation can solve specific management problems related to both resource protection and to providing visitors with a safe and enjoyable recreational experience.

RESEARCH ON BENEFITS TO MANAGEMENT

During the 1980s, reports of interpretation helping to meet management goals continued to accumulate. Interpreters focused more closely on specific interpretive strategies to solve management problems. For example, Cunningham (1985) reported ways that interpretation enhanced safety in the U.S. national parks, and Harrison (1982) and Sharpe (1988) presented practical suggestions for using interpretation to reduce vandalism.

Observations and anecdotes provide only some of the evidence. During the 1980s, the quality of the data supporting interpretation as a management tool improved. Researchers answered the call for empirical documentation of benefits. In one Corps of Engineers study (Fritschen, 1985), distributing an interpretive brochure reduced tree damage and littering by 50 percent. Adding an enforcement message to the brochure had a small marginal effect. Adding a positive personal contact (without any enforcement message) to brochure distribution achieved a reduction of 80 percent.

Another study showed that interpretation significantly increased compliance with certain boating safety rules. On Detroit Lake, Corps of Engineers interpreters used posters, flyers, decals, signs, radio broadcasts on message repeaters, and newspaper articles promoting boater safety. As a result, boaters increased compliance with lake safety markers; speedboats in marked danger zones went down 53 percent; and water-skiers violations dropped 77 percent. Posters and signs on site had the greatest impact (Fritschen, 1984).

A third Corps study (Oliver, Roggenbuck, and Watson, 1985) documented reductions in depreciative behavior at Corps of Engineers campgrounds with interpretation. Similarly, at Shiloh National Military Park, Vander Stoep and Gramman (1987) documented a decrease in depreciative behavior associated directly with interpretive messages.

Roggenbuck and Berrier (1982) documented successful dispersal of wilderness campers using interpretation.

Cable, Knudson, Udd, and Stewart (1987) measured attitude changes as a result of exposure to interpretive messages at an Environment Canada interpretive center. They found small but positive changes in attitude toward the forestry agency message and toward forest management policies, even after relatively brief visits.

Another value comes from simply acquainting people with the natural resources. Getting people to use and enjoy the property may require interpretation. Penaloza (1987) concluded from a study of Wisconsin citizens that "information is the key to fuller use of state parks," including what experiences they offer, how to develop new interests and skills at parks, and how to use them. Her sample showed that 35 percent of the respondents (residents with a drivers license) visited the state parks in that year.

VALUES TO THE AGENCIES

The agencies and organizations that manage large ecosystems and that preserve and present history to the public require continual feedback from the public. When the feedback is from well-informed people, the inputs are often assumed to be wise. When the people are poorly informed, they may not even know the identity of the agency that is supplying them with recreational opportunities, wood products, clear water, historical and cultural preservation, or any number of other services or products. Survival of public land agencies and cultural organizations often depends directly upon effective interpretation of their messages. If at least the politicians and prosperous citizens do not sense their value, agencies have little chance to fulfill their mission.

Simply put, it is in the agency's interest to let the public know what it has, what it is doing, and why. A long-term investment in interpretation should create more good will and support than short-term, expensive advertising or public relations campaigns.

NATIONAL PARKS

In 1984, managers in the national parks heard from Director William Penn Mott that if you want to get the money, you have to tell the people about the parks—and that's interpretation. An application of this occurred in Everglades National Park, where urban and agricultural water diversions had priority over the water left in the slowly flowing "river of grass" that sustains park flora and fauna. Ranger Jack Morehead and colleagues decided to get better information out on water and the timing of its flows. The strategies included (1) bringing in high school and junior high students to tell them about it; (2) interpreters talking to the press about the consequences of altering natural water flows and changes (threats) to the ecosystem; (3) interpreters talking to legislators; (4) producing a new folder with a message on how to protect and preserve the water quality and flows for the Everglades. In other words, interpretation provided information for enlightened decision making. Enlightened managers use it; others perhaps haven't hit the hard issues of survival yet. Morehead's effort succeeded, with new respect evident for the water regime that flows into the Everglades. He moved to Alaska parks and used similar techniques there.

Most agencies and industries recognize this as a survival need. Many see it as a public education obligation related directly to their functions.

FOREST PRODUCTS INDUSTRIES

For at least half a century, the American Forest and Paper Association (formerly named the National Forest Products Association) has produced educational films, booklets, slide shows, posters, and kits to help children better know their natural environment. The Association's development and sponsorship of Project Learning Tree since 1973 represents a commitment to environmental education. The Association's firm policy of keeping the information objective and nonpromotional reflects the belief that, in the long run, accurate information and preparation for decision making is more productive than propaganda.

The Association President, Barry Cullen (1992), further emphasized the need for informative interpretation—not propaganda. He said that several issues have made the Nineties the "Decade of the Environment." A danger comes from the level of public knowledge: " . . . the public's new found environmental commitment is based on emotion . . . not facts." A 1991 Roper survey found that most Americans expressed a high level of concern about the environment but "very few could back those concerns up with any hard knowledge. . . . Roper found that those it surveyed—even avowed environmentalists—were able to answer only a third of the survey's questions correctly" (Cullen, 1992). Forest industry representatives actively support the value of interpretation. Their interest arises from the large forest holdings and the need for public goodwill and sanction to manage the lands for sustained wood production. Some forest products companies have long had the foresight to employ a few naturalists and historians. Interpreters, when given the facts and not asked to be company shills, have already been effective in getting issues in perspective and allowing the public to see forest management and industries in more than the tabloid emotionalism used by even "respectable" big-city newspapers. Were it not for interpretations of liability law, more interpretive centers and trails would exist on industry lands. The Redwoods Council in California provided several exhibit centers and public trails before a judge ruled that they must protect themselves from all lawyers who might wish to sue for damages to all visitors as if they were invitees.

The wood products industry faces a dilemma: the public's concern about forests has triggered a tide of regulations, legislative proposals and court actions. Cullen (1992) pointed out that there is little interest in the facts that the industries own but 15 percent of the nation's commercial forest land yet plant almost half of all the trees installed nationally each year—far more than all of the public agencies combined. A few suggestions for getting industry messages across to the public appear in Box 4.1 (page 80).

BOX 4.1: INDUSTRIAL FORESTRY INTERPRETATION

Richard Lewis, president of the American Pulpwood Association, suggested industries should use interpretation to deal with the perceptions of the urban public when they drive by a timber harvest area:

1. **Use informative signs at every harvesting or forest management area**. The signs don't have to be big and expensive, but must provide the basics: what's happening, how it's being done, and the company or agency responsible (with a telephone number).
2. **Explain natural disturbances**. The effects of a fire, tornado, or storm may be obvious to the company, but not to the public. Signs should explain what happened and when, especially when the area is in or near a park, wilderness area, or scenic lookout.
3. **Seeing is believing**. The most effective way to show that a forest does grow back is to explain its history. For example, a sign could state "Harvested 1970, thinned 1992, next harvest 2010." Assure the visiting public that the area is under stewardship, which may predispose them to future harvest.

Source: Cullen (1992)

Does Interpretation Pay Off as a Management Tool?

MANAGERS BELIEVE IT DOES

In a 1981 survey of county, state and federal natural resource property managers, more than 90 percent said interpretation aided the agency (Table 4.1). They believed that interpretation would increase public support and assist in meeting goals for the property. Interpreters were perceived to be part of the management team, not isolated in their function (Cable and Knudson, 1983).

In another survey, Braley and Hanna (1980) found that 68 percent of respondents (two-thirds of them are managers) had used interpretation as a management tool, primarily for resource protection. Sharpe and Gensler (1978) and Griest (1981) contended, however, that misunderstandings between managers and interpreters inhibited the use of interpretation to help resolve management problems. Nevertheless, using interpretation as a management tool dates back to the early days of the modern profession.

Both the National Park Service and the Forest Service of the United States began their interpretive programs in response to management motives. Yosemite and Yellowstone National Parks faced threats by vandals and commercial interests. In 1919, NPS Director Stephen T. Mather was fighting off lobbying efforts to allow gambling in Yosemite. The gamblers took their defeat by threatening to cut off Congressional appropriations for national parks. Mather saw the need for an informed citizenry to lobby against these and other

TABLE 4.1 BENEFITS OF INTERPRETATION AS SEEN BY 103 NATURAL RESOURCE PROPERTY MANAGERS

Question	Yes %	No %	Unsure/No Ans. %
Would you expect interpretive facilities/programs to:			
• Decrease poaching?	38	62	0
• Decrease vandalism?	51	47	2
• Decrease other forms of misbehavior?	59	39	2
• Increase carrying capacity?	51	46	3
• Increase public support/cooperation?	93	6	1
• Assist meeting goals of the property?	93	7	0
• Offer no benefits to the property manager?	1	99	0
Assuming you had sufficient funds and personnel would you like to have more interpretation on your property?	90	10	0

Source: Cable and Knudson (1983)

threats. In 1920, he personally financed a vigorous interpretive program in Yosemite. The 1920 visitors heard from Ranger-Naturalists of the anti-park lobbying in Washington, followed by a suggestion for action: "If you want a part in this war, send even as little as a postcard to both your Senators, your Representative" (Goethe, 1960). Correspondence flowed into Washington clinching the park funding. Even today, one of the main objectives of national park interpretation is to develop support for the service among visitors.

Likewise, Forest Service Chief Richard McArdle recognized the value of interpretation to management. In 1960, the Multiple Use-Sustained Yield Act directed the Forest Service to manage its then 185 million acres for recreation, water, grazing, wildlife, and timber. The complicated decisions and policies involved in this blending of uses is difficult for the public to understand. McArdle established a major interpretive initiative to explain the new Act and the Forest Service, under the name "Visitor Information Service" in 1961.

Nevertheless, the national forest system—the whole profession of forestry, in fact—has a public image problem. Interpretation can help to overcome it. Until 1991, its environmental role got only weak agency interpretive support, seldom in a proactive manner. The forestry profession could more effectively interpret its dedication and long involvement in wilderness preservation, endangered species protection and habitat protection, ecological diversity preservation, wild and scenic river protection, and production of wood so the forest will remain.

Interpreters believe in supporting management through their work. Hooper and Weiss (1990) found that 82 percent currently used interpretation as a management tool. Nearly 80 percent had personally seen other interpreters do so effectively. About half reported receiving training on this aspect of interpretation. Barriers to its use were: time (15 percent), money (13.5 percent), and lack of management support (10.4 percent). The proportion who reported managerial barriers was the same level as those who lacked management support reported by Cable and Knudson (1983).

WHEN THE BUDGET CRUNCHES

With the endorsement of interpretation as a management tool, reported earlier, many interpreters feel perplexed by the weak financial support they sometimes get from upper management. Cox (1992) asked: "Why then do we not receive the funds to do our job and when budget crunch time comes we are considered nonessential and are the first to be cut?" This plaintive cry comes occasionally from interpreters at federal, state, county, and city levels. It may not be so frequent at private agencies, where public acceptance of the programs is the source of income.

To attempt an explanation may just add to the long series of discussions in which interpreters often flagellate themselves for a variety of faults. These include not enough data-keeping, poor accountability, lack of cost-effectiveness studies, lack of political clout, not painting a clear public picture of what we do, and not telling management of all the jobs and image-making done by interpreters. Solutions of each of these may help alleviate the problem, but the relative marginality of interpretation probably relates to something more basic than that. It seems to go back to the hierarchy of needs proposed by Maslow (1954) and management's (mis)perceptions of the survival value of interpretation.

When the budget drops, cuts have to be made. This allegedly happened in Indiana State Parks in 1992. The response: drop all the seasonal park naturalist positions (and other summer jobs). The press reports quoted Director Jerry Pagac: "We're looking at ensuring that restrooms are clean. . . . Safety is a paramount concern to us. . . . We don't want to do anything that jeopardizes the safety of the public. . . . obviously the facility would still be open, and I think that would be our bottom line."

In this case, survival (staying open) came first, along with health and safety needs, just as Maslow's list suggested. This included survival of the permanent staff, among them the ten permanent interpreters. But the cut eliminated the seasonal naturalists—part of the core program—at a time when state parks obviously needed skilled "advocates" to assure strong public understanding and support. Many a business leader would say that the company most needs its marketing/sales department during tough times. Interpreters meet the higher, more refined needs of visitors, indeed, but they also serve agency survival needs. For the agency, interpreters may boost public support by presenting the agency in its best light, by presenting the parks in their full values, and by providing the richest possible level of visitor experience.

In response to similar federal belt tightening and accountability discussions of the 1970s and 80s, interpreters placed new emphasis on management benefits to justify maintaining their programs in parks and forests. For some of them, this was a bitter pill; they visualized interpretation as a service to the visitor that could stand on its own. Its goodness seemed so obvious to them that no one would question its important role. Surely, they thought, no one should ask for measures of productivity or tangible benefits—there is no way to measure the high quality of interpretive experiences. Not so, say the theory and recent practice. Ways exist to estimate the quality, benefits, and efficiency of interpretation, even as it relates to management. It starts with questions of how to succeed at influencing visitor attitudes and affecting their behavior.

TURF TALK

Each museum has its own themes and educational purposes. Each natural resource agency has different policies and management objectives. Sometimes, apparently friendly rivalry exists among them. Visitors, often confused by the variations among federal agencies and state and local institutions and agencies, ask questions about the differences. Sometimes, poorly informed employees who have a limited notion of another agency's practices respond as if their agency were morally superior to another. For example, individual National Park Service employees have publicly refuted the idea that forests are renewable; they advocate widespread preservation for forest lands, apparently rejecting the idea of sustained use of forest resources, even on national or private forests. Some have been heard to misstate the functions of other federal and state/provincial agencies. This, of course, makes a poor impression on informed visitors, misleads uninformed visitors, and constitutes improper interpretation of government actions.

Preservation policy applies to most national and state park lands as well as to over one-sixth of the U.S. national forests (33 million acres of wilderness plus primitive and special areas) and parts of the BLMs national resource lands. Preservation is not, however, the only policy operating, legal, or valid in the U.S. and Canada. Rejection of other agencies' legal mandate does not provide useful interpretation. People have opted for diversity in the management of their large public lands estate, recognizing that preservation of some lands and wise, sustained use of other resources can operate side by side.

Interpreters play a vital role in shaping public perception of the resource and the managing agency. Front line interpreters need to understand controversial issues facing the agency and learn to effectively communicate these to visitors. The interpreters serve as the advocate (lawyer) of the agency or museum—but not in an antagonistic sense. They must have the information—the whole truth—or they can do damage to the agency, inadvertently.

Interpretation can assist management in explaining issues that face an agency or owner. It helps protect the resources through preventive education. It helps market the agency, both through on-site programs and outreach programs.

Interpreters are the image-makers of the agency. They carry the message to the public of the value of the resources being managed for the public. A 1988 study sponsored by the National Parks and Conservation Association, a private, nonprofit group that defends the parks but not necessarily the Park Service, confirmed these statements. It said that National Park Service interpreters form an important link between the resources and the visitors. They develop the positive image of the NPS. A positive image helps rally support for the parks. A national park system cannot survive intact in the future without interpretation efforts. The conclusion of the study called for a management approach that recognizes and rewards professional interpretation (Cox, 1992).

DIFFERENT LEVELS OF AGENCY SUPPORT

The value of interpretation didn't achieve immediate or sustained recognition from all public or private agencies. The Forest Service operated for many decades with spurts of interpretive efforts, then started a roller-coaster support process. The Bureau of Land Management only started in recent decades. The Fish and Wildlife Service vacillates between enthusiasm and indecision on how environmental education services should operate. The Army Corps of Engineers had a slow, steady progression of commitment and activity, with a recent burst of activity, even without new funding. In the National Park Service, interpretation received recognition from the beginning of the Service.

Although several states and counties have hired interpreters every summer since the 1920s, others have only recently become dedicated supporters of interpreters. Likewise, the museum business has held widely differing views on the value of interpreters; education, always on the list of functions in most museums, only recently gained high priority across the board. Camps vary considerably. Although "Cap'n Bill" Vinal and, later, Steve Van Matre provided high-profile advocacy of environmental interpretation/education in youth camps, many still give "nature counselors" only second rank billing, training, and support. Top interest often goes to wranglers, waterfront directors, and sports counselors. Yet, other camps focus on natural and cultural history, seeking to develop excellent interpretive programming.

Theoretical and Practical Bases for Attitude and Behavior Change

To answer the issues of when, how, and why interpretation succeeds, we need a theoretical framework can help guide experimentation and analyses. Only then can we achieve a scientifically sound understanding of human behavior and how to influence it.

INTERPRETATION AS PERSUASION

Interpretation often takes the form of persuasive communication. Interpreters attempt to develop or change attitudes and behavior toward the resource base or toward history and culture. A speaker always seeks to persuade the audience, even if for nothing more than to consider the facts as the speaker perceives them. Administrators often hope that the interpreters will persuade the public to support agency policy. Many of the principles of effective interpretation are common with the bases of persuasion theory.

A comprehensive summary of literature related to persuasion, attitudes, and the attitude-behavior link suggested several key facts (Eagley and Himmelfarb, 1978). Here are three processes experienced by the listeners or receivers of messages.

1. People don't receive all the facts aimed at them. Information availability and reception is a key component of the persuasion process. Not all of the information presented remains quickly available to the recipient, who experiences gaps in attention, doesn't comprehend some of the message, or may not remember everything comprehended.

2. People accept only some information received. The internal process of acceptance or rejection of information affects persuasion and attitudes. What determines acceptance or rejection? Many things do, including the content of the message, the context, and the attributes of the communicator. Usually, if information is rejected, it is gone—out of the mental system that forms attitudes and decisions.

3. People evaluate the new information they've accepted. Information integration occurs after the individual accepts information. The integration process is affected by the perceiver's valuation of the importance of the information, prior attitudes, and other recalled items of information.

These three processes focus on the listener. On the other side of the communications process, interpreters are senders of messages. They can use several principles of persuasion that give their messages greater likelihood of being integrated into the minds of the listeners. There is no simple formula for success, no set of rules. These are some guidelines, stated in terms of probabilities for relative success (Verderber, 1978).

1. Consider audience needs and attitudes. Persuasion is more likely to occur when a speaker has a clear speech objective that considers audience needs or attitudes. The objective is a clearly worded statement that calls for belief or action. You may identify audience need levels with one of Maslow's categories: physiological, safety, belongingness and love, esteem, or self-actualization. First, help meet the lowest level needs (e.g., is it safe to be here?), then build up to meet higher needs.

   Audience attitudes can be defined by three characteristics: direction (favorable or unfavorable), intensity (strong to weak) and salience (very important to not very important). If a presentation is inconsistent with an attitude or if an objective does not meet a need, the persuasive task requires patience, skill, and persistence. Achieving the objective is most difficult under these four conditions (Verderber, 1978):

   a. if you ask for major turns from existing attitudes or beliefs,

   b. if the cost in effort or difficulty is large (it's better to show how easy it is to follow up on your proposition),

   c. if the audience is highly ego-involved with an attitude you seek to change, and

   d. if the change is basic (e.g., to stop eating meat is more basic than to switch from beef to chicken and fish).

2. Apply several methods to make your message persuasive. Persuasion is likely to occur when the speaker uses several means of persuasion (Verderber, 1978).

   a. Present information, describing and demonstrating what something does or the facts about a situation.

   b. Project credibility, which is the perception that the communicator possesses qualities such as competence, good intent, character, and personality that cause the audience to like, trust, and have confidence in the interpreter.

   c. Use reasoning through presentation of logical reasons, explaining the "why" of situations or requests.

  d. Develop motivation through language that is adapted to the needs of the audience, and touches the emotions.
  e. Respect ethics. Audiences usually have some common attitudes about ethical behavior; they reject the ideas of a communicator who violates them. Some examples are lying, name-calling, grossly distorting or exaggerating, and condemning ideas or people as if by gossip without information.
3. Anticipate audience opinion and organize accordingly. Persuasion is likely to occur when the speaker organizes material according to expected audience reactions. Three general classes of audience reaction or attitude are normal: no opinion, in favor, or opposed to the persuasive message. Each calls for a different strategy.
  a. If the audience has no opinion, they either need information or are apathetic. The interpreters strategy seeks to get them the important information and/or to break them out of their apathy.
  b. If the audience is in favor of the interpreter's proposition or accepting of his or her theme, the interpreter's efforts can focus on bringing the audience to the point of specific decisions or action. Instead of just echoing beliefs (preaching to the choir), crystallize attitudes, recommit the audience's direction and equip them to carry out a specific course of action.
  c. If the audience is opposed to the interpreter's point, he or she should approach the topic indirectly for hostile groups, creating common ground and planting seeds. For a slightly negative group, he or she may use a more direct approach. In both cases, the speaker may seek common ground as to what everybody wants (e.g, healthful, clean water) and criteria for such wants. Then, show how the proposed actions will satisfy it, perhaps contrasting it with other less valid alternatives.
4. Allow enthusiasm and concern to come through. Persuasion is more likely to occur when the speaker demonstrates conviction without fanaticism.

DEFINING PERSUASION PURPOSES

Interpreters limit their persuasiveness unless they define their purposes in clear terms. They need to form the goals that managers seek into precise behaviors that they expect from the visitors after the interpretive activities. The concerns of management might include:
  • resource protection and management, including wilderness,
  • protecting and maintaining visitor facilities,
  • water quality protection,
  • visitor protection, and
  • public information and awareness about current issues, such as spruce mortality.
    These concerns are not objectives, but they can lead into them. Here are two examples of behavioral objectives. They describe outcomes from defined interpretive activities, i.e:
  • After reading this brochure and viewing this video on backcountry camping practices, visitors will be able to list and explain the reasons for safely disposing of organic wastes as well as repeating the three-point test for wilderness campsite clean-up.
  • After this program, all the visitors will be able to describe two reasons that some of the spruce trees are dying and explain why the foresters aren't spraying to prevent it.

Visitor needs, expectations, and desires may directly affect the purposes for persuasion. Unless the audience is ready to listen and enjoy the activity, their reception will not be optimal. Their concerns may not relate to management's objectives; rather they might include:

- creature comforts/necessities, such as food, shelter, restrooms,
- safe, enjoyable recreational opportunities,
- exciting recreational opportunities,
- friendly, helpful service, and
- educational opportunities.

An interpreter planning to be persuasive must remember these types of concerns/goals and provide for them. Only then can visitors fully focus on the higher order management problems.

INTERPRETER CREDIBILITY AND PERSUASION

Persuasion theory involves several components involved in individual acceptance and integration of information. Among the factors, these affect listener acceptance of the message (Eagley and Himmelfarb, 1978):

1. Information availability—Not all the information presented is available to the recipient.
2. Salience of significant others—The listener reacts to the communicator and/or other participants.
3. Message characteristics and content—Normative ideas may agree or conflict with previous beliefs of the visitor; the medium used, the context, and type of appeal (e.g., fear, humor, factual) affect listener acceptance.
4. Delivery characteristics—Rate of speaking, verbal and nonverbal expressions of confidence, diversity of vocabulary, and physical appearance.

Interpreters can use all of these factors to enhance their credibility, effectiveness and persuasiveness. More about applications of these persuasion factors appears in subsequent chapters, especially in discussions of effective speaking and writing techniques. Much literature presents various persuasion theories and applications. Manfredo (1992) provided an excellent treatment of this field of study in his book, *Influencing Human Behavior: Theory and Applications in Recreation, Tourism, and Natural Resource Management.*

INTERPRETATION AS BEHAVIORAL GUIDE

Intuitively, it seems that producing behavior change is a matter of increasing knowledge and fostering desirable attitudes. This is reflected in the popular maxim at the head of the chapter—long an unofficial mission statement for many field interpreters.

Wagar (1976) formalized this relationship in a "Hierarchy of Objectives" that presented behavior changes as dependent on attitude changes and attitude changes as a result of retention of information that is achieved by attentiveness (Figure 4.2, page 88).

Attentiveness leads to enjoyment and appreciation. If one achieves success in overcoming the initial obstacles to effective interpretation (i.e., attracting and holding people's attention), then "our probability of success at the higher levels is greatly increased, even if such success is not yet directly measurable" (Wagar, 1976). Not everyone agreed. Although this made sense intuitively, no empirical data supported Wagar's model.

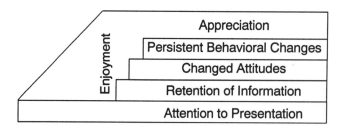

FIGURE 4.2
A hierarchy of objectives: To change attitudes, interpretation must hold the audience's attention and convey information; behavior changes may depend on attitude changes (Wagar, 1976).

DO CHANGED ATTITUDES CHANGE BEHAVIOR?

Psychologists have argued back and forth about the effect of attitudes on behavior as their research measurements produced different results. Doubts about the linkage between attitudes and behavior came up in social psychology literature.

Until the 1960s, researchers studied attitudes as "the most theoretically rich and empirically active area within social psychology" (Eagley and Himmelfarb, 1978). By the early 1970s, however, many social psychologists regarded the attitude concept as almost useless. This view developed primarily from the literature of the 1960s which emphasized the inability of attitudes to predict behavior reliably. For example, Wicher (1969) reviewed 30 studies and found little evidence to indicate a relationship between attitudes and behavior. Others thought a link existed but that it was often masked or altered by methodological or explanatory variables.

Then, in the 1980s, Fishbein developed the "Theory of Reasoned Action" to directly predict and explain the behavior of individuals. This theory changed many peoples' attitudes about attitudes.

THE THEORY OF REASONED ACTION

As the name implies, this model applies only to reasoned or rational action. It assumes that human beings use information in a rational way to make a behavioral decision (Figure 4.3). The model traces the causes of individual behavior back to beliefs (Fishbein, 1980).

Each of four successive levels of analysis, from beliefs to behavior, provides a more comprehensive understanding of the factors underlying the behavior:

1. **Personal attitudes** are a function of personal beliefs and evaluation of the outcome of the behavior. In turn, personal beliefs and evaluations develop from information one has about the world.

2. **Subjective norms** also affect intentions. They are determined by beliefs about what significant others think the person should or should not do and by motivations to comply with salient others. Social or group norms and their degree of motivation on

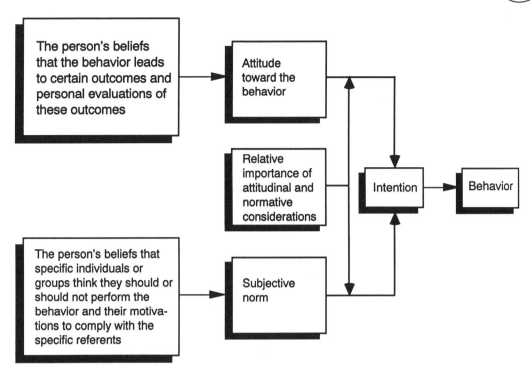

Note: Arrows indicate the direction of influence

FIGURE 4.3
Factors determining a person's behavior based on Fishbein's theory of reasoned action.
(adapted from Fishbein, 1980)

the individual to comply thus have great importance. The perceived wishes of others may be partly affected by the interpretive presentation and its implied or explicit normative content.

3. **Intention** results from some combination of personal attitudes toward the behavior and subjective norms. The relative weight of these two key factors—attitudes and social norms—varies with the intention; for some intentions, attitudinal considerations may be more important, while in other cases normative considerations determine the intention.

4. **Behavior** is guided by intentions, although intervening circumstances may temporarily or permanently modify them. Fishbein (1980) emphasized that for accurate predictions of behavior from intention it is important to:
   - carefully define and observe behaviors, that they not be general categories or outcomes, but specifically identifiable behaviors of the same category as the intention;
   - carefully define intentions in terms of all of the behavioral alternatives a person perceives as available.

Heed three cautions when using and interpreting Fishbein's model. *First*, although behavior ultimately links to beliefs, the linkage is not direct. Therefore, it is inappropriate to try to predict intentions or behavior directly from beliefs. Any attempt to predict while skipping a level in the model is not meaningful; the intervening relationships should be empirically described.

Secondly, while going from behavior to intention, from intention to attitudes and norms, and then to underlying beliefs, one can gain increased understanding of the factors determining the behavior. It does not follow, however, that a person gains in ability to predict behavior because of the effects of the intervening levels. For example, knowing intention may allow prediction of behavior; knowing the intention's determinants (attitudes and norms), however, will not improve the accuracy of the predictions because the effects of these two determinants are mediated by the intention.

A *third* caution concerns the level of specificity of definitions of attitudes and behaviors. Predicting specific behaviors can rarely arise from general attitudes. Lack of consistency between the levels of attitude analysis and behavior has been identified as one of the major reasons why researchers have not been successful in predicting behavior directly from attitudes (Fishbein, 1980). In addition, people sometimes fail to distinguish between behaviors and occurrences that arise from those behaviors, and between single actions and behavioral categories (e.g., turning down a candy bar and going on a diet).

INTERPRETATION AND ATTITUDE CHANGE

The Wagar (1976) "Hierarchy of Objectives" suggested that one can infer attitude changes from measures such as attentiveness and comprehension. Fishbein's model identified beliefs and evaluations as determinants of attitudes and attitudes as precursors of intentions. These determinants develop from information, whether correct or incorrect.

Communication, such as interpretation, can facilitate integration of new information into changes of beliefs which may affect changes in attitudes. Therefore, interpretation can affect people's attitudes. If one observes attentiveness and comprehension in a visitor, however, attitudes will not necessarily change. The interpreter is simply measuring the signals that suggest reception of the information. Even if people receive information, they may not integrate it into existing beliefs. Even when persuasion effectively changes a belief or value, it may not change the related attitude; any attitude may be the result of several different beliefs. Thus, it may not be valid to infer attitude changes from observations at more basic levels. This may explain the mixed results observed in environmental education studies of the knowledge-attitude relationship.

The inability to demonstrate a change in attitude does not necessarily indicate an unsuccessful interpretive effort, however. An individual's interpretive participation accumulates knowledge gradually. Every interpretive event won't produce radical change of mind; several beliefs may have to change before an attitude changes. Also, the audience receiving the interpretive messages may already possess the desired attitudes. In this case, interpretation reinforces these existing appropriate attitudes.

WHY BEHAVIOR DOES NOT ALWAYS CHANGE

According to Fishbein's model, it should be possible to observe changes in behavior as a result of changes in attitudes. Exceptions will occur, of course. Listeners' subjective norms may be so strong or conflicting with the message as to not allow for changes in intentions. Even though a strong correlation exists between intentions and behavior, it is not a perfect correlation. Some people do not have the ability to, or are prevented from, carrying out their intentions.

Another block may come from failures of attention, comprehension, and memory. Not all information presented by an interpreter gets through to the listener—a gap in reception. Some is heard, but forgotten—a gap in post-event information availability.

Assuming attention and comprehension occur, allowing information to be received, then the recipient either accepts or rejects it. If the listener accepts the information, then it may be integrated and valued by its importance, considering prior attitudes and other re-called information.

EXTERNAL VARIABLES

Throughout the literature, many other variables have been shown to affect behavior. The theory of reasoned action does not deny the importance of other "external" variables such as demographics, extant attitudes, and personality traits. However, it holds that they influence behavior indirectly by influencing the attitudinal and normative considerations that ulti-mately determine that behavior.

Although some of these variables are not under the control of interpreters, they should be important to them since they affect the reception, acceptance, and integration of informa-tion. By knowing the characteristics of visitors, it is possible to aim the persuasive mes-sages more effectively to accommodate the special needs of visitors. Figure 4.4 (page 92) shows the relationship between external variables, persuasive messages, interpretation, and the theory of reasoned action. This expanded model integrates into Fishbein's model of in-dividual differences (e.g., gender, education) which have been shown to be correlated with environmental attitudes (Gifford, Hay and Boros, 1982).

OPPOSING THEORIES AND RESEARCH

Although the Theory of Reasoned Action received wide acceptance, some park profession-als remain skeptical. That is probably healthy, since most theories change and develop with experience and time. The challenges to the current version fall into two categories: (1) imagined or real failings of current interpretation programs to reduce undesirable behavior and (2) lin-gering doubts about the linkage between attitudes and behavior.

Two of the most common criticisms included in the first category are that interpre-tation reaches too small an audience to have a significant effect on the entire resource and the audience reached usually doesn't include the people causing the problems (Harrison, 1982). This statement suggests that interpreters often end up "preaching to the choir." Al-though that may be true, both of these observations criticize interpretive strategies and indi-vidual performance rather than the underlying theory. The problems could be reduced by

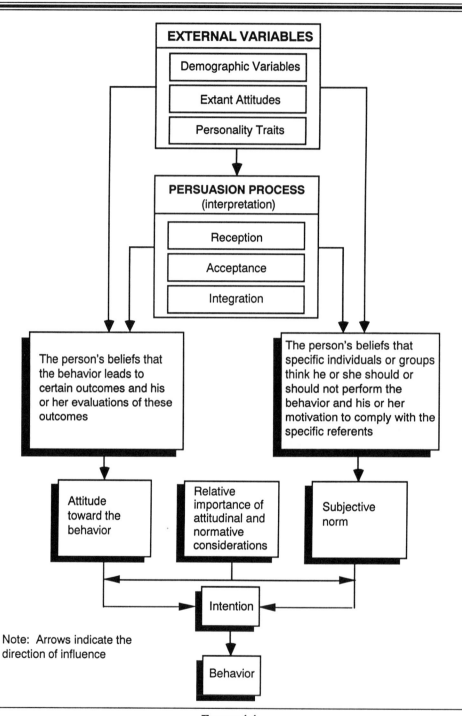

FIGURE 4.4

An extension of Fishbein's theory of reasoned action, showing indirect effects of external variables and persuasive communication behavior. External variables can affect beliefs, evaluations, and, when present, the persuasion process (adapted from Fishbein, 1980).

communicating with more or different audiences, by directed interpretation or more mass media emphasis. Moreover, "preaching to the choir" has great value, in that it reinforces existing appropriate behaviors.

A more serious challenge to the idea of interpretation as a management tool arises from the uncertainty regarding the relationship between behavior and attitudes. Historically, many perceived weaknesses with the attitude-behavior link were the result of problems in specification and measurements of attitudes and outcomes (Cable, Knudson, and Theobald, 1986). Likewise, other apparent weaknesses may have come from ignoring the role of norms which, according to the Theory of Reasoned Action, can influence behavior as strongly (or stronger) as attitudes.

SELF-PERCEPTION THEORY

An alternative theory from the social psychology literature offers a completely different perspective of the attitude—behavior linkage. This "self-perception theory" states that behavior causes attitudes—just the opposite of the relationship between attitudes and behavior proposed in the Theory of Reasoned Action. The self-perception theory proposes that, as individuals participate in a particular behavior, they develop an explanation for their behavior from observing and evaluating themselves, their beliefs and feelings. Freedom and choice are important to most individuals, so one tends to attribute behavior to one's own internal motivation (perceiving that the choice of action was voluntary, rather than to avoid penalties or to follow the crowd unthinkingly). Over time, the individual forms beliefs and attitudes that reinforce the behavior.

In the application of this theory, if park managers wanted to reduce an undesirable behavior, rather than using interpretation to educate the public about the ramifications of the behavior, they would post and enforce regulations about the behavior. Initially, some people would adopt the desired behavior out of fear of being penalized for breaking park rules. However, in time, the individual will attribute it to personal choice; eventually the person would develop attitudes and beliefs to justify that behavior.

McAvoy and Dustin (1983) made a strong case for this approach of using direct, coercive management to insure the appropriate behavior. In this context, they suggested that interpretation could assist visitors to internalize the rationale for the direct controls, so the visitors can attribute their conduct to internal motivations. Interpretation's role is to influence the development of appropriate attitudes and behaviors with direct management measures.

This theory applies best to situations where vigorous enforcement of behavior becomes critical due to safety or resource/exhibit protection.

Philosophical Challenge

*The soul of a man is an all encompassing yet unknown factor with which we
deal, day in and day out. If we can somehow reach the soul we need not fear
whether our guest be a day laborer or a college president!*

*We seldom feel, however, that our exhibits are responsible for the ultimate
result in this direction.... The visitor will determine the educational result in
so far as his individual understanding is concerned.*
—Carr, 1931

SHOULD WE CHANGE ATTITUDES?

Interpreters often see themselves as people who try to make a difference, attempting to lead
others to develop stronger civic or environmental ethics. The objectives of interpretation
programs often include the goal of changing attitudes and behaviors, either explicitly or im-
plicitly. Historical interpreters often seek to heighten civic pride, increase cultural sensitivity, and/or reduce tensions among racial or ethnic groups (Hall and James, 1992).

Hendee (1972a) and many other observers have noted the "missionary aspects" of environmental education and interpretation. In one study, 99 percent of the nature center directors surveyed hoped to change environmental attitudes of the people involved in their programs (Holtz, 1976). Knapp (1972) expressed the belief that environmental attitudes and
values "hold the keys to the future of mankind and the quality of life on this planet." Van
Matre (1988) chastised environmental educators and interpreters because they had not systematically addressed "how life functions ecologically, what that means for people in their
own lives, and what they are going to have to do to change their lifestyles in order to lessen
their impact upon the earth."

On the other hand, many interpreters strive to be nonconfrontational and find that discussion of persuasion is discomfiting, perhaps even distasteful. These may protest that they
are not trying to persuade anyone—they just present the objective facts and let visitors make up
their own minds. (Those who protest most along these lines often turn out to be the truest propa-
gandists of all.) Indeed, most agencies insist upon objectivity and nonadversarial approaches.

The protest could have validity, if one understands persuasion only as nonfactual, emotional, confrontational, unpleasant or somehow undesirable. Being argumentative or unpleasant, however, normally has the effect opposite of persuasion. Persuasion seldom succeeds if a speaker seeks to reverse thinking by 180 degrees. Effective persuasion can be
gentle, friendly, and factual. The term persuasion too often gets confused with images of
phony sales pitches, propaganda, and appeals to our lower nature. The persuasive communication of interpretation almost invariably works on a positive, constructive, uplifting level.

Some professionals, however, still contend that even the goals of affecting attitudes and
behavior may not always be appropriate. For example, some question the appropriateness
of government civil servants using the taxpayer's money to change the taxpayer's attitudes.
They ask, should public servants do things "for people" or "to people?" (Peart, 1980; Foley
and Keith, 1979). They argue that, although privately sponsored interpreters may seek

to change attitudes, public interpretive programs should serve by providing proper information and experiences, thereby allowing visitors to make their own intelligent decisions. Ah, yes, but what better way to persuade than by providing that "proper information" and offering those experiences that provoke people to make their own decisions? It's persuasion by a sweeter name and interpreters can't avoid it. Interpreters are in the business of affecting how people think (Figure 4.5). They are not in the brainwashing or propaganda business, however. The distinction is important. Hendee (1972b) said that interpreters should increase knowledge and participation rather than "closing minds by trying to specify attitudes." Moreover, because of the difficulty in measuring attitudes, he suggested that interpreters should "cease their preoccupation with attitudes as a criterion to evaluate their efforts and concentrate on providing knowledge." In another article, he stated that interpreters should " . . . aim first at transmitting knowledge and facts and, subordinate to that, at changing attitudes, values, and cultural perspectives" (Hendee, 1972a).

FIGURE 4.5
Sometimes simple messages can affect behavior; this thought-provoking label in the District of Columbia seeks to reduce pollution of a famous seafood resource base.

Presenting information and facts in itself stimulates the process by which attitudes change. Current attitude theories and measurements find that interpreters will change some attitudes by sticking to the facts, the stories, and the images. That seems to be just the point made above—the inappropriateness of heavy-handed propaganda or inelegant behavioral modification techniques that may masquerade as interpretation. Persuasion theory and attitude theory suggests that the most effective means of encouraging behavior modification is with a very light, factual touch that allows the visitor to develop the thoughts into personal reasoning, attitudes and behaviors.

Any time that an agency talks about changing attitudes, it opens itself up to charges of elitism or arrogance. This implies to cynics that agency personnel regard the values and attitudes of the "unconverted" public as inferior to their own.

Few if any interpreters regard their public as ignorant or inferior. Rather, they see their job as one of helping elevate consciousness of a place or event with which most visitors have limited familiarity. According to Dabney (1988), Freeman Tilden considered interpreters as " . . . engaged in a field essentially of morality—the aim of man to rise above himself and to choose the option of quality rather than material superfluity." However, Tilden defined how the teaching of morals need not be elitist nor narrowly arrogant (Dabney, 1988):

> . . . we shall not teach morals as such. We use our vast natural and historic resources to show what true morals are. We do not tell people what they must do, but what they can do; not what they must be, but what they can be . . . .

This can be called the ethics of interpreting ethics—probably a necessity for survival in a world that is seemingly facing ecological disaster.

Do park and forest agencies want interpreters to persuade people that the environment is worth protecting, that there are good reasons for management decisions, that a museum's historical message and collection offer useful clues to past and present culture? Does the environmental interpreter have a commitment to guide people to lessen their impacts on the land, to respect the miracle of the humblest of species, to assure protection of plants and animals in danger of extinction (Figure 4.6), and to see the complex interconnectedness of an ecological system? Does the interpreter at national memorials seek to impart a sense of inspiration in the national heritage? If so, they are in the business of persuasion, most of it uplifting, pleasant, gentle, and civilized.

If interpreters do not seek to change people through their function, their purpose becomes that of a butler and court jester, providing superficial courtesy and light amusement.

THE MISUSE OF INTERPRETATION

Inappropriate messages (propaganda) and inappropriate delivery (proselytizing and intruding) comprise two misuses of the opportunity to interpret.

Just as any management strategy, interpretation can be abused as a tool. As managers become more aware of the powerful role interpretation can play in shaping attitudes and modifying behavior, it has been used as a propaganda tool of the agency on some occasions. Managers have modified, embellished, or even eliminated interpreters' messages. In the

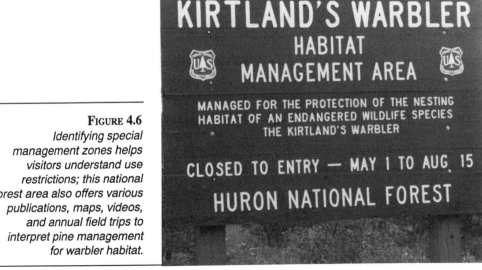

FIGURE 4.6
Identifying special management zones helps visitors understand use restrictions; this national forest area also offers various publications, maps, videos, and annual field trips to interpret pine management for warbler habitat.

worst cases, they have told interpreters to lie to the public. At one county park, interpreters weren't allowed to discuss water quality problems in a river that was in violation of public health standards where the parks department operated canoe trips. Likewise, an innocent question by a student on a class field trip to a national park went unanswered, as the interpreter indicated that, by answering the question, he would put his job at risk.

On the other hand, managers may need to modify or eliminate some messages. For example, one state dismissed an interpreter after repeated complaints from visitors. Personal zeal about overpopulation caused the interpreter to tactlessly admonish parents with more than three children that they had gone too far, and they were putting the world in peril. While the point has validity, the personal attacks built a barrier against any effectiveness that this or other interpreters might have offered.

Interpreters may find these situations surprising and uncomfortable. They may not know how to sort out the pragmatic and ethical ramifications or how to handle them. Is this a form of censorship which should concern interpreters? Or is it merely a matter of agency loyalty or being a "team member?" Certainly, in a private corporation, employees often are not free to discuss specific information. Should the motives favoring the organization be considered? Some misinformation is directly self-serving, in order to enhance park visitation and hence revenues. At other times, misinformation seems to be merely politically expedient.

At times misinformation may help protect a scarce resource. For example, an interpreter may deny the presence of a rare raptor nesting in the area to reduce the chance of bird watchers or falconers disturbing the birds. Interpreters must decide whether the situation and the long-term consequences balance out in consonance with their sense of ethics. Some will choose to make a dramatic move over what seems to others to be an insignificant situation. Others will persevere because they feel that they can do more positive good for the citizens and the agency by staying on than they can achieve by demission, perhaps resulting in discontinuity of what may be a precarious interpretive position. Michael Frome (1982) wrote an essay entitled "To Sin by Silence" in which he challenged interpreters to speak out even when it may cost them their jobs. Others might counsel supporting administrators and work vigorously towards change from within.* Both attitudes have their times and places.

Cases of misuse of interpretation need not imply rejection of it as a management tool to persuade people to think or act differently. Any communication strategy or medium can be applied in an unethical fashion. However, this important issue should be a matter of much introspection by every interpreter. Under what circumstances, if any, would you knowingly disseminate misinformation? Under what circumstances, if any, would you risk losing your job?

As interpreters promote the management applications of their work to administrators, there could be greater pressure to use it only as a management tool, thus losing the essence and spirit of interpretation as a tool to enrich recreational experiences (Dustin and McAvoy,

---

* If Benjamin Franklin and George Washington had stormed out of the Continental Congress after questions of principle were decided against them, the flimsy confederation might have lingered for many decades as thirteen squabbling, precarious colonies. In the long run, they stayed in control of their flare-up passions and saw their stronger, long-range passions for a functional, free nation turn into reality.

1985). In this case, interpreters might become mere disseminators of information; the art of interpretation could be reduced to those tasks that guarantee specific and measurable results. In extreme cases, these fears are legitimate.

Pragmatically, however, to ensure the survival of interpretive programs, they must help resolve management (not just the manager's) problems and their outcomes must be documented. The interpreters must work to remind themselves and their administrators that as public servants, their primary work enhances and enriches the lives of the visitors, while protecting the resource. Interpreters who truly love their resource, their job and their visitors will probably keep this perspective. The challenge for all interpreters is to assist in meeting management goals without compromising the traditional values and philosophy of interpretation.

Summary

The interpreter represents the organization or agency, by helping visitors understand the goals of the museums, park or other resource. A major by-product of interpretation shows up as public interest and support for the organization. Thus, interpreters serve as image-makers of their organizations, communicating the organization's role in protecting valuable cultural and natural resources for the public.

According to the Theory of Reasoned Action, interpretation can change beliefs and evaluations which make up attitudes. It can influence perceived norms which, along with attitudes, affect behavioral intentions. In cases where visitors already have appropriate norms and attitudes (e.g., when you are preaching to the converted), interpretation can serve to reinforce and extend them to new applications.

In the context of the "self-perception theory" interpretation's role as a management tool promotes the development of desired attitudes and behavior by encouraging the internalization of existing behaviors generated by direct regulation.

Should one theory or the other guide planning of interpretive strategies? It may depend on the setting. McAvoy and Dustin (1983) noted that direct regulation should be used only when absolutely necessary. Settings where direct regulations would be necessary could include areas experiencing overuse, user conflict, or depreciative behavior in which the primary managerial objective is to protect a pristine or ecologically fragile resource base. In such situations, the "self-perception theory" could guide interpretive efforts aimed at complementing the direct regulation of behavior. In areas where the primary objective is to serve large numbers of recreationists it would be desirable to use the Theory of Reasoned Action to prompt changes in attitudes and behavior.

When he was Chief of Interpretation for the National Park Service, William Dunmire (1976) delivered a paper that reviewed the many managerial benefits of interpretation. His thesis stated: "Interpretation should be employed by management as the primary means of achieving all management objectives directly affecting the public." He further remarked that he had little difficulty persuading managers in the field to place interpretation high in their priorities. Rather, the budget examiner and others far removed from the parks were the hardest to sell. Fifteen years later, administrators say the same; most managers know the many values of having interpreters in their parks, but it is a hard sell to some bureaucrats and legislators.

Today, however, psychological theories and empirical studies complement the scores of anecdotal success stories. The study of persuasive communication and its application to interpretation indicates the increasing depth and breadth of the interpretive profession in the last decade. Interpreters now have theoretical foundations and experimental evidence to support and direct their efforts. Their work and beliefs are no longer just "folklore," hopes, or assumptions. Armed with this evidence, interpreters should effectively convince taxpayers, donors, park managers, and bureaucrats, including those away from the parks, refuges, and forests, of the values of interpretation.

Without interpretation to bring the managers and the people together, there is little chance of integration and full achievement of functions of many public agencies and facilities. Sustained public support requires understanding, sympathy, and active backing for agency policies and programs. Interpretation is THE place where the exchange between the park management and the public happens. Interpreters need to work closely with administrators and agency division personnel to assure that the messages going to the visitors actually do support management objectives.

> *Everyone who works for the National Park Service is a resource manager, regardless of his or her job. Every decision we make and every action we take affects the cultural and natural resources entrusted to our care by the American people. We are all involved in the protection of park resources, while providing for the enjoyment of the visiting public.*

> —TEAM Resources course brochure, 1992

Literature Cited

Braley, M. and Hanna, J. (1980). The use of interpretation as a management tool. In *Proceedings, National Workshop, Association of Interpretive Naturalists*. Boston, MA.

Cable, T. T. and Knudson, D. M. (1983). Interpretation as a management tool—The manager's view. In *Proceedings, National Workshop, Association of Interpretive Naturalists*, West Lafayette, IN: Purdue University.

Cable, T. T., Knudson, D. M. and Theobald, W. F. (1986). The application of the theory of reasoned action to the evaluation of interpretation. *Journal of Interpretation*, *11*(1):11-26.

Cable, T. T., Knudson, D. M., Udd, E., and Stewart, D. J. (1987). Attitude changes as a result of exposure to interpretive messages. *Journal of Park and Recreation Administration*, *5*(1):47-60.

Carr, W. H. (1931). *Trailside actions and reactions*. New York, NY: American Museum of Natural History, School Service Series No. 5.

Clark, R. N., Burgess, R. L., and Hendee, J. C. (1972). The development of anti-litter behavior in a forest campground. *Journal of Applied Behavior Analysis*, *5*(1):1-5.

Cox, W. E. (1992). Challenges for the nineties. *Interpretation, (Fall-Winter)*:1-4.

Cullen, B. (1992). Meeting the challenge: NFPA in 1992. *NFPA in Focus, (Jan-Feb)*:4-5.

Cunningham, R. L. (1985). Visitor safety interpretive survey. *Trends*, *22*(4):37-39.

Dabney, W. D. (1988). Travels with Freeman. *Journal of Interpretation*, *12*(1):T7-T8.

Dillon, C. (1991). Interpretation and the protection of Zambia's wildlife. In *Proceedings, National Interpreters Workshop*, NAI. Vail, CO.

Dunmire, W. (1976). Stretching recreation dollars through interpretation. In D. M. Knudson (Ed.), *Managing Recreation Resources for Century III*. W. Lafayette, IN: Purdue University.

Dustin, D. and McAvoy, L. (1985). Interpretation as a management tool: A dissenting opinion. *The Interpreter, 16*(Spring):18-20.

Eagley, A. H. and Himmelfarb, S. (1978). Attitudes and opinions. *Annual Review of Psychology*, *29*:517-554.

Fishbein, M. (1980). A theory of reasoned action: Some applications and implications. In H. E. Howe and M. M. Page (Eds.), *1979 Nebraska Symposium on Motivations*. Lincoln, NB: University of Nebraska Press.

Foley, J. P., and Keith, J. A. (1979). Interpretation in Canadian national parks and related resources—To what end? In *Conference II, Canadian National Parks Today and Tomorrow*, University of Waterloo, Ontario.

Fritschen, J. A. (1984). Interpretation for management. In *Supplements to a Guide to Cultural and Environmental Interpretation in the U.S. Army Corps of Engineers*. Vicksburg, MS: Environmental Laboratory, Recreation Research Program, Instruction Report R-84-1.

Fritschen, J. A. (1985). Interpretation research in the Corps of Engineers. *Trends, 22*(4):26-28.

Frome, M. (1982). To sin by silence. *Journal of Interpretation, 7*(2):41-45.

Gifford, R., Hay, R., and Boros, K. (1982). Individual differences in environmental attitudes. *Journal of Environmental Education, 14*(2):19-23.

Goethe, C. M. (1960). Nature study in national parks interpretive movement. *Yosemite, 39*(7):156-158.

Griest, D. L. (1981). "Factors contributing to and effects of manager-interpreter conflict: An analysis of U.S. Fish and Wildlife Service support for interpretation." Columbus, OH: Ohio State University, M.S. Thesis.

Hall, E. and James, D. (1992). The education program at Jefferson National Expansion Memorial celebrates the 75th. *Interpretation, (Fall-Winter)*:20-24.

Harrison, A. (1982). Problems: Vandalism and depreciative behavior. In G. W. Sharpe, *Interpreting the Environment (2nd ed.)*. New York, NY: John Wiley & Sons, Inc.

Hendee, J. C. (1972a). Challenging the folklore of environmental education. *Journal of Environmental Education, 3*(3):19-23.

Hendee, J. C. (1972b). No, to attitudes to evaluate environmental education. *Journal of Environmental Education, 3*(3):65.

Holtz, R. (1976). Nature centers, environmental attitudes, and objectives. *Journal of Environmental Education, 7*(3):34-37.

Hooper, J. K. and Weiss, K. S. (1990). Interpretation as a management tool: A national study of interpretive professionals' views. In *Proceedings, National Interpreters Workshop*, NAI, Charleston, SC.

King, L. M. and Tabata, R. S. (1992). Hanauma Bay educational programs: Interpretation as a park management tool. In *Proceedings, National Interpreters Workshop*, NAI, San Francisco Bay Area, CA.

Knapp, C. E. (1972). Attitudes and values in environmental education. *Journal of Environmental Education, 3*(4):26-29.

Mackintosh, B. (1992). Interpretation: A tool for NPS expansion. *Interpretation, (Fall-Winter)*:10-13.

Manfredo, M. J. (Ed.). (1992). *Influencing human behavior: Theory and applications in recreation, tourism, and natural resources management*. Champaign, IL: Sagamore Publishing, Inc.

Maslow, A. (1954). *Motivation and personality*. New York, NY: Harper & Row, Publishers, Inc.

McAvoy, L. H. and Dustin, D. (1983). Indirect versus direct regulation of recreation behavior. *Journal of Park and Recreation Administration, 1*(4):12-17.

Oliver, S. S., Roggenbuck, J. W., and Watson, A. E. (1985). Education to reduce impacts in forest campgrounds. *Journal of Forestry, 83*(4):234-236.

Peart, B. (1980). An application of the Foley-Keith objectives framework to interpretation activities. *Journal of Interpretation, 5*(2):6-9.

Penaloza, L. J. (1987). Who uses our parks: Results of the 1986 recreation survey. *Research Management Findings*, (8).

Reilly, W. K. (1991). Our national parks: Toward a new era of protection. Keynote speech, 75th Anniversary Symposium of the National Park Service. Vail, CO: (unpublished).

Roggenbuck, J. and Berrier, D. L. (1982). A comparison of the effectiveness of two communication strategies in dispersing wilderness campers. *Journal of Leisure Research, 14*(1):77-89.

Sharpe, G. W. (1988). Reducing vandalism through interpretation. In *Proceedings, National Interpreters Workshop*, NAI. San Diego, CA.

Sharpe, G. W. and Gensler, G. L. (1978). Interpretation as a management tool. *Journal of Interpretation, 3*(2):3-9.

Spears C. J. (1992). Using the press in controversial issues, In *Proceedings, National Interpreters Workshop*, NAI. San Francisco Bay Area, CA.

Van Matre, S. (1988). Environmental education: Mission gone astray. *Mini Journal of Interpretation (NAI), 1*(1):4, 6.

Vander Stoep, G. A. and Gramann, J. H. (1987). The effect of verbal appeals and incentives on depreciative behavior among youthful park visitors. *Journal of Leisure Research, 9*(2):69-83.

Verderber, R. (1978). *Communicate! (2nd ed.)*. Belmont, CA: Wadsworth Publishing Co.

Wagar, J. A. (1976). Evaluating the effectiveness of interpretation. *Journal of Interpretation, 1*(1):1-7.

Weaver, H. (1982). Origins of interpretation. In G. W. Sharpe, *Interpreting the Environment (2nd ed.)*. New York, NY: John Wiley & Sons, Inc.

Wicher, A. W. (1969). Attitudes vs. actions: The relationship of verbal and overt behavioral responses to attitude objects. *Journal of Social Issues, 25*(4):41-78.

The Clients

Understand the customers and what they seek—that stands as a first rule of most successful businesses, especially those producing services. In the museum and interpretation business, the visitor/customer/client comes first, even before the artifacts get displayed. It hasn't always been so.

Interpretation is one of the most intensely personal services. It involves people in complex thought processes to understand their surroundings and history while enjoying themselves. Yet, relatively few systematic studies analyze interpretive "visitors" to specific areas. As one interpreter asked at a national workshop, "Do we even know how well the owners of public lands and facilities like being called visitors?"

Serving Clients

Consumer-driven philosophy of product and service delivery is a hot topic now. The focus in management has shifted from technology, product, or operations as the driving force to the primacy of the customers. The approach is not new to interpretation management. It has long been suggested for industrial management by Peter Drucker, Theodore Levitt and Philip Kotler (Walters and Bergiel, 1989). The essence of the philosophy boils down to making decisions only after carefully considering consumer behavior and preferences.

THE REAL BOSS OF THE INTERPRETIVE OPERATION

The consumer-oriented marketing approach first tries to determine what clients want, then provide services to meet those wants. The final evaluation focuses on the quality of satisfaction, not just on how much was produced or earned. The client is the real boss of the agency or the company. This marketing approach is a state of mind, an attitude that is appropriate for all interpretive operations. It says that:

> *We are not in charge; the potential user is.*
> *We don't promote programs; we solve problems.*

> —Howard and Crompton, 1980

Programs themselves are not marketable. Only their benefits have a value—the response of the consumer to the interpretation. The program serves as a vehicle conveying a benefit. "If an agency defines its business in terms of specific programs, it is likely that it will miss opportunities to serve its clientele" (Howard and Crompton, 1980).

The alternative approach focuses on the product or service. Produce it and then persuade the customer to buy it (some call this selling, as contrasted to marketing). With the product-oriented perspective, suppliers decide what a park agency or interpretive company can do best, then offer it to the public on a take it or leave it basis, hoping that the public accepts and uses it.

This sort of product orientation usually doesn't focus on facilitating recreation experiences, but on the management of a visitor center. It is less concerned with service to the community and more with supervision of the staff, facilities and grounds. Many park and recreation professionals for whom interpreters work have strong resource or agency orientations. Their intellectual training and focus is necessarily on the site, facilities, and agency policy more than on the delivery of services. This is not peculiar to one professional academic preparation or government agency. Neither does it fall into the simplistic and often inflammatory dichotomy of people-oriented vs. resource-oriented thinking.

PRESERVING AND USING PARKS

Within the National Park Service, for example, some people insist on the primacy of preservation of the resource while others say visitors come first. It's a rather silly distinction; most recognize that the Congress mandated a real balance between the two. In practice, the interpreters deal with both foci, seeking to enrich the visitor experience, meeting real needs and desires, while directing the experiences within the bounds of reason, so the visitor will seek to enhance or protect the resources. The interpreter must know and use the resource thoroughly and carefully, in a way that has the greatest appeal and learning potential for visitors.

To put the matter simply, the astute interpreter will actively and reflectively seek the visitor's point of view while developing programs. The customer is king, but not an absolute tyrant. The interpreter can't and wouldn't want to ignore the resource. The interpreter has to know what's special, interesting and curious about the place, the region or the processes being interpreted. The interpreter offers a clear idea of the key values of the place.

FOREST SERVICE GUIDELINES

Long ago, the Forest Service published for its employees six basic principles of good visitor contacts:

1. *The Visitor Is Important.* In fact, recreation visitors are the most important people you will meet in the forest. Why?
   - They own the forests.
   - They have a right to be there.
   - The existence of the national forests depends on how they feel about them.
   - That goes for salaries, too.

2. *Service Is What We Give.* The word is in the name of the organization and information is a key service to forest visitors. It's not an option, but a must; not a special favor, but part of the work.

3. *Be Receptive.* Be encouraging; be friendly; give the visitor your full attention; make their contact a good experience.

4. *Be Helpful.* Take time to help find answers. "That's not my department" doesn't make it as an answer.

5. *Be Accurate.* Carry and use maps and brochures effectively.

6. *Be Informed.* Read the maps and brochures; find answers to common questions. Make up a reference book. Know the management activities as well as the interpretive facilities and programs in the area.

Studying Visitor Behavior

To observe the actions and reactions of city-bred people, left to their own devices in open country, is enlightening.... Their behavior sometimes passes all understanding as it changes rapidly from the ordinary to the extraordinary. We have been observing them for a number of years and find it a fascinating study.

—Carr, 1931

Visitor analysis and adaptation of exhibits and programs to their tastes has long been part of the practice of the profession. Visitor studies in museums and visitor centers since the late 1920s and various analyses in parks and forests give a theoretical basis of how they use the facilities and their apparent preferences. Interpreters use a number of marketing and communications principles to determine audience characteristics and preferences for selecting interpretive media and designing programs.

ANALYZING THE AUDIENCE

Every interpreter probably asks reflexively: Who's the audience? What works with them? What won't or can't they respond to? Grinder and McCoy (1985) pointed out that each audience is a small "culture" unto itself. Some have members who know each other very well and have well-developed relationships. Their interpersonal rivalries, friendships and behavior norms can override the relationship that the interpreter tries to set up with individuals. For example, school classes form tight little civilizations (some of them rather barbaric).

Other groups come together rather randomly and have little or no "cultural" structure. They often become very responsive to the interpreter. Then, if they become regular visitors, they may form their own subculture—a condition that interpreters might encourage, without making it exclusive.

Many techniques exist for studying the existing audience and the potential clientele (Figure 5.1, page 106). First come applications of marketing theory to interpretation. Then come studies of needs of particular groups.

FIGURE 5.1
Visitors come as families and alone, from very young to very old, from many nations and cultural backgrounds.

SEGMENTING DEMAND

Sociologists have had a busy time in recent years doing recreational and travel studies based on marketing theory. One favorite technique is to segment the demand side of the market, that is, to divide customers into descriptive groups (almost always four quadrants). Individuals are placed on a grid, or analyzed in clusters, based on some set of demographic or group characteristics. Thus, young males who camp and travel in packs of three or more can be segmented from extended families of three or four generations including both sexes who are picnicking. The value of this—with more elaborate categories—comes when a park manager can see the current composition of the clientele and compare it with the kinds of facilities and programming available. The interpreter can see if the visitors to the center and programs match those of the park in general, then try adjustments in programming or self-guiding facilities to reach those who are not getting the interpretive messages.

To carry this further, the interpreter could interview representatives of the groups that are not being reached, to determine directly what kinds of activities might be appropriate for them. The challenge comes in determining the type of questions to pose to get honest and helpful answers.

Putting on Their Shoes

Before starting to develop and package programs, put yourself in the shoes of the visitor—and the nonvisitor. What questions about this place spark people's interest? Why are some people not coming? Is there some service that could reach out to them—not to get them to buy the park or museum interpretation, but to enrich their sense of place, of joy in their surroundings, of elevating their sense of belonging and identity? To explore the possibilities, several approaches may be used, as explained in the following paragraphs.

METHOD 1:
BE A FRESH VISITOR YOURSELF

To see a new place as a visitor might, study it as if it were an unfamiliar place to you. The first visit or the first few weeks are crucial—before you begin to take things as routine or before you are involved with the agency or company culture. After a while, you will adopt many of the company reasons, excuses and other logic that cause things to be a certain way. At first, however, you can bring an innocence and awe as well as a critical mind to the task. Remember your initial confusion as to where you were and how to get to the next place—these are visitor barriers to comprehension of interpretive messages. Think of visitors driving into the general region who (probably) will not know of the interpretive opportunities lying in wait for them. Will the family in a private resort know about the State Forest hikes and campfires just down the road? Are they welcome? Does it cost? Wear the visitors' shoes for as long as you can, taking notes and talking little. Keep the notes. Ask a few discrete questions but avoid insulting your colleagues with intemperate criticism. With time, make the changes that seem to fit. Remember that the freshness of perspective wears off quite rapidly as you become part of the area.

METHOD 2:
GO SOMEWHERE ELSE TO REFRESH YOUR VIEW

Looking at a neighboring facility as a customer may stimulate your critical faculties. Go not as a professional interpreter visiting a colleague but as a perceptive visitor seeking answers and experiences, with normal questions about what's happening and what's this and that. Again, note-taking causes you to review your first impressions, even after they may have been modified and seem trivial (they probably aren't trivial to the visitor). Review your own operation with these questions in mind.

METHOD 3:
CALL IN A CONSULTANT OR OTHER OUTSIDE OBSERVER

A friend or paid consultant can do two things for agency personnel. First, they provide their own fresh and hopefully expert impressions and opinions. An experienced consultant may quickly assess a situation and offer suggestions for improvement of service, as well as finding defects. Often, the staff knows of these, but the outside opinion may settle differences of opinion. It may focus or clarify the problems and may direct the staff toward reasonable improvements in service. Second, consultants can efficiently survey visitors (or nonvisitors or neighbors), getting responses that may be more candid or to the point than an agency employee could elicit. Consultants come in many guises and for many prices. Know what you want done—identify your goals—and find out who can do it effectively. Sometimes, a Cooperative Extension Service specialists can do a job quickly for no cost; they will tell you when you need outside help.

METHOD 4:
ASK THE VISITORS

Check regularly with visitors to inquire about their expectations, interests, preferences, and questions can provide a sense of what they seek. This will take special effort—one that is appreciated. It cannot be just a question period at the campfire program nor just a chance encounter although both could reveal some important ideas.

Why do some local residents come to a local nature center or museum? Why do others stay away? Conjecture in the park office won't answer these questions definitively. A suggestion box or entries in a guest book will shed only a glimmer of light on the topic. To put the clients in charge of the agency, they must be contacted and heard, directly.

The interpreter who wants valid information will take time (or money) to survey and interview clients and nonclients about what they seek or would seek. Use statistical sampling principles, such as population definition, random sampling, adequate sample size and representativeness, plus stratification and replications over time and space.

Door-to-door sample surveys may work well for local parks. Interviews with selected people at the gates or doors of a facility may help in other cases. Sociologists and other researchers often hand out questionnaires at the gates, hoping to get back enough returns in the mail so they can declare it a meaningful study— and it works for many. Many other methods can answer questions about what consumers want from interpretive programs. Masses of data may not be as desirable as personal sensitivity and regular refreshment public contact on the part of the interpreter. The attitude that the interpretive program is driven by visitor needs is the key.

METHOD 5:
WATCH THE VISITORS

Time and movement studies reveal how visitors use a museum, or how much they read on a trail. Counters, clickers, videos, and samplers can record how often and how long people view expensive exhibits, which ways they move, even whether or not they stay long enough to get the message. Perhaps more important, just watch and listen, taking notes of daily observations. It may affect your jaded stereotypes of who shows up and what interests them (Box 5.1).

BOX 5.1: OBSERVATIONS SHATTER STEREOTYPES

At one nature center I was studying, I saw many visitors wearing tattoos, under-shirts as outerwear, black t-shirts, leather jackets, interesting jewelry, and similar "identity badges." Their language suggested they'd had little formal education in the natural sciences, and they'd missed a few classes in using their native tongue.

I watched and listened as they looked at exhibit cases with their children. The conversations suggested profound interests in animals and plants. They asked provocative and riveting questions of their children and each other with enthusi-asm. They answered the kids' questions with joy, excitement, and positive rein-forcement. More listening revealed that many of these people enjoyed fishing and hunting; they spent many weekends in forests and parks. Many of them knew a lot about nature and enjoyed learning more. They read labels aloud.

Few of these people went to interpretive talks; they seldom went on conducted hikes. But they thoroughly enjoyed the exhibits, as they proved in exit interviews. Yet this market segment (lower education level, high experience level) wasn't tar-geted or even clearly identified by the interpretive program. Literature, personal assumptions and general observation suggest that this group wasn't likely to be interested in interpretation. Observational consumer analysis over many days, however, revealed that many active participants came from this little-known seg-ment of the market.

—DMK

VISITOR PREFERENCE STUDIES

> When and why do we ask people what they think and want, instead of giving them what we have or believe is good for them?
> —Harris, 1991

When specific interpretive alternatives exist, visitors will express their preferences when asked. The alternatives may relate to times of programs, means of presenting information, styles of type, or choices of topics in visitor center exhibits. Travel programs and special events may also be put to a preference "vote" through simple questionnaires or interviews. Others use focus group interviews (see Chapter 19).

As one example of simple visitor study, cave interpreters listened to visitors. Management used the results to make big financial decisions. Three years of prefer-ence studies asked what kinds of tour through the cave visitors preferred. Of three types of delivery—(a) guided walking tours, (b) self-guided tours with stationed guides, and (c) self-guided with taped interpretive messages—none enjoyed a clear preference by visitors.

When visitors had a choice of walking to the cave entry or riding a tram, they pre-ferred the walk. When the cave discontinued the tram, the walk weeded out the one to two percent who couldn't have made the cave visit physically. As a result the number of stretcher removal cases dropped from one every 2-3 weeks to one case in four sea-sons (Gilbert, 1977).

Interpreting Over Barriers

On the social front the parks provide one of the few truly democratic facilities for enjoyment and inspiration of all of the people. To the extent that we become inclusive in our welcome, understanding, accommodation, and interpretation of all constituent populations . . . we reduce fragmentation and strife.
—William Brown, 1971

Much concern about serving all populations infused national law in the past twenty years. Assuring equal access to facilities and programs includes dealing with physical, economic, racial/cultural, educational, age and other barriers that keep arising. Laws say that public agencies—or those financially tied to government by assistance or tax breaks—should assure equal access to virtually all people. The most rigorous of these, Canada's recent Multicultural Act and the Americans with Disabilities Act of 1991, applied the previously existing regulations of federal agencies to provincial, state, local, and private organizations.

WE ARE ALL DIFFERENT

This book refers generically to visitors and audiences. Any implication of the existence of an average visitor oversimplifies reality (Figure 5.2). Each visitor brings along a personal set of experiences, interests, knowledge, ability, and personality. Yet, interpreters often refer to the public, the visitor, the average family as convenient abstractions.

FIGURE 5.2
Japanese high school students and their translator seek to understand the Carroll County Farm Museum in Maryland.

If one limits their thinking to the "average" or "typical" family, he or she may build a form of social or physical barrier to participation in interpretive activities. By choosing certain activities, locations, subjects, words, or attitudes, interpreters effectively bar participation to some members of the community. By not addressing barriers to participation, interpreters limit their audiences and fail to fully accomplish their missions. More importantly, nonparticipants miss opportunities to secure the personal benefits that interpretation offers.

Physical barriers limit access by the elderly and physically handicapped. Some ethnic groups sense limits on their participation. Nonparticipants either (1) do not know about the interpretive opportunities, (2) they want to participate but encounter real or perceived barriers, or (3) they do not perceive value in participating. Regardless of the reason for nonparticipation, interpreters can try to make everyone aware of the opportunities, eliminate barriers, and understand the needs and values of all those who can be served. Many government agencies devote special resources to serving these populations.

QUICK BARRIER THEORY

The many barriers inhibiting full leisure participation fit into three major categories (Smith, 1985). They are not all related to physical or mental limitations; some are purely personal, psychological, or attitude phenomena.

- Intrinsic barriers, resulting from an individual's personal limitations involving physical, psychological, or cognitive disabilities, include several situations that may inhibit desires to try interpretive service:
    - —Skill/challenge gap, where the person's skills may seem inadequate to allow enjoyment of an activity.
    - —Physical dependence on another person or machine.
    - —Psychological dependence on support groups for encouragement.
    - —Health problems and chronic limitations, such as range of movement, allergies and hyper-reactions to poisonous plants, sun, insects, hemophiliac limitations on contact or rough activities.
    - —Social ineffectiveness and related self-image problems.
    - —Lack of knowledge of programs, facilities, and recreation resources to make informed choices may inhibit a person's desire to try interpretive service modes of transportation and support services.
- Environmental barriers, involving external forces that impose limitations on an individual with a disability, including the following:
    - —Attitudes of family, friends, or strangers, including negative behaviors toward people who are different, paternalistic behaviors that set persons apart, and apathetic behaviors that ignore needs and concerns of disabled people.
    - —Architectural structures that don't allow access, shutting out some.
    - —Natural obstacles such as hills, rocks, snow, sand, and even trees that limit use of the environment unless access designs make them less of a problem.
    - —Transportation barriers that keep a person from traveling to a site.
    - —Economic barriers from low income and high expenses produce less discretionary money for leisure pursuits.
    - —Rules and regulations may limit some activities by people with certain disabilities, although many of these were eliminated by recent laws.
    - —Barriers of omission, such as lack of interpretive services providing access, lack of publicizing appropriate services, lack of education or training for leisure and interpretation skills.

- Communications barriers, resulting from sender and/or receiver failures, arise when the two parties fail to link up. The most obvious cases are people with sight and/or hearing impairments. Although an interpreter may be speaking so most people can hear and showing slides that most can see, some people will have difficulty and may become frustrated with the program offerings.

TEENAGE CLIENTS

It may take time and patient probing to discover why interpretation "just isn't cool" for some teenagers, and how it can be made attractive, especially when they are around their peers. Extreme self-consciousness and striving to conform to imagined or real group norms seems to go with adolescence. So does the breaking away process, as the youth seeks gradual independence from parental connections.

Yet, those teenage years comprise a peak learning time—a period when the mind can comprehend many complexities and see a global view for the first time. This youthful life stage represents an opportunity to build the constructive ideals of responsible behavior toward the natural world and maybe even toward the valuable structures, artifacts and sites of history.

The physical challenges of the environment stir many youths to adventure, risk recreation, and a sense of oneness with the world, providing experiences that last a lifetime in memories. Once, the lessons of hunting, trapping, and working the woods with dad were rites of passage for most boys. Today, the interpretive naturalist may be the only person that a youth meets who really can provide the deep-woods knowledge to inspire deeper probing for revelation and self-actualization. Yet, most "cool" kids seem to avoid interpreters—and most interpreters can't figure out how to change it. The interpreters who have solved this riddle report positive responses and a sense of accomplishment.

The answers seem to lie in the application of learning theory along with imaginative mixtures of fun, adventure, sociability, and interpretive techniques (Figure 5.3). Teenagers may need to be offered programs that let them participate independently of their parents, associated with others of their age or a little older. Then come the rewards for the even tougher job of getting kids excited about historical interpretation. Living history seems to do it as well as anything.

FIGURE 5.3
Talking exhibits can involve teenagers with a favorite implement.

ETHNIC GROUPS

Some ethnic groups rarely avail themselves of interpretive opportunities. In a sort of self-fulfilling prophecy, interpreters don't develop programs for these groups because the groups don't attend interpretive programs. Although interpreters may never overcome all of the cultural and social barriers which limit participation, the better interpreters understand their constituents, the better they can serve them.

Recent research regarding African-American and Hispanic participation in outdoor recreation and interpretation suggests some of the problems and solutions. Each of these two large groups of people includes subgroups that vary greatly one from another. For example, U.S.-born, Mexican, Central American, and Caribbean-born Hispanics may differ markedly in their recreation values and behaviors. Within any of these origins, individuals and families differ markedly in economics, culture, and tastes and resent stereotyping as much as do Anglos. However, some generalizations from research on these categories provide some basis for approaches to stimulating greater participation in interpretive services.

Research on Hispanics by the USDA Forest Service (Simcox and Pfister, 1991) revealed two important findings about national forest visitors in southern California:

- Some Hispanic immigrants have little formal education. This affects the use of interpretive signage, brochures, maps, and other media, even when written in Spanish (Figure 5.4). Different word nuances among different Spanish-speaking countries can also create some amusing and possibly embarrassing situations.

- Interaction with extended family and friends ranks as extremely important when visiting a site. Thus, large groups picnic together, breaking the planned mold in many parks of single family picnic sites (for 5-6 people maximum). The groups most commonly have three characteristics: (1) strong family orientation, (2) strong social focus of the recreational activity, and (3) presence of children.

FIGURE 5.4
Bilingual interpretation serves many visitors and residents alike in the southwestern U.S.

Although few Hispanics participated in nature-related recreation in two urban national forests, they seemed open to trying the activities (Chavez, 1992). For example, only 28 percent had been on a natural history hike, but 78 percent said they might try it. Likewise, 4 percent had been on a "camera safari" but 76 percent might try it. Apparently, some kinds of barriers or alternative preferences limit participation in such activities. Fullfilling children's interests might encourage such participation.

Research on African-American preferences and participation in interpretive related activities include surveys and focus groups in Missouri urban areas (Wallace and Witter, 1990). This work revealed the following attitudes about interpretation:

- Fear of wild animals and fear of racial intimidation served as major barriers to outdoor recreation participation. The people preferred well-lighted areas where authorities kept track of who went in and out—places where nature and humans could be controlled.
- They preferred areas offering chances for group interaction and social exchange where they could feel welcome.
- They would prefer hiking a nature trail without a guide if they had a map, someone knew where they were and would come for them if they did not return.
- Respondents had an interest in visiting nature centers, particularly those with hands-on exhibits. They also expressed interest in what the centers could do for their children.

A study of Chicago households also found that African-Americans preferred developed sites and meeting people (Dwyer and Hutchison, 1990). They travelled shorter distances than whites, resulting in a stronger urban park orientation, perhaps partly due to family finances. This study also explained differences in rates of participation between white and African-American populations. Two viewpoints currently produce much debate: the marginality viewpoint suggests that differences derive from the generally lower socioeconomic position in society, while the ethnicity view suggests that differences are a product of racially based culture preferences. Dwyer and Hutchison's data supported both marginality and ethnicity perspectives.

Meeker, Woods, and Lucas, (1992) hypothesized that—seemingly in a remarkable oversimplification—unlike European cultures where peace and fulfillment came from the land, African-Americans have found humiliation and misery there. The latter look on the land with hatred rather than love. Meeker cited Eldridge Cleaver to the effect that African-Americans "measure their own value according to the number of degrees they are away from the soil" and that one of the worst insults is to be called "farm boy" or somehow to be linked to an agrarian environment.

Caron (1989) assessed African-American concerns about environmental issues and found a moderate acceptance of a proenvironment perspective, comparable to that of whites. Toxic waste and other health risks from pollution seemed most salient. She noted that, although the absolute level of environmental concern compares to that of whites, it may be less of a concern than more urgent survival and acceptance issues such as poverty and discrimination. This relative concern may lead to the assumption that African-Americans think environmental issues have little importance. Caron (1989) concluded, however, that environmental and conservation organizations shouldn't dismiss African-Americans as potential clients and allies.

NATIVE AMERICANS

A generation ago, Meeker first wrote that national parks were places of humiliation for Native Americans, who were often displayed and exploited there (Meeker, 1992). Although truth abides in that statement, it most certainly ignored the many parks where American Indian heritage got very sensitive treatment and where long-term direct collaboration with neighboring tribes and communities existed. These types of relationships have expanded rapidly in recent years, with increasing participation by many American Indians leading interpretation work today.

Wilson Hunter, Jr. of Canyon de Chelly National Monument won the 1991 national Tilden Award for bringing greater cultural sensitivity and union to southwestern interpretation. He established the Tsegi Guide Association and training program for the Navajos who accompany all visitors into Canyon de Chelly. He stressed pride in the land and in personal heritage, helping build bridges of understanding between Navajos and the public, as well as with the National Park Service. He helped his trainees express views in graphic ways that all people may comprehend. For example, he described creation as a woven Navajo rug. It is beautiful; it took a long time to weave the threads into the intricate pattern. If we unravel it, it loses its integrity.

Hunter also helped found the Council for American Indian Interpretation. When he visited Venezuela at the International Parks Conference in 1992, he encouraged native groups throughout Latin America to more clearly interpret their cultures within their own nations.

Today, in the U.S. and Canada, growing numbers of villages and tribes offer their own recreation and interpretive facilities. Some of them focus on their religious traditions. Others explain their history, cultural traditions, outdoor skills, music, and current living conditions through museums, tours, pow-wows, and other services.

INCLUSIVE INTERPRETATION

How then should interpreters respond to the two factors of ethnicity and socioeconomic barriers? They may surely identify and address distinct ethnic preferences, while at the same time trying to reduce social and economic barriers.

For Hispanics and African-Americans, providing programs and well-developed sites that accommodate large groups would address some ethnicity needs. Likewise, attracting families to nature centers and programs may start with attracting their children. The ethnicity perspective also points toward topics and activities of interest to a particular population which could be linked to other messages on those topics.

An approach to reduce economic barriers of transportation could take interpretation into the streets, schools, churches, community centers and parks close to the target population. Nature-Mobiles and History-Mobiles, with portable exhibits and activities, extend many interpretive centers and museums. Often, interpreters can coordinate the scheduling of in-museum or in-park programs with the availability of public transportation.

Making people feel welcome and safe reduces social barriers. Even though a nature center would seem to represent a safe, family-oriented site, focus group participants said they probably wouldn't visit without an invitation. Several said they needed an indication of being welcome and secure. Invitations through churches, schools, social clubs and selective mass media could be effective. Several participants suggested that young African-Americans trained to teach other minority children and the presence of minority staff would make them feel more welcome (Wallace and Witter, 1990).

Innovative programs reduce barriers by taking messages to the people across ethnic barriers by tailoring programs to the needs and preferences of specific audiences (White, 1991), as indicated in Box 5.2.

BOX 5.2: ROBIN WHITE: PLANTING SEEDS IN A CONCRETE JUNGLE

Robin White grew up in an urban housing project in Gary, Indiana. By the age of 12, she led a gang, eventually spending time in a "girls' home." The turning point in her life came when she joined a Young Adult Conservation Corps team at the Indiana Dunes National Lakeshore. She became a cooperative education student at the Lakeshore and earned a B.S. degree in criminal justice.

Ms. White became the "Outreach Coordinator" at the Indiana Dunes. She developed partnerships with community groups and crafted sensitive programs for those who do not usually visit parks. Her target audiences included probationary juveniles, gang members, physically disabled, senior citizens, groups from Gary's low-income housing projects, groups from mental health centers. The programs emphasized the value of natural environments and cultural heritage preserved at the Dunes. She got inner city youth and nature together. She worked with more than twenty community groups in the Chicago-Gary corridor, drawing 1,500 people to environmental education programs. Her gang intervention workshops in the park involved more than 200 rival gang members (White, 1991). One took rival gang members into the park on overnight field trips called "Moonlight Dunelight." This experience resulted in some of the young people dropping out of the gangs and leading more productive lives.

In 1991, Robin went to Petroglyph National Monument as "Urban Outreach Environmental Education Specialist." She brought the diverse cultures of Albuquerque to the park and developed programs specifically for them. One cooperates with an intervention and substance abuse program, exposing at-risk youth to the environment, enhancing self-development, learning the concept of teamwork, expanding leadership skills, breaking down social barriers and developing deductive reasoning skills.

Robin believes that for young people to invest themselves in any productive activity, organizations must "speak their language and catch their imagination." The goal of her program is to plant seeds of greatness in our youth. She planted these seeds first in a concrete jungle and now in the desert, watching them grow and bear fruit.

Sources: cited material, interview and correspondence

Meeting the needs of ethnic groups also means getting the stories straight when interpreting. More than half of the almost 200 historical areas of the National Park Service focus on the contributions of ethnic minorities and/or women (Mackintosh, 1987). However, most of the traditional interpretation at these sites came from a strictly Eurocentric perspective. Many of the messages contain stereotypes (Sanchez, 1990) that can insult and repel many people.

The problems haven't all disappeared with greater general sensitivity and legal maneuverings. Misinformation and myth in the Alamo still implies that heroes were more melodramatic than in real life and that Mexicans were invaders. Lindo (1991) reported little progress at multicultural programming and services in Canada, with attempts being made as still in the awkward phase.

As interpreters move toward a more balanced and accurate approach, they need not inflate or overly dramatize what was previously ignored (Mackintosh, 1987). Some misinformation, given out by overzealous interpreters, tries to atone for past sins of omission. "Accuracy, appropriateness, perspective, and balance are universal requirements, regardless of subject matter. As long as these essentials are adhered to, the expanded interpretation of minorities and women will continue to inspire national park visitors" (Mackintosh, 1987).

FOREIGN VISITORS

Tourists from other countries increased dramatically over the past ten or fifteen years. Most tourists to the U.S. come from Canada, Germany, Mexico, and Japan. Most visitors to Canada come from the U.S., Hong Kong, Japan, France, and Germany.

At some museums and parks, signing and staffing require the use of multiple languages. Most major attractions have at least brochures and maps available in three or more languages. Loaned audio cassette tapes, recorded in various languages, offer one of the most popular and efficient ways of interpreting to foreign clientele.

The key to successful interpretive efforts boils down to knowing the visitors. International studies of visitors indicate some definite preferences and travel patterns. For example, a majority of Japanese visitors arrive at a park, forest, or private attraction in tour buses, disgorging 30-60 visitors at a time in a visitor center or museum. Many of these groups have common interests, such as employer, occupations or study interest. Many are highly motivated to learn about the environment and culture. By tradition, they also wish to shop for meaningful gifts for relatives and friends at home (Machlis, Field, and Van Every, 1992). And, of course, this country's citizens are famous for their consistent use of the fine cameras that they produce.

Japanese, French, and German tour groups usually arrive with a translator or two, allowing some ease of interpretation. However, the interpreter must adjust the presentation. Having everything said twice slows down the presentation and doesn't allow for highly interactive presentations. Much humor can be lost in translation, especially puns, irony, and local events. Physical demonstrations of things that don't require a lot of explanation plus direct participation in simple skills usually turn out as more productive than long talks.

Many visitors who arrive as tour groups don't fit into "normal" programming schedules or styles. Therefore, they are too often welcomed to the visitor center and left to their own devices. The bus company then recommends a 15-20 minute stop, which prevents much significant interaction with the resource. If a visitor center or museum gets very many tour groups, the interpreters might introduce special programming to serve these people with brief, well-prepared high-involvement interpretation that could be the highlight of their tour—something beyond a normal rubber-necking stop.

PHYSICALLY DISABLED VISITORS

I am calling on America to meet a great challenge: achieving the full acceptance and participation in all aspects of life for our 43 million citizens with disabilities. The signing into law by President Bush last year of the Americans with Disabilities Act has strengthened this commitment.

> —James Brady, Vice-Chairman,
> National Organization on Disability;
> former Press Secretary for President Reagan

On July 26, 1990, President Bush signed the Americans with Disabilities Act (ADA—PL 101-336). This sweeping, long civil rights law extends federal protection and specifies standards for the elimination of discrimination against visitors with disabilities.

The ADA states that everyone, regardless of disability, should have full enjoyment and equal opportunity of public services, facilities, employment, and goods. An individual with disabilities is a person who has a physical or mental impairment that substantially limits one or more major life activities or has a record of such impairment. The law mandates that policies and practices accommodate such individuals. Accessibility must be anticipated and assured in new or remodeled facilities. The law and its predecessor, the Rehabilitation Act of 1973 (for federal installations), applies to all facilities except private clubs and religious organizations.

Failure to comply with the ADA may result in grievances and civil rights law suits. The best defense comes from a strong relationship with the disabled community and demonstration of good faith efforts to comply with the law (Stevens, 1992).

Creative approaches developed after the 1973 law. For example, the U.S. Fish and Wildlife Service arranged with the Job Corps to reconstruct National Wildlife Refuge facilities to comply with the law. Similar cooperative arrangements might be possible for local agencies with Job Corps or similar Vocational Skills Training Program.

HOW THE ADA AFFECTS INTERPRETATION

The following examples illustrate situations considered discriminatory under the ADA (McGovern, 1993):

1. Camps cannot assume that an individual with disabilities would not want to climb rocks or climbing towers or that it would not be safe and therefore prohibit participation. When safety arises as a concern, the agency must conduct an individualized assessment to determine whether accommodations can allow safe participation.
2. Allowing an individual with disabilities to register for an orienteering program but failing to identify accessible orientation points is discriminatory. If a program is open, it must make accommodations for the disabled.

3. An interpretive facility which offers 100 programs but only ten for people with disabilities would be considered discriminatory. Interpretive programs for people with disabilities must be equal to those programs for people without disabilities.
4. Programs must occur in the most integrated setting possible. If staff members don't learn techniques to reduce negative interaction among people with and without disabilities, they might be found in violation.
5. Requiring the disabled to attend the 10:00 a.m. museum tour when others go on throughout the day would be considered discriminatory.
6. Charging higher fees or surcharges to visitors with disabilities to recover the cost of compliance or accommodations violates the ADA.
7. Rules, policies, and procedures must enable a person with a disability to meet eligibility requirements. For example, a person should be able to register for a program in advance by telephone or FAX rather than having registration on a first come-first served basis at a remote site.
8. Agencies must provide auxiliary aids such as raised letters, special signage (Figure 5.5), signers for the deaf, or cassette tapes to facilitate communication.
9. Structural changes to facilities or other methods of making an activity or program accessible must be undertaken to prevent violations.

FIGURE 5.5
A bronze, raised relief model helps most visitors to grasp the design of Ft. McHenry in Maryland.

These demands seem onerous in some cases. What does not have to be provided under ADA? Agencies do not have to provide personal services such as carrying an individual with disabilities, feeding, toileting, or changing their clothes. Also, an "undue burden clause" states that an agency need not provide reasonable accommodation if it causes undue burden such as fundamental alteration in the nature of the program, economic burden, or administrative burden. However, according to McGovern (1993), this test will seldom be met.

INTERPRETING FOR AN INDIVIDUAL WITH DISABILITIES

In light of these restrictions and requirements, how should an interpreter proceed? If an organization complies with the ADA, it will have a coordinator. This person works to make specific interpretive facilities and programs accessible.

A wealth of available literature describes how to remove physical barriers or design accessible facilities. The U.S. Department of the Interior and the Department of Justice, along with the Architectural and Transportation Barriers Compliance Board (ATBCB) offers guidelines for accessibility in parks, playgrounds, and similar areas. Site design guidelines for accessibility abound in the professional park literature (e.g., Hultsman, Cottrell, and Hultsman, 1987, Trapp, Gross, and Zimmerman, 1991).

The National Recreation and Park Association has taken the lead in offering ADA workshops and publications for park settings. Some of the best sources of information are individuals with disabilities who live in the local community.

For many years, interpreters have made attempts—many of them misguided—to serve special populations. Yambert (1981), after long experience as a pioneer in this field, outlined the predictable sequence of stages that historically took place as interpreters tried to meet the needs of the disabled:

1. Highly visible, but often incomplete adaptations of facilities to make them accessible, including Braille trails, ramps, toilets, and clever signs.
2. Self-serving publicity campaigns extolling the virtue of the work. In some instances more effort would go into the publicity effort than would go into the operation or maintenance of the facility or program.
3. Bureaucratic disillusionment when the individuals with disabilities did not flock to the facilities and programs.
4. Personal disappointment when the individuals with disabilities who did visit told us about our inadequate efforts either verbally or by not returning.
5. Eventual abandonment of the programs and reduction in maintenance of the facilities or use of the access sites as "tour stops" to show what was being done for the disabled.

INTEGRATING DISABLED INDIVIDUALS INTO INTERPRETIVE PROGRAMS

The ADA broke tradition by focusing on integrating the individual with disabilities with the nondisabled rather than on providing expensive and seldom-used special facilities. Integration is not just mandated by the ADA; this cost-effective approach meets the needs of visitors. The idea of separate tours, hikes, programs or facilities offends many individuals with disabilities because it focuses on their inabilities rather than on similarities with other people.

Braille trails, popular in the 1970s, illustrate the wisdom and efficiency of integration. Gregoire and Wobig-Freimund (1987) reported findings that, after years of infrequent use and expensive maintenance, visitors with visual impairments would rather use regular trails to emphasize their similarity to nondisabled visitors. Moreover, the visitors with visual impairments almost always accompanied sighted people, thereby rendering the Braille signs unnecessary.

Instead of Braille, small and inexpensive changes to existing trails, such as a raised and textured map of routes and landmarks, can produce multiple benefits. This increases the number of trail options for the visitors with visual impairments. They use existing trails, allowing chances for the disabled to interact with nondisabled. Likewise, a hard-packed trail surface benefits many visitors—those with visual impairments, those who use wheelchairs, the older adult, small children, families with strollers, and any visitors with difficulty in walking, such as those wearing sandals.

Besides integration being "the law" and being cost effective, Gregoire and Wobig-Freimund (1987) listed several other reasons for providing for it:

- It's a civil right.
- The disabled learn social skills when integrated [so do the rest of us].
- Integration provides opportunities for building self-esteem.
- Integration enhances the quality of life for the disabled.

THINKING AND ACTING APPROPRIATELY

The following seven practical suggestions for integrating the individual with disabilities into interpretive programs may guide the interpreter (Lais, quoted in Gregoire and Wobig-Freimund, 1987).

1. Respect each person's dignity in gestures, language, and action. Involve them in all aspects of an interpretive program, but not unctuously. Provide challenging yet success-oriented options to mixed ability groups. At any level the tasks should be meaningful. When referring to an individual with disabilities, emphasize the person by name.

2. Open lines of communication: be open and honest about assessing a situation and talking about feelings and attitudes. Talk with individuals before the program to learn how to meet their particular needs in certain situations. Ask for suggestions when deciding on an issue that affects them. Never indicate that you understand someone when you do not. Ask the person to spell out or rephrase information that you do not understand; take time to communicate.

3. Establish patterns for integrated decision-making or answering questions. Make decisions with individuals, not for them. Answer questions asked of you. Do not answer questions asked of the individual with disabilities; this may seem helpful to you but to them it may seem to discredit their intelligence, insights, and judgement. Assign leadership responsibilities equally in a group among participants with or without disabilities.

4. Emphasize the value of effort and nonphysical accomplishments. Recognize the value of roles that individuals with disabilities take in the group. For example, a person responsible for overseeing appropriate safety measures has as much importance as the person carrying equipment.

5. Focus on group challenges. These tend to equalize everyone's participation. If the group goal is to identify 20 species of birds, visitors with visual impairments can contribute by hearing distinctive bird calls and visitors with hearing impairments can contribute with sightings. Disadvantages would arise from an individual competition, but each can make positive contributions and be successful in a group challenge.

6. Develop social relationships among participants. Use structured activities that involve individuals with or without disabilities in cooperative tasks.

7. Delineate and delegate tasks. Break down tasks into parts to find activities for each member of the group to accomplish. For example, in a group exercise to develop a key to tree identification, visitors with visual impairments may separate the leaves based on leaf shape, size and type of margin, while other group members may be asked to describe leaf and bark color and other visual characteristics.

To sum up this section, interpreters working with disabled individuals as part of a visitor group can focus on good teaching methods, on getting people to participate, and learn by building on their own prior knowledge and skills. The interpreters will avoid offending people if they avoid acting overly solicitous, if they avoid limiting the individual by personal feelings or assumptions or words. Treat them as people who have learned to deal with some impediments every day. Offer pride; don't take it away by doing for them what they can do and have done for years. Let them say when they need help. Don't be cruel—either by excessive kindness or by ignoring or dismissing them.

OLDER ADULT VISITORS

In learning theories, the needs of children receive much attention. This section discusses how to meet the needs of the people at the other end of the age spectrum. More than 25 per cent of Americans (62 million) are over 50 years of age, nearly 30 million of them are over 65 (McCormick, 1991). This age group will continue to grow in numbers and mobility. The older adult will make up an increasingly important audience for interpreters.

At some times of the year, they make up the majority of visitors in parks, forests, and vacation attractions. Not restricted by school schedules, they can avoid summer crowds by traveling in the fall, winter and spring. During these off-season periods, interpreters can focus their attention on serving the rather sophisticated needs and abilities of this age group.

Elderhostel programs throughout the world attest to the eagerness to learn and travel. People over 60 go to these week-or-longer intensive courses for both recreation and interpretation. They get exposure to some of the leading teachers and professional people in whatever area they visit, challenging those lecturers or crafts persons to put forth their best efforts.

Although seniors do experience physical changes that affect how they recreate, they don't all act frail and feeble. Many are active athletes and have great endurance and enthusiasm. Unfortunately, many others slow down considerably as muscles lose tone and bones lose calcium and other ravages of carefree living catch up to them. Geiger and Ellis (1991) identified the three most common ailments as arthritis, hearing loss, and visual impairment. The following strategies can mitigate the effects of these ailments:

1. **Arthritis.** This condition, along with several related ones, limits mobility and dexterity. Hard, smooth surfaces make it easier to get around. On trails, gentle slopes (5 percent) and frequent benches make walking more appealing to those with limited conditioning stamina or mobility.

2. **Hearing loss.** The awareness of the interpreter to the difficulty some people may have with hearing will reduce embarrassment of those who hesitate to ask you to speak louder. Watch for visual clues such as lack of eye contact, failure

to respond readily to questions. The simplest remedy involves speaking louder. "Assistive Listening Devices" such as AM or FM radio, infrared or induction loops can amplify sound signals and enable visitors to better hear talks and audio visual productions. Captioning on films helps the hard of hearing, the foreign visitor, and it reinforces or clarifies the message for all visitors. Because many people won't ask for captioning, use the captioned version all the time to maximize its benefits.

3. **Visual impairment.** As a person ages, the pupil size decreases, making it necessary to have more light to see well. Exhibits and pathways need to be well-lighted for older visitors. The ability to read small print often decreases with age (although recent developments in lens replacement makes vision nearly 20/20 in many older people.) Reading small print becomes difficult, as does distinguishing colors. Those who wear bifocals (not necessarily the older adult) prefer signs placed on exhibits at 3.5 to 5.5 feet in height in order to avoid cricks in their neck (Figure 5.6).

FIGURE 5.6
This well-lit but shiny exhibit reflects lights and adjacent pictures on the polished surfaces, impairing clarity; placement of text above eye level adds to the difficulty of reading through bifocals.

OLDER ADULTS PARTICIPATE

Older visitors make up a large part of the audiences for daytime interpretive programs. Bultena, Field, and Renninger (1992) found regular levels of 25-35 percent of audiences were people over 60 years of age. Sometimes they reached 65 percent in the three national parks studied. Park staff consistently underestimated their numbers.

The older campers studied felt more ambivalent about evening programs. Many found them uninformative and redundant. They often conflicted with the "early to bed, early to rise" schedules of many seniors (Bultena, Field, and Renninger, 1992). Although some did not like disruptions from other people's children, they enjoyed taking their own grandchildren to evening programs. Without grandchildren present, evening programs attracted the older adults less.

Many elders seek more sophisticated information than an introductory interpretive talk or an old nature video will provide. Because they stay in one place longer than younger people, they may quickly exhaust the interpretive offerings in the area, unless allowed to choose some progressively deeper programming. Interpreters who limit themselves to two or three talks per season, repeated on a cycle, may sound fairly smooth but won't be very interesting to long-term visitors. Seniors tend to have good knowledge about the park resources and exhibit strong environmental commitments. Therefore, they often find the interpretation to be superficial, uninformative, and unchallenging. As this segment grows, the wise interpreter will provide opportunities for greater depth and diversity of topics, many of them involving individually-matched activities.

Some additional recommendations for interpreters wishing to serve older adults (Bultena, Field, and Renninger, 1992) include:

1. Interpreters need in-service training for sensitivity to the needs, characteristics and orientations of older visitors, to dispel myths and stereotypes.
2. Special age-graded programs for seniors could allow more appropriate information exchange, provide social interaction with peers, and eliminate distractions such as disruptive children.
3. In-depth presentations or publications for knowledgeable, repeat visitors would serve a wide audience.
4. Comprehension of subject matter could be enhanced by interpreting concepts such as succession and eutrophication to emphasize the life cycle processes in ecosystems, social systems and human life.
5. The elderly offer tremendous sources of relevant historical information about the area. Some have scrap books and data in their files. Many have hobbies, talents (e.g., photography, storytelling, craft skills) that can apply to programming. Programs that encourage the participation of older adults may lead to volunteering, where they often do outstanding jobs.

Summary

Interpreters by nature usually accept individual differences and react sensitively to people's needs. Yet, an interpreter's job also encourages them to use their abilities to their fullest extent to simultaneously challenge their clients to experience new things and use their own abilities. To succeed, the interpreter needs to study the characteristics of the potential and actual audience. Several sociological techniques can aid in these studies. People who don't get to the facility also deserve study by interpreters, to determine how to extend the message farther or to appeal to a wider audience.

A way that requires interpreters to expand their sphere of influence involves reaching out proactively to segments of society that typically feel barred from many interpretive experiences. Cultural minorities, teenagers, older adults, and individuals with disabilities may participate more readily when efforts to welcome and better serve them come from the interpretive staff.

One must know their visitors and potential visitors. If one knows them, one can serve them.

Literature Cited

Brown, W. E. (1971). *Islands of hope*. Arlington, VA: National Recreation and Park Association.

Bultena, G., Field, D. R. and Renninger, R. (1992). Interpretation for the elderly. In G. E. Machlis and D. R. Field, *On interpretation (rev. ed.)*. Corvallis, OR: Oregon State University Press.

Caron, J. A. (1989). Environmental perspectives of blacks: Acceptance of the "new environmental paradigm." *Journal of Environmental Education, 20*(3):21-26.

Carr, W. H. (1931). *Trailside actions and reactions*. New York, NY: American Museum of Natural History, School Service Series No. 5.

Chavez, D. (1992). Recreation knowledge and participation of Hispanics. *Recreation Research Update, 5*(1):(n.p.) (USDA Forest Service, PSW Research Station).

Dwyer, J. F. and Hutchison, R. (1990). Outdoor recreation participation and preferences by black and white Chicago households. In J. Vining (Ed.), *Social science and natural resource recreation management*. Boulder, CO: Westview Press.

Geiger, R. A. Jr. and Ellis, W. K. (1991). Attracting senior visitors to your programs and facilities. In *Proceedings, National Interpreters Workshop*, NAI. Vail, CO.

Gregoire, J. and Wobig-Freimund, T. (1987). Bridging the gap: Gateways to integrating individuals with disabilities into natural and historic programs and environments. In *Proceedings, National Interpreters Workshop*, AIN. St. Louis, MO.

Gilbert, S. (1977). A study of visitor tour preferences at Lewis and Clark Caverns. In *Proceedings, National Cave Management Symposium*. Albuquerque, NM: Adobe Press.

Grinder, A. L. and McCoy, E. S. (1985). *The good guide: A source-book for interpreters, docents and tour guides*. Scottsdale, AZ: Ironwood Press.

Harris, N. (1991). Conceiving the art museum: Some historical observations for the Getty colloquium. In E. Walsh (Ed.), *Insights: Museums, visitors, attitudes, expectations*. Los Angeles, CA: J. Paul Getty Trust.

Howard, D. R. and Crompton, J. L. (1980). *Financing, managing and marketing recreation and park resources*. Dubuque, IA: William C. Brown Company, Publishers.

Hultsman, J., Cottrell, R. L. and Hultsman, W. Z. (1987). *Planning parks for people*. State College, PA: Venture Publishing.

Lindo, P. R. (1991). Interpretation in a multicultural society. In *Proceedings of the Heritage Interpretation International Third Global Congress*. Honolulu, HI.

Machlis, G. E., Field, D. R., and Van Every, M. E. (1992). A sociological look at Japanese tourists. In G. E. Machlis and D. R. Field, *On interpretation (rev. ed.)*. Corvallis, OR: Oregon State University Press.

Mackintosh, B. (1987). Interpreting minorities and women in the national park system. *Trends, 24*(4):38-40.

McCormick, S. (1991). The greying of parks and recreation. *Parks and Recreation, 26*(3):60-64.

McGovern, J. N. (1993). The Americans with Disabilities Act: This law will change public parks and recreation in Kansas! *Kansas Recreation and Park Association annual, (Jan. 16)*:13,16.

Meeker, J. W., Woods, W. K., and Lucas, L. W. (1992). Red, white, and black in the national parks. In G. E. Machlis and D. R. Field, *On interpretation (rev. ed.)*. Corvallis, OR: Oregon State University Press.

Sanchez, J. P. (1990). *The Spanish black legend: Origins of anti-Hispanic stereotypes.* Albuquerque, NM: University of New Mexico, Spanish Colonial Research Center/National Park Service, Publication Series No. 2.

Simcox, D. and Pfister, R. (1991). Hispanic values and behaviors related to outdoor recreation. *Recreation Research Update, 3*(2):(n.p.) (Forest Service, PSW Research Station).

Smith, R. W. (1985). Barriers are more than architectural. *Parks and Recreation, 20*(10):58-62.

Stevens, K. (1992). Americans with Disabilities Act: An overview for interpreters. In *Proceedings, National Interpreters Workshop*, NAI. San Francisco Bay Area, CA.

Trapp, S., Gross, M. and Zimmerman, R. (1991). *Signs, trails, and wayside exhibits: Connecting people and places.* Stevens Point, WI: University of Wisconsin Stevens Point Foundation Press.

Wallace, V. K. and Witter, D. J. (1990). Urban nature centers: What do our constituents want and how can we give it to them? In *Proceedings, National Interpreters Workshop*, NAI. Charleston, SC.

Walters, C. G. and Bergiel, B. J. (1989). *Consumer behavior: A decision-making approach.* Cincinnati, OH: South-Western Publishing Co.

White, R. (1991). Planting seeds in a concrete jungle. In *Proceedings, National Interpreters Workshop*, NAI. Vail, CO.

Yambert, P. A. (1981). Are we handicapping the handicapped? A second look at architectural and attitudinal barriers. In *Program Papers, National Workshop of the Association of Interpretive Naturalists and Western Interpreters Association*. Estes Park, CO.

The next nine chapters describe principles, theories, and practical approaches to delivering interpretation in its many forms. These include several sets of well-proven principles that describe the aims and methodology of interpretation. This section also discusses useful principles of communications, persuasion, and learning.

Interpreters use a wide array of media and techniques for presenting their messages to diverse audiences. The chapters on mass media, print, exhibit centers and museums, and self-guiding methods describe how to interpret without being present—nonpersonal interpretation. The next three chapters describe personal interpretation methods and skills used, when the interpreter guides the visitor, presents talks and pictures, gets into historical context, or uses drama, music, poetry, and art to directly develop and convey messages.

This section sums up the key skills that interpreters need and use to do their principal work—providing people on-site and off-site with interpretive messages. Although it suggests ways of presenting environmental education interpretation, the details of that procedure are left to specialized books on environmental and outdoor education. This section illustrates the complexity of the interpretive profession, as well as the rich range of talents arrayed within it.

A Wetlands Institute, Inc., interpreter explains sea animal ecology.

THE ANIMALS IN
THIS TANK
ARE RESTING.
PLEASE
DO NOT TOUCH

Traditions, Principles and Challenges

A country is measured not by population alone, not by wealth, not by power, but by the mental attitude of the people. . . . When we better understand Nature's call, we shall hear her say: Come and visit me and bring your children; I have beautiful things to show you, and stories to tell that you will never forget. . . . Come and get acquainted with me, and I will give you health and strength and inspiration. Let me train your children to see and hear things as they are. I will make your boys and girls efficient, I will give them high ideals, and fit them to be the fathers and the mothers of future noble men and women.
—Mrs. J. D. Sherman (1917)

Interpretation ranks among the highest of callings. The quote above, from Mrs. Sherman's address to the 1917 National Parks Conference, demonstrates the educational and inspirational underpinnings of early interpretive efforts. People then, just as now, sensed the power of the tool we now call interpretation. They saw it not as just something optional or nice or convenient. Interpretation serves as a vital means to inspire a strong mental attitude toward life and a vigorous, civilized nation. Interpreters bring people to a closer understanding of the creation and of human culture. People will surely draw inspiration from well-developed interpretive programs. They will gain ability to perceive their culture, their natural surroundings, and their fellow humans.

This chapter presents the history and principles of interpretation as expressed by several leaders of the profession. The traditions demonstrate the constancy of underlying purpose, despite the vicissitudes of time, of changing public policies, and of the growth of the profession in many different types of institutions and businesses.

INTERPRETATION—AN OLD PARKS TRADITION

National Parks in the early years provided accommodations including one that had an educational bent—an intellectual accommodation for the natural curiosity of the visitor. The idea was to make the visit interesting and enjoyable, not just comfortable.

Parks people realized quite soon that their visitors wanted and needed guidance. The early visitors to western parks were well-to-do but usually inexperienced in the forest. Yosemite National Park Acting

Superintendent Colonel Forsyth noted in 1912 that "Hundreds of people come in here that have never been on a horse or a mule." A Grand Canyon ranger noted in 1917 that about 100,000 of the 116,000 visitors "had to be taken care of" (Makruski, 1978).

These visitors not only had little experience but also little familiarity with natural (or historical) phenomena. They sought and paid for guide service, often tipping informative guides handsomely. In the absence of organized professional interpretation, some of the wranglers, hotel employees, and drivers merely posed as interpreters, often improvising interesting tales and fascinating explanations that had little to do with reality.

The Wylie Camps provided private interpretation with a professional approach. This company offered tent shelters and guided tours in Yellowstone as early as 1883. Before 1883, Mr. Wylie published illustrated guidebooks to the park. The camps were portable until 1894, when Wylie set up permanent platforms for the tents. The employees were carefully selected for their intelligence and training, including college professors, high school teachers, geologists, and college students. Their jobs were to serve the guests, entertain them, and interpret to them. The company insisted on enlightenment, not tall tales. It also insisted on enjoyment. Evening campfires were accompanied by an organ, songs, and stories. Daytime visits provided focused activities in the park, something beyond just gazing around. They called it educational entertainment.

Interpretation concerned the military caretakers of many of the early parks, long before the National Park Service took over in 1916. Army park guards often enlightened tourists. Their commanders sought enlisted men familiar with ornithology and zoology. With time, they developed knowledge of the curiosities and history of the park (Makruski, 1978, from 1911 NPS meeting proceedings). In Yosemite, Lieutenant F. Pipes led botany field trips in 1904. General S. B. M. Young reported in 1907 that "a visiting tourist should always be favored by an intelligent and courteous answer" (Makruski, 1978).

Principles and Departures from Principles: Enos Mills and Freeman Tilden

Enos Mills, writer, resort owner, and intellectual "nature guide," led people through what is now Rocky Mountain National Park from 1889 through the early 1920s. He also traveled the nation as a lecturer, friend of Presidents, and lobbyist for stronger interest in nature by the public and the Congress.

Mills distinguished the "nature guide" from the horse wrangler or hunter type of guide. "Natural history has been incidental to all previous types of guides, while to the nature guide it is the essential feature of every trip" (Mills, 1920). He claimed that a nature guide is neither an ordinary type of guide nor a teacher. The methods of formal education in those days were not seen favorably by Mr. Mills. He thought they were too rigid and structured to stimulate interest among the students. He insisted that nature guiding should be more inspirational than informational: "People are out for recreation and need restful, intellectual visions, and not dull, dry facts, rules, and manuals" (Mills, 1920).

Mills' "formula" for the best nature guiding (paraphrased, 1920) seems to apply equally well to historical and cultural topics:

- Discuss facts.
- Appeal to the imagination and the reason.
- Give flesh and blood to cold facts.
- Make life stories of inanimate objects.
- Deal with principles rather than isolated information.
- Give biographies rather than classifications.

In the late 1950s, Freeman Tilden wrote down some rather intertwined, poetic and inspiring "principles of interpretation" that seem quite parallel to those of Mills. Tilden's (1967) principles have guided interpreters for nearly 40 years (Figure 6.1). They have stood the test of time, perhaps because of their lucidity, perhaps because of their slight inscrutability that rings with a sense of truth. These principles serve as guidelines for performance, for evaluation, and for training, even though they offer great difficulty in definition and quantification. The following presents brief paraphrases of the first half of Tilden's book (1967):

FIGURE 6.1
Freeman Tilden in 1969. (NPS, M. Woodbridge Williams)

I. Any interpretation that does not somehow relate what is being displayed or described to something within the personality or experience of the visitor will be sterile.

—Appeal to the visitor's first interest.

II. Information, as such, is not interpretation. Interpretation is revelation based upon information. But they are entirely different things. However, all interpretation includes information.

—We prefer a knowledge of humankind to a mere acquaintance with their actions.

III. Interpretation is an art, which combines many arts, whether the materials presented are scientific, historical or architectural. Any art is in some degree teachable.

—The story's the thing.

IV. The chief aim of interpretation is not instruction, but provocation.

—Through interpretation, understanding;

—through understanding, appreciation;

—through appreciation, protection.

V. Interpretation should aim to present a whole rather than a part and must address itself to the whole person rather than any phase.

—Wisdom is not a knowledge of many things but the perception of the underlying unity of seemingly unrelated facts.

VI. Interpretation addressed to children should not be a dilution of the presentation to adults, but should follow a fundamentally different approach. To be at its best it will require a separate program.

—Information, not ecology, sociology, or theology. In other words, kids absorb facts and instances, not abstract processes.

Tilden taught that love of the place and love for the visitors constituted the key or priceless ingredient—the overriding principle of interpretation (Tilden, 1967):

> If you love the thing you interpret, and love the people who come to enjoy it, . . . you not only have taken the pains to understand it to the limit of your capacity, but you also feel its special beauty in the general richness of life's beauty.

Tilden taught that interpretation sometimes involves judicious silence. He noted that some scenes need no words, that "reporting" the beauty of a scene might reduce the opportunity for inspiration. Sometimes the scene interprets itself, so interpret but do not impose (Figure 6.2). Curmudgeonly Harold Ickes agreed. Secretary of the Interior from 1933-1945, he had much to do with current recreation and interpretive policy. He wrote " . . . that [national] parks are for those who will appreciate them and not merely for hordes of tourists who dash through them at break-neck speed in order to be able to say that they have been to Glacier or Yellowstone or some other park." Despite his hope to instill appreciation, he thought museums had "no place in the parks at all" and took a dim view of eager interpreters who did not allow beauty to speak for itself (Ickes, 1938):

FIGURE 6.2
Beauty often needs no interpreter's intervention. (NPS, Richard Frear)

We have too much of a disposition not to allow people freely to enjoy the parks for what they can get out of them for the refreshment of their spirits and the good of their souls. Our guides insist on describing the beauties and the wonders of nature in trite and uninspired words. Nothing makes me want to commit murder so much as to have someone break in on a reverential contemplation of nature in which I may be indulging by giving me a lot of statistical or descriptive information relating to what I am looking at.

Applying Teaching Theory for Interpretation

Education teaching theory of today includes an approach now called "constructivist." Put very simply, it involves building new knowledge, values, and beliefs upon each individual's earlier constructs of knowledge and values. It recognizes that people learn in different ways, so that each person's new "construction" may differ from those of other people. The principles of Mills and Tilden seem to suggest that interpretation has long used this philosophy. Perhaps "teaching" outdoors promotes this approach.

Mills, Tilden, and modern constructivist educators apparently have roots that go far back, perhaps with some different emphases. One who seemed to embody the principles was Maria Montessori, whose name still appears on many preschools. This Italian educator developed a philosophy that focused on individual learning. "Dr. Maria Montessori believed that no human being is educated by another person. He must do it himself or it will never be done. A truly educated individual continues learning long after the hours and years he spends in the classroom because he is motivated from within by a natural curiosity and love for knowledge" (Wolf, 1969).

FIGURE 6.3
Put an old bottle in context to capture young imaginations and then encourage them to think.

Modern constructivists often suggest keeping classroom lecturing to a minimum and individual interaction with problems and real objects to a maximum. The interpreter can apply this to adults as well as children, using the outdoors or museum objects to do much of the teaching (Figure 6.3). The technique requires preparation of materials, questions, tasks, activities, and situations in which people can act. It cannot be done without careful planning. The approach requires that the interpreter focus on ways that visitors may learn instead of concentrating solely on what to say or do. The interpreter plans with less thinking about self and more about the clients as the thinkers, the doers, the learners.

Applying Communications Theory

Communication is the essence of interpretation. Interpreters use communications principles in public contact, talks, guided activities, signs, exhibits, audiovisual programs, publications and other means of presenting interpretive information. They try to get the message from their head into the visitor's head, so it becomes a stimulus and working tool for further inquiry and curiosity by that visitor.

A person's reaction to word selection, tone of voice, actions, attitudes, mood, personality and appearance determines much about the learning process. A negative reaction to any one of these reduces acceptance and message effectiveness (Verdeber, 1978).

The interpreter must be conscious of their own image and presence, but not distractingly self-conscious. Focus on the visitors' receptivity and reception of the messages. Attention to feedback from the visitors—their body language, questions, and interest—help the interpreter adjust the presentation to achieve its objectives.

HOW INTERPRETERS COMMUNICATE DIRECTIONALLY

The communications process can be seen as unidirectional or multidirectional (Haas, 1977). Unidirectional communication prevails in most interpretation. The interpretive message or messenger provides stories, information, images and ideas to the visitor through various media, with little feedback from the audience. Examples include self-guided interpretive trails, most exhibits, guided walks, and campfire talks. Although visitors may offer some feedback, relatively few people ask questions or exchange information. Unidirectional activities meet many of the needs and desires of many people (Haas, 1977). They comprise the most common forms of interpretive programming.

The multidirectional approach involves a high level of interchange among the participants. They exchange or relate their own experiences, knowledge, feelings, and discoveries among themselves. The interpreter often serves as a facilitator and process guide more than as a performer or expert. The activity is less formally structured. People can feel they are part of the activity; they can learn something for themselves. There is more social interaction. This method may be of great value in some cases. In other situations, it may be distracting to those who "want to learn something" about technical phenomena, without having to "play games." If done in an appropriate manner and without causing discomfort, the multidirectional approach may work superbly. The telling difference may be in whether or not it gets easily-embarrassed adults to participate without coercion. It requires special preparation by the interpreter—the strategy works best when good tasks and questions are thought out ahead of time.

GROUP STRUCTURE FOR INTERACTIVE COMMUNICATION

These two general approaches can be achieved through use of several different structures of groups. The Division of Interpretation (1976) of the National Park Service described seven group structures seen in interpretive events. Each structure has an appropriate function. In most interpretive events structures change during the activity; often three or more structures occur during a single hike or program, sometimes spontaneously, often by plan. The illustrations and brief comments below give an idea of how these work. The first is unidirectional; the next two are variants from unidirectional. The last four are forms of multidirectional group interactions.

1. **Didactic structure:**
   The interpreter informs
   the listeners with a speech,
   film, audiovisual presentation,
   sign. *On this tour, I will tell
   you about . . .*

   1.

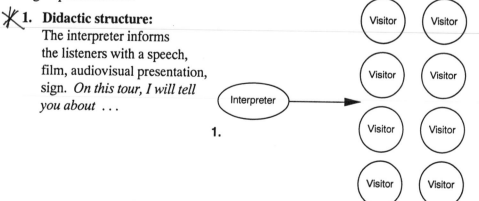

2. **Tutorial structure:**
   The interpreter listens and helps
   individuals in progress on tasks.
   *Let me see how you are coming
   along and help you over any
   barriers.*

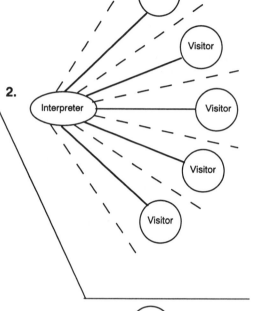

2.

3.

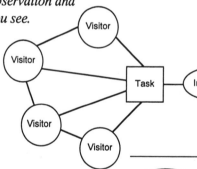

3. **Individual task structure:**
   Task Interpreter assigns tasks to individuals,
   then moves among them to assist. *Each use your
   power of observation and
   list birds you see.*

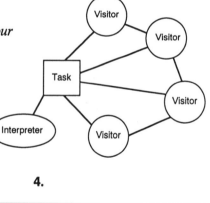

4.

5.

4. **Small group task structure:**
   Interpreter assigns tasks to groups,
   checks on progress, provides for
   reporting. *The Texas group will study
   this tree; list all forms of life you find on
   the tree. Then compare your list with
   other group.*

Project
IDEA

5. **Conference structure:**
   Interpreter allows free discussion
   among visitors, then stays out of the way.
   *Let us take a few minutes at this view point for you
   to talk among yourselves.*

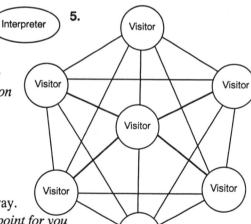

6. Group meeting structure:

Interpreter enters as a member of conference structure, raises a problem but stays nonjudgmental listening and clarifying: We have so many deer in the park that they have overbrowsed the vegetation. *I would like you to discuss how we might handle that problem.*

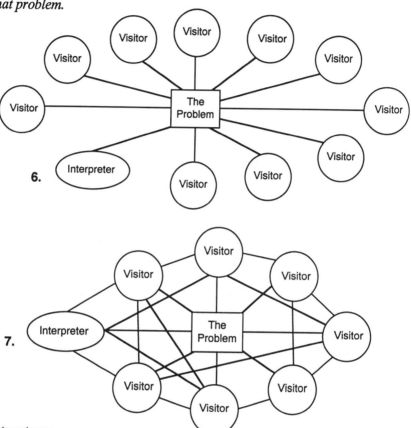

7. Socratic structure:

Interpreter poses questions, promotes discussion/dialogue, elicits higher levels of thought, refocuses, adds data for visitor use and requires them to justify their ideas. *Look at the leaves on these two trees. How do they compare? Why is one droopy and discolored and the other healthy-looking? How can we apply this at home?*

Each of these approaches has value and validity, although most impersonal and much personal interpretation use the didactic approach out of practicality and necessity. The effectiveness of a program can grow by including participatory segments. A talk, walk, tour, or museum lesson will often mix two or more of these seven approaches. For example, in a single one-hour program, an interpreter might mix a short demonstration segment (structure 1) with a participatory activity from Project Learning Tree (structure 4) and a discussion to "solve" an historical mystery (structure 6).

Other examples follow (from Haas, 1977). After a campfire talk or slide presentation (structure 1), visitors may be invited to stay to talk with knowledgeable individuals (a form of structure 5). This is especially effective when the experts are members of a cultural group (e.g., hula dancers, craftspersons, rock climbers, Navajo singers/drummers) who have just presented a program on the subject. If they can have an after-program starter or something visible to prompt continued discussion, they will draw a significant proportion of the audience to stay around and interact.

Another opportunity comes during guided nature walks (structure 1) when participants are asked to sit quietly for a few minutes and then report what they heard, saw, smelled, or felt (structure 3). They may be directed to observe a tree, mountain ridge, or clouds, then describe images they saw. The activity guides people to learn and discover for themselves and to relate their experiences, feelings, and knowledge to others in a simple manner.

RESPONSES TO INTERPRETER

People's responses and understanding of interpretive messages depend upon their reactions to: (1) the person who interprets, (2) the location, (3) their own physical or emotional conditions, prejudices, and experiences.

Interpreters often have great motivating power over visitors by their position of relative authority, force of personality, and apparent superior knowledge of the local environment. Simply put, they are authority figures and that makes them credible. The credibility can be eroded by presenting invented or erroneous information, by actions that suggest insecurity (e.g., annoyingly nervous laughter, rudeness, failure to take leadership). Among factors that persuasion theory suggest as affecting credibility are: rate of speaking, diversity of vocabulary, physical appearance (including uniform, smile, and posture), plus verbal and nonverbal expressions of confidence (Eagley and Himmelfarb, 1978). All of these factors can be used by interpreters to enhance their effectiveness and persuasiveness.

Another way the individual affects response is through simple courtesy and consideration of others. This allows most interpreters to face groups without inadvertently offending them. Negative "habits" such as intoxication from alcohol or other drugs are offensive (and grounds for immediate dismissal in most agencies). Others just reduce interpretive effectiveness. A few examples of simple distractions and discourtesies that generate negative feelings among virtually all audiences can be easily altered by the interpreter:

- wearing baseball-type caps indoors and out, often with advertising and stains; "hats off" works much better unless you are wearing a uniform hat outdoors.
- chewing gum or tobacco; smoking.
- failure to use effective antiperspirant.
- repetitive use of uninformative utterances such as "umm," "uh," "like . . . " and "you know."
- failure to speak loudly enough for all to hear (or, occasionally, speaking too loudly).

The location may strongly affect reception and acceptance. The place establishes a mood. The interpreter who seats his or her audience so they face the historic buildings being discussed provides an excellent backdrop for her talk. The place may also include distractions, however. The low passage of helicopters or jet planes may reduce attention to bird calls or historical crafts. Lights can ruin an evening program. An onslaught of mosquitoes can distract from the best-prepared small group discussion of wetlands.

Visitor characteristics and attitudes often make communications difficult. Most of these barriers are beyond the control of the interpreter. Sometimes communication is tough because visitors come with strong preconceptions about the topic or the agency. Some come to programs with personal distractions, some of them as compelling as a wet baby in the backpack. A few individuals may create their own personal barriers to understanding. Some play psychological games and try to figure the interpreter out, suspecting your motives or assuming that what they say and what they mean are two different things. Still other people have real handicaps in reading, hearing, or perceiving. Many foreign visitors will have trouble with colloquial English.

MESSAGES

Although Marshall McLuhan (1964) persuaded North Americans that "the medium is the message," the content and characteristics of messages also persuade, thereby affecting changes in attitudes and behavior.

Messages carry normative components, probably even in the most objective presentations. They suggest behaviors and attitudes that are either acceptable to or advocated by the interpreter. If the messages conflict with previous beliefs of the visitor, the normative message and supporting evidence must be very persuasive to produce a change in the visitor. If the beliefs of the interpreter and the listener are in concert, the visitor will probably accept the suggested actions or attitudes.

Other factors associated with the message include: the type of appeal (e.g., fear, value-discrepancy), the medium of communications used, and the context of the message (Eagley and Himmelfarb, 1978). Interpreters often incorporate these into many of their programs. Witness the common use of fascination with snakes to attract attention and to lead into broader interpretive themes.

Message content may not be accepted simply because it cannot be understood. For example, a newly arrived visitor will have a tough time with directions that use local place names (to the old Ross House, over the second cattle guard, then up toward Hawk Mountain along Mosquito Branch for 60 rods—you can't miss it). Or try something like this (far-fetched) interpretive desk suggestion for an afternoon visit to a Latin American visitor who has studied English diligently with textbooks: *Go out on the loop road around the sheep meadow. When you come to the overlook take five to hand-feed the chipmunks and jays. Then work your way over to Trail Ridge and on up to Alpine Visitor Center. Check out the cool interpretive exhibits and the super view. Do not forget your U-V shades. Take the tundra trail up top and get an eyeful of the cute little cushion mosses. Then . . .* The interpreter now has one befuddled visitor with a sense that English is an impossible language.

Many ways exist to confuse visitors. Communications theory tries to teach us ways to reduce the confusion and maximize the transfer of ideas, thoughts and procedures. The interpreter's job of communicating vital concepts and provoking new levels of seeing, searching, and enjoying the environment is no simple task. It requires theory, considerable practice, and plenty of evaluation. The key is to engage the mind of the "audience" member in a lively process of idea exchange. That process can take several forms and follow any of several techniques.

Roles of Interpretation

Any interpreter can seek to achieve three goals: (1) make the interpretive offerings so productive that they become the central feature of a visit, (2) reach every visitor on the property and the nonvisitors that support the facility, and (3) promote the power of perception among all clientele so they see the world in a more meaningful way.

THE CENTRAL EXPERIENCE

Try to make interpretation into the central visitor experience—the key part of a visit to a natural or cultural resource area. The interpreter serves as the property's official host. The job: guide people to richer experiences appropriate to park purposes. Promote perception; enrich recreation. Interpretation should offer the biggest and most important activity that a visitor seeks on an outing—and that could go for everyone, even the family reunion picnickers. If it is properly interpreted, they will tell the out-of-town relatives the story of the trail or explain the exhibits in the museum of their esteemed local park.

This seems a bit idealistic, perhaps, but it need not remain so. An interpreter who lets the program slide into the back of the park where only a few visitors go can think of this as a warning. There are ways to make every museum, every camp, every park into a place for meaningful interpretation without making it unpleasant.

THE INTERPRETIVE CLIENTS = EVERYONE!

To make interpretation the central experience is to get the message across effectively to the greatest number of people who will receive it voluntarily. The greatest number of people are not limited to those who seek out the interpreter in the "Tuckaway Nature Center." Potential customers are not only those willing to go on a hike scheduled at the interpreter's convenience.

Studies of Indiana state parks found that a maximum of 17 percent of visitors present in the parks at the time participated in evening programs, with only 5 percent of the park visitors attending guided walks. A maximum of 24 percent of the visitors participated in the interpretive programs or museums (Herbert, 1974; Knudson and Vanderford, 1980). This suggested that three of every four visitors were not interested in interpretation or that interpreters were not actively seeking to provide the services and facilities at the most appropriate places and times.

The "clients equals everyone" concept does not imply that an interpreter must run up to all visitors, guide them by the arm, and say, "Come with me to the central experience." Instead, interpreters use a variety of subtle means to allow choices for the visitor to participate in some kind of interpretive service. Interpreters make resources readily, easily and conveniently available. Many messages may be silent and waiting. Nonpersonal devices set up at places visitors normally go may have the best effect: signs, exhibits, short self-guiding trails, books, postcards, and other media (Figure 6.4). Personally conducted interpretive programs start at places and times convenient for visitors; this may stimulate impulse participation. In many historic sites or historic villages, interpreters station themselves at key sites, encountering virtually every visitor who strolls through the area, offering explanations and demonstrations of the key themes of the area.

FIGURE 6.4
Much interpretation allows visitors to encounter places at their own pace, along roads and trails, and in museums.

In other words, make interpretation available where people gather. It cannot be limited to the pretty nature center hidden back in the forest two miles away from the beach on a side road. A park with a popular beach should have interpretation available at the beach. That does not mean that the nature center or historical programming must be on the beach, but do not reject that alternative out of hand. It does mean that signs, brochures, and aquatic interpretation certainly should be readily available to adults and children at the beach and other places where they go. This way, the interpreter reaches out to a majority of the visitors who otherwise may not perceive an opportunity to learn more about the resource.

When it is done right, they will respond. It may take many tries to get the right combination. The interpreter does not stalk the visitors, forcing them to participate in a "clap-hands-hike-the-beach-pick-up-shells game." Instead, well-placed information and programs offer visitors the ready opportunity to learn about where they are and what is important there, allowing them to voluntarily participate and learn.

While at historic sites or museums, it is relatively easy to implement this concept. In natural areas, it may not be so easy, especially if the interpreter is used to playing second viola (something nice in the background, blending in but attracting little attention) instead of first chair solo trumpet. The interpreter can help meet the challenge by trying a number of solutions. Several strategies have worked at bringing out visitors.

1. *Advertise and inform people about the programs.* Reyburn and Knudson (1975) showed that simple in-park advertising and personal contact increased attendance significantly. Enrich the well-prepared programs with a little music (loud for a minute or two) and humor to get more word-of-mouth advertising.

2. *Devise programs that offer continuing interest.* As the audience changes, the approach will have to change. As some people return to the park repeatedly, they will find less interest in repeat programs. On the other hand, repeat visitors can become involved in an active program that progressively prepares them to appreciate the full story of the site. This kind of programming comes to fruition in only a few parks and forests, but frequently in museums.

   Art in the park programs draw repeaters who practice by drawing, painting or photographing the property. An expert artist who comes to critique and instruct, draws repeat visitors. Photographic hikes and clinics often attract visitors who learn to see the park from a different perspective. Kodak offers this free service in leading national parks. A local camera shop might do a monthly workshop in a county park in hopes of boosting local sales. Teaching and practicing crafts, quilts, and other skills will draw adults and children. Social interpretation programs draw old time musicians, steam farming enthusiasts, and Civil War buffs. Folk festivals draw visitors year after year. The junior ranger/naturalist programs at many state facilities bring in repeat visitors and assure progressively deeper experiences.

3. *Select the menu of offerings to fit visitors.* Museums and visitor centers are often the most-attended interpretive offerings. Sedentary or passive kinds of interpretive programs draw more people than hikes and other active programs (Knudson and Vanderford, 1980). Some interpreters, however, draw dozens of people on hikes through their promotion, starting points, and promises to be gentle.

4. *Provide self-guiding trails with brochures or signs.* This can reach people at their own convenience without the uneasiness that some feel in following a naturalist or being "trapped" at a talk. Convenient well-identified, self-guiding facilities will get the messages across to many more people than an interpreter can ever hope to reach personally (Figure 6.5).

FIGURE 6.5
Self-guiding walkways can get visitors into the subject, both literally and intellectually. This Canadian forest route uses signs and taped messages.

5. *Use action and discovery activities, along with development of camping skills, identification, other woodcraft activities in nature parks, and historical sophistication in cultural parks.* People remember what they do in a park or museum or camp as much as they remember the place itself. In many parks, visitors probably participate in picnicking and swimming. Do they also interpret at this place? Does the interpretation make it easy for them to do it?

To gauge program effectiveness and payoff, the interpreter can ask the following questions:

1. Are people coming to the programs, using the exhibits, brochures, signs and self-guiding tours? Numbers do matter, like it or not.
2. Are visitors involved in active interpretation or just being told? Quality involvement matters, too.
3. Are interpretive programs, trails, brochures, and facilities central to the site experience, not just a side show or babysitting service?
4. Do the programs interpret the *genius loci*, the special character, and themes of the property?

When the answer is no to any of these, new opportunities exist for stronger interpretive efforts.

One maxim of this work recognizes that interpretation is a visitor activity. Although interpreters often speak of interpreting for the visitor, in reality the visitor's mind does the perceiving and interpreting of artifacts and nature and context. The professional interpreter facilitates these perceptions by providing experiences, information, special books, trails, exhibits, and many other methods to develop the interpretive skills of each visitor.

Perception: Chaos or Pattern?

> To promote perception is the only truly creative part of recreational engineering.
> —Leopold, 1966

The key job of the interpreter might be boiled down to one of helping people perceive more acutely the world around them, the cultures that preceded and coexist with their own, and the ways they can affect the future ways in which humans live in this world.

On one hand, the interpreter helps people gain some understanding of the unusual and curious places of the land and the people that inhabit[ed] it, trying to impart a sense of wonder in the mind of the perceiver. The "mysteries" and unique features of plains, islands, canyons, and cities help give the area a special character (Figure 6.6).

On the other hand, the interpreter helps people gain new perspectives on the commonplace and new understandings of the world around them. One way is by seeking patterns in nature. Many visitors seek help in perceiving patterns that characterize tree species or architectural styles. Many seek even more subtle patterns. Here, the artistic and scientific mind can blend together nicely.

FIGURE 6.6
An aluminum sign helps visitors find patterns and features of Yosemite Valley (NPS).

Nature should be viewed without distinction. All her processes and evolutions are beautiful or ugly to the unbiased and undiscriminating observer. She makes no choice herself—everything that happens has equal significance. Withering follows blooming, death follows growth, decay follows death, and life follows decay in a wonderful, complicated, endless web the surface beauties of which are manifest to a point of view unattached to vulgar, restricting concepts of what constitutes beauty in nature.

—Porter and Gleick, 1990

For some reason, the identification of patterns in a complex, variable world became known as the "science of chaos." From it, Benoit Mandelbrot, a mathematician, invented fractal geometry and fractal relationships. This mathematical inquiry seeks uncanny, subtle, intricate structures in places that some see as disorderly or without significant pattern. Of course, the laws of physics and physiology have long recognized such patterns. Examples of structure appear in talus slopes, in grasses strewn in a meadow, in cracks of a dry mud bed, in ice, in lichen blotches on a tree trunk, in the trees themselves (well-studied), and in the clustering of galaxies. These apparently chaotic textures have long intrigued artists and photographers, who recognize patterns and repetitions within them.

Mandelbrot saw rhythms in the shapes of rocks and plants, in the life of a river, in cloud dynamics and in the interfaces between two fluids. These are not disorderly phenomena. Many interpretive naturalists have explained or pointed out to their clients these often-overlooked patterns. It is fascinating that so few people see the patterns without help. Traditionally, scientists looked for a more conventional order in nature and treated the erratic as a side issue, an unpredictable kind of marginalia. Now many scientists look more directly at the irregularities.

The "new science of chaos" contends that seeming irregularities can be contemplated, sorted, measured, and understood. Mandelbrot's (1977) credo: "Clouds are not spheres, mountains are not cones, coastlines are not circles, and bark is not smooth nor does lightning travel in a straight line." He asks us to scrutinize, rather than dismiss, the apparently formless, to "investigate the morphology of the amorphous."

Some "chaotic patterns" worthy of study by naturalists include:

- a model or picture of a human lung; it is a "tree" of ever-smaller tubes.
- a cloud—one of many clouds; weather forecasters have known their patterns for millennia, but few of us study them for order or meaning now.
- a river; draw the basic shape of a river—not as a line but as a tree; this pattern (dendritic) repeats itself wherever nature drains land of water; in some places it resembles a twisted tree; in others it is long and almost straight [why do streams meander?].

An interesting photography tour or slide show may be based on images of the unconventional geometry of untamed, undomesticated, unregulated wildness. One of the finest photographers of this genre is Eliot Porter. He wrote that we usually notice flowers, autumn foliage, mountain landscapes, and other summits of nature's displays. Underlying them, patterns and slow, quiet processes pass almost unnoticed. "Yet, how much is missed if we have eyes only for the bright colors" (Porter and Gleick, 1990). Porter had photographed the order of nature for years, usually in close-up details. Then he noticed that his photos emphasized the random chaos that exists—"a world of endless variety where nothing was ever the same."

Gleick, author of the book *Chaos*, stated (Porter and Gleick, 1990) that:

> Nature paints its scenes without regard for conventional order, for straight lines or Euclidean shapes. Luckily so—the human mind seems to take as little pleasure in a straight line as in pure formlessness. The essence of the earth's beauty lies in disorder, a peculiarly patterned disorder, from the fierce tumult of rushing water to the tangled filigrees of unbridled vegetation.

The scientific training of the interpreter emphasizes the order and pattern of history, culture, and nature. The idea of seeing chaos may seem daunting and confusing. The idea of making it interesting and meaningful to people may seem counterproductive to many who have tried for decades to inculcate a love of and respect for the sequences of succession and the predictability of natural reactions to human intervention.

It need not be so fearsome, however. Gleick used the term chaos not to confuse but to draw attention to cultural change—people now see beauty in more than the tamed, the arranged, the dressed up and trimmed down. Formal gardens, mechanical structures, geometrical terraces are not the only places to see beauty. A more complex, sophisticated beauty lies in wild, natural arrangements—"untamed, undomesticated, unregulated wildness."

This is something quite familiar to most naturalists and most profound students of history. They have long seen beauty in such complexity. Most are at the next level of sophistication, having learned the orderliness of such apparent chaos—except that they know they have only grasped a little of the order while feeling comfortable with the wildness. In other words, nature interpreters and many historical interpreters have long since accepted the thesis that beauty is in the hard-to-perceive order of the universe. They probably prefer the random mosaic of natural wildness to the tamed order of gardeners and engineers. They feel comfortable with the rhythms of nature, varying and irregular as they may be. They see and feel and sense the beat of a different drummer, that is greater than mere people, more powerful than human machines, and has existed longer on this planet than our species.

Limited experimental evidence confirms these speculations about wildness. For example, Morton Arboretum clients and volunteers ranked 20 color photos of arboretum scenes, ranging from natural forests, formal gardens, plant collections, and open fields (Schroeder, 1993). Highly manicured, formal landscape scenes got the lowest ratings. Dense forests with natural-appearing trees and shrubs had the highest ratings.

What to Interpret

Selecting the approach and subject of interpretation involves identifying major themes that will identify the character of a place (its *genius loci*). It also involves an approach referred to here as total programming—presenting the interpretation in many ways to many people, both those who come to visit and those who do not. Key concepts of interpretive programming help define the program and subject matter. The interpretation effort will often be faced with controversial issues and philosophies. Facing these issues requires careful preparation of factual presentations that allow for differences of opinion and outlook and of fair presentations that can turn the interpretive center into an issues resource center—a place for community involvement in a creative and constructive manner.

Emphasize *Genius Loci*

Each park, forest, museum, camp, historic building, and cave has its own characteristic values and uniqueness. A site may be representative of an ecological, geographic, historic or architectural phenomenon (Figure 6.7).

A visitor should have the central experience of understanding these special or representative values. The interpreter explains and translates the values to the visitor, thus enriching the experience by presenting the essence of the reason for the property's designation or existence.

FIGURE 6.7
The "Fog Woman Group" helps identify the genius loci *of Sitka, Alaska's cultural character (NPS, W.S. Keller).*

Genius loci means the particular character of the place. The place (locus) may refer to a historic building (Windsor Castle) or a large ecosystem (the tundra or the Chihuahuan desert). The distinctive nature (genius) defines the place's significance. The *genius loci* may be due to a unique quality—the only or the last of this type—or a representative character— typical of old-growth forests or part of the Canadian Shield. Some refer to this as a sense of place or a sense of presence. American Indians often report sensing the spirit of the place in a tangible way. A sensitive, scientifically-trained mind can perceive and describe the sun's radiation, the water seeping down, the trees growing, the rhythms of natural process. An effective interpreter will help clients perceive the life and interrelations among the plants, rocks, waters, and sky—all tied together.

Interpreters find and study this special character so they can define it for visitors, tell its stories, legends, history, and nature. These can then be related to the rest of the world, allowing the visitor to take information and skills home to better interpret the personal environment, to better comprehend the variety and diversity of the nation.

Alexander Pope advised: "Consult the genius of the place in all." Frederick Law Olmsted consistently and broadly did so in his park planning work, setting the controlling theme for a design in the situation and circumstances of the site (Jordy, 1974).

Once, many years ago, a naturalist at a state park consistently ignored *genius loci*. His park featured sand dunes and forests. On most days, visitors who expected to learn something about the dunes would have felt sadly disappointed. For example, the interpreter did not show up for an afternoon demonstration because some rain clouds appeared and he assumed it might rain (it did not). The evening program he offered was a Disney movie about woodlots, which might have been appropriate elsewhere but had nothing to do with dunes or dune forests. The next day, an afternoon program offered a short hike into the dunes, but it never got over the hill toward the beach, where dune-forming action was going on; he said little about the dunes process. Further, the whole interpretive program reached only a few people staying near the remote edges of the campground. It never got to the thousands who were at the beach actually enjoying the dunes.

A visitor cannot be forced to participate in interpretation. However, this interpreter did not even invite them. He put no signs or leaflets or announcements about interpretation at the beach. He had no beach hikes, no beach campfires, no beach demonstrations, no beach interpretive exhibit boards, not even directions to the rather remote nature center. So this interpreter failed in two ways—he did not focus on the major characteristic of the park and he did not actively offer his services or products to the visitors.

Another observation involved an evening talk by a Zion National Park interpreter on geology. The odd thing was that the naturalist showed slides of Grand Canyon National Park, with no tie-in or comparison to Zion. No one in the audience understood the speaker's sense of *genius loci* but some speculated that his previous assignment interested him more than his current park.

To apply the concept of *genius loci*, explore the following ideas for themes.

1. *Interpret the name of the park and its significance.* Visitors will all have some exposure to the name and many will want to know more about it. Unfortunately, too many interpretive centers and brochures say nothing about this headline topic. Often, the name will describe a key character and special flavor of the place.

2. *Inventory the natural features.* The dominant ones such as lakes, cliffs, peaks, or large animals attract attention and serve as major interpretive features related to immediate visitor interests. For example, an outstanding fishing stream or lake can prompt the interpreter to discuss fishing and fish, easing into aquatic ecology, the food chain, and related land ecology. Sometimes, more subtle or sweeping themes may come from careful observation of the area, e.g., continental glaciation and how it made this place so flat.

3. A *third major theme identifying the character of the place comes from history*. The human story of the area can be fascinating if developed properly, with care and with flair.

For one small battlefield park, three major themes followed this pattern: (1) the battle culminated a conflict of cultures; (2) the land, creek, marsh, wildlife, and vegetation gave life and joy to American Indians and modern residents; (3) the history of European settlement and notable political and religious events this battlefield represents.

In developing thematic characteristics, don't just copy ideas from elsewhere. If a good idea fits, adapt it to the particular characteristics of the place. Visitors who travel to various Civil War battlefields or several lakes and forests in the north woods enjoy hearing something different, not reruns of the same general material.

To apply the concept of *genius loci* to interpretive efforts, the interpreter may take several specific actions:

- Analyze all the visitors—their home environs, interests, skill levels.
- List and think about the questions which visitors often ask.
- Do an interpretive inventory of the main features and stories about an area.
- Write down the character of the place, then translate it into the main interpretive themes and concepts.
- Develop interpretive programs to illustrate these themes, some programs in broad terms and others rather detailed.
- Try schedules and activities at various times to find the most suitable combination for attracting visitors.
- Recognize and adapt to differences among visitors and offer an array of methods to deliver interpretive information.
- Ask visitors what they consider the most interesting and significant aspects of the place that added to their experiences.

Total Programming

Interpretive programming extends beyond walks, talks, and evening campfire programs. It seeks to involve visitors in a series of activities, such as those facetiously suggested in Box 6.1, to offer visitors a complete experience. This does not mean that the visitor surrenders the entire visit to the interpreter, although that happens in some total immersion programs such as Outward Bound and many camp programs.

BOX 6.1: ONE DAY PROGRAMMING TO "IMPROVE" THE VISITOR

NATURE DAY AT IRON MAN STATE FOREST

8:00 a.m. --------------------	Mandatory 18-mile nature walk.
12:00 p.m. (noon)	Vegetarian potluck lunch—bring your own greens from the survival part of the walk.
1:00 p.m. --------------------	Afternoon Acclimatization: Get in touch with nature on our Swamp Slog—two hours of really feeling the environment.
3:00 p.m. --------------------	Slide Lecture by the head ranger: "Wood Ticks of the Midwest."
4:45 p.m. --------------------	Quiz and evaluation forms.
5:00 p.m. --------------------	Formal dismissal—"Here is to your better nature."

[Note: Do not do it this way! Think of the visitor.]

Total programming does cover all the bases. The interpreter provides the visitor with a full menu of self-guiding and open-ended opportunities that offer the chance to partake fully from a rich array of interpretive facilities, events and processes. The visitor to a fully interpreted park or museum or camp may encounter many levels of learning and skill development. The diversity of activities, programs, and ever-ready self-guiding facilities allows the person to completely immerse in interpretive recreation, just as one would in the sport of fishing or hunting or mountain climbing.

The programming includes exhibits, events, and printed material, designed to meet the needs of general audiences while also providing specific opportunities for children, the older adults, teenagers, foreign visitors and families. Total programming goes beyond the visitor center or the interpretive setting. It includes mass media, tours, and one-on-one interactions. Quality interpretation seeks to reach the whole of the clientele—on site and at home. It covers the entire subject matter and territory—without being diluted. It uses many sources, experts, and opportunities to extend the expertise of the interpreter.

The average person spends the equivalent of 27 years of a lifetime in leisure. How is it used? What is the role of the interpreter in making this 1/3 of a lifetime more meaningful, in making the citizens more environmentally constructive? America's work culture and focus has yielded to leisure culture at least partially. In recreation, our culture will flourish or die. Quality, not quantity, has become the key watchword. Interpreters are now among the key shapers of culture—guides to our future relationships to the land. They can help lead society to a meaningful, constructive relationship with its environment. There has never been a time when more historians and naturalists were working; there have never been more visitors to our natural and historic areas, and they are seeking more than amusement. The interpreter can help assure that visitors to recreation areas and museums will find more to do in the place than merely pass time.

 If you treat an individual as he is, he will stay that way, but if you treat him as if he were what he could be, he will become what he could be.
—Goethe

KEY CONCEPTS

- Know the park and service area; become its information center and reference for history, art, or nature.
- Reach all property visitors with interpretation.
- Try to make interpretation the central experience of each visitor.
- Reach beyond
  —to the nonvisitors that can serve the support base.
  —interpret the total context, not just the park.
- Use many media and approaches (people learn differently).
- Provide interpretation at all times (i.e., personal, nonpersonal, inside-outside, take-home).
- Provide life-long interpretation, provoking clients to become truly happy amateur experts.

All the interpretation need not be easy to absorb or simplistic. It can offer gradations of intellectual challenge. It can include some information that suits beginners and some that satisfies experienced people who try to continuously expand their knowledge.

Interpretive programs are not all available to visitors in automobiles, by television or radio or movies, nor all in exhibit centers. The interpretive effort often includes many approaches. Any museum or interpretive center can offer a menu of many choices, many media, in several places. The point is that the complete interpretive program has many facets. It reaches different people in different ways—some in the visitor center or museum, some out in the garden, forest, or park, some in their homes, some in their cars, and/or some in the library.

The richness of experience and some of the rewards of interpretation may come partly from the effort made by the customer. Some of it is best learned by the individual during an experience that may be designed by an interpreter but accomplished when the participant is alone.

Interpretation should be readily available and accessible to every visitor on a property as well as to those outside of it.

> It is not so important that we be taught but that we be given the wish to learn.
> —Anonymous

How to Channel Interpretation

The tradition of professional interpretation started with personal contact and interaction. Mr. Wylie in his Yellowstone camps, the professors and foresters in California who led resort and national park lectures and hikes and answered questions at the museums, and Enos Mills, leading his resort customers up Long's Peak or along a stream, formed the "nature guiding" tradition that led to modern interpretation. Early museum curators and owners emphasized labels and guided tours to interpret the exhibits. Today, however, the interpreter faces a wide array of methods to reach interpretive clients. Among them are very clever impersonal media that can supplement the personal approach. Opinions about which approach works best will long be discussed among professional interpreters.

MEDIA PHILOSOPHY

Interpretive programming involves a menu of subjects and activities. The interpreter chooses the medium of presentation for each of them. Modern technology offers an array of equipment and tools that baffle any interpreter giving top priority to subject matter and visitors. The interpreter chooses among many, based on advantages, purposes and costs (Box 6.2).

GADGETS

Tilden (1967) wrote a chapter, *Of Gadgetry*, in which he confessed that "the gadget has come to stay, and will be used to a much greater extent than is now the case." That means more projectors, sound installations, tapes, visitor-operated gadgets, and quality motion pictures. However, Tilden asserted that "...such a mechanical device can never deliver anything better than what some person thought, prepared, spoke, or otherwise personally performed." "There will never be a device of telecommunication as satisfactory as the direct contact ... with that something which flows out of the very constitution of the individual in his physical self."

BOX 6.2: WHICH MEDIA TO USE? (COUNTRYSIDE COMMISSION, 1980)

Personal	Written	Audiovisual
Flexible	Easy—may enrich later	Compare before and after
Limited duty time	Souvenir value	Show different time scales
Not always available	May bring income	"On duty" always, some sans staff
Variable performance	Can become litter	Consistent high performance
Expensive	Inflexible, no change	Expensive, specialized personnel
	Visitor must read	Specialized environment for some
	Short messages only	Strict maintenance

Tilden's philosophy about mechanical things leaned heavily toward personal services and for good reasons based on his years of field observations. The multiple cases of interpreters being mastered by their mechanical servants plead for prudence in becoming nonpersonal interpreters. Tilden (1967) issued a very good warning that many investors in interactive computer displays have learned the hard way (Figure 6.8):

> No institution should install any mechanical devices until it knows that such gadgets can be adequately, continually, and quickly serviced. No matter how good they may be when they are working properly, they are a source of shame and chagrin, as well as an imposition on the public, when they are allowed to be more than briefly inoperative.
> —Tilden, 1967

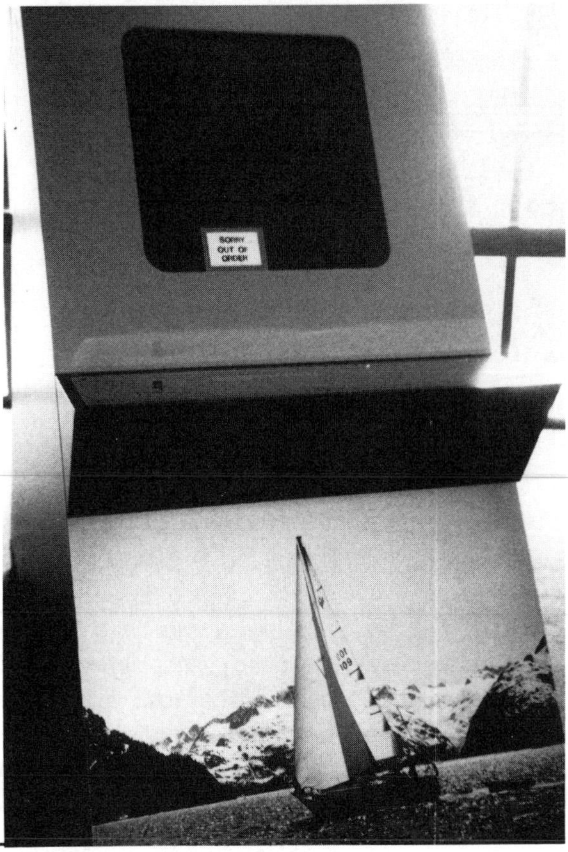

FIGURE 6.8
The electronic age often has its limitations in interpretation.

INTERPRETATION RANGES WIDELY:

... from clip art to virtual reality,
... from Ben Franklin's press to robotics,
... from first person role playing to complete abstraction.

The opportunities for expression proliferate (Figure 6.9). Visual interpretive materials range from the very simple and inexpensive paste-in line drawings to high-tech images of virtual reality and whatever will come after it. Black-and-white clip art goes hand-in-hand with photocopiers and computer scanners. It has become a cottage industry for artistic interpreters who sell their drawings at reasonable prices. The potential for future uses of technology and old-fashioned equipment demonstrations seems endless. Caution and care in keeping the visitor in mind are of primary concern. Interpretation is not gadgets, but some gadgets can enhance interpretation.

FIGURE 6.9
The penultimate gadget—a John James Audubon robot gestures and talks in the Whitewater Forest, Hamilton County, Ohio.

Controversial Issues Interpretation

Virtually every museum, park, forest, historic district, wildlife refuge, or industry faces one or more critical issues (Figure 6.10). Each of these institutions exists in a community, county, or state where critical issues of the environment, architecture, historic preservation, or art call for resolution or improvement of conditions.

The issues may relate to the past, the present, or the future. They may involve both natural and cultural resources. They may include local, regional, or global scales.

Interpretation addresses these issues more and more. As part of the mission to tell the whole story or to relate events in one place to everyday life, interpreters address controversial issues in a rational, factual manner—sometimes with passion.

They interpret racial tensions and slavery at Martin Luther King, Jr. National Historical Site and Harpers Ferry National Historical Park, among others. They demonstrate how heavy metals accumulate in the food chain at Everglades National Park and Indiana Dunes National Lakeshore. They speculate about overpopulation and agricultural practices at Mesa Verde National Park and Bandelier National Monument. At the Tippecanoe Battlefield County Park, the theme "hoe vs. bow" describes land use conflicts between advancing European American farmers and Native American hunters/farmers.

More critical issue interpretation seems desirable. Until the past 10-20 years, most interpretive programs avoided controversial subjects. Interpreters offered ecology or history lessons in the field or around the campfire. They explained a property's grandeur or special features. They discussed the forest or refuge management in broad and positive terms. They identified the area's trees and rocks and birds; they still do and should continue to do so. Property managers and museum curators may have encouraged this neutrality. Many of them saw interpretation as entertainment, promotion, or safety lessons. Park Superintendents and Forest Supervisors seldom have seen themselves involved in maintaining active, meaningful interpretive programs that give their staff a direct line to the public. Interpretation has been nice but seldom vital in the minds of many administrators.

Today's visitors, however, look for more than basic lessons in displays, brochures, talks, or films. They engage the historian in the antecedents of the modern woman's movement. They ask the naturalist about biodiversity and oxygen in the atmosphere. They want to know how the well-known cultural and environmental concerns relate to their children. They want to know what to do about local problems—what will do some good. They look for an informed person to lead them to the best literature and presentations. They look for evaluation of what they have heard or read in the news. They want an apolitical analysis of

FIGURE 6.10
*The private Adirondack Museum used current debates about the Adirondack Park Agency
to summarize a century of controversy about park policy.*

current issues and long-range trends. The interpretive center or museum has the opportunity—no, a duty—to become such an information center. To do so properly, the interpreter will have to call upon many resources, selecting outside experts wisely, forming an advisory and program committee from among volunteers. Then, controversial issue interpretation can proceed as a community service, using some of the strategies and cautions listed below.

RELIGION AND INTERPRETATION

Don't mention religion. This advice urges keeping social peace in families, at community picnics, and at social dinners. An interpreter can mention religion (and politics) but should avoid arguing or advocating a point of view. History of religious groups in a community makes one of the most fascinating interpretive topics—and the distance of time may make it relatively noncontroversial. The "Quaker corner" of one midwestern county contains the first school (still standing), an underground railroad "station," and an annual festival—all worthy of interpretation. The same county has a strong Irish Catholic component (including a cathedral), a plethora of Presbyterians, and a former Methodist camp (now a county park) that hosted traveling Chatauquas and famous evangelists.

But you cannot avoid religion if you talk about geology, the extinction and development of species, glaciers, Native Americans, Egypt, Greece, dinosaurs, stars, the sun, or anything else that involves estimates of past times. You can step carefully and prevent inflammatory statements, but your carefully-chosen words will still produce varying responses among your listeners.

That is because some religious people have chosen to attach specific years to God's works of creation (calling themselves literal creationists). Other people say they know how and when evolution occurred (strict evolutionists—some call them naturalists). Just why this passion to fix times and methods has such importance (is it hubristic?) is seldom discussed, but the resulting debate is bitter. Some call it a difference between science and religion. The roots of the debate go back in the history of human intractability for many centuries. Galileo lived under house arrest and could not write about the earth moving around the sun due to a similar 17th century debate. In modern times, similar but different arguments still rage, leading to complications for interpreters of the natural scene. Imagine the quandary of the naturalist at Dinosaur National Monument or the Petrified Forest National Park, where the fossils stand out so clearly, but well-educated visitors hold strong and differing opinions about when they got there.

Complications arise from the split in opinion among the United States population. The interpreter is going to say something that will be questioned by one group or another. For example, geologists estimate the age of the rock strata of the Grand Canyon as long before some people say God created the earth. When it comes to dinosaurs, the dates do not jibe with some creationist views, although some seem more concerned with apes than dinosaurs. Certainly, even the words creation, evolution, mutations, and maybe even adaptation to changing climatic conditions can raise emotional and negative responses among members of the interpretive audience. Dealing with this in a diplomatic and neutral way seems to be the most effective response. Estimates of the age of the earth are just that. Science does not deny the existence or creative power of God (although some scientists seem to). Rather, many scientists attempt to discover more about the processes used to form the earth and the universe. Even theorists with strongly opposing views seem to agree that those processes occurred before humans appeared, before people comprehended the earth as a round ball circling the sun, and before they developed literal western language and linear thought patterns.

Apparently, however the polarization will not go away. A Gallup poll indicated that many people in the audiences that interpreters seek to influence could be emotionally upset by statements about creation and about evolution. Sheler and Schrof (1991) reported that a 1991 poll showed that 47 percent of all Americans hold a strict creationist view, 40 percent hold a centrist view, and 9 percent have the view that God had no part in human development from less advanced forms of life (Table 6.1).

TABLE 6.1
PERCENTAGE OF AMERICANS WHO IDENTIFY WITH DIFFERENT CREATION VIEWS
(GALLUP POLL, NOV 21-24, 1991)

Categories*	Strict Creationist[†]	Centrist**	"Naturalist"[††]
✳ All Americans	47	40	9
Men	39	45	12
Women	53	36	7
College grads	25	54	16
< Hi-school diploma	65	23	5
Whites	46	40	9
Blacks	53	41	4

* A small percentage in each category was undecided.

[†] Strict Creationists say God created people pretty much in their present form at one time within the last 10,000 years.

** Centrists say *Homo sapiens* developed over millions of years from less advanced forms of life, but God guided this process, including human creation.

[††] "Naturalists" or strict evolutionists say *Homo sapiens* developed over millions of years from less advanced forms of life; God had no part in this process.

POLITICS AND INTERPRETATION

Never discuss politics. This old family solidarity admonition applies to interpretation as well. Politics arouses emotion. It splits families. It can prevent friendships. Some of us assume that a person of the opposite party is not only flawed but also to be ignored, ridiculed, or converted.

Therefore, an interpreter may unnecessarily imperil his or her credibility and distract positive thought by gratuitously referring to twelve years of Republican rule, 50 years of Democratic Congresses, or Clinton tax madness. Likewise, mention of the Governor, the Mayor, the Prime Minister, or ineptness of any party probably clouds the real message to be offered.

In the U.S., some people still feel disturbed when an interpreter says the North beat the South 130 years ago. A senseless argument still crops up over whether or not the War Between the States was fought over slavery. Even cute references to British-American historical conflicts can put off some visitors. While almost anything political may offend someone sometime, there is no sense in messing up a good message with irrelevant or diversionary talk about side issues. What happened to people's sense of humor? "None of your business" in terms of politics, if you are an interpreter. Of course, if the themes or subjects are political tenets or persons, objective facts, rich stories, and maybe a bit of well-considered humor can help send the themes home with visitors. But tact remains essential.

That does not suggest that interpretation should be "safe," avoiding all aspects of controversy. It only says that tact is better than being "funny" or "just kidding" or bellicose, especially about the touchy subjects such as politics and religion. Add to the list the topics of race, national origin, gender, and other areas that call for common courtesy and respect. Do not allow courtesy to serve as an excuse to make interpretation ineffective. Instead, use courtesy to lead people to knowledge about how to act appropriately in relation to other people, their country and environment.

WILDLIFE REHABILITATION: AN ISSUE WITH AN OPPORTUNITY

With animal rights believers butting heads with sport hunters, any talk or exhibit about wildlife carries explosive potential, as well as being a top attention-getter (Figure 6.11).

Wildlife rehabilitation centers, often attached to interpretive facilities, provoke controversy. They require high expenditures for cages, flight pens, feeding, veterinarian services and routine care and cleaning. They require specialized permanent personnel. To be effective, they require an interpreter. Yet live animals provide interpreters the best visual aids available and can help emphasize important messages about environmental stewardship.

Among the problems, rehabilitation centers seem to stimulate new arrivals just by their availability. Children and adults seem to actively search for wounded or "orphaned" animals to take to the center. Unless interpreters screen firmly and diplomatically, the center can become a dumping ground for all sorts of pets. One place run by a kind-hearted woman in Chicago contained monkeys, macaws, alligators, and other refugees from warmer climes, along with local squirrels, songbirds, and skunks. It was not a pretty sight or smell, and there was little time for skillful interpretation.

Some claim that rehabilitation centers may create some erroneous subliminal interpretive messages in

FIGURE 6.11
Raptor rehabilitation requires much work and has strong appeal for visitors at Carrie Murray Environmental Center, Baltimore, MD.

the minds of clients. One is that rehabilitating individual creatures might somehow benefit a species or population. The romantic/heroic act of working with one animal can eclipse the more important principles of habitat management to let wild animals take care of themselves (Manes, 1990). The same concern for one animal requires diplomacy when it has little chance to survive and/or release back to the wild becomes an issue. The pet question arises as attachment grows with hand-feeding, naming, and teaching rehabilitative behavior (Baker, 1988).

On the other hand, rehabilitation centers create public enthusiasm, a mostly positive image of the agency, increased opportunities to interact sincerely with citizens at a very serious level, invitations to visit camps, clubs, and schools, and openings for discussion of wildlife habitat management. The site will get increased visitation, often increasing the number of repeaters; an Oklahoma state park nature center saw visitation soar by 400 percent in five years after a rehabilitation center started (Baker, 1988). Interpreters have the chance to discuss the needs of animals. They can dispel the "Bambi" paradigm of forest life. They can also provide information about parasites, disease, teeth, talons, training and clean-up work, thus dispelling the idea that it is fun to raise wild animals. The negative impact of exposing wild animals to humans will come up, too.

A tactful interpreter, sensitive to people who go out of their way to show concern about animals, yet honest about injured animals and wildlife habitat, seems vital to making wildlife rehabilitation a positive and beneficial interpretive experience. Without a high level of interpreter/visitor interaction, the center may have negative educational effects (Baker, 1988). Manes (1990), while warning against exploiting live wild animals for interpretation, declared that:

> Rehabilitation efforts are valid if they provide unreleasable specimens that are properly employed to foster public understanding and appreciation of wildlife resources and issues. . . . A park interpreter . . . can guarantee program participation by carrying a live owl through campgrounds when promoting a program about raptors. . . . Rehabilitation programs do put to use animals that would otherwise be lost from human benefit—perhaps a valid form of conservation.

Controversial issues such as religion, politics, and using live animals for education constitute only a bit of what may stir interest. Resource management also comes up in local and national debates. Visitors expect interpreters to explain the facts and perhaps opinions about how resources may be best managed. Interpretation serves as an active, influential part of the management team. The greatest responsibility for this teamwork rests with interpreters (Maynes, 1992). They need to do careful research and read widely on all sides of the issue. Inviting subject-matter authorities to discuss the various points of view and facts with staff and perhaps with visitors will provide good background.

PROVOKING THOUGHTFUL ANALYSIS AND SOLUTIONS

Talking about critical issues takes but one step. In some cases, maybe it is enough. In other cases, the interpreter will feel compelled to seek to stimulate a change that would help resolve the problem. In recent years, the interpretive profession discussed its value in terms of what changes it has made. As Steve Van Matre has said in many speeches, our work is in vain if we do not see results, if we do not walk more lightly on this earth, if we do not modify our understanding and behavior to make us better citizens of our environment (Van Matre, 1988). Interpreters are basically educators—agents of change. Not all change involves controversial issues, but that is where a good share of it occurs. And controversy can get people's attention. The interpreter presenting facts and artifacts in a rational way can encourage visitors to reason with evidence.

Many years ago Freeman Tilden (1967) wrote about relating an interpretive theme to people's lives back home, but there is still work to be done. Tilden promoted provocation, shunned propaganda. The techniques of stimulating people to think about subjects is the key to getting them to examine issues (Brown, 1971). The interpreter uses provocation as a basic tool. To provoke public involvement in environmental issues and action, the interpreter can use three approaches advocated by Brown (1971):

1. Use the story-line approach to describe the physical environment and social processes. Demonstrate the potential of the site to involve the public in the resource; the interpreter serves as the expert and guide, getting the people started with historical and scientific information presented in understandable ways.

2. Facilitate use of the museum or park as a clearinghouse for exchange of environmental information and discourse. Offer programs by invited speakers, conduct research, and maintain a reference service; the interpreter plays the roles of organizer, chairperson, and reference librarian.

3. Host public forums that may lead to improvements. Allow the citizens to talk to each other, while the interpreter provides a setting for the forum. Brown (1971) explained that this strategy is low-risk—the interpreter does not act as a lone wolf howling into the wind about problems. The interpreter is not haranguing an audience, prophesying doom, inviting opponents to attack his or her authority or person.

This three-stage structure can stimulate the public to do its own exploring, thinking, and concluding, using the cultural or natural resource base (e.g., museum, park, science center) as a community setting and catalyst. The search for information can encompass the full breadth of public concern, presenting facts on all sides of an issue. The interpreter thus shifts the burden of interpretation to the public—making them interpreters of the local, regional or national scene—the goal of strong, durable interpretive programs.

Local issues that environmental interpreters can explore with their clientele include forest management; wildlife population dynamics, predators and hunting; atmospheric alterations; water use and abuse; soil erosion; farming practices; and sewage disposal. The interpreter will face several challenges in this process of working with controversial issues, such as:

- how to describe management concerns in a positive, enjoyable way.
- how to present and allow various opinions and viewpoints on the subject, even if the interpreter has a strong opinion.
- how to involve visitors in finding their own solutions.
- how to get administrators and board members to reduce their reluctance to have interpreters deal with controversy.

Seek out examples of other cases where interpreters have dealt with critical issues. They can provide guidelines for positive approaches. Use questioning strategies and positive examples to help visitors develop their own solutions rather than feeding them the company line. Evaluate to make sure the interpretation increases the effectiveness of the take-home message.

Values of Programs

Beck (1986) hypothesized several ranks of common nature-oriented interpretive programs according to the value they offered the visitor. He assumed that more direct involvement with objects produces a higher level of more valuable experiences. To put it simply, shaking the prime minister's hand has higher value than seeing her picture in the paper. This philosophy has long served as a tenet of interpretation, but has insufficient experimental evidence to prove it. Museum curators likewise value the original artifact and personal interaction with it as a highlight experience. Colin Turnbull (1981) identified the frustrations of many "tourists that are carefully kept at a distance from . . . the animals, the land, the people. They are denied the opportunity many of them sought."

The hypothesis suggests, for example, that auditorium programs offer lower level interpretive experiences to visitors than programs that are active and allow for involvement with the cultural or natural resource.

Movies or slide shows, for example, may contribute to management goals, and understanding of the site, but they provide little stimulation or reward to the visitor because of the indoor setting, the technological requirements of the program, and the passive, remote nature of the visitor's involvement with the interpreter. Beck ranked them low in value. An evening campfire program affords a higher level interpretive experience. The outdoor setting and informality may allow for greater intimacy between the interpreter and audience, but visitors generally sit and listen passively.

The following categories of interpretive programs rank higher because they promote active visitor involvement and the potential for application of higher level thinking skills:

Interpretive demonstrations involve visitors directly in the experience. They learn "through the use of original objects, by firsthand experience" (Tilden, 1967). Members of an interpretive audience may actively examine a nugget of gold, an owl pellet, an arrowhead, a caribou antler, or learn Native American or pioneer skills—the "primitive skills in pioneering travel and subsistence" (Leopold, 1966).

Nature walks have high value because they, too, offer firsthand learning experiences about the cultural and natural features of the land.

This very loose ranking could be useful if given numerical values, so cost-effectiveness comparisons can become meaningful. Yarde (1989) tried to get at this through a short questionnaire on program value, quality, or effectiveness. He asked 70 permanent and seasonal interpreters in the Midwest (mostly Indiana and Michigan) to independently assign relative values to different types of activities. These state, local and federal natural history interpreters used the general hike or tour as the basis, with a weight or value of 1.0. If they felt that people get twice as much benefit from a slide show as from a hike, the weight for a slide show would be 2.0.

Table 6.2 indicates the mean score, standard deviation, and 95 percent confidence interval (based on a t-value of 2 corresponding to n = 60 and α = .05).

TABLE 6.2 AVERAGE PROGRAM VALUE WEIGHTS ASSIGNED BY INTERPRETERS.

Activity	n	Mean	SD	95% CI
Demonstration	62	1.452	.4207	1.56-1.34
Living Interpretation	62	1.406	.4405	1.57-1.35
School programs	61	1.228	.4405	1.34-1.11
Junior Naturalist	59	1.112	.4973	1.24-0.98
Talks	61	1.085	.2863	1.16-1.01
Roving interpretation	62	1.045	.4272	1.15-0.93
Nature Center time	63	1.027	.4120	1.13-0.92
Guided hikes	70	1.000		
Camp fires	61	0.993	.4486	1.11-0.88
Special events	59	0.849	.5556	0.99-0.70
Mass media	63	0.787	.4542	0.90-0.67
Self-guiding trail	64	0.769	.3328	0.85-0.69
Brochure	64	0.734	.3168	0.81-0.65

Source: Yarde (1989)

This information suggests that the demonstration and living history programs ranked as the most valuable interpretive methods, while brochures and self-guiding trails had the least (but still high) value to the visitors. The opinions seem to emphasize the value of personal interaction over nonpersonal services—perhaps to be expected as the opinion of those who provide personal services. These rankings provide an hypothesis that deserves further study. Theoretically, the visitors' opinions of benefits provide the true measure of value. Measuring them, however, becomes methodologically difficult, partly because visitors may not have experience with many of the activities.

Summary

The interpretive profession has grown in the fertile ground of museums and parks through many decades of careful cultivation. Enos Mills and Freeman Tilden formalized the principals that describe how to get messages across to people by applying communications and teaching theories.

Interpretation aims to serve as a central experience for museum and park visitors as well as extending the major messages to all citizens. Interpreters define the special character of a place and then offer total programming for skill growth related to major themes. The interpreter seeks to bring people into more intimate contact with their natural and cultural surroundings.

Literature Cited

Baker, R. E. (1988). "Wildlife rehabilitation as an interpretive tool." In *Proceedings, National Interpreters Workshop*, NAI. San Diego, CA.

Beck, L. (1986). A hierarchy of interpretive programs. *The Interpreter* (Winter):18-20.

Brown, W. E. (1971). *Islands of hope*. Arlington, VA: National Recreation and Park Association.

Countryside Commission. (1980). Audio-visual media in countryside interpretation. Chettenham, Gloucestershire, England: *Countryside Commission Advisory Series, No. 12.*

Division of Interpretation. (1976). *A personal training program for interpreters*. Washington, DC: National Park Service.

Eagley, A. H. and Himmelfarb, S. (1978). Attitudes and opinions. *Annual Review of Psychology, 29*:517-554.

Haas, G. E. (1977). Recreation and parks: A social study at Shenandoah National Park. Washington, DC: *National Park Service, Scientific Monograph Series, No. 10.*

Herbert, M. E. (1974). "System for measuring visitor participation in interpretive programs in Indiana State Parks." West Lafayette, IN: Purdue University, M. S. Thesis.

Ickes, H. L. (1938). Letter to Jens Jensen (Container 222, Ickes Papers, Library of Congress), quoted in Mackintosh, B. (1985), Harold L. Ickes and the National Park Service. *Journal of Forest History, 29*(2):78-84.

Jordy, W. H. (1974). The genius of the place. *New York Review of Books, 21*(10):33-37.

Knudson, D. M. and Vanderford, M. E. (1980). Participation in interpretive programs by state park visitors. *Journal of Interpretation, 5*(2):20-23.

Leopold, A. (1966). *A sand county almanac; with other essays on conservation from Round River.* New York, NY: Oxford University Press.

Makruski, E. (1978). "A conceptual analysis of 'environmental interpretation.'" Ph.D. dissertation, Ohio State University. Ann Arbor, MI: University Microfilms.

Mandelbrot, B. (1977). *The fractal geometry of nature*. New York, NY: W. H. Freeman & Co., Inc.

Manes, R. (1990). Creating public misconceptions. *Human Dimensions in Wildlife Newsletter, 9*(1):12-14.

Maynes, B. (1992). Interpreting significant issues. *Ranger (Journal Association of National Park Rangers), 8*(1):24-25.

McLuhan, M. (1964). *Understanding media: The extensions of man*. Toronto, ON: McGraw-Hill, Inc.

Mills, E. A. (1920). *The adventures of a nature guide*. Garden City, NY: Doubleday & Co., Inc.

Porter, E. and Gleick, J. (1990). *Nature's chaos*. New York, NY: The Viking Press.

Reyburn, J. H. and Knudson, D. M. (1975) The influence of advertising on attendance at park programs. *Journal of Environmental Education, 7*(2):59-64.

Schroeder, H. W. (1993). Preference for and meaning of arboretum landscapes. *Visitor Behavior, 8*(1):13-14.

Sheler, J. L., and Schrof, J. M. (1991). The creation. *U. S. News and World Report, 111*(Dec. 23): 56-64.

Sherman, Mrs. J. D. (1917). Women's part in national parks development. In *Proceedings, National Parks Conference* (Jan. 2-6).

Tilden, F. (1967). *Interpreting our heritage (rev. ed.).* Chapel Hill, NC: University North Carolina Press.

Turnbull, C. (1981). Tourism as pilgrim. *Natural History, 90*(7):76-81.

Van Matre, S. (1988). Environmental education: Mission gone astray. *Mini Journal of Interpretation,* (NAI) *1*(1):4, 6.

Verderber, R. (1978). *Communicate! (2nd ed.).* Belmont, CA: Wadsworth.

Wolf, A. D. (1969). *A parents' guide to the Montessori classroom, Leaflet No. 1.* Altoona, PA: Penn-Mont Academy.

Yarde, N. (1989). "Cost effectiveness of interpretive programs, personnel and agencies." M. S. Thesis, Purdue University.

Foundations:
How People Learn

If he is indeed wise he does not bid you to enter the house
of his wisdom but rather, leads you to the threshold of your
own mind.

—Kahlil Gibran

This chapter, rooted in educational theory, assists interpreters in their
quest for effective methods of performing their craft. An understanding
of how people learn enables interpreters to structure worthwhile and
valuable learning experiences. Acquaintance with educational theories
gives interpreters guidelines for communicating more relevantly.

Effective interpretation, just as effective teaching, changes people's
information bases, skills, and attitudes. In other words, interpreters "cultivate people's minds," by affecting their knowledge, their attitudes, their
beliefs, and presumably their subsequent actions. Unlike traditional
classroom education, interpretation integrates a spirit of recreation and
interaction with real objects or environments. Perhaps that's a major advantage that interpreters have over classroom teachers.

DOES INTERPRETATION EQUAL EDUCATION?

Most writers strive to say that interpretation differs from education, yet is
educational (Makruski, 1978). Mills (1920) and Tilden (1967) emphasized that the interpreter, although pedagogical, is not pedantic. Interpretation differs from "schooling." Yet, people learn from it.

No doubt should exist that interpretation *is* educational. Museums
use the terms education and interpretation almost interchangeably—and
they are not referring just to school children. The National Parks agencies of the U.S. and Canada refer to the educational roles their interpreters undertake. As early as in the 1917 National Parks Conference, education occupied a major portion of the agenda.

Some confusion can exist in terminology, however. In some museums and nature centers, the staff refers to *educational* programs when
talking about services to school groups and *interpretive* activities being
those for informal audiences on site. These have some convenience
value but do not preclude the cross-over of the terms.

The practice of interpretation of natural and cultural resources involves and uses many education principles.

Receiving and Processing Information and Ideas

To get started on the theoretical constructs of learning, individuals begin with some basic physical and psychological principles that add up to saying people learn with anatomical and mental parts (modalities) and from different kinds of internal learning processes (domains). Humans use all their senses to learn. Research suggests that people absorb general information through the five senses in the following proportions (Countryside Commission, 1980):

Sense	Percent
sight	— 75
hearing	— 13
touch	— 6
taste	— 3
smell	— 3

The next question asks how do people process and "learn" the information that they receive? How do individuals retain and recall it? Several theories and hypotheses try to explain the answers.

MODALITIES OF LEARNING

Researchers seem to agree that humans use four principal modalities as they learn (Christensen, 1990). They are the visual, auditory, kinesthetic, and symbolic/abstract modalities of learning.

1. Individuals learn through *visual* means, through art, sculpture, graphics, and mapping.
2. The *auditory* mode involves patterned sound such as speech, music, song, rhythmic patterns.
3. *Kinesthetics* relates to movement, tension, and contraction of the joints, muscles, and ligaments, sensed through the nerves; physical action expressed by the body excites the mind-brain system of most people.
4. *Abstract codes and symbols* help individuals learn from real things or imagined things, generally through reading, writing, and arithmetic.

Interpreters frequently use all four of the modalities of learning. They help people touch, lift, and manage real objects, thus involving kinesthetics. People hear the sounds of the natural surroundings, they see the real things, and use the abstractions of words and numbers to explain, compare, and measure them. The visitor's entire range of senses and learning modalities can get involved. The interpreter who does this employs education at its most powerful and most versatile.

LEARNING DOMAINS

While using several receptors of information and ideas, the learning domains construct divides our learning skills into three basic domains in which all people operate:

The *cognitive domain* involves knowing information, recognizing elements of the landscape and putting them together in an understanding way, or developing concepts.

Common ways to reach this domain include talks or lectures, written labels or brochures, charts and exhibits.

The *affective domain* involves feeling, learning at the emotional level, developing and expressing attitudes or sentiments. Common interpretive approaches include discussion, photography, paintings, music, and drama.

The *kinesthetic domain* uses motor skills, a sense of motion, or physical development. The interpreter may use participatory activities, hiking through the swamps, or physical skill practice sessions.

Interpreters seek to expand the knowledge, attitudes, and skills of people through appropriately mixing domains, according to the subject matter and visitor/learner development. For example, before adults can learn the cognitive lessons that might be found on an interactive computer, many have to overcome the affective barrier of dealing with the computer; they need the motor skill to get the machine to operate. Despite all the claims of user-friendliness, computers can leave many people embarrassed or puzzled.

Weak cognitive skills in reading and calculating preclude some from receiving the full message. With about 20 percent of the U.S. population being relatively illiterate or having reading difficulties, exhibits or brochures with emphasis on written material alone may be a problem for one visitor in five. They just will not understand written messages. Probably 95 percent of the visitors will not read any one particular message, according to systematic observation in exhibit centers (Ham, 1992). Exhibit planners can help overcome this by making the objects and graphics tell the story through the sequence and display of objects.

Major Learning Theories

This section describes several different models or theories of how people learn. Some theorists suggest that learning abilities are age-related. Others describe learning strategies. Others use the currently popular theory of constructivism that states that humans build on what they know and have experienced.

COGNITIVE DEVELOPMENT THEORY

Cognitive development theory suggested that children, teenagers, and adults will respond to interpretation according to their own level of cognitive maturity. Piaget (1952, 1955), a Swiss psychologist, noted that intelligence develops in a specific sequence as people progress from childhood.

First comes development of sensorimotor skills, when infants put objects together, separate them, and begin to see them as groups. Then, to their kinetic muscular intelligence, they add language to slowly develop symbolic mental perceptions, but without a sense of cause and effect. In the third stage, abstract thinking develops but only operates in the presence of concrete objects. Finally, maturity develops with pure abstract thinking, apart from objects; theories, processes, and purely verbal teaching make sense. Simply put, this hierarchy specifies that concepts develop from simple to complex and from concrete to abstract.

Individuals learn differently at different stages of life. Piaget (1952) described learning at four stages of childhood, at about ages birth to two years, two to seven years, seven to eleven years, over eleven years (Table 7.1). Of course, individual children develop at different rates. Tilden's sixth principle of interpretation reflects that children and adults learn differently and have distinct capabilities. Tilden (1967) recognized that interpretation addressed to children "should not be a dilution of the presentation to adults, but should follow a fundamentally different approach." Piaget's levels of cognitive development may be used to design interpretive materials and methods for various age groups.

TABLE 7.1 PIAGET'S STAGES OF COGNITIVE DEVELOPMENT

AGE	DEVELOPMENT STAGE	ABILITIES
0-2 years	Sensorimotor	Develops organized patterns of behavior and thought (schemes). Use sensory and motor activities, primarily.
2-7 years	Preoperational	Masters symbols (words). Centers attention on one characteristic at a time. Cannot mentally reverse actions.
7-11 years	Concrete operational	Generalizes from concrete experiences. Unable to mentally manipulate inexperienced conditions.
> 11 years	Formal operational	Able to form hypotheses. Deals with abstractions. Solves problems systematically. Engages in mental manipulations.

Source: Adapted from Pomerantz (1990).

Stage 1. The first stage in Piaget's model includes infants and toddlers from birth to two years. At this early level, toddlers learn through sensory and motor activities in the sensorimotor developmental stage. Recent research suggests that infants may "learn" much more than previously thought. Toddlers can learn bird names and flowers very quickly. Parents and interpreters can introduce them to experiences in nature, helping them to feel comfortable in an outdoor setting, thus putting them in the environment to learn.

Questions children commonly ask relate to the stages (Piaget, 1955). The first types of questions are related to place and name. These questions of very young children can be identified as where, what, and who questions.

Stage 2. In the second or preoperational stage, two to seven-year-olds master symbols or words. The child can focus attention on only one characteristic at a time, so interpretive programs designed for children in this age range should concentrate on one central idea. As Ralph Waldo Emerson observed, "To the young mind everything is individual, stands by itself. . . . Later remote things cohere and flower out from one stem"(Tilden, 1967).

After age two, when and why questions start coming out, sometimes with irksome frequency. These are questions of cause and time. Piaget (1955) noted several meanings for the why questions. He called "why" the "maid-of-all-work" among questions (Box 7.1).

Three big groups of whys exist, according to Piaget's construct:
* those of causal explanation, including finalistic.
* those of motivation.
* those of justification and later (ages 7-8) logical justification.

BOX 7.1: WHAT "WHY" MIGHT MEAN

A child's earliest why's come from the heart—more affective than intellectual (Piaget, 1955). They indicate disappointments more than curiosity, e.g., the favorite—why can't I? Then, somehow, the child passes to curiosity in general. Next in the developmental line come more subtle interests such as the search for causes.

A three-year-old boy might ask "Why do the trees have leaves?" He may want any of at least four types of answers. The first two are those that an adult questioner would expect:

1. finalistic or functional—"to breathe with," or
2. causal or logical—"because . . . all vegetable relatives have leaves."

In the child's mind, at least two other possibilities exist for the inquiry:

3. anthropomorphic—who put the leaves on?—"God did" may be a satisfactory answer, or
4. purposive or utilitarian—what use are leaves to us, or to the tree?

When an interpreter or a parent hears those *why* questions, they might ponder the many alternative ways to answer. Of course, they may also have the lingering thought that another purpose for *why* could be to get attention or maybe to annoy adults just for fun.

Stage 3. Piaget's concrete operational stage includes children from seven to 11 years of age. Preadolescents tend to limit their thinking to those things they have experienced concretely and directly. This suggests that interpretive programs for this age group focus on those aspects of cultural and natural history that can be directly experienced. For example, a multi-sensory approach (i.e., seeing, hearing, smelling, touching, tasting) which allows for personal examination of various qualities of an interpretive site would be appropriate for this age range.

Stage 4. The formal operational stage covers people over the age of 11 years in Piaget's hierarchy. At this stage of cognitive development youths can solve problems systematically and deal with abstractions. At this level, adolescents engage in mental manipulations and form hypotheses. This stage coincides with Tilden's seemingly arbitrary demarcation of 12 years of age as that which separates programming for children from that of adults. At this level, interpretation can challenge youth in more sophisticated cognitive ways.

Overall, interpreters can apply Piaget's theory by:
a. offering thoughts and information consistent with how the children in the audience can process it, and
b. using different interpretive techniques that fit the different levels of cognitive development represented in an audience.

For example, abstractions or cause-and-effect relationships may prompt responses from adults, whereas children will not comprehend the discussion. A nature hike or museum tour that does not progress in some orderly, story-like fashion may surpass the abilities of young children (Grinder and McCoy, 1985). This does not mean that interpretation for mixed age groups should aim at the lowest common denominator. With mixed audiences the interpreter can offer a variety of age-appropriate interpretation to meet the needs of all members of the group.

Bettelheim (1989) built on Piaget's scale of development to focus on how young children perceive their world. "To the child, there is no clear line separating objects from living things . . . " Piaget explained that, to an eight-year-old, the sun is alive because it gives light and it wants to give light. "Even a twelve-and-a-half-year-old is convinced that a stream is alive and has a will, because its water is flowing. The sun, the stone, and the water are believed to be inhabited by spirits very much like people, so they feel and act like people" (Bettelheim, 1989).

A child's thinking remains animistic until puberty, said Piaget (Bettelheim, 1989). Children are sure that animals understand and feel. They think rocks, trees, and animals can tell us things if we tune into them. It seems reasonable to expect answers from those objects which arouse our curiosity. "In animistic thinking, not only animals feel and think as we do, but even stones are alive . . . " (Bettelheim, 1989).

SOCIAL COGNITION THEORY

When people attend interpretive programs, they interact with each other and the interpreter in patterns that correlate with their ages. Their social actions seem to relate to their sense of self and society. An interpreter can prepare for different levels of social interaction by understanding this age-stage theory of how children see others. This theory may help in averting frustration and in designing activities for young children.

Robert Selman outlined five stages of development (approximately ages 3-6, 5-9, 7-12, 10-15, ≥ 16) which describe how children relate to the people around them (Muuss, 1982). The overlap among the age ranges allows for different individual rates of development.
1. The egocentric perspective of ages three to six refers to children consumed by their own points of view, not comprehending perspectives different from their own.
2. The subjective perspective of ages five to nine, allows for the possibility of other perspectives than one's own. These children judge others based on physical observations. They do not really understand different points of view easily.
3. By the time children reach the age range of seven to twelve, self-reflective thinking occurs. They can understand another person's perspective and evaluate their own behavior. At this stage they broaden their awareness that other people may have widely differing values, ideas, and points of view.

4. The mutual perspective, ages 10 to 15, refers to shifting beyond a personal point of view and the perspective of another person to that of a neutral third person. Thus, they perceive concepts in the context of the larger social system.

5. At age 16 and beyond, a full social view emerges which takes into consideration a wide array of different perspectives—known as the in-depth and societal perspective-taking stage.

The upshot: children and young adults relate to others, including interpreters and the other members of an interpretive group, in a variety of ways, according to their different levels of interpersonal understanding. Interpreters may plan programs with reference to both the intellectual development (Piaget's theory) and the social maturity (Selman's theory) of the youth that they serve (Grinder and McCoy, 1985).

BLOOM'S TAXONOMY

Another refinement of the descriptions of the ways that people learn may also help interpreters. A model known as Bloom's taxonomy describes a six-level process that hypothesizes how individuals acquire, assimilate, and apply information. Over time, they move up the learning scale from such routine tasks as memorization to higher level thinking skills such as analysis, synthesis, and evaluation.

The application of this educational theory to interpretation highlights the values of interpretive programs that incorporate higher level thinking skills through active visitor involvement. The following overview (derived from Bloom et al., 1956) describes the process from the lowest to the highest levels of thought.

1. *Knowledge* refers to recalling a fact in the same form as it was learned from memory. This most basic method of learning is teacher-centered.

2. *Comprehension* means that a learner knows and understands the information and can translate it. Learners at this level can explain what they have learned.

3. *Application* takes ideas from several sources and relates them to new situations. At this level the teacher role becomes more facilitative.

4. *Analysis* refers to the breaking down of ideas into component parts to discover distinguishing characteristics or relationships. The student critically examines information to determine assumptions or draw conclusions. The teacher in this instance serves as a resource.

5. *Synthesis* refers to creating new ideas using existing information in unique and different ways. Learners can create, design, compose, and formulate.

6. *Evaluation* appraises or judges information based upon one's command of the material. At the levels of synthesis and evaluation the teacher serves as a sounding board for ideas.

Bloom's levels of learning apply both to the classroom and to the design of interpretive programs. Depending upon an interpreter's audience, programs may be slanted toward lower or higher levels of thought. The interpreter's role changes accordingly. In the transition from simple to more complex thought processes the interpreter shifts from the focal point of knowledge transmission to a facilitative role.

Educators strive to develop self-sufficient learners by providing the environment in which to be curious and learn. Similarly, interpreters seek to provide visitors with progressive levels of development, ultimately leading toward self-initiated discovery (Beck, 1986). Some aspects of history or wild nature are best discovered on one's own (Risk, 1982). With experience and guidance, many mature visitors can operate well by analyzing, synthesizing, and evaluating.

MORAL DEVELOPMENT THEORY

Educational theorists have also defined various stages of moral development, an understanding of which may also be useful to interpreters. Lawrence Kohlberg (1971) devised six stages of moral development which provide an overview of how people arrive at the moral choices they make (Table 7.2).

TABLE 7.2 KOHLBERG'S SIX STAGES OF MORAL DEVELOPMENT

STAGE	PRINCIPAL CONCERN
Preconventional morality	1. Fear of punishment 2. Maximizing pleasure/minimizing pain
Conventional morality	3. What significant others think 4. What society thinks
Postconventional morality	5. Justice and fairness 6. Self-respect

Preconventional morality or the **morality of the child** includes the first two stages. Fear of punishment characterizes *Stage One morality*. An appropriate decision—e.g., not stealing a piece of petrified wood—arises out of a concern for the consequences of getting caught. Fear of punishment still motivates *Stage Two morality*, but here the person makes a conscious evaluation of whether a certain behavior is worth the price of getting caught. Automatic compliance with regulations does not occur in this instance. The decision-maker weighs the benefits of the desired action versus the costs of getting caught.

The next two stages make up **conventional morality** or the **morality of the parent**. They represent the moral level of most people. Concern for being an upstanding member of the family and the community dominates. *Stage Three* represents an evolution of behavior beyond selfish considerations that define preconventional morality. This stage of moral reasoning extends beyond the individual to include the well-being of family and friends. *Stage Four* extends concern to even broader applications; moral decisions expand to encompass the general welfare of society as a whole.

Postconventional morality or the **morality of the adult** includes the final two stages. *Stage Five* represents a shift back to the individual, but not in the same sense as ego-centered preconventional morality. Rather than passive acceptance of societal norms, this stage depends upon individual evaluation of the appropriateness of conventional morality. *Stage Six* produces a way of life that fosters self-respect with the individual taking complete responsibility for his or her actions. It represents conviction of purpose and a commitment to ethical principles.

Kohlberg believed that people cannot skip stages in their moral development, but rather advance in their morality one step at a time. Interpreters can use this to steer park visitors toward environmentally responsible conduct. For example, an interpretive message often carries the "why" of keeping a reasonable distance from (and not feeding) the wildlife. To meet the various moral possibilities of the visitors interpreters serve, they could design informational programs that would assure effectiveness across all six stages of moral development. Messages could target a suitable moral stage of development and expose visitors to the next higher stage of moral reasoning.

Of course, a person can make the same choice after starting from any of the six stages. If the behavior is the same, does the motivation behind it really matter? Dustin (1985) suggested that it does, for three reasons:

1. Making moral choices based on reason and understanding is better than making them based on fear and ignorance.
2. Feeling responsible for one's actions is better than feeling irresponsible for them.
3. Answering to oneself is better than answering to others.

Kohlberg found that as people advance through the six stages their decisions become more consistent. This implies for interpreters that a child (or adult) who behaved one way in the presence of a uniformed employee and the opposite way in the absence of the employee may evolve into someone who behaves consistently and responsibly regardless of the employee's whereabouts. Furthermore, if interpretive messages are well thought out and justifiable to the public, the advanced moral thinker can be expected to support them.

Figure 7.1 shows an example of the application of Kohlberg's theory in the design of a multi-dimensional interpretive message to safe-guard fragile Anasazi cliff dwellings and granaries in the American Southwest. Note the correlation with Table 7.2.

Do Not Go Beyond This Sign
Violators Will Be Prosecuted
You are standing before a gift from the ages.
It is a priceless reminder of our human heritage, of our link to the past.
This pueblo is fragile and irreplaceable.
Enjoy it from a distance so that your children and
your children's children can enjoy this gift as well.
They and your ancestors, the Anasazi, will be forever grateful
for your concern for the future and respect for the past.

FIGURE 7.1
Sign appealing to several moral levels (Dustin, 1985)

Although Kohlberg's conceptualization received wide support in the literature, two criticisms of his work deserve mention. First, his theory is based largely on hypothetical situations. Second, he based his stages of moral development on studies of men. Carol Gilligan (1982) offered a different developmental scheme for women who behave with reference to their care and concern for others. Still, the two developmental models do not differ much and the overall perspective provided by moral development theory has much to offer the designers of interpretive messages (Christensen and Dustin, 1989).

LEARNING STYLES

The theory of learning styles suggests that different individuals learn in different ways and that students can be successful if they are allowed to learn according to their own manners. In practice, learning style theory serves as a framework for teachers who seek to accommodate different types of learners. Likewise, interpreters can benefit from a knowledge of how different people most effectively take in and process information.

The best-known research on learning styles (Keirsey and Bates, 1978) grew out of the work of Carl Jung and identified four basic temperaments of different individuals by Greek names. Keith Golay (1982) built on this foundation in describing four basic types of learners, using more clinical hyphenated adjectives, shown in Table 7.3, and estimating their proportions in the population.

TABLE 7.3

FOUR TYPES OF LEARNERS AND ATTRIBUTES (GOLAY, 1982)

Actual-Spontaneous Learners (38 percent of the students)

Physical involvement	Bold	Fun loving
Stimulating the senses	Expending energies	Function-lust
Realistic	Adventuresome	Excitement
Immediacy	Competitive	Free-spirit
Spontaneity	Challenge	Risk
Contest		

Actual-Routine Learners (38 percent of the students)

Social belonging	Preparing	Planning
Caretaker	Conserving energies	Practical
Giving service	Being decisive	Standards
Obligation	Step-by-step order	Sensible
Responsibility	Routine	Rules
Stable	Policies	

Conceptual-Specific Learners (12 percent of the students)

Developing intelligence	Ingenuity	Depth
Being capable	Critiquing	Objectivity
Possibilities of principles	Explanations	Exploring ideas
Impersonal analysis	Predictions	Categorizing
Being concise	Technical details	Classifying
Building systems		

Conceptual-Global Learners (12 percent of the students)

Understanding self	Insightful	Breadth
Self-actualization	Appreciative	Subjectivity
Possibilities in people	Imaginative	Integrity
Empathetic	Speculative	Idealistic
Developing relationships	Global	Inspirational
Personalizes learning		

1. The action-oriented *Dionysian Temperament* is characterized by an existential approach to life. Dionysians are enthralled by the physical and sensual world. They enjoy challenge and willingly take risks. Golay (1982) called these *Actual-Spontaneous* learners. They have the least interest in cultural and intellectual matters or in acquiring knowledge for its own sake. Traditional learning situations (lectures, for example) bore this type of learner who prefers gaining knowledge through direct experience. This learning pattern makes up about 38 percent of the population.

2. The *Epimethean Temperament* recognizes the social nature of humans and tends to relate to others in terms of their status. The Epimethean does not like to be rushed into things and goes to great lengths to plan and organize to avoid uncertainty. They can also be called *Actual-Routine* learners. They prefer a structured schedule with clearly defined procedures. They hold traditional instructors/lecturers in high esteem. These learners set high standards in executing a task and their school work tends to be meticulous. This pattern makes up another 38 percent of the population.

3. The *Promethean Temperament* thoroughly enjoys thinking and learning. A passion for discovery distinguishes the Promethean from the other types. Prometheans like to collect, organize, and classify objects as well as solve problems. These people come under Golay's nomenclature as *Conceptual-Specific* learners. This kind of person strives to understand, explain, and predict through a research-orientation. These learners can focus on a single point for an extended period of time. Following structured and routine tasks does not captivate this type of learner, which makes up 12 percent of the population.

4. The *Apollonian Temperament* is people-oriented, not in terms of social institutions as is the case with Epimetheans, but rather in terms of individuals and their relationships to one another. Apollonians consider life as a process of self-discovery. This category coincides with *Conceptual-Global* learners. These Apollonians seek the significance of events and try to discover the meaning and relationship of learning to his or her own personal life. *Conceptual-Global* learners also make up 12 percent of the population.

Identifying these classes of individual learning differences have produced positive results, as well as some vigorous discussion and creative ways of working with them. The theory and follow-up trials have led to five key findings (Brandt, 1990):

- Variety in learning style does exist among individuals.
- The concept applies to all areas of education.
- There are different ways to apply the theories.
- People who learn best by different styles can be equally intelligent.
- Some approaches for accommodating learning styles in schools can produce impressive short-term gains in achievement and can affect staff and student morale.

In classroom application of the concept, teachers use questionnaires to distinguish students according to learning style. Then they tailor learning experiences accordingly, both individually and for groups with similar styles. Many teachers who take their classes outdoors discover that an inattentive, "slow" child becomes alert, quick and enthusiastic when learning from the real world in a tactile way—a way that fits that individual's learning style.

In interpretive settings, with ephemeral audiences, interpreters cannot thoroughly test the people to discover their learning styles. However, knowing of the diversity of temperaments and learning styles should help in structuring interpretive programs. By using aspects of each of the four styles, interpreters can build programs that take into account the needs of all program participants (Strang, 1992). Orchestrating interpretive programs to meet the needs of diverse visitors also results in innovative and stimulating events. The interpreter can introduce information through a person's particular learning style and help the individual "stretch" by learning through other styles as well (O'Neil, 1990).

COGNITIVE MAP THEORY

Cognitive map theory provides a foundation for understanding how people assimilate information, code it into simplified units, and store it in relation to other information. Cognitive maps, then, resemble mental structures which contain information about how the environment is organized. As a result of these organizing functions, cognitive maps serve to facilitate the absorption and comprehension of details (Neisser, 1976). These maps provide the mental scaffolding for organizing otherwise fragmentary pieces of information into a meaningful structure.

As it relates to interpretation, cognitive map theory matches external stimuli with an individual's internal models in order for meaning to occur. Hammit (1981) observed that cognitive map theory correlates to Tilden's (1967) first principle of interpretation:

> Any interpretation that does not somehow relate what is being displayed or described to something within the personality or experience of the visitor will be sterile. Tilden continued: The visitor ultimately is seeing things through his own eyes, not those of the interpreter.

To best relate to and serve visitors, the interpreter must strive to understand the cognitive models that visitors possess and to present information in those terms. This will often require the use of comparisons, contrasts, analogies, and metaphors (Hammit, 1981).

In addition to relating to existing cognitive models that each visitor holds, the interpreter can also try to create a basic cognitive map for first-time park visitors. Research conducted by Richard Knopf (1981) at Gettysburg National Military Park suggested that cognitive map formation early in an interpretive experience can aid in assimilating more information. To apply this, prior to immersing visitors into a novel cultural or natural environment, an interpreter could present an overview of the entire setting. An effective cognitive map defines the bounds of the environment to be explored and gives the visitor a sense of clarity. According to Knopf (1981):

> It allows details of the interpretive message to become more relevant, it yields the capacity to see where the interpretive message is heading, and, most significantly, it gives one the ability to predict—to guess and fill in pieces of the picture that have not been made explicit.
>
> In large and complex interpretive settings, different activities and programs can be designed to build upon one another and interpretive managers should determine which order of visitation should be promoted to provide for optimal interpretive experiences.

PROSTER THEORY

Recent advances in understanding the human brain led to the "proster" theory, developed by Leslie Hart (1983, 1991). It builds on findings from a number of disciplines including the neural sciences, ethology, brain evolution, and computer science. Hart synthesized this work into a theory of learning with educational applications. Basically, proster theory applies to creating learning situations that are brain compatible.

According to Hart (1991), the human brain acts aggressively, not passively, as was long believed. Through rather "intensely aggressive" action, the brain steadily makes sense of the world by extracting patterns from huge amounts of input [perhaps making order of chaos]. Several principles of proster theory relevant to interpretive applications follow:

1. Effective learning environments are characterized by the absence of threat. (The neocortex, the newest part of the brain and nearly five-sixths of the whole, does not function well under pressure. Processing in this portion of the brain is cut short and the much older limbic system exerts more influence when a person feels threatened.) Learners need to feel secure and at ease for effective learning to take place.
2. Encourage the basic skills of communication (oral and written) by purposeful use.
3. Give learners freedom to manipulate materials in hands-on situations that provide large amounts of input to the brain.
4. Emphasize exposure to reality, not to contrived situations.
5. Address learning through performance, not through the answering of questions.

Consistent with learning style theory, proster theory advocates applying the "smorgasbord principle" which permits broad recognition of, and allowance for, individual differences. In interpretive programming, a variety of strategies should be used to meet the wide range of needs of those who are participating in the event.

Strategies for Learning

In addition to research conducted on the dynamics of learning as it relates to the educational theories discussed above, there are several systems specifically designed for application in outdoor settings. Most methods of implementing the theories of learning have not been written down as formal procedures. Among those that have been written up, the following seven stages or concepts of learning have been applied in environmental education (Figure 7.2, page 178).

THE SEVEN STAGES

A seven stage hierarchy of learning in the outdoors was presented by Phyllis Ford (1981). It should work well in museum settings, as well as in the outdoors. She suggested specific strategies that are appropriate for advancing levels of cognitive, social, and moral development. In this scheme, the various stages apply to all ages; they do not correlate with specific age ranges. According to Ford, people require a progression of activities to acclimate them to outdoor settings before they can advance to learning that deals with concepts and, ultimately, the formulation of a philosophy regarding our relationship to natural settings.

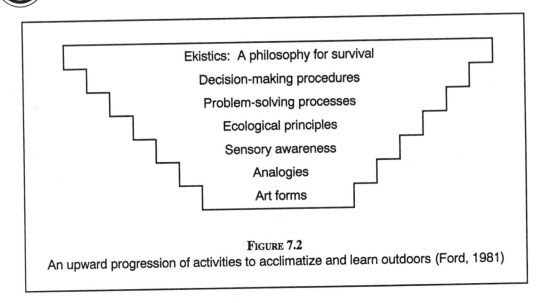

FIGURE 7.2
An upward progression of activities to acclimatize and learn outdoors (Ford, 1981)

The three lower levels of the hierarchy—art forms, analogies, and sensory awareness—help individuals to gain a basic familiarity and level of comfort in the outdoors. The four higher levels—ecological principles, problem-solving, decision-making procedures, and ekistics (a philosophy of the interrelatedness of nature and humanity)—build from this basic comfort with nature and advance from acquisition of knowledge to the development of a life philosophy. This environmental philosophy develops as a logical progression in an individual's cognitive and moral development.

At the earliest stage of learning, exposure to art forms develops awareness of the variety of shapes, colors, patterns, and forms found in nature. At the second level, analogies consist of descriptions of various items in terms useful in forming images. Analogies assist with understanding and retention of information. For example, Josh Barkin, naturalist with the East Bay Regional Park District in California, described organisms capable of building their own roads, traveling over the roughest terrain, and navigating with the use of retractable periscopes. Over the course of a nature walk his charges would discover that he was referring to the banana slug—a seemingly unlikely candidate for such interesting characteristics.

Sensory awareness encompasses the third level of learning in outdoor settings. The application and appropriate use of all the senses provides for a greater understanding and appreciation for the natural environment. This category matches Piaget's concrete operational stage of cognitive development. The first three stages provide a foundation of comfort and understanding necessary for the next sequence of stages of conceptual development.

The fourth stage, ecological principles, deals with universal concepts such as food chains, predator-prey relationships, adaptations and the flow of energy. With this background, problem-solving processes, the fifth level, may be introduced. The learner applies ecological principles to solve problems, such as the construction of a four-tiered food chain of animals observed on a field trip.

The sixth stage, decision-making, allows for critical analysis of environmental problems and the skills necessary for personal involvement as a citizen. This stage can consist of simulation games and role-playing in hypothetical situations. In stage seven, a personal philosophy develops regarding the connection between humans and nature. This sense of inter-relatedness, called ekistics, is consistent with the "land ethic" advocated by Aldo Leopold (1966) in *A Sand County Almanac*. This last stage emphasized moral and attitudinal, rather than intellectual, advancement. Evidence from several different studies (e.g., Rejeski, 1982; Pomerantz, 1990) confirms that a progression of attitudes that people hold toward nature culminates in a sense of stewardship for the land.

This hierarchy closely parallels the seven key principles of the curriculum framework in the design of Project Learning Tree prepared by the Western Regional Environmental Education Council (WREEC, 1975). These principles organize environmental education activities according to seven similar levels of cognitive and moral development. Similar principles form the conceptual framework of Project WILD activities (WREEC, 1983), as illustrated in Box 7.2. Both programs were recently revised but use similar principles.

BOX 7.2

Components of the Conceptual Frameworks of Project Learning Tree and Project Wild

Project Learning Tree	Project Wild
Environmental Awareness	Awareness and Appreciation
Diversity of Forest Roles	Diversity of Wildlife Values
Cultural Contexts	Ecological Principles
Societal Perspectives on Issues	Management and Conservation
Management and Interdependence	People, Culture, and Wildlife of Natural Resources
Life Support Systems	Trends, Issues, and Consequences
Lifestyles	Responsible Human Actions

Flow Learning

Joseph Cornell (1989) developed a slightly different interdisciplinary approach to nature education based upon established educational principles and his years of experience as a nature educator. Flow learning consists of a four-step sequence of games and activities that harmonize with human nature and flow from one to another in a logical manner (Figure 7.3, page 180). As he suggested in a previous book, a sense of joy should permeate all experience in nature (Cornell, 1979).

The goal of flow learning is to provide all participants with a deep and uplifting experience. The first step *awakens enthusiasm*. This stage is meant to be playful and fun. Although teens and adults tend to be more skeptical than children, appropriate games and activities can generate interest and enthusiasm without bending the dignity of the participants. The second step *focuses attention*. Having generated enthusiasm it concentrates attention so that people become more alert and observant. Cornell suggested that the key is to isolate one of the senses and devise a way for participants to concentrate on it. This helps to settle the group down after the playful first stage while also enhancing their awareness of the environment. Focused attention inspires an inner calm that promotes the third step of the sequence which is called *direct experience* (Figure 7.4). During this stage people become directly involved with the natural setting and a sense of wonder and reflection is awakened through personal discovery. The fourth stage *shares inspiration* to strengthen and clarify individual experiences. In this last step, people not only talk about their own experiences but are exposed to the insights, adventures, and ideas of great naturalists such as Aldo Leopold, Rachel Carson, and John Muir. This tends to draw the group together and sets the stage for future enriching experiences in nature. Cornell (1989) provided representative nature activities that are appropriate for all ages and that correspond to each of the four stages.

STAGE	PURPOSE	QUALITY	BENEFITS
1	Awaken enthusiasm	Playfulness and alertness	• Builds on children's love of play. • Creates an atmosphere of enthusiasm. • A dynamic beginning gets everyone saying "Yes!" • Develops full alertness, overcomes passivity. • Creates involvement. • Gets attention (minimizes discipline problems). • Develops rapport with the leader. • Creates good group dynamics. • Provides direction and structure. • Prepares for later, more sensitive activities.
2	Focus attention	Receptivity	• Increases attention span. • Deepens awareness by focusing attention. • Positively channels enthusiasm generated in Stage 1. • Develops observational skills. • Calms the mind. • Develops receptivity for more sensitive nature experiences.
3	Direct experience	Absorption	• People learn best by personal discovery. • Gives direct, experiential, intuitive understanding. • Fosters wonder, empathy and love. • Develops personal commitment to ecological ideals.
4	Share inspiration	Idealism	• Clarifies and strengthens personal experiences. • Builds on uplifted mood. • Introduces inspiring role models. • Gives peer reinforcement. • Creates group bonding. • Provides feedback for the leader. • Leader shares with a receptive audience.

FIGURE 7.3
Stages of Flow Learning (Cornell, 1989)
reprinted with permission of the sharing nature foundation

FIGURE 7.4
Children learn by observing details, preferring tangible, real things to abstract concepts and theories.

Summary

The educational theory presented in this chapter serves as but an introduction to some of the best-known work by educators and researchers. The material selected seems to hold particular relevance and application for interpreters. Defining the different ways people learn and develop has attracted the attention of some imaginative theoreticians. They have produced many models and hypotheses, creating some potential for confusion among interpreters and teachers. For practical purposes, the interpreter needs to read these ideas, then develop programs and methods that respond to the most sensible ideas, try them out, adjust them, and use them to advantage.

Pond (1993) compiled a list of learning concepts from educational theory, interpretive research, motivation theory, and other related disciplines. The following condensed version of some of these gleanings has application for interpreters and provides a summary of much of the theory covered in this chapter:

1. People process information differently.
2. Learning is influenced by the degree to which people are motivated to learn in meeting their individual needs.

3. A person's sense of comfort and security has a bearing on his or her capacity to learn.
4. The degree to which people care about and remember information is influenced by how they feel about the person facilitating the experience.
5. People tend to learn more easily when many of their senses are employed.
6. People tend to remember what they do, are less likely to remember what they see or read, and are least likely to remember what they hear.
7. A variety of approaches to a subject enhances the learning process by making it more interesting and by meeting the needs of diverse learners.
8. Self-discovery is a powerful motivator.
9. An organized presentation of information and activities offers a more conducive way for people to learn.
10. Repetition can effectively facilitate learning.

Continual attention to developments in the educational field should prove fruitful for interpreters who wish to stay abreast of methods, techniques, and strategies that will improve their interpretive efforts. More importantly, the interpreter can use one or more of these models to plan strategic learning schemes. Develop programming as a "smorgasbord" to serve up varied offerings that match different learning styles and stages of development. Develop a sequence of experiences, such as the four-step flow learning model. This moves professionals beyond simple "walk and talk" interpreters, allowing them to serve as a true museum or environmental educator for all people.

> The ultimate purpose of the national parks is the education and inspiration of the people . . . that idea infuses our entire cause from top to bottom. . . . One of the destinies of our national parks, then, is to become the great school houses for nature and science of this American people.
> —Yard, 1917

Literature Cited

Beck, L. (1986). A hierarchy of interpretive programs. *The Interpreter, (Winter)*:18-20.

Bettelheim, B. (1989). *The uses of enchantment.* New York, NY: Vintage Press.

Bloom, B., Engelhart, M., Furst, E., Hill, W., and Krathwohl, D. (1956). *Taxonomy of educational objectives. Handbook I: Cognitive domain.* New York, NY: David McKay Company, Inc.

Brandt, R. (1990). On learning styles: A conversation with Pat Guild. *Educational Leadership, 48*(2):10-13.

Christensen, H. and Dustin, D. (1989). Reaching recreationists at different levels of moral development. *Journal of Park and Recreation Administration, 7*(4):72-80.

Christensen, J. (1990). Interpretation can target everyone. *Legacy, 1*(1):11-15.

Cornell, J. B. (1989). *Sharing the joy of nature.* Nevada City, CA: Dawn Publications, Inc.

Cornell, J. B. (1979). *Sharing nature with children.* Nevada City, CA: Ananda Publications.

Countryside Commission. (1980). *Audio-visual media in countryside interpretation.* Chettenham, Gloucestershire, England: Countryside Commission Advisory Series, No. 12.

Dustin, D. (1985). To feed or not feed the bears. *Parks and Recreation, 20*(10):54-57, 72.

Ford, P. (1981). *Principles and practices of outdoor/environmental education.* New York, NY: John Wiley & Sons, Inc.

Gilligan, C. (1982). *In a different voice.* Cambridge, MA: Harvard University Press.

Golay, K. (1982). *Learning patterns and temperament styles.* Newport Beach, CA: Manas-Systems.

Grinder, A. L. and McCoy, E. S. (1985). *The good guide: A source-book for interpreters, docents and tour guides.* Scottsdale, AZ: Ironwood Press.

Ham, S. H. (1992). *Environmental interpretation: A practical guide.* Golden, CO: North American Press.

Hammit, W. (1981). A theoretical foundation for Tilden's interpretive principles. *Journal of Environmental Education, 12*(3):13-16.

Hart, L. (1983). *Human brain and human learning.* New York, NY: Longman Publishing Group.

Hart, L. (1991). The "brain" concept of learning. *The Brain Based Education Networker, 3*(2):1-3.

Keirsey, D. and Bates, M. (1978). *Please understand me: An essay on temperament styles.* Del Mar, CA: Prometheus Nemesis Books.

Knopf, R. (1981). Cognitive map formation as a tool for facilitating information transfer in interpretive programming. *Journal of Leisure Research, 13*(3):232-242.

Kohlberg, L. (1971). Stages of moral development as a basis for moral education. In C. M. Beck (Ed.), *Moral Education: Interdisciplinary Approaches.* Toronto, ON: University of Toronto Press.

Leopold, A. (1966). *A sand county almanac; with other essays on conservation from Round River.* New York, NY: Oxford University Press.

Makruski, E. (1978). "A conceptual analysis of 'environmental interpretation.'" Ph.D. dissertation, Ohio State University. Ann Arbor, MI: University Microfilms.

Mills, E. A. (1920). *The adventures of a nature guide.* Garden City, NY: Doubleday, Page & Co.

Muuss, R. (1982). *Theories of adolescence.* New York, NY: Random House, Inc.

Neisser, U. (1976). *Cognition and reality.* San Francisco, CA: W. H. Freeman & Co., Publishers.

O'Neil, J. (1990). Making sense of style. *Educational Leadership, 48*(2):4-9.

Piaget, J. (1952). *The origins of intelligence in children.* New York, NY: International Universities Press, Inc.

Piaget, J. (1955). *The language and thought of the child.* New York, NY: World Publishing, Inc.

Pomerantz, G. (1990). Understanding children's perceptions of nature through developmental theory: Implications for interpretation. *Legacy, 1*(3):12-19.

Pond, K. (1993). *The professional guide.* New York, NY: Van Nostrand Reinhold Company.

Rejeski, D. (1982). Children look at nature: Environmental perceptions and education. *Journal of Environmental Education, 13*(4):27-40.

Risk, P. (1982). Conducted activities. In G. W. Sharpe, *Interpreting the Environment (2nd ed.).* New York, NY: John Wiley & Sons, Inc.

Strang, C. (1992). Educational Theories and Program Design. *Legacy, 3*(4):18-22.

Tilden, F. (1967). *Interpreting our heritage (rev. ed.).* Chapel Hill, NC: University of North Carolina Press.

Western Regional Environmental Education Council. (1975). *Project Learning Tree activity guide K-6.* Washington, DC: American Forest Foundation.

Western Regional Environmental Education Council. (1983). *Project WILD elementary activity guide.* Boulder, CO.

Yard, R S. (1917). Educational day (introduction). In *Proceedings, [U.S.] National Parks Conference,* Jan. 2-6.

Interpreting to the Masses

Put it before them briefly so they will read it, clearly so they will appreciate it, picturesquely so they will remember it and, above all, accurately so they will be guided by its light.

—Joseph Pulitzer

Many interpreters work for organizations that seek to serve more than visitors to their museum or nature center. Their employer is an entire community, region, state or nation. To offer interpretive service just to those individuals who visit a site only partially fulfills their mission. Perhaps the people who need the message most will seldom visit museums or other interpretive sites.

Mass communication provides one way to spread the interpretive message beyond the property or museum. Mass communication can be defined as "the process of using a mass medium to send messages to large audiences for the purpose of informing, entertaining, and persuading" (Vivian, 1991). Mass media include books, newspapers, magazines, radio, television, and movies. If used effectively, they can educate the public and shape public opinion. The leaders of political revolutions know this and invariably attempt to control mass media systems.

Interpreters can use these media by doing something as simple as sending in an announcement for a "community calendar." Or they can take full advantage of newspapers, radio, and TV by creating regular features for news or entertainment. Thus they can serve a much larger audience than they will see at their museum or visitor center. Through mass media, the interpreter may truly reach out to the whole community.

This chapter discusses the mass media in general, then presents detailed approaches to the electronic media. Chapter 9 will discuss the print media in more detail.

PHILOSOPHY

One can interpret to more than the visitors who seek out the historian or naturalist. Interpreters can serve the entire community, not just those who show up at the museum or park or refuge.

A museum or agency's purpose usually says something about serving the entire community, state, or nation. To restrict that to only those who seek out their place may be unnecessarily restrictive. Perhaps the best interpretation of the function statement (charge) implies involving all the people in the message. Perhaps those who "need" interpretation most are those who wouldn't normally go to the museum or other site.

The Smithsonian Institution provides a good example of this philosophy in action. It produces a fine magazine that gets into homes and libraries across the nation. Its traveling exhibits take the museum on the road (sort of like a bookmobile from a library). People from Pueblo, Peoria, and Portsmouth who may never get to a Smithsonian museum will see some of the artifacts and receive interpretation. Radio broadcasts and television clips from the Smithsonian also interpret the museums' findings, to help fulfill the mission as the *National* museums—not just 15 museums in Washington, DC, and New York City.

WEAKNESSES

Mass communication only offers a one-way form of communication with no immediate feedback. Unlike personal interpretation, one cannot see if his or her audience looks bored, confused or excited. The mass audience voluntarily receives messages—usually in private. While a person attending a campfire program, slide show or hike might feel compelled to stay until the end due to politeness, the mass audience can tune out or turn off instantaneously without concern for politeness or decorum. Capturing and maintaining the attention of listeners, viewers, or readers presents a challenge. Moreover, mass media relies heavily on ever-changing technology. Mass media's dependence on equipment and specialized expertise makes it expensive.

Each medium has its strengths and weaknesses. The sweeping, panoramic images that enthrall theater audiences may go unnoticed when seen on small TV screens. Likewise, newspaper stories usually cannot compete with riveting television coverage of people fighting raging forest fires to protect Yellowstone National Park. On the other hand, less dramatic but equally important events such as the destruction of historic buildings, forests, and scenic vistas by poor air quality may come across better in a print medium. Dialogue with sound effects or visual images may keep people glued to their radios or TV but may fall flat if published in the morning paper. Details of a new state park policy may have little impact on a radio or TV audience but allow newspaper readers to examine it carefully.

Theorist Marshall McLuhan (1964) divided media into two categories — hot media and cold media. He categorized books, newspapers and magazines as "hot media" because they require a high degree of thinking. He also considered movies a "hot" medium because the large screen and darkened viewing rooms shut out distractions and command the full attention of the viewer. Radio and television are "cool" media because they can be used without much intellectual effort or involvement. Radio, as background noise is "cold." However, radio "warms" when it involves the imagination of the listener as in radio drama. Television has many of the same characteristics as movies but because it does not overwhelm viewer's senses like movies he considered it "cool." The importance in McLuhan's distinction is that the harder a person works to receive a message from the medium, the more they remember from it (Vivian, 1991). So, people can remember more from a story they read in the paper than they can if they merely heard the story on the radio. The trick for interpreters is to entice people to expend the effort and get involved intellectually with the message. This chapter presents theories and ideas to help interpreters use the media, both hot and cold, more effectively.

A MODEL OF MASS COMMUNICATION

The Concentric Ring or HUB Model (Vivian, 1991) provides one useful description of mass communication. In this model (Figure 8.1) the communicators code messages by putting their thoughts into symbols, such as the written word or visual representations. The message then moves away from the center just as a ripple would if a pebble were dropped into water. After being coded it encounters gatekeepers—persons who can stop or alter a message. They include producers, editors, or censors. Gatekeepers decide which messages are broadcast or printed. For example, magazine editors sort through hundreds of articles to select only a few for their publications. Once past the gatekeepers, the message appears in a medium.

Regulators comprise the next force that influences the message. The U.S. Federal Communication Commission (FCC), citizen's groups, trade and professional organizations, libel laws, and theater licensing laws can all serve as regulators that influence the message.

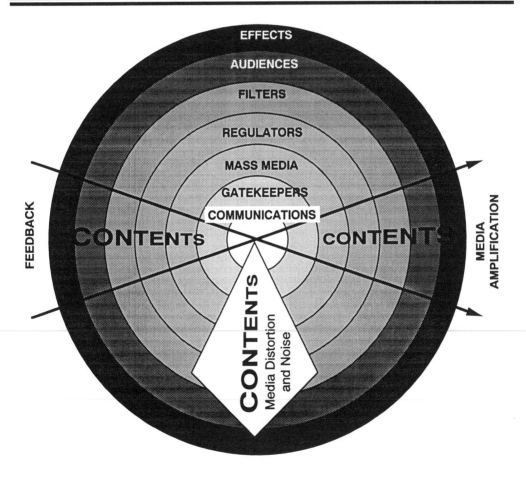

FIGURE 8.1
HUB Model of Mass Communications (Vivian, 1991)

Filters serve as the next message modifiers. These can be: informational filters if the sender and receiver do not have a common understanding of the symbols; physical filters if, for example, the audience is fatigued or cannot hear well; or psychological filters when the experiences or perspective of the receiver affect the message. For example, a hunter and an animal rights advocate may hear the same interpretive news release and come away having received two completely different messages.

The pointing arrows in Figure 8.1 show that the communicators can be influenced by feedback from the receivers. Audiences can tune out certain messages and demand others. The outward pointing arrows indicate that mass media can "amplify" messages. This is accomplished by conferring status on people or events merely by covering them. The media can fuel public reaction (positive or negative) to issues and make a previously obscure person or place a household name.

One of the biggest mass media events involving interpreters was the Yellowstone fires in 1988. That year, many other fires of similar magnitude threatened and claimed more human lives and developments. Yet, the media treated the Yellowstone fires as more newsworthy. Opponents of National Park Service fire policy used the opportunity to question it publicly. Messages depicting "blackened moonscapes" amplified unfounded predictions of regional economic and ecological disaster. The "effects" ranged from an outpouring of goodwill from private citizens to politicians asking for Director William Penn Mott's resignation for overseeing a flawed policy. As the fires went out, so did the media attention. Director Mott kept his job. Within a short time, people realized that the fires were not economic nor ecological disasters, but rather part of the natural processes that have acted upon the area for centuries. The Yellowstone fires illustrated the power of the media and the importance of understanding the operation of the model.

WORKING WITH THE MEDIA

The first step toward successful media relations involves getting to know the right people and developing a friendly, rather than an adversarial, relationship with them. When it is time to send a message, better results can be obtained by talking to a person with a name, not just a "station" or "newspaper." For radio or TV, contacts include the program director, news director, or the person responsible for public service announcements. At the local newspapers identify the relevant editors (e.g., managing editor, city editor, outdoor editor, feature editor). Get acquainted with regional correspondents for the wire services or networks. Make appointments with the key people in the local area. Make sure they know who and what is represented. Then establish a "contact" person and provide them with a day and night phone number so that the newsperson can call in the event an unexpected news story occurs. Get the appropriate day and night phone numbers for reporting news stories to the media.

Whenever possible personally deliver materials to the stations or papers. Be prepared to briefly explain the "cause" and the message being delivered. If the media personnel do not have the time to listen an explanation or read a story, leave a business card with the material and thank them for considering it. Don't ask when the material will be used or how many times it will be used. If there is uncertainty about whether it will be used, check back after several days to see if a decision has been made. Pick up any tapes or film that are not used; generally such items are not returned. When they air or print the material, appreciation can be expressed by sending a thank-you letter to the responsible parties.

When dealing with reporters, never say anything that would not look good in print or sound good on the air. There is no such thing as an "off-the-record" comment. An appropriate response to a question for which the answer is not known could be "I do not know, I'll check it and get back to you," rather than "no comment." Reporters appreciate honesty and diligence. Some reporters take offense when a person asks to read their story before it is printed. Offer help if questions arise later in the writing or editing of the story. If reporters do botch up a story, open criticism of them will be counterproductive. Rather, invite them to meet to explore the subject in greater depth. If they do not botch it up, send them a thank-you note congratulating them on such a fine job.

Do not be concerned if editors or broadcasters rewrite or condense a story—that is normal. If the material is never used or if the media personnel call frequently to fill in gaps in the information then there is cause for concern. Learn from mistakes by assessing the use of the materials submitted. Are they consistently modified in some way? Are they being used at all? If consistent problems arise, approach the editors and ask how their needs for information can be better meet.

Don't play favorites when sending out news items. Treat all the stations and papers in the area equally by providing them with the same information. One good way of keeping all the media outlets in the area informed is to develop a mailing list and send them copies of the newsletters and other routine mailings.

The Print Media

Newspapers, books, magazines, and pamphlets get wide use for interpretation. Many national and state parks and museums produce their own quarterly or monthly tabloids to provide schedules and feature articles that describe their attractions. Cable and Udd (1990) found that anglers in Michigan and Kansas most often received water quality information from newspapers. Likewise, Ostman and Parker (1986/87) found that residents of Ithaca, New York, most often used newspapers for getting environmental information. Books rated as the most "believable" medium, although they seldom received mention as a source of environmental information. Magazines, newspapers, and pamphlets were all judged to be more believable than TV or radio.

Daily newspaper circulation in the U.S. reached a record 62.8 million in 1988, but proportionally fewer people buy newspapers. The circulation decline came primarily among evening newspapers, as people have turned to television for their evening news. Although the readership base is eroding, newspapers still have the advantages of being portable and providing indexed, specialized content. Newspapers also provide the most in-depth coverage of news.

Magazines provide another good outlet for interpretive material. Most magazines maintain relatively small staffs, relying on contributing editors and free-lance writers. This provides an opportunity for interpreters to access this medium. Magazines typically focus on specialized subjects and therefore target specific audiences. Rather than using a shot gun approach inherent in other media, interpreters can submit articles to the magazine aimed at the audience they want to reach.

News Releases

Interpreters often provide newspapers with information through news releases. Before preparing a news release, make sure that the message really amounts to "news." News reports recent events of fairly wide interest. To be financially successful, newspapers must provide helpful, practical, relevant and important information to the audience presented in an interesting and entertaining manner. The following criteria can help determine if the information rates as newsworthy (Fazio and Gilbert, 1981).

Timely—An event should have just happened or be about to happen. Or it may relate to other events of current interest. An example of the latter: an item on Christmas tree cutting in early December.

Human Interest—Certain story characteristics hold special interest to people. Elements including violence, animals, old age or youth, sex, conflict, suspense, sympathy or uniqueness attract people's attention.

Proximity—The information should relate to the community served by the publication being considered.

Prominence—Well-known people or places attract attention. For example, the visit of a well-known dignitary to a park or museum may be a newsworthy story.

Consequence—Something of importance to the readers is newsworthy. For example, hazardous water conditions in a park may affect local readers.

If the information an interpreter wishes to communicate contains most of these criteria then it probably is newsworthy. If so, a news release should be prepared and distributed.

To write a news release, first collect and verify all the facts, making sure to include the traditional who, what, when, where, how, and why questions on which news reporters and editors focus. Once the facts are at hand, write the text in the "inverted pyramid" style (Figure 8.2). This means that the key facts appear in the first paragraph preferably within the first three or four lines. The next paragraph should present the next most important facts. More detailed explanation of the first two paragraphs follows until all the information is given. Editors typically start cutting at the end of a story to trim it to fit in the space available, working their way up. The release should be written so that it will make sense regardless of where the editor cuts it.

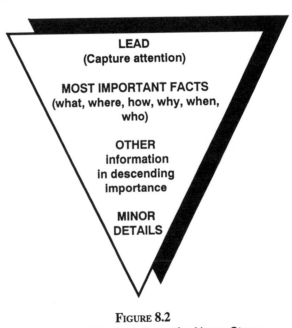

Figure 8.2
Diagram of the Structure of a News Story

Words, sentences and paragraphs should be kept short. Use action verbs. Since releases often do not reach the editor the same day they are written, the "when" question should be answered carefully. Terms such as today, tomorrow, this weekend, and next week lose their meaning after the release sits on the editor's desk a few days or otherwise gets delayed.

Include the following information at the top left corner of the release: your name, agency, address, phone number, and a short headline. Specify a release time or date. Indicate "For Immediate Release" unless there is a specific reason to delay the announcement. Center a headline over the text of the body of the release. Indicate that photographs (usually 5" x 7" or 8" x 10" black-and-white prints) accompany a story. Figure 8.3 illustrates the heading of an agency news release that roughly follows most of the guidelines. Releases often go out in packets containing several news stories (e.g., six per week). Agencies send such packets on a regular and routine basis, so news directors can plan on using them frequently.

Dateline. . . .

ALL OUTDOORS

MISSOURI DEPARTMENT OF CONSERVATION	*Weekly News*
JERRY J. PRESLEY, Director	*Stories*

1. Pretend Pals for Prairie Poultry (w/pic)	FOR IMMEDIATE
2. Capitol Plans Peregrine Apartments (w/pic)	RELEASE
3. Welfare for Winter-Weary Wildlife	Mailed: 4/16/93
4. Sapsucker Sighting Sensational	
5. Outdoor Calendar	

News contract: Jim Low, Jefferson City Missouri, (314) 751-4115

"The life of every river sings its own song, but in most the song is long since marred by the discords of misuse."—Aldo Leopold, *A Sand County Almanac*

1. Pretend Pals for Prairie Poultry (w/pic)

MILAN—If someone spotlighted you right in the middle of a romantic interlude, grabbed you and put you into a box, drove you hundreds of miles from home and then opened the box, what would you do?

If you had wings, you'd probably fly until you dropped. That's what many prairie-chickens do under similar circumstances. So, before the Missouri Department of Conservation (MDC) opens the doors on prairie-chickens imported from Kansas, the MDC does everything it can to make them feel at home in Missouri.

(more)

DATELINE. . . .All Outdoors

FIGURE 8.3
First Page of a News Release Packet

An easy-to-read release reduces the chance of errors creeping into the story. The following courtesies help assure the clarity and accuracy of a story when it appears:
- use only one side of standard size paper (8 1/2" x 11").
- type the release using either double or triple spacing.
- leave wide margins and space at the top for comments.
- if more than one page, type (MORE) at the bottom
- end all pages with complete paragraphs.
- at the top left corner of following pages type an abbreviated identification (e.g., last name) and the page number.
- type end marks (###) after your last sentence.
- fasten pages together with paper clips.

FEATURES

Another way to get a story in print is to write a feature article. For example, an interpreter wants to tell people about all the surprising discoveries of an archæological dig just completed at a local site. He or she features a strong human interest component, e.g., the people who lived at the Butternut Lake campground for 50 centuries. The interpreter writes a draft containing the essential facts of the dig. Usually newspaper or magazine staff reporters or editors will write the final version of features, with the guidance and help of the archæologist or interpreter.

Finding the best outlet for the story helps maximize its impact. A good place to start is with local or regional publications. Most states have a magazine published by the Department of Natural Resources or an equivalent agency. Annual reference books such as *Writer's Market* provide names of contacts, phone numbers, addresses, submission instructions, and other important information for hundreds of magazines. These books also provide tips for getting an article published.

The Electronic Media

It is trickier to write the spoken word for radio or TV than for print. For broadcast media, one writes for the tongue of the announcer and the ear of the listener. Unlike newspapers, brochures, and other printed material, the audience cannot go back and read the text a second time. An absolutely clear text helps the audience "get it" the first time. The first sentence ("lead") attracts the attention of the casual listener, and then the most important information is relayed. If one starts immediately with the most important fact, one may miss the attention of the casual listener. Remember, there is no instant replay for newscasts! The listener needs to be alerted to what's coming; then the key facts can be reviewed at the end.

The following helps both the announcer and the listener:
- Use contractions and nontechnical words to make the speaking sound more natural.
- To make reading easier for the announcer avoid abbreviations by spelling out names of states, months, and days. Abbreviations are acceptable when commonly known and pronounced as a word (e.g., NEPA). When they should be read as individual letters, separate them in the copy with hyphens (e.g., C-C-C).

- Construct sentences so the announcer can breathe and speak naturally. Sentences should sound conversational. Text should be read aloud to see if it works.
- For a difficult name the actual spelling should be included along with the phonetic pronunciation in parentheses.
- Minimize the use of quotes. They can confuse and slow down the announcer.
- The announcement or script should be timed carefully to assure that it fits within the allotted time frame.
- Write out words (e.g., dollars, cents, percent) rather than using symbols to make it easier for the announcer to read.
- Spell out numbers from one to ten. Use numerals for 11 to 999. Write out the words hundreds, thousands, millions, billions (e.g., two hundred, 20 thousand). Use numerals for all times and dates.
- As with all professional writing, it must be proofread—more than once—and if possible have another person check it over.

RADIO INTERPRETATION

Radio offers the most widespread mass medium available, with 2,043 radios per 1,000 people in the U.S. (Vivian, 1991). In the U.S., 95 percent of all cars and 99 percent of all households have radios, averaging 5.5 radios per household (Radio Advertising Bureau, 1984). Radio serves as the first source of news each day for 56 percent of Americans over 12 years of age; 83 percent of Americans listen to radio sometime in an average day; and 96 percent listen in an average week (Radio Advertising Bureau, 1984). Radio's greatest advantages come from its potential to reach many people regularly, and its inherent flexibility in targeting specific audiences.

Ostman and Parker (1986/87) found that radio ranked ahead of books and pamphlets as a source of environmental information with 12.7 percent using it "very often" and 20.5 percent never using it.

Radio stations aim at narrow audiences, based on age cohorts, musical or news interests, and even language groups. In large cities such an abundance and diversity of stations exists that one can target stations with very specific types of audiences. Advertising data describes the size and characteristics of the audience. Stations featuring expanded news coverage or talk shows have audiences geared toward listening to messages rather than music. Such audiences may be highly receptive to messages.

News Releases and Public Service Announcements

News releases for radio stations should be written using the "inverted pyramid" structure, as those for newspapers. However, news releases for radio stations are shorter than those sent to newspapers. Shorter stories are more likely to be broadcast. With the fast-paced radio format, a news editor will usually cut to the lead, allowing only minor details. If a release requires too much cutting, it may not be used at all.

Sometimes unanticipated newsworthy events happen at museums and parks. By the time a news release could be prepared, distributed and used, the story is "old news." When a "hard" news story breaks at a facility, the radio station's news desk should be called. They may want to interview someone over the phone or send a reporter out to cover the story.

Another way of accessing radio air time is through public service announcements (PSAs). In the United States, radio and television stations, licensed by the Federal Communications Commission, must devote a certain percentage of their air time to nonprofit public service organizations. Many community organizations submit material to be broadcast free of charge during this allotted time. Competition for free air time is fierce since most stations are deluged with PSAs. Moreover, with the deregulation of radio in the 1980s, the percentage of time devoted to PSAs has decreased. However, many PSAs received by radio stations are poor quality material. If an interpreter can submit a PSA that is exciting, colorful and professional quality, it has a better chance of being used.

Here is how interpreters can get their messages used as a PSA:

- Call the station and find out who is responsible for public service programming; learn deadlines or special requirements for submission of PSAs.
- Second, identify and limit the subject to one specific idea for the PSA.
- Next, write a short, simple, factual statement, to focus on answering the traditional questions of who, what, when, where, and why. The PSAs length should be either 10 seconds (20 -30 words), 20 seconds (40-60 words), 30 seconds (70-80 words), or 60 seconds long (150-200 words). The shorter the PSA, the more likely it is to receive air time. However, the most critical concern is that the who, what, when, where, and why are covered adequately in the announcement.

Type and double-space the announcement. At the top of the PSA include: name and address of your organization, name and telephone number of the person preparing the copy, the length of the PSA (e.g., 10 second announcement) and the release date (i.e., date for broadcasting). For quick airing, indicate "For Immediate Release."

Most organizations submit PSAs in written form, to be read by a station announcer. However, some organizations have the specialists and equipment to tape their own announcements. Other organizations contract with a private production studio or radio station to produce their PSAs. Sound effects greatly improve the effectiveness of radio PSAs. In the "theater of the mind," appropriate sound effects make mental images more vivid and memorable. Most stations and studios have a wide selection of sound effects available to choose from.

Radio Features

Many interpreters have the opportunity to air features on a daily or weekly basis. This is particularly common with small town stations. These broadcasts range from one-minute fishing or star-gazing reports to half hour call-in shows dealing with complex natural resource issues. To build an audience the show must be on the same days and at the same time so listeners know when and where to find it. Usually these types of regularly broadcast shows are aired as a public service, but sometimes sponsors will back them.

Several formats exist for such radio programs. A speaker can merely present information or interpret as a monologue. This format is best suited for brief programs (1-5 minutes). The Missouri Department of Conservation produces "Nature Notes" consisting of 52 episodes for a once-a-week series (Box 8.1 contains two sample scripts). These programs go, at no cost, to radio stations that will broadcast them (usually typed in upper case letters and double-spaced.

BOX 8.1: WEEKLY NATURE NOTES RADIO RELEASES, MISSOURI DEPARTMENT OF CONSERVATION

ZCZC PRDCT0344

STATIONS, HERE ARE YOUR NATURE NOTES FOR THE MONTH OF JUNE, 1993. IF YOU HAVE QUESTIONS OR SUGGESTIONS FOR NATURE NOTES, CALL RICHARD THOM, MISSOURI DEPARTMENT OF CONSERVATION, (314) 715-4115 EXT. 193

JUNE NATURE NOTES - WEEK ONE
SPITTLE BUGS BY CHRIS HUMPHREY

SPRING CAN DELIGHT, AS FLOWERS BLOOM AND BIRDS NEST. BUT ONE EVENT OF SPRING MAY PROMPT DISGUST. IN MANY FIELDS AND ALONG ROADSIDES, IT CAN LOOK LIKE SOMEONE, OR MANY SOMEONES, HAD SPIT EVERYWHERE!

THE SPIT-LIKE FOAM THAT HANGS ON PLANT STEMS ACTUALLY COMES FROM AN IMMATURE INSECT, APPROPRIATELY CALLED A SPITTLEBUG. IF YOU GENTLY CLEAR AWAY THE SPITTLE, YOU WILL LIKELY FIND ONE OR MORE TINY, GREEN SPITTLEBUGS.

TO MAKE THE FOAM, THE SPITTLEBUG CLINGS, UPSIDE DOWN, TO A PLANT STEM. AS IT DRINKS THE PLANT'S JUICES, THE BUG SECRETES A SUBSTANCE WHICH RUNS DOWN ITS BODY AND IS WHIPPED INTO A FROTH.

THE FROTHY SPITTLE PROVIDES A MOIST HOME THAT PREVENTS THE IMMATURE INSECT FROM DRYING OUT. IT MAY ALSO PROTECT THE BUGS FROM PREDATORS THAT WON'T SEARCH THROUGH THE UNPLEASANT OR DISTASTEFUL SPIT FOR THEIR FOOD.

WHEN THE SPITTLEBUG REACHES ITS ADULT STAGE, IT LEAVES ITS FROTHY HOME AND JUMPS ACTIVELY FROM PLANT TO PLANT. THE ADULTS FEED IN THE SAME MANNER AS IMMATURE SPITTLEBUGS, BUT NO LONGER CREATE OR LIVE IN SPITTLE.

WHEN YOU SEE THE SPIT APPEAR IN A NEARBY FIELD OR ROADSIDE, EXAMINE IT AND SEE IF YOU CAN FIND THE SPITTLEBUG.

THIS NATURE NOTE IS PROVIDED BY THE MISSOURI DEPARTMENT OF CONSERVATION.

JUNE NATURE NOTES - WEEK FIVE
DRAGONFLIES BY CHRIS HUMPHREY

MANY PEOPLE ARE AFRAID OF DRAGONFLIES. MAYBE IT IS BECAUSE THEIR NAME SOUNDS THREATENING, OR PERHAPS IT IS BECAUSE THEY ARE RELATIVELY LARGE INSECTS. BUT YOU NEEDN'T FEAR THE DRAGONFLY. THOUGH DRAGONFLIES ARE FEROCIOUS PREDATORS, THEY ARE HARMLESS TO PEOPLE.

A DRAGONFLY IS BUILT FOR HUNTING. IN OUR AREA, MOST DRAGONFLIES HUNT OTHER INSECTS, ESPECIALLY MOSQUITOES. SOME DRAGONFLIES HUNT FROM PERCHES, WAITING FOR INSECTS TO FLY BY, THEN DART OUT TO CATCH THEM. OTHER DRAGONFLIES CATCH AND EAT INSECTS ON THE WING. THEY CUT UP THEIR PREY WITH SHARP MOUTH PARTS.

THE QUICK, MANEUVERABLE FLIGHT OF A DRAGONFLY RESEMBLES THAT OF A HELICOPTER. THE DRAGONFLY HAS TWO PAIRS OF WINGS, AND EACH PAIR WORKS INDEPENDENTLY. THE DRAGONFLY CAN FLY FORWARD, BACKWARD, SIDEWAYS, UP, DOWN, AND EVEN HOVER. ONE DRAGONFLY WAS CLOCKED AT 60 MILES PER HOUR. DRAGONFLIES CAN'T FOLD THEIR WINGS FLAT AGAINST THEIR BODIES. EVEN AT REST, THE WINGS JUT OUT DISTINCTIVELY.

THE DRAGONFLY'S HEAD IS MOSTLY COVERED BY TWO ENORMOUS EYES MADE OF MANY LENSES; THIS HELPS IT TO SEE BETTER THAN MOST INSECTS. A DRAGONFLY CAN TRACK INSECTS AS THEY FLY THROUGH THE AIR AND SPOT PREY FROM ALL DIRECTIONS.

THE DRAGONFLY'S LONG LEGS ARE USED TO CATCH AND HOLD FLYING INSECTS.

OVER 400 SPECIES OF DRAGONFLIES OCCUR IN NORTH AMERICA. SOME EAT TADPOLES AND SMALL FISH. OTHERS DEVOUR HUGE NUMBERS OF MOSQUITOES. WE DON'T NEED TO WORRY ABOUT THIS ULTIMATE PREDATOR, BUT INSECTS BEWARE!

THIS NATURE NOTE IS PROVIDED BY THE MISSOURI DEPARTMENT OF CONSERVATION.

Preparing such short features is similar to preparing any other interpretive talk. As with radio news spots, sound carries the whole message, so appropriate background music and sound effects should be used whenever possible. The key difference between preparing a radio feature and preparing an interpretive talk is that on the radio you are on a strict time budget. If your radio spot is a minute too long it will definitely be noticed!

For longer features (15-30 minutes), a common format is the interview. The host interpreter talks with guests such as other park staff, policy-makers, or local experts on a particular salient topic. Box 8.2 presents tips on conducting successful interviews.

BOX 8.2: INTERVIEWING TECHNIQUES FOR RADIO AND TELEVISION

1. Prior to the interview, "do your homework" and get background information about the guest and the topic.
2. Be at the studio to welcome your guest well before air time. Identify the key points that the guest wants brought out in the interview. Remind your guest about the nature of the audience.
3. Begin by quickly introducing your guest. Explain the guest's relationship to the program and provide background information that will interest the audience and make the guest seem more personable.
4. The first question should serve as an "ice breaker" and should establish the credibility of the guest. Allow the guest to talk about himself or herself briefly (e.g., "How did you get interested in this topic?" or "What brings you to town?").
5. Arrange the questions in a logical order (e.g., chronological, geographical, simple to complex, by species).
6. Keep the questions short. The audience should hear the guest, not the host.
7. Do not ask questions that will bring a simple "yes" or "no" answer and do not ask "how many" questions that may produce only a number for an answer.
8. Avoid long monologues. Keep the spotlight on the guest.
9. Listen to what your guest is saying and appear interested.
10. Make short transitions from question to question, if at all possible. Use the preceding answer as a spring board into the next question.
11. Avoid double-barreled questions. Ask only one question at a time.
12. Do not routinely restate interviewee's answers by saying "in other words." Clarify ambiguous answers, however.
13. Keep it conversational and friendly. Do not ask surprise questions about unrelated topics and avoid potentially embarrassing questions unless previously arranged.
14. Seize control of the interview near the end so you do not have to interrupt the interviewee to end the show.
15. End with a summary of the main points you want the audience to remember or the specific actions you desire them to take.
16. Always conclude by thanking the guest and by repeating the name, title, and affiliation.

Adapted from Fazio and Gilbert (1981)

If an organization does not have its own show, it can often get the feature story on the radio through someone else's show. Most stations have weekly or daily talk or interview shows that focus on stories of local or regional interest. When talking to the program manager or the producer of the talk show, present a brief overview of the feature story and the ideas for the show. If they accept the offer to be on the talk show, prepare a suggested opening statement for the host and a list of questions the host can use for the show. They may not stick to information provided for them, but it is one more thing that can be done to help assure that the information you want communicated actually goes out over the air waves.

Being Interviewed

The earlier interviewing tips applied to the interviewer. Being interviewed, on the other hand, requires other skills. Not all interviews are friendly. Often the interviewer tries to uncover "hard news" rather than focusing on a feature story that had been selected. Sometimes reporters will want to conduct a telephone interview. How can a threatening situation be turned into a positive one for an organization? Blank (1990) presented the following four steps for improving one's performance in an interview.

1. *Do Your Homework.*

   Get to know the interviewer's expertise and prejudices. Review the subject; make sure you know your organization's position on the subject. Familiarize yourself with all sides of an issue, not just your side. Find out about the audience; assess how the issue or subject affects them. Try to aim your responses to the interests and perspectives of the audience.

2. *Focus on Your Most Important Message.*

   Prepare to give your most important message in a few short sentences. If you want to give facts and statistics, provide them in a "media packet" containing fact sheets. It helps save time and assures accuracy when the reporter has some "hard copy" for later reference. Speak only about what you know — don't speculate. Sometimes you lose credibility if you drift from topic to topic.

3. *Pay Attention to What Is Happening During the Interview.*

   Eliminate all distractions and interruptions during an interview. It's not only courteous to do so, but you need to concentrate on the interview. Listen to the questioner's restatement of your comments. Watch for nonverbal clues. Avoid saying more than you should. A very friendly interviewer may get you talking and then feature what you consider a peripheral idea or opinion. Remember, "off-the-record" comments may become news.

4. *Check Your Smile Before Beginning.*

   Blank (1990) referred to smiles: he wasn't just talking about looking good. Rather, he was encouraging people to prepare for an aggressive interviewer. No matter how obnoxious you might find the interviewer, calmly project your organization's dignity and your personal dignity.

Appearance matters even if you do not appear on TV. Most reporters come from backgrounds significantly unlike most interpreters. And, they certainly work in different worlds. Although it's not necessarily fair, people judge by appearances. If interpreters want to be taken seriously by the mainstream, they must not look as if they want to be outside of it. If interpreters are unwilling to forego their personal self-expression through unconventional appearance, they risk building barriers between themselves and their audience. This is why many organizations have dress codes or require uniforms to be worn while on duty.

LOW WATTAGE RADIO:
TRAVELER INFORMATION STATION

Traveler Information Stations (TIS), low-wattage radio stations, broadcast information at AM frequencies at either 560 or 1610 on the dial. Interpreters tape short messages that play continuously over one of these frequencies. These stations are extremely successful taking the information to where the people are—in their cars! TIS orients visitors to fees, accommodations, weather, the schedule of interpretive programs, or safety as they approach the park. Upon entering a park, it can call attention to and interpret a specific feature.

Although TIS units are not cheap, the cost per visitor contact is usually very low, because they reach many people. At Yellowstone National Park, about 75 percent of the people entering the park tuned in to the TIS broadcast (Fazio and Gilbert, 1981). This is a much greater than the percentage of visitors who read park signs. The messages can be changed easily, even daily.

The message must be brief. A technician must be available on staff or a contract basis to provide reliable and prompt repair service. If the TIS is not operating, it will frustrate the visitors and create negative feelings about the organization as they try unsuccessfully to find the broadcast.

A frequency authorization from the FCC must be obtained, and these requests are granted routinely. TIS units can be mounted in a building or on a free-standing, waterproof and vandal resistant unit. Common power sources for TISs are AC, battery, or solar. Signal strength is limited to 10 watts. The signal may range from a 1/4 mile in hilly terrain to 5 miles in areas more conducive to broadcast.

Like all interpretive efforts, successful implementation depends on thorough planning.
- Identify the purpose, specific message, and the audience (e.g., first-time visitors? repeat visitors? winter visitors?).
- Find the most appropriate location to deliver that message (e.g., inside or outside of the park, at the entrance, exit, campground, or at a specific feature).
- Determine the travel times in the receiving area and the length of the message. Ideally, keep messages designed for moving cars short enough to allow for the occupants to hear it twice before moving out of the broadcast area.
- Place signs to allow lead time for the person to locate the designated channel. Typical signs merely say "Park Information — Tune AM 530" (or 1610). More specific signs such as "Wildlife Viewing Information" or "Campground Information" may entice more listeners.

Visitors find TIS a convenient, efficient way to receive information. It can provide helpful and interesting information that will enhance the visitor's experience. TIS provides potential for more communication of interpretive information and may increase greatly with technological improvements.

TELEVISION

Around the world, 750 million TV sets provide in-home entertainment, news, information, and interpretation. *UNESCO's 1988 Statistical Year Book* estimated that there are nearly 200 million TV sets in American homes (one per 1.3 people), and 30 million in the United

Kingdom (one per 1.9 people). Less than six percent of U.S. homes lacked television sets in 1990 (Clark, 1990). This medium will continue to grow with developments in technology such as high definition television and expanded cable service which will offer up to 500 channels!

Television shows action and emotion well. It is at its best when there is action taking place. Part of the magic of television is its ability to condense time. In a few seconds or minutes TV can represent something that may have taken an hour or even years in actual time. The human mind fills in the gaps of time.

Television also has several disadvantages. It requires special equipment, facilities and trained personnel so production opportunities are not as readily available as other media. Also, the pace of a television program is predetermined and cannot be adjusted for different viewers unless the program is on videotape.

The size of the screen limits both the size of the audience that can watch and the type of information that can be broadcast. A rule of thumb suggests that one person per diagonal inch of screen can view a TV at one time. For example, about 25 people can view a 25-inch television screen. Larger audiences require more than one TV screen. Because of the limited size and resolution of television screens, it is difficult to show detail on TV. Maps, floor plans, anatomical drawings and the like show up better in print media or exhibits where they can be studied closely.

In one study, television was second only to newspaper in frequency of use for environmental education; however, the use of television as a source of environmental information decreased with the education level of the audience (Ostman and Parker, 1986/87). Moreover, television generally was not considered a believable source.

Television News Releases and PSAs

As with radio, when a "hard" news story breaks you can alert the news desk at the TV station. They may choose to send out a reporter, film crew, or ask you some questions over the phone. For less immediate items, submit news releases and PSAs. Send visual images with the writing, whenever possible. A video or matching 35mm color slides can accompany the PSA. Use horizontal slides to match the 3 units high by 4 units wide proportions of television screens.

The written script contains a column describing the visual image (slide or video) with the text in the adjacent column. Figure 8.4, page 200, presents an example of a PSA for television. The cover letters that accompany the PSAs and news releases should stress the timeliness and importance of PSA; this may make a difference in air time.

Television Features

Interpreters sometimes appear as guests on TV shows or host their own television program. Some shows are produced at local TV stations as a public service. Cable TV has increased the opportunities for getting messages on TV. Many cable TV companies dedicate a channel for community service programming. This may be as simple as a Community Calendar text that scrolls across the screen or it may contain regular half-hour features. Some natural resource agencies produce their own television shows. For example, the Missouri Department of Conservation produces a yearly 13-week TV series of 1/2 hour shows called Missouri Outdoors. Each episode contains three short video stories about a variety of

AUDIO	VIDEO
The chickadee checkoff is putting your dollars to work for nongame wildlife. By checking line 26 on your state income tax form, you can help build a better future for hundreds of wildlife species. One way your donation helps is by paying for the planting of trees, which are so important to many kinds of nongame wildlife. March is wildlife heritage month in Kansas. The theme this year is: Forests—more than just trees. I invite you to join one of the many celebrations taking place around the state. It's a good opportunity to discover the many ways wildlife can enrich your world. . . as well as the many ways your support of the chickadee checkoff. . . can make a difference.	Hummingbirds at nest Chickadee in tree Income tax form Governor Mike Hayden Tractor-draws tree planter Ladder-backed woodpecker Trees at sunrise Governor Mike Hayden Fonts: "Chickadee Checkoff Protecting our Wildlife Heritage"

FIGURE 8.4
A Script for a Kansas Public Service Announcement Spot

natural resource related topics. For many years, Indiana's state interpreters produced weekly half-hour shows that were heavily oriented towards nature interpretation (Weis and Knudson, 1980).

Because television is a visual medium there are several special tips when preparing to be on a television show. Keep props simple. Use visuals that are legible, attractive, and in 3" x 4" proportion. Wear something comfortable but appropriate for the theme. Get advice on chroma-keying colors. Plan for eye contact; avoid hats, caps or sunglasses. Keep the microphone at least six inches from your mouth.

Start off the program with something unusual or provocative to get the audience's attention. Focus on the visual nature of the medium—show things. Avoid monologues. Talk casually, yet alertly. You may use cue cards or an outline, but don't read a script on the air. Look at the guest/host or look directly at the camera. Address the audience as a single person rather than a group. Rehearse.

The host keeps track of the time, sets the pace, and makes the transitions and necessary adjustments to have the program end at the right time. Both guest and host should have some extra material to use if the show proceeds faster than anticipated.

As with other interpretive media, focus on a particular theme in each program or, in the case of longer programs, a theme for each segment, rather than producing a show that superficially covers many topics. Interpreters often write the script and plan the visuals or props. Although it may be appropriate for interpreters to plan the content of the show, they should defer to experts about other matters on the set. The professional technicians, directors and producers determine the best way to create and deliver a program.

Video and Film

Most natural resource agencies have video or film libraries available for interpreters to use in park programs. Videos have replaced most 16mm films as VCRs have replaced 16mm projectors in schools and homes. Many organizations responded to this change in technology by transferring their 16mm films to videotape.

Some large agencies make their own films to loan or broadcast through TV. A case in point: for over 50 years the Missouri Department of Conservation (MDC) has produced interpretive films which they distribute on a free-loan basis throughout the state or for sale outside the state. Most recent MDC productions are 20-minute videotapes. The diverse titles include "Blooming Secrets," "The Snake's Tale," "Creating an Urban Oasis," and "Streams: The Force of Life."

Quality productions such as those of MDC require professional people and special equipment beyond the resources of most interpreters. It is difficult and expensive for a nature center staff to produce footage that looks professional. Producing a professional-looking video is expensive and once the production is started there is no turning back. So, two questions need to be answered before jumping into a video project: (1) Is video the best medium for this message? (2) Is a new video cost-effective?

Videos are portable and easily accessible since most schools and homes now have VCRs. Unlike television broadcasts, videos can be stopped, replayed or fast-forwarded to meet the needs of the audience. Videos can condense time. Because the sound is usually recorded separately, multi-lingual versions of videos can be made easily. Many commercial videos are readily available on the subjects of history, culture, and environment topics. Check catalogs and other agencies to see if a similar video already exists. If so, it is almost always better to purchase a copy of an existing video than to make a new one. If a tape comes close to what is needed, it may be more cost-effective to add a new opening or closing, or incorporate parts of it into another video. Of course, permission to use materials from existing videos must be acquired from the originating person or agency and a credit or acknowledgment should appear in the final product (Dillon, 1990).

Video has several disadvantages. First, it is expensive. An industry rule-of-thumb is that it costs about $1,000 - $2,000 per minute of finished product. A 10-minute video may be $2,000 per minute and a 60-minute video $1,000 per minute (Dillon, 1990). A cheaper price quote may result in an inferior product unworthy of your organization and the profession. Videos cannot easily be changed. If you are going to spend $15,000 on a video you want it to be used for many years, so do not do one on a topic that will become out-of-date. Avoid making videos from slides—a video without action is essentially a very expensive slide show.

Getting Started

If the decision is made to produce a video, one needs to determine what the video will look like and who will do the work. There are several different approaches to communicating information with video:

The Expert on Camera—

A knowledgeable person explains the topic while on camera. While this is a simple tape to shoot and edit, the format can be deadly. There is a common practice to never show a person just speaking for more than 15-30 seconds. Camera (eye) movement following objects in the speaker's hands, diagrams, or having the narrator walk as he or she talks help keep the audience's interest.

Interview With Expert—

A relatively simple production, but without props or illustrations this can bore viewers unless the subject is intriguing.

Voice Over Video—

This format uses an unseen professional narrator speaking over a pretaped video. Television nature shows and documentaries use this format most frequently.

Role Playing—

This uses actors playing roles to show different situations and historical periods—a difficult format for amateurs to do well.

Animated Graphics—

This approach displays electronically produced graphs, charts, and drawings on the video with narration. As computer graphics and video technology both become more sophisticated, the possibilities for using animated graphics increases.

Script Preparation

Scripts should be prepared before any video is shot. Within the script, indications of visual material should coincide with the text. Everything does not have to be spoken; pictures and sound effects also communicate information. An accurate outline of a proposed script contains timed minute and second notations for each item. Pages should be divided down the middle with the spoken words on the right and a description of the video shot on the left. One can estimate the time needed by reading the script aloud and including time for silent actions, pauses, and transitions.

The total length of the video depends on the type produced. Dillon (1990) recommended the following video lengths:

Orientation videos—

Three to five minutes. Audiences at orientation videos often stand and expect to move on to something else shortly.

Videos for Auditorium Use—

Ten to fifteen minutes. Because the audience sits in a formal setting, they expect more detail and will tolerate a longer video that interprets a particular subject. Normal attention spans are short; prime time television shows consist of seven-minute segments broken up by commercials.

Souvenir Videos—

Thirty to sixty minutes. People seldom buy a video that is shorter than 30 minutes. Souvenir videos that interpret remote or off-limit locations that visitors cannot see are useful and popular. Most major attractions now have commercial videos that interpret their key features.

Getting it Done

Once the idea for a production is formed, it is time to hire a production company. If an organization has a TV production staff one can merely work through normal defined channels. The producer will determine how much can be spent and how to spend the available money. Items such as in Box 8.3 should be specified in the contract.

BOX 8.3: FACTORS AFFECTING COMMERCIAL VIDEO PRODUCTION

- **Access** - Where is the crew allowed to go? Who has to be with them? Are there sensitive areas that are off-limits?
- **Actors** - Professionals or amateurs?
- **Copies** - How many copies are included in the price?
- **Copyrights** - Permission must be acquired to use copyrighted material. Will this project be copyrighted? In whose name?
- **Costumes** - How authentic do they need to be?
- **Credits** - Who will be listed and under what title?
- **Crew** - How many? What positions are necessary?
- **Delivery date** - Be sure to specify the due date and penalties for missing the deadline.
- **Editing time** - This is the time-consuming process of putting the film together and is a significant portion of the cost.
- **Equipment** - Will you need specialized equipment (e.g., lighting, dollies, cranes, tracks). It is best to figure this out early; changes and last minute additions can be expensive.
- **Format** - What format will the final product be in? One inch, 3/4 inch, 1/2 inch VHS, 1/2 inch Beta, and 1/2 inch PAL are just some of the choices.
- **Hiring approval** - If you want to retain hiring approval for the crew and the talent, specify this in the contract.
- **Insurance** - How much and what kind of insurance is required?
- **Length of finished product** - How long will the program be?
- **Locations** - Is there a cost or permit involved? Many places require a fee, insurance, or bonds.
- **Music** - Who is paying for it? Where is it coming from? You can not just play John Denver songs in the background of your video. You can play you own original music or you can perform public domain music (e.g., Mozart, Stephen Foster music). However, you cannot use the Chicago Symphony Orchestra playing public domain music. You may buy music from music library companies or commission someone to write and perform a music score for your video.
- **Narration** - Who selects the narrator? Will it be a professional or amateur?
- **Number of cameras** - Multiple cameras may be needed, especially for live events. Each additional camera costs extra.
- **Props** - These can run into a lot of money, or remain simple and inexpensive.
- **Releases** - Needed for talent in many locations. Who handles this paperwork and the accompanying legal details?
- **Script** - Who writes it? Who has the final say? Is the cost included in the original price?
- **Sets** - Are any needed? Can locations do?
- **Shooting ratio** - More tape is used for documentaries than for scripted scenes. Don't reuse old tape for professional products.
- **Special effects** - This includes wipes, dissolves, and fades. These cost extra and should be discussed in advance.
- **Titles** - These can be expensive and there is a charge for each.
- **Transportation** - Who supplies the vehicles? Are overnight or other travel costs involved?
- **Union regulations** - Union rules could dictate the number of workers and affect the cost.
- **Unused footage** - Who keeps it and who can use it.

Adapted from Dillon (1990)

Dillon (1990) advised using care when choosing a production company. Some people buy a camera and work out of their basements or garages and call themselves a company. Study the company, its equipment, and its facilities. Lists of former clients can be used to seek out references. Recent examples of the company's work should be examined. Prospective directors should be interviewed to assure a level of comfort and responsiveness from the director about the proposed production. Once the director is on the set he or she is boss. Any disagreement on the set will undermine the director's authority and has the potential to cause major problems.

MAKING YOUR OWN VIDEO

With the proliferation of camcorders many interpreters are tempted to make their own video for use in the nature center. The urge often passes after a few attempts. The quality won't be suitable for TV when using normal 1/2 inch or 8 mm tapes. Production requires more than just shooting nice pictures. Editing even the simplest videos requires considerable time. Adding sound, titles, and refinements requires more time and equipment than most interpreters can gather.

In some situations, however, creating your own video with your own equipment can work well. Recording specific local phenomena or events, such as parts of an important speech, the birth and nurturing of a rare animal in a zoo, a gathering of cranes at a refuge, a look inside a cave, or a group planting trees on a fire-scarred area, can be worked into interpretive talks. If done carefully, training videos, short clips for exhibits, or videos to show to local public groups (e.g., schools, civic groups, community meetings, agency officials) can be satisfactorily produced in-house.

Two situations call for "home video." One involves capturing ephemeral events that won't be filmed otherwise. The other involves a targeted audience with an inherent interest in the subject. These people will be more tolerant of an amateur production than a general audience. Of course, a captive audience is no excuse to make an inferior video. If the video is poorly done, the audience won't give you the opportunity to capture them again!

Equipment

The following equipment suggestions may help as you make your own video (Frank, 1993).

- *Camera* —Currently, the camcorder format of choice is 8 mm, for its ease of operation and compact size. VHS camcorders are quite popular, but better resolution and brighter colors are achieved with S-VHS (Super VHS) system. Standard VHS produces only 245 lines of resolution whereas S-VHS produces 440 lines. S-VHS is still greatly inferior to the 1 inch tape (used in network TV shows, best commercials) or 3/4 inch tape (used by local TV stations, local commercials, news clips).
- *Telephoto lens* —You need a 10 to 1 or larger zoom lens, particularly if your subject is wildlife.
- *Tripod* —A good "fluid head" tripod will make your video look more professional. Hand held images will look unsteady and amateurish. When you don't have time to set up a tripod, use a "bean-bag" camera support to steady the camera. The bean bag conforms to the shape of the bottom of the camera and to the top of whatever it is resting on (e.g., car door). This may help get some steady video of wildlife.

- *Microphone*—An external microphone (i.e., one not attached to the camera) with a wind screen prevents unwanted sound. Wind screens are foam "gloves" that fit over the microphone eliminating annoying wind sound. The external microphone eliminates unwanted noise and picks up the sounds of nature which will enhance any outdoor video. If a person is speaking on the video, use a lapel or necklace type microphone. A cheap lapel microphone is much better than the microphone on the camera.
- *Miscellaneous* —Always keep extra batteries, cables, and microphones available to save frustration and prevent losing once in a lifetime shots. For outdoor videotaping, take along an all-weather protective cover to keep moisture and dirt out of the equipment.

Editing makes good video images into useful tapes. Yet, few interpretive facilities purchase their own editing equipment. The most primitive editing uses two VCRs, merely recording desired segments to a blank tape in the desired order. The cuts between segments usually look rough and obvious. Most organizations that shoot their own tape take it to an editing studio. If you take your tape to the studio, you will most likely find an enthusiastic technician who is tired of doing supermarket commercials (Burke, 1990). An editing session involving four PSAs cost Burke's agency about $2,000. The reports received from TV stations airing the PSAs indicated that they received about $250,000 worth of air time!

Techniques

The following techniques make videos look more professional.
- *Follow the script.* A logical sequence of scenes reduces the need for editing.
- *Resist the temptation to pan and zoom.* Most amateur videos contain dizzying amounts of these "unnatural" actions. Instead, treat scenes as if you are using a still camera; before moving, turn off the camera, establish the new shot, and then resume filming. Zooming may be acceptable when something interesting begins happening in a wide shot. You can zoom in (slowly!) to the object of interest. Pan slowly only to follow an animal's movements.
- *For scenery or when no action takes place for 10 seconds or more, sequence shots in the following manner:* wide, medium, close-up, and repeat until the scene changes. This breaks up the monotony of the scene. If something moves in the picture, no shifts are necessary.
- *Allow people or wildlife to walk out of the picture at the end of a scene.*
- *Use a dissolve for difficult transitions and to indicate the passage of time.* In dissolves, one picture gradually disappears and a new image gradually appears over it.
- *Try to illuminate the subject evenly unless some special effect is desired.* Bright days are usually best. For wildlife in a forested area, however, overcast days produce more even lighting under the trees and animals will be less likely to be hidden in shadows. Avoid overcast skies in the background because the diffuse light will cause the lens to stop down and the subject will become too dark. In bright situations, the sun behind the subject will stop down the lens and produce a silhouetted or completely shaded subject. To bring the subject into normal exposure, manually open the camera's iris.
- *You may want to use manual focus most of the time.* Auto-focus may constantly search for a subject among the scenery and creates a distracting, pulsating picture.

- *Set the recording speed for the fastest possible speed SP (Standard Play), rather than SLP (Super Long Play).* The quality of the picture is superior on SP.
- *Shoot more than enough video to allow for easy editing.* When recording speakers, start the tape and count to 10 before the person starts to speak, then let the tape run about 5 seconds after the person finishes. It's a good idea to shoot "cut-aways." These silent reaction shots of people's faces or close-ups of pamphlets or objects can be used to cover up poor edits or make a visual transition in the video.

Summary

Print media and the electronic mass media of radio, television, and video provide interpreters with powerful tools for reaching many people with interpretive programming. By regularly using radio and television spots, announcements, interview appearances, and features, the interpreter can reach a large number of people that otherwise might seldom hear interpretation of their natural and cultural resources. Mass media carry messages off-site to the "unconverted," allowing interpreters to "preach" to more than the already converted "choir."

The complex technology associated with these media make them challenging to use effectively. Likewise, the unseen audience gives no direct feedback to let the interpreter know whether or not the message is getting across. Therefore, interpreters can and should use the expert help available. This allows the interpreter to focus on message content and its development to maximize the use of interpretive principles. Because of the inherent strengths and weaknesses of each medium, it is wise to use several combinations of media to communicate and reinforce messages. Audiences may be missed if just one medium is used.

The interpreter seeks to develop effective messages and materials. When they fit mass media delivery systems, the ideas should be taken to the mass media professionals. They'll listen and guide the production. The mass media professionals control the media; the interpreter controls the essence of the message. Broadcast news will boil down the message to a few key phrases and images. Features or extended programs will allow more elaboration on the subject. Videos can tell the whole story.

When using mass media to communicate interpretive messages or when responding to media interest in a major event, such as the Yellowstone fires, consider the components of the communications model. Who are the gatekeepers and regulators? What filters, distortion, and noise might interfere with the message? Is there amplification or feedback? By combining knowledge of the communications industry with intriguing, interpretive messages, the success of communication efforts can be assured.

With a few phone calls, personal visits, some friendly follow-ups, and hard work to properly prepare good material, a message can have an impact on a wide audience. By using mass media, more members of the community, state, or nation that employs interpreters can be served as opposed to relying on on-site personal interpretation. Greater attendance may be generated at interpretive programs that use mass media. Mass media can generate awareness and support of resources, their values, and the agencies that administer them.

Literature Cited

Blank, G. B. (1990). How to be your best in a media interview. In *Proceedings, Society of American Foresters National Convention*. Washington, DC.

Burke, A. R. II. (1990). Future visions in video. In *Proceedings, National Interpreters Workshop*, NAI. Charleston, SC.

Cable, T. T. and Udd, E. (1990). Effective communication of toxic chemical warnings to anglers. *North American Journal of Fisheries Management, 10*:382-387.

Clark, K. R. (1990). The "big three" become "just three more." *Britannica Book of the Year*. Chicago, IL: Encyclopædia Britannica, Inc.

Dillon, C. (1990). So you want to make a video? In *Proceedings, National Interpreters Workshop*, NAI. Charleston, SC.

Fazio, J. R.. and Gilbert, D. L. (1981). *Public relations and communications for natural resource managers*. Dubuque, IA: Kendall/Hunt Publishing Company.

Frank, R. (1993). *Extension communication guide to producing videotapes*. Kansas State University Cooperative Extension Service.

McLuhan, M. (1964). *Understanding media: The extensions of man*. Toronto, ON: McGraw-Hill, Inc.

Ostman, R. E. and Parker, J. L. (1986/87). A public's environmental information sources and evaluations of mass media. *Journal of Environmental Education, 18*(2):9-18.

Radio Advertising Bureau. (1984). *Radio facts*. New York, NY: Radio Advertising Bureau.

Vivian, J. (1991). *The media of mass communication*. Needham Heights, MA: Allyn & Bacon, Inc.

Weis, C. and Knudson, D. M. (1980). Naturalists and the mass media: Reaching beyond the parks. *Journal of Environmental Education, 11*(4):41-44.

The Printed Word

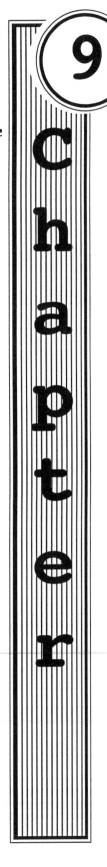

Anything that is not writing is easy.
—Jimmy Breslin

Writing is the hardest work in the world not involving heavy lifting.
—Pete Hamill

No one likes to write, everyone likes to have written.
—William Zinsser

These quotes from prominent writers should not discourage but, rather, console those writing in moments of discouragement. One who finds writing difficult is probably normal. And yet, the written word can be powerful, profound, and compelling. It can enrich lives. It can change the course of history. Written accounts of the western U.S. by early explorers generated interest in what would become our first national parks. Writers garnered support for our first state parks, our first wilderness areas, and our public forests.

An interpreter's writing (Edwards, 1979) breathes life and color into the whole sweep of Canadian identity in just a few phrases:

> Canada is rocky seas of mountains and magnificent tables of plain, thousands of leagues of spruce woods and fertile miles of farms, frozen white oceans and cities dominating the earth as far as the eyes can see. Canada is foggy wet coasts and dry cold deserts, rolling golden grasslands and valleys ablaze with autumn leaves, lonely surf-girt islands and towns teeming with people. This land is many lands each worth knowing. To glimpse this diversity is to feel some of the meaning of being Canadian.

Written communication can stimulate patriotic pride, educate, entertain, and persuade. It was Rachel Carson's written words in *Silent Spring* that energized the environmental movement which began in the 1960s and continues today. This chapter presents ideas to help interpreters write more effectively so readers can catch their enthusiasm and learn their provocative messages.

The Interpretive "Library"

Interpreters use a wide range of written materials to get their thoughts across. Most fall within the categories of: *books, brochures, catalogs, trail guide booklets, maps, trail signs,* and *museum labels.* In addition, writing creates the basis for most talks, guided hikes, interpretive tours, exhibits, and audiovisual presentations.

From books to brochures, exhibit labels to trail signs, interpreters write messages and desire that people read them. Some writing aims at visitors in a museum or park. Documents can serve as guides to see and understand the original objects in the exhibits, or along trails. Other printed materials aim to prepare those who have not yet arrived. Still other items serve those who came, saw, and wanted to know more after they left. Some techniques and guidelines for writing and editing these types of publications comprise most of this chapter. The sometimes painful, sometimes joyful process of writing should be made easier after reading the suggestions here.

Writing Techniques for Effective Interpretation: A Quick Preview

> *All writing is communication; creative writing is communication through revelation—it is the Self escaping into the open.*
> —Strunk and White (1979)

The art of interpretive writing involves using artful language precisely. The process can be rather simple by doing the following:

- Pinpoint the story.
- Relate it to the interpretive theme.
- Write succinctly and colorfully.
- Tell the story so someone can enjoy reading it.

Achieving success in this process is easier said than done (Figure 9.1). There are several techniques that serve people well. Some of them appear below in both generalities and specifics.

Two keys—brevity and simplicity—remove the biggest barriers to clear writing. A wise

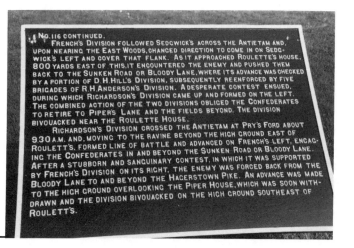

FIGURE 9.1

An old Civil War explanation— try to concentrate for three sentences—hard to read, hard to follow, and hard to comprehend what happened (TTC).

and successful wildlife writer, Dr. Durward Allen, suggested to his students one simple guideline: never put more than one idea in a sentence. If you wish to express two ideas, use two sentences. Three other simple guidelines work well for writers. To capture and keep the reader's attention:

1. Use short words.
2. Use short sentences.
3. Use short paragraphs.

Add to these some guidelines for word selection:

4. Employ action verbs; use "to be" verbs sparingly.
5. Appeal to the five senses when appropriate.
6. Use accurate, colorful words.
7. Think rhythmically when combining and choosing words.

Then, edit, edit, and edit again.

Nowhere do these rules suggest that writing should sound choppy or simplistic. There is no need to restrict yourself to three word declarative sentences. Variety in sentence length, arrangement, and form adds interest. Elegance of expression need not suffer for clarity or simplicity. The simplest writing, however, is often the most elegant.

Nevertheless, elegance is not the first goal of an interpreter. Readership is. An interpreter writes so people will read the messages, understand the precautions, and enjoy the significance of the resource or artifacts (Figure 9.2).

FIGURE 9.2
More modern wayside signs at Antietam Battlefield use photos, drawings, brief quotes and easily-read writing (TTC).

How to Write Effectively

Despite all the fine books that describe how to write, the authors feel compelled to select and summarize some of the most useful advice that may help interpreters do their jobs well. Some claim that the art of writing arises from individual peculiarities and impulses. Yet, the techniques described below can surely improve almost anyone's writing. Clearly, writing can be learned. Practice, criticism, and vigorous editing will tire, anger, confuse, and help all writers.

PREPARING TO WRITE

Three prerequisites to writing require one to:

1. *Know the purpose.* As one begins an interpretive writing effort, define the objectives to direct the content and organization of the writing. This reduces the chance of drifting to other topics or providing unneeded information (Figure 9.3).

2. *Know the audience.* To effectively target messages one must consider the demographic characteristics of the audience, such as age, place of residence, and education. Referring to local landmarks in a brochure about the geology of a park will not work if the audience comes mostly from out of state. Likewise, the interpreter needs to know what the audience might already understand about the subject matter. Most importantly, one must know what interests the readers—something that touches their personality, experience or ideals (Tilden, 1967).

3. *Know the subject.* Not only does the interpreter need to know enough information about the topic to make the communication worthwhile, but also enough to interpret the material. Beyond the basic facts, the interpreter shapes and forms it into a message for the audience—information converted into revelation that is fun to read.

Tilden (1967) observed that adequate interpretive writing comes from "90 percent thinking and 10 percent composition." Knowing what one is writing about, why one is writing it, and to whom one is writing allows the writer to accomplish the 10 percent composition effectively and with confidence.

FIGURE 9.3
A "Just the Facts" sign uses economy of words with lettering and frame that help tell the story.

Mission San Xavier Del Bac

Bac. Where water runs into ground. Early name of settlement. Father Kino, S.J. first visited Bac in 1692. Built first chapel in 1700. Present church built by Franciscan Fathers 1783-1797.

GIFT SHOP →

THE WRITING PROCESS

Once an interpreter has carefully addressed the three prerequisites of writing, then it is time for him or her to start putting words on paper. Writers write by stringing words together, one word at a time.

> The greatest masterpiece in literature is only a dictionary out of order.
> —Jean Cocteau

Outline and Draft

First, keeping in mind the purpose and audience, one should jot down a brief outline of the main points in a logical order. This can serve to keep the writer headed in the right direction.

Next, write the rough draft quickly. Plunge right in and try not to stop until the end of the outline is reached. Do not stop to deliberate over particular words or to check spellings or precise punctuation. If the right word or idea is elusive type a series of question marks (???) or asterisks (***) in the space and move on. Likewise, if more than one word or idea is appropriate, type both of the choices and mark the location with asterisks. These markers allow one to easily locate the problems later. There is nothing more daunting to a writer than a blank piece of paper or blank computer screen. Fill it up fast. Write more than is needed; the excess can be edited out later.

Constantly refer to the outline to stay on track. Because an outline is analogous to a skeleton, writing the quick draft is sometimes called "fleshing out" the outline or adding meat to the bones.

Why this frantic strategy of writing quickly? Haste helps to capture fleeting ideas. If one stops to ponder a problem he or she risks losing their overview and momentum. This strategy allows one to write enthusiastically. Tilden once said that "Whatever is written without enthusiasm will be read without interest." It is difficult to write enthusiastically if one is continually getting bogged down with word choices or punctuation problems.

Revising and Polishing

All professional writers revise their manuscripts. The story of Abraham Lincoln writing the Gettysburg Address on the back of an envelope while riding the train to Gettysburg is a myth. He worked on the speech for over two weeks, and revised it at least five times. He probably revised the speech again on the train. (He did not write it on an envelope either.) Ernest Hemingway revised the last page of *Farewell to Arms* 39 times before he was satisfied with the wording. Interpreters should keep that in mind when tempted to rush their brochure to the printer.

The first revision should focus on fixing the big mistakes, such as misspellings, typos, and obviously inaccurate or awkward passages. This removes the rough edges from the manuscript. Polishing the text consists of a series of revisions to address the problems marked earlier and make other more subtle improvements in the text. It is often more efficient to focus on a different kind of problem during each revision rather than trying to correct every possible type of problem on the same pass through the manuscript. In each of these revisions try to find the best words to communicate decisive, unambiguous ideas. These three tips will expedite the polishing process:

1. *Read the manuscript aloud repeatedly.* This is particularly helpful to identify punctuation problems. Trust your ear to judge what sounds correct.
2. *Lay the manuscript aside for several days between revisions.* It gives one a fresh perspective on the writing and he or she is more likely to read what is on the paper rather than what one thought he or she wrote.
3. *Ask someone else to review the manuscript.* Make sure the reviewer is impartial and will give an objective opinion. An honest review by a friend or colleague before going to the printer could save one much embarrassment later.

Style

Much writing goes unread. Both content and style influence whether people will read written material. Interpretive writing about subjects interesting to the reader and treated in a fun way will more likely be read.

Writing style wraps itself in mystery. To discuss style opens avenues for argument. Style affects the sound of the words on paper and in the mind. Strunk and White (1979) claimed to have no infallible guide to good writing, no inflexible rule that can steer one to becoming a clear writer: "Who can confidently say what ignites a certain combination of words, causing them to explode in the mind?" In fact, these authors recommended that "to achieve style, begin by affecting none . . . Style will emerge from careful, honest writing."

Despite the mysteries of that personal phenomena called style, certain guidelines and techniques mentioned below help make a writer more effective without stifling individuality.

Perhaps the simplest guideline to effective writing follows the "3 Cs of Communication"—be CORRECT, CONCISE and CLEAR.

Correct writing enhances readability and credibility. Writing riddled with errors in grammar, spelling, or punctuation shows that the writer does not know any better or does not care. Likewise, the content must be correct too. Unfortunately some interpreters have dealt loosely with the facts in an effort to simplify the subject or make it more interesting. Use accurate, up-to-date references, backed by data or other references to assure correct information.

Gender inclusive writing has become standard. Avoid pronouns that identify one sex (i.e., he, his, she, her) when referring to both sexes. Avoid exclusive pronouns by using the plural form. For example, "The interpreter must make sure he welcomes visitors." can become "Interpreters must make sure they welcome visitors." Also, names of occupations and positions contain some gender-free alternatives (e.g., reporters rather than newsmen; chairperson rather than chairman). Failure to write inclusively may offend and alienate readers, distract from the message, and reduce credibility.

Concise writing improves readability and contributes to clarity. The following 10 tips present ways to improve the conciseness and clarity of writing text:

1. *Keep sentences short.* Sentences between 15 and 20 words usually make reading easier. Sentences longer than 30 words often are confusing. Condense wordy phrases by eliminating needless words. Limit a sentence to one idea. Box 9.1 gives examples of reducing needless words.

2. *Vary the length of paragraphs but keep all of them relatively short.* Even one hundred word paragraphs can look intimidating in narrow brochure columns. One rule of thumb is to limit paragraph length to no more than 15 typewritten lines.

3. *Replace hard words with easy words.* Hard words are generally those with three or more syllables. But some short words are considered hard (e.g., aerial), and some long words are easy (e.g., beekeeper). Read the text aloud to identify hard words. Box 9.2 gives examples of simple words replacing hard words. Can the hard words in the following sentence be replaced with easy words to make the same point? "It has been posited that a high degree of inquisitiveness proved lethal to a feline."

BOX 9.1: CUTTING WORDY EXPRESSIONS AND PHRASES

INSTEAD OF	USE
a number of	some
at the present time	now, at present
due to the fact that	because
for the purpose of	for, to
in the amount of	for
in the near future	soon
on a quarterly basis	quarterly
the month of June	June

Diluted Verbs

DILUTED	STRONGER
give consideration of	consider
make preparations for	prepare
make use of	use
is applicable to	applies to
is indicative of	shows
undertake an analysis	analyze

Redundancies to Avoid

pleased and delighted	absolutely complete
stimulating and interesting	reduce down
review and comment on	circular in shape
help and support	most unique
alternative choices	subject matter
join together	future plans

---

4. *Use verbs rather than nouns or adjectives made from them.* For example, say "increased" rather than "experienced an increase," or "I recommend" rather than "I make a recommendation," or "we intend" rather than "our intention is."

5. *Use active voice rather than passive voice.* "The fox ate the rabbit." is more concise than "The rabbit was eaten by the fox." People are used to reading sentences structured: subject, verb, object. Passive voice reverses the order to: object, verb, subject. This makes sentences longer and less clear.

6. *Use positive words rather than negative words.* Say what things are rather than what they are not. Rather than "The exhibit won't be ready until Monday" say "The exhibit will be ready Monday." Also, replace double negatives with positive statements (e.g., replace "not unimportant" with "important"). Double negatives require unnecessary mental gymnastics.

7. *Avoid sentences that begin with "It is" or "There is."* Make these sentences more active and concise. Unless "it" refers to something mentioned earlier, "it is" tangles sentences, encourages passive voice, and delays meaning. For example, rather than "It is my understanding that the program was effective", write "I understand that the program was effective." One can often eliminate "There are" or "there is" without

losing meaning. Rather than "There are some trails that are closed," write "Some trails are closed." The authors found an even worse example, "It is important to remember that there are some trails that are closed."

BOX 9.2: Everyday Words to Replace More Difficult Words

FOR THIS	TRY THIS
appreciable number	many
assistance	help
has capability	can
consequently	so
endeavor	try
equitable	fair
expedite	hurry, speed up
indicate	show
magnitude	size
methodology	method, way
preclude	prevent
terminate	end
timely	prompt, in time
utilize	use
consequently	so
nevertheless	still
aforementioned	the, that, those
heretofore	until now
notwithstanding	in spite of

---

8. *Keep related words together and unrelated words apart.* This improves clarity. For example, "A small bird in the tree" is clearer than "A bird in the tree that was small."

9. *Beware of dangling modifiers.* These words or phrases have nothing to logically modify or seem to modify something in a word that it cannot possibly modify. Examples: "Tacked to the bulletin board, the interpreter read the activities schedule." "Having been run through the computer, the interpreter used the statistics in the exhibit."

10. *Be definite and specific.* This approach will stimulate and hold the reader's interest. Instead of " a period of inclement weather set in," write "it rained every day for a week." Or instead of "the rabbit went through the grass," one can be more specific and dramatic by replacing "went" with words like "leaped," "darted," or "sprinted." Use a thesaurus, if necessary, to help select the best word.

Rating Readability

Several quantitative formulas allow one to assess readability. The two most popular are the Flesch Index (Flesch, 1949) and Gunning's Fog Index (Gunning, 1962). Government agencies and corporations often use these techniques to help assure that their clientele will find their publications readable. These tests use sentence length and word length to estimate the ease of reading. Most newspapers and popular publications seek to write for an imaginary 5th to 8th grade level. Most best-selling books and much of the Bible are 7th or 8th grade level; Plato's Dialogues range from 4th to 8th grade. So, even deep subjects can be "readable."

Flesch (1949) also developed a "Human Interest" index based on personal words. The more personal words used, the more human interest the writing may carry. Personal words include: specific individual pronouns, gender-specific words, group words, dialogue-type "spoken" sentences, questions, commands, requests addressed to the reader, exclamations, and incomplete sentences whose full meaning is inferred.

These indices are available as part of many computer software packages that evaluate grammar and style. The essence of the method to calculate the FOG Index (Gunning, 1962) follows. Refinements appear in the original publication. To make the calculations, select a sample of writing at least 100 words long then:

1. Count the words; then divide the total number of words by the number of sentences for the average number of words per sentence.

2. Count the number of words of three or more syllables in your sample. Do not count
   (a) capitalized words;
   (b) combinations of short, easy words such as bookkeeper;
   (c) verbs that gained their third syllable by adding -ed or -es, such as created.
   Add this number to that derived in step one.

3. Multiply the total by 0.4. This number gives you the FOG Index. It corresponds roughly to the number of years of schooling a person would require to read and understand the passage easily.

Neither the Flesch nor the FOG test assesses organization, layout, accuracy, or content. Therefore, a poorly written piece could score well on the readability scales. Moreover, these tests try to assess the ease of a reading, not its desirability. Content must present an interesting topic in an interesting way if one expects people to read it.

STRUCTURE

Just as buildings have foundations, frames, and roofs. Likewise, written pieces have their structure or "architecture," with beginnings, middles, and ends. The "look" of each will vary according to the purpose and creativity of the architect/writer. Just as architects plan their projects, accomplished writers lay a plan for how a piece will begin, where it will end, and how they will get from the beginning to the end.

Interpreters often have the opportunity to write in the style of feature articles—journalistic stories that entertain and inform (Hay, 1990) with a specific design to engage the reader's attention. Feature articles appear in newsletters, magazines, or newspapers. The approach also appears in brochures, interpretive signs, and booklets.

The structure of feature-type stories contains the four components described as follows (Hay, 1990):

The Lead—The lead captures the reader's attention, indicates the article's general nature, and persuades the reader to continue. Although the lead's information relates to the rest of the article, it does not have to contain the most important points or facts (as it should in a news article). In the lead, writers use different techniques. Many focus on a person whose experience ties into the story. Sometimes quotes work well as part of a lead by humanizing subjects which otherwise might seem dry. Catchy anecdotes also work well. These mini-stories have their own beginning, middle, and end. Make sure that the end of the lead anecdote links with the rest of the main story. Feature articles for newspapers have shorter leads than stories written for magazines or newsletters because of space considerations. Leads for interpretive signs or exhibits may be only a few words long.

Transition—This "capsule statement," "bridge," or "nut paragraph" ("nut graf") tells the reader what the subject is and why he or she is writing about it. Many writers compose a one or two sentence thesis statements before they begin writing because it helps them organize and focus their thoughts. Often, this appears as the key element in the transition paragraph. As the name implies, this paragraph moves the reader smoothly from the lead into the body of the story. This requires some careful crafting, particularly if he or she has a good, startling, or gripping lead.

Development—This constitutes the body of the article where one makes their points or discusses the issues. This requires a logical order. Choose an order that makes sense for the topic. Chronological order works well for "how-to-do-it" stories, stories showing cause and effect, or reports of historical events. Deductive order (taking the reader from familiar information to unfamiliar concepts) works well for scientific writing, where one may have to introduce difficult concepts. An inductive order would draw general conclusions from specific facts. Regardless of the order chosen, each paragraph in the body should have a brief, but smooth, transition to the paragraph before and after it.

Strong Ending—Save a real gem for the last paragraph. It can include a powerful quote or observation. It may or may not refer back to the lead, but it can summarize the article in a colorful and powerful way.

The Print Media

Interpretive writing appears in a variety of formats including: brochures, newsletters, signs, labels, booklets, and newspapers. Each format presents special advantages and challenges. General advantages and limitations of publications appear in Box 9.3. Brochures, signs and labels, and newsletters are discussed in more detail below.

BROCHURES

Brochures are the most commonly used form of written interpretation. Government agencies and private organizations produce dozens of interpretive brochures each year. Some professionals believe that too many brochures are produced and this glut diminishes the effectiveness of this medium. Certainly the tons of brochures being stored in parks and museums around the world suggests that many brochures go unused. This, however, should not serve as an indictment of the medium. Rather, it should challenge interpreters to produce attractive, useful, and popular brochures instead of wondering where to store them. The challenge should become how to keep an adequate supply.

As with all interpretive media, using brochures has advantages and disadvantages.

Advantages

Many of the advantages of brochures result from their usefulness for off-site interpretation by communicating in several ways outside the park or museum:

- Distribute off-site at locations such as libraries, schools, restaurants, motels, gas stations, rest stops, and other parks or museums.
- Mail promotional and educational brochures to inform potential visitors about the programs/facilities. Such mailings not only entice people to come, but help them prepare for a rewarding visit. Educational brochures can be sent to interested people who cannot visit.

BOX 9.3: ADVANTAGES AND LIMITATIONS OF PUBLICATIONS FOR INTERPRETATION

Advantages of publications:
Relatively inexpensive per copy
Easy to revise
Transportable by visitors
Visitor can use at his or her own personal pace and place
Handy for interpreters to use—at the desk and in the field
Excellent for new areas with few facilities
Can condense a lot of information within them, allowing visitor to select
Good for sequential stories and date-related information
Allow illustrations of ideas and concepts
Stimulate ideas that lead to other media, books, etc.
Good way to handle translations for foreign visitors
Good protection against court cases
Souvenir value
Can produce income for agency or its partners

Disadvantages or limitations of publications:
Supplies may run out; people who paid to get in are miffed
Many people cannot read maps (about 50 percent)
Too small to substitute for large displays
Not good for showing movements over time (geology or troop placements)
Maps and similar graphic material may be quite expensive unless produced in large
     quantities (3,500-20,000 copies minimum, depending on detail and colors)
Publication contents are not real objects, so they do not substitute for exhibits or
     trail-side specimens
Hard for some elderly to read.
Can cause litter, especially if there are many different pieces/bulletins for any one site
Some are too big to handle or to fold
Can discourage intended audience with too much detail.
Can produce a poor image, if poorly done

—Adapted from notes by Bruce Hopkins, Harpers Ferry Center,
National Park Service

- Visitors take brochures off-site to read later or to keep as a memento of the visit. This "souvenir value" may recall the value of the visit, just as brochures read later may reinforce earlier messages and aid retention of information.

Other advantages of brochures include the following:
- Low cost, compared to other media. Costs vary depending on the quality of the paper, the use of color, and the number printed.
- Available to the public continuously. As long as people can access a brochure rack or box, they can enjoy interpretation, even when no staff members are present.
- Reduce the burden on information desk staff by providing answers to the most often asked questions.
- Self-paced. People can slow down, speed up, go back to the beginning, or stop reading at their own choosing.
- Low impact on resources. Reduce litter potential by keeping a clean, well-maintained area. Also, a high quality, useful brochure seldom appears on the ground. Place collection boxes at the end of trails, to encourage return of unwanted trail brochures for reuse. Finally, a small charge imputes some value to the publication and reduces the chance that it will end up as litter.

Disadvantages
- A surprising number of people cannot read easily. Others dislike making the effort to read while doing something else such as riding or walking.
- Brochures are a "cold," impersonal medium. Readers cannot ask questions or discuss; interpreters get little feedback to evaluate the effectiveness of the brochure.
- Brochures do not present complex and dynamic topics well.

SIGNS AND LABELS

Interpreting through the use of signs and labels presents many of the same opportunities and challenges presented by using brochures. They are always "on-duty," available to the public, and allow self-paced interpretation. They have an advantage over brochures in that they provide good opportunities for visitors' photos. By using a permanent sign interpreters do not have to be concerned with keeping the brochure boxes or racks full. However, unlike brochures, signs and labels have no off-site values. Unless carefully planned, signs can have a negative impact on site aesthetics. Their permanence makes them difficult and costly to revise.

NEWSLETTERS

Most interpretive organizations have a newsletter. Newsletters play an important role in providing regular communication with friends of the organization. They may also provide the public an opportunity to communicate with each other and the organization. The organization can use newsletters to educate and entertain their public, solicit volunteers and specific donations to meet other needs, and call attention to staff, volunteers, and others deserving recognition.

Because newsletters often provide an organization's most regular and tangible contact with people, they create, maintain, and reinforce the organization's image. Newsletters make a convenient item to send to other agencies, politicians, mass media reporters, and others to whom the organization wishes to be visible.

Like other print media, newsletters should be attractive and inviting to read. Because they visually represent the organization they should look professional and consistent in appearance, so that over time they are immediately recognizable. Newsletter content typically includes: a column written by the editor, some form of feedback items, feature articles, a calendar of events, short news items, and membership or subscription information.

Most organizations do their newsletters in-house. With the advent of personal computers and desktop publishing software, it is possible to produce professional-looking newsletters out of the back room of a museum or nature center.

Design Tips

The design of printed material greatly influences whether something is read, as does the writing itself. Zehr, Gross and Zimmerman (1990) described the "nuts and bolts" of creating interpretive publications in a useful handbook. Trapp, Gross and Zimmerman (1991) also prepared another useful handbook of ideas for trail signs and wayside exhibits. These books and other references available from agencies such as the National Park Service and USDA Forest Service offer specific information about materials and design criteria related to the various print media.

One conceptual design tool that indicates the readability of a publication or sign/label text can be expressed in an equation called "The Fraction of Selection" (Schramm, cited in McIntosh 1982):

Fraction of Selection = Expectation of Reward / Effort Required

The higher the value of the fraction (high reward/little effort), the greater is the likelihood of the text being read. The lower the fraction (lower reward/high effort), the smaller the likelihood it will be read. In other words, people engage in a momentary benefit/cost analysis to determine if it is "worth it" to stop and read the text. The interpretive writer seeks to maximize the numerator (expectation of reward), while minimizing the denominator (effort required). To do this, consider both content and design. If the design is poor, people probably will not get to the content. The following tips help increase the expectation of reward and reduce the effort required.

DESIGN TIPS—BROCHURES

These first three design factors will enhance the expectation of reward:

Title—Catchy titles improve the chances that a brochure will be picked up. Questions, provocative statements, or a bit of humor all will affect use positively.

Color—Bright colors command more attention. Choose colors appropriate to the subject. For example, red helps emphasize a brochure warning of hazards, while orange seems logical for a brochure on fall colors, and blue fits a brochure about water.

Layout—Besides the title, an attractive layout strongly influences whether a person will pick up the brochure.

The next considerations affect the perception of "effort required."

Layout—Keep paragraphs short. Break up the text with subtitles, photographs, or other graphics. People would rather look at an illustration than read. Remember the cliché: "a picture is worth a thousand words." Leave enough "white space" to achieve a clean, uncluttered appearance.

Margins—Wide margins may increase the length of paragraphs but if the lines are too long readers may have a difficult time moving from line-to-line smoothly. About 65 characters is a rule of thumb for the maximum width of text. Very short lines make the text appear choppy and smooth reading becomes difficult.

Font—Each font conveys a feeling, so carefully select a font style that is appropriate for the subject. Also, select fonts that are easy to read, usually a serif typeface for the text, because they help the eye flow from word-to-word. Avoid fancy, script fonts. Interpreters may wish to consult a professional printer to help with their decision. Once a font is selected, stick with it throughout the publication.

DESIGN TIPS—SIGNS AND LABELS

All of the factors mentioned above for brochures apply to designing signs and labels (Figures 9.4 and 9.5). In addition to those considerations, several other factors must be addressed.

Contrast—Lettering must contrast with the background to be read easily. Typically, dark letters on a light background are more readable than light letters on a dark background. The reverse to this rule works for signs placed in a dark environment, such as in deep woods, or in a cave, or even for night visibility.

Lighting—Provide adequate lighting for indoor signs and labels. Light causes photo-chemical reactions that can damage the objects being interpreted, such as valuable artifacts. Therefore, museum designs normally avoid windows in exhibit areas. Yet, to interpret an object requires clear visibility and an easily read text. To deal with this dilemma, focus spotlights (track lighting, usually) to illuminate the text and, indirectly, the objects. New, cool lighting and fiber-optic systems help protect artifacts despite direct illumination. Also, filters can be placed on the lights to reduce some particularly destructive wavelengths such as ultraviolet.

Sometimes glare or poor angles create problems. Shiny exhibit surfaces and glass can create distracting reflections. Dull finishes reduce the amount of glare, thereby making the sign more legible. Also, to prevent glare consider the angle of the sign relative to the light. The best reading surface to line of sight angle is 90 degrees, but this may produce a reflection off the reading surface. To eliminate the glare, change the lighting or tilt the reading surface slightly.

Lettering—Again, use fonts large enough to read them easily from the appropriate distance. For most museum exhibits, a minimum of 24 point size works well for text on indoor exhibit signs, as does 18 point type for captions (Trapp, Gross and

FIGURE 9.4
Signs in the Alaska Zoo use several sizes of lettering and offer compact, interesting messages.

FIGURE 9.5
Three levels of text state (a) the theme, (b) simple orientation to the four sets of images, and (c) specific explanations of each set.

Zimmerman, 1991). Use both upper and lower cases for ease while reading; re-place signs written with all capitals (Figure 9.6). Detailed lettering should be kept below eye level to avoid neck craning for people who use bifocals.

Times—A serif type-face

THE LODGEPOLE PINE LIVES ONE OF THE MOST INTERESTING STORIES IN ALL THE FOREST WORLD. IT IS A PIONEER TREE, ONE OF THE FIRST AND MOST SUCCESSFUL TO TAKE POSSESSION OF BURNED-OVER AREAS. IT IS MOST EASILY KILLED BY FIRE, YET EVERY FOREST FIRE THAT SWEEPS ITS TERRITORY PROVES AN ADVANTAGE TO IT.

The lodgepole pine lives one of the most interesting stories in all the forest world. It is a pioneer tree, one of the first and most successful to take possession of burned-over areas. It is most easily killed by fire, yet every forest fire that sweeps its territory proves an advantage to it.

Helvetica—A sans serif font

THROUGHOUT THE WEST IN THE LAST FIFTY YEARS THE NUMEROUS FOREST FIRES HAVE ENABLED THE LODGEPOLE TO EXTEND ITS HOLDINGS GREATLY. A COMPLETE CESSATION OF FOREST FIRES WOULD ALMOST EXTERMINATE IT. IT MAY BE SAID TO COOPERATE WITH FIRES, SO CLOSELY IS ITS LIFE INTERRELATED WITH THEM.

Throughout the West in the last fifty years the numerous forest fires have enabled the lodgepole to extend its holdings greatly. A complete cessation of forest fires would almost exterminate it. It may be said to cooperate with fires, so closely is its life interrelated with them.

FIGURE 9.6 COMPARISON OF TYPE FACES AND LETTER CASES (TEXT FROM MILLS, 1920)

DESIGN TIPS—NEWSLETTERS

Specific recommendations on materials and production of newsletters appear in the booklet by Zehr, Gross and Zimmerman (1990). They also suggested the following general prin-ciples of newsletter design.

Format—Lay out the sequence of articles or sections of a newsletter; then stick with a consistent design. This will help readers to easily follow the logic and key points of the publication.

Length—Keep it short, preferably no more than eight pages. If it gets much longer, people are less likely to read it, thus wasting effort.

Nameplate and Masthead—The nameplate should be catchy and colorful. It should immediately connect the reader to the identity of the organization. The masthead contains the information about the newsletter such as volume number, the issue, and name of the organization; sometimes it includes the name and address of the editor(s), and board members, as well as a listing of what is inside.

Columns—One column across the entire page is easiest to format and gives a business-like appearance. Two columns work well for newsletters with long stories. They appear simple and uncluttered. The lines are longer than those in three column newsletters so they require less eye movement and less hyphenation. Three column newsletters are best for short stories or very brief news items. They also allow for the most flexibility in size of illustrations or photos.

Summary

The art of interpretive writing involves using artful language. Creative writing employs language that helps paint word pictures. It makes connections that allow readers to turn abstract letters and words into pictures in their minds. It builds bridges over which ideas may travel smoothly, making the journey from the page or label into the brain. It expresses ideas clearly, without deformation or distraction (Figure 9.7). Effective writing creates images that focus the readers' attention and interest, excite the imagination, provoke the deepest curiosity, and incite the true joy of greater perception.

The pen may be more powerful than the sword, but only if you know how to use it. Box 9.4, page 226, consolidates many of the principles and suggestions that will help a writer prepare messages that will have a high likelihood of being read and understood. The process of learning to write never ends. Hemingway once said about writers, "We are all apprentices in a craft where no one ever becomes a master." As with other skills, however, writing will improve with practice. The tips and principles in this chapter should speed the improvement of anyone's writing.

A powerful pen can stimulate most people's latent inclination to read. Interpreters face the challenge to write signs and labels with phrases that seem to reach out and grab people. They also must aspire to design publications that people find easy to pick up and hard to put down. Printed interpretation provides many opportunities to affect the visitors and the rest of society. An active writing program is indispensable to any complete interpretive effort.

The difference between the right word and the almost right word is the difference between lightning and the lightning bug.
—Mark Twain

FIGURE 9.7
Care in punctuation can clarify messages.
(NPS, Ronald G. Warfield)

BOX 9.4: Summary of Clear Writing Guidelines

ORGANIZATION

- Use headings and subheadings (these tell the reader what is coming next and break up long columns).
- Present only the most important information.

LANGUAGE AND STYLE

- Use short sentences: not more than 25 words.
- Use short paragraphs: not more than 60 words.
- Write in the active voice, not passive voice: *Read the instructions before beginning* seems easier to understand than *instructions should be read before beginning.*
- Use concrete examples to illustrate a point: *You get Vitamin A in dark green leafy vegetables and deep orange vegetables* is less concrete than *spinach, carrots, and squash are vegetables that have Vitamin A.*
- Avoid clichés and jargon: *Labels let you in on the inside* may be too abstract. *Container labels can tell you a lot about what's inside the package* is better.
- If you must use a technical unfamiliar word, explain the word with a simple definition or example.
- Repeat new or unfamiliar words several times to make them more familiar to the reader.
- Use positive statements: *Follow safe practices* is better than *Do not follow unsafe practices.*

DESIGN

- Use a left-justified margin.
- Use larger, easy-to-read type for text (10-12 point).
- Use upper and lower case letters—this style is easier to read than all capitals.

Source: Schuster and McAllister (1993).

Literature Cited

Edwards, Y. (1979). *The land speaks: Organizing and running an interpretation system.* Toronto, ON: The National and Provincial Parks Association of Canada.

Flesch, R. (1949). *The art of readable writing.* New York, NY: Harper & Bros.

Gunning, R. (1962). *New guide to more effective writing in business and industry.* Boston, MA: Industrial Education Institute.

Hay, V. (1990). *The essential feature: Writing for magazines and newspapers.* New York, NY: Columbia University Press

McIntosh, P. A. (1982). Signs and labels. In: G. W. Sharpe, *Interpreting the Environment (2nd ed.).* New York, NY: John Wiley & Sons, Inc.

Mills, E. A. (1920). *The adventures of a nature guide.* Garden City, NY: Doubleday, Page & Co.

Schuster, E. R. and McAllister, D. W. (1993). *Writing for a changing world; Reaching low literacy audiences with print material.* St. Paul, MN: University of Minnesota, North Central Regional Extension Publication No. 475 (folder).

Strunk, W. Jr. and White, E. B. (1979). *The elements of style (3rd ed.).* New York, NY: Macmillan.

Tilden, F. (1967). *Interpreting our heritage (rev. ed.).* Chapel Hill, NC: University of North Carolina Press.

Trapp, S., Gross, M., and Zimmerman, R. (1991). *Signs, trails, and wayside exhibits: Connecting people and places.* Stevens Point, WI: University of Wisconsin-Stevens Point Foundation Press.

Zehr, J., Gross, M. and Zimmerman, R. (1990). *Creating environmental publications.* Stevens Point, WI: University of Wisconsin-Stevens Point Foundation Press.

Exhibits and Museums

The most common perception that many people have about interpreters is of the uniformed guide at the head of a rugged trail, ready to lead a hike out onto the tundra of Alaska, into the towering redwoods, or around a Civil War battlefield. With wit, charm, and active intelligence, backed by a card file of enchanting stories, the ranger faces the visitors (or lack of them) ready to entice them into the mysteries of a complex location.

That image sketches only a partial picture of the interpreter of today. Interpretation also happens in museums, visitor centers, and entire villages full of characters who tell their story to the modern wayfarers who may pay to enter a special world. Often, the visitors arrive looking very "modern," which can give the interpreter an opening to bring them into the spirit of the historic time. For example, in one village, a male tourist bedecked in shorts, T-shirt, tennis shoes, and camera, stepped into a restored 1847 men's clothing store. The "proprietor" good-naturedly commented that he saw the poor fellow as "walking around town in his underwear, badly needing a good set of our new ready-made clothes and a silk hat to look proper on the streets of Harpers Ferry."

This chapter discusses the different kinds of museums, visitor centers and exhibits that interpreters use to get across their messages.

BASIC TERMINOLOGY

Exhibits come in all sorts of forms. Some are paintings or photographs in an exhibition. Some are living trees, swimming dolphins, or wayside signs placed in the foreground of an interesting outdoor scene. Some exhibits explain or model an industrial process visible through a window. Often they are panels, models, or an arrangement of real objects placed within a building (Figure 10.1, page 230).

Museums or Visitor Centers contain exhibits—or at least some of them. Some integrate the theme of the subject matter into the architecture. Others appear to be temples of treasures, secure places to carefully view the wonderful works of the masters or the diverse masterworks of nature. Others serve, literally or figuratively, as cathedrals, where one can reverentially review the glories of church history, art, music, or architecture. Cathedral-like forests often inspire attitudes of awe, especially when visitor centers at the entrance to their park present exhibits that give one pause.

FIGURE 10.1
Old Cars—the real thing—comprise part of a transportation museum at Luray Caverns in Virginia.

Centers and Museums

In the U.S., 7,000 museums interpret all aspects of life and its various curiosities. Another 1,500 museums in Canada, several hundred in Mexico, and at least 5,000 museums in Europe, including Britain's 2,000, combine to make up a tremendous cultural resource. Here, interpretation is the *raison d'être*, allowing people to learn about their local environment and history or about cultures from afar. The museum tradition thrives on all continents, with vigorous, long-term efforts throughout Latin America, Southeast Asia, Japan, China, Australia, and New Zealand. In Africa, some of the oldest and newest museums exist. Due to the current rapid growth of tourism in equatorial Africa, many new visitor centers and museums are focusing on tourists. The former USSR and eastern Europe, until recently, made museums out of many churches and opened up the treasures of the Czars and kings to public view. Recent changes and financial instability in these countries may set back museum work for a while.

The simplest classification of museum collections divides them into three types: art, historical, and science museums. The diversity of museums and collections defy such neat and simple classification, however. These museums cover art, science, natural history,

history, industry, religious groups, trades, professions, and transportation. Specialized museums exist for children and about farms. Others feature automobiles, glass, native peoples, cowboys, police, sports heroes, and loggers. They include planetaria, aquaria, herbaria, botanical, and zoological gardens.

The background of the word museum ("temple of the Muses," Gk) suggests some of the diversity of themes found there. The Muses of Greek mythology were the nine daughters of Zeus and Mnemosyne. Each presided over one of the arts to inspire mankind: Clio, Muse of history; Calliope of epic poetry; Erato of love poetry; Polyhymnia of sacred song; Euterpe of music; Thalia of comedy; Melpomene of tragedy; Terpsichore of dance; and Urania of astronomy.

Museums exist in national and state parks, in forests, in the heart of swamps, in city parks, in modest homes, storefronts, mansions, and major downtown edifices. Some are entire villages or towns. Others are scattered cabins, barns, and chapels united by interpreted walking and driving routes. One is in the outdoor space beside a newspaper plant, the Scranton (PA) Newseum; another graces the lobby and spacious halls of a podiatrist's office. In the word's most expansive form, national parks are said to be huge outdoor, living museums. This chapter focuses on the structures (some without roofs) that are normally identified as visitor centers and museums.

MUSEUM OR VISITOR CENTER?

Only a few of the U.S. "visitor centers" are listed by the American Association of Museums. These visitor centers occur throughout our public forests, parks, refuges, and along highways. Most of them have interpretation as a centerpiece.

Visitor centers and museums can be split into two categories or lumped as one rather diverse group. The basic interpretive concepts do not differ much, so they are treated together here. The distinctions that exist can be boiled down to the approach toward the subject matter.

1. The museum contains original objects, brought in for display and study in a convenient place, often close to where people live or travel. The objects often come from afar.

2. The interpretive center introduces original objects, places, or ideas that are found outside the door; it is a portal to the living museum

FIGURE 10.2
Visitor centers provide windows on and portals to the resources. (NPS)

beyond it (Figure 10.2). Both serve as orientation and educational institutions to the greater world around them. The visitor center at a natural or historical resource area serves to make the visit more meaningful, with the focus on the outdoors or historic phenomena (Figure 10.3).

FIGURE 10.3
The Forest Service's Portage Lake Visitor Center gets into its theme.

3. Another kind of interpretive facility is the historical structure or site, located wherever history put it, often accompanied by a separate visitor center or museum. In most cases, the battlefield or building itself serves as a form of museum but not always as a shelter for artifacts.

4. A related facility that is somewhat interpretive is the tourist information center. It offers mainly accommodation and attraction information, orienting visitors to recreational and interpretation opportunities. Most of these are neither museums nor interpretive centers as such. Some, however, contain interpretive exhibits. Their location is a function of travel patterns, at the portals of a state or province, or major road junctions of a local area. A few use historical buildings as their venues.

Museums are "in the serious business of trying to make objects speak effectively." What museums do is take objects out of context (collected) and then try to restore context to "allow them to speak directly to visitors, even carry on a dialogue with them." The client is an important part of the dynamic of the object. A key evaluative question asks if your restored context is appropriate to its different audiences (Spock, 1990).

History of Museums

To collect and conserve and exhibit curious, precious, and beautiful things seems to go with human nature. Although modern public museums seem to be somewhat new, the basic idea of exhibiting collections of things goes back to ancient times. The Greeks who went to the Delphi Oracle carried statues and other gifts that were kept in Treasuries, or temple-like warehouses. Today, many of these treasures can be seen in museums near the ruins of the treasury buildings at Delphi and other points throughout Greece (and in European museums). The same is true of Egypt and China and other ancient civilizations that have not been totally ravaged. On the Acropolis in Athens, one of the prominent buildings bears the name pinakotheke—a gallery featuring collections of paintings that honored the gods.

Chinese, Japanese, Muslim, and Christian tombs, temples, mosques, and cathedrals served as repositories for relics and art work considered precious. In medieval Europe, princes, dukes, kings, and bishops were avid collectors. Many European royal private collections featured works of art. The objects served as a form of prestige and accumulated wealth that could be used to raise funds for military campaigns and other state expenses. The relics of Christiandom were involved in a lively economic trade (Lewis, 1990). One result of the Crusades was the transfer of pillaged Middle Eastern art works to western Europe.

Colonization of Africa likewise produced numerous natural, mineral, and cultural specimens for the growing number of show places in Europe. Back in the seats of power, the people could see the wonders of the far-flung "empires." The collections and their study did much to advance science and to broaden knowledge of the diversity of the world. Colonial museums were also developed in central and southern Africa, notably in Zimbabwe (1901), Uganda (1908), Kenya (1909), Mozambique (1913), and various cities of South Africa (Lewis, 1990). Most newly-independent African nations recently started to advance their own museum traditions; they are proceeding with enthusiasm, despite weak funding in most cases. International agencies help with some of the financing and technical assistance.

Natural history became of major interest with the growth of international commerce. Exotic curiosities seemed to attract the most attention. In Italy, 250 or more natural history collections were recorded in the 16th century, including an herbarium of Luca Ghini at Padua (Lewis, 1990). Other early museums appear in Table 10.1 (see page 235) to illustrate the diversity of purpose and wide distribution of museum efforts.

The educational value of many museums became evident in the Victorian period. Vogel (1991) noted that Victorians were the great museum builders. "They sought to collect and assemble materials, to categorize and organize them to try to comprehend the technological, cultural, and natural information explosion." The sheer bulk of information the century generated, the sheer pace of scientific advance it maintained, required new organizational schemes to make sense of the flood of new data (Vogel, 1991). The Victorians developed displays of natural specimens in schools and universities. "They organized museums to satisfy their curiosity and to instruct themselves."

Local museums throughout England received support through national subsidies. They received Parliaments' authorization to collect and display local historic, artistic, industrial and natural features.

In Russia the revolution of 1917 ushered out the "royalty" of the Czars and ushered in an egalitarian philosophy. For at least two reasons many royal collections were opened— first, politically, to demonstrate the opulence of the oppressive Czars and secondly to encourage education and culture for all the people. The artifacts of history and culture of the states were displayed and interpreted for all to see at little or no cost. Any pre-1990 visitor to Moscow and Leningrad could not help but be impressed at the long lines of museum attendees, even in cold weather. Likewise, the numbers of palaces, churches, and other buildings used as museums was impressive.

The Wagner Free Institute of Science, in Philadelphia, pioneered as a strongly educational museum. William Wagner sponsored its construction (1859-1865). He believed that popular education was a powerful instrument for bettering society. His Institute began as an educational endeavor; the auditorium held a key role as the site of lectures by 19th-century leaders; the museum was intended to illustrate the lecture programs (Vogel, 1991). The exhibits included one of the first American direct visual comparisons between monkey and human bones (1880). The exhibit design drew attention first to the striking similarities and then to the subtle variations that comprised Darwin's Law of Natural Selection. The philosophy of educating the public, even using controversial findings, thus enjoys a long tradition.

National museums now represent part of many nations' cultural identities. Since the middle 1800s, one could ask "what's a good country without a national museum?" In 1802, the Hungarian Assembly founded a national museum in Pest, using private collections. Many others followed, throughout central and southern Europe. By 1846, an Englishman's gift to the U.S. started the national museum complex named for the benefactor, James Smithson. One of the first large publicly owned museums developed in 1852 as the Victoria and Albert Museum, featuring decorative arts and crafts. It still operates in London, as the first of the modern public museums (Grinder and McCoy, 1985). Today, most nations have one or more national museum. Likewise, most states*, provinces, counties, and cities have one or more public museum to promote education about the area. Now in at least two-thirds of the world, the question is "what's a good city or county without a local or regional museum?"

Most counties of 100,000 people or more will have at least an art museum, a historical museum, and some sort of nature center, supported primarily by local taxpayers and donors. In addition, there are few North American local park systems of any size or significance that do not have their own visitor centers or museums featuring natural or cultural history of the area.

Modern museums and interpretive exhibit centers are largely products of the late 1700s and early 1800s. Great Britain's Parliament acted in 1753 to establish the public British Museum. France opened royal collections to the public in 1789. These spearheaded the move from private aristocratic collections to public access.

Interpretive or educational museums in the U.S. trace back at least to painter-collector-public educator Charles Wilson Peale in Philadelphia. He opened his Museum of Natural History in the mid-1780s, with the patronage of Thomas Jefferson. Peale's rather eclectic collection included scientific curiosities, mounted animals and birds, patriotic symbols and his paintings of the heroes of the American Revolution (Vogel, 1991). Peale's museum attracted many who became influential in their own right, including painters George Catlin and John James Audubon.

Peale's museum started in his home, then moved to the American Philosophical Society and subsequently to the State House (now known as Independence Hall). Many decades later, P. T. Barnum bought the collections (Vogel, 1991). Peale's museum helped create an informed public that the new nation needed for success. The key was that it was not a museum for the elite or for one man's private collection. Peale reached out to educate the public, to offer knowledge, a chance to see the real things, beyond what one could see with personal resources.

---

* The State of Pennsylvania alone maintains 28 state museums, widely scattered, and helps support 31 others. Wisconsin has eight state museums in various parts of the state each representing a different major subject. Additionally, most towns and cities and many private groups have their own museums throughout these two states.

TABLE 10.1 EARLY MAJOR MUSEUMS

ESTAB-LISHED	NAME	LOCATION	KINDS OF EXHIBITS AVAILABLE
1471	Museo Capitolino	Rome, Italy	Paintings, sculpture
1565	Galleria degli Uffizi	Florence, Italy	Art
1635	Musée d'Histoire Naturelle	Paris, France	Outdoor gardens, botany, zoology, geology, comparative anatomy
1650	Rosenberg Slot	Copenhagen, Den.	Castle, arms, crown jewels
1683	Ashmolean Museum	Oxford, England	Art, archæology
1694	Natural History Museum	Berne, Switzerland	Africa and Swiss mammals alpine natural history
1731	National Museum	Dublin, Eire	Art, industry, history
1748	Naturhistorisches Museum	Vienna, Austria	Minerals, natural sciences, prehistory
1759	British Museum	London, England	Natural history, writings, multi-topical
1761	Museo Nacional Chile	Santiago, Chile	Prehistory, history, military, anthropology
1778	Central Museum of Indonesian Culture	Jakarta, Indonesia	Cultural, art, natural history
1785	Salon del Prado	Madrid, Spain	Art
1786	Peale Museum	Philadelphia, USA	Art, natural history
1793	Louvre	Paris, France	Art
1804	New York Historical Society	New York, USA	General American history
1812	Museo Argentino de Ciencias Naturales	Buenos Aires, Arg.	Science, native music (2 million exhibits)
1812	Academy of Natural Sciences of Philadelphia	Philadelphia, USA	Natural history
1818	Museu Nacional do Brasil	Rio de Janeiro, Brazil	Architecture, paleontology, ethnography, art, geology, natural science
1823	Brooklyn Institute of Arts and Sciences	New York, USA	Music, fine arts, architecture
1824	Museo Nacional	Bogotá, Colombia	History, conquest/colony
1827	Australian Museum	Sydney, Australia	Nat. history, ethnology, palæontology, minerals
1836	Alte Pinakothek	Munich, Germany	Paintings and sculpture
1846	Smithsonian Institution	Washington, DC	Multi-museum group
1860	Univ. New Brunswick	Fredericton, NB	Natural history of Canada
1862	Munic. Museum & Library	Guayaquil, Ecuador	Local history and culture
1872	Tromsö Museum	Tromsö, Norway	Scientific expedition collections
1894	Norsk Folksmuseum	Oslo, Norway	Open air folk crafts, village, Ibsen home

Source: adapted from Hall-Quest (1962) and Lewis (1990).

The educational function was atypical of many early museums. When wealthy individuals collected and stored precious metals, art, or artifacts in castles or churches, few people saw these treasures. Later, display took precedence and then interpretation/education became important. The move away from private collections to public education was most clearly marked by the opening of the British Museum with a stated mandate that its collections were "not only for the inspection and entertainment of the learned and the curious, but for the general use and benefit of the public" (Lewis, 1990).

The architectural design of many older museums reflects the Treasury influence of ancient times. Only in the twentieth century did the architecture reflect the new emphasis on public education (Figure 10.4). The use of natural materials and architecture that blended into the landscape of national parks led the way toward museums that focused on visitor use and relevance to the environment being interpreted.

The number and size of museums grew rapidly in the 20th century. In England, dozens of private museums, garden centers, and animal collections attract paying visitors. So do hundreds of local and county museums as well as several impressive national institutions. By 1990, there were about 7,000 museums in the U.S. listed by the American Association of Museums and many more small collections and interpretive centers of public agencies not included in the list. History and art top the list of favorite themes, followed by natural history. Then come many specialized collections such as automobiles, agricultural implements, ethnic culture, and many other specific topics. The types of museums range from scantily-labeled collections of miscellaneous "old things" to the dynamic and carefully researched "talking exhibits" in the dozens of theme museums at Walt Disney World.

GOVERNMENT MUSEUM DEVELOPMENT

Many early government interpretive museums and visitor centers started with private impetus and funding as well as from individual curators or rangers taking the initiative. Of course, the classic example is the Smithsonian Institution, established with the 1846 bequest from James Smithson, who had never seen the United States. Smithson saw the museum as an interpretive medium "for the increase and diffusion of knowledge among men." Today's 14 museums and the National Zoo support a large research component as well as many diverse educational/interpretive programs, publications, and traveling exhibits.

Another key example is the case of the National Park Service. Ranger Frank Pinkley started a collection of artifacts and structural information at Casa Grande in Arizona in 1901, long before there was a park service or any official effort to set up museums. National Park Service exhibits and museums officially began in Yosemite National Park, where Ansel Hall started the collection of natural materials and cultural artifacts in 1920, opening it to the public that summer in the ranger office. Its growth and popularity led to a move to Chris Jorgensen's old artist studio. A few years later, J. D. Rockefeller, Jr. supplied the funds to build a larger, new museum in the valley.

Congress acted slowly to fund the National Park Service's early efforts (1918-24), although agency officials believed in the idea of park interpretive museums. NPS Director

Stephen Mather wrote in his 1920 annual report to the Secretary of the Interior: "One of the most important matters to receive earnest consideration is the early establishment of adequate museums in every one of our parks" (Burns, 1941). Nevertheless, it took financial support of private groups for public park museums to begin. Their success finally convinced the U.S. Congress that interpretive museums were popular and important. Among the notable early contributors, besides park rangers and superintendents, were the Yosemite Museum Association, the American Association of Museums, the Carnegie family and the Rockefeller family (Table 10.2). The private philanthropy did not end when the government finally formalized the National Park Service in 1916 and gave it some museum funding in the mid-1920s. When Hall became chief naturalist of the national parks in 1923, Carl P. Russell replaced him at Yosemite. Russell continued to work with exhibits. In 1933, he became the first head of museums for the National Park Service. By 1935, he hired several young men with backgrounds in anthropology, botany, and entomology (Ralph Lewis, 1992). They worked under Depression-era programs, usually on contract with no permanent status. They moved from park to park, making plans and installing exhibits. Many of their rustic designs still stand, now often protected as historic buildings.

TABLE 10.2 SELECTED EARLY NATIONAL PARK MUSEUM STARTS AND THEIR FUNDING SOURCES

FACILITY	START	FUNDING SOURCES
Mesa Verde Museum	1918	NPS, Mrs. Stella Leviston, CCC, PWA
Yosemite Valley Museum	1920	Yosemite Museum Assoc, AAM*, CCC, PWA, NPS
Mammoth Hot Spgs, Yellowst	1920	NPS, AAM*
Crater Lake-Information/Museum	1921	Kiser Studio, NPS
Petersburg VA museum	1925-40	NPS, CCC
Yavapai Point trailside museums	1926	AAM, Carnegie, et al.
Montezuma Castle Museum	1927-35	NPS, in private buildings
Hawaii National Park	1927-39	NPS, HI Volcanic Research Association, George Lycurgus
Mount Rainier	1928	NPS
Yellowstone—4+ museums	1928	AAM*, NPS
Lassen Volcanic	1929	NPS, Mr and Mrs. B. F. Loomis
Crater Lake-observation station	1930	NPS, Carnegie
Rocky Mountain Museum/Information	1931	NPS, Jonas Bros., Colorado Museum of Natural History
Many parks	1933-41	PWA, CCC, WPA, some private money through NPS

Abbreviations: AAM = American Association of Museums;
(*) = funded by Laura Spelman Rockefeller Memorial;
CCC = Civilian Conservation Corps;
NPS = National Park Service (Congressional funding);
PWA = Public Works Administration;
WPA = Works Progress Administration.

Source: Burns (1941).

The excitement of the ride on the museum administration wagon comes from the frequent variation in funding. Federal, state and local government funding often stays in low, slow gear, with occasional spurts of generous speed, while the museums operate at a higher speed. Private donations of funds and personal time and talents make possible more rapid progress. Although government funding supposedly may suffer fewer ups and downs than the private infusions of capital, election year variations often reveal cuts by officials trying to exhibit their tax-saving prudence or generosity to show their concern for public culture and education.

What's a Museum Do?

In 1895, George Brown Goode defined a museum as " . . . an institution for the preservation of those objects which best illustrate the phenomena of nature and the works of man, and the utilization of these for the increase of knowledge and for the culture and enlightenment of the people" (Burns, 1941).

Goode also said museums are agents of change—"passionless reformers." Passion motivates many specialized modern museums however; they seek to influence minds toward a particular point of view. For example, Chicago's Peace Museum unabashedly presents a strong point of view; curators developed its exhibits to passionately advocate pacifism. Visitors learn of the icons and issues that drive pacifists and may be persuaded to "reform." An art museum that did not somehow advocate the value of art would seem particularly dry, as would a nature center that didn't somehow nurture admiration and care of the natural environment.

THE NATURE OF MUSEUMS

Modern museums serve as interpretive environments, first and foremost. Museums must be beautiful—visually attractive. Museums must convey a message—visually intelligible. A design or exhibit can be beautiful but unintelligible; a poor floor plan or exhibit arrangement may cause confusion or mislead the viewer.

Museums function primarily as places for people, not just places for storing artifacts and collections. Indeed, the things stay in an exhibit much longer than the people stay in the exhibit hall, but the reason they lie there is to tweak people's minds, to pique their curiosity, to provoke them into further study or research, and to help them leave the museum with a new sense of perception.

The museum that serves as an on-site visitor center usually seeks to excite people about what lies outside. It produces so much interest that they cannot resist going forth into nature or into the historical milieu beyond the walls to see for themselves the phenomena described within. This type of nature center is a gateway, an entry lock, and an introduction to some real place just beyond the doors. It prepares the mind and spirit to see more and perceive more, to put things in context. The museum also serves as a reference collection, so visitors can return and check on their finds, and focus their observations into a more complete, integrated image of time, space, interrelationships, and diversity.

FUNCTIONS AND OBJECTIVES

The functions that characterize a museum, according to National Park Service museum expert Ralph Lewis (1976), include these three:

- It assembles and preserves objects.
- It provides opportunities for object-centered research.
- It interprets through contact with the real things in it.

The British Museum (Natural History) expressed similar terms to state its objectives (Chalmers, 1989):

> The Museum's objectives are firstly to discover and make available to the scientific community the information contained within its collections of natural objects and secondly to entertain, interest and educate children and adults in natural history.

Interpretation in museums and visitor centers brings the objects and the people together in a meaningful way. The people see and study real objects (Figure 10.5). Object-based learning has several advantages over word-based learning. Among them, objects emphasize the role of things in our own lives; "Things form our world and are as significant to us as language for comprehending it; they aid us in obtaining food, water, warmth and shelter . . ." (Durbin, Morris and Wilkinson, 1990). Objects help us link our lives to other societies, past and present. Objects also provide a concrete experience that illuminates abstract thought.

Objects help motivate a desire to know, and create a need to learn more. Objects provide creative and emotional stimulus for art, writing, or drama. Real objects, as compared to abstract ideas, aid the memory through physical sensations. Finally, everyone can use objects, whether they can read or not (Durbin, Morris, and Wilkinson, 1990).

FIGURE 10.5
Historic homes and farms often show processes of everyday life.

People go to museums and exhibit centers for many reasons, including some that are mundane and some that are functional. Art museum director Thomas P. F. Hoving once described in personal terms the biggest motives for going to any museum (McDarrah, 1967):

> Presumably, you are relatively aware of your daily surroundings. If you are also a bit curious as to how it is that your life runs along particular lines, and that you are surrounded by particular objects, and that certain things seem beautiful to you—if you are just a bit curious about the condition of man—then you are a museum person. Not every day, but every once in a while you feel like seeing something other than your four walls. These are the times that you go to a museum.

Services offered by museums range widely. Those commonly available at large museums for the general public, students and researchers include the following:

Library
Bookstore/gift shop
Books, brochures, research reports printed by the museum
Member reception rooms; occasionally, overnight rooms
Restaurant, lunch room
Audiovisual collections and equipment, with slides, photographic prints, films, and models
Research staff and programs
Exhibit loan services, circulating exhibits to schools; mobile exhibit vans
Exhibit space for borrowed exhibits and programs
Reference and information retrieval service (computerized)
Lecture halls/studios with classes, staff lectures, visiting talks
Auditorium sometimes used for plays, recitals, films
Guided tours of museum and grounds
Personal interpretive services on the museum floors
Field excursions and travel club programs.

EXHIBITING CONTROVERSY

One of the opportunities for natural history or history exhibits comes when a scientific controversy arises. Black (1992) described a 1987 exhibit in the then British Museum (Natural History). A vigorous discussion about the origin of birds was led by Sir Fred Hoyle and Chandra Wickramasinghe, who alleged that archæopteryx, the earliest known bird, was a fraud. Instead of taking a position on one side or the other, the museum presented both sides and let the public sense the debate, judge the evidence and reach their own conclusions. To represent one side, the museum science staff wrote an analysis of the questioned specimens. Then, the arguments of Hoyle and Wickramasinghe were put beside them in an interesting exhibit.

"Almost every natural history museum uses the diorama to present a glimpse of some aspect of the natural world" (Black, 1992). These recreated mini-habitat groups let visitors glimpse environments that most will never see first hand (Figure 10.6). Black (1992) criticized them as being "valid but romanticised reminders of the past . . . " seldom labeled as such. He saw opportunities lost in the absence of mention of the disruptions that occur in these habitats by human intervention, by housing developments, elimination of fence rows in farms, extending agriculture into new areas of Africa where spraying American chemicals allows elimination of disease-carrying flies. He also criticized insect and bird displays that show hundreds of species without raising questions about species definition and relationship, about the species disappearing, about habitat destruction, and about the species yet little known. In other words, the museum research staff does many things and is concerned about many issues that are seldom discussed. This same idea can be tied to evolution charts, which often look like clear highways with neat exit ramps to major groups of animals; somehow the primates and humans often end up at the top of these charts of the descent of *Homo sapiens*. The controversies, the alternate theories, the debate about the rate and timing of changes, the gaps in the record, the doubts about relationships lead well-read visitors to regard the evolution chart as quaint, dogmatic expression of one version of a theory.

Providing facts and objects for the public to weigh may be the best service that a museum interpretive program can provide; Black (1992) asked:

> As the world changes around us at a bewildering pace . . . what role should our public institutions play? Should we be passive, presenting what used to be or what may still rarely be? Should we be activists presenting information on extinction as an accelerating process and the reasons behind that acceleration? Or should we try . . . to present the facts, all the facts available please, in the expectation that our visitors, given information, are indeed capable of reaching their own conclusions? We must recognize, however, that these conclusions . . . may not be those that we had intended. . . . I believe that we must nevertheless opt for the latter course.

It surely does not seem wise to make the museum/interpretive staff out to be the arbiters or authorities of scientific endeavor. If they are careful and competent scientists, they will qualify their enthusiasms and treat many of their conclusions as tentative hypotheses. Yet, Black (1992) noted that museum interpretation may often be more pedantic than open: "There is no doubt that in the United States, as in Britain, pedagogy poses an acute problem in museums of natural history." The controversies raging around many current issues on natural

FIGURE 10.6
Animals at an African water hole stand in a life-sized habitat diorama at the Denver Museum of Natural History.

history, not to mention human history, often receive little coverage in museum public programs. Things are presented as fact when, indeed, there is a lot of interesting controversy about the topic perhaps running nightly on television news shows.

Diverse Museums for Diverse Purposes

RURAL AND AGRICULTURAL MUSEUMS

Several score museums in North America fall into the category of farm or agricultural museums. Hundreds of others are village museums with farming life as a feature.

These museums defeat the lament that history is boring. They show what happened to the commoner, they strengthen a sense of heritage. These museums contain people who resemble those of the period by using artifacts or replicas. They come out from behind the glass into a human environment, no longer separated from their time or function (Alegre, 1978).

They all feature the physical evidence of the rural way of life in some past era. Many of them include a small village with buildings devoted to various trades and professions important to survival and comfort in a rural village (Figure 10.7). They also include at least one farmhouse, tool shed, house garden, and small field. A barn, several farm animals, a corral,

and pasture give a sense of the important role of animals.

Some agricultural museums give a sense of farm life as isolated and distant from others. In many, the emphasis on buildings more than fields and pastures keeps visitor interest alive, providing variety and a flow of interesting exhibits (Table 10.3, page 244). These museums compact into a relatively small area the many aspects of rural life, providing the visitor the opportunity to see in a few hours what the farmer may have experienced in a week or a month or more.

FIGURE 10.7
A Plimoth Plantation roofer pauses to interpret his raw materials and technique.

Buildings typically include:

Farm/ranch house	Cook kitchen	Outhouse
Chicken coop	Barn	Mill (e.g., grist, saw)
Shed for agricultural	Church	Lawyer's office
implements (usually many of them)	Doctor's office	Pharmacy/Apothecary
Blacksmith shop	Cooper's shop	

Some historical farmsteads limit themselves to only the buildings that were on the site at the time of residence of a famous person. One example is the Ethan Allen Homestead in Vermont, where the house and barn are the only historical structures. Nearby are a large interpretive building and the offices/shops of the Winooski Valley Park District; they clearly

are not historical in color or style and provide little confusion with the farmstead itself. John Brown's Farm, near Lake Placid, likewise features the house, barn, fields and gardens of the original farm (Figure 10.8). Support buildings hold the office (no interpretive center) and home of the manager, painted and somewhat apart, allowing the visitor to imagine the rural character of the area, despite the Olympic ski jump structures on the near horizon.

FIGURE 10.8
John Brown's farmstead near Lake Placid, NY, provides a very simple glimpse of one aspect of his complex life.

The fields and pastures are usually small, not in proportion to their critical function as the principal areas of production of agricultural income that supported the family. Rather, they serve as interpretive fields and gardens, where methods and crops can be demonstrated to visitors.

TABLE 10.3 SELECTED AGRICULTURAL/VILLAGE MUSEUMS IN THE U.S. AND CANADA

PLACE	NAME OF MUSEUM (OWNER)	BUILDINGS	PERIOD	ATTENDANCE
Colorado	White House Ranch Historical Site (Municipal)	3 open	1860-1907	63,000
Delaware	The Delaware Agricultural Museum (State)	11	19th Century	25,000
Massachusetts	Old Sturbridge Village (Private)	40+	1830s	500,000
Maryland	Carroll Co. Farm Museum(County)	11	1800s	80,000
North Carolina	Tobacco Farm Life Museum (Private)	4	1900	
Nova Scotia	Ross Farm Museum	10	1800s	28,000
Nevada	The Farmers' Museum, Inc. (Private)	12	19th Century	90,000
Ontario	Black Creek Pioneer Village (Municipal)	33	1860-67	216,000
Saskatchewan	Western Development Museums (Private)	30 buildings 4 locations	1920s	N/A
Utah	R. V. Jensen Living History Farm (University)	7	1917	15,000
Vermont	Billings Farm & Museum (Private)	4 major	1890	57,000
Wisconsin	Stonefield Village (State)	38	1890s	14,000

In Westminster, Maryland, the Carroll County Farm Museum converted the abandoned county "poor farm" into an educational resource. The land and buildings went to the County Park and Recreation Department. A volunteer Board of Governors operates the property as a very active living history agricultural farm museum. The large alms-house serves partly as offices and partly (six rooms) to represent a farm residence. Costumed interpreters explain the house features, play the organ, and get people thinking about the implements of everyday living. Outside, the men's dormitory rooms now house different crafts and offices. A blacksmith, a collection of interpreted farm vehicles and instruments, live farm animals, gardens, and several craftspersons add to the color and interest. The "general store" sells many of the crafts products. On the 140 acres are pastures and woods, a pond and creeks, all connected by interpreted nature trails. The exciting part of this museum is its dynamism. It is not a place to visit but once in fourth grade or just when the British relatives come visiting. Active programming and monthly changes in some exhibits offer plenty of information. During the period from April through October, there are sixteen special events plus three week-long living history camps for 9 to 12-year-olds. After a late October closing, the farm museum nine-day Christmas open house starts the holiday season after Thanksgiving. Each of the special events offers several carefully interpreted activities, often bringing in specialists to work with the regular interpretive staff.

These are some of the events:

Jubilee (Older Americans)	Fiddlers Convention
Maryland Beef Festival	Therapeutic Recreation Day
Steam Show Days	Maryland Wine Festival
Blacksmiths' Day	Fall Harvest Days
Victorian Tea Party in Flower Garden.	

All activities and visits to the farm carry a charge.

At Patrick Point State Park in northern California, Sumêg, a Yurok Village, interprets the area's Native American past and ties it to the people of today through ceremonies, dances, and direct involvement in rough and tumble games. On special occasions, acorn soup, elk and salmon barbecue, canoe building, and traditional gambling games are available. After years of budget cuts, setbacks and struggle, the village dedication finally occurred in September, 1990. Its recreated buildings, dance rings, fields, and pools have been busy every since. The Sumêg Advisory Committee approves all facilities, programming, and Environmental Living Programs.

Many private villages preceded these two examples. In 1891, Artur Hazelius founded the Skånsen Folk Museum, an open air Swedish museum. Hazelius felt that the structures and farm implements alone presented only a dry shell of the past, so he added appropriately dressed people to demonstrate and tell the story. The concept has spread to Africa, India, Indonesia, Europe, and the Americas (Alegre, 1978).

In the 1920s, the Rockefeller family funded Colonial Williamsburg. Every year, it takes several hundred thousands visitors into a bygone era, so they can better understand where and why they are now, as well as who once lived here. Colonial Williamsburg usually seems to operate at a loss, but at great benefit and technical and inspirational support to the others who seek to put on this type of programming. Its staff pioneered many restoration methods.

Near Plymouth Rock lies another private village that recreates the past (Figure 10.9). Plimoth Plantation takes the visitor into the 1600s with its architecture, clothing, and economy. First person portrayals include many accents from the various parts of Great Britain. These people are backed by an extensive research and training program. They represent the unsung heroes of Plymouth—the roofer, the milkmaid, the indentured servants, the mothers and children, and, often, Elder Brewster. Someone explains that Govenor Bradford is off governing and that Miles Standish is out on a surveying job, but he should be back this evening, if you care to wait. Meanwhile, there's work to be done, such as gardening, milking, preparing the stew, weaving, blacksmithing, and keeping over 30 buildings in repair.

In Indiana, a large 1830 farm and rural village at Conner Prairie operates privately through an Earlham College foundation. It takes visitors of all ages back to school under the stern, vigorous tutelage of a schoolmarm

FIGURE 10.9
Plimoth Plantation employees use first person interpretation, adopting the work, dress, accent, and knowledge of a 1627 settler near Plymouth Rock.

who reminds the class when regular payment by the parents comes due. A blacksmith hammers and argues with his wife, a maid offers a look into the Conner House, and a dozen villagers do their daily chores, interrupting their work to talk with visitors. A sturdy, weathered fence screens the village from the modern entry building with its exhibits, sales center and fine dining room. Nearby, a naturalist conducts a variety of programs about uses of plants and animals in the early days.

FIGURE 10.10
Morwellham Quay provides a chance for visitors to dress in vintage clothing and offers photographic/video mementos of the experience.

Acadian Village, New Brunswick, Canada, celebrates the return of the Acadians from "Cajun" Louisiana (1780-1880). Expelled in 1755 for refusing to swear allegiance to Britain, some filtered back. The 3,000-acre marsh and village show how deprived but persistent people reclaimed the swampy seaside with canals and dikes to grow hay and food. Forty buildings and pioneer skill demonstrations are based on careful research by the provincial government.

Morwellham Quay, Devon, England, is a commercial outdoor living history museum, reviving an old mining and shipping town, with costumed interpreters and sales persons of the past century (Figure 10.10). It offers dozens of experiences such as horse-drawn wagon rides, a tram tour through a tin mine, and a photo opportunity while wearing Victorian clothing.

On a smaller scale, Pioneer Village in Worthington, MN, rebuilt a 19th century agricultural settlement of 30 buildings. The Nobles County Historical Society shows off the church, school, lawyer's office and log house.

South Park City in Fairplay, CO, also contains 30 buildings; they resemble the shops, professions, and industries of a 19th century mining town. The original brewery, mining equipment and narrow-gauge railroad join with the buildings to re-create the three street town.

In Kentucky, Daniel Boone's village of Boonsboro is kept alive in a state park. In rural Arizona, a ranch called Pioneer Arizona relives the cowboy life as a private interpretive effort. Massachusetts' venerable Old Sturbridge Village, South Carolina's Middleton Plantation, and Des Moines' Living History Farms represent the many outstanding efforts—mostly self-supporting or foundation supported—to bring past events alive.

A sampling of other interpretive villages and agricultural museums:

The Loyalist Farm, Upper Canada Village, Morrisburg, Ontario
The Farmers Museum, Cooperstown, New York
Ontario Agricultural Museum, Milton, Ontario
Old Bethpage, Old Bethpage, New York
Colonial Pennsylvania Plantation, Edgemont, Pennsylvania
Quiet Valley Living Historical Farm, Stroudsburg, Pennsylvania
Amish Farm and House, Lancaster, Pennsylvania
Pennsylvania Farm and Museum of Landis Valley, Lancaster, Pennsylvania
Oxon Hill Children's Farm, Oxon Hill, Maryland
George Washington Birthplace, Washington Birthplace, Virginia
Turkey Run Farm, McLean, Virginia
Westville, Lumpkin, Georgia
Agrirama, Tifton, Georgia
Shakertown, Pleasant Hill, Kentucky
Pioneer Farmstead, Great Smoky Mountains National Park, Tennessee
Lincoln Boyhood Home National Memorial, Lincoln City, Indiana
Greenfield Village, Dearborn, Michigan
Mississippi Agricultural Museum, Jacksonville, Mississippi
Gibbs Farm Museum, Saint Paul, Minnesota
Agricultural Hall of Fame and National Center, Bonner Springs, Kansas
Old Cienega Village Museum, Santa Fe, New Mexico
Pipe Spring National Monument, Moccasin, Arizona
Living History Farm, Des Moines, Iowa
Camillus Nelson State Historical Farm, Sacramento, California
Pioneer Museum and Haggin Galleries, Stockton, California
Bybee-Howell House and Pioneer Orchard, Portland, Oregon
Kipahula Living Farm, Hana, Maui, Hawaii.

ROLES OF VISITOR CENTERS

Visitor centers in the natural or historical environment play a key role in the interpretive process. The prime objective is to give visitors information on the spot which will encourage going out and seeing for oneself, rather than lingering inside as in a city museum or library (Beazley, 1971). They usually serve as the portals through which visitors enter the interpretive experiences of a resource.

They serve as headquarters for interpretation—the place to check on what, when, and where things are going to happen—the starting point for interpretation. They also may house the reference collection for visitors who, having experienced the resource at some level, want to come back for more information, check details, verify their personal interpretation or identification of the land. This last function dominated the early National Park museums and led to the parks being called museums. Over time, their orientation role grew and their reference role diminished; with these changes came the name "visitor center." Curatorship of large collections is usually not possible in most field interpretive visitor centers.

In some cases, the museum is the resource itself. "A historic building authentically furnished and exhibited becomes a museum" (Lewis, 1976). This occurs in most historic homes, e.g., James Whitcomb Riley house; in ruins of earlier cultures, e.g., Mesa Verde; and in many military installations, e.g., Fort Knox State Park in Maine. The structure itself becomes a specimen, one that also must handle streams of visitors. Under the principles of accuracy and authenticity, the building's doors, stairways, windows, carpeting remain in or are restored to historic condition. On the other hand, laws and ethics require a system of access for visitors with limited mobility. Reinforcement for durability and interpretation to handle hundreds of visitors per day also will modify the historic conditions somewhat (Lewis, 1976). The need for balance of appropriate preservation and interpretive use often produces ingenious solutions and compromises.

Museum Philosophy

Appropriations for [museums] are as much a duty of the government as for any other purpose connected with the true welfare of the people. . . . It is requisite that our public should have free access to museums.
—James Jackson Jarves (1864)

Museum professionals have long discussed the tension between protecting research collections and using artifacts for education. Curators thought of themselves as the key professionals and restricted themselves to collections and exhibit design. Educators came later and were often regarded as a strange, nice, but perhaps less necessary breed—teachers in the museum. This perception changed in most museums. Curators of Education now work as partners with other professionals in making major decisions and designs. The educational function dominates the thinking of many museums and all interpretive centers.

Yet, the discussion continues. The museum is an effective social instrument, with the aim of preserving and presenting "cultural goods" and stories involving art, history, or environmental themes.

Museums have implicit responsibilities with natural and cultural heritage to:
- collect and preserve the past,
- record and educate the present, and
- provide perspective and inspiration for the future.

George Brown Goode (1888) wrote that "the people's museum should be more than a house full of specimens in glass cases. It should be a house full of ideas, arranged with the strictest attention to system." A well-designed museum can cultivate the powers of observation. Even casual visitors can make discoveries for themselves.

DEFINING THE CLIENTELE

Should a museum reach the entire public or is it an institution for the few who are prepared (and interested) to use it? In this democratic period, most societies have opened museums to all comers. The free or low-cost museum opens the option of seeing and studying the works, the stories, the science of the past, along with opinions about the present and future to everyone. Thus, scientific and artistic knowledge was opened to all, and no longer confined to aristocratic classes. In the early days, this may have been more symbolic of democratic principles than a reality. Physical admission did not necessarily open or prepare the minds of many to comprehend the museum experience. However, with growing public education, museums became more accessible to the public.

This philosophy came long ago. The influential George Brown Goode (1888) declared: "The museums of the future in this democratic land should be adapted to the needs of the mechanic, the factory operator, the day laborer, the salesman, and the clerk, as much as to those of the professional man and the man of leisure." In other words, he said, "the public museum is, first of all, for the benefit of the public."

Museum professionals usually seek to balance their efforts in adding knowledge (research) and extending knowledge (education or interpretation). Many visitor center staffs seek primarily to extend knowledge, by interpreting the resource by which they stand. Seldom do they have an ongoing research function except for the purpose of improving interpretation effectiveness.

There is a great deal of introspection by the museum profession, which is evident in the various journals and books about the subject. Among favorite subjects are uneasiness about the museum's relationship to the general public. Closely related is the influence on programming and collections by professionals, wealthy members of the public, and the "general public."

EXHIBITS AND ARTIFACTS

FIGURE 10.11
Artifacts gain meaning when placed in their context of use, even if in the abstract.

Objects or artifacts have great importance in museums and visitor centers. In a decorative arts museum, a chair goes in a case or on a pedestal. The curators feature the chair so visitors may admire its grace, workmanship, wood, style, and age. In an interpretive exhibit, the same chair goes behind a table to create the sense of a room. The essence of this historic room experience consists of context (Figure 10.11). The objects have importance in an interpretive exhibit, but once in the room, the context takes over to produce the experience. People relate easily to spaces; they understand a room.

Furthermore, when possible, the room should relate to the primary park/site theme. The room becomes a springboard to developing a stronger sense of the central interpretive theme. Thus, the main product consists of an experience of a place's character, not just an individual piece of furniture or crystal.

People will stand in line for 20 or 30 minutes to see the Hope Diamond at the Smithsonian. That one object has enough "celebrity value" to make it a feature. So does Babe Ruth's locker from Yankee Stadium, that is on display in the Baseball Hall of Fame in Cooperstown, NY. On the other hand, an original caned chair by Abner McKay in an Appalachian museum or a set of china donated by Mrs. Ball and used by her prairie pioneer grandparents have less intrinsic pull; their chief value may be in the context of a room, showing the style of the living environment in which the pieces were commonly found, emphasizing, in the case of the chair, how people fabricated their own furniture from local materials and, in the case of the china, how people guarded select, treasured articles as they travelled over rough routes to settle the West.

ORIGINALS OR REPRODUCTIONS?

Historic interpreters and museum curators often share intense concern with authenticity. That concern extends to all exhibits, including textiles and papers. Even the authenticity in methods of manufacturing and invisible details capture the attention. The frontier reenactor who worries about fabric and stitching in his or her underwear has clearly moved beyond drama and superficial impressions. The concern is with an abiding human interest in things that are real.

There is a certain inspirational value in original artifacts that affects the intensity of an interpretive exhibit. Facsimiles and reproductions may provide the same or more educational opportunity. But somehow the human psyche responds with greater interest in the presence of originals of some things. The real Declaration of Independence at the National Archives draws hundreds of thousands of viewers per year, although reproductions are available to read in virtually every home, in any large U.S. dictionary and in many school books. Original uniforms of the Royal Canadian Mounted Police in several Canadian museums seem to have greater value than the many facsimiles available. So do original jewelry, stone weapons, and everyday implements used by Native Americans, the ancient Celts, the Romans, and the ancient Benin Kingdom of West Africa. In fact their value is high enough to incite collectors to expend much time and energy in their pursuit.

Exhibiting or using original artifacts is not always practical, however (Figure 10.12). Especially when educational activities allow people to touch artifacts, they must be very abundant and replaceable, or they may be reproductions. It is not the economic worth of originals that dictates this. "In general, reproductions are likely to be as costly as period pieces" (Lewis, 1976). Instead, it is the intrinsic, nonmarketable value of originals that makes them irreplaceable.

Some materials obviously do better than others in exhibits and use. Silk deteriorates within 30 years, regardless of how well it is kept. That suggests that reproductions of silk clothing are essential for any historical collection. On the other hand, stone survives millennia. When stone implements abound, originals may be used for both exhibits and participatory activities. Wood and paper fall somewhere between these extremes; with care, both can last for centuries with relatively little deterioration. If handled frequently, however, some kinds of paper can disintegrate quickly.

Heavy visitation creates a stream of foottraffic in a historic building. In the Abraham Lincoln home in Salem, Illinois, a steel I-beam now holds up the floor to sustain the constant stream of people. The reproduction carpet in his Springfield home cost $100 per yard and imitates the wall-to-wall carpeting of Lincoln's day.

When using reproductions of artifacts, "museum ethics require that visitors be told in an effective manner the true nature of reproductions" (Lewis, 1976). Clear, permanent marking on the bottom or other inconspicuous place prevents mistaking them for originals. That may prompt a story in itself—the ten top hats in a Harpers Ferry store came from a London firm that still makes them—at $300 each. The reproductions of wooden chairs in the Russian Bishop's home in Sitka, Alaska, came from a small factory in St. Petersburg that still can make them in the knock-down style that allowed convenient shipping to serve the Czar's far-flung empire. Clearly, reproductions may cost much more than originals.

Sometimes, authenticity conflicts with fiercely held modern attitudes, creating a practical dilemma for interpretive administrators. In the mid-1800s, the only women to enter a men's clothing store were seamstresses who quickly and discreetly delivered the clothing they had sewn at home. Women did not work behind the counters nor did they appear in the store with their husbands. Such indecorousness surely would have embarrassed the male customers. It just was not done. Nevertheless, from time to time, female interpreters show up in period clothing to interpret a store from behind the counter in at least one U.S. national park, as a practical compromise to scheduling, skill, and the gender balance of the staff.

Spittoons were part of all stores where men gathered, yet, in this same store, interpreters put them away, out of sight. Very few visitors seem to request them, but gentility or modern bias against the "filthy habit" has compromised some of the authenticity. On the other hand, chamber pots appear in virtually every preplumbing bedroom on display in museums and historic homes. Some take pains to bring the pot out from under the bed, as if to emphasize the beauty of the porcelain or to make it clear that not everyone ran out into the nighttime snow.

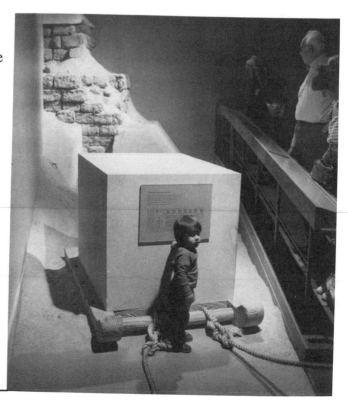

FIGURE 10.12
A replica of a building block and wooden sledge at the Field Museum of Natural History gives visitors a chance to sense the size and weight experienced by the pyramid builders.

How People Visit Exhibits

The behavior of the museum visitor offers an inexhaustible stock of problems.
—Edward Stevens Robinson, 1928

The initial question for museum and exhibit designers boils down to figuring out what people seek and understand, how they move through museums, what they see and miss in exhibits. People are very selective and have different approaches to viewing exhibits. Most of them do not grasp the total message or story in one or two visits—surely not upon entering the door. A museum will produce more understanding people if it offers a range of opportunities, and a variety of styles and modes for learning.

THE VIEWERS AT THREE SPEEDS

One simple division of exhibit viewers divides them into three levels of viewing speed: the skaters, the strollers, and the studiers. Each of us who visit museums act in each of these roles at different times.

The skaters (aliases: streakers, speeders, and scanners) pass by the exhibits with little apparent attention or interest in anything except perhaps the themes. Some use the skating approach to get the lay of the land, and to reconnoiter for topics of interest for later study. Others are scanners, getting the "table of contents" in a short time. Some are just in a hurry. Others are harried by children, parents, or tour directors. Some just are not interested in looking at anything but the big picture. They read the headlines, sometimes. Skaters scan, then skedaddle.

The strollers get the big picture in slightly more detail, because they pick up the major themes and some of the details. The museum text writer keeps some of the key ideas in large print for them. They may stop and look at details of some exhibits, but generally, they will skim through the museum selectively, seeing most of the exhibits but getting only the key ideas and most compelling facts. Strollers skim, then slip out.

The studiers read the fine print and examine every object—at least in areas of special interest to them. They make the exhibit planner happy with their intense interest (even when they report errors). If the exhibit is designed without them in mind, they may also become barriers to traffic as they park in front of a panel full of interesting details. Studiers stay.

Most museum or exhibit visitors demonstrate all of these tendencies at some time—often during a single visit. Of course, there are the purists—the people that are in and out of a nature center in three to five minutes, announcing that "there ain't nuthin' in there 'cept some stuffed birds and kiddy games." There are slow strollers—often pushing baby strollers—who wander attentively or dreamily, only occasionally engaging themselves with the messages but picking up on the visual imagery. Only a few visitors are pure studiers. Instead, people selectively study exhibits or objects that hold special interest for them.

VISITOR BEHAVIOR STUDIES

Research about museum visitor behavior goes back many years. A series of studies in the 1920s and 1930s produced a base by which much museum design has been measured for decades. Observing more and speculating less; watching the visitors more and talking about them less; using measurable and useful questions—these guidelines were behind these studies by Robinson (1928) and others. They documented answers to apparently simple but measurable questions, avoiding psychological or physiological techniques that might leave more doubts than answers. Among the studies' simple questions were:

- What do people do when they come to this exhibit?
- How long do they stay?
- Is there an easy and natural manner for prolonging their stay?
- What do they look at?
- What do they pass by?
- How can the visitor's behavior be influenced through the location, size, or color of exhibits?

The data came from discretely observing visitors with a stopwatch and small notebook in hand, noting what they looked at and for how long. Researchers stopped no visitors to ask what their aesthetic experience had been or other revelations because " . . . we know from sorrowful experience that they are sure to be more false than true" (Robinson, 1928).

The American Association of Museums published several Studies in Museum Education during the 1920s and 1930s. DiMaggio, Useem, and Brown (1978) reviewed 250 studies, mostly in the 1970s, offering data on audiences at cultural institutions and events. (In general, the public that "consumes" culture is more educated than the norm, and have higher incomes and higher status jobs; education seems to be the persistent key feature.) The work is modernized, confirmed, and modified in *Visitor Behavior* and other current publications as well as in many unreported studies done internally by museums. Several general observations based on these studies describe how visitors view exhibits. The observations have value for museum and exhibit designers.

1. Visitors enter a display area and tend to turn right, then go around the room counterclockwise. Museum and supermarket designers have known for a long time that about 65 to 75 percent of people go right, then move counterclockwise, given the choice (Melton, 1935). (Ice skaters and roller skaters circle their rinks the same way, as do runners on a track—reversing the direction requires special mental and physical effort.)

2. Position affects the number of viewers. Paintings in an art gallery " . . . immediately to the left of the entrance received less attention than any other group of paintings in the gallery, and the paintings immediately to the right of the entrance received more attention than any other group . . . " (Melton, 1935). In some cases, the difference between the two positions was three-fold. A similar pattern exists for natural history exhibits. However, Porter (1938) found that an open mount or illuminated habitat case at the end received attention compared to the first case on the right of the entry.

3. Viewers do not study all the pictures in an art show or all the exhibits in an interpretive center. The percentage of visitors who examined the first and last exhibit cases in a natural history museum, (by subject): First case: Gorilla 78 percent, Kodiak Bear 36 percent, Evolution of the Horse 26 percent; Last case: Skeletons of Apes and Man 74 percent, Black Bear 52 percent, Geologic History Chart 8 percent (Porter, 1938). The same happens in zoos and art galleries. Robinson (1928) reported that no two visitors looked at the same number of pictures in any of four art museums. On average, in a large museum with about 1,000 paintings, they stopped to look at about 10 percent of the paintings they passed.

4. Visitors do not look at any exhibit for long. On the average, works of art get only a quick glimpse. Measurements in four art museums produced averages of 7 to 18 seconds per picture observed (Robinson, 1928). That included only cases where the visitor stopped before a picture; it included the time to read the label and look at the art work. Adler (1968) found that, of visitors who stopped for ten seconds or more at a rather poorly lighted, uncolorful but informative exhibit on Indian bag weaving, most (57 percent) spent less than 30 seconds viewing it. Only 13 percent stayed longer than 60 seconds. (The human brain is a quick, remarkable thing!)

5. Viewers read only some of the labels. Only four brief labels were read by 50 percent or more of the visitors on the whole first floor of the Peabody Museum through two years of observations (Porter, 1938). One experienced observer put it clearly: "Visitors do not really like reading labels. If the label is over 50 words, it will probably not be read" (Veverka, 1989).

6. Most visitors don't remain in the exhibit rooms very long. Getting through the exhibit area apparently is as important as completing observations of the exhibits themselves. Visits to the large Peabody Museum of Natural History varied from 3 minutes to 50 minutes, with an average of 21 minutes (Porter, 1938). The gallery exits compete with the objects on display for the attention of the visitor (Melton, 1936). When the entry and exit are the same portal, visitors tend to look at more paintings in a room, including those on the left wall.

   However, not all museums hold visitors for the brief average of 20 to 30 minutes of many forest and park interpretive centers. Larger museums (often with high entry fees) keep people for hours. Old Sturbridge Village (Massachusetts) and others sell tickets that allow a second day's free entry. Many customers buy two and three day tickets to Walt Disney World and Disneyland—facilities combining amusements and educational exhibits. The Adirondack Museum (New York) holds visitors attention for at least 3-4 hours—some for an entire day. So does the huge Shelburne Museum in Vermont. The Baseball Hall of Fame provides so many rich interpretive experiences that people stay inside the buildings for a minimum of an hour; the average may be two to three hours, as well as real fans staying four hours or more.

7. Variations in display methods can lengthen interest in specific exhibits. Porter (1938) identified peaks of interest wherever there were variations in the mode of display. She found the frequency of stops ranging from none to ten

at cases of uniform size and arrangement, as compared to 21 to 32 at the illuminated habitat cases.

8. Exhibit observation time increases for large, moving, close, and easily visible objects or animals. Parsons (1965) found that audiences responded better to well-filled exhibits than simple ones; "they wanted not only to see more specimens, but apparently they understood more, learned more, and enjoyed it more when there was more to see."

9. Colors add interest but aren't essential for success. Simple colors—even black and white—did as effective a job of communicating as did exhibits with up to eight colors in an anthropology museum (Parsons, 1965). Visitors commented that the black and white exhibit was "too plain" but they rated it well on other aspects.

10. Attentiveness flags with time in the exhibit area.

EFFECTIVENESS

> Just because the visitor looks doesn't mean the visitor has learned or benefited. . . . It is difficult to appraise what actually does occur . . . [yet] objective appraisal is essential if the museum is to make serious claim to an educative or culturally significant role.
>
> —Lucy N. Nedzel (1952)

Many museums try to measure their educational results. Some have ambitious goals. Stapp (1990) reviewed the historical and recent literature to conclude that museums have relatively limited roles as a stabilizing or change agent. "With all our talk about humanizing, socializing, enlightening, and the like, we in the museum business have perhaps laid claim to too vast a field for conquest. The museum holds but little chance of directly ameliorating social injustice through public education by objects . . . "

The realities of the museum visit, reflected by Stapp, came from careful observational research that goes as far back as that in the Peabody Natural History Museum at Yale University in the 1930s. Porter's (1938) research summary indicated that visitors have their own way of thinking and viewing exhibits.

When the individual records were examined, it was found that the route taken by the average visitor was the reverse of that planned in the Guide Book, 24.4 percent of the exhibits were examined, 10.9 percent of the labels were read, and the average time taken by the visitors for reviewing the history of life on the earth during the past 500,000,000 years was 21.4 minutes. These numbers are enough to humble the grand designs of those who would revolutionize the nation through an important museum exhibit. The numbers cannot discourage the exhibit preparator nor the educator, however. Rather, they can guide the techniques to be utilized to communicate at least some of the message to the public.

Even people's reasons for visiting museums are difficult to pin down. Graburn (1977) postulated three types of experiences that are sought by different museum visitors. Some seek a reverential experience; others, associational; and still others, educational. If one is limited to these three theories involving museum experiences, one has a diversity of goals that defy measurement by a common formula or satisfaction scale.

Museum Programming

People seek museums for education of a special kind—a museum serves as an interpreter and interlocutor to educate the nonverbal, intuitive, or synthetic aspect of people. This is very difficult to measure and document (Stapp, 1990). Museum professionals have long discussions about their roles as educators and agents of social change and/or stability. The key to getting messages across, however, seems to evolve from visitor involvement in the exhibits and interpretive activities of the institution.

Many ways exist to get visitors involved in museums. Here are a few:

- The Hagley Museum of Delaware conducts archæological site work that offers live interpretation. As volunteers unearth and clean artifacts, they interpret their work to visitors.

- The same museum staff started a graduate level course with the University of Delaware on "Historical Archæology and Museum Interpretation." First offered in 1985, it was a National Endowment for the Humanities Exemplary Course (Orr, 1989).

- The timber company train at Laona, Wisconsin, doesn't just sit on a siding for people to see the machine once used in railroad logging. It loads people into train cars (at a few dollars per ride), cranks up the steam, and takes them through a bit of the company's managed forest. Then they get out to wander around an old farmstead, pet and feed the livestock then perhaps take a short pontoon boat ride through the company's wetlands or a wagon ride through the big trees—all for a small additional price—before they climb aboard for the short train ride back to their modern automobiles. These visitors are not looking at pictures or replicas of the logging days. They get out into an actively managed forest, feed real animals, smell real train smoke, and move around in a real-world "museum," slightly different from what they normally see.

- Art on Tyneside, a 1992 exhibit in the Laing Art Gallery, Newcastle-upon-Tyne in Northumberland, England, interpreted its collections of silver, glass, ceramics, paintings, and costume to tell 300 years of art history in the area. It used scenic recreations, interactive computers, and other devices, sounds, smells, and models including a talking tugboat. A 1,500-word narrative, written at the 12-year-old level in four local languages, was accompanied by cartoons. Several access devices aided audiences with disabilities, including nonreflective glass, a closed-captioned induction loop for the video, and a raised floor-track. Hands-on opportunities exist in this art museum: visitors can sit in an 18th-century coffee house to read a 1757 newspaper, arrange a building facade with classical architectural elements on a magnetic board, or get into a role-playing quiz (Millard and Phillips, 1992). Visitation grew by 70 percent over the previous year. As expected, some critics found the exhibit inappropriate for high culture, and even debasing of the art (Millard and Phillips, 1992). Unlike study collections (and many displays), the glass, silver, ceramics, costumes, and paintings were combined in chronological settings—interpreting an impression of changes that took place in the culture without breaking the culture into compartments. Time will tell whether the considerable cost (£300,000) will produce and sustain higher visitation levels and whether the text was targeted at the proper age and intellectual level to attract all visitors (Millard and Phillips, 1992).

- The dioramas at Mesa Verde, which are over 60 years old, small, have no moving parts, and are considered "out of fashion," still interpret the theme of family/community life in an arid, dramatic environment. The modeled images stimulate the imagination vividly, enabling one to step outside and "feel" the flat mesa-tops and steep cliffs as places to live and work, allowing modern visitors to project themselves into the distant past (Figure 10.13).

FIGURE 10.13

Miniature dioramas of Mesa Verde Anasazi communities draw more visitors of all ages than any other exhibit in the park's museum.

These four very different museums encourage the involvement of all senses where possible. New facilities can use their ideas to provide for touching, smelling, hearing and tasting, as well as seeing. If an artifact is too delicate, use replicas that people can handle. Interpreters have often allowed visitors to use specimens or replicas to grind and taste cornmeal with a mano and metate, or to write with a quill pen, or to don articles of period clothing. They have added to static visual exhibits with audio devices and the sounds of specimens, such as a rattlesnake, songbird, or blacksmith's hammer. Appropriate odors enhance interest in a period kitchen, a granary, and even a medieval street scene. The two learning principles these examples present are that (a) people remember what they do more easily than what they just see and (b) people learn through reinforcement by using several senses.

Exhibit Planning and Design: Exhibits That Affect Visitors

Good displays and exhibits may orient the visitor before a forest or factory or park tour or enrich a visit as a post-tour extension. In museums, where the exhibits comprise the destination, their composition and quality make or break the whole experience.

CRITERIA FOR EFFECTIVE EXHIBITS

What qualities make a good exhibit? Here are some judges' comments about winners in a recent competition of the American Association of Museums (Kelly, 1990):

> A splendid exhibit combining outstanding research, design, and interpretation ... Sophisticated, complex concepts are made accessible and easy to understand. ... Clear evidence of sound research. ... Takes a popular subject and provides a broad range of information, effectively presented. .... Emphasized visual affinities rather than chronology and eschewed labels, providing instead a confrontational, experiential relationship between visitors and art.

Criteria for this award include originality of concepts, suitability for presentation as an exhibition, evidence of thorough research, and success in conveying a message through content, design, and programming. In other words, criteria should include:

1. A good concept—a theme that's novel.
2. An appropriate topic that can be exhibited.
3. Careful "homework," i.e., library, field, and expert study to get the facts straight.
4. Contents—e.g., artifacts, graphics, writing—that convey a message clearly.
5. Design and layout of the exhibits to convey the message clearly.
6. Providing a visitor experience that conveys the message clearly.

UNIQUENESS TO THE PLACE

Should every visitor center look alike? Most visitors appreciate uniqueness and something special. Highly mobile visitors can develop ennui from sophisticated well-designed exhibits and centers that all look the same. Excellent posters to aid in identification of birds, butterflies, tree leaves, and flowers appear in most U.S. nature centers—gifts of the USDA Forest Service. The only trouble with them is that they cover the nation, not the local area. Some exhibits should be unique to every center—exploit the locality. Beazley (1971) suggested these:

- The place—What's special about it? Why is there a museum or center here? This can be partly explained by siting and designing the building appropriately, as well as effective displays and programs.
- The staff—Interpreters have individual character and special skills that are worth featuring. Robot rangers who spout an agency script more tailored than their uniforms are neither particularly interesting nor memorable. Individual enthusiasm, originality, and devotion to the place come through as positive attributes.
- Topical data—Weather forecast, tide times, bird migrations, flowers in bloom, local archæological finds, a farmer's old (or current) diary, catastrophe news as oil spills can go on the bulletin board; visitors can add news of bird sightings, flowers in bloom to a chalkboard or special log book.
- Local events—Posting local entertainment, lectures, rodeos, dog shows, regattas, festivals, services in nearby and interesting churches, civic and social events—all add to the "local color" opportunities for the visitors which enrich interpretation.

COMMON ELEMENTS

Some things will be common to many exhibit centers. Local identity can be maintained if the common agency materials aren't allowed to overwhelm. Samples of common elements:

1. Anything alive—Bees, ants, fish, farm animals, birds at the window, people at work, and plants in terraria or planters are interesting. Once, wild animals in captivity were featured at state and local parks. Today, most interpreters prefer to build observation blinds or offer walks to see special wildlife habitats.

2. Rugged instruments—Binoculars, magnifying glasses, telescopes, and other equipment to aid perception of the environment by enlarging visual powers enhance observation.

3. Fire—Campfire programs and a cool-season fireplace or a wood-burning stove enhance comfort and create a sense of memorable hominess.

4. The story of land use in the area—Economics and ecology of former occupants along with current stories of land restoration add human interest to an area.

5. Models—A working mill, a still, a bird in flight, even tools that visitors can handle or archæologists at work, help interpret how things operate.

6. Visitor-operated quiz panels—Lights or hinged solutions boards can be lifted to reveal answers allow the visitor to know whether their answers are correct or not. Often simple construction and operation of solution boards is best.

7. Life cycle of an animal—An in-depth description of one species of animal can be effective and individualized.

8. Mounted animals—Children are fascinated with the opportunity to stroke the fur of common animals. Roadkills and a local taxidermist can add meaningful, replaceable displays.

9. Objects and panels.

10. Dresses and costumes.

11. Outdoor sculpture.

12. Brief facts that stop visitors in their tracks, e.g., dates when two or three species became extinct.

13. Personalized text.

TYPES OF EXHIBITS

Dioramas or habitat groups are miniature or life-sized scenes featuring three-dimensional figures and objects placed in front of a painted background (Figure 10.14). A diorama may be as simple as a stuffed bird on a twig placed in a corner case with the background painted as a forest scene. These are popular in large wildlife displays in the American Museum of Natural History, Field Museum of Natural History, Denver Museum of Natural History, and Texas Museum of Natural History. Dioramas require much more information and research to accomplish than do techniques such as writing or two-dimensional representation (Lynn, 1976). Scholarship must be accurate. Craftsmanship gives it appeal; with it, a diorama becomes an unsurpassed teaching instrument. It attains even more teaching power when accompanied by a taped or written explanation.

Cycloramas were, before movies and television, very popular attractions. Very large paintings of complex scenes such as Civil War battles (e.g., Gettysburg, Atlanta), wrap 100-300 feet around the inside of a circular building. Viewers stand in the middle of a mostly darkened

FIGURE 10.14
Stuffed magpies and an eagle stand on sand in front of a painted river in a diorama at the Denver Museum of Natural History.

room following the action of an event by a narrated sequence of selective spotlighting of key features on the painting. They sometimes take dioramas to a grandiose, circular scale by placing scaled figures of people, horses, houses, vegetation, rocks, and fences on a sculptured foreground that represents the land's formation; this blends artfully with the perspective of a painting in the background. Only a few of the several hundred cycloramas that once existed remain in operation.

Relief Models/Maps receive heavy use for orientation purposes in most visitor centers and many museums. Informal observation suggests that these often become the most popular exhibit in the museum (Figure 10.15).

FIGURE 10.15
A relief model of Lake Pleasant defines the shape of the landscape and the outline of the enlarged Arizona reservoir.

Simulated Immersion attempts to immerse the visitor in a feeling of being transported to another time and place, (mentally discounting the reality of the museum location), so the exhibit becomes more meaningful. Bitgood and Patterson (1986) described the enhanced impact of exhibits designed to involve visitors both physically and mentally. Studies of immersion experiences at the Anniston Museum of Natural History (Bitgood, Ellingsen, and Patterson, 1990) indicate that the kinds of exhibits that produced a feeling of immersion include realistic looking animal mounts or casts, vegetation, thematic backgrounds, recorded or real sounds, clever use of films and slides, predators and prey posed in apparent conflict, a walk-through approach for caves, forests, villages, and several other three-dimensional devices.

Hands-on Exhibits are designed more and more to allow the visitor to touch, feel, and manipulate something in the scene (Figure 10.16). Kinetic participation, puzzle-solving, and actual feeling of how something works should increase the interest and learning experience more than mere observation. The manipulation may be as simple as lifting a flap or pushing a button to find an answer to a written question about the exhibit. It may be simply testing one's strength. From crayons to computers, children and adults may express themselves in modern museums. Discovery rooms in museums and nature centers draw thousands of children per month to the boxes full of puzzles and games (Figure 10.17).

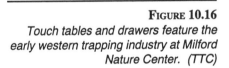

FIGURE **10.16**
Touch tables and drawers feature the early western trapping industry at Milford Nature Center. (TTC)

Exhibits behind glass, flat-work diagrams and mounted artifacts or specimens will continue to have the dominant place in most museums. But when the visitor can become physically involved with an exhibit or artifact, its impact can often be dramatically enhanced.

Planetaria, aquaria, beehives and wildlife windows bring the outdoors inside to provide excellent visibility for processes and phenomena that otherwise can't be seen easily.

Interactive art exhibits in science and history museums proved effective in holding the attention of visitors; therefore, art museums tried this technique. Trials prove that there is physical attention. Visitor comments and behavior indicate that interactive exhibits seem to increase intellectual activity (Hyde and Smith, 1992). A test exhibit of drawings and paintings had some simple questions about the characteristics of 22 pairs of drawings, e.g., showing two pictures of a young woman, asking "which is by her father; which by a man attracted to her?" It also encouraged quick self-portraits by providing mirrors and drawing materials. The images could then be put on a screen which become a very popular part of the display.

FIGURE 10.17
Discovery drawers of Meadowside Nature Center, Rockville, MD, contain children's activities.

Time-lapse video monitoring indicated that 80 percent of all visitors took part in this "Behind a Painted Smile" interactive section, while 24 percent viewed adjacent British watercolors of landscapes (both were equally publicized). Those who "took the quiz" spent an average of 10-15 minutes in the interactive "Smile" exhibit; the landscapes held them for two to five minutes (Hyde and Smith, 1991). Visitors said that they enjoyed the intellectual activity added to passive observation in the "Smile" exhibit and two subsequent "challenge captioning" hangings.

The art history approach to exhibitions has long indicated that there is a single correct meaning for the work of art—i.e., the artist's intent is somehow reported. An interpretive explanation of western U.S. art at the Smithsonian in 1991 created considerable protest. The new explanation attributed dark secret meanings in the pictures of Remington and others by finding the "real" meanings of their work to be oppression and prejudice. The controversy created interest in the exhibit. The controversy seemed to arise from the interpreters underestimating the sophistication of their audience. The interpreters wrote as if the viewers' only impressions of western U.S. history came from Roy Rogers movies. The idea was presented as if all Americans thought that the West was "won" by nice people with noble motives. The writers "educating" American viewers emphasized things that most children learned in the middle years of school, if not elsewhere—prejudice, attempts at genocide, greed, and land-grabs were part of life on the frontier.

ANIMALS—DEAD OR ALIVE?

Zoos and aquaria, of course, feature live animals. Animals bring in the crowds as waiting lines at Sea World, Busch Gardens, and the National Aquarium of Baltimore testify. Should interpretive centers and museums do the same? This controversy has seen sharp swings in the past few decades. At present, most nature centers have no caged animals except for snakes in glass cases, fish and turtles in aquarium tanks, and enclosed beehives in the building.

Live animal displays were once very popular portions of nature centers. In fact they did and still do dominate public attention in some centers. Where the practice has been abandoned, older visitors often return and ask what happened to the elk, bison, raccoons, etc. Live animal displays are less than popular with many interpreters and park administrators due to the fact that they require considerable effort and prove expensive. Since it began in 1901, the Horniman Museum in England had an aquarium. It still does. "Living Waters" cost £300,000 (over $500,000) to remodel a room 9 feet by 60 (Wheaton, 1992). Quality live animal units cost a lot of money, equipment, and staff time. This is a major deterrent. Unless the staffing and funding are available for full-time care of a zoo or aquarium, it seems less than likely to succeed.

An ethical deterrent exists in some places. If a park visitor center is to be the portal to the natural features and wildlife of the park, it somehow seems inconsistent that the local animals should be featured in cages. Although visitors can presumably see what they are going to look for in the woods, that is more wishful than factual. However, stuffed and mounted road-kills in the museum allow visitors to identify a well-lighted specimen, with a chance for careful study and questions to the resident naturalists. If the exhibit designers are careful, they can even display mounted animals in a way that is photographable without reflecting front glass or distracting backgrounds. Good photos are a great souvenir in which a visitor can take pride and they make a fine incentive for return visits.

EXHIBIT PLAN

Generally, three components convey messages and provide the context:
1. the object,
2. the text, and
3. the design.

These three components make up the interpretive language of exhibits.

Language can be expressed in a document that becomes the exhibit script. The script goes into a notebook or onto index cards. It states the theme, objectives and character of the exhibition, lists every exhibit panel or case, details of each item, and the text of the words to be printed as signs, labels, and guides (Beazley, 1971).

Planning for the three types of viewers requires a layout and strategy that:
1. quickly informs the "skaters" of the big messages—so they get at least something from their quick visit and may want to return for a closer look; this is usually done with brief headlines and dramatic use of artifacts and illustrations that emphasize the basic themes;
2. provides the "strollers" with easy-to-read brief explanations of key artifacts and concepts—so they can quickly get the sense of the stories behind the themes. These images and messages answer the big questions and prompt interest in further observation. This level usually includes medium-sized type with brief nontechnical messages and a few key artifacts or demonstrations for each major theme; and
3. offers the studiers more details including some reference-type information in an unobtrusive, uncluttered way that, by its relatively small type and careful location of artifacts, is inviting but almost "invisible" to those seeking only the big picture.

FIGURE 10.18
The Smithsonian Naturalist corner allows personal study of corals, bones and hundreds of other natural things.

Many museums offer fourth and fifth levels as well that include:

4. public hands-on study collections in back rooms and books for further study (Figure 10.18)
5. courses, specialized lectures, and seminars.

EXHIBIT LAYOUT

Every exhibit presents many basic options that affect display arrangement. For example, how should objects be displayed, e.g., chronologically, in related groups, as species? How many objects should appear: isolation of single objects to give immediate impact and elegance or groups of related objects to provide more coherence and comprehension? How much can objects be handled: can object touching and manipulation work, or must they be protected against theft, dust, and humidity?

Focusing and restricting the field of vision can help the viewer's concentration (Beazley, 1971). If a museum or zoo does not aid field of vision by arrangement and lighting, the visitors will have to do it on their own. Studies of visitor behavior show that people select exhibits and objects that dominate by size, movement, and visibility. In a museum space, this can be aided by lighting and arrangement that add depth and vividness to the scene.

One study suggested the use of zoned visitor flow patterns. Three zones include (de Borhegyi, 1965):

A. areas of constant crowd flow with terse, repetitive exhibits;
B. areas of crowd stoppage with easily digestible general exhibits; and
C. areas of variable crowd flow that allow visitors to make leisurely choices among simple and complex exhibits.

Crowd flow pressure principles suggest that exhibits can be most effective when placed where people will most likely read them. Specifically, here are four principles useful for exhibit arrangement.

1. Unless there are guiding structures, museum visitors almost always turn to the right, follow the outside walls, moving from right to left, but reading labels left to right. The result is a slow, rather jerky pattern of flow. Easier reading, better information retention and better flow may result by deflecting visitors to the left at the entry and establish a clockwise flow. Since early studies of museum visitor behavior (e.g., Melton, 1935), traffic patterns have generally been laid out in a counter-clockwise

fashion that recognizes the natural tendency to circle to the left. A study by Adler (1968), however, noted that visitors then approach a panel or case from the right. His data suggests that those who approached a test case from the left learned more than those who approached from the right, presumably due to normal left-to-right reading pattern in English. The people from the left also spent more time observing the exhibit (43 seconds versus 28) than those approaching from the right.

2. In areas of smooth crowd flow, terse, repetitive exhibits with limited introductory material for all visitors should be used (de Borhegyi, 1965). Even the "skaters" should comprehend these messages as they move past—e.g., a single easily-read sentence covering the overall theme of the display.

3. Where crowds can or do stop, general conceptual displays for a general audience should be provided. These may be mostly visual with writing that gives the key concepts and short explanations, e.g., a lead paragraph or display communicating the main idea.

4. Out of the main flow of traffic, where flow speed varies, there is a choice to provide simple or complex exhibits, e.g., complete exhibits with a headline, and a lead paragraph followed by a few statements or paragraphs for study by the more interested visitors.

PRINCIPLES FOR EXHIBIT SEQUENCE

Carefully program the sequence of displays, with the general theme and messages clearly described. Use a process rather than a static approach. The designer works with a sequence of viewing experiences, not a specific display. The total viewing experience becomes paramount to any particular scene.

a. Provide a framework of understanding for specific displays.

b. Vary the mood and rhythm of the display experience; use humor or textural effects to vary exhibits and make them more striking.

c. Design some exhibits in the sequence to arouse the visitor's curiosity and make the topic personally relevant. An audience needs motivation for the effort of viewing displays (de Borhegyi, 1965).

Study visitor response and learning. It "should be the backbone of future exhibit planning and programming. Without them, museums will fail in their function to provide mass education and will become simply glorified warehouses, recreational facilities, or exclusive clubs for the learned" (de Borhegyi, 1965).

Museum/Visitor Center Design

The ideal is to interpret the place to the visitor in such a way that the place wins; the means of interpretation must not impinge on its special character or the genius loci.
—Elisabeth Beazley (1971)

Visitor center/museum design affects the interpretive experience. The discussion below relates primarily to facilities that introduce and interpret a much larger historical or natural site. The building itself can convey part of the message and express the theme. Architecture and design are therefore interpretive tools (Stephen, 1980). A visitor center serves people and the property, not the architect. Rather than standing as a signature building, it harmonizes with the resource, provides a usually modest, esthetically pleasing exterior. Minimal interior size guidelines relate to the number of visitors per hour at peak times. For most agencies, the center must be accessible by all, energy efficient, constructible at a low cost, and have a low impact on the site. First and foremost, however, comes the experience offered to customers during a visit to this portal of the site.

The prime interpretive objective is to allow the visitor to orient and to focus on the resource. The first requisite is to give an instant impression of the *genius loci*, to enhance the visitor's perception of where they are and why they came. Most visitors will not know. Some come into a building to find a restroom or to get out of the rain or the cold. Others come reluctantly or out of curiosity with no real preparation. They see the visitor center as a place that will tell them "Why are we here?" in terms of content. Even the informed person will enjoy a brief statement of the theme or special character of a site. A good example is the imprecise but eloquent headline at the Wright Brothers' Memorial in Kittyhawk, NC— *Here Man First Flew*.

ENTRY AND THEME

In visitor center design, focus on the entry and the big theme. The theme is a dominant concept—a guide to the place and the parts of it. Avoid "mind-scatter" in the entry. The entry theme should:
- intrigue without perplexing the visitor.
- offer a clear message that illuminates the repeat visitor.
- provoke but not be cute.
- use humor unless it becomes a stale joke.
- be profound but not obscure.

A compact, lively, nonbureaucratic, and enduring set of guidelines came from Britain (Beazley, 1971): "To be of any use these [field] centres must be both stimulating and enjoyable; well-sited and thoroughly well-designed; shipshape, simple and direct in character, not plush, rich or ritzy."

Basic facilities in the design might include the following:

Entry or gathering area	Parking for vehicles
Information desk	Picnic area/refreshments
Staff workroom/offices	Restrooms
Storage	Litter collection facilities
Exhibition space	Reading/discussion space
Sales area/bulletin distribution	Play area
Meeting room/auditorium	Group work area
Outside trails and study areas	Covered porch or patio

Another common facility is a bird observation room with sound from a secluded out-side feeding area. Outside amphitheaters are popular in the arid regions for evening programs. Some places have large indoor projection rooms for frequent orientation films and slide shows. A few parks have these projection rooms with a mini-planetarium.

Some centers have opted for an open plan where interpreters are exposed to the public at all times, presumably to increase ready visitor contact, but then the interpreters can not find means to escape for concentrated work.

It is important to offer private space where the interpreter can work in isolation from visitors on program preparation, scheduling, telephone calls, laboratory work, change shoes and clothes, and store papers, personal books, valuable cameras, binoculars and micro-scopes safely. The danger develops if a timid interpreter turns troglodyte—seldom being accessible to the visitors. Discipline plus generous, comfortable, space behind the information desk, where two or three people can work comfortably, will help draw even recluses from their recesses back into the mainstream of public contact work.

AUDITORIUM DESIGN TIPS

The following recommendations and preferences provide guidelines to evaluate plans for interpretive auditoriums (adapted from Countryside Commission, 1980). These facilities may as well be constructed for multiple purposes, e.g., films, videos, slide shows, personal talks, demonstrations, workshops, and even parties. The simpler and more flexible the design, the greater the net economic benefit in most cases. Only when a room will be heavily and almost constantly used for a single purpose (e.g., a daily dose of eight to 20 showings of orientation audiovisual or video) should it be outfitted exclusively as a theater.

Physical Concerns

- Seating should not be too close to the screen (front row should be set back two times the height of screen); not too far back (rear row set back less than eight times height of screen); not too oblique an angle from the screen; ideal seating is width of three times by length of four times. Tiered or sloping seats serve best. Each seat uses a floor area of 535 mm x 915 mm (22 inches by 36 inches).
- Darkness is key, and windows are undesirable; use light-proof coverings where windows exist, and light trap partitions in front of doors. Avoid venetian blinds—they let in light, make noise in wind, and cannot be automated easily.
- Ventilation should offer 30 cubic meters of fresh air/person/hour (900 cubic feet).
- Ceiling height aids in good acoustics, size of picture, and quality of ventilation.

Acoustics

- If reverberation is less than one to two seconds after one hand-clap you can expect problems especially with loudspeakers. Seek reverberation from the ceilings and side walls; try to absorb sounds on the back wall, floor, and seats.
  - Hard rear walls often cause trouble—add fabric or sound absorbers.
  - Side walls with alcoves and recesses increase reverberation.
  - Hard-backed seating (unless upholstered) causes problems.
  - A rigid floor calls for a carpet that absorbs reverberation.

- Clap once; if the sound is "dead," higher frequencies of voices will not reach the corners of the room. Reverse some of the above.

Projection

- A matte white wall reflects evenly up to 45° angle. Spraying with a special coating gives a pearl-like finish producing double the reflected light. Glass beaded screens give high reflection for 10-15° on either side. In a multi-purpose room, the white wall offers the greatest flexibility and attractiveness.
- Rear projection systems work well where ambient light is fairly high. The rear-projection system produces no shadows, and equipment isn't visible. This system can be bulky up front, but mirrors can fold the light path with light loss of only 10 percent per reflector. This system distributes light less evenly than reflected projection.

Projected Image Formats

- If you expect format variety (highly likely), a square or large rectangular white wall allows for flexibility—even multi-image programs. Curtains can adjust edges, or images can bleed off the edges for sharp boundaries.
- Shape

	Height:Width
Square (110, 126, Superslide, Hasselblad)	1:1
Cinema film/filmstrip/overhead	3:4
35 mm slides	2:3
Wide screen cinema	1:2/1:2.5/1:3
Video	4:5

Slide Shows

- Slide shows offer excellent picture resolution; they are cheap, flexible, and easy to update.
- Single image; one-projector shows are easy to prepare, present and alter but produce black intervals between slides.
- Two projectors with a dissolve unit for overlapping single images create smoother, more professional shows; music on tape with dissolve cues can make the show automatic. These take careful preparation and set-up but give a professional impression when managed correctly. (They date back to the Victorian lap dissolve technique with a mechanical iris and "magic lantern" slides.)
- Three or more projectors add more slickness at the cost of more complications. Multiimage slide tape shows and multimedia (slide-movie-video) require expensive tailor-made computer programs that are entertaining but seldom justifiable for educative purposes. They require special permanent set-up, offer higher probability of breakdown, and the interpreter has little picture or script flexibility. These impressive, flashy, sometimes very emotional shows seldom possess interpretive value greater than single or double projector presentations.

Museum Administration

Museum and visitor center administrators face many policy and management decisions including structure and organization, governing mandate, governing body, monetary support and problems, membership organizations, space and housing requirements, and security of collections and exhibits.

Marketing and development comprise another major area of responsibility including publicity of the museum's programs and development of funding resources. One of the keys to success in running museums comes from developing "buy-in" by the public and community leaders. The balancing act between public interest and professional control over programming, exhibitions, and operation details requires skill and good sense.

WHO OWNS AND INFLUENCES MUSEUMS AND CENTERS?

Both private parties and public agencies support museums and visitor centers. Many public museums operate with state, provincial, local and national government funding. In addition, most federal, state and local land-owning agencies provide hundreds of visitor centers with exhibits that interpret the features and phenomena of their properties; some centers are operated cooperatively by private associations.

Among private museum and visitor center operators, industries interpret their history, the operation of their factories, their products and their forestry practices. Others are in the museum business for profit—some as small family collections and others as major corporations.

Most private museums in the United States, however, operate as not-for-profit organizations. This gives them important tax breaks; it allows private donations to their facility to serve as income tax deductions. It also puts them into the public sector at least partially. Legally, therefore, these museums are vested with public interest. Public support, even if by the indirect subsidization of tax benefits for its donors, suggests that the purpose and mandate of these is to serve the public. If not, their tax exemptions should be scrutinized.

The question remains of who controls or affects museum programming and collections. Are they genuinely popular, serving the common person, or are they more controlled by an elite, active group? Public agencies aside, most are and always will be controlled by the "benefactors," whose financial gifts keep the voluntary agency museums (e.g., art, history and nature societies) open. The influence of these people arises from their social, political, financial, and philosophical interest as well as their active participation on museum boards and committees. In many communities, work on the art association board or as a governor of the historical society is expected of "leading citizens" and representatives of local industries. These people put their money and time where their hearts are. Only a few of them, however, seek to become dictators of taste or policy.

The so-called general public—the vast body of culture consumers and nonconsumers—pays the taxes that also support many museums and enable the "generous" gifts from the wealthy (without the general public paying taxes, the benefactors would not find their gifts to be deductible, and reducing their tax payments). But most members of the general public can usually vote on museum policy and programming only with their feet. They can stay away or make visits. Many who stay away are "voting" out of ignorance—they know nothing of the museum or its contents and may have little or no interest. If attendance falls, the museum managers cannot say with certainty that the cause is some policy or other; it may be economic conditions, new leisure time attractions, or other factors. Thus, the benefactors' influence forms the ideals of most museums, with guidance and help from the citizens whose inclination, available time, and popularity encourage them to donate their time as board members and volunteers. Of course, the museum staff persuades and cajoles the board in forming much of the policy and philosophy. But the staff members walk very gingerly on the thoughts of the board and benefactors. They use gentle, massaging persuasion, rather than abrupt, sharp breaking of tradition, or else donations dry up and one's job status changes.

The call for a genuinely popular museum has gone out in several countries over the years. In the U.S., leaders who wrote of their search for the ideal museum that somehow comprehends and serves the general public in all the positive ways included: George Brown Goode 1888-1897, John Cotton Dana 1914-1920, Paul Rea 1932, Thomas Adam 1937-1939, Francis Henry Taylor 1945, Theodore Low 1948, Alma Wittlin 1970, Emily Dennis Hary and Bernard Friedberg 1971. As Stapp (1990) put it, "identifying the public's expectation of and experience in the museum has proceeded . . . disjointedly and haphazardly at best."

COLLECTIONS

Museums collect artifacts. Even without a collections staff or policy, artifacts would arrive at the museum. Hundreds of local museums consist of cluttered collections of what appears to be miscellany, donated after attic and barn cleanings or left over from auctions. The staff—often volunteer—struggles just to keep track of what is where, how to identify it by donor, and how to somehow get it into public view.

The major tasks of curators involve acquiring and rejecting, preserving, restoring and securing specimens. Then they decide whether and how to exhibit them. The interpreters focus on how to use the collections for public education and enjoyment. The skill, patience, and money invested in the objects are justified only by the use they receive. Such use may be for research, reference, or interpretation to the public. The major interpretive use comes through exhibits.

To select the objects to be shown—and maybe to be accepted as gifts—use the interpretive themes as criteria. Carefully select objects, photographs, maps, and other graphics that best illustrate each theme. Do not choose to accept materials just because they are "interesting" or "unusual."

Collections Acquisition and Management

Accessing, cataloging, information retrieval, collecting laws, care-storage-use of collections—all comprise part of collection work. Rejecting artifacts becomes a large part of the work of small local museums and public visitor center exhibits. This difficult discipline exacts an emotional toll from the museum staff, unless there is a strong and firm (yet somewhat flexible) policy as to what kinds of items are of interest and how potential donors may be involved tactfully in the decision.

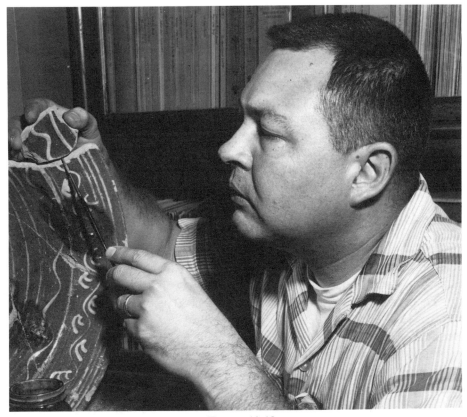

FIGURE 10.19
Some artifacts have special value and requiring special repair—a first step in re-
vealing the story of a historic site. (NPS, Jack E. Boucher)

Conservation

Conservation, preservation, and restoration of artifacts requires special skills, but cannot be ignored as an immediate and integral part of museum operation. The National Park Service has an entire Division of Conservation that stores and restores all kinds of equipment, furnishings, clothing, and other artifacts. Any large museum also has a conservation workshop or a contract with a professional conservator/restorer (Figure 10.19).

Interpreting Collections

People learn from exhibited objects. Seeing an object brings realization to the words interpreters apply to it. Displayed in context, the objects help communicate ideas. Their interpretive power develops in various ways (Lewis, 1976):

   a. the exhibit shows how the object works or how people use it.
   b. the exhibit invites comparison by placing the object with similar objects.
   c. the exhibit groups the object with other things that normally accompany it.

Combined with labels, objects should become meaningful and serve as symbols for a more abstract idea or a link with some person or event.

EXHIBIT ROTATION POLICY

Besides regular "permanent" exhibits, most museums and visitor centers offer short-term exhibits as well. Many visitors to local and state parks, museums, and nature centers make repeat visits. By knowing their visitation patterns, one can plan the exhibit rotation accordingly. Highlight seasonal changes or mark an anniversary to emphasize timely aspects of the interpretive theme. If some exhibits are displayed too long, they lose much of their value. To counteract this, the Pratt Museum in Homer, Alaska, for example, regularly changes one of its four major exhibit areas by featuring recent paintings or photographs by local artists. This helps maintain local interest and may help stimulate the artistic productivity in the community.

HOURS OF OPERATION

It's just common sense that "Open 9 to 5, Monday through Friday" cannot be the best policy for recreation area visitor centers or museums for leisure time use. It's unrealistic for city museums also, due to the fact that it would prohibit the working population from visiting the facility. For decades city museums have hosted about 50 percent of their visitors on Sundays (Porter, 1938).

Beazley (1971) suggested an alternative schedule for British field facilities: "Information centres and field museums near holiday centres will be popular in the evening when visitors often have little to do after high tea or dinner. ... Staffing can be a major difficulty but an unmanned centre is better than a bolted door."

Yet, amazingly few government agencies employ anyone clever enough to arrange hours so the naturalists and museum attendants can be available when most of the public has the time to visit the facility. In a few places, difficulty arises involving labor unions and contract rules—if so, it would seem time to get rid of the rules or the union. Union-bound Chicago and Philadelphia city museums and nature centers, however, have overcome this problem and offer services when people can visit.

Another excuse suggests that there are not enough people visiting the site to justify opening on weekends or evenings. That could mean either that no one really measured "off-hour" visitation or that the visitor center shouldn't have been built in the first place. Weekend openings seem most likely to draw in visitors than do "bankers' (or bureaucrats') hours." The name *visitor* center might offer a clue as to the appropriate policy orientation.

EDUCATION AND INTERPRETATION AS ADMINISTRATIVE PRIORITIES

Education gets high priority in some museums, but not always. Several observers have commented on the art museum profession in Britain. The observation may apply to some degree in other types of museums.

> In many of Britain's galleries debate centres on the merits of different wall colors, types of lighting, how high or how densely pictures should be hung, and whether sculpture or furniture should be included in the rooms with the

paintings. These institutions are concerned primarily with display; the disputes are those of interior decorators and architects, and education is marginalised...Surely no one can sensibly argue that galleries should relegate education to the margins of their activities, but many do. Some dispute whether there should be information in the galleries at all, and in those galleries that do allow their careful creations to be marred by texts, the labels are often so half-hearted, ill-thought and badly written that they do little to communicate the intellectual curiosity and aesthetic pleasure (let alone the excitement and enthusiasm) that their authors feel for the objects they are supposedly interpreting.

—Davies, 1992

Peer-group pressure may intimidate professionals who attempt to move interpretation into the center of art and history museums. Attacks for considering the wishes of the public rather than curatorial orthodoxies have been printed in *Museums Journal* as recently as 1991. As an example, art galleries and museums may suffer from a cultural snobbery that surrounds the fine arts.

"For a very long time 'fine art' has been a social indicator: a symbol of status, wealth or education" (Spalding, 1992). Fine art is unique or limited, not reproducible. Therefore, art works can be possessed. Possessors are often fond of showing off what they have—at least to those who will appreciate and not depreciate the value of that which is owned.

Art curators are part of the system. They usually come from upper-middle-class families and have a background in art. Even if they do not,

they are quickly absorbed into the art-world scene and, like all professionals, usually spend most of their time working for the respect of their colleagues, rather than for the general public. So the priesthood is formed, and in the art world it is tied to the seductive world of wealth and dealers, and classy restaurants, the famous and the freaky, so it becomes all that more enjoyable to be in the scene. And Joe and Josephine Public get quite forgotten. And the whole thing becomes a sort of charade tied to the coat tails of the art market, when no one talks seriously about visitor figures or interpretation...Because art speaks for itself, don't you know? And if you don't, do you really think you ought to be here?

—Spalding, 1992

Spalding (1992) suggested that "Public art galleries are not at the fringe of art, but at its cutting edge." He recommended going out and meeting the audience where they are. He suggested learning from Disney—though art galleries may have a more difficult job. Art museums are not in the entertainment business—or the education business. They do not entertain or teach. They are in the communication business. Museums provide a direct experience in an increasingly second-hand world. They have seldom done enough to exploit that direct experience value. It was and is not always or universally so. Art galleries have a long philanthropic, educational tradition. Since its 1820s founding, the National Gallery in Britain has offered popular, low-cost guidebooks. There were explanatory labels at the National Portrait Gallery by the 1870s. The Whitechapel Art Gallery reported on its first five years in 1906, explaining that its first exhibition had a one-penny catalogue that "aimed at linking the subject to the experience of visitors" and a group of "volunteer watchers" described the pictures to visitors who didn't know how to use the catalogue (Davies, 1992).

According to Spalding (1992), in the British art world, the term interpretation has come to imply some sort of caste system, an us-and-them approach, a priesthood dispensing cultural improvement. He emphasized, however, that art interpretation isn't just for those in the club. Therefore, when writing a label, designing a display, choosing an object, making an interactive exhibit, commissioning a video or a computer game, you communicate as one human being reaching another. "All interpretation, all the work of museums, is nothing more, nor less, than people communicating with people" (Spalding, 1992).

> For most people, pictures do not speak for themselves; for an even larger number the thinking behind gallery displays is an impenetrable mystery. Hanging pictures is an act of interpretation (although perhaps not quite the great creative act that some curators think), and galleries should explain to all the aesthetic and intellectual principles that inform their approaches, rather than leaving them to be discovered only by the initiated.
> —Davies, 1992

Curators acquire collections; their ultimate responsibility is to communicate; the collections exist to communicate and adding to them should improve the ability to communicate. Conservators become responsible for the care of collections so the curator can give communication a top priority. Administrators seem to be moving toward much greater support of education and interpretation as the top priorities of their museums and visitor centers.

Summary

The role of maintaining the nation's heritage in a living, visible form provides cultural continuity and reference points. Historical museums, homes, farms, and villages offer much more than nostalgia. They help tie people to their roots, allow them to understand how their forebears lived. Some historical and anthropological museums give a time dimension to the modern world dramatizing that only the past few generations of *Homo sapiens* have had electric lights, fast cars, bulldozers, and televisions; until very recently, no human beings felt they needed such trappings.

Some technology museums and theme parks predict how humans may live in the future. They may give the audience pause to wonder if people will become robot-like brains who exist only to push buttons and procreate or if individuals may use technology to enhance their skill and thoughtfulness and worshipfulness while on this earth.

Most museums, nature centers and park visitor centers suggest how people might better live in the present, and how they might understand the processes of life around them. All of them seek to enhance the experience of living now, how they might most constructively use their leisure time, and how they may more completely and intelligently enjoy our natural and cultural environment.

Literature Cited

Alder, T. S. (1968). Traffic pattern and exhibit design: A study of learning in the museum. (M.S. Thesis, Univ. of Wisconsin-Milwaukee) In *The Museum Visitor, Publications in Museology*, No. 3, Milwaukee Public Museum.

Alegre, M. R. (1978). *A guide to museum villages: The American heritage brought to life*. New York, NY: Drake Publishers.

Beazley, E. (1971). *The countryside on view*. London, England: Constable.

Bitgood, S. and Patterson, D. (1986). *Report of a survey of visitors to the Anniston Museum of Natural History*. Jacksonville, AL: Jacksonville State University, Psychology Institute, Technical Report No. 86-50.

Bitgood, S., Ellingsen, E., and Patterson, D. (1990). Toward an objective description of the visitor immersion experience. *Visitor Behavior, 5*(2):11-14.

Black, C. (1992). Evolution and all that. *Museums Journal, 92*(2):16-17.

Burns, N. J. (1941). *Field manual for museums*. Washington, DC: National Park Service.

Chalmers, N. (1989). Defining our mission. *Museums Journal, 88*(4):186-187.

Countryside Commission. (1980). *Audio-visual media in countryside interpretation*. Chettenham, Gloucestershire, England: Countryside Commission Advisory Series, No. 12.

Davies, M. (1992). Display priorities. *Museums Journal, 92*(2):27.

de Borhegyi, S. F. (1965). Testing of audience reaction to museum exhibits. *Curator, 8*(1):86-93.

DiMaggio, P., Useem M., and Brown, P. (1978). *Audience studies of the performing arts and museums: A critical review*. New York, NY: National Endowment for the Arts, Research Division, Report 9.

Durbin, G., Morris. S., and Wilkinson, S. (1990). *A teacher's guide to learning from objects*. London, England: English Heritage.

Goode, G. B. (1888). Museum-history and museums of history. In: *Report of the U.S. National Museum for 1897, part 2*. Washington, DC: GPO, 1901.

Graburn, N. (1977). The museum and the visitor experience. In C. Draper (Ed.), *The Visitor and the Museum*. Berkeley, CA: Lowie Museum of Anthropology, University of California.

Grinder, A. L. and McCoy, E. S. (1985). *The good guide: A source-book for interpreters, docents and tour guides*. Scottsdale, AZ: Ironwood Press.

Hall-Quest, A. L. (1962). Modern museums. *Collier's Encyclopedia, Vol 16*:722-734.

Hyde, M. J. and Smith, C. R. (1991). Rethinking "the public": The role of emotion in being-with-others. *Quarterly Journal of Speech, 77*(4):446-466

Jarves, J. J. (1864). *The art-idea*. New York, NY: Hurd and Houghton.

Kelly, J. (1990). Concept and content share the honors in these winning exhibits. *Museum News, 69*(6):71-73.

Lewis, G. D. (1990). Museums. *The New Encyclopædia Brittanica, Vol 24*:478-490.

Lewis, R. (1976). *Manual for museums*. Washington, DC: National Park Service.

Lewis, R. (1992). *Personal Communication*. Washington, DC: National Park Service.

Lynn, J. A. (1976). Reconstructing a Maine lumber camp of 1900: The diorama as a historical medium. *Journal of Forest History, 20*(4):191-202.

McDarrah, F. W. (1967). *Museums in New York.* New York, NY: F. P. Dutton & Co., Inc.

Melton, A. W. (1935). *Problems of installation in museums of art.* Washington, DC: American Association of Museums, New Series, No. 14.

Melton, A. W. (1936). Distribution of attention in galleries in a museum of science and industry. *Museum News, 14*:6-8.

Millard, J. and Phillips, D. (1992). Art history for all the family. *Museums Journal, 92*(2):32-34.

Nedzel, L. N. (1952). "The motivation and education of the general public through museum experience." Chicago, IL: Ph.D. dissertation, University of Chicago.

Orr, D. G. (1989). *Historical archæology and museum interpretation: An exemplary course.* Wilmington, DE: Hagley Museum and Library, Occasional Paper.

Parsons, L. A. (1965). Systematic testing of display techniques for an anthropological exhibit. *The Museum Visitor, 8*(2):167-196.

Porter, M. C. B. (1938). *Behavior of the average visitor in the Peabody Museum of Natural History, Yale University.* Washington, DC: American Association of Museums, New Series, No. 16.

Robinson, E. S. (1928). *The behavior of the museum visitor.* Washington, DC: American Association of Museums, New Series, No. 5.

Spalding, J. (1992). Communicating generously. *Museums Journal, 92*(2):28-31.

Spock, M. (1990). Context and commitment (debate). *Museum News, 69*(5):66-70.

Stapp, C. B. (1990). The "public" museum: A review of the literature. *Journal of Museum Education, 15*(3):4-11.

Stephen, G. (1980). Architecture as an interpretive tool. In *Program Papers, AIN National Workshop.*

Veverka, J. A. (1989). Where is the interpretation in interpretive exhibits? *Proceedings of the 1989 National Interpreters Workshop,* NAI, St. Paul, MN.

Vogel, M. J. (1991). *Cultural connections: Museums and libraries of Philadelphia and the Delaware Valley.* Philadelphia, PA: Temple University Press.

Wheaton, P. (1992). The age of aquaria. *Museums Journal, 92*(2): 22.

Self-Guiding, Nonpersonal Interpretation

11

Chapter

Interpretive services are often put into one of two bags—personal services or nonpersonal, unattended services. This chapter considers the kinds of nonpersonal services and methods and the values of delivering them.

The first sections describe some of the opportunities and problems of interpreting through gadgets, including some of pending utility but still of very high initial cost. The philosophical question of first-hand or electronic interpretation comes up for debate.

The second part of the chapter describes more prosaic signs, brochures, and other means of letting visitors conduct themselves around exhibits and trails. Most museums, zoos, some factory tours, and large expanses of public and private recreation lands depend on visitors to guide themselves, using labels, brochures, or signs as their main source of interpretive information. The work on these facilities has every bit as much importance as working on personal presentations. In fact, in many cases, the nonpersonal work will reach far more people and stay with them longer than brief personal encounters with historians, naturalists, or archæologists.

"Gadgets" or Personal Interpretation?

The merits and limitations of personally conducted interpretation and the use of mechanical gadgets, and written and graphic messages have received much attention and debate. The discussions often sound as if interpretation were either personal or nonpersonal. Of course, in reality, interpreters use both in some combination. Each has its strengths and advantages. In agencies such as the U.S. Fish and Wildlife Service, the Forest Service and the Army Corps of Engineers, with very large and scattered properties and somewhat variable funding of interpretation, self-guiding facilities that do not depend on the presence of an interpreter can reach people at all times. These agencies have an interpretive mix that depends less on personal interpretation. National Parks and many State Park systems weigh in on the side of personally-delivered interpretive efforts, with supplementary nonpersonal approaches.

Personal interpretation has the most value where flexibility is necessary, when many different questions have to be answered, and where the individual's personality or character is an essential ingredient.

"In some instances nothing is, or can be as good" (Countryside Commission, 1980). An interpreter of Native American heritage with proper, authentic attire rivets listener attention and gives stronger credence to the story of a historic battle than do signs, slide shows, or museum exhibits. The personal approach also helps characterize the agency as attentive and service-oriented.

On the other hand, there are some limitations inherent to personal interpretation, which can be partially erased through publications, mechanical "gadgets" and signs. The interpreter has a limited duty-cycle and seldom repeats a message within a day, except at the information desk. The interpreter is not always available at a site but visitors may arrive at any hour. The interpretive personnel may offer variable performances. Finally, interpreters may be expensive, although they may also be quite cost-effective since they can stimulate literature sales, guide visitors for strategic use of time, and attend to emergency needs promptly.

FIGURE 11.1
A computer game aids understanding a rocket launch in a NASA interpretive facility.

HOLOGRAMS, HYPERMEDIA, AND VIRTUAL REALITY?

To keep up with the times, interpreters must communicate through what kids and adults enjoy—say those who take on the task of pushing interpreters into the modern age (Figure 11.1). Of course, many interpreters already lead the pack and innovate frequently. Others seek to keep us in the woods—at the historical roots, by offering direct, simple participation and visitor involvement. Churchman (1992) asked, "Are they going to be able to figure out how they fit into the universe by using a joy-stick?"

Clearly, technology affects interpretation. Videos give us wonderful moving pictures of birds, mammals, and tree growth, at least on a small screen. Computers inhabit many interpretive centers and allow some interactive games—but is it really interpretation? Beyond videos and computer games, some workers have developed ways to use holograms to help us see all sides of an image. As soon as it becomes less expensive, virtual reality will be part of commercial and private interpretive centers. Imagine a virtual reality feature incorporated into the recent Smithsonian exhibit on the tropical rain forest which offers a vivid experience of traveling through the Amazon. The new development of hypermedia may lead interpreters and their audience into serious study of whole systems of wildlife habitats, forests or global climates by allowing the visitor to simulate different management techniques and then observe the unfolding of the outcome based on massive ecological inputs—far beyond the simple choices of outcomes in game boards or computer games of today. In a retrospective interview, Sharpe noted (Bevilacqua, 1993): "The replacement of the live interpreter with a machine in some situations was probably inevitable. Millstone or milestone? Perhaps it's a bit of both."

Many interpreters believe that personal interpretation gives "the real thing." They argue that one-on-one contact, in the woods or with the original artifacts, provides the authentic experience that allows for true interpretive communication. The naturalist or historian meeting the people allows direct and personal questions for real "show-me" field experiences that lead to greater understanding. This brings one to firsthand experiences, holding, touching, smelling, examining the real essence of nature, the real artifacts of history, and a true sense of place.

DO WE *HAVE* TO WALK ON THE HALLOWED GROUND? DO WE *HAVE* TO GO TO THE WOODS?

> I like to play indoors better 'cause that's where all the electrical outlets are.
> —4th grader (Churchman, 1992)

If interpreters get away from the personal approach (e.g., limiting interpretation to the exhibit, the videotape, the book, the question-and-answer computer program), the customer may never need to leave home, or certainly not have to leave a building. The dazzle and ease of technology can distract from the thrill of real encounter, the patience of long waiting, the discipline of observing and thinking for oneself. It can also lead to a real fear of things natural, as teachers and interpreters near big cities have long noted. Interpreters even see land-grant university students who actively avoid going outside, even when they are caught somewhere rural, especially hiking, canoeing, or otherwise risking wet or dirty shoes.

A BIT OF GADGET PHILOSOPHY

Yet, the field of interpretation employs many mechanical devices, from pictures and slides to virtual reality. What proper role should these devices play? How far should interpreters go? Some claim interpreters must compete with the home video game and commercial TV or kids will find us hopelessly uninteresting and out-of-date. Others argue that a slower simpler pace—something they cannot get from a wire and electron bombardment at home— may be the appeal, and distinction of interpreters. They call for purity, simplicity, and dissociation with the artificiality of technological entertainment—give them the real thing, not a flickering picture.

Professional practice usually lies somewhere between. Freeman Tilden (1967) wrote that:

> . . . in the field of interpretation, the gadget has come to stay, and will be used
> to a much greater extent than is now the case. There will never be a device

of telecommunication as satisfactory as the direct contact not merely with the voice, but with the hand, the eye, the casual and meaningful ad lib, and with that something which flows out of the very constitution of the individual in his physical self.

Tilden (1967) also made several still-valid observations about choosing and using mechanical devices as means of serving visitors.

- "A good device is far better than no contact at all," but poor interpretation by a gadget may be worse than none.
- "A good result by device is better than a poor performance by an individual." On the other hand, "A poor interpretation by mechanical means is worse than a poor interpretation by personal contact."
- Maintenance plans and financing should come before installation.

When gadgets come, before putting them in place, promptly instigate a plan to service the device so it operates constantly. Too many computers, electric answer boards, sound devices, and other pieces of mechanical equipment work well for a few months, then go out of service for lack of maintenance know-how. This makes them terrible investments. They do not have perpetual life and operation and require systematic maintenance. An interpretive gadget or sign that does not function serves the organization and people negatively. Those that work well and that are backed by competent, quick repair technicians can supplement personal interpretation, often in very effective ways.

GADGETS OF NONPERSONAL INTERPRETATION

"Gadgets" could be a very broad category—everything in the nonpersonal interpretation area, from signs and labels to sophisticated interactive electronic devices. For convenience, signs and exhibits are discussed separately. Among gadgets that could be included in this category are:

- quizboards with simple flaps (Figure 11.2) or complex electronic light and voice boards.
- all types of audiovisual programs, including computer-driven 12-projector slide/movie shows now available with sound; most centers can give effective

FIGURE 11.2
Visitors young and old get involved with questions above, and answers under the flap, at Indiana Dunes State Park.

programs with a two-projector plus dissolve slide show, synchronized with music and narration.

- talking trees, triggered by electric eyes or treadle pads located along a trail (a pine has been telling its story for over 30 years at Trees for Tomorrow in Wisconsin).
- holograms and real models (Figure 11.3).
- hypermedia to simulate the earth's crust or wetlands, an interactive computer tied to video segments.

FIGURE 11.3
A fixed model of Ted Williams somehow demonstrates the graceful swing that got him into the Baseball Hall of Fame.

Virtual reality will soon become inexpensive enough for museum and nature center use. It can isolate a person entirely from nature, yet give a near-natural sensory experience. If a person dons a helmet and gloves, he or she can now seem to fly through a "forest" while in a shopping mall. The potential for interpretation seems exciting, but the idea seems repulsive to many field interpreters. The selection of appropriate and desirable programming will require imagination, judgement and wisdom. The explanations of tree physiology, fall color change and abscission through virtual reality seem to have great potential, as would the recreation of historic events, such as the Civil War, the exploration of the Arctic, or the understanding of the tensions and cooperation between British colonists and American Indians. Virtual reality can simulate a personal trip inside a tree, beneath the ground, where roots and moles encounter, or through the magma tubes beneath Yellowstone. Similar trips through historical events, such as Lincoln's assassination or the extended treks and transcendence of Fra Junipero Serra, could make history into memories more vivid than movies or novels can produce.

More Gadgets for Interpretation

- Audio messages in caves or along trails. The visitor carries a battery-powered head-phone and tape player. A system of inductive loop aerials along the route activates the tape when the visitor arrives at the various features described. Carlsbad Caverns has used this system to release its rangers from "tour guide" duty so they can meet visitors along the trail and answer deeper questions than the height, name, and color of the formations.
- Listening posts at audio stations along trails, in museums, and in factory tour routes contain tape players. Visitors push a button or break a circuit to start the continuous loop message, received through a loud speaker, phone, or ear cone. Note: "More people will listen to a short message than a long one" (Countryside Commission, 1980).
- Models of the landscape—a cave, a village, a farm, a factory draw people—some of whom struggle to understand them. These orientation and interpretation magnets deserve consideration for any area with topography or complicated sets of buildings. They are tough to keep clean and dry. Builders should over-design any electrical or mechanical devices in the model.
- Lighting with spots, floods, and shadows are keys to effective interpretation through exhibits. Polarized, ultraviolet black-lighting, and colored lights allow special effects. Fiber-optic lights offer illumination with minimal fixture space; small "ropes" of fibers can start behind a wall, wrap into the corners and margins of the case, then emit a light from the tip to discretely illuminate an exhibit without visual intrusion or heat from fixtures and bulbs.
- Pepper's ghost (old) and modern holography (relatively new) create three-dimensional models by visual and artistic effects. The old ghost makes apparent changes in a model with light and mirrors—something that politicians have referred to for decades. They still appear in some museums. Holography uses continuous wave laser beams to make a moving 3-D image on a nearly flat surface. So far, its expense limits its use among interpreters but mass-produced holograms now appear on credit cards, National Geographic magazine, baseball cards, and even a few postage stamps.
- More traditional gadgets that facilitate visitor perception include binoculars, telescopes, periscopes, magnifying glasses, and microscopes. Lasers to measure distances and aid in the precise locations of objects may see increased use in some interpretation.
- Closed-circuit television and video presentations allow many programming possibilities. The many new nature videos have substituted for movies in most interpretive centers. The enthusiasm that many interpreters have about creating their own videos usually wanes before the first production reaches completion. Closed-circuit television, however, can provide immediate viewing of animals, factory work, or crafts-making in process.
- Portable CD-ROM players, when commercially feasible, will allow a visitor to carry to the field an audio-visual encyclopedia of information about birds, trees, ferns, or fish. For example, a bird watcher seeing a long-legged wading bird will be able to

key its characteristics into a small fanny-pack unit, and up will pop the range of possible identifications on a tiny screen.

Audio packages for computers now can imitate a variety of bird songs and other sounds in nature (e.g., weather, animals). New products on the market in the mid-1990s make possible coordination of pictures with realistic computer-generated sounds. With touch-screen features, the computer station user in a museum can hear an historic pronouncement, get involved in the replayed sounds of an exciting event, or gain enhanced understanding of nature's sounds.

Blow-up zoom capabilities coupled with sound packages would permit on-command explanations of many natural and industrial processes. Imagine the value of seeing the process of water movement and nutrient absorption into root hairs of a tree, followed by the water "climbing" the tree through the cells and eventually doing its cooling work by transpiring from the leaves. On a factory tour, the process of engraving circuits in tiny chips and describing in a simple way the chemical reactions that turn iron ore into steel can be explained with the help of computer stations. By locating them within view of the real process, the visitor can quickly seek more detailed explanations on the spot. That could provide much more satisfying interpretation than the often inaudible shouted explanations by a guide standing in front of a blast furnace or assembly line. Previously, the visitors were left to ponder a complicated chart on the wall or to go home and look up the details in the encyclopedia, never really being able to directly associate the essence of the process with the specific points they saw in the factory.

Other questions that may best be described by computer programs and random access memories with compact disks (CD) that the visitor can easily manipulate include:

- How does a lake "turn over" every year? What happens to the fish and other life in the lake as these major temperature inversions and mixtures occur?
- What makes creeks and rivers meander?
- Who did what to whom in a complicated political assassination?
- Where did the different regiments march and fight in the Battle of Antietam? Where did Colonel Marvin Smith fall?
- What really goes on in a nuclear reactor that is making electricity?
- How did the Model T assembly line operate?
- What are the population dynamics of snowshoe hares in the Arctic and what animals are involved in it (beyond statistical abstraction)?

ELECTRONIC INFORMATION

Even basic procedures and research information can become more accessible through computer developments. Storage of agency manuals and regulations is now going to CD-ROM (Compact Disk Read-Only Memory). Libraries have led the way, with most abstract services now available on quick-access CD database systems. A CD-ROM disk can hold over 600 megabytes of information on a device that occupies about the same physical space as a diskette. (Today's high-density diskettes hold about 1.4 megabytes.) Many agencies have regulations, manuals and handbooks that they update annually. They must now reproduce and mail volumes of paper to numerous sites around the country (e.g., the Forest Service has 155 national forests with 450 district offices). Static information can now be set to CD-ROM which can reduce more than one hundred thousand pages of text to a single disk. Then, annual updates are mailed out on another disk. Faster electronic mail may soon eliminate having to ship even voluminous update disks.

The advantages include the elimination of paper shuffle and the drastic reduction of shipping costs. The scanning potential in disk information allows rapid access without shuffling through many manuals. When the update disk arrives, they may be kept for reference. After several years, large databases (major manual systems) can be reissued completely which will eliminate the need to insert new sheets in old notebooks. Future technology will probably increase the flexibility of this procedure. The cost of equipment for writing a CD-ROM has dropped dramatically in the early 1990s (e.g., from $30,000 in 1991 to $5,000 in 1992), making it feasible for companies and agencies to cut their own disk.

Conceivably, scientific and historic information for a state park system would wait in a file, readily accessible to all the interpreters as they prepare presentations or exhibits. It could be indexed by subject matter, allowing quick access to the most accurate current information. Of course, it would require someone who understands interpretation to keep information current. Perhaps this offers a commercial or academic opportunity, maintaining a team to summarize interpretive information and transmitting it promptly to interpreters.

"Gadgets" may open an interpretive can of worms. Questions of cost, durability, maintenance, and updating must precede acquisition. An even larger question is one of appropriateness. Buying a gadget just because it is new, state-of-the-art, the wave of the future, on the cutting edge, or "powerful" tells colleagues that the purchaser has succumbed to the seduction of vanity, rather than using intelligence or concern for the visitor experience. There will always be interpreters who would rather have a new gadget for its one-upmanship rather than for its serviceability. They can cost an agency millions of dollars in foolish experimental whims with little or no benefit to the public seeking solid interpretation. On the other hand, where they really meet a planned objective or need of the interpretive effort, they may well be worth the investment.

Self-Guiding Features

Self-guiding devices allow any visitor or local resident to enjoy interpretive services at any time, on their own schedule, at their own pace. These nonpersonal services require that the interpreter reach an individual through any of a number of media—exhibits, written labels, taped messages, videotapes, graphics and art, booklets and brochures, and even computer-based systems.

Museum and zoo curators and interpreters use self-guiding devices as their standard approach. The staff designs exhibits, arranges objects to encourage viewing, and writes copy for labels, brochures or catalogs and hopes the visitor will pay heed to the work. These people construct an environment, an arrangement, that provides for a visitor experience—the physical context. The visitor then brings to that physical environment two other factors—the personal context and the social context (Dierking and Falk, 1992). Similarly, in a park or forest, the interpreter prepares a route through a woods, along a river, or up a ridge, locating existing objects that help tell the story, elucidating the theme. Then comes the publication of a written trail guide or the interpretive signs to go along the trail, to form the link between the visitor and the resource.

KINDS OF NONPERSONAL UNATTENDED SERVICES

The USDA Forest Service uses at least 21 different kinds of nonpersonal services and facilities (Box 11.1). Other agencies offer a similar mix of opportunities. Another type of booklet offers airplane "tours," which allow passengers to refer to maps, photos, and text about the landscape beneath them. The same can be offered for train trips, a ship's passage, and interstate highway travel. In several cities and counties, bicycle tours with brochures lead riders to key historic sites, parks and attractions.

BOX 11.1: NONPERSONAL SERVICES OF THE FOREST SERVICE

After-hours displays: Conveniently located information at stations and offices.

Campground bulletin boards: Interpretive notes and information strategically located where campers consult them easily.

Exhibits: Thematically-designed, three-dimensional artifacts, models, devices, specimens, including text or audio messages.

Displays: Thematically-designed, two dimensional wall displays of maps, photos, art and text, indoors and out.

Wayside exhibits: Roadside or trail side signs interpreting the site or management activity; may include signs, pull-off, parking, walks, platform and interpretive panels.

Interpretive signs: Thematically designed signs in kiosks, along trails and at scenic roadside areas; of wood, metal, porcelain, embedded fiberglass, always available to interpret.

Information stations, unstaffed: At major road entry points to forest; much information, including changeable current information.

Kiosk: Small, roofed outdoor structures with orientation, information and/or interpretive displays.

Publications: Complex information and interpretation, sold or distributed free.

Free material: Interpretive and informational brochures, small maps, newspapers, posters, pins, patches, pencils, etc.

Sales material: Interpretive and informational books, brochures, large maps, slides, posters, videos, calendars, games, etc., sold by a nonprofit association.

Newspaper guide: Interpretive guide on tabloid-sized newsprint, including articles, maps, schedules, illustrations, stories.

Brochures: Small publications, free or sold, that interpret features or processes.

Map tear sheet: A one-page visitor guide map on a glued pad, usually provided free.

Recreation opportunity guide: Catalog of hikes, climbs, ski routes, etc. with map and brief narrative to orient and inform visitors.

Self-guided trails: Short, pleasant hikes with interpretive brochures, signs, or audio-cassettes.

Auto tours: Interpretive tours along a road, often with booklet, tape, signs, or guide.

Radio transmission: Limited area broadcast of visitor orientation and information.

Sensory device: Exhibits using senses of touch, smell, hearing and taste to interpret, e.g., temperature control devices, touch tables, scratch and sniff displays.

Relief model: Three-dimensional topographic scaled map of land forms and features.

Interactive video: Monitor with touch screen, buttons or control sticks showing information menus, learning games, maps.

Other more common nonpersonal unattended services include auto byways, aquatic interpretation, and self-guided trails, each of which is described in more detail below.

Uptown, downtown, all along the river may be three local self-guiding brochures for a community's walking or bike tours. Country tours along old railroad beds or bike rides from park to park provide other opportunities. In the brochure, list rest stops, rest rooms, food, and local color.

AUTO BYWAYS

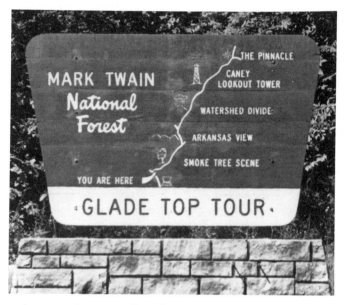

FIGURE 11.4
New Scenic Byways sometimes follow older auto tour routes, inviting visitors to drive forest roads.

The Forest Service recently established a system of over 100 National Scenic Byways to better interpret historic and scenic features of the national forests. The Plymouth Division of Chrysler Corporation collaborated financially and in advertising. On some routes, the Forest Service carefully interprets stops along the historic or scenic routes. On others, a general brochure tells of a few characteristics that visitors can encounter as they drive. These interpretive driving tours represent a long tradition of making the roadside more interesting to those who enjoy nature from the seat of their conveyance (Figure 11.4).

Highway interpretation holds potential for commercial interpreters. A few booklets by touring companies, oil companies and state tourism councils mention features and businesses along a highway route. Kansas produced a beautiful booklet of watercolors in 1990, to illustrate the nature and color of the landscapes along the interstate highway. The artistic colors did much to alert the traveler to the normally-overlooked subtle beauty of the Kansas landscape.

Wisconsin's "Rustic Roads" system gets people off the main traveled roads onto some of the most scenic back routes. Most states designate "scenic routes" of some kind on their highway maps by using dotted lines along some of the most attractive routes. When there is interpretation, it usually consists of cast iron markers (Figure 11.5) identifying the historical significance of a community or home or site. These markers, erected by state/provincial or county historical societies in virtually all parts of the U.S. and Canada, are valuable resources for interpretation. Unfortunately, visitors have difficulty reading most of these signs; they often sit at the edge of town on the busiest streets with no place for pulling off to read them.

New Mexico and other western states built many scenic roadside areas with beautiful routed interpretive signs to explain some feature visible from the road. Many of these described cultural facts about a Native American village, an immigration route, a cattle ranch of note, or some recent historical event. Others showed natural phenomena such as a caldera, a volcanic cone, a canyon, or a special vegetation community.

Self-guiding brochures show routes and describe points of interest. The road and brochures (or audiotapes loaned or bought for car players) lead visitors to historical and natural features. Several different tours allow short or long, diverse experiences in various parts of a county or region or within a large park. Interpreting local color helps visitors and residents get to know a county intimately. Unique little facts, interesting people, stores, homes, creeks, and factories help to make it fascinating.

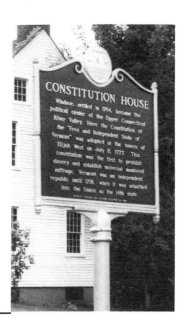

FIGURE 11.5
Cast metal plaques mark many historic sites throughout the USA.

AQUATIC INTERPRETATION

Canoe trails, boat trails, and underwater trails interpret aquatic environments such as rivers, lakes, and ocean bays/reefs. Booklets keyed to landscape features or numbers marked on the shore interpret some waterways. In wider waters, floating buoys have numbers or messages. Several "trails" for snorkelers or scuba divers interpret ocean reefs.

At Hanauma Bay in Hawaii, about 2 million visitors come each summer. A few thousand take the knee-deep guided hike to learn about the fish and coral; many tens of thousands use the displays on the beach on their own (King and Tabata, 1992).

Underwater snorkeling trails exist at two Virgin Islands locations (Figure 11.6) and at John Pennekamp Reef State Park in Florida, among others. Here, visitors looking through snorkeling masks read brief porcelain

FIGURE 11.6
A snorkeling trail at Buck Island Reef, Virgin Islands, points out coral features with underwater signs. (NPS)

signs fastened to the shallow bottom and near the reef, learning first-hand of the plants, animals and rocks that occur in the area. These usually do not exceed a quarter mile (or 500m) and seldom get into very deep water.

Other trails in other places take people into or onto deeper water. The Rogue River, in Oregon, has a complete river guide folder. One side of the folded sheet shows a large map of the Wild and Scenic segment. Also on the map, interpretive messages (in black) and information on mileage, landmarks, and river conditions (in blue), keyed to numbers on the map, help boaters see the river more clearly (Harrison, 1977). The map, printed on waterproof paper, folds down to pocket size. (Other than folded maps, a river guide may use accordion folds or a scroll format.) Paddlers can read about outdoor manners, boating safety, and recreation facilities, as well as interpretive sections on the history, vegetation, and wildlife of the Rogue River.

Other approaches for getting the interpretive messages across include printing messages on a buoy; printing a number on a buoy or flag that corresponds with a small guide booklet; using landmarks correlated to booklet text, or using tape-recorded messages.

Many wetland trails interpret from a boardwalk. For example, the Patuxent River Park in Maryland has a floating boardwalk traversing a marsh, plus a tall observation tower near the river to allow views of ducks and geese (Harrison, 1977).

Minnesota State Parks offer a self-guiding river canoe trail on the St. Croix which interprets aquatics, wildlife, and riparian ecology (Harrison, 1977).

In Michigan, a river canoe route on the Huron River started and ended at the Oakwoods Nature Center. Anchored plastic milk bottles served as floating markers at the stops of this "Walk in the Water Trail." Messages interpreting the river features were printed on these buoys along with the trail emblem and the Huron-Clinton Metroparks logo. This method has several advantages over brochure dependent interpretation (Wooley, 1979):

1. Paddling to the buoy and picking it up to read gets some visitor involvement and interest.
2. Some element of suspense and anticipation exists without a map; the buoy messages give directions to the next stop, giving a treasure hunt sort of angle to the trip.
3. Paddlers do not need to carry maps or brochures.
4. As river conditions change, messages can be moved around and changed easily.
5. The buoys cost little and can be made fairly attractive.

Three small pocket-sized leaflets interpreted the different seasons, while giving instructions and orientation about using the one-mile trail. For more information, a general pamphlet on the Huron River interpreted the watershed, geology, animals, and human history along the river in some detail. Landlubbers walked the Riverbank Trail.

TRAILS—THEMES AND CONTENT

In almost every natural and cultural history area, the title "Nature Trail" invites visitors to stroll in the woods and learn a thing or two about what's there. Self-guided trails often interpret through brochures keyed to numbers, by a discovery-based brochure, or by signs and labels placed strategically along the trail. In places where tape recorders can be checked in and out conveniently, visitors may carry audio messages with them. In Box 11.2, elements of a general interpretive trail suggest how a nonthematic approach often develops. This is not necessarily a recommended nature trail.

Although the "recipe" in Box 11.2 appears on the trails of many successful nature centers, most evaluators would suggest a more original, more thematic approach. To do this, pick a theme and feature the stops so they relate to it and develop its whole story. Some trails with a thematic approach have the following titles: *Keen Eye Trail* (Figure 11.7), *Prairie Lane, Kipuka Puaulu Trail (islands of forests), Walk in the Footprints of Time, Butterfly Trail, Tropical Terraces, Duff'n Stuff Trail . . . a guide to exploring the forest floor.*

BOX 11.2: GENERIC NATURE TRAIL—A COMMON RECIPE

Mix ingredients to suit local site conditions and sequences. A set of 15-20 stops on a half-mile or 1-km trail often includes the following:

"Welcome. Leave only footprints; take only pictures."
- a rotting log (text on recycling)
- a stump and its rings (text related to historical events and how trees grow on the outside and tips only)
- a tree with a cavity (den trees for wildlife)
- five or more tree names on labels or a tree finder device.
- leaf litter (recycling and nutrient cycles)
- acorns, nuts, and berries (human and animal food)
- poison ivy (leaves of three, but no problem for deer)
- creek or pond life (aquatic succession, maybe)
- lightning strike on old tree (spiral growth form and forces of nature)
- the forest community (intertwined destinies; interdependence)
- the food chains (producers, consumers, predators)
- succession of the forest (change is inevitable)
- signs of people (environmental ethic)
- history of the property (human stewardship or deterioration)
- microclimate (cool forest versus hot open area)

These simple themes suggest that the signs or brochure will feature various facets of that general topic throughout the walk. These may include such simple topics as trees, animal food and shelter, geology, wetlands ecology, where Lincoln walked, or the Cradle of Forestry Trail in North Carolina. Write themes as provocative, complete sentences.

In a property with several thematic trails, interpreters can introduce the system of trails with one general trail—a foretaste of the opportunities and an introduction to the character of the place. This trail might have two or three stops that cover geology, another two to five on plant ecology, a few on forest management, and a couple on wildlife habitat.

BROCHURES OR SIGNS ALONG THE TRAIL

To get the information across to visitors, use either labels or signs in the woods, along the trail or place numbers along the trail, keyed to a booklet or folder that is available at the trail head (Figure 11.8).

The booklet-number approach has several advantages and one big disadvantage that can be overcome (Figure 11.9). Advantages include:
1. relatively low cost

2. little visual intrusion in the forest
3. easy-to-include diagrams, maps, lists
4. souvenir-reference value
5. easy to produce translated copy for foreign visitors.

The main disadvantage occurs when the brochures or booklets are not available at the trailhead for the visitor (Figure 11.10). Without them, the visitor may have a nice walk, but miss out on the interpretation. Unfortunately, in practice, the printed guide type trails often require a visitor to go to the office (unknown place for most visitors—and seldom close by for a family on foot) to get a trail guide. Results—many interpretive opportunities are lost, leading to less enriching experience for visitors.

The approach of putting up interpretive signs along the trail, at the stops, also has advantages and disadvantages. One is that the interpreter and the visitors need not be concerned about a booklet. Another comes from exact location of the sign. Interpreters can orient it so visitors look directly over the sign at the object being interpreted (Figure 11.11). Likewise, visitors will see the sign easily, whereas they might pass by a numbered post without noticing it.

FIGURE 11.7
The Keen Eye Trail guide promotes powers of observation at 14 numbered stops on a loop behind headquarters of Kenai National Wildlife Refuge.

FIGURE 11.8
A simple painted number on a rock may be enough to indicate interpretive features keyed to a booklet, such as this low budget first version of the Kenaitze tribe's trail on the Chugach National Forest, Alaska.

FIGURE 11.9
Self-guiding trails may offer several brochures on different topics. (TTC)

FIGURE 11.10
At the start of a self-guiding trail, visitors pick up a brochure that interprets numbered stops along the path.

FIGURE 11.11
Cast metal signs along a winding trail describe the site of stockaded old Fort Calgary, Alberta.

Disadvantages to a signed interpretive trail include the relatively high cost for most durable, high-quality signs. This can be overcome by using coated paper signs attached to an attractive board that allows for easy replacement (Figure 11.12). On remote trails, transporting large signs and keeping them maintained can be difficult. Likewise, replacement costs may cause administrators to balk at modifications, even though things along the trail have changed. This can also happen if 5,000 once-accurate trail booklets are sitting in storage.

FIGURE 11.12
Trailside messages printed on weather-proof paper and stapled into wooden signs allow seasonal changes and quick repair. Plastic paper provides durability in all weather and computer graphics can allow flexible layouts.

TRAIL DESIGN

A few basic concepts make interpretive trails work well; violating them sometimes causes people to miss the point or not accept the interpretation.

1. Plan on-site by getting to know the area thoroughly. Then go through the following steps:

    a. Clearly define the theme, purposes and objectives. This can be kept flexible since knowledge of the site will increase, but the interpreter must know the theme, purpose or objective before he or she starts writing

    b. Identify stations (temporary markers) that will relate the theme and help accomplish the objectives; make sure the object of the interpretation will be there in the future (i.e., avoid bird nests, bear dens, logs, spider webs, and other ephemeral phenomena).

    c. Study the sequence of points so it provides a logical story and flow of thought.

    d. Get someone else to review the ideas. When the final version is complete, the stations should be marked clearly but unobtrusively.

    e. Decide on the medium—e.g., signs, brochures, cassette tapes, audio stations along the trail, or audio devices with induction loops.

2. Now write the interpretive message with clarity, simplicity, and brevity by putting the key information in a story form. Avoid trite questions and phrases. Use imagination in headlines. Keep it brief and lively. Strive for less than 50 words per stop. Review, evaluate, refine. Print only a few of the brochures at first, so the organization can test and revise the brochures before final printing.

3. Identifying plants or animals may be an important objective for an organization, e.g., at a botanical garden, historical garden, arboretum or zoo. If so, interpretation should not be limited to just the names. Write about the values, uses, physiology, reproductive strategy, natural distribution, adaptations, and/or culture.

4. Make the interpretive trail a loop that closes on itself, bringing the walker back to a clearly identifiable starting point. Any loops that spin off the trail should also close on themselves. Avoid D-shaped loops. They confuse people, even with good directional signing.

5. Trail length should stay fairly short, but appropriate to the location and the needs of most patrons. Length usually ranges from 200 to 500 yards (meters), but some popular trails are up to two miles long (3.5 km).

6. Provide benches in a few spots, usually with good views and along steep slopes.

7. Interpret about 10-20 stops, varying with the length of the trail. Ten stops or signs fit an average quarter mile trail (Pilley, 1990).

8. Place signs so people can find them easily, read them without straining, and see the feature interpreted. Try to place your first two stops fairly close to the start of the trail. This gives the visitors assurance that they are on the right trail. Space the other stops so that there are not worrisome long gaps between any two. After sharp turns or intersections, set up a stop or directional sign ahead, within view, to keep people going the right way.

9. Look for other ways to use the trail, so repeaters may find new information in different seasons. Spring wildflower lists, winter resident birds, a leaflet on why leaves change color, a winter folder on hibernation and dormancy, timber harvesting practices, and other topics can supplement the basic trail guide.

10. Maintain the trail regularly. Keep brochures in the distribution box or signs in their places. When damage occurs, fix it quickly.

SIGNS AND WAYSIDES

Interpretive signs and wayside exhibit signs offer advantages in communicating with visitors. The term wayside simply means an outdoor exhibit panel that interprets a particular feature or event. They use graphics and a limited amount of text. The key is the presence of graphics, not text. A wayside exhibit may be one panel on a nature trail or a series of up to 15 panels under a kiosk roof (Figure 11.13). The principles of writing remain the same as for other interpretive stops.

FIGURE 11.13
Wayside exhibits mounted at an angle allow ease of reading and intrude little on the natural scene. (NPS, Hakala)

Signs and wayside exhibits stand ready, always on the job, rain or shine, day or night. They do not need rest, coffee breaks, battery charges, or special attention. Their courtesy and patience remain constant, as good at the end of the day as at the beginning. They make more visitor contacts than all other programs and activities put together—with the possible exception of the brochure handed out at the gate. The visitors can enjoy them at their own pace, by themselves, or even ignore them. They can be inexpensive without looking cheap.

Even the most expensive outdoor signs or wayside exhibits, properly placed, can produce low cost per visitor contact hour. They also can be beautiful depictions of geology, history, and botanical comparisons that get the key messages across (Figure 11.14).

FIGURE **11.14**
A sheltered group of signs from three agencies provides orientation and interpretation at the entry to San Luis Valley, Colorado.

Signs need not create a clutter of confusion or visual pollution; they need not appear at every parking area, building or beautiful view. Proper sign placement can be determined by answers to these questions:

1. Does the site have something people can see or hear that needs explaining? Examples: a large burn or blow-down; strange and interesting features such as peaks, waterfalls, odd plants, geological columns; historic ruins or buildings; a reforestation project; a helipad; a wilderness area boundary.
2. Is there something interesting at the site that visitors will probably miss if it is not pointed out? Examples: a glacial moraine; new tree growth in a harvested forest; a restored prairie; a historic event that occurred there; special management work not obvious to a casual look.
3. Will people get more out of their experience at this site if they know what kind of property it is? Sometimes, identifying the land as a special public place heightens an experience.
4. Do we need to help visitors figure out where they are on the property at this point? Example: how to get somewhere; how to get back where they came from; where they're going; or how this location relates to the whole forest/park/refuge.
5. Would it help visitors at this point to explain a rule or boundary, rather than just posting it?

If you answer yes to at least one of these questions, then answer the next three:

6. Will enough visitors see the sign to make it worthwhile?
7. Does this make one-too-many signs in the area?
8. Is this spot really all right for a developed site—safe, convenient, practical for stopping?

If an interpreter decides he or she needs an interpretive sign, planning can begin. First, define a clear and simple objective—a statement of what the sign should do, in terms of what the visitor will get from it. Seeing and reading the sign has to be interesting and enjoyable, or there's no point in putting it up.

Then check the agency's policy or procedures for guidelines on quality, construction, and design. Nothing can blunt creative enthusiasm more than uncaring administrative roadblocks or apparently unnecessary procedures. Even most large agencies, however, allow some flexibility for interpretive signs (Box 11.3).

BOX 11.3: PLANNING GUIDELINES FOR WAYSIDE EXHIBITS

Site survey: Choose a location where visitors pass or congregate, where the feature is visible year-round, at a feature visitors have asked about, at a feature that can be explained with graphics and in less than 50 words (National Park Service guideline—often exceeded).

Choose materials and size: Wood, metal, porcelain, fiberglass, and Plexiglas™ all work. Design the size and orientation. NPS uses 16 by 20 inches up to 42 by 20 inches.

Production: On your own or with professional contractor, price materials, gather photos and artwork. Write brief text blocks and specify type sizes and styles: usually serif, with 72 point for headlines (theme), 24 to 36 point for summary (key sentences, phrases or subthemes), and 18 to 20 point for text details and captions.

Mount: Low profile angle is customary (Figure 11.13); the angle offers ease of reading for people of various heights and blends into the landscape at a distance. An audio post on one side can blend nicely.

A quality interpretive sign will be first-rate only if done by people who know what they are doing (e.g., Box 11.4):

- Someone who understands interpretation should coordinate the project.
- Someone who knows the site and who can write interpretively should write the text.
- Someone skilled in landscape architecture or recreation resource design who's been on the site should design the parking location and place the sign.
- Someone skilled in graphic arts who has been on the site should design the sign.
- Someone equipped to produce the actual sign in a professional way should complete the project.

A good temporary sign will usually serve much better than none at all, when the best sign cannot be made in time. Too often, administrators who do not understand interpretation will argue that no sign should be put up unless it is the ultimate. This can leave visitors without the information and perhaps with safety dangers while the wheels of appropriations and contracting grind slowly. It may be worth discussing, politely and insistently.

BOX 11.4: SIGN PRODUCTION CONTRACTORS

Among many fabricators of wayside signs and museum exhibit panels, the following have shown particular interest in serving U.S. interpreters.

Badger State Industries, Madison, WI
Color•ad, Manassas, VA
Dahn Design, Seattle, WA
Deaton Museum Services, Minneapolis, MN
General Graphics, Cumberland, MD
Genesis Graphics, Escanaba, MI
Great Big Pictures, Inc., Madison-Milwaukee, WI
GS Images, Hagerstown, MD
Interpretive Exhibits, Inc., Salem, OR
Interpretive Graphics, Salt Lake City, UT
KLB Exhibits, Missoula, MT
Pannier Graphics, Warminster, PA
Raymond Price Associates, Frederick, MD
The Graphics Group, Staten Island, NY
Wilderness Graphics, Inc., Tallahassee, FL
Winsor Porcelain Enamel Display, Olympia, WA

SIGN TYPES AND MATERIALS

Over the years, sign materials have varied greatly, although the principles of sign-making art remain rather consistent. Current technology makes it possible to produce a detailed, colored sign, including drawings, fine photography, and varied text on material that resists weathering, fading, and vandalism, at least to some degree (Trapp, Gross and Zimmerman, 1991). The cost may be several thousand dollars per four-foot-by-four-foot sign, but many agencies find that these are cost-effective in reaching and informing visitors who carry away a positive impression (Figure 11.15).

Signs can be made on wood, paper, plastic, fiberglass, metals, acrylic, and glass. Each medium requires special methods and has its advantages (Table 11.1).

FIGURE 11.15
Porcelainized sign panels offer high durability, brilliant, nonfading colors.

TABLE 11.1 SIGN MATERIALS AND COMPARATIVE ATTRIBUTES

Sign Material	Cost	Durability	Repair	Photos	Frame	Color	Copies
Porcelain enamel: enamel surface on steel	High	Very high no fade	Easy clean even paint	Yes	Need	Yes, full range	Expensive
Fiberglass embedment	High	High may fade	Wax the scratches	Yes	Need	Yes	Inexpensive
Silk-screening on acrylic base	High	High scratches	Not easy	Yes	Need acrylic	Yes	Easy
Metal-micro images	High	High will not fade scratches	Eyebrow pencil	Yes	No	Shades of gray	Expensive
Wood, paint, carve rout, sand-blast	Lo-Hi	Medium-High	Easy	No	No	Paint	= original
Laminated or "plastic" paper	Low	Medium (often temporary)	Replace easily	Yes	Yes	Yes (box)	Easy, cheap
Vinyl adhesives plastic base	Medium	Medium scratch easily	Medium	No	Yes, acrylic front	Limited	Easy, cheap
Mold-cast aluminum, plastic, concrete	Medium (variable)	High	Not easy	No	Usual	Paint	Expensive, = original

Adapted from Kuehn, 1993.

LABELS AND SIGNS—GENERAL GUIDELINES

William H. Carr (1932, 1933) discovered, by experience, some simple rules for trail and museum labels or signs. His advice from 60 years ago still has validity and a certain charm. Modern writers use similar guidelines (e.g., Trapp, Gross, and Zimmerman, 1991).

1. Make labels concise—25 words or less. If you have more to say, put it on several signs. For most visitors, "individual short tags will be read where long ones will only hide the landscape" (Carr, 1932).
2. Do not pack labels with technical terms—even though the writer may think nearly everyone would or should know them. This sample label contains twenty words, but would have failed for nine out of ten persons, according to Carr (1932):

THE WOODCHUCK
A common rodent of the fields—hibernates in Winter.
Lives on plant food and inhabits self-made burrows.

Words such as rodent, hibernation, and self-made burrow may require explanation. Carr proposed separating this message into four labels—one key and three auxiliary—to tell the woodchuck story.

THE WOODCHUCK
A courageous inhabitant of fields and pasture lands, living in country districts in the face of its principal enemies—gun, man and dog.

A RODENT
The plant-loving woodchuck is related to . . . squirrels and mice. It has two gnawing, or rodent, teeth in front of upper and lower jaw.

WINTER SLEEP
The woodchuck sleeps, or hibernates, during cold months. It curls up in a furry ball and lets the snow fall unheeded.

THE HOME
Woodchucks dig or burrow in the earth, forming passageways and nest spaces. The burrows spell safety in time of danger.

3. Place the labels as close to the object as possible, or on it. Wires or cord may connect the label and the specimen to help a visitor locate it. Most should go on posts or separate stands, e.g., directions or quotes or poems. Some labels may be "hidden" to require some physical effort to find them—under a lid or a sliding cover.
4. Write the labels to offer information and, more importantly, to stimulate ideas, and invite observation. For example, encourage bringing seeds, or other materials back to the museum to examine under the microscope or magnifying glass [where allowed].
5. Listen to the visitors; observe their reactions; rewrite the labels.

To sum up these guidelines, these few words of Carr (1933) seem appropriate: "In order to interest and inform the visitor, it is needful to tell him salient facts in few words. It is a case not so much of what one would like to tell, but rather what the reader would like to be told."

Trail label writing—for signs or for entries in a booklet—requires clarity, simplicity and interest. Long ago, Lutz (1926) put the principles neatly. Labels should be "written in a language that ordinary people understand." They need to be chatty, colloquial, and educational. He suggested using three parts in sequence in the label:

Open the subject simply.

Develop its more complex ideas.

Close with a short summing up or by a few questions.

A label contains more than names. The trail label or brochure entry educates and entertains when it involves the emotions. Try to get some "kick" out of the label. Select words with emotional and physical punch, smoothness, music, and lightness to get across different points with different emotions. Think of the subtle images that the sounds of words can make. Some words lighten and brighten the spirit, just from seeing or hearing them in combination. Some produce nostalgic feelings that could help tie a person to a place or exhibit, e.g., the crackling campfire, marshmallows, a full moon and good friends.

Other words and phrases create suspense, anxiety, awe, curiosity. The "word artist" must practice, playing with words, testing their power. Put them together in different ways for different effects. It is not just the sounds, either. The meanings of words also excite our imaginations.

> The deeds we do, the words we say,
> Into still air they seem to fleet,
> We count them ever past;
> But they shall last,—
> In the dread judgement they
> And we shall meet.
> —John Kebble, *The Effect of Example*

Once the labels are up, reevaluate them and take appropriate action. Lutz (1926) recommended ". . . taking down things that do not seem to serve their function of interesting, and putting up things which would both interest and educate . . . but not so much that the average visitor would be confused or get tired." He likened a self-guiding trail to taking a walk with a friend and discussing interesting things in an agreeable way, telling stories when and where it was proper to do so.

The need for accuracy should be obvious—it seems pedantic to say it—but years of reading interpretive brochures prove that it must be said again: check your spelling, punctuation, grammar, factual accuracy, placement of pictures and legends, and meanings of any words that you barely know. Proofread the copy before printing it. Get several objective, independent people to proofread it. Then fix the errors—enough will show up after all of this to prove that you're human. A low-budget trail leaflet does not serve as an excuse for carelessness with language or looseness with facts.

MONUMENTS

Early military site interpretation consisted of battlefield monuments to the regiments or individuals who fell or fought there (Figure 11.16). The names and dates were enough, perhaps, when the nation was smaller, when the events were fresher in the collective memory. As new generations came to visit, the monuments appeared to clutter the battlefields with stone details that did not give the whole picture. Even at Gettysburg and Antietam, a foreign visitor would find it hard to tell who fought and why, how their deployments were moved, where the battle flowed or what the significance of the place was. Was it just where brave soldiers died and where Abraham Lincoln gave a memorable, brief oration?

Fields full of obelisks suggest a powerful kind of story; modern interpreters have used mostly self-guiding and a few personal methods to tell it. They started with a huge cyclorama painting at Gettysburg. At Antietam Battlefield in Maryland, huge paintings by a battle participant show several scenes, each now placed in line with a matching view from the visitor center. Later, interpreters made troop deployment charts and maps—some of

FIGURE 11.16

"We are inclined in America to think that the value of monuments is simply to remind us of origins. They are much more valuable as reminders of long-range, collective purpose, of goals and objectives and principles. As such even the least sightly of monuments gives a landscape beauty and dignity and keeps the collective memory alive."

—J.B. Jackson, "Concluding with Landscapes"

them now electronic marvels. The tapestry of methods to sort out the chaotic pictures of battle includes self-guiding brochures, auto-tour tapes keyed to numbers along the roads, wayside signs and models, visitor center models, maps, films, and books.

The monuments remain. Once the big story is told, their meaning enriches the site, rather than detracting from it. They show hard evidence of the depth of emotion felt by earlier generations at the losses of battle. The paucity of Southern monuments remind us of the rancor that remained, as well as the new poverty of the South after the War. When the visitor gets the big story, the old monuments and cannons seem not to clutter so much as they stand there "speaking" as abstract reminders of troops, some of whom spent the last moments of their lives at those spots.

Summary

This chapter started with some questions about gadgets and reality. Clever electronic devices can help people see the world more holistically. They can help people imagine the consequences of their actions on society and nature. They can play back the splendid oratory of Dr. Martin Luther King, Jr. and replay the music of summer birds in winter. They can quickly show phenomena that require months, even years, to develop.

Yet, people can become slaves to their toys, isolated from reality by the devices' realistic images. Interpreters can surely use the latest innovations to convey meanings. But they should never permit these gadgets to keep people from the real things. If interpreters do not give people direct experiences with real things, who will? If society's members do not get in touch with reality, do we end up with an unrealistic society?

Personal contact may often provide the highest quality of interpretation. However, nonpersonal media such as signs, brochures, audio devices, and other methods tied to the land or the museum artifacts may often reach more people. Because everyone has a chance to use nonpersonal media almost anytime, the reproduced words and images get to a very broad audience (Figure 11.17).

To make these media effective, one must write effectively, using brief, understandable messages. Where possible, accompany them with graphics that relate exactly to what is seen on the ground. Plan trails, tours, and other methods of getting visitors in contact with the resource so that they will be provoked to study carefully, to look beyond the paper or sign, to see reality and sense its complexity. Through varied self-guiding devices, help make the visitor into a true interpreter—a person who learns to translate what is seen into something meaningful and personal.

Figure 11.17

Humor can make a self-guiding trail more intriguing. (NPS)

Literature Cited

Bevilacqua, S. (1993). Milestones, millstones, and stumbling blocks. *Legacy, 4*(4):24-26.

Carr, W. H. (1932). *Trailside family*. New York, NY: American Museum of Natural History.

Carr, W. H. (1933). *Blazing nature's trail (2nd ed.)*. New York, NY: American Museum of Natural History, School Service Series No. 3.

Churchman, D. (1992). How to turn kids green. *American Forests, 98*(9&10):28-31, 60.

Countryside Commission. (1980). *Audio-visual media in countryside interpretation*. Chettenham, Gloucestershire, England: Countryside Commission Advisory Series, No. 12.

Dierking, L. D. and Falk, J. H. (1992). Redefining the museum experience: The interactive experience model. In: *Visitor Studies: Theory, Research, and Practice, Vol. 4*, Collected Papers, 1991 Visitor Studies Conference, Ottawa. Jacksonville, AL: Center for Social Design.

Harrison, A. (1977). *Interpreting the river resource*. Washington, DC: USDA Forest Service.

Jackson, J. B. (1984). *Discovering the vernacular landscape*. New Haven, CT: Yale University Press.

King, L. M. and Tabata, R. S. (1992). Hanauma Bay educational programs: Interpretation as a park management tool. In: *Proceedings, National Interpreters Workshop*, NAI, San Francisco Bay Area.

Kuehn, D. M. (1993). *Developing interpretive signs for visitors*. Oswego, NY: SUNY Sea Grant.

Lutz, F. E. (1926). *Nature trails and experience in outdoor education*. New York, NY: American Museum of Natural History, Miscellaneous Publication No. 21.

Pilley, E. T. (1990). Self-guided trails/tours: An alternative. In *Proceedings, National Interpreters Workshop*, NAI, Charleston, SC

Tilden, F. (1967). *Interpreting our heritage (rev. ed.)*. Chapel Hill, NC: University of North Carolina Press.

Trapp, S., Gross, M. and Zimmerman, R. (1991). *Signs, trails, and wayside exhibits: Connecting people and places*. Stevens Point, WI: UW-SP Foundation Press.

Wooley, F. J. (1979). "River interpretation: Development of an on-water trail." Ann Arbor, MI: University of Michigan, M. S. practicum report.

Performance Interpretation

If you smile at me, I will understand,
because that is something everybody,
everywhere does in the same language.
　　　—Crosby, Stills, and Nash ("Wooden Ships")

The two previous chapters focused on nonpersonal interpretation via exhibits and self-guiding trails and tours. This chapter concentrates on personal delivery of interpretive messages from information desk duty to roving interpretation. In addition, it provides the "nuts and bolts" of preparing and delivering interpretive talks and walks.

The key to personal or performance interpretation is the skill of the interpreter. As noted by Hilker (1974): "The principal instrument used by the interpreter is himself [or herself]. Despite the obviousness of that statement, sufficient effort is seldom made to hone the instrument." The individual directly contacts the audience in a number of methods, several of which are described below.

Information Desk Duty

Many interpreters begin their careers as seasonal employees with a primary duty of fee collection or information desk duty. Fee collection involves making monetary transactions with visitors as they enter the park and answering basic questions about the area. Information desk duty, which most often occurs at ranger stations or park visitor centers, provides orientation and information to visitors (Figure 12.1).

Although information duty sometimes gets tedious, it plays an essential role in an

FIGURE 12.1
Desk duty requires knowledge, patience, and cheerful sensitivity to people's needs.

interpretive setting because it offers visitors information they need for a safe, enjoyable, and life-enhancing experience. Furthermore, visitors' first contact with information personnel can strongly influence their impressions of an area. From the proper perspective, information duty can be rewarding work—after all, interpreters are being paid to talk with people who have come to them in a spirit of leisure and personal enrichment.

Edward Abbey (1968) listed the three most common questions that visitors ask: "Where's the Coke™ machine? Where's the restroom? How long does it take to see this place?" According to Maslow's hierarchy of needs (Chapter 3), people have to satisfy their basic needs prior to addressing higher order needs, as reflected in more sophisticated questions. Understanding this will help interpreters to remain patient and friendly when it appears that refreshment, relief, and an assessment of how long they have to stay dominate the people's interests. (Indeed, the interpreter also needs patience and friendliness to respond to orientation and information questions when meeting people at presentations of interpretive talks and walks.)

Despite these basic questions, sufficient opportunities arise for information desk personnel to interpret the park's attributes. Although some visitors move through quickly, others will want to learn more about the place. Whether visitors ask more penetrating questions depends a great deal on whether or not they feel secure, comfortable, and welcome. Interpreters can eliminate interpretive productivity by turning off the visitor.

Information staff, then, should be easily available to visitors as they enter the facility, greeting them with a genuine welcome. In many settings the information personnel approach visitors to indicate their availability to answer questions. Emerging from behind a desk or counter removes both a physical and psychological barrier and allows for more personal communication.

An interpreter should attempt to treat each visitor contact as a new situation, even though he or she has just heard a popular question several times. Interpreters should try to actively learn about each individual so that they can structure their responses to that person's interest and experience. An interpreter needs to discover the purpose of someone's visit; he or she cannot assume they already know. The responses will vary according to whether people have come to relax, fish, hike, watch birds, take scenic photographs, or some other activity. Also, find out if the visitor has been to the park before, to help in terms of background information to provide or experiences to suggest.

When appropriate, sensitize visitors to the values of the setting. Introduce the major interpretive themes—the significance of the area. Explain how visitors should conduct themselves to avoid damaging the site (Ham, 1992).

Although the purpose of information duty is to talk to people, interpreters must not allow any one visitor to dominate their time. He or she will need firm tactfulness with visitors who just "shoot the breeze"—out of respect for other visitors who may require his or her expertise.

When confronted by a difficult or angry visitor, remain calm. Do not take an abusive person's behavior personally. Listen carefully to the person and try to understand the situation. Attempt to correct the problem and fill out a complaint form if necessary.

A few other points that information personnel should keep in mind include:

1. Know the resource. It is essential that an interpreter know about his or her museum or interpretive site and the surrounding area. They should know the answers to common questions and where to find the answers to more unusual questions. Strive to

interpret the information relating what is being explained to something within the experience of the visitor. For example, while answering a simple inquiry about a campsite, they could call the visitor's attention to an interesting plant, animal, or geological feature that can be seen at that location (e.g., the campsite with the three redbuds in bloom). Furthermore, as a resident in a certain setting interpreters should constantly renew their own capacity for the complexity and wonder of the place (Beck, 1989). The interpretation will remain fresh and visitors will sense enthusiasm. Good interpretive supervisors will allocate sufficient time for continued learning about the resource, both for the sake of the interpreter and the visitors.

2. Interpreters should admit when they do not know the answer to a question. Their training and personal interest in the area will prepare them to answer the vast majority of questions. Still, occasionally he or she will not have the answers. In these instances he or she may refer to a more seasoned employee or supervisor, look up the information, or make a phone call. If the interpreter still cannot turn up the answer, the visitor will know that he or she tried and that the answer is not readily available. For detailed orientation and information, many visitor centers and administrative offices keep notebooks, filled with important information for quick reference by information personnel or visitors, arranged according to category, e.g., food and lodging, emergency services, regional attractions, on-site interpretive opportunities (Box 12.1).

3. Provide hand-outs. Brochures and other hand-out material give the visitor something to take for further reference. These inexpensive materials generally focus on interpretive programs and other park activities (often in the form of a park newspaper), natural history (such as bird lists), safety considerations (often half-page flyers), and near-by attractions (generally promotional materials).

4. Use maps. Because many visitors are new to the area, make reference to maps when giving directions.

5. Know how to respond when emergencies occur (they will). Information personnel should be familiar with basic first aid and CPR. Further, they should know who to contact in case of an emergency they cannot handle. Supervisors should cover site-specific emergency procedures early in training; a sequence of actions should be posted or readily available.

6. Provide after-hours information. On an outdoor bulletin board provide up-dated weather, safety precautions, important park regulations, emergency phone numbers, and visitor procedures information during times the visitor center is closed. Some parks use computer programs to provide this and similar information.

7. Interpreters should not take themselves too seriously. Some information personnel (and interpreters in general) become brash and arrogant or just plain dull over time. Remember that interpreters will meet and guide many people of great skill, accomplishment and education. They just happen to have information and experience that can help them enjoy their museum or forest or camp. Whatever the visitor's background, the customers deserve your courtesy and respect, even if they are temporarily nervous or upset. That is, after all, the nature of the job.

BOX 12.1: AN INFORMATION CHECKLIST

Visitor information notebooks can be organized according to various topics of interest as follows:

AUTOMOTIVE SERVICES
- Gas Stations
- Towing
- Repair Shops

EMERGENCY SERVICES
- Ambulance
- Hospitals (with maps)
- Fire Station
- Police or Sheriff

FOOD AND LODGING
- Bed-and-Breakfast
- Grocery Stores
- Restaurants
- Camping and RV parks
- Hotels, Lodges, Motels
- Youth Hostels

GENERAL SERVICES
- Banks
- Churches
- Sewage Disposal
- Veterinarian
- Camera Stores
- Ice Vendors
- Souvenir Shops

NATURAL AND CULTURAL FEATURES
- Cultural and Historic Information
- Natural History Information
  (i.e., geology, plants, animals)

ON-SITE INTERPRETIVE OPPORTUNITIES
- Interpretive Guidebooks
  (i.e., reference and sale items)
- Programs (i.e., schedules, topics, and locations)
- Self-Guided Opportunities
  (e.g., trails, wayside exhibits, audio tours)

OUTFITTERS, GUIDES, AND OTHER RECREATION
- Climbing Instruction
- Golf Courses
- River Trips
- Diving
- Horse Rentals
- Swimming

REGIONAL ATTRACTIONS (with travel distances and times)
- Art Galleries
- Monuments
- Scenic Drives
- Wine Tasting
- Museums
- Other Parks (local, state, federal)
- Theaters, Outdoor Dramas

SAFETY HAZARDS
- Dangerous Wildlife
- Site-Specific Hazards
  (e.g., cliffs, flash floods, thermal pools)
- Poisonous Plants

TRANSPORTATION SERVICES
- Airlines
- Car Rentals
- Taxis
- Travel Agencies
- Bus Schedules
- Sightseeing Tours
- Trains

Roving or Station Interpretation

Roving interpretation refers to the stationing of interpreters in high use areas for informal individual contacts with visitors (Figure 12.2). Station interpreters work at a particular spot, often in a museum, in the front of a visitor center, or along a walking route. Often, they demonstrate a craft or special skill related to the theme of the interpretive program. Sometimes, they teach the skill to visitors as they come by. In other cases, they present a short talk or explanation of a phenomenon at that point (Figure 12.3)

FIGURE 12.2
A volunteer roving interpreter shows a tarantula to the visitors at the Arizona Sonoran Desert Museum.

Roving interpreters roam about or set up a small portable work table, interpreting to people about the site or about nearby exhibits in a museum. This approach works well near a major museum exhibit or at an outdoor overlook, where people concentrate to see a certain feature. For example, at Cabrillo National Monument, in California, interpreters go to the whale overlook where they help visitors to spot gray whales that are migrating south during the winter months. They discuss natural history of the gray whales and answer other questions about the park.

A common practice among roving interpreters is to carry a small pack with items such as first-aid supplies, maps, binoculars, field guides, and other resources that may be useful to help visitors or interpret the area. A small box or folder with exhibit materials, identification charts, and

FIGURE 12.3
Roving interpretive contacts sometimes turn into talks to large groups, such as on popular Cadillac Mountain in Acadia National Park.
(NPS)

free brochures help interested visitors get deeply involved (Figure 12.4).

Visitors may not immediately understand that the roving interpreter came to the site to talk to people and answer their questions. Many visitors could assume that interpreters have

FIGURE 12.4
Interpreters set up temporary stations in the Arizona Sonoran Desert Museum to add detailed information about exhibits as visitors circulate through the outdoor museum.

other business, so they may hesitate to approach them. Therefore, approach visitors (gently) or otherwise "open the store" to let them know of your availability.

Because roving and station interpreters locate where many people congregate, they often see violations of regulations, such as collecting shells in a tidepool area, picking wildflowers, or feeding the wildlife. Wallace (1990) recommended a three-point nonthreatening sequence when contacting visitors who have committed minor infractions. First, provide a descriptive account of the observed situation. Talk about the infraction in the context of the resource without reference to agency regulations. Second, explain the impact of the action on the resource as well as how the action impinges upon the enjoyment of the resource by other visitors. Third, provide the visitors with an assessment of how the situation can be remedied.

This three-point interaction emphasizes the values of the setting and the consequences of the actions, rather than reprimanding someone for violating regulations. It tries to inculcate the reasons that a behavior is important. The focus centers not on the enforcer or getting caught, but on the resource and what happens to it. Thus the interpreter seeks to change behavior by "revealing the authority of the resource" (Wallace, 1990). This approach works especially well for visitors who are simply unaware of what entails responsible behavior in a natural or cultural setting (Hendee, Stankey, and Lucas, 1990; Gramann and Vander Stoep, 1987).

Most interpreters enjoy roving duty because they interpret features first-hand, spontaneously, and to individuals. It requires considerable knowledge and flexibility, so experienced personnel do the job best. From the perspective of park management it provides good public relations to people who otherwise might not come in contact with an interpreter. Roving interpreters often give visitors current information about hazards such as inclement weather or dangerous wildlife. They can also feature special ephemeral interpretive opportunities, such as a mayfly hatch, a shad run, a historical reenactment, or a celebration.

Lewis (1980) suggested that roving interpreters provide "mini-walks" to groups of people interested in a short, guided tour of the area or a section of the museum. Although "mini-walks" are informal and impromptu orientations, they may use many of the principles listed in the following sections titled "The Interpretive Talk" and "Interpretive Walks."

CAVE INTERPRETATION

Station interpretation methods have become more popular in caves. Combining it with personally conducted special tours gives greater flexibility and interest (Woods, 1977). With visitors using self-guiding headsets, the interpreters have greater opportunity to station themselves along the way to address individual questions, adapting to each visitor and exploring key features and processes in detail, according to each visitor's needs and wishes. Thus, each cave can better feature its individual characteristics, providing visitors more than "just another cave tour."

Most commercial and public cave tours have explained the lighted, paved path and formations, a sort of "gee-whiz, ain't it beautiful" kind of sightseeing with an underground novelty. Guides invariably explain the names of formations, using both popular and geological terms (Smith, 1977). They almost always describe how water dissolves limestone to form stalactites and stalagmites by dripping and drying. These standard inclusions in any cave tour result in some travelers saying that they've already been in a cave; they need not go again. Rather than pointing out the uniqueness and providing a discovery approach to learning about caves, some guides parrot a standard script that could almost be used universally, with adjustments for order and local names of formations (e.g., the Queen's Veil, The Emperor's Throne, the Devil's Caldron, the Emerald Pool).

The Interpretive Talk

Interpretive talks may take place almost anywhere. The personality of the interpreter enters as a major component concerning the success of any given talk.

Most commonly, talks occur in relatively formal settings such as auditoriums, outdoor amphitheaters, museums, and on visitor center porches. Less formal talks, although no less professional, are given "on-site" in historical, archæological, and natural areas (Figure 12.5). Josh Barkin, with the East Bay Regional Park District in California, was well-known for his innovative "gutter" talks—that is, interpretation of what is found in sidewalk gutters!

FIGURE 12.5
Interpreter Cem Basman offers an outdoor talk at Beall Woods State Park, IL.

The talk can take the form of 10-20 minute "porch talks" on the patio or back porch of the interpretive center; "theater talks" of variable length, usually not more than 45 minutes, in an indoor or outdoor theater; or "evening campfire talks" of 15 to 45 minutes that headline or supplement an evening program. A variety of other talk possibilities exist, on- or off-site and of varying lengths.

Talks also occur on ships, buses, trams, trains, and other modes of transportation within an interpretive area (Figure 12.6). Interpretive walks employ the same principles as talks along with some additional considerations.

FIGURE 12.6
The skipper of the Danny J, out of Homer, Alaska, interprets birds, bays, fish and fjords.

A visitor chooses to attend a talk and can decide to leave at any time. A "noncaptive" audience expects an informal, nonacademic, and enjoyable presentation. An effective interpretive talk may encourage visitors to attend other programs and will fill them with interest and excitement about the place they came to visit. On the other hand, a poorly executed talk can discourage visitors from seeking to experience more.

Many people have weakly developed listening skills. Although they may hear what is said, they do not necessarily process and retain it. What an audience is told and what a member of it actually retains goes through a multiple-step communications process proposed by Grater (1976):

1. What the speaker knows about the subject.
2. What the speaker thinks he or she told listeners about the subject.
3. What he or she actually told them.
4. What the listener heard about the subject.
5. What the listener actually actively listened to.
6. What the listener understood about what he or she said.
7. What the listener retained about the subject initially.
8. What the listener remembered later.

Apparently, the average person retains only about 10 percent of what a speaker offers if there is an attempt to absorb the message (Grater, 1976). Therefore, choose a few key ideas on which to concentrate on so that the audience does not become overloaded with information.

BASIC QUALITIES OF EFFECTIVE SPEAKING

An effective interpreter shares many of the same characteristics and uses many of the same techniques of any competent public speaker. Books on how to speak in public generally include the following qualities of good speakers and speeches.

Amiability. Effective communication begins with an open, friendly, and good-natured demeanor on the part of the speaker. Because interpretation takes place in recreational settings, aloofness and extensive solemnness are not appropriate. This does not suggest that interpreters, who offer important messages, should act like comedians, but rather that they exhibit genuine friendliness, good humor, and concern for the well-being of visitors.

Enthusiasm. As the old adage goes, enthusiasm is contagious. Interpreters who seem energetic and truly excited about what they discuss create an atmosphere of inspiration. This affinity both for the subject being interpreted and the people who have gathered to hear the message can capture and hold the attention of the audience. Of course, the reverse is also true. An interpreter's lack of enthusiasm can put an immediate damper on the spirit of an audience.

Confidence. Good speakers radiate self-assurance and poise. Interpreters have the advantage of a certain level of initial credibility because of the agencies they are affiliated with and the uniforms or identification many of them wear. Virtually every interpreter builds up a sense of anxiety just prior to a talk. An elevated adrenaline level can benefit the talk because the interpreter becomes more alert and focused on the task at hand. Interpreters can control various outward signs of nervousness, such as fidgeting, slouching, using a podium as a "crutch," saying "uh" in excess, avoiding eye contact with members of the audience, crossing both arms across the chest. Colleagues and supervisors can alert less experienced interpreters to how they portray a lack of confidence and help eliminate those habits.

Delivery. For good delivery, speak conversationally. Interpreters should strive to speak with (not at or down to) the audience, personally and informally, as he or she would with smaller groups. Informality does not preclude rigorous preparation; rather, it avoids the appearance of rigor mortis. Use simple, vivid words and illustrations to make a point.

Several delivery faults turn off listeners. Some inexperienced speakers tend to talk in a monotone; this reduces listener comprehension (Knapp, 1972). Speech that is consistently too fast or too slow, too loud or too soft, too insistent or too docile can frustrate and irritate members of an audience. Varying the rate, volume, and force of speech, within reasonable limits, will increase the attentiveness of the listeners. So will a natural use of appropriate gestures. Avoid slang or profanity. Likewise, do not resort to potentially insulting references about people or places—even good-natured jibes at states, universities, or towns can offend some people.

To improve speaking habits, study closely and emulate particularly effective public speakers. Compare them to video or audiotapes of recent efforts.

Organization. Confidence and good delivery skills depend on a strong grasp of the subject matter. Furthermore, a well-prepared program lends itself to increased self-assurance. The interpretive talk should flow in an orderly sequence and the transitions within the body of the talk should be logical. Use a few appropriate cues (numbers, transitions) that tell the listener that the talk is moving forward in an orderly way. This will help the audience follow the presentation without becoming lost.

A good interpretive presentation entails a great deal of research, thought, care, and rehearsal. An audience will sense when a speaker has committed substantial effort to the work. The effort counts, however, only when the final product turns out to be fun, effective, and informative.

Ideally, give interpretive talks without using notes. Reading from paper or cards may distract and interrupt eye contact with members of the audience. Some interpreters may be tempted to write out and memorize their talks. Unless the speaker has a special talent, this will cause the talk to lose its spontaneous and conversational tone. It can also be a disaster if the interpreter forgets any segment of the presentation and finds it difficult to get back on track.

An effective approach is to organize an outline, memorize the major headings, and then talk about each of the sections in order. This allows for a more conversational tone. It also provides a degree of flexibility depending upon the specific needs of any particular audience. A small card or two listing the major points and a quote or two may be unobtrusive while giving the interpreter a sense of security.

COMPONENTS OF AN INTERPRETIVE TALK

A. The Theme

Each presentation that you develop will focus on a certain topic. Topics may start out as broad as geology, wildlife, desert ecology, human history, and so on. The topic refers to the general subject area of the talk. In contrast, the theme represents the message to be conveyed. The theme, in a sentence, provides a concise cognitive overview of the central idea that you reveal in more detail in the full presentation.

The following characteristics are used to develop and define themes (paraphrased from Lewis, 1980):

1. State the theme concisely, simply and clearly in an active sentence.
2. Convey the one central idea, or overall message of the presentation.
3. Base the theme upon topics related to the property's resources.
4. Word the theme in an interesting, provocative manner.
   Examples of themes developed by National Park Service trainees in a short course demonstrate these characteristics:
   - Lafayette Park serves as the focal point of First Amendment rights.
   - The actions of our nation's third president were responsible for the development and settlement of the West.
   - A rodent played a big part in the discovery and exploration of the American West.
   - Animals at Hurricane Ridge in Olympic National Park must adapt to severe winter weather or die.
   - The most polluted national park area in the U.S. has the most plant species per acre.
   - The absorptive qualities of snow can save your life or take it away.

The theme dictates the kind of information needed to construct the program. Furthermore, because the theme is shared with an audience early in the interpretive presentation, it aids in providing organizational structure and clarity for the audience. Therefore, the theme should clearly focus on the key concept that visitors will take from the presentation. It serves as the take-home message, the unifying idea, or the motif of the presentation. Talk themes usually relate directly to the attributes of a particular site, camp, or museum. They usually derive from themes stated in the interpretive prospectus.

People comprehend and remember information most efficiently when they hear or read the theme at the beginning, according to research findings (Thorndyke, 1977). By introducing the theme early, the questions "Why is this important?" and "Why should I listen?" are answered.

B. The Introduction

The introduction of a talk provides the audience with key information, including the theme, that will help them understand the balance of the presentation. Many effective communicators make use of a "grabber" in the introduction to catch the interest of the audience. This strategy employs the use of a quotation, an anecdote, humor, or conundrum related to the theme.

The introduction (1) defines the purpose of the presentation, (2) creates a cognitive map to help visitors follow the talk, and (3) creates a favorable atmosphere. In practice, a speaker begins his or her talk by welcoming the group to the park, introducing himself or herself clearly, announcing the theme of the program, giving a quick preview of what's about to happen, and suggesting how long it will take.

C. The Body

The introduction should flow smoothly to the body of the talk. The theme is developed within the body. The body consists of a logical sequence of information cued by key ideas and transitions. The key points are revealed as the text develops. List and enumerate major ideas to help the audience perceive the organization. It helps them listen and comprehend.

Public speakers may make use of a number of rhetorical strategies to most effectively and interestingly convey a message (Box 12.2). The body of a talk should have these characteristics:
- Narrative quality—A story approach that pulls people along.
- Cohesiveness—Based upon a sequential outline and the effective use of transitions.
- Suspense and climax—This can be accomplished by posing a question and revealing the answer.
- Completeness—Relate your specific subject to the larger whole.

D. The Conclusion

In the introduction the audience is told what the speaker is going to do. In the body of the talk speakers do what they said they would. In the conclusion speakers tell the audience what they did. Speakers strive to make the presentation more memorable to the audience in the conclusion. "Well, that's about it" serves as a poor excuse for a vivid and inspiring conclusion. Another poor one: "OK, any questions?"

The conclusion, then, summarizes the talk's key points and restates the theme. Make the conclusion direct and unambiguous. If possible, have a final tactic that brings the subject to a dramatic close—a quote, a story, a poem. An interpreter at Denali National Park, for example, concluded his evening auditorium programs by reciting Robert Service poetry about the wonders of the Far North. Dr. Martin Luther King, Jr. ended the most famous speech of our time with a quote that summarized his theme and carried its own dramatic impact: "Free at last! Free at last! Lord, God Almighty, we are free at last!"

End the talk with a bang, then stop. If a conclusion runs on after an impressive statement, the magic vanishes. Leave people inspired, wanting to learn and experience more.

Finally, the speaker should always make himself or herself available after the program to answer individual questions. He or she can also provide the more interested visitors with recommendations for gaining even deeper perspective on the subject.

BOX 12.2: RHETORICAL STRATEGIES FOR "SPICING THE PROGRAM"

Stories. Illustrate your message with stories to captivate the interest of your group. Make the whole interpretive message a story.

Anecdotes. Concise and pertinent biographical stories should somehow relate to the theme of the presentation.

Quotations. Quoting others briefly, particularly those who are associated with the cultural or natural history of the area, can add interest and color to a talk.

Examples. Examples give the audience detail and specifics to help understand the broad points or context of the message.

Analogies. Explain something by making a comparison to something similar that is more familiar to the audience.

Metaphors. Give a name or quality to something when it literally does not fit, but figuratively describes it, e.g., "an icy glance."

Similes. Similes use the words "like" or "as" to relate characteristics of two items.

Current News Events. Use of current news events at the local, state, national, or international level to relate to site history or as an example of a key point.

Repetition. Repeat key phrases to create powerful, memorable messages. In Martin Luther King's most famous speech he started eight sequential paragraphs with the statement "I have a dream."

Humor. Humor, used appropriately, can loosen up the audience and the speaker and drive home some key points.

Adapted from Kawasaki (1991)

Illustrated Talks

Illustrated talks employ all of the principles previously covered for interpretive talks. In addition to spoken words, illustrated talks offer the added dimension of visual aids. Although excellent interpretive talks can be conducted without visual aids, the use of slides, props, overhead transparencies, flip charts, chalkboards, and cloth boards can make presentations more understandable and interesting to the audience.

The first task is to develop an effective narrative that stands on its own. Words alone can create vivid pictures. For example, most people having read a book and seen a movie based on the book will say that the book was better. This is because the imagination of the reader comes into play in the reading process creating vivid images and details.

After developing the talk, determine if visuals will enhance the prepared materials. If visuals will make the talk more comprehensible and entertaining—use them. If visuals will distract the audience or result in a more complex message—avoid them.

Regardless of the type of visual aid there are several guidelines that should be kept in mind. Most important, make sure that everyone in the audience can see the visual aids. The object or the chart displayed should be sufficiently large so the people in the back row can see it. If one can hear oneself saying "Maybe all of you cannot see this, but . . ." then that prop should be set aside for a smaller audience. To be most effective, visuals should be simple and straightforward. Complex drawings or illustrations may only confuse the audience. Use the visual only for the length of time that the commentary corresponds to it. Once the visual no longer offers relevant information it should be removed or replaced; otherwise, it serves only as a distraction.

Although some find it a difficult habit to break, avoid talking to the visual; face the audience, even in the dark. A speaker's toes should point at the audience, as he or she stands on firmly planted feet. Then, whenever a speaker twists to see the picture, his or her body will spring back into proper position.

SLIDE SHOWS

Among the most commonly used illustrated talks is the slide show (Figure 12.7). Interpreters present slide shows both indoors, such as in a visitor center auditorium, and outdoors as part of the evening program as discussed in the following section and Box 12.3.

FIGURE 12.7
Slide talk at an Acadia National Park campfire event. (NPS)

BOX 12.3: SIMPLE TIPS FOR QUALITY SLIDE SHOWS

- Use the best slides that can be acquired—focused and properly exposed.
- Use images with good composition.
- Use pictures that do not confuse the audience.
- Use slides which illustrate the point being discussed.
- Use a title or theme slide and an end slide when appropriate.
- If available, use a series of images, progressing from overview shots to close-ups.
- Avoid showing any one slide for too long. The audience will lose their focus on the flow of your talk.
- Avoid playing music while narrating slides at the same time. Generally, use music with slides at the introduction or conclusion of the program.
- Arrange slides so they convey the theme of the talk, e.g., a seasonal progression of images for a presentation on seasons.
- Avoid all but the simplest of maps, graphs, and charts.
- Pause during the talk at important points to let the words sink in a bit.
- Use moments of pause to strengthen the speech. The narrative may lead up to a slide or a series of slides that do not require words. This technique can be powerful when well-orchestrated.
- Start an outdoor evening slide show only when the sky is dark enough so the slides can be clearly seen.

In developing a slide show, work out the entire outline and narrative before illustrating the talk with slides. A common problem for inexperienced interpreters occurs when attempting to develop a talk around a set of slides that they previously picked out. Now, realistically, most speakers use some combination of these two approaches. They outline the talk, then fit in slides, then fill in details of the narrative to match the slides. Take plenty of good slides (Box 12.4). Keep them dry and clean.

A recent three-night visit to a major national park revealed the apparent poverty of the park slide collection. In three different evening talks by three different interpreters plus two other automated slide presentations, at least 20 slides appeared in all programs. The ingenious interpreters used them to make different points, however.

As with all programs, the speaker must arrive early. With slide presentations this is especially important because he or she must set up his or her equipment. Obviously, familiarity with basic problem-solving techniques such as changing a projector bulb or releasing a jammed slide can have high value. Know the equipment well before trying to use it in the dark under pressure. Ideally, a speaker will finish setting up prior to the arrival of most visitors. This way the speaker can focus on the talk rather than fiddle with equipment.

Once warm-up activities are conducted and the program is introduced, turn down the lights. Always start and end with a picture or a dark screen. A glaring white screen breaks the mood, distracts an audience and gives children (and some adults) the irresistible opportunity to make shadow figures with their hands. Newer slide projectors are designed so this cannot happen. Two-projector dissolve units allow smooth transitions from slide-to-slide, giving a presentation a more professional look.

Stand in front of the audience, without obstructing the view of the screen, rather than behind with the equipment. Use a remote (cord or cordless) device to advance the slides. Talk toward the audience and not toward the screen, although it is natural to glance at the screen occasionally.

Know the narrative and slides well enough to have the order memorized. Remember that the slides do not drive the talk. The slides illustrate the narrative. That thought should help prevent any use of the phrases "this slide shows . . . " or "Here is a picture of . . . " These weak transitions strongly suggest that the slides are running the interpreter's mind. Common sense also suggests (to some) that a speaker need not show all of his or her slides. The bear that's a mere black dot or the overexposed image or the blurry flower add nothing to public understanding. They can be stored temporarily in the "never use" file until it is realized that wishful thinking will not improve them; then they can be incinerated. A number of excellent references for developing professional slide presentations include Lewis (1980) and Ham (1992), as well as inexpensive Eastman Kodak booklets available through local camera shops (Box 12.4).

BOX 12.4: Basic Photography Tips

- Be certain that the subject is in focus. In wildlife photography focus on the eyes.
- When a slide comes back from the developer out of focus, just throw it away.
- Check for proper exposure. If a slide comes back too light or too dark, just throw it away.
- Attempt to take photographs that tell an interesting story.
- Take pictures in rich light, in the morning or evening, but not just at dawn or dusk.
- Attempt artistic photographs. The best compositions (such as those by Eliot Porter, David Muench, and Philip Hyde) elicit emotional responses.
- Strive for a visually simple photograph. Decide not only what to include but choose what to eliminate that might detract from the composition (see photos by the three artists listed above).
- Avoid cutting your photo in halves, e.g., with the horizon. If you include the horizon, make sure that it is horizontal (or at least that the camera is level).
- Avoid placing the subject in the exact middle of the composition—use the "rule" of thirds, putting key subjects and lines off-center.
- Bracket important shots to insure proper exposure. Take one photo at the light meter reading, then take the exact photo again at one f-stop lighter and one darker.
- Remember the difference between a good photographer and an average photographer; a good photographer throws out or incinerates the average slides.
- Read a detailed discussion of professional methods for the interpreter such as John Shaw's *The Nature Photographer's Complete Guide to Professional Techniques* (1984).

Evening Programs

An evening program gathers people—something like moths to a flame—if they know about it, if it is attractive to them, and if it is close enough so they can easily get there.

The evening program provides a contact point for inviting overnight visitors to explore and to use other interpretive services. It helps them get acquainted with other visitors and the staff. For example, interest in a hike the next day may grow if new acquaintances will be there or if the hike leader has talked with them. People sometimes participate for the social interaction as much as for the information.

Evening "campfire" programs need not include flames and wood, although that adds to the color and character of them. Start the fire about a half hour before the program. Make sure dry wood is available (to keep smoke to a minimum) and some kind of extinguishing device lies at hand to prevent unwanted spread of the flames. Avoid putting the fire in the center, where it will reflect on the projection screen; likewise, do not put the fire ring up-wind of the audience, the projection screen, or the speaker.

The evening program, to a certain degree, is a social event and can help visitors experience a good time and feel comfortable in their new temporary surroundings. Just as with any social occasion, it requires planning and careful preparation.

Many traditional strategies promote interaction among audience members. Some are done too often and may come off as artificial stimulants to sociability. The most common device is asking people where they are from. This approach, although perhaps trite to some, may lead to discussions with visitors from foreign countries or from in-common states.

Another ice-breaker activity (it makes some people uncomfortable) requests visitors to shake hands with and introduce themselves to people seated nearby. This appropriate courtesy, however, can have obvious benefits. It sets the program apart from, say, going to the theater and gets people acquainted who may be spending several days together.

Group singing can help relax and unite people without coercion. The most challenging aspect of this activity is to somehow make it consistent with the theme of the program. Ideally, choose songs to fit the main message of the event. Keep the singing portion of the program relatively brief. A serious visitor coming to a program about geological strata could be put off by a 20-minute song fest. Three or four well-known selections that relate to the topic of the evening, even in a humorous way, may be most appropriate.

To accommodate people who may not know the words to songs, show them on a screen or provide song sheets. Another popular strategy is the "lead line-repeat" method where the audience repeats the key lines sung by the leader.

Sometimes, a guitar-playing interpreter may do a little singing to set a mood or wind up a program; this can lead to a participatory event as the audience joins in. The key to successful song leading is your enthusiasm, so relax, get into it and lead with vigor if music is to be included as part of the program.

Be aware that many visitors will be perfectly content without any social events. The singing and similar activities, however, if conducted thoughtfully and in moderation, can have the benefit of developing a sense of community and fun.

EARLY ARRIVALS

The key to success in working with early arrivals is a calm, friendly interpreter who initiates contact and is inclusive of others as they arrive. Interpreters have been observed using these specific techniques:

- Conduct some simple activities using natural materials—such as acorn cup or grass whistles.
- If there is going to be singing, get the early arrivals practicing so they can help lead the fun parts (e.g., motions, rounds, percussion, strange sounds). Their early involvement attracts other people and gives some forewarning that the program will soon be underway.

- Play some music appropriate to the theme of the program. Make it loud enough to remind campers that something will start soon; keep the aural intrusion short, however, to prevent irritation.
- Create some demonstration packs that relate to the interpretive site and allow early arrivals to examine them and carry them around. These can include a Civil War soldier's pack, a miner's grubstake pack, a modern backpack equipped for five days in the wilderness, a fire-fighter's pack, a horse or mule pack, or a bicycle pack for a three-day ride. Other display items related to the topic of the program would also be appropriate.

Guided Travel

Moving around a museum, a zoo, a camp, a forest, a refuge, a factory, even a wilderness with a guide comprises conducted activities (Figure 12.8). The personal interpreter shows the visitor the artifacts or environment, weaving a walk or ride into a whole story. The abstractions stop at the beginning of the tour. The interpreter leads visitors to art works, exhibits full of artifacts, or the trees and plants of the forest, explaining them in ways that provoke the visitor to investigate them in detail. Make guided travel relevant and enjoyable. People want to enjoy the experience.

FIGURE 12.8
Guided auto tours on Crater Lake Rim Drive were popular many decades ago. (NPS)

Bus tours in Denali (Figure 12.9), elephant trains in Yosemite National Park, CA and Sabino Canyon, AZ provide low-impact ways of presenting the resources to many people while talking with them about their specific interests.

INTERPRETIVE WALKS

Walks, hikes, and tours often symbolize interpretation to many people (Figure 12.10). Nature walks and history tours need descriptive names to attract people. *Nature walk* sounds rather vague and either too scientific or too taxing for kids, depending on your experience.

History tour scares off some just because of a fear of history. More thematic titles, giving an intriguing name should attract more. Examples from Montgomery County, MD, nature centers include: Trees are Terrific, Litterbug!, Creatures of the Night, Search for Spring, Stones and Bones Tour, Spring Amphibian Search, Incredible Edibles, Garden Tour: Old Roses, Slip & Slop Stream Search, Fox Trot Night Hike.

FIGURE 12.9
Commercial bus tour guides in Denali National Park help visitors spot and understand wildlife.

In historic homes, archæological sites, and environmental education centers, guided tours or hikes often make up the central visitor experience. Other places may offer only one or two escorted hikes or tours per day, relying on self-guiding trail brochures, wayside signs, visitor center exhibits, and auto tour booklets for much of the interpretation.

Guided hikes and tours may run into logistical problems in some areas. Visitation to these programs, generally

FIGURE 12.10
Interpreters acquaint others with how fellow species function and where they live.

open to all comers, may fluctuate greatly. For example, a 6 a.m. bird hike may draw only a few visitors. A 1 p.m. walk may have 60 hikers on a nice day and only a few hardy souls on a hot summer afternoon. Some interpretive agencies set limits on the number of people that participate to maintain a level of quality that is associated with the interpretive experience. Guides limit walks to the Betatakin cliff dwelling at Navajo National Monument in Arizona to 25 people. Likewise, only 25 can go on a guided walk within the Fiery Furnace at

Arches National Park in Utah. Larger groups may diminish the quality of the experience. Small groups allow for more personal attention from the interpreter and a more intimate tone (Figure 12.11). Concerns for safety and resource protection also come into play.

Approaches to Presentations

In preparing a hike or other program, the interpreter develops an introduction, body, and conclusion just as for interpretive talks. The introduction should include the theme, time, distance, ending point, difficulty of terrain, type of clothing and supplies needed, and other pertinent information.

Several different techniques may contribute to the making of a good hike, tour, or talk. Grater (1976) boiled these down to four common methods, each related to different learning principles, as follows: telling, telling and showing, drawing out, and telling-showing-drawing out.

1. In the basic **telling** approach, the guide leads the group to preselected points along a route, gathers them, tells about the features of the stop, then moves on to the next destination. Although questions and answers occur, most of the action is leader-directed. This method is often used on structured building and factory tours, cave tours, historical building visits, archæology walks, and museum tours. On nature and geology walks, it may be a major component. This approach best suits the "actual-routine" learner (Chapter 7).

    Strengths: The telling method offers a clear focus on the subject; it presents information in a mostly uninterrupted sequence. It allows efficient control of the group and the length of time allotted to the event, which is important at popular attractions, or for traveling groups with tight schedules.

    Weaknesses: This approach offers little opportunity for visitors to broaden the scope of the topic. The learning comes primarily from listening. Compared with the following strategies there is little group involvement. Finally, interpreters can fall into mechanical, rote presentations.

2. **Telling and showing** adds interesting demonstrations and activities to the telling approach. Several good demonstrations during a walk provide worthwhile additions,

FIGURE 12.11
Talks with small groups allow audience participation.

especially if they involve audience participation. The interpreter can get participants to act out or pantomime natural processes. For example, people can act out the parts of a tree: the taproot, lateral roots, heartwood, sapwood, phloem/cambium, and bark. Cornell (1989) called this activity "Build a Tree" and suggested that it has the "magical" power to create camaraderie as well as teach tree biology.

A demonstration could also involve improvised role playing in historical situations. Grater (1976) described how four children became the "firing crew" at an inert cannon, going through the disciplined processes involved in preparing and firing it with military precision as commanded by the interpreter.

At Denali National Park and Preserve some interpreters who presented sled dog demonstrations lined up visitors to represent the lead dog, swing dogs, team dogs, and wheel dogs according to their functions. Role playing can both demonstrate the procedure and entertain the entire group. Then the real dogs get into harness and show how vigorously they pull. This approach suits "actual routine," "conceptual specific," and "conceptual global" learners.

Strengths: Properly planned there can still be reasonable control of the group, the time, and the topic focus. Opportunity exists for visitor involvement and group interaction with more or less predictable results.

Weaknesses: As with the "telling" method, visitors provide minimal contribution to the content of the program.

3. The **drawing out** approach requires an alert, informed, and confident interpreter. To give the walk a focus, the interpreter defines a theme such as survival foods or insects in the forest. In this context, the group explores to find things of interest. As a visitor locates something, the interpreter employs questioning techniques. Through the use of thoughtful questions, the interpreter draws out possible answers and draws the group toward more intimate observation of the phenomenon. Questions such as "Why do you think we only find these insects inside the logs?" will lead the group to ponder possible answers and often to raise other questions. The interpreter serves as the director of the investigation. This method is most appropriate for "actual spontaneous" learners.

Strengths: In this approach the walk becomes the group's. Members encouraged to explore gain information through direct experience. The interpreter skillfully asks questions and makes connections. The high degree of visitor involvement usually leads to personal satisfaction and enhanced learning by doing and investigating.

Weaknesses: The "drawing out" part of the method takes time, so specific topic and distance goals must remain flexible. The interpreter's skill, adaptability, and mature judgment affect the success of the outcome. Depending upon the cognitive level of the group, some questions may be difficult to answer; unsuitable answers or hypotheses may require tactful rescues of the persons involved. The program may seem somewhat unstructured to those visitors who learn best from straightforward organization.

4. **Telling, showing,** and **drawing out** combines the three previous methods and tends to be the most effective. The leader combines verbal messages, demonstra-

tions, and discovery methods at appropriate places along the walk. This approach most consistently matches diverse visitor learning styles and tends to be the most exciting.

Strengths: This approach includes visitor participation in several different ways. The interpreter orchestrates a well-balanced program using various learning styles.

Weaknesses: The combined approach requires more detailed planning and design than the other methods.

Effective hikes differ from ineffective ones in the details of courtesy to the visitors as much as in the information and learning theory used. Most interpretive manuals have lists of "dos and don'ts" for guiding people. They all focus on what interpreters often call "common-sense" courtesy. To relate with visitors better, interpreters must put themselves in the visitor's place. This can be accomplished by attending interpretive walks other than their own, and figuratively via, self-awareness on their own walks. Only then can the interpreter develop an awareness as a visitor and determine how he or she wishes to be treated in turn.

Risk (1982) provided a number of suggestions for leaders of interpretive walks, condensed and adapted as follows:

1. Inventory the area. Interpreters should become intimately familiar with his or her trail or route and each of the stops he or she planned along the way. An outline that lists each stop and the key ideas to be made can be especially helpful.

2. Keep stops brief. Most stops should last between five and seven minutes. Several may take only one to two minutes. A few stops may be longer, to conduct an activity, to tell a story with meaningful implications, or to give the group a sense of peace and solitude. Heat, terrain, weather, and physical condition of the audience will affect stop length and frequency. For example, at mountainous Big Bend National Park, interpreters beat the heat by walking slowly and talking in shady spots for about five or ten minutes per stop.

3. Stay in front. Here, the pace of the walk can be controlled by the interpreter to keep the group together. When an interpreter stops he or she should bring everyone together before starting an explanation.

4. Face the group. Talk to the group, not to the object which is being interpreted. Look around and talk to everyone, not just to those who are nearest. Also, stand so group members have their backs to the sun.

5. Be sure that everyone can see. Arrange each stop so that everyone in the group has the opportunity to see what is being interpreted. Invite children to get closer since adults are able to see over them.

6. Speak with enough volume. Consider the size of the group and environmental conditions (such as wind) and speak loudly enough so that everyone can hear.

7. Know when to be quiet. While observing wildlife, a spectacular overview, a sunset, or moonrise it is appropriate to be quiet and let the visitors enjoy the moment quietly. They do not need to hear that it's beautiful, "cool," great, or unbelievable.

8. Be flexible. If an interpreter sees something of interest that is not a part of his or her agenda, adapt so that visitors have the opportunity to witness the event of the moment.

Audience Assessment

As you design each type of program, focus on the kind of audience that you expect and plan accordingly. Several generalizations about audiences may serve as guides (Horn, 1980).

1. The audience is made up of individuals, free to withhold or give their attention.
2. People have varied backgrounds and temperaments. They may have strongly held beliefs or experiences that cause them to disagree with the interpreter's assumptions or theories, e.g., on questions of how and when the Creation occurred, historical geology, or perspective on historical events.
3. The members of the audience have normal intelligence and vocabulary. Remember that there are relatively few professional foresters, wildlife biologists, archæologists, historians, and geologists among the U.S. population. Nonspecialists will not understand lapses into professional jargon. However, they will comprehend the key concepts if they are explained vividly in nontechnical language.
4. Audience attention is widely scattered—members do not all await an interpreters words of wisdom. One of the challenges is to focus their attention.
5. The attention and interest span of the audience is short. Interpreters seek to hold and renew their interest throughout the talk, as well as by previewing, presenting, and reviewing the key points. Most people cannot concentrate on a subject longer than 10 minutes, but highly motivated groups often maintain their interest for up to 30 minutes.

Visitor studies of the museum or park clients will give the interpreter a sense of whom he or she would normally expect. In the half-hour preceding the program, as the interpreter makes early arrivals feel welcome, he or she assesses and reassesses visitor impressions. Make adjustments in the approach according to who shows up. Interpreters might answer the following questions as they assess the early arrivals. To whom am I speaking? What common characteristics and differences do they possess? Where do they come from? How long have they been here and what have they seen? Have they been here before?

Promoting Participation

Participation by visitors can be encouraged by various techniques. Getting people to handle objects, make observations, discuss findings, express opinions, and develop skills often requires special techniques. Preparing for demonstrations and participatory exercises call for special planning. Questioning techniques likewise require practice and careful thought. Participation does not just happen naturally for most interpreters.

Although first-hand experience and observation characterizes interpretation, many interpreters talk so much that the visitor has little or no chance to participate. Talking is relatively easy—and necessary. Structuring and promoting participation requires more planning, but can be rewarding in visitor response. With practice, getting visitors to participate, look, ask, and talk becomes relatively easy.

Direct experience helps words gain effectiveness. If someone does something or sees an object, an interpreter's words have more impact. For a talk, use specimens, demonstrations, visual aids, or even an on-site visit (Boulanger, Smith, and Smith, 1973). On the trail, make sure the visitors can participate actively. Use questioning techniques. Make listeners active to get active listening. Talk less; do more. Ask them to discover how many kinds of trees live in a defined area. Give them a reasonably solvable mystery that relates to the main subject. Demonstrate actions through audience participation.

Strang (1990) advocated methods of enhancing sensory capabilities through several group exercises, e.g., wide-angle vision, seeing in three dimensions, focused hearing, scanning, and eventually seeing purely. He suggested that these exercises can apply to all the senses, helping people become more a part of the landscape. This enhanced awareness may be valuable to many kinds of historical and natural interpretation.

USING QUESTIONS AND DISCUSSION

Most interpreters seek audience reaction by calling for questions or discussion at some time in their presentations. Often, when the request comes at the end of the talk and the response is uninspiring. Perhaps the audience thought the talk or hike lasted too long. Maybe it was too pedantic or confusing—questions might just prolong the agony. Perhaps the visitors suffer from cold, hunger, or other discomfort; the interpreter is more likely to be comfortable than the audience. More than likely, however, the interpreter simply did not use an effective strategy to prompt questions or discussions.

To get interplay with the audience, first provide for physical participation. Use more than words.

- First, give them direct contact and experience with living things or artifacts, so they can react to something. Let them touch, measure, name, describe, or vote about it.
- Second, motivate and focus their thoughts and actions on the relevant topic.
- Third, prompt them with provocative, open-ended questions.

Avoid use of:

 a. discussion-killing questions with one-word answers (yes-no, 1811, Lincoln); they often begin with is, when, what, who or where.
 b. trite lead-offs that threaten to reveal low ability (*Can you . . . , Who knows . . . , Did you know. . .*) or lack of experience (*Have you ever. . .*), watch out for their cousin (*How many of you. . . .*); these usually get half-hearted hand-raising responses, not real involvement.

As much as possible, use questions that start with how, why, what's happening. Ask for comparisons, evaluations, inferences, problem solving, relationships and applications. An example is: *"How might you use this plant to help you survive in the wilderness?"* (Boulanger and Smith, 1973). To answer such questions, the respondent must think creatively; answers go beyond yes, no, right, wrong.

Four categories of questions allow the interpreter to tailor the questioning strategy to meet different objectives (Grinder and McCoy, 1985; Boulanger and Smith, 1973):

1. Memory questions require
   - factual recall of specific information
   - descriptive recall of processes or experiences
2. Probing or convergent questions ask one to analyze, expand, or clarify response to a preceding question, e.g.,

- Seek clarification or elaboration.
- Increase critical awareness by justifying response.
- Refocus response—what are the implications?
- Prompt or hint to help answer a question.

3. Higher order questions require use of ideas and creative thought processes to emphasize concepts, principles and problem solving. Some of them are called judgemental questions. These questions ask for evaluations, inferences, comparisons, applications of concepts, problem solving and cause-and-effect relationships.

4. Divergent questions are open-ended, requiring exploration of the unknown. They encourage branching thoughts that extend the imagination.

Using this array of questions can help provoke new thinking and active participation. A general strategy, as outlined in Box 12.5, usually focuses on emphasizing the higher order and divergent questions. However, a sequence of questions, moving from type one, systematically through type four, seems to encourage sustained attention and participation (Grinder and McCoy, 1985; Hammerman, Hammerman, and Hammerman, 1985).

BOX 12.5: GENERAL RULES OF QUESTIONING

1. Distribute questions widely among your visitors so many may speak. If necessary, redirect a question to several visitors to bring them into the discussion.
2. Balance the kinds of questions asked by using factual, probing, higher order, and divergent questions as appropriate.
3. Encourage visitors to give detailed responses. Ask questions that require such answers and follow with probing techniques.
4. Allow ample time to think over a question (pause for at least five seconds).
5. Ask clear and coherent questions. Frequent rephrasing should not be necessary.
6. Encourage your visitors to confer with each other as well as with you.
7. Ask questions that require more than a yes or no answer.

Evaluating the Performance

After a talk, hike, or other activity, evaluate. That is, assign value to the work. Determine how the value may increase for the next performance; enrich the next audience by pondering positively.

Evaluation for an interpretive programs may come from three sources: the audience, a colleague, and yourself. Carefully observe the audience during a walk or talk to determine if people are paying attention. If visitors are talking with each other, fidgeting, or leaving the program then something is obviously wrong. Adjust. If they are too tired or too frisky on a hike to listen to the message, change the pace or the number and length of stops. Although you could survey visitors regarding their reaction to a particular program, this is seldom done.

A skillful, honest colleague or supervisor may serve as the best critic. The interpreter will have to help create a noncompetitive and nondefensive environment in order to get constructive criticism. Even if it hurts, accept it with grace. If the supervisor does not offer to give evaluation, insist upon it as a professional necessity. How else can one develop unless someone else observes and makes suggestions?

Most frequently, interpreters will have to rely upon him- or herself. Tape or videotape the presentation when possible; play it back to be one's own critic. After each session ask yourself some key questions. Several forms exist, e.g., Lewis (1980). Interpreters can make their own simple rating sheet with this set of six questions by keeping written track of suggestions or comments for future presentations:

1. Did the speaker hold the audience's interest all through the talk?
2. Did the audience get any new ideas?
3. Were favorable attitudes developed toward the area and agency?
4. What were the weakest points of the talk?
5. What were the strongest points of the talk?
6. Did the speaker put himself or herself into the talk completely from the audience's point of view?

When one evaluate oneself, two contrasting tendencies that do not constitute evaluation should be avoided. One focuses only on negative faults—the "I'm a failure—I'll never be any good" lament. The other asserts, unwaveringly, that "it went really well; they really liked it"—the cheerleading self-delusion. Seek to reinforce and reuse what worked best, drop problems from the presentation, and introduce or strengthen material where gaps or confusion existed. Chapter 19 offers a more detailed discussion of evaluation from both a practical and philosophical standpoint.

Summary

The interpreter serves as the key image of the agency or company or museum. As far as the public is concerned, this may be the only professional person they encounter during their visit. Therefore, as the person in charge and representing your organization:

1. Look good—in uniform, grooming, posture, mannerisms.
2. Speak clearly, conversationally and in a friendly, courteous way. Enunciate and project with adequate volume.
3. Organize and prepare well but do not read your presentations; do not recite them. Do converse with the audience. Know the facility and area intimately.
4. Address and face the whole audience; interact with the clients. Avoid distractions, such as pacing, fast talking, and "nonword" filler sounds.
5. Project enthusiasm, pride, and courtesy as the host or hostess and the ambassador of the place.

This chapter focused on the personal services work of the interpreter. Whether providing information via desk duty, roving interpretation, or any of a variety of tours, demonstrations and talks, the interpreter strives to serve visitors in a professional manner. Although specific principles apply to each of these functions, quality interpretation starts with attitude, including qualities such as amiability, enthusiasm, confidence, conversational delivery, and organization. The interpreter aims to enrich and excite people regarding the magic of the place they have come to visit. Personal services comprise key tools for fulfilling that responsibility.

Literature Cited

Abbey, E. (1968). *Desert solitaire*. New York, NY: Simon and Schuster.

Beck, L. (1989). Conversations with Barry Lopez: Musings on interpretation. *Journal of Interpretation, 13*(3):4-7.

Boulanger, F., Smith D., and Smith, J. P. (1973). *Educational principles and techniques for interpreters*. Portland, OR: USDA Forest Service General Technical Report PNW-9.

Cornell, J. (1989). *Sharing the joy of nature*. Nevada City, CA: Dawn Publications, Inc.

Gramann, J. and Vander Stoep, G. (1987). Prosocial behavior theory and natural resource protection: A conceptual synthesis. *Journal of Environmental Management, 24*:247-257.

Grater, R. K. (1976). *The interpreter's handbook: Methods, skills, and techniques*. Globe, AZ: Southwest Parks and Monuments Association.

Grinder, A. L. and McCoy, E. S. (1985). *The good guide: A source-book for interpreters, docents and tour guides*. Scottsdale, AZ: Ironwood Press.

Ham, S. H. (1992). *Environmental interpretation: A practical guide*. Golden, CO: North American Press.

Hammerman, D., Hammerman, W., and Hammerman, E. (1985). *Teaching in the outdoors (3rd ed.)*. Danville, IL: Interstate Publishers, Inc.

Hendee, J., Stankey, G. and Lucas, R. (1990). *Wilderness management*. Golden, CO: North American Press.

Hilker, G. (1974). *The audience and you: Practical dramatics for the park interpreter*. Washington, DC: National Park Service.

Horn, E. L. (1980). *Talk tips*. USDA Forest Service..

Kawasaki, G . (1991). *Selling the dream*. New York, NY: Harper Business.

Knapp, M. (1972). *Nonverbal communication in human interaction*. New York, NY: Holt, Rinehart and Winston, Inc.

Lewis, W. J. (1980). *Interpreting for park visitors*. Philadelphia, PA: Eastern Acorn Press.

Risk, P. (1982). Conducted activities. In G. W. Sharpe, *Interpreting the environment (2nd ed.)*. NY: John Wiley & Sons, Inc.

Shaw, J. (1984). *The nature photographer's complete guide to professional field techniques*. New York, NY: American Photographic Book Publishing.

Smith, S. Q. (1977). Interpretation at Mammoth Cave. In *Proceedings, National Cave Management Symposium*. Albuquerque, NM.

Strang, C. A. (1990). Advanced awareness techniques. In *Proceedings, National Interpreters Workshop*, NAI. Charleston, SC.

Thorndyke, P. (1977). Cognitive structures in comprehension and memory of narrative discourse. *Cognitive Psychology, 9*(1):77-110.

Wallace, G. (1990). Law enforcement and the authority of the resource. *Legacy, 1*(2):4-8.

Woods, J. G. (1977). An interpretive concept for Nakimu Caves. In *Proceedings, National Cave Management Symposium*. Albuquerque, NM.

Historical Interpretation

[Landmarks] stand for continuity, community, identity,
for links with the past and the future. In the contemporary
American community these roles are what counteract our
mobility and fragmentation and forgetfulness of history.
—Jackson, 1984

History seldom tells itself. Relics, forts, barns, villages, and battlefields all serve as reminders of things in the past. Without interpretation, however, the real significance of a place's history remains obscure. Exhibits, films, booklets, signs, and—most engaging—live interpretation can make historic places come to life. Interpreters turn back the pages of time to create a bond between visitors and the memorialized events, people, and objects for which a site was established.

People relish opportunities to briefly return to antiquity. Change in a "modern" world tears at people's roots. As just one example, people treasure seeing the pleasant character of their neighborhoods, unchanged, throughout their lives (Cromie, 1979). Pursuing knowledge and experiences related to the past—the language, dress, mannerisms, and way of life of our forebears—is a powerful human desire. It is clear that "the majority of people are interested in history to one degree or another. They may not visit research facilities or know where to search for historic data, but they have made a common practice to visit areas of historic significance" (Killen, 1969).

There are many reasons why people are attracted to historic sites. These places satisfy a desire people have to learn more about their own roots. Many people are interested in tracing past relatives to various historic places, including battlefields, historic villages, or Ellis Island (an immigration station in New York Bay) to gain a sense of the feelings and experiences of their kin. Others have their interests aroused in school or through various media including books and movies. Still others seek history as a hobby with particular interest in forts, lighthouses, presidents, or a certain historic period. And there are those who are simply intrigued by anything that offers a better understanding of our place in the world (Figure 13.1).

Interpreters collect pertinent data and then prepare for the interpretation of a place in the form that is most valuable and provocative to the visitor. Interpretation should relate what is being displayed and to the background and experience of your audience. Tilden (1967) provided a good illustration from the Witte Museum in San Antonio,

Texas—a label about the skeleton of a mammoth: "Prehistoric mammoths were here in Texas just a few thousand years ago. They roamed the plains in great herds . . . The chances are that they browsed right where you are standing right now."

Interpretation such as this brings visitors directly into the picture. Historical material should be presented in such a way that people will feel inspired by and drawn into places, objects, and ideas from another time.

FIGURE 13.1
An interpreter wearing period dress describes the operations of locks on the C&O Canal to a steady stream of visitors.

HISTORIC SITES

Historical interpretation covers many kinds of places, from railroad yards and historic districts to vast tracts of open land, from the homes of the immensely wealthy to the hovels and cabins of the poorest. It also includes monuments and markers that define a location where something interesting happened in the past (Figure 13.2).

FIGURE 13.2
A "cannon talk" at Petersburg Battlefield, Virginia, describes the long, last siege of the War Between the States.

The diversity of interpretive places enriches our understanding of how societies developed and how they can continue to live on this earth. Three examples (Box 13.1) and several photographs portray some of the diversity.

BOX 13.1: THREE HISTORICAL PLACES

1. Shelburne Farms, on Lake Champlain in Vermont, once served as shelter for William Seward and Lila Vanderbilt Webb. Frederick Law Olmsted helped design the grounds. Today the 1899 "house" serves as an inn and restaurant amidst a major environmental education center and working educational dairy farm on 1,000 acres of pasture and forest. The interpretive staff teaches students, educators, and casual visitors about agriculture and the environment: "The mission of Shelburne Farms is to preserve, maintain, and adapt its historic buildings, landscape and productive farmland for teaching and demonstrating the stewardship of natural and agricultural resources" (Shelburne Farms, 1992).

2. At Fort Missoula's Historical Museum, the Missoula Chapter of the Montana Society of American Foresters recently organized a forestry interpretive area. It explains forest protection, forest management, fire science, and wood products. It includes a display of how wood gets from the forest to the market, both now and in the past. A 1923 steam locomotive sits beside other logging equipment that shows how logs were transported from the woods to the mill. The large exhibit area was made possible by contributions from civic groups for the signs and donations by various industries (Heilman, 1993).

3. In southeast Texas, not far from Houston, the George Ranch Historical Park advertises itself as a "great adventure in living history." The 474-acre headquarters unit recalls the thousands of acres of coastal prairie where longhorns, shorthorns, and Brahmans grazed and where cotton, sorghum, and other cash crops were cut with horse-drawn farm implements. Role-playing guides show the town house as it was in 1896, and offer opportunities for visitors to help in domestic activities. The headquarters ranch house represents the late 1930s. The demonstrations of ranch life and methods show how several generations operated this successful spread for cattle, crops, and petroleum.

As machines replace skill, they disconnect themselves from life;
they come between us and life. They begin to enact our ignorance of value—
of essential sources, dependences, and relationships.
                                         —Wendell Berry, *The Unsettling of America* (1977)

Authenticity

The interpretation of historic events seeks to present authenticity—in clothing, buildings, information presented, details of conversation, even accents and phrases. A great deal of research goes into creating an accurate program that includes events of the age, clothing styles, and the prevailing attitudes of the time (Hook, 1987).

Sources, which often prove useful in the search for relevant and authentic data, include agency experts, private consultants, libraries, museums, historic societies and long-standing members of the community. If an interpreter uses legend, rumor, or hear-say, then he or she must mention it as such, perhaps as part of the "color" of the site. If an item is a replica, it is important to convey that to the audience. The task of the interpreter is to present an honest portrayal of events. Perhaps the most "fundamental issue" for interpreters at any site is historical integrity (Warder and Joulie, 1990).

Visitors to historic areas generally lack detailed knowledge regarding the actual site, the period or era depicted, or of preceding or subsequent events associated with the place. Because an interpreter cannot realistically present a complete course in history to the visitor, he or she must provide an abbreviated interpretation of the broad picture of key events and issues. Although it is important to present a "whole" story, the focus should be on the significant qualities concerning the particular site. A combination of site-specific interpretation along with the significance of the place in a broader history may pique the curiosity of visitors to make the effort to discover more about both the site and its historical era on their own.

Of course, interpreters will find that many visitors have inaccurate pictures of history. Much of the misinformation that visitors hold may be corrected through quality interpretation. Yet, according to White (1969), it is counterproductive to expect to "fulfill the sacred mission of correcting every error in fact that the visitor holds . . . Not only is such a thing a physical impossibility, but in trying to do so we would probably destroy any chance of that visitor gaining anything meaningful from his [sic] visit."

Interpretation of Common People

In reading [pioneer women's] diaries we come closer to understanding how historical drama translates into human experience. Through the eyes of women we begin to see history as the stuff of daily struggle.
—Lillian Schlissel,
Women's Diaries of the Westward Journey (1982)

Much historical interpretation now focuses on common people, vernacular architecture, and everyday folk skills. This "new social history" is a recent change from the long concentration on heroes and nationally significant events (Figure 13.3). Even at battlefields, interpretation now often deals with the soldiers and civilians as much as the generals. This approach is referred to as "looking at history from the bottom up." It does not eliminate the hero or national significance of the events being interpreted but rather relates them to the common experiences of everyday people. Special interest in women, ethnic minorities, urban history, and rural living balance traditional interests in political and military events and luminaries. As this is a rather recent phenomena, Weber (1988) cautions against skewing events in "the interests of a general 'evening up' of the interpretive score."

The Jefferson National Expansion Memorial in St. Louis, Missouri, provides a fine example of interpreting common people. This outstanding museum beneath the arch at St. Louis presents the history of the west using five main methods (Capps, 1992).

1. Exhibits tell stories of mountain men, explorers, buffalo hunters, soldiers, Native Americans, cowboys, miners and farmers. Ordinary objects sit beside pictures or drawings that include them as part of the landscape. Direct quotes tell of past experiences. Huge museum space allows visitors to walk among the artifacts and images, and sense their interwoven nature.

2. Programs are designed so interpreters may describe topics such as what caused people to go West, what preparations they made, and what it was like to be on the trail for six months. They discuss how the various Plains Indians groups wove spiritual beliefs into their lives, how they hunted bison, and how they made teepees. Soldier life on the frontier makes up another facet—how did soldiers spend an ordinary day; how did they feel about where they were; what did they eat?

3. Interpretive media provide a third avenue for sharing western history. Brochures, a newspaper, bulletins, and slide packages allow more in-depth interpretation that can be taken home. These are based on current historical research and are written for the lay person.

4. Education programs serve tens of thousands of students (preschool-12) and the staff also sends materials out to teachers. The goal is to help students experience western history for themselves. Participatory techniques and hands-on objects extend learning beyond textbooks. A full day in a "frontier classroom" gives a vivid idea of what school was like back then. Handling items made from bison bones and hide, drilling like a soldier, or wearing real cowboy working gear can produce long-lasting images.

    The museum sends out packets of slides for each of the groups of frontier people along with historical information and a bibliography. There are also traveling trunks of clothing, tools, games, videotapes, mounted photographs, maps, and teacher handbooks that allow a school to set up lessons and temporary exhibits. A special program celebrates racial and religious diversity in the settling of the West and the development of St. Louis (Hall and James, 1992).

5. Special anniversaries and annual observances rely on special efforts. The 1976 U.S. Bicentennial gave interpretation a big boost at this site. The 1992 Columbus Quincentennial featured Spanish heritage of the American West.

Each year, the museum offers western themes related to Black Heritage Month (February), Women's History Week (in March), and Native American Week (in November). Surely, the year 2003 will make this gateway a featured interpretive center to celebrate the Louisiana Purchase of 1803.

FIGURE 13.3
Professor Richard Pawling relives 1905 as miner Frank Kehoe for audiences who engage his services. He portrays a wide range of common people to bring "History Alive!" (Tim Tannous)

Another example of focusing on the ordinary comes from the story of how the Great Smoky Mountains National Park got its museum collections (Tardona and Manscill, 1992). Everyday items were left behind as mountain people abandoned the land they sold to the National Park Service. Ranger Philip Hough picked up their leftovers—e.g., implements, dishes, tables, and other objects—starting in 1930-31. To the amusement of some of their colleagues and neighbors, Hiram C. Wilburn and Charles Grossman collected everything from architecture to "trash" during the Civilian Conservation Corps era.

The rebuilt and refurnished homes and barns of Cades Cove and Oconaluftee, plus exhibits at four visitor centers, now use those structures and artifacts to demonstrate how the mountain people lived just 60 to 70 years ago. The stored collections are now outstanding research sources that are utilized by 500 people per year for baseline and reference information.

Ethnic and Cultural Interpretation

[Anglos] think of time as linear, flowing from past, to present, to future like a river, whereas the [Pawtucket-Micmac Indian] Nompenekit thinks of it as a lake or pool in which all events are contained.
                        —John Hanson Mitchell, *Ceremonial Time*:
                        Fifteen Thousand Years on One Square Mile (1984)

Ethnic and cultural interpretation is often conducted by people of different backgrounds from the subjects of the interpretation. For decades, in the United States and Canada, Anglo-Americans (Anglos) have dominated the interpretive corps of public agencies. They have explained—mostly to other Anglos—various aspects of Native American cultures, the conditions of African-Americans during the days of slavery, the Russian Bishop's home in Alaska, the Spanish forts and missions from Puerto Rico to California, and the village life of Hawaiian Polynesians (Figure 13.4). The interpretation often has been excellent and almost always well-intentioned. Yet the work may have been unavoidably biased, without any prejudicial intent.

Gradually, however, interpretive programs accounted for and included other cultural perspectives as well (Figure 13.5). Many agencies make major efforts to bring in employees from the culture being interpreted. For example, interpretive supervisors in Canada and the U.S. now seek Native Americans to help interpret the perspectives of Native American culture. Likewise, African-Americans, Hispanics, and Orientals often give their versions of cultural perspectives about parks and memorials dedicated to their people. On southern battlefields of the War Between the States, men with southern accents and uniforms explain the equipment, horses, and maneuvers of the Confederate Army (Figure 13.6).

Implicit in this approach is the need to make sure that the individuals selected aren't just typecast and assumed to know their own culture. A Native American interpreter must be sensitive to and aware of Native American history as well as being capable of developing interpretive programs that transmit the culture.

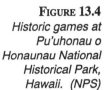

FIGURE **13.4**
*Historic games at
Pu'uhonau o
Honaunau National
Historical Park,
Hawaii. (NPS)*

FIGURE **13.5**
*Historical role playing
thrives at living history
events such as the Cabrillo
Festival in San Diego.
(NPS)*

FIGURE **13.6**
*The War Between the
States gets a
southern
interpretation at
Petersburg National
Battlefield. (NPS)*

NATIVE AMERICANS

> The Power of the World always works in circles, and everything tries to be round.
>
> —*Black Elk Speaks* (Neihardt, 1961)

Strong interest in the life of American Indians has been evident since the Colonists landed. At first, the Native Americans provided guidance in survival and agricultural skills. As the "new Americans" moved west, they often saw "Indians" as impediments to settlement and expansion. The various tribes could not help but see the growth of numbers and hunger for land possession as a threat to their ways of life and existence.

Despite the image presented in many books and movies, however, the relationships among the different peoples were often tolerant, sometimes friendly. The pitched battles with the invading white settlers were relatively isolated instances until the big push westward. Three or four decades of open hostility—when the western frontier was pushed back with military assistance—captured the literary imagination, overshadowing nearly three centuries of usually peaceful coexistence (albeit to the continuous disadvantage of the Indians).

Starting in the early part of the 20th century, strong popular and intellectual interest in native peoples developed with preservation of architectural structures in Casa Grande (Arizona), Mesa Verde (Colorado), and Bandelier (New Mexico), among many others. These areas plainly revealed that the former residents had highly developed community structures, clever architecture, technical agriculture, and sophisticated religion (Figure 13.7).

FIGURE 13.7
An interpreter explains the calumet at its origin, Pipestone National Monument in Minnesota. (NPS)

Interest in learning and presenting information about Native Americans grew rapidly in the past few decades. Many Anglo citizens sensed the importance of learning more about those who lived on this continent prior to settlement by "new Americans." That the newcomers had a brutal effect on both the land and native people is an understatement (Lopez, 1990). Now, many people seek to find some of the wisdom of the natives who lived in a mostly harmonious relationship with the land.

Interpretation by park and forest rangers of Native American cultures and by tribal interpretive organizations led to several workshops and guidelines for greater sensitivity and awareness. The National Association for Interpretation (NAI) has led in the effort. Several key NAI members in the Southwest formed the Council of American Indian Interpretation which became a nationwide section of the Association. With reference to this Council, Brown (1990) suggested that "conventional interpretation could not convey the substance and nuance of cultural differences and perspectives." He continued, "Only occasionally, and with great difficulty, could [conventional interpretation] communicate the distinctive world views of ancient and modern Indians; their relationships to landscapes; their spiritual integration with all of nature; their human arrangements, aspirations and rewards."

Now national and regional workshops, meetings, and publications encourage appropriate approaches to interpreting cultures other than one's own. A listing of guidelines for American Indians awareness appears in Box 13.2.

BOX 13.2: GUIDELINES FOR PRESENTING THE NATIVE AMERICAN PERSPECTIVE

A panel discussion on American Indian Awareness in Wisconsin State Parks produced the following guidelines, offered by members of different nations (La Mere, 1991):

1. Do not lump all American Indians into one category as "Indians." It is better to refer to a specific tribe or nation. Remember each nation or tribe is different. Seek information on the tribe or nation you are describing.
2. Avoid the statement: "Back when the Indians were here . . . " There are Native Americans living in every state of the union and most metropolitan areas.
3. Should I dress up in traditional dress? This is up to the interpreter, but one should not copy the dress of another. Each item of dress, including colors, designs, and ornamentation, has a significant meaning for that person. It is probably best to avoid dressing up.
4. Where do I go to find accurate information? Your best place to start is by contacting tribal members. They will probably have a person responsible for archival and historical information. Also use the State Historical Society, local library, historians in the community and university. Be cautious of books that lump all Native Americans together.
5. Avoid interpreting anything to do with the religion of the people, stories you have not been given permission to retell, and information which you question or cannot verify.
6. Involve the people in the planning and presenting of their own culture. Make contacts by attending powwows, contacting tribal offices, and involving Native Americans at your facility.

These suggestions apply to both non-Indians and Native Americans. Members of a tribe find themselves having to do considerable research to include the diverse history and customs of their own people. Even if one speaks only from personal experience and feelings, preparation and organization are vital to successful interpretation.

It has been asked, "Can a non-Indian interpret Indians?" Wilson Hunter (1990), a Navajo, answered: "No, one doesn't have to be an Indian—but it helps." He explained that all over the National Park Service, interpreters make sense of traditions, religions, and life ways different from their own. The non-Indian interpreter can become an expert on hogans and deliver moving programs. "But in the final analysis, he lacks one ingredient that can contribute so much to interpretation: he did not live in one." The Navajo interpreter from the hogan, on the other hand, can speak of family, of stories told in the hogan, as well as of the institution that the hogan represents. In the telling, this interpreter talks about more than the hogan, expressing the personal life in and around it. The interpreter becomes part of the story, imprinted in the mind of the visitor as an indelible, personal part of the resource and experience.

Not all stories are so successful. A less than satisfactory case that has long plagued the National Park Service was the hiring of Crow interpreters at the former Custer Battlefield National Monument in Montana. The goal was to develop a stronger Indian perspective on the battle (Mangum, 1990). But "Indian" perspective is neither singular nor definitive. The Crow were Custer's scouts and traditional enemies of the Cheyenne and Sioux. The victorious combatants were mostly Sioux (a diverse group in itself) and Cheyenne, but there are no monuments to their dead and, until recently, little emphasis on their success at this important site. Interpreters from those victorious nations did not relish working in a park surrounded by the Crow reservation, even after the Custer Battlefield was renamed the Little Bighorn Battlefield.

Interpretation has changed to a more sensitive approach. It takes into account diverse cultural points of view by explaining the stories of several sides of cultural conflicts, economic development processes, and everyday living.

Methods of Historical Interpretation

Historical interpretation uses several methods, both personal and nonpersonal. Data from 122 historic sites, museums, and living history associations in the United States (Warder and Joulie 1990) showed that 95 percent used personal methods of interpretation (Table 13.1). Guided tours were the most popular interpretive method, used in 84 percent of the sites, with uniformed interpreters in 73 percent. Interpreters wearing period clothing or costumes worked on less than one-half the sites (43 percent); first-person living history was used on only 38 percent.

Coincidentally, 95 percent of the sites used nonpersonal services. The most common methods included museum displays (88 percent) and publications (87 percent). Audiovisual programs were offered at 70 percent of the sites. Audio devices were the least used (37 percent) method of interpretation assessed by this study. Their relatively meager use suggests their ineffectiveness under these circumstances. For example, when money and personnel were short at Fort Laramie, they tried audio messages in the off-season, only to find that people walked away from them.

TABLE 13.1 INTERPRETATION METHODS USED AT 122 HISTORIC SITES

Method	Total Cases	% of Sites
PERSONAL	116	95
Guided Tours	103	84
Uniformed Interpreter	89	73
Period Clothing	53	43
Living History	46	38
NONPERSONAL	116	95
Museum Displays	108	88
Publications	106	87
Audiovisual	85	70
Audio devices	45	37

Source: adapted from Warder and Joulie (1990)

Most of the methods mentioned in Table 13.1 have been addressed in previous chapters with the exception of living history and costumed interpretation.

LIVING HISTORY AND COSTUMED INTERPRETATION

"Making history come alive" through living history and costumed interpretation provides a balance between education and entertainment. These approaches offer excellent ways to convey emotional content and give some sense of realism, as well as to provide real fun to visitors (Figure 13.8).

FIGURE 13.8
Frontier pastimes often involve the paying customers at the Feast of the Hunters Moon, Indiana.

Interpreters may work in first-person style (playing a role directly as an individual of the period) or third-person (wearing period clothing but speaking about, not as, historic individuals). The National Park Service defines the first-person style as living history and the third-person style as costumed interpretation. Other organizations use living history as a broader term to cover both first- and third-person interpretation in period clothing.

Relatively few parks and museums successfully use first-person interpretation throughout. Plimoth Plantation in Massachusetts is one of the outstanding examples (Figure 13.9) of success of first-person interpretation. Here, the visitor enters a village of people talking with 17 accents/dialects of English, wearing the clothes of the early 1600s, and discussing the current events of those days. Actors know nothing of "future" events, persons, customs, or names. For example, in their conversations with visitors, the name "United States" has no relevance; the Massachusetts Bay Colony and the new King Charles were the political realities.

First-person interpretation requires considerable research and practice. Therefore, some places maintain a flexible program with some interpreters working in first person, but most using third person. Most Old Sturbridge Village interpreters speak as modern persons who

FIGURE 13.9
Plimoth Plantation militia conducts regular drills as modern visitors stand aside.

dress and work as if in 1830s conditions (Figure 13.10). A few enter into first-person discussions with other interpreters in specific locations, such as women working in a house, chatting with visitors about sewing, cooking, and town gossip.

At Fort Laramie National Historic Site, Wyoming, first-person interpretation is encouraged when the interpreter feels comfortable in the role. Other costumed interpreters use modern comparisons and analogies. A few contract interpreters who really lived as if in the past, even in the off hours, have become part of the park legend. They enjoyed first-person work so much that they stayed in character day and night, sometimes to the surprise of late-arriving visitors. Body odor and ribald behavior unbecoming a modern interpreter linger in memories and tales of Fort Laramie's staff. First-person interpretation has the advantage of involving the visitor and communicating the essence of the era very quickly, at least to those with the imagination to immerse themselves,

FIGURE 13.10
Old Sturbridge Village employees garden with 18th century plants and clothing.

even as observers. The third-person approach enables a rich experience for those visitors who need to make comparisons with their own modern experiences and understanding to contrast with past conditions.

There is no doubt that the public enjoys living history. According to research conducted by Jones (1991), 95 percent of the public attending living history programs in museums judge them to be better than traditional exhibits in "presenting historical information in a meaningful and enjoyable manner." Tens of thousands pay to participate in weekend festivals throughout the U.S., Canada, and England.

Summary

People have a strong affinity for contact with history. Historical interpretation, through various methods, makes history come alive. Living history and costumed interpretation bring visitors directly into the picture. As White (1969) noted, "the charm of the living history demonstration lies in the ease at which visitors become involved with the events of the past . . . . With seemingly no effort at all they become involved with the scene and its captivating history—and at that moment . . . [enter] the highest plane of interpretive communications—personal experience."

> *The world exists for the education of each man. There is no age, or state of society, or mode of action in history, to which there is not something corresponding in his own life.*
> —Ralph Waldo Emerson

Literature Cited

Berry, W. (1977). *The unsettling of America: Culture & agriculture.* San Francisco, CA: Sierra Club Books.

Brown, W. E. (1990). The storytellers. *Legacy, 1*(3):20-21.

Capps, M. A. (1992). The National Park Service and the evolving interpretation of western history: Jefferson National Expansion Memorial as a case study. *Interpretation* (Fall-Winter):13-16.

Cromie, A. (1979). *Restored towns and historic districts of America.* New York, NY: E. P. Dutton.

Hall, E. and James, D. (1992). The education program at Jefferson National Expansion Memorial celebrates the 75th. *Interpretation* (Fall-Winter):20-24.

Heilman, E. G. (1993). Forestry at Fort Missoula: Bringing history alive. *Journal of Forestry, 91*(4):50.

Hook, E. (1987). First person living history. In *Proceedings, National Interpreters Workshop,* AIN. St. Louis, MO.

Hunter, W. (1990). Can a non-Indian interpret Indians? *Contact* (Southwest Region Interpreter's Newsletter) 8 (July-September):13.

Jackson, J. B. (1984). *Discovering the vernacular landscape.* New Haven, CT: Yale University Press.

Jones, D. (1991). Making your interpretation vibrant: Living history and drama in museums. In: *Proceedings, National Interpreters Workshop,* NAI, Vail, CO.

Killen, R. (1969). The middleman. *Rocky Mountain-High Plains Parks and Recreation Journal, 4*(1):15-18.

La Mere, K. S. (1991). American Indian interpretation from an Indian perspective. In *Proceedings, National Interpreters Workshop* NAI. Vail, CO.

Lopez, B. (1990). *The rediscovery of North America.* Lexington, KY: University Press of Kentucky. (n.p.)

Mangum, N. C. (1990). Custer Battlefield as a symbol of cultural differences. *Contact* (Southwest Region Interpreter's Newsletter), *8*(July-September):10-12.

Mitchell, J. H. (1984). *Ceremonial time: Fifteen thousand years on one square mile.* Boston, MA: Houghton Mifflin.

Neihardt, J. G. (1961). *Black Elk speaks.* Lincoln, NB: University Nebraska Press.

Schlissel, L. (1982). *Women's diaries of the westward journey.* New York, NY: Schocken Books.

Shelburne Farms. (1992). *Calendar of events.* Shelburne, VT.

Tardona, D. R. and Manscill, K. L. (1992). Museums, museum curators, and technicians: Their role in interpreting natural and cultural resources. *Interpretation* (Fall/Winter):16-17, 20.

Tilden, F. (1967). *Interpreting our heritage (rev. ed.).* Chapel Hill, NC: University of North Carolina Press.

Warder, D. and Joulie, R. (1990). Historic site interpretation: Past, present and future research. In *Proceedings, National Interpreters Workshop,* NAI, Charleston, SC.

Weber, S. (1988). Angels or agitators? Avoiding stereotypes in the interpretation of women. *Trends*, 25(1):45-48.

White, T. E. (1969). Making interpretation fit. *Rocky Mountain-High Plains Parks and Recreation Journal*, 4(1): 23-30.

Arts in Interpretation

You must entertain to educate.
                    —George Bernard Shaw

People perceive resource and historic values emotionally as well as intellectually and scientifically. It seems that human nature first reacts emotionally, then applies intellect to understand or explain a situation (Cantu, 1990). People use emotions first, and intellect second. Interpreters and managers, can use both emotional and intellectual approaches to communicate resource information and issues. Performing and visual arts have long been the media of interpretation (Figure 14.1). Professional interpreters, even those tied to once-stuffy federal agencies, increasingly use the arts judiciously for the interpretive messages they can convey.

A growing development in the interpretive profession emphasizes innovative methods that include interpretive theater, storytelling, and music. Some of these approaches have been explored by trail-blazing interpreters to complement traditional performance interpretation (Chapter 12) including various methods of historical interpretation

FIGURE 14.1
An artistic and dramatic way to depict a common interpretive theme—the food pyramid—adorns Coyote Point Museum, San Mateo County, California.

(Chapter 13). Now, in many instances, these methods make up entire programs. The use of the "arts" in interpretation is becoming more sophisticated in its mission to entertain, educate, convey culture, and make emotional impacts. Theater concepts are increasingly being used in parks, zoos, museums, and aquariums (Covel and Thomas, 1992).

Interpretive Theater

CONCERNS AND SOLUTIONS

Although interpretive theater is on the rise (Hughes, 1993), administrative apprehension continues about the costs, skills, and equipment necessary for a quality program. Interpretive theater refers to dramatic performances in the popular sense, with or without a theater stage. These presentations range from the elaborate and costly to the basic and inexpensive.

Cost will vary widely depending upon the approach taken. Cromie (1979) suggested, "In smaller park agencies we too often adopt the attitude we have no personnel qualified or facilities available to produce interpretive devices. However, if we make an attempt to produce even a modest interpretation, we may be surprised at the ingenuity and talents of our own people, in this work."

At the Monterey Bay Aquarium costs were under $2,000 for a theater program that has served more than 60,000 visitors in its first two seasons (Covel and Thomas, 1992). In this instance volunteers did most of the program development and delivery, and elaborate sets were considered unnecessary.

In other cases, costs can mount substantially; they may include specialized equipment, props, costumes, and in-house or professional salaries. Equipment, like funding and talent, will vary according to your needs. Auditoriums with a stage and elaborate light and sound systems can enhance a performance but are not necessary. Indeed, much of living history takes place on the premises of the historic site.

Skills, too, may vary according to the professionalism of the program. Specialized skills include scriptwriting, directing, and acting. These skills require either staff time (assuming the talent exists) or consultants. Interpreters may develop a script with current staff, advertise for script submissions, commission a writer to meet your needs, or purchase an existing script. A director and actors, if not on your staff, may come from a local high school or college drama department, or a community theater group.

Covel and Thomas (1992) suggested the following time estimates for each of the four major steps of integrating theater into the interpretive program. These will vary according to the sophistication of the overall program, perhaps especially the talent search.

1. Develop program concept. (Three months)
2. Research and scriptwriting. (Three to six months)
3. Talent search. This includes recruiting, screening, and selecting a director, actors, and technical support crew. (Two months)
4. Construction of set and rehearsals. (Two to four months)

A suggested production checklist for planning effective interpretive theater appears in Table 14.1 (adapted from Jones, 1991).

TABLE 14.1 A PRODUCTION CHECKLIST FOR DRAMA

_____	Idea
_____	Audience needs and expectations
_____	Program outline (i.e., events and characters)
_____	Facilities and equipment
_____	Costumes and props
_____	Budget preparation
_____	Fund raising if appropriate
_____	Staff assignments
_____	Contracts if appropriate (e.g., playwright, director, consultants, actors)
_____	Organizing research materials
_____	Reviewing and rewriting script
_____	Auditioning
_____	Planning rehearsals and preparing actors
_____	Rehearsals
_____	Production schedule
_____	Publicity
_____	Evaluation

OUTDOOR DRAMAS

Outdoor dramas offer the ultimate interpretive theater—a story on or near the historic site, performed in the elements, presenting the character of the place or the people who made history there in a holistic way. Outdoor theater dates back to the Classical Greeks, where people could learn more about their religion and ritual. Modern outdoor dramas may be as elaborate as the Greeks offered, with 100 actors, real horses, boats, burning cabins or tents, and plenty of action by the actors. Three of the most venerable interpretive dramas are near Branson, Missouri, Lubbock, Texas, and Manteo, North Carolina. They all struggled financially for about five years before they began to break even.

Shepherd of the Hills had operated as a commercial business for two decades before country singers even found Branson, Missouri. (Now, the drama is just one of dozens of shows in town, with musical entertainment centers producing clogged roadways for miles around.) The drama recounts a wonderful novel that, in the 1920s, interpreted isolated rural life in southern Missouri. The theater opened in 1960; it operates all summer, six nights per week. The theater holds 3,000 or more to watch a cast of 80. It helps preserve the Ozark dialect and living patterns.

In Palo Duro Canyon, the Texas Panhandle Heritage Foundation interprets the historic struggle between cattlemen and farmers at the turn of the century. A three-stage amphitheater seats 1,650 people six nights per week to watch *Texas*, which has been on stage since 1965.

In North Carolina, the Cherokee Historical Association puts a cast and crew of 130 to work six nights per week during the summer in a 2,800-seat theater. They have performed *Unto These Hills* since 1950. This drama interprets the taking of Indian lands in the late 1700s through the exile from the mountains in the early 1800s. The story features a family that hid, avoided the Trail of Tears, and remained in the region as part of the remnant Cherokees.

These large, elaborate productions exceed the vision and patience of most communities and interpretive agencies. Instead, the normal interpretive drama involves one or a few actors or storytellers interpreting through drama something that relates to the site. Other kinds of cultural performances also may be presented in museums and parks under the ægis of the interpreter. However, in this chapter the authors focus on only those that help interpret the themes of the place.

LEE STETSON ON INTERPRETIVE THEATER

Lee Stetson, a professional actor, has performed more than 50 major roles, from Shakespeare to Simon. He is best known in interpretive circles for writing and performing several portrayals of the life of John Muir at Yosemite National Park and throughout the country for more than a decade (Figure 14.2). The closing keynote address of the 1988 National Interpreter's Workshop was his performance of "Conversation with a Tramp: An Evening with John Muir." Stetson related the following qualities for developing an effec-

tive dramatic presentation (summarized from Beck, 1989):

For a show to work requires the most rounded characters possible. In addition to reading all of John Muir's books and articles, Stetson read every source written about Muir to learn more about his style of living. He noted the value of looking for aspects of the character's life that show the faults, foibles, and funny moments that all of us experience. Incorporating these aspects of the character enriches the show enormously.

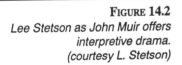
FIGURE 14.2
Lee Stetson as John Muir offers interpretive drama.
(courtesy L. Stetson)

To provide another element of authenticity, Stetson concerned himself with what a 75-year-old man is all about, as this was the moment in time he chose the action to occur. Likewise, he insisted on attention to detail in the development of costuming and props. These accessories often make a big difference and allow the character to shine.

Stetson believes that lighting and sound effects should be reduced as much as possible in park theater. He noted that, "In most parks people are trying to get away from the kaleidoscope of images that assail them in the city. I think there is a visceral connection between a live performer and the audience" (Beck, 1989).

Stetson contended that it is not absolutely essential that interpreters have extensive dramatic training. He advised that the quality of acting derives from the degree to which the character feels those things that are being portrayed. The preferred way to convey a message is for the character to show, rather than tell. There must be a commitment to delivering the joy, the anger, and the overall passion of the character. Using the full gamut of emotions, from laughter to sorrow, is essential in eliciting a reaction from the audience. Stetson advised, "The character must be moved, to expect the audience to be moved also." A major difficulty is working on the acting techniques which allow one to become fully engaged in each and every moment. Furthermore, nonactors find it difficult to sustain a show over a long period of time.

However, interpreters need not develop a full-length production from scratch. They can develop smaller projects that lie within the capabilities of most interpreters. These demand less in terms of research, script writing, and dramatic endurance. This approach allows interpreters to hone their skills over time and to continue adding segments in the development of a larger production over a couple of years. Large park operations might also consider dramatic training. This way, interpreters can gain the expertise necessary for bringing theater into the parks.

The other approach, of course, brings professional actors into the parks on some type of contract. Based upon his association with Yosemite, Stetson sees a logical future for arts in the parks—from theater to storytelling to music. At Yosemite, the Muir shows pay Stetson's salary, a technician, promotion, and other costs. The shows' ticket receipts bring an infusion of surplus funds into the Yosemite Association to sustain other conservation efforts. This contract arrangement, then, has proved tremendously successful.

Stetson favors using the arts in parks to inform and inspire people. He said:

> I am passionately convinced that art can serve to enhance our moral sensibilities and to promote in many a sense of environmental integrity. It used to be that our place on this planet was well claimed by the feelings of the people who lived here. Indigenous peoples, once naturally contained and nourished by the environment, integrated and celebrated that environment in their art, dance, music, community rituals. Their daily art evoked their values, aspirations, understanding, and their thoughts. The things we still need to learn are very old things we once knew well.

Stetson acknowledged the power and transforming qualities of art to move people. The greatest insight he gained from the study and character enactment of John Muir is the great hunger on the part of the public to hear a simple truth eloquently told. Ultimately Stetson emphasized (Beck, 1989): "The arts are a medium for gentle awakening of the unconscious good people and we desperately need more unconscious good people becoming conscious."

MODEST DRAMA

Numerous interpreters who are not professional actors don costumes and characters to get across their messages. Sometimes they present a whole program as "Critter Man" by Denny Olson, a variety of characters by Will and Sarah Reding, or many others. Other times, they present a skit or brief segment of their programs in a persona other than their own. These "modest dramas" may be very convincing, very humorous, and highly motivating. They can stimulate sight, smell, touch, hearing, and maybe tasting. They can involve the audience in the action. The drama seems to produce memorable concepts and information.

Keys to success seem to be (Reding, 1981):
1. developing the character, considering his or her whole existence and social environment,
2. believing and immersing into the character,
3. costuming that is authentic to the character and the period,
4. practicing,
5. using audience reaction,
6. developing the believability of make-believe,
7. acting whole-heartedly with professionalism, and
8. evaluate.

Interpretive actors have been observed portraying characters who had messages about weather, the water cycle, wildlife, recycling, insects, and many historic or mythological characters, e.g., Gwaltney and Pawling's (1992) living history characters.

MUSICAL DRAMA

In Kananaskis Country, a region of Alberta's provincial park system, a story of interpretation put to music may inspire others to try musical drama. About one in six people in the park overnight (mostly campers) showed up for evening interpretive programs. Then, almost by accident, the interpreters tried a skit or two to accompany traditional talks. Now the skits have evolved into interpretive plays with original songs—musical theater as interpretation. The interpreters cannot wing it any more. They script, rehearse, and critique the skit ahead of time, incorporating accurate information with entertainment. They work harder, and produce fewer types of programs, yet reach more people.

The results showed success, both in direct ways and in the numbers. On hikes the next day, many adults commented on enjoying the skit in the program. Many children and adults later recalled and recited the songs and details of the message—one day, one year and even three years later (Mair and Landry, 1991).

More visitors showed up. From 16.5 percent of the potential audience, attendance jumped to 32.3 percent in one year (1985). This figure remained stable until 1989, the year when more music was used in the programs. Then attendance jumped to 38.6 percent. In 1990, attendance was 44 percent and in the summer of 1991, almost 53 percent of the campers were making it to the evening programs, as documented by the research of Mair and Landry (1991).

The lesson that music can help people remember messages comes as no surprise to anyone who has listened to advertisements on radio and television, where companies put big money on public attention and response, even from unwilling audiences.

Music

Right-brain communication not only helps attract the public; it also reinforces intellectual messages in the "other half" of the human mind (Figure 14.3). Many types of music can be used in interpretation. One possibility is to use authentic

FIGURE 14.3
Music from the past, played on period instruments, enriches historical interpretation.

music as played or sung by the people of the period that are being interpreted. Traditional music and dance brings the audience in direct contact with different lifestyles or people. Folk songs document history—"a direct interpretation of people as they saw themselves and their times" (Cantu, 1990). A well-planned narrative that weaves together the music can relate the entertainment aspect to the educational theme (Barry et al., 1992).

Music as part of interpretation goes way back in history. In the early days of Yellowstone, Wylie Camps used songs and performance as an integral part of every evening campfire. Interpreters have long employed Native American singers, as well as players of guitars, banjos and accordions to enrich campfire programs in some national and state parks. Musical backgrounds to slide shows now can be produced in house with a little effort and the right (inexpensive) equipment.

"Singing for ecology" also livens up interpretive events, especially with spirited adults and children. Performances usually include audience participation. Billy B. performs in front of painted backdrops, focusing attention to trees, bays, and photosynthesis with high-energy fun that gets the audience up, laughing, and moving to the scientific lyrics of his songs (Hutcherson, 1993). Bill Oliver and Glen Waldick use a variety of props in their repertoire of songs ranging from creation stories ("Turtle Island") to John Muir ("Muir Power to You"). A West Coast group called "The Banana Slug String Band" performs zany music, with costumes and choreography and plenty of environmental messages. Rita Cantu, a Forest Service interpreter, and Doug Wood, a commercial musician, both sing and talk from a scientific base to promote environmentally-sensitive behavior.

Another use of music comes from Longwood Gardens, a high-tone private demonstration/interpretation center in Pennsylvania. It contains 350 acres of outdoor gardens, woodlands, an historic mansion, and conservatories. It also offers 300 performing arts events each year. An outdoor theater uses large, old trees as a natural backdrop. The Longwood musical accouterments include what is billed as one of the world's mightiest pipe organs. While most people pay to see flowers and plants in beautiful designs, they also get superb musical concerts, as well as ballet, drama, sculpture, and illuminated fountain displays.

On a more modest scale, Indiana State Parks offer several cultural events in six or eight heavily visited sites as an adjunct to the regular interpretive program. Hoosier woodwind and string quintets, bluegrass performers, choral groups, and others who can perform outside or in a picnic shelter draw in campers and lodge guests for a bit of culture. Additionally, several of the naturalists use folk music performance and participation as part of their evening campfire events.

How Music Interprets

Songs can work in several ways: (a) to get words and facts to stick in the minds of participants, (b) to paint a picture in the imagination, and (c) to reach the emotions of a person. Schuch (1992) suggests that "for environmental songs to really make a difference for the long haul, we need to look for ways to make them meaningful to the heart as well as informative for the mind."

Some songs evoke strong emotions which make them memorable. Others are catchy tunes that are remembered long after a performance. Songs can also work very effectively with children. Earth tunes (songs about science and nature) include "Spiders and Snakes" which teaches children about the usefulness of spiders and snakes and helps them to overcome fear, and "Dirt Made My Lunch," which shows how almost everything people eat is connected through the food chain and depends on soil (Miche, 1992). Solid information hung on the framework of a story and expressed through music produces both emotions and stronger memory (Mair, 1992).

Storytelling

Storytelling can be a powerful means for conveying information about cultural and natural history. Stories have the potential to hold the attention of large, mixed-age audiences. Because the images of stories are vivid in the minds of listeners, they retain what they have heard. Furthermore, storytelling is a relatively straightforward and inexpensive interpretive technique (Box 14.1).

Whole cultures have persisted through centuries, passing their rituals, beliefs, skills, and perceptions from generation to generation through stories. The Council for American Indian Interpretation chose the pueblo storyteller as its symbol (Brown, 1990). Stories in many forms comprise the core of interpretive speech, writing, and audiovisual materials.

Most interpreters faithfully follow Tilden's (1967) dictum that "the story's the thing." Unfortunately, after establishing that interpretation is an art, using artistic forms and methods while drawing upon all of science, Tilden said precious little about stories. Yet, the "story-line" approach is often emphasized as a key to effective interpretation. Brown (1971) claimed that "the interpreter must be explicit" when using the story-line approach to illuminate the visitor's world, "because educators hold little faith in the transfer of meaning from one universe of discourse to another, unless transition is made very clear."

Susan Strauss makes a living working with interpretive stories (Figure 14.4). She revives (and sometimes revises and invents) stories based on characters of Native American and rural folk societies. Strauss (1992) reminds people that speaking, especially story-telling, is a musical as well as a literary art.

FIGURE 14.4
Expressive hands, a mobile face, and a flexible voice enrich and enliven Susan Strauss' interpretive stories.
(courtesy S. Strauss)

BOX 14.1: THE STORY AND THE INTERPRETER—SOMETIMES ONE AND THE SAME

For most of us, a simple object can hold stories and memories that reveal something of us. Wilson Hunter (1990) told of one case in which a sensitive interpreter revealed something of people and culture through personal narratives.

"An interpreter at Canyon de Chelly developed such a story around the prosaic cradle board. Her purpose was to take her audience beyond the obvious, that the board is made of certain materials and is used in such-and-such a way. She tells how the person who makes a cradle board does not just find a well-shaped branch or bush and simply cut it down. Certain things must be said and done before removing these things from nature. Prayers are involved, and the necessary proprieties are observed. A child will start his life and begin the process of learning who he is on this cradle board; it must be a good board. And after it has served its purpose, it must not be discarded as if it had no value. It is something lent by nature, and must be returned to nature in the appropriate way.

"In the taking and the returning, one must be cognizant of the importance to maintain a harmony with nature.

"In other words, a perceptive and understanding interpreter tells not only what a cradle board is, but what it means. In so doing, one brings out of that simple and common object something of the Indian's world view, what things are important, and why."

Poetry's possible, too. Many cultures, including those of African, European and North American origins, use poetry to express deep feelings, reactions to the landscape, expressions of joy and laments of misery. Native Americans often use them to teach about ethics and religion, as in this one from *Songs of the Tewa* (Spinden, 1976).

SONG OF THE SKY LOOM

O Our Mother the Earth, O Our Father the Sky
Your children are we and with tired backs
We bring you the gifts you love
Then weave for us a garment of brightness
May the warp be the white light of morning
May the weft be the red light of evening
May the fringes be the falling rain
May the border be the standing rainbow.
Thus weave for us a garment of brightness
That we may walk fittingly where grass is green
O Our Mother the Earth, O Our Father the Sky.

Poems and stories have many traditional purposes: to pass on from one generation to another the values, ideas, standards of behavior, ideals, dreams, and folk wisdom of a culture (MacCarry and MacCarry, 1991). In America, a wealth of folklore includes American Indian myths, plantation slave folk tales, sea chanteys, and legendary stories of folk heroes. The earliest folk tradition in this country developed from the Native Americans. Among the common themes of native legends are explanations of how things came to be. A version of how the earth was formed offers an interesting interpretive possibility (Robinson, 1985):

The Great Spirit searched through all the animals of the sea to find the right one to carry the mud to form the earth. Finally, He found Grandmother Turtle, piled mud high on her back, and the first piece of earth was formed. Because of her help, the turtle is the only animal today who is at home beneath the water, within the earth, or above the ground. But for all times, the Grandmother Turtle and her ancestors must move very slowly, for they carry the weight of the world on their backs.

Poems read during interpretive programs can evoke a special feeling or give a little spice to the presentation. Having people write poems provides a creative exercise that provokes close observation of nature or exhibits. In environmental education groups, the follow-up reading of haiku or cinquain or diamante "poems" also provide great fun and fine openings for reviewing ecological concepts.

For the early settlers in this country survival took much of their energy. Yet they created legends and ballads to describe the vast frontier and its wildlife. Some of these are educational, while others (such as Paul Bunyan and Pecos Bill tales) amuse and entertain listeners who yearn for simpler and more innocent times.

Winslow (1983) offered several principles for effective storytelling, summarized as follows:

1. Use original myths, legends, and stories to maintain authenticity.
2. If original stories are unavailable to suit your purposes, then diligently research your subject and assemble a story. Sources may include journals, local newspapers, older members of a community, and books on geography, travel, and history.
3. Create a mood to tell the stories: choose an appropriate site, dress up in authentic costuming, and use artifacts or facsimiles.

4. Become involved in the story through use of expressions and gestures. Mime the story as you talk.

5. Use a full range of vocal expression, volume, tempo, and sound effects.

Storytelling can serve as the basis for an entire program. It can also be incorporated into a traditional campfire program or nature walk. This works especially well when the interpreter takes cues from the environment and uses stories to explain certain natural phenomena (Yemoto and Mortan, 1981). According to storyteller Susan Strauss (1988), "in the world of interpretation, the job of the storyteller is to bridge the gap between human beings and the natural world."

Art

Art museums thrive on interpretation. Many local art museums also actively train their publics in art skills, from photography, painting, and sculpture to art appreciation. Most offer lectures, short courses, and international tours to bring people and art together. Many small museums make strong efforts to promote interpretive skills among their members. One of these, *ArtSmart*, comprises three sets of lessons to interpret art to children and adults.

ArtSmart programs supplement the outreach program of the Greater Lafayette Museum of Art, Indiana. The first unit, with 150 slides and accompanying text, introduces Indiana artists and artworks to school children and adults. A second stage seeks to engage the visitor in critical thinking about what constitutes an effective work of art—not to rate one artwork as better than another. It urges viewers to trust their own sense of why one art work appeals more to them. A third stage in this progressive program fosters connoisseurship and esthetic discovery. It displays work of contemporary local artists and teaches methods of assessing quality, effectiveness and creativity of pottery, painting, and lithographs (Theobald, 1992).

Artists in the Parks have long brought painters and photographers into parks to teach by example and demonstrate their skills (Figure 14.5). The Adirondack Museum shows a superb exhibit hall full of paintings from the early years of the great forest preserve—the artists came on their own. Since then, national and state/provincial parks in the U.S. and Canada have maintained cooperative arrangements of mutual benefit to the park (publicity), the artist (sales), and the public (learning from artists).

FIGURE 14.5
Sculpture illustrates an interpretive theme of Black Hill Regional Park, Montgomery County, Maryland.

from artists). Eastman Kodak regularly supports company or free-lance photographers in parks. They give daily photo walks, including suggestions on seeing photographically, and evening slide programs.

Putting it All Together

An effective blend of music, drama, art, and stories occurs at Harpers Ferry National Historical Park on the Fourth of July. A group of volunteers from Frederick, Maryland, comes in period dress to put on an old-fashioned Fourth of July stump-speaking event as if it were in 1860. Park interpreters in period dress join the crowd. As "residents" of a town with loyalties divided between the North and the about-to-secede South, the speakers stand on a porch and vigorously present both sides in a civilized debate; the organist plays music; the performers and audience sing songs appropriate to the day; and the event closes with the (then) national anthem, "Columbia, the Gem of the Ocean." Tourists in modern garb drift right in to the listening area and generally become engrossed in the event, just as they would have in 1860.

The introduction of music and theater was found to increase attendance in Kananaskis Country interpretive programs in Alberta's Rocky Mountains. Perhaps a combination of theater, story, and music is ideal for engaging an audience emotionally, intellectually, and physically.

The use of the arts in interpretation has proven to be extremely effective in attracting and serving visitors. Some speculation (e.g., Mair and Landry, 1991) suggested that this style of programming is more attractive to the "unconverted"—those people who are not necessarily interested in the environment. Drawing a larger and broader segment of the population to interpretive programs may well stimulate widespread concern about cultural and environmental issues. It is likely that there will be continued growth of the arts in interpretive programming.

> *The interpretive arts bring to many a temporary vitality and a sharing of one another's truth. I am passionately convinced that art can serve to enhance our moral sensibilities and to promote in many a sense of environmental integrity.*

> —Lee Stetson (Beck, 1989)

Literature Cited

Barry, D., Bernardo, C., Farwell, R., and Fonfa, L. (1992). Using traditional music in interpretive programs. In *Proceedings, National Interpreters Workshop*, NAI. San Francisco Bay Area, CA.

Beck, L. (1989). Lee Stetson on interpretation. *Journal of interpretation, 13*(6):6-7.

Brown, W. E. (1971). *Islands of hope*. Arlington, VA: National Recreation and Park Association.

Brown, W. E. (1990). The storytellers. *Legacy, 1*(3):20-21.

Cantu, R. (1990). Gaia calling: Interpreting critical resource issues through the arts. In *Proceedings, National Interpreters Workshop*, NAI. Charleston, SC.

Covel, J. and Thomas, T. (1992). Interpretive theater programs: Getting started. In *Proceedings, National Interpreters Workshop*, NAI. San Francisco Bay Area, CA.

Cromie, A. (1979). *Restored towns and historic districts of America*. New York, NY: E. P. Dutton.

Gwaltney, W. and Pawling, R. (1992). Getting it right: Excellence in living history. In *Proceedings, National Interpreters Workshop*, NAI. San Francisco Bay Area, CA.

Hughes, C. (1993). Interpretive theater is on the rise. *Legacy, 4*(2):34-35.

Hunter, W. (1990). A cradle board and a culture. *Contact* (the Southwest Region Interpreter's Newsletter), 8 (July-September):12-13.

Hutcherson, A. (1993). Billy B. brings trees alive. *Tree Farmer,* (Winter):9.

Jones, D. (1991). Making your interpretation vibrant: Living history and drama in museums. In *Proceedings, National Interpreters Workshop*, NAI. Vail, CO.

MacCarry, B. and MacCarry, N. (1991). How storytellers contribute to a better understanding of cultural diversities. *Legacy, 2*(2):6-7.

Mair, S. and Landry, C. (1991). Musical theater in interpretation: The Kananaskis Country model. In *Proceedings, Third Global Heritage Interpretation Congress*. Honolulu, HI.

Mair, S. (1992). Interpretation for everyone. In *Proceedings, National Interpreters Workshop*, NAI. San Francisco Bay Area, CA.

Miche, M. (1992). Earth tunes and nature notes: Songs about science and nature. In *Proceedings, National Interpreters Workshop*, NAI. San Francisco Bay Area, CA.

Reding, W. (1981). "Yas eenya oyaka." In *Program Papers, National Workshop*, AIN-WIA. Estes Park, CO.

Robinson, L. (1985). As legend has it—The use of folklore in environmental interpretation. *Trends, 22*(4):46-47.

Schuch, S. (1992). Reflections on doing "environmental songs" with kids. *Mason-Dixon By-Line* (NAI Region II Newsletter), *15*(3):1,4.

Spinden, H. J. (1976). *Songs of the Tewa*. Santa Fe, NM: Sunstone Press.

Strauss, S. (1988). Story telling and the natural world. *Journal of Interpretation, 12*(1):4-7.

Strauss, S. (1992). Voice: The guardian angel of the interpreter. In *Proceedings, National Interpreters Workshop*, NA., San Francisco Bay Area, CA.

Theobald, S. A. (1992). *ArtSmart: New vistas II*. Lafayette, IN: Greater Lafayette Museum of Art.

Tilden, F. (1967). *Interpreting our heritage (rev. ed.)*. Chapel Hill, NC: University of North Carolina Press.

Winslow, W. (1983). Storytelling—An interpretive tool. In *Advances in Interpretation: National Workshop Proceedings*, AIN, Purdue Univeristy. West Lafayette, IN.

Yemoto, L. and Mortan, S. (1981). Be a better bard. In *National Workshop Program Papers*, AIN-WIA. Estes Park, CO.

Section IV

The remaining chapters focus on organizing and operating interpretive programs, in a logical, business-like manner. This section starts with a chapter on planning that considers the basic philosophy of interpretation. This sums up many ideas presented earlier—whom interpreters try to reach, the importance of reaching them, the need to serve as many people as possible and how to do it.

The next two chapters look at interpretation in a business-like way. First, a client-oriented service ethic leads to agency goals stated in terms of visitor experiences and social objectives. Second, interpretation marketing and finance keep the operation going.

Interpretive personnel management has long suffered from benign neglect. The professional societies and the government agencies recognize the need to improve the status and pay of those who interpret the most valuable resources of the nation. The interplay of professionals, seasonals, and volunteers provides excellent service as well as a few administrative problems which can be solved.

Evaluation techniques and philosophy integrate directly into any worthwhile interpretive program. Administrators can use evaluation as a positive, reinforcing, developmental procedure that interpreters will welcome. When administrators fail, the interpreters themselves can evaluate and improve their productivity by self or peer evaluation. This chapter describes several techniques used in the business community for evaluation of performance and total program productivity. It also advocates using neutral but expert observers to assess the general impression and performance of the organization.

The last chapter reviews the development of the profession of interpretation and points to its future opportunities. A vision of interpretation as a full-service, lifelong learning program takes us beyond the stereotype of a one-talk, one-walk naturalist in a park where visitors come once in a lifetime. Instead, the future can fulfill the dream of Enos Mills to have an interpreter in every community, perhaps in every park and every neighborhood.

Planning, design, evaluation and effectiveness of interpretation start with the visitor to be served. (LB)

Interpretive Planning

This chapter discusses the process and purposes of planning for interpretation. After reading it, the interpretive planner should be able to develop a strategy that works for a particular situation. The idea of using themes as a core of planning should become meaningful and active. The study of this chapter should help in the understanding of the interpretive prospectus used by the National Park Service and other agencies. The chapter also describes briefly an approach to master site planning that uses interpretation as the starting point and core of the plan. Several examples of planning processes used in major federal agencies appear as guidelines. Of course, every small museum and park system will have its own special requirements and will develop its own specific proposals.

The key message of the chapter is that interpretive programs and facilities proceed from careful planning (Figure 15.1). A plan considers the clients, defines the *genius loci*, states themes, and prescribes interpretive methods and media.

FIGURE 15.1
Interpretive planner Bruce McHenry gets down to work.

What Planning Means

Planning involves a series of processes and ideas. Boiled down to a few words, planning simply means to:
- Think ahead
- Prepare
- Develop process and action
- Develop concept and detail
- Imagine
- Coordinate

An interpretive plan or prospectus defines what and how a property or organization will tackle the task of presenting its stories to the public. It requires thought before action. A plan guides and coordinates the work of the various interpreters.

The process of planning for interpretation:
- considers the clients who come to a facility or area, as well as those it serves beyond the property.
- defines the special value, significance, and purpose of the place.
- sets up key goals, so interpreters know what they're trying to do and evaluators can determine how well they do it.
- outlines the approaches taken to interpret the facility, from themes to the personnel, methods, and media to use.
- prescribes the best mix of the methods, media, and messages.
- gives broad, general guidelines for a new or revised exhibit center and arrangement, trail schema, and other facilities.
- sets a style for the facility—the signs, the publications, the correlation of personal and nonpersonal services, the balance of efforts on-site and off-site.
- considers timing and financing of new developments.

Terminology and Meaning

Two terms, plan and prospectus, mingle on these pages. They mean about the same thing to us. To some the prospectus means more of a specific document (various forms exist). A plan can be something a little more intangible and broad, including a document and the mental processes involved to complete the task.

In the interpretive profession, some people might wish to make a sharp distinction between the two, on the basis of timeframes, content or intent. No harm comes from that, as long as you can figure out the terminology of a particular consultant or agency.

The National Park Service (NPS) currently uses the term *prospectus* as a prescription of the media to be used in a park—deciding when and where to use signs, brochures, exhibits, audiovisual devices, and computers (Figure 15.2). Oddly, but with purpose, a NPS prospectus does not include personal interpretation. The reason is that the prospectus serves as a guide to the Harpers Ferry Center for development of the nonpersonal media for a park. It is something like a physician (interpretive planning team) writing a prescription (prospectus) for the pharmacist (Harpers Ferry Center) to fill for a client (the park). But such a document is only part of a full interpretive plan.

The NPS prospectus process (gradually being revised) leaves out the important values of providing a guideline and reference for how to balance personal interpretation with the impersonal media efforts. The park staff and administration know what exhibits and gadgets, and audiovisual materials they should get in the future, but the overall picture of how the park will be interpreted and how many people are optimal requires another NPS planning effort. This usually is expressed in an annual "statement for interpretation" that specifies staffing needs for the coming year.

Outside the National Park Service, the interpretive prospectus usually includes the whole range of defined goals and the ways to accomplish them. The interpretive prospectus for other agencies defines the optimum combination of personal and nonpersonal services, the key themes and strategies to develop, and the means for developing and implementing them. The process also puts a premium on considering the visitors or customers—their needs and preferences.

A prospectus tries to define (a) the customers the interpreter expects or seeks and (b) what the visitor should take home with them. It may define several audiences—those who come and those interpreters reach. It targets the audience and strategies for reaching it.

It recognizes and defines visitor circulation by setting up interpretive facilities and programs to fit the circulation. It creates the sequence(s) of experiences.

Without a prospectus, one can imagine confusion, division of efforts, and lack of a sense of purpose.

Figure 15.2
An interpretive prospectus records long-term plans for presenting the key messages.

Developing an Approach to Interpreting a Natural Resource: A Consulting Strategy

To take interpretive planning down to the basics, imagine yourself as an interpretive consultant on a foreign assignment. For the next few paragraphs, visualize yourself sitting in a little hotel in a steamy rural province of a foreign country. Outside the window lies a provincial park. You do not know the flora or fauna very well. You do not know much about the geology, limnology, ecology, culture, or history of the area, although you have a reasonable background in these areas.

The provincial government pays you well, plus expenses, from their debt-laden public treasury, to advise on how and what to interpret. They are quite hopeful that ecotourism will pay off for them. Your opinions and recommendations are obviously important. It is time to outline your report and some key questions that you will ask tomorrow when the small park staff meets with you. What do you do? What is your approach? Panic is not acceptable behavior.

Obviously, the government did not bring you here to turn you into an expert on the local animals and plants and ecosystems. They do not plan on your going to the library for months of self-education or writing interpretive booklets. Nor do they expect to pay you as an anthropologist or historian to study the human story of the park. They hired you as an interpretive planner—one who can look at the park as a visitor and as a professional, one who can see the staff and resources and help adapt to the conditions and suggest ways to provide effective, responsible interpretation. They want a realistic vision of where they can go, what they can do, and how it will benefit their society. They need a document from you that will help them persuade their legislature to dedicate funds to the park's interpretive effort. They may even ask you to provide some rough cost figures and a calendar of development.

In other words, the government wants the interpreter to do what he or she surely needs to do at home, as well. For interpreters who have sat in similar hotels or huts, looking at similar parks—through the Peace Corps, World Bank, universities, or as consultants—the foreign experience immediately focused their attention on what they could do, usually in a short time. To approach this work, an interpreter needs to develop a sense of the vital questions in planning and define a planning process.

The Essential Elements: Vision, Change, Conflict, Risk, Challenge

A National Park Service planner, Fred Babb, uses these five key words to define planning work. *Vision* requires that interpreters design and paint a picture that people can understand and buy into. A need for *change* precedes a need for a plan; plans usually call for some kinds of change in the interpretive mix or methods and direct how to go about it. *Risk* and *conflict* come with any change; planners may as well learn to work with them. The *challenge* is to facilitate and coordinate the planning process, then to present a plan to the owners and to implement it with the staff.

The planning process serves as a means to achieve an end—the vision. Too often, interpreters start with problems of today rather than a vision of how they want things to be. The problems include things as mundane as—what to do about the water leaks, how to change the typeface on the brochures, getting an amphitheater, to reducing accidents at the overlooks—all important means, but not the vision. If the problems get top billing, the tail wags the dog. The staff sees what needs to be fixed and figures that the interpretive prospectus should say to patch it up. Too many fix-it requests can kill the planning process, unless the leader of the team can keep bringing the focus back to accomplishing the vision.

Try zero-based planning. Mentally, wipe the slate clean. For a moment, ignore programming that "we've always done." More realistically, define current programming and facilities as the status quo alternative in the array of possible recommendations. Think broadly, dream, think analytically, believe in what the organization is doing, dare to take a risk. It can be mentally liberating. It need not be irresponsible in the final outcome to spend a few moments seriously writing about what could be achieved given a larger staff or different facilities. Try to avoid thinking of the staff or buildings as the end product—think of what the group wishes to produce for the clients whom it serves.

GENIUS LOCI

Define the essence of the place—its character—its special qualities—its significance—to get the planning process started (Figure 15.3).

A sense of place or *genius loci* expresses itself locally, globally, and cosmically. Annie Dillard (1974) wrote about the natural forces at work or play in her isolated mountain valley. She let her mind sense what was near, then related it to what is beyond. She perceived everything from cicadas and water to the air moving across her valley to interplanetary winds out in that vast space above the atmosphere people breathe. This may seem a bit too broad for an interpretive vision but it starts to define the character of a place.

FIGURE 15.3
A sculpture captures the complexity of John Brown, clearly identifying the interpretive theme of this farmstead in New York.

JOHN BROWN
1800 – 1859

Allow change to enter the thoughts of planners. Maybe fresh approaches will get to more visitors. Allow conflict of ideas to occur only during planning, under the control of constructive discussion. Run the risk of considering various alternatives—even some that may seem impractical. They may lead to more practical ways to achieve similar results. The challenge consists of interpreting for every client and potential clients so they sense vibrance in what is going on now and what has gone on in this place. Interpreters seek to make the significance of the place come alive in each of their clients.

Themes and Planning

DEVELOPING STATEMENTS OF THEMES

This is the process of selecting the best, most important, most relevant, most interesting, most appropriate subjects and concepts to be interpreted. It is usually a narrowing or focusing process.

Anyone who works hard on an interpretive site can find many possibilities for interpreting natural and historic phenomena in the area. With careful observation and research on the area, the list of possibilities can become extensive. By talking to a few other talented interpreters or visitors, the list can grow even more. Such a list of brainstorm ideas may be useful as a backup whenever someone despairs about the lack of things about which to talk. In the case of repeat or long-term visitors, the list may give a source of diverse possibilities that an interpreter can use.

Unless the special character of a place is very evident, it may be difficult to narrow the topics down to a few themes that the visitors can comprehend. Visitor time and interest may be limited. The interpreters seek to select the topics that must be interpreted so that visitors can receive consistent topics and messages. The basic purposes have to be researched to prevent the development and reiterating of "legends" and other serious factual errors.

Selection of subjects and key concepts often starts from the board of directors or legislature. They define the general values of the place—the *raison d'être*. For example, the property may be set up to interpret a subject such as 19th Century mining technology, colonial furniture, or old-growth bottom land forest communities. The concepts to teach may be the immigration patterns of the West, the economic activity of the colonies, the adaptability of certain tree species to wetlands.

A classic example of thematic development is the chain of concepts about the natural environment used by Van Matre for a boys' camp. This chain is a group of selected concepts that form the basis for experiential interpretation during a camp session:

This chain of concepts serves as an introduction to the ecology that is defined as "the study of all living things in their relation to one another and to their environment; an investigation into homes and communities" (Van Matre, 1972).

THE WEB OF LIFE
|

*Light, air, water, and soil are the
elements of life,*
|

Life is divided into producers, consumers, and decomposers,
|

Everything is becoming something else,
|

Everything has a home,
|

*Homes in a defined area form a community,
Inhabitants of these communities live together in competition,
cooperation, or neutrality,*
|

Man is the chief predator.

PURPOSE AND INTERPRETIVE POLICY

The statement of purpose of a site is important in restoration and interpretation policy. It defines why the site was saved—why it is to be restored. There are often secondary objectives, but they are by-products, not keys to decision making.

Acquiring historic buildings always raises the question of what to do with them. The usually fast, emotional, and urgent campaign to "save the building" is over. Now, how will the site or facility communicate its values to the public? Two broad answers exist: (a) restore to past condition for it to be an interpretive building, or (b) adapt the building to another use.

Restoration uses include two categories of interpretation (Alderson and Low, 1985):

1. documentary and
2. representative.

A documentary building is a structure focused on a specific person or event, (e.g., a tavern where Revolutionary battle plans were designed, or the restored home of an inventor). The building's importance derives from what happened in that exact place at a particular time or because of who lived there. Its restoration and interpretation in specific terms related to the person develops strong importance. An example includes the various structures associated with the childhood and later life of Lyndon Johnson, in Texas, where restoration to particular years in his life became the focus of the National Park Service.

A representative building is a typical structure of the period, or of the way of life of people in that period, e.g., a tavern interpreting the functions of an 1830 inn, for food, lodging, and socializing; a typical federal style home in the Midwest (names of owners are interesting but incidental). Old Sturbridge Village in Massachusetts stands as a collective example of a representative rural community-farm complex. It consists of buildings moved in from all over New England to re-create the essence of a New England village; this village never existed historically.

TEAM PLANNING

To define a vision requires a team, including the park (or museum) management staff and interpreters. The team also should include upper administrators, perhaps a political leader, and potential users. An outside planner should usually chair the team and coordinate the process, just to prevent suppression of thought among staff or local citizens due to hierarchy status. Each team will operate differently; some combinations of people do not work well. Sometimes a planner steps back as leader if there are personality conflicts.

The team can be flexible in size as the work progresses. At some steps, local or general public input may swell the number of people involved. At times of writing, the core team will do most of the work, with assigned sections and plenty of revision, or with one or two doing most of the drafts and the others checking, editing, and refining.

A team completely from inside the organization has limitations, unless it is a large organization. Even so, a few independent planners who "do not understand" the system or are outside the tradition may bring in fresh perspective of great utility. A team composed of only outside consultants may crank out a prospectus very astutely and quickly, but the lack of internal responsibility can mean that no one ever will read the plan with true understanding or will implement it. Astute consulting planners insist that key agency personnel and local leaders participate fully in the planning process. They structure the steps to optimize local "buy-in" opportunities.

Planning Processes

If you give a planning group a clear process to follow, then things go faster. With the emphasis on government-citizen interaction, planning groups often get unwieldy and group decisions take a lot of time. For an interpretive plan, with a lot of creativity required, a small group taking input from others may be the most efficient method of proceeding. Sometimes, the imaginative spurts of one person become essential to define the vision, suggest the alternatives, and/or justify the choice and direction, with the group refining, adjusting, and finally endorsing the plan.

Many different linear planning processes exist. For example, one commonly used general planning sequence follows these five steps:

1. Define the problem, so everyone starts from the same point.
2. Analyze the problem, in terms of its basic facts and constraints.
3. Suggest solutions or recommendations as alternatives.
4. Establish criteria for analysis and comparison of alternatives.
5. Select the solution and describe it so it can be implemented.

That process gives some major points and may seem to be orderly. In practice, even these five steps will overlap and change order. Discussions get people involved in solutions before the problem gets well-defined. Often, an interpreter cannot really analyze the problem until some ideas of solutions and alternatives arise.

Planning provides a way of making choices about how to achieve a vision or final outcome. Therefore, it is not the planning process that is important. It is just one of many ways of getting to a plan. Each person will eventually develop his or her own favorite procedure. Here is another list, for comparison (others follow). It shows three stages where administrative/public/staff participation will help get buy-in.

1. Determine and state the scope of the plan.   *Get buy-in.*
2. Develop the vision by discussing opportunities, needs, dreams, expectations, the resource's significance, its purposes, and its administrative mandate.   *Get buy-in.*

   > *Note: The vision states what interpretation should be on the site. It does not refer to what is wrong on the site.*

3. Define objectives, as realistic stepping stones to achieving the vision.
4. Set out visitor and resource management facts and concepts.
5. List the important issues.
6. Develop alternatives.   *Get buy-in.*
7. Choose and develop the recommended alternative.

Again, a linear process appears. Most people do not really function in straight lines when they are being creative. One experienced planner says he operates in linear fashion with occasional holistic, round bursts of inspiration. Developing (writing or drawing) these inspirations drive the planning team along its linear path toward completion.

All interpretive planning considers two key components in parallel: (a) the visitors or clients and (b) the resources or facility. The interpretive planner can use the following approaches to planning in each of these categories.

VISITOR EXPERIENCE PLANNING

First and foremost comes the visitor experience. This is the essence of the interpretive plan's vision. The approach to interpreting a museum, forest, park, or reserve starts with what the clients seek. Interpreters need to present a practical philosophy that leads to a strategy, themes, and messages. The themes are those ideas so important that every visitor leaves with them imbedded in the mind.

Then, this should lead to alternative techniques of presenting the interpretation. Your value is in helping define the interpretive philosophy, setting the strategy, and identifying the types of themes and messages that will help the agency achieve its interpretive goals. The visitor experience really boils down to how the visitor interacts with the resource or museum. The interpreter provides brochures, exhibits, information, talks, films to help make the interaction possible. On the planning team, then, the interpreter and selected visitors describe how visitors interact with the resources and how interpreters can better promote favorable, productive interactions.

Consumer Orientation

Public agencies providing natural and cultural resource areas have made impressive progress in using social and behavioral sciences. Economics and marketing now focus first on consumers and the products they desire rather on the products first and how to get the consumer to buy it. Likewise, interpreters can define recreational needs and interpretive opportunities in terms of what the visitors may desire—what kind of recreational interpretive experiences they might seek. To discover this requires more than just leaving it up to the interpretive planner to somehow know or divine it. It requires public input at early stages of planning. Before writing down planning assumptions, ask the customer, usually in a formal way. The consumer-oriented outcome can be called the desired experiences and the experience opportunities (Pulsipher and Parker, 1980). Then follow-up with various stages of input by visitors. An interpretive planning team could serve itself well by including one permanent member who acts as a visitor advocate.

An early consideration is to define the visitors that come now and the ones that are expected or targeted.

1. Are they local and/or outsiders? What languages do they speak? What is their cultural context and interests?
2. How do they arrive? By tour bus, school bus, foot, horse, auto, train?
3. How long and where do or can they stay? Are they visiting out of a tourist hotel complex across the island or will they camp in the park?
4. To visit the resource well, what must they do? Backpack or ride for several days? Descend into a cave or mine? Be out at night? Stop by for an hour or two during the day? In other words, to get the essence or the immersed experience—the real value of the place—what should interpreters offer/require in terms of time, movement, equipment and guided services? Might it be a three-day safari, a week-long expedition across the glaciers to observe rare species, an elevator trip or hike into a huge cavern, or a tour of a factory with safety precautions?

Involve visitors in the planning. A few might serve on the planning team, at least at critical points. Collect the available visitor data from the interpretive staff or their consultants. Ask front-line staff for their observations of visitor needs and desires—ask them independently of the back room administrators. If needed, conduct interviews with visitors or request responses to questionnaires, that focus on what this place does for them and what it might do. Beware compiling a list of minor complaints; search for the big picture that will lead to stronger service. When alternatives are developed, visitors (e.g., the museum's history society) might be asked to comment or vote in an advisory capacity.

To be honest, it is unusual to start out a planning process with a sit-down-write-it-out statement of what the visitor experience will be. An interpreter may have to start by getting into the subject through facts, on-the-ground study, visualizing, studying pictures, reading of the place. Some individuals "surround" the subject, then go straight to the solution. Others use a Russian nesting doll approach, starting with the world then working down to a specific place or person of interest. This could be called the step-wise shrinking context. Others would reverse the process, starting with the particulars of a case, then working up to how it relates to the world. These creative, imaginative approaches come from confessions of professional planners. Whatever their inner thought processes, they know how to express the visitor experience clearly.

Personal-Nonpersonal Services Planning

Given the vision and visitor experience statement, the team can focus on what kinds of mix between personal (guided) interpretation and those mechanical and self-guided services to use. Various alternatives arise, from personal to nonpersonal. Then, the balance of these alternatives derive from study of costs and staff and the nature of the messages. Where the messages should be available day and night, the presentation will probably be nonpersonal. When the messages are in remote or little-used places, nonpersonal messages usually seem appropriate. Personal interpretation has its role where guiding, questions and answers, flexible learning, and encouraging visitor action are desired.

RESOURCE-ORIENTED PROCESS

While the visitor comes first, in many (most) cases, the resource itself requires a separate analysis. The following simple process focuses strictly on the resource. A parallel audience analysis can be blended into this process before the recommendation stage.
1. Inventory existing facilities and programs.
2. Inventory interpretive opportunities, resource inventory data (e.g., forest inventory, artifact accessions records).
3. Study the agency/owner objectives and emphases.
4. Develop and recommend alternatives for interpretation.
5. Prepare an interpretive action plan for all facilities and programming.

FROM VISION TO THEMES

The visitor will carry away certain themes. The themes express the broad vision of what the museum, park or forest represents—what serves as its central messages. The planner sometimes sees the big picture first, as a so-called vision of the character of the place. Then the vision gets broken down into one to four major interpretive themes.

Models of Interpretive Planning

Interpretive planning by different agencies uses variations on the approaches presented above. The Bureau of Land Management and the National Park Service procedures follows. The Forest Service's approach to Visitor Center planning follows.

BUREAU OF LAND MANAGEMENT MODEL

A simple planning model, used by the Bureau of Land Management (BLM) for 10 years for an entire property or just a small program, is the modified Peart Woods Planning Model, shown on page 372 (Figure 15.4).

FOR THIS MODEL, THE ELEMENTS INCLUDE:

WHY?   *Goals and objectives.*
WHAT?   *What are the resources to interpret?*
WHO?   *Visitor analysis.*
HOW?   *How, when, and where to conduct programs or install interpretive media and services.*
SO WHAT?   *Evaluation.*
I&O   *Budget, phasing, staff needs, and other needs to carry out the program.*

FIGURE 15.4
BLM INTERPRETIVE PLANNING MODEL

This model can help develop the outline for the interpretive prospectus, changing it to meet individual planning needs.

The steps that define an interpretive planning process can include these five used by the Bureau of Land Management:

A. Formation of planning team.
   1. From the public sector.
   2. From the private sector.
B. Interpretive inventory.
   1. Audience analysis.
   2. Cultural and natural resources.
   3. Current interpretive services.
C. Preparation of the plan.
   1. Area overview.
   2. Goals, objectives, and themes.
   3. Program components.
D. Implementation requirements.
   1. Personnel.
   2. Equipment.
   3. Site development.
   4. Maintenance.
   5. Time schedule.
   6. Program budget.

E. Monitoring and evaluation.
    1. Plan monitoring.
    2. Effectiveness evaluation.
    3. Plan revision.

NATIONAL PARK SERVICE INTERPRETIVE PLANS

The following lengthy discussion describes probably the most structured interpretive planning system in the U.S., that of the National Park Service. Despite its apparent rigidity, many variations occur from park to park, and from planning team to planning team.

The players involved include: (1) Park Staff, (2) Regional Office, (3) Harpers Ferry Center for interpretation (HFC), with various divisions, and the (4) Denver Service Center, with various kinds of park planners and specialized analysts (DSC).

The sequence involves the following steps.

A. Each *park requests* planning, preferably for both:
    1. a General Management Plan, outlining overall park land and facility planning (a refinement of what is called the master plan by many agencies).
    2. an Interpretive Prospectus, consisting of analysis, identification, and prescription of four major components:

    > Park story
    > Themes
    > Objectives (i.e., desired outcomes/futures) and
    > Media (e.g., visitor center, trails, waysides, films/videos).

    The request goes to the Regional Office, gets prioritized and then waits in line at the Denver Planning Service Center (DPSC) and Harpers Ferry Center (HFC).

B. *Conceptual planning* is done by a team made up of park staff, the DSC, HFC, and usually a regional office representative. The Harpers Ferry representative usually comes from its Division of Interpretive Planning. Increasingly, interpretation and visitor experiences take a leading role in the planning process. As the key output of a park visit, the identification of interpretive values and the park's reason for being serve as primary guidelines for the plan. (Before 1960-65, Master Plans focused almost exclusively on physical facilities such as buildings, utilities, and roads, with park values and prominent features as an important consideration. There was little writing about ecosystem problems, the flow and sequence of visitor experiences, and contacting and informing the visitor except as incidentals or afterthoughts.)

C. This leads to *Exhibit Plans (indoors)* by the HFC Division of Exhibit Planning & Design and *Exhibit Plans (outdoors)* by the HFC Division of Wayside Exhibits.

D. *Production and installation* of exhibits (and rehabilitation) becomes the responsibility of the HFC Division of Museum Production, with some outdoor installation by Wayside Exhibits.

E. The exhibits/interpretive plans get support *by specific plans, designs, and developments* such as:

1. Audiovisual shows	Division of Audiovisual Arts*
2. Exhibit information photos, art	Library and Photo Archive, Division of Audiovisual, Exhibit Planning
3. Publications (e.g., booklets, brochures, maps)	Division of Publications
4. Artifacts, furnishings	Division of Historic Furnishings, Division of Conservation.

NATIONAL PARK SERVICE APPROACH

The National Park Service in its current planning mode uses four steps to define the interpretive methods that will be used in a park.

1. **The park story:** From the park master plan or General Directives, determine the park's key values and story—what makes this park special? Why was it established? What are the main elements or people who comprise the character and history of the park? What kinds of questions are visitors likely to ask when they come here? This first major step in interpretive planning determines and defines the key story of the resource (e.g., park, forest, museum, factory, monument). What is the major value being preserved or told about? Why do people come here—or what would draw them here if they knew about it? It may be as obvious as a pivotal battle, a major invention, the fishing, the deep canyon. It may be as ordinary as a beautiful stream accessible to the public at this point. If it is the latter, the story may be about that stream and this valley, how it was formed, how it flows, its recovery from pollution, its fish and other life. The story could be about the trees that grow along the river and the bird life that inhabits them.

2. **Themes:** Define the one or more major concepts or themes that are to be the focus of the interpretive presentations (e.g., signs) to be used in the park. For example, Harpers Ferry National Historic Park does all their interpretation around four interrelated themes: (a) the industries that made the place important, (b) John Brown's raid, (c) the Civil War events that pivoted around the area, and (d) the story of black families and education in Harpers Ferry. The next step is to define the theme that the interpreter will follow in presenting the story—the key idea that the visitor should carry away. Sometimes, there is more than a single theme. Each gives broad scope to the interpreters and the exhibit-makers. For example, the African-American history of the town goes from well before the Civil War to the early education of blacks at Storer College, to modern day families depicted in one of the exhibit complexes (Day and Larsen, 1991).

3. **Objectives:** Delineate the skills or knowledge that the visitors will be able to demonstrate upon completion of an interpretive visit to the property, in fairly broad terms (not program-by-program in the prospectus).

---

* The names and organization of divisions within the Harpers Ferry Center change periodically.

The third step identifies the objectives to carry the theme statement into outcomes that an interpreter expects the visitors to achieve after a visit. They start with the phrase: The visitor will be able to . . .

4. **Media:** Select the strategy to be used in interpretation, emphasizing the nonpersonal devices, such as signs, wayside exhibits, audiovisual presentations, museum or visitor center exhibits, restorations, brochures, booklets, or maps. A new or expanded visitor center may be called for; here, its need and general character are defined.

In this fourth step, the plan focuses on the methods to be used to achieve the objectives. Often this includes a visitor center with exhibits that feature the story and its themes, developed in ways to achieve the objectives. The methods also include audiovisual programs, signs, brochures, walking tours, personal interpretation of various types, special viewing points with wayside signs and exhibits, special programming and information, publications, and maps.

The logical fifth step is the planning of personal services interpretation. In the National Park Service, this is currently included in an annual Statement for Interpretation, which analyzes the entire program, recommends staffing and productivity, and other current needs, e.g., equipment replacement, updated audiovisual materials, signs. The Statement for Interpretation goes to regional offices for review and approval.

In the NPS model, the prospectus stands as the basic guide for interpretation for up to 10 years, by focusing almost entirely on the general concepts and the relatively permanent (long-term) interpretive devices and facilities. The more flexible programming of personal services and special events comes through an annual planning process where, presumably, flexibility also exists to make necessary alterations and improvements in some of the more permanent media. The only problem with this approach is that the prospectus might not reflect the full range or character of the interpretive effort to be made in the park. It is not an "under-one-cover" document which provides a new employee or regional coordinator a picture of the whole effort.

VISITOR CENTER PLANNING—FOREST SERVICE STYLE

National Forest interpretive facilities that require development costs over $250,000 must seek approval. The USDA Design Center in Washington reviews them for process, technique, and construction alternatives. The Chief of the Forest Service and USDA officials also approve them.

To get started, the Region submits a short (less than 20 pages) Interpretive and Design Prospectus and cover letter to the Chief to request a review and project approval. It contains the following elements:

Purpose of Facility

Basic Marketing Information

- audience-projected visitation
- projected length of stay

Interpretive Programs and Facility Objectives

- what visitors will do, feel, and know after using this facility

Functional Uses of the Facility
- information/orientation area
- exhibit areas
- audiovisual requirements
- administrative uses
- interpretive sales areas

Scale of Development
- estimated square footage of facility
- operation and maintenance plans and considerations
- estimated costs

Suggested Media Treatments

Simple Site Plan (if available)

After a response (the goal is a four-week response time), the region and forest may proceed with more detailed planning. Some of the keys or principles in planning include:

1. Make sure to provide enough space without waste.
2. Choose the theme and subthemes critically.
3. Consider the audience throughout the process.
4. Carefully consider what is worthy of display; avoid too much material; do not tell too much.
5. Seek a good design with visual appeal that emphasizes the main points.
6. Lay out the design both visually and by narrative; combine the key elements in a logical manner.
7. Use visual materials such as artifacts or replicas, photos, drawings, maps, charts, and graphs.
8. Study the message; know your subject; describe it briefly but enough to get the message across; use humor where appropriate.
9. Make all lettering big enough to read easily at an average viewing distance for that facility; make labels and text brief but appropriately informative; separate the text into small portions to facilitate reading.

VISITOR CENTER APPROPRIATIONS

The Forest Service expressed concern about the high capital investments and annual operation and maintenance costs of its visitor centers and similar facilities. In the fiscal year (FY) 1992 budget, Congress earmarked $18 million dollars for visitor center construction. That money came out of recreation management funds. The result reduced the ability to operate and maintain existing visitor facilities, including other visitor centers. A system-wide strategy for the development of visitor centers seems more sensible and financially responsible than the continued ear-marking of projects promoted by Representatives for their districts.

REHABILITATION PROGRAMS

Major rehabilitation of existing facilities or exhibits require planning. Often a prospectus coincides with a rehabilitation program. Then, the NPS interpretive planning team usually wipes clean the slate of ideas and exhibits, and starts over with the exception of using functional buildings and roads and trails. The National Park Service seldom keeps older exhibits in its prospectus planning process, so the planning process may as well start at ground zero. New exhibit climate control allows better care of artifacts. For example, bright lights in closed cases produce high temperatures, which then cool at night. This contributes to deterioration of the artifacts and fading of colors.

NOTE: A CONTRARIAN WARNING

This text emphasizes brevity in writing and exhibits. When planning most interpretive centers, interpreters make an effort to counteract the tendency to tell people everything they know by "putting a book on the wall." Perhaps the guiding rule should be to write as much as people will actually read while standing up, if interested (some visitors will not read anything—not even Entry or Exit). Consider how long people may stay in the specific facility and how often they might return and whether they might use it for reference.

For example, a visitor center planned for a destination campground will probably draw visitors several times, if there is enough information. On rainy days, it could become a major attraction for the whole day. If the only text is at the headline level and the themes are so few that there is no detail or diversity, it is kind of like offering "feel-good" advertisements for cars—you may be attracted to the picture for a minute, but you're given little information. People say "I've been there; nothing ever changes." Think of the huge picture panels of a forest and lake scene with a trade-show eye-catching but uninformative slogan such as "Your National Forests—Lands of Many Uses." On the other hand, a much more satisfying and enriching Bureau of Land Management panel stood in the Anchorage airport (where many people spent 5 to 10 minutes reading). It explained and showed BLM surveying projects, uses of LANDSAT information, and the property run by the BLM in Alaska. The slogan-type information was there to catch the person walking to a plane; for those with more time, smaller type and illustrations gave a very positive image—an agency spending its money to inform, not just to propagandize.

A visitor center planned for repeaters and long-time campers should probably contain more complete and detailed exhibits and writing than one which serves primarily as a 10-minute pass-through introduction to a park, forest or refuge. A county park or campground nature center may fall into the repeater category.

Plan such a center to offer more activities that require time and study, give the long-term visitor some chances to examine and read at leisure, with tables, microscopes, reference books, tools, and suggested projects. Interpreters at these centers can plan their activities to include crafts, investigations, outdoor skill development—for adults as much as for children. Provide a center that prompts visitors to come back for more, at least in places where repeat visits seem likely.

Implementation

No battle plan ever survives contact with the enemy.
—Ancient military proverb

The lack of fidelity to plans, once the action starts, usually distresses the planner and cause the manager to wonder about the lack of prescience of those planners. Things change; conditions require new responses, unanticipated in the plan. Elected officials need to enhance their images or to respond to certain groups, sometimes at the cost of the best-laid plans. It is a universal phenomenon.

Plans hopefully provide a foothold in the rush of events. As a museum exhibit gets rushed to completion, builders, electricians, carpenters, and other preparators often make changes—some inadvertently—in the plans drawn on paper. Likewise, an interpretive plan may call for a certain mix of activities and programs; when one type does not work well, the interpreters may drop it, as if by public demand.

The key job requires a plan that states key principles and clearly explains the necessary details, without descending into minutia. The next key requires a plan that the implementers will read and later return to as a reference. Often, planners seem to write and draw for themselves, rather than for the busy manager who needs quick-to-find, easy-to-read, clear-to-show sections that lay out the interpretive plan in just enough detail to clearly convey the ideas and approaches, written to stimulate and guide the imaginations of interpreters and their supervisors.

Summary

Bucy (1991) summarized the interpretive planning processes into two phases, each containing several components.

PHASE I: The Background Questions

Goals: What end results justify the expenditure of time, money, and other resources?

Audience: Who are the target audiences? What are their needs, expectations, and limitations?

Opportunities: What significant sites, facilities, collections, stories, and events are available for use in the interpretive program?

Parameters: Under what circumstances must the components of the interpretive program be created (e.g., time, money), and under what conditions must they function (e.g., weather, vandalism, competing stimuli)?

PHASE II: The Planning Decisions

Themes: What messages should be sent?

Media prescription: What topics or stories should be used to send the messages? What media [or personal services] should be used? What sites should be developed?

Priority: Which components should be developed in which order?

These ordered categories give a start; they're a guide to gathering information and making decisions. Above all, planning requires the right information. The planner is an information seeker-and-finder. The best planners are often those who have the skill to get and use the best information—those who know how to gather, perceive, and comprehend the information, then transmit it so it leads to effective decisions. They get the feel of the place, the sense of what is important about it (and some experienced planners seem to do it outside of the constructs listed above). The guidelines here allow the planner to ask the right questions, in the right order, to get the right information. They also allow clear communication of the planning process to those who help make, fund, and implement the decisions.

An interpretive prospectus provides a thorough analysis of (1) the purpose and special qualities of the area, (2) the opportunities for interpretation, (3) the expected visitors and their activities, and (4) the interpretive experiences the interpreter can provide them. There is no formula for an interpretive prospectus. Each property, museum, county, or factory should be approached as a unique resource with its own outline. Yet all planning models have similar characteristics and components (Bucy, 1991):

- Establish goals.
- Define and analyze the circumstances under which the goals must be attained.
- Examine the options.
- Select solutions that work under these circumstances.

A plan can conform to an output orientation. Specifically, identify products and services intended to result from implementing the plan and then the process components.

Write this in the form of mission statements and objectives along with the ways to measure the outcomes. In other words, write the objectives in terms that allow measurement of the outcome (consumer experiences).

In the planning process, eliminate potential conflicts among objectives at both higher and lower levels by fitting the property interpretive plan into district, regional, and adjacent community plans or activities.

Literature Cited

Alderson, W. T. and Low, S. P. (1985). *Interpretation of historic sites (2nd ed.)*. Nashville, TN: American Association for State and Local History.

Bucy, D. E. M. (1991). Tourism vs. environmental integrity and livability: Using interpretive planning to solve tourism management problems. *Legacy, 2*(4):10-14.

Day, M. and Larsen, D. (1991). Personal battlefields: The African-American exhibit—a valuable educational tool. In *Proceedings, National Interpreters Workshop*. Vail, CO.

Dillard, A. (1974). *Pilgrim at Tinker's Creek*. New York, NY: Harper & Row Publishers, Inc.

Pulsipher, G. L. and Parker, T. C. (1980). Integrating interpretation into land management planning: A Forest Service case study. In *Proceedings, National Workshop, Association of Interpretive Naturalists*. Cape Cod, MA.

Van Matre, S. (1972). *Acclimatization*. Martinsville, IN: American Camping Association.

The Business of
Interpretation

16

Leadership = Doing the right thing.
Management = Doing things right.
—Stephen R. Covey

This chapter focuses on managing interpretive services to deliver a quality product that effectively achieves the desired benefits. It deals with administrative philosophy and methods to deliver a quality service to the public that will also benefit the agencies involved.

The chapter should enable the reader to:
- identify sound management principles that can work for managers of interpretive programs.
- develop and use a business-like philosophy for interpretive supervision and administration.
- employ effective management and marketing techniques for interpretive organizations.
- set and achieve agency/company goals in terms of visitor experiences and social objectives.

The following concepts draw heavily on the writings of Tom Peters and his collaborators in two business management books (Peters and Waterman, 1982; Peters and Austin, 1985), as well as a few other popular business management writers. The principles presented here have become goals for both public and private organizations. They are based upon study of America's best-run companies.

Certainly, some interpreters of poetic bent may feel uncomfortable with the notion of treating interpretation as a "business." Some got into the field precisely to escape business environments, to get back to nature or history, and to deal with fundamental facts and rhythms of life, not the artificial abstractions and deadlines of balance sheets and bureaucracy. Nevertheless, disdain for business-like management, marketing and revenue generation will seldom produce an abundance of operating funds and supporting salaries, let alone capital for expanding the museum building, providing parking, or annexing the neighboring wetlands or historical properties. Indeed, the consequence of a cavalier attitude toward commerce may be a dearth of dollars (or pounds or pesos). Money does not usually comprise the major goal of interpretation but it provides one means for reaching the goals.

Indeed, interpretation is a business. Regardless of the nature of your personal motivation and commitment, apply ethical business methods and principles to help you serve as a more effective interpreter. A business approach can make more interpretation available to the public at the right times and places.

Many interpretive programs rely on direct or indirect revenue generation. Attendance is often the measure of success and value. Therefore, interpretive services, as any other service-oriented business, must attract and keep customers. This, by necessity, leads to questions of marketing, customer relations, and evaluating service. Interpreters can improve the management and delivery of their services by analyzing their customers, delivery schedules, and cost effectiveness. Being "business-like" should not be perceived as an insult to the environment or to history or art but rather as a high compliment.

WORK HABITS TO DEVELOP FOR LEADERSHIP

Covey (1993a) studied leadership throughout the centuries. He concluded that many effective leaders have in common seven attitudes or habits. Covey recommends that leaders:

1. Be proactive: Initiate, create a vision, empower others, take responsibility for your own actions. This is one of the key characteristics of a supervisor as compared to an employee.
2. Begin with the end in mind: Think of how you want to be remembered at your funeral. To do the right things, create the action in your mind, then pave the road for others to follow. Make sure your people get the skills and information to get the job done. Get them involved in important decisions.
3. Put first things first: Prioritize, delegate, adjust if priorities change. Say no—you cannot do everything yourself. You can find those who can do it for you; give them jobs. Devote time to what is important, but not necessarily urgent.
4. Think win-win: Think with an abundance mentality; avoid the scarcity syndrome (win-lose). Seek the best alternative for mutual benefit. This involves true cooperation and sharing, clear expectations, resources, accountability, and the consequences of performance.
5. Seek first to understand, and then to be understood. Listen to understand, not to reply. Create meaning—that is communication.
6. Synergize: Make the whole greater than the sum of its parts. Put talents together, giving value to differences between people's skills and interests.
7. Renew yourself, sharpen your skills. The basis of what we do is enthusiasm. Balance renewal of the physical, mental, emotional, social, and spiritual areas of life.

The quality of leadership defined by these habits provides the foundation for meeting standards of excellence in the work place. Enthusiastic and effective leadership manifests itself in the passion for work shown by employees and the quality of service offered through interpretive programs.

A Framework for Interpretive Organizations

Peters and Austin (1985), in their book *A Passion for Excellence,* present these model components as a framework for strong organizations: (a) care of customers, (b) constant innovation, and (c) turned-on people—all connected by the critical element of leadership (Figure 16.1). This model is the basis of this chapter.

FIGURE 16.1
COMPONENTS OF STRONG ORGANIZATIONS

Customer Care

Business leaders put a lot of emphasis on customers or clients. Their slogans have become part of international popular business lore. Most of the ideas can apply as well to interpreters. Several statements quoted by Peters and Austin (1985) illustrated the concern interpreters might develop for their clientele.

> *Probably the most important management fundamental that is being ignored today is staying close to the customer to satisfy his needs and anticipate his wants. In too many companies, the customer has become a bloody nuisance whose unpredictable behavior damages carefully made strategic plans... "*
> —Lew Young, Editor-in-Chief, *Business Week*

> *Consumers are statistics; customers are people.*
> —Stanley Marcus, Chairman Emeritus, Neiman-Marcus

One of the basic characteristics of America's best-run companies involves staying close to the customer—learning their preferences and catering to them (Peters and Waterman, 1982). Excellent organizations all define themselves as customer service businesses, regardless of what product or service they actually provide. In fact, most excellent companies seem *obsessed* with some form of service, often to a seemingly unjustifiable degree of commitment.

If a provider of a service does not understand the customer, he or she will not understand the business. This applies directly to every interpretive sign or program. Tilden's first principle is to relate the subject matter to something within the personality or experience of the visitor. To do this an interpreter must know the personalities and experiences of his or her visitors. Then treat them accordingly with courtesy, perception, and listening. Edwards (1979) said to keep the visitors in the forefront—even ahead of the boss, whose wishes may seem like a waste of time to the customers.

COURTESY

Any organization *can* act courteously to its clientele (Box 16.1). However, surprisingly few actually commit to courtesy. Today, common courtesy is really uncommon! Peters and Waterman (1982) found that "thinly disguised contempt" (TDC) toward customers prevailed in many businesses that they studied.

Some TDC also exists in the field of interpretation. The administrator who provides little funding, training, or supervision of young interpreters declares disregard for a key customer service. The middle managers who refer to the "dickey-birders" or the "let's pretend" historical interpreters imply contempt for front-line customer service, even if they excuse it as insider humor. The museum docent who sees the public as a nuisance is in the wrong business—even as a volunteer. A naturalist or historian referring to visitors as interruptions of work on "important" projects is another sign of TDC. Others include reference to clients in less than complimentary terms such as the "mindless masses," "bratty kids," "dumb dudes," or even "tourists."

By contrast, at one of the top recreation businesses, disparaging words are rarely heard. At the Disney Corporation, every person who comes on a property is a Guest. Should one write the word at Disney, he or she would better capitalize the "G." A typical Guest interacts with 73 Disney employees per day. That puts Disney's reputation on the line 10 million or more times per day, just in the two U.S. theme parks (Peters and Austin, 1985).

Negative impressions come from the interpreter who argues with a visitor, who exhibits impatience in answering "stupid" questions, or who presents a careless physical appearance. All send signals of thinly disguised contempt for the visitor. On the positive side, sincere courtesy can make a powerful impression. Courtesy is paramount for Scandinavian Air Services (SAS). The president of the company identified "moments of truth" when SAS employees meet passengers—"unique, never to be repeated, opportunities to distinguish ourselves in a memorable fashion from . . . our competitors" (Peters and Austin, 1985).

Courtesy in interpretation is a major reflection on an organization. The interpreter often provides the only meaningful personal contact for the visitor to a museum or park. Remembering this, the enthusiastic interpreter may want to be as visible as possible where the visitors congregate—circulating through a campground, standing unobtrusively at key points in a museum or park—available to greet and help visitors to develop a strong positive impression of the park. This is being the good host—that "uncommon" common courtesy. This is interpreting "beyond the program." The ways of doing this include informal personal presence sometimes and nonpersonal surrogates through signs, exhibits, brochures, and other media all of the time.

BOX 16.1: WATCH WHAT YOU SAY

Ever wish you hadn't said something? I was closing the visitor center on a winter evening while employed at Cabrillo National Monument on Point Loma in California. This was whale watching season and we were getting many phone calls since we were at the peak of the annual migration. From our whale overlook you could see southbound gray whales. The phone rang just as I was locking the last door. A cooperating association employee answered the phone, then summoned me saying, "this person wants to know about the whales."

We were closed. It was the end of a long day answering questions about whales. A friend was waiting for me so we could leave together.

The person on the phone asked a number of questions: "Where are the whales coming from?" (The Bering and Chukchi seas off the north shore of Alaska.) "Where are they going?" (To the lagoons of Baja California where they mate and the pregnant females bear their young.) "How far do they travel?" (Up to 12,000 miles round trip, the longest migration of any mammal.) There were countless other questions with no end in sight.

My friend was getting impatient and was motioning to me to end the conversation. Yet the gentleman on the phone persevered: "What are the chances of my seeing one of these whales out there at the park?"

I responded—impatiently, carelessly—that the chances were excellent as we were at the peak of the season, sighting 20 or more whales per day. I continued, "in fact I guarantee that you'll see a whale if you come within the next week, you're patient, and the sky is blue."

I then explained to the caller that the park had long been closed for the day, but that he could call in the morning, ask for Larry Beck, and I'd be delighted to provide further information.

Still, he persisted, "One last question. What are my chances of seeing Gigi?"

Gigi was a young gray whale, captured by Sea World 10 years previously for study, then released when, at seven tons, she had outgrown her tank.

I said, "Who knows! You might spot Gigi, swimming with a calf at her side and raising a tail fluke in celebration of her 10th birthday."

"That's great," the man said, "thanks so much."

I had forgotten the incident until a few days later when I caught sight of the *front page* of the newspaper. I had been talking to a reporter. The article, among national and international news, was titled: "It's Time For A Whale of a Story."

And it read:

San Diego (UPI)—Larry Beck, park ranger at Cabrillo National Monument, "guarantees" visitors that if the sky is clear in the coming week, they'll see a majestic California gray whale on its annual migration to Baja California. And if the whale-watcher is extra lucky, he may spot "Gigi," the most celebrated gray whale of all with a calf at her side and raising a tail fluke on the occasion of her 10th birthday.

There is a lesson here. Even at the end of a long day of answering the same questions, be patient. And never, never, never say anything that you wouldn't want to see on the front page of a major newspaper.

—LB

A personal campaign for courtesy could require committing one 10-minute act of uncommon courtesy to a customer each day (Peters and Austin, 1985). If every person on a typical interpretive staff did this, visitors to the site would receive thousands of special courtesies each year. Probably no better way exists to build public support for a program (Box 16.2).

BOX 16.2: TOTAL QUALITY SERVICE FOR EXCELLENCE

---

by Bob Jennings, Director, Oxley Nature Center, Tulsa, OK

There's Excellence and then there's EXCELLENCE.

So, you've moved into your new million dollar Visitor Center. You've spent a ton of money on exhibits designed by the best consultants. You've hired the very best, most creative staff you can find. You're ready to show the world excellent interpretation, right? Not necessarily.

To EXCEL you have to pay attention to the "day-to-day" details—the people things. You do not want visitors to remember a person at the front desk who was bored, distracted, or irritated. In addition to excellent interpretation, we need a few other little actions to clearly show our attitude to "total quality."

As a municipal facility we get phone calls that should go to the zoo or another park. We give the caller the right phone number, but first we see if we can answer the question ourselves and offer to help follow up.

We do not, and will not, have one of those phone systems that answers calls like this: *Ring... Ring... Hello, you have reached the Ferndock Nature Center. If you have questions about hours of operation, push 1. If you have questions about fees, push 2. ... If you need information on the phases of the moon, push 142.* If you call us, we're going to answer the phone, because you're important to us! And we want to serve you.

At our centers, we make it a point to see that every visitor who hits the front door gets spoken to—just a genuine greeting and an offer to help.

Our building is arranged so the front desk attendant can see the entire exhibit hall. This allows us to watch how visitors interact with the exhibits. We can learn which displays work and which do not. We also make ourselves available if a visitor needs assistance. We have a "Feel This" box and a "Smell This" box with no labels. This was purposeful. As soon as they ask "What is in that yellow box, anyway?" we've got them where we want them . . . talking to us!

And when they leave we speak to them again—to welcome them to come back. In other words, we try to let people know that they are important to us and that we do really want them to come back. We do not want our visitors to feel as if they were invisible to us.

At the core of it all, I believe, is the matter of personal commitment to provide friendly and competent service. I don't think you can be truly professional unless the professionalism goes all the way to the bone. There is a line from a song that says, "Whatever your hands turn to do, you must do with all your heart." Remember that.

For a long time I resisted when people would tell me that interpretation is just like a business. I knew it wasn't. It was something grand and noble, a sacred trust, and I was fortunate to be carrying the flame. Yet, I've learned that a good interpretive program must operate just like a successful business—at least in terms of customer satisfaction.

We spend time and energy getting big things right; we can't forget the important little things. A smile, a helping hand, attention to questions must accompany magnificent programs. In the business world, it's called SERVICE. What are you going to call it?

PERCEPTION

Customer perceptions demand attention from interpreters and administrators. Many administrators claim that their difficulties with the public are "merely perception" problems. They are correct; in reality, perception is all there is. Reality is only what an individual perceives. People perceive service or quality in their own terms, in their own milieu, out of their own immediate and past experience. As society urbanizes and first-hand environmental knowledge diminishes, perceptions by "the public" could endanger the forests and other natural resources that sustain the same public. Edwards (1979) noted that:

> . . . many loud voices now commenting on environmental issues are from minds completely innocent of relevant knowledge. Inevitably they can advocate the ridiculous or the disastrous while believing they champion ecological salvation. And the appalling thought here is that as we become increasingly urban with more and more voters living as city recluses out of touch with the realities of the green landscapes that make our cities possible, we will become a nation of voters ignorant of the country's basic needs. There is surely no easier or surer way to destroy a nation.

An interpreter or administrator may believe that the customers' perceptions are unfair. An airline executive once lamented that when the public sees coffee stains on the seat-back tray, they unfairly assume that engine maintenance is done poorly. He has a point, but is not the doubt still there? The best managers accept the point that customer perceptions may be unfair. Rather than complaining about it, they use the "guilt by association" thought pattern as a positive tool to influence perceptions. Perhaps the only real distinction of successful service firms such as McDonald's, Disney, and Marriott is that they are the world's greatest "coffee stain" cleaners. They do not allow customers to see a "coffee stain" and partly because of it help to create a positive impression about other aspects of their operations (Peters and Austin, 1985).

In a forest interpretive operation, a bad experience on an interpretive hike could cause an "unfair" leap in logic to the perception that the other interpreters are poor or that the resource management is also poorly done. On the contrary, a fine interpretive experience could incline one toward the perception that the forest or refuge has fine management in all aspects. Likewise, an art museum docent who misinforms visitors about painters may reflect upon the authority of the entire museum staff. Therefore, maintain excellence in *all* aspects of the interpretive operation.

Perceptions—even ill-founded ones—can last a long time. Once formed, an interpreter may have little opportunity to change them. He or she may have lost the opportunity to serve that person or family again. If an interpreter is not serving people, he or she is out of the interpretation business (Figure 16.2).

Clearly, the interpreter must know something of the perceptions of the visitors. To do so requires evaluation and simply talking to the customers regularly—being where the customers are and communicating with them (but not annoying them). Most of all, it requires listening to them.

LISTENING

Excellent organizations listen well. An interpreter cannot know his or her clients unless he or she hears what they think. Most of them will not speak unless the interpreter encourages them. Casual observation of visitors at programs and collection of attendance data may give some idea of the general pleasure value of interpretive programs but does not measure the success of the program (Edwards, 1979).

According to Peters and Austin (1985), manufacturer of medical equipment, Castle Corp., has one approach to getting in touch with customers. Three mornings each week, each executive gets a "Daily Dose of Reality" sheet with a recent customer's name and phone number. A quick call to ask about satisfaction with the product has three benefits: it lets the customers know they are important to the company; it uncovers problems before they become major irritants; it gives company managers a reminder of the importance of the real world and contact with the real suppliers of their salaries. If museum, park, forest or other administrators regularly contacted recent visitors about the interpretive (and other) programs, what might be the reaction?

FIGURE 16.2
Colonial Williamsburg, a private, nonprofit corporation, welcomes thousands of visitors every day to the late 1700s, and maintains a superb public image.

Complaints can be opportunities to develop better relationships. But for every complaint, there are about 50 people who do not bother to tell an interpreter they are mad. The number may go up to 2,000. Peters and Waterman (1982) suggest that each angry person has 250 acquaintances and 100 of them will hear about the bad experience they had with an organization. And some of those—

maybe 50 percent— will then tell 100 of their acquaintances. These figures may be exaggerated for any single interpretive experience, but they make the point that bad news travels faster and farther than good.

Interpreters need to ask themselves how easy it is for people to complain to them. Do the interpreters share IBM's philosophy of "the joy of complaints," seeing them as golden opportunities? How well do they listen when the complaints come in? The Forest Service has long had a Good Host program. They try to make sure that each employee—even once-sour clerks—treats each visitor as a guest of the forest. Recent emphasis on customer service by this federal agency rededicates the Forest Service to listening better. The idea aims beyond gracious reception of complaints and seeks to elicit feedback on products or services. For this to succeed it must operate all the time, not only during public hearings on a new plan or major development.

Many managers in one survey thought that customers do not want to be bothered (Peters and Austin, 1985). However in every case studied, the customers overwhelmingly appreciated the attention they received and gladly took advantage of it. Through recent history, companies that allowed their customers to "push them around" have done well. Customer comments can provide ingenious ways of improving products. Blue jeans came from an idea of one of Levi Strauss' customers. Years later, another customer developed the faded blue jeans and convinced the company the style might sell. Likewise, most of IBM's early innovations, including their first computer, were developed in cooperation with a big customer—the U.S. Bureau of the Census.

Can the public improve an interpretive product? You bet! They are full of ideas for programs or exhibits that they'd like to see. Some interpretive consultants who are planning new facilities or themes first visit with local residents who both know the area and use the facilities. Long-term area residents often inspire ideas that enrich local history interpretation. A visiting amateur botanist or a fisherman often can suggest an idea about the resources that the interpreter missed. The visitor is king or queen to be served intelligently by the interpretive program. Long may they reign and benefit from the interpreter.

The same lesson was restated by L. L. Bean, an old-fashioned modern retailer, with the slogan posted throughout the offices in Freeport, Maine (Figure 16.3).

WHAT IS A CUSTOMER?

- A Customer is the most important person ever in this office ... in person or by mail.
- A Customer is not dependent on us . . . we are dependent on him [sic].
- A Customer is not an interruption of our work . . . he is the purpose of it. We are not doing a favor by serving him . . . he is doing us a favor by giving us the opportunity to do so.
- A Customer is not someone to argue or match wits with. Nobody ever won an argument with a Customer.
- A Customer is a person who brings us his wants. It is our job to handle them profitably to him and to ourselves.

FIGURE 16.3
L. L. BEAN POSTER TEXT

Constant Innovation

A second part of the model of successful organizations promotes "constant innovation" (Peters and Austin, 1985). Interpreters usually fall into the category of highly creative people. Many are innovative as well. Most people do not distinguish between creativity and innovation. According to Harvard's Theodore Levitt (Peters and Waterman, 1982), creativity is thinking up new things; innovation is doing new things.

Society suffers no shortage of creative people. The shortage is one of innovators. Creativity does not automatically lead to innovation. Creative people often tend to pass the brass tacks work to others. The creative idea-maker may even create inertia problems. They can pepper everybody with proposals, just enticing enough to arouse interest but too brief to address how to use them or how to implement them. Rare are the people who have the know-how, energy, daring, and persistence to implement ideas.

Successful interpretation requires innovation. Certainly excellent interpretation seems to be associated with innovative ideas. But people also need the good, solid, practiced interpreters who do not ignore the fundamentals. One fundamental is to remember the steady customers—repeat visitors—with new ideas and refreshing looks. Sites that have had the same displays exhibited for decades or have been offering the same old programs may be neither successfully fulfilling their mission nor garnering much public support.

STIMULATING INNOVATION

How can interpretive managers stimulate innovation? The key principle: promote autonomy and entrepreneurship. These two terms imply independence and self-reliance, and energy to take risks and a stake in the outcome. Innovators are usually individuals who grab an idea and run. A new idea will die if there is no backer or champion of it. The person who "likes" an idea, commenting that it would be "nice" is probably not its champion. It takes special involvement and energy to implement new ideas, and overcome the resistance that change provokes among any agency's many non-innovators.

It also requires patience, persistence, and the ability to express ideas in ways that are rational to the organization. Innovative-type people may seem impatient, impulsive, irrational (or at least unable to express themselves in terms of the organization's internal interests). They therefore may be perceived as not very serious, perhaps even slightly unstable to the "steady" go-by-the-book types. They therefore may not get promoted, rewarded, or even hired in organizations that do not understand what innovation is about.

When they do get hired and have freedom to take risks, champions of ideas become pioneers—the ones crazy enough to move out ahead of others, even into territory seen as dangerous or inhospitable. Managers of many successful companies have rich support systems for innovation that allow pioneers to flourish and even compete with one another. These companies allow the mythology and hero structure to go to employees, beyond the normal hierarchy figures. They do not give them "just enough rope to hang themselves with" but, instead, supply assistance so the innovators can survive to get the job done.

DEALING WITH FAILURES

Good failures are misdirected quality efforts or well thought-out missteps—not sloppy stabs in the dark. Striving for interpretive innovation offers no excuse for sloppiness, inaccuracy, or poor quality work. Therefore, innovation requires discipline, definition of aims, and evaluation of past efforts. It also requires action. The best managers love experiments and are as intrigued with the ones that fail as they are with the successes.

An over-riding principle is that successful organizations have the ability and willingness to accept failure (Peters and Waterman, 1982). A person who is not making mistakes is probably not being innovative. Innovation is a game of chance in some ways. There are odds that new ideas will not always succeed.

The idea of rewarding failure is too challenging for some bureaucratic minds. They imagine risks rather than seeking opportunities. They fear failure rather than aspiring to achievement. They rationalize inaction and introduce ponderous "considerations" that cool off or squelch the fiery drive required for much innovation. Successful interpreters, like successful businesses, have to take their risks and lumps, however. Innovative progress comes from those who move ahead, not by those who wait for a smooth, well-marked road.

The pain and consequences of failures seem to soften with frequent, frank, and friendly communication. Failure is most costly when little evaluation or adjustment occurs, that allows small mistakes to grow into serious impacts. Thus, risk can be managed and minimized.

The National Association for Interpretation annually provides open forums for exchanging innovations and ideas that work. These interpreters share their successes with peers, to inspire and educate each other and to receive their peer's approval or acceptance. The organization gives awards for the best brochure of the year, the best video program, and so on. Perhaps in the future these interpreters could follow the lead of Hewlett-Packard Corporation, by giving positive awards for the five best failures of the year. These awards might stimulate the creative and innovative profession of interpretation.

Turned-On People

Small autonomous teams or groups seem to be more innovative than larger groups when given the means and authority to implement the ideas (Peters and Waterman, 1982). This may not be the most creative structure for new ideas, but even in interpretation, further development and implementation of the ideas may be more successful with two or three heads than with one. When successful, group brainstorming and experimentation can be very productive. On the other hand, in some cases, committees are legendary for killing good ideas or slowing the idea's implementation. Individual innovators will work in different ways, but it seems likely that a sequence of individual-group-individual-group may work very well in interpretive planning and other innovations.

Internal competition drives many excellent organizations, rather than the rule-driven, committee-driven, or boss-driven behavior typical of most bureaucracies. Internal competition between individuals or groups is a powerful management strategy to foster innovation (Peters and Waterman, 1982). How well this can work in an interpretive organization may vary with the type and number of interpreters.

Autonomy among enthusiastic individuals may produce a rather chaotic scene. Managers seek to allow autonomy while maintaining control where it counts. A system of informal but intense communications provides the key to this apparent anomaly. The exact techniques are several: regular meetings without agendas or minutes, coffee klatches, or other discussions with free flow of ideas. The people talk to each other frequently and do not feel intimidated by the president or chairman of the board. The happy result is that intense, informal communication serves as a tight control system while the open communication promotes rather than constrains innovation. Genuine concern, not criticism or personnel reporting forms, prompt questions and ideas from outside the group. Peters and Austin (1985) have called this "management by walking around." Others might call it creative chatter about new ideas. Where controls and forms rule the process, individuals can hide out or get away with almost anything once they figure out the paperwork.

Entrepreneurship involves rewards for risks. Although most interpreters are not literally entrepreneurs, given a chance by wise leadership they can easily develop a sense of "ownership" in the success of the organization. The individual who takes a chance on innovation and excellence will be more likely to try it again if some social, ego, or financial reward arises for the effort. Open celebration of successes by managers increase the incentive to take new risks. The history of the organization has to demonstrate that the agency supports such risks, even if success comes only after repeated failures.

The best managers have contempt for inaction—whatever the excuse. As General George Patton said, "a good plan violently executed right now is far better than a perfect plan executed next week." Keep them moving. Keep them trying. Keep them informed and up-to-date technically as well as theoretically. Keep the interpreters excited about their work and the organization will produce visitors who feel they've been served well and enriched by their experiences.

ARE HAPPY PEOPLE WEALTHY?

It may seem odd that finances have not been the central topic of this discussion of the business of interpretation. Many interpreters can claim they do not have the time or resources to be innovative. Most can (and do) claim to be underfunded and very good at scrounging, scraping and improvising. Perhaps the interpretive ground is then fertile for innovation. Ken Olsen, President of Digital Equipment, noted that in the history of his company, "not a single substantial, commercially successful project had come from an adequately funded team. They always came from the scrounging, scraping, underfunded teams" (Peters and Austin, 1985). This does not imply that the people who are grindingly underpaid will be the most productive. It simply suggests that the latest in equipment, fancy offices, and help may not be conducive to creative imaginations. On the other hand, constant concern, short-handedness, and tension about low pay, no assistance, and budget scraping can likewise distract from focusing on the job of getting the messages and skills to the people in the best way.

Good results may be born of improvisation and low budgets. One nature center, observed on a professional tour, had old facilities and lacked professional displays. A typical program skit involved audience participation. Using cardboard scenery, costumes and masks made of paper plates, pie pans, coat hangers, and paper bags, plus an amusing, educational skit produced no apologies or complaints from the staff. The interpreter said that even if they had a big budget they would still use these materials. The children play with such materials at home; they learn that they can produce similar skits at home. Bigger and more expensive are not necessarily better. Creating a quality program at virtually no cost is an example of innovation.

Total Quality Management: Application of Principles

Many of the principles described in the preceding pages have been applied in a management philosophy called Total Quality Management (TQM). In recent years, many American businesses and government agencies have adopted TQM. The unifying principle is total dedication to customers in order to meet their needs and exceed their expectations. Customers seem to be best served by employees who demonstrate enthusiasm about their work and understand the importance of quality service.

Total Quality Management seeks to empower the work staff by loosening the traditional bounds of narrowly prescribed working specialties. It intends to help employees buy into the enterprise, stimulating ideas and improvements from all levels. Empowerment of employees involves setting up supportive structures and systems that reinforce newly delegated responsibility and authority. The boss' job is to provide a clear sense of desired results, guidelines, accountability, and a coaching style to help and facilitate (Covey, 1993b).

FOREST SERVICE PILOT STUDY

A notable illustration of the principles of Total Quality Management comes from the USDA Forest Service. Indeed, Forest Service applications of TQM in a national pilot study won prime time features on Tom Peter's PBS television special, "Excellence in the Public Sector."

The National Pilot Study began in 1985, when the Chief of the Forest Service loosened the management structure on three national forests and a research station. Pilot units had maximum flexibility to operate, including full delegation of authority and freedom to change or eliminate any process or regulation, as long as the action was legal (USDA Forest Service, n.d. a and n.d. b, provided the following information).

Budgets were allocated by lump sum, affording tremendous latitude over the traditional 55-line item structure which carried specific restrictions concerning use. Traditionally, the funding received for any one function could be spent only on that function. For example, if a range manager had $5,000 left over at the end of the year and a recreation manager needed an extra $5,000 to paint all the picnic tables and improve a campground, an exchange was unlawful, even within the same national forest. Furthermore, the money not spent on range functions had to be returned to the U.S. Treasury. So, the agency either spent the allotted money on range or gave it back, recognizing that the function might get less the next year if it went back to the Treasury. By contrast, the lump sum budget empowered managers to shift funds as deemed necessary at the field level. Furthermore, they could retain savings to be spent on additional high priority work and for employee bonuses or incentives.

The TQM pilot program encouraged units to try new ideas, even at the risk of failure, which was considered a learning experience. Finally, this approach to change worked from the bottom up, to the extent that all operational improvements came from the employees themselves.

Following the pilot success of the Mark Twain National Forest, the Eastern Regional Forester requested similar status for all the forests of the region. Employees at all levels were given increased freedom to make changes. In fact, more than 12,000 proposals came in to eliminate outdated rules, streamline procedures, and otherwise improve quality of employment. This resulted in increasing levels of creativity, innovation, and motivation. At the same time, the Region's customers received more responsive service.

In 1987, the Eastern Region added to its commitment to change with the "Team Excellence" initiative. This used integrated teams to stimulate the synergy and innovation that arises from teamwork. Communications, information sharing, and working relationships flourished across hierarchical boundaries. Shared leadership also extended throughout the organization, to a degree that all employees felt encouraged to become leaders regardless of their positions.

Productivity had increased dramatically at the pilot sites and public service improved since decisions became more responsive as a consequence of less red tape. There was also an upsurge in morale and organizational spirit. In 1989, Chief Robertson acknowledged the success of the TQM Pilot Study and signed the new Forest Service Management Philosophy (Box 16.3).

BOX 16.3: FOREST SERVICE MANAGEMENT PHILOSOPHY

THE FOREST SERVICE IS A WORKPLACE WHERE—

- All directions, procedures, and operations begin with a focus on the needs of our customers.
- Quality results count; process is secondary.
- People are important, trusted, and empowered by being given the fullest authority and responsibility consistent with their capabilities.
- People have the opportunity and operating flexibility to exercise independent judgment.
- Individual skills and cultural diversity are valued and sought out as important assets of the organization and key resources for solving problems.
- Managers provide a climate where responsible risk-taking is encouraged and rewarded, and failures are acceptable learning experiences.
- Creativity, innovation, and entrepreneurship are viewed as critical to our success and fostered at every level of the organization. Pilot testing new ideas on the cutting edge is a traditional mode for remaining competitive.
- The manager's role (both line and staff) in the organization is one of guiding, educating, advising, and encouraging rather than regulating and controlling. The tone of direction is shifted from "limits and controls" to one of "promoting people's full potential—expanding and encouraging ideas and skills."
- Nonconformists, risk-takers, and innovators are encouraged and are a key to meeting the challenges of a changing future.

Source: *Chartering a Management Philosophy for the Forest Service*, signed by F. Dale Robertson, Chief, Dec. 19, 1989.

To facilitate the cultural evolution of the agency, the Eastern Region, in 1991, developed a new set of evaluation criteria for all regional leadership positions. It specified expectations in terms of philosophy, vision, teamwork, communication, and knowledge of human and natural resources to be certain that leadership embodied the principles set forth in the Management Philosophy. The first two criteria indicate the type of leadership called for (USDA Forest Service, n.d. a):

Philosophy. Commitment to fostering a leadership environment built on customer service, quality results, and empowerment of people.

Vision. Skill in promoting innovative, nontraditional approaches to the organization and operation of resources to accomplish the Forest Service mission.

Overall, the Forest Service model built upon the premise that people are the key resource in every organization. To motivate employees to buy into a mission, they must see how it fits with their own values. These values include responsibility, development of individual skills, rewards, challenging work, and a sense of trust.

With the elimination of most bureaucratic hurdles, employees became more effective, with more time to spend on their work as well as more time "on the ground." For example, managers had additional time assessing forest needs through on-site field visits.

One of the other pilot units, Ochoco National Forest in Oregon, provided a good illustration (USDA Forest Service, n.d. b). Overall productivity increased 25 percent the first year and an additional 35 percent during the second. People learned to have fun and the quality of work improved. Employees coined the phrase: "The army wins and loses together." Increased time on the ground for managers ranged from 10 to 20 days per year. Employees who were traditionally office-bound found time to work in campgrounds, post mile markers on forest roads, collect campground fees, back up fire lookouts, build fences, and pile slash. One 15-year veteran said, "I'm no longer just an office worker. Now I'm a Forest Service worker."

When a campground was scheduled to be closed due to budget constraints, a group of administrative employees (mostly budget analysts) took it upon themselves to save the campground. As they had been relieved of some of their routine duties by the reduction of administrative red tape, they learned about campground operations and maintenance. When the summer season arrived, the group adopted the unfunded campground and provided the necessary upkeep in their spare time. The public, in effect, received extra recreational opportunities at no extra cost to the taxpayer.

In addition to the adoption of diverse duties specified above, interpretation is an excellent area for expansion. Indeed, it allows a natural extension of duties for employees wishing to contribute to public understanding and appreciation of "their" national forest. Imagine the various talents and areas of expertise available for enhancing visitors' experiences! Imagine the increased support for interpretation both within the agency and out!

Applying the principles of TQM worked well for the Forest Service. They produced higher morale, better quality work, and greater overall productivity. They also brought about a new awareness of public needs. The approach has required listening to customers in the form of symposia, special demonstration projects, and learning centers. These have brought together the diversity of viewpoints regarding the nation's forests (DeLaney, 1993).

This philosophy is people-oriented and the tone of the new direction seeks to expand possibilities—the field is larger and boundary markers fewer. Hence, the possibilities for meeting challenges are greatly enhanced. Finally, a thrust toward continuous improvement through people-empowerment and customer service goes on, in the pursuit of excellence.

Summary

This chapter has suggested adoption of a business-like philosophy for interpretive management and supervision. To apply this management philosophy, managers should act proactively in their quest for high quality interpretive facilities and services for the public. They should prioritize and delegate so their efforts focus on excellence. They should seek to synergize, to make the whole greater than the sum of the parts. They should make the work environment one that generates staff enthusiasm, creativity, and high levels of service to customers.

In this scenario, managers promote innovation by providing autonomy in the work place and promoting a spirit of entrepreneurship. They accept failures when they are thoughtful attempts to achieve. They encourage "turned-on" interpreters who commit to high quality customer service and innovation. These characteristics that work well in business and government organizations can work with striking results in the highly creative interpretive arena. Undoubtedly, the best interpretive organizations will subscribe to the importance of empowering employees and serving customers with professionalism and profound courtesy. A business-like orientation in no way weakens the interpretive mission. It makes it stronger.

Literature Cited

Covey, S. R. (1993a). *Personal leadership application workbook*. Provo, UT: Covey Leadership Center, Inc.

Covey, S. R. (1993b). Career wisdom for the '90's. *USA Today* (June 1, 1993):5B.

DeLaney, B. (1993). Total quality management in the public sector. *Quality Engineering*, 5(4):583-588.

Edwards, Y. (1979). *The land speaks: Organizing and running an interpretation system*. Toronto, ON: The National and Provincial Parks Association of Canada.

Peters, T. J. and Austin, N. (1985). *A passion for excellence*: *The leadership difference*. New York, NY: Random House, Inc.

Peters, T. J. and Waterman, R. H. (1982). *In search of excellence*: *Lessons from America's best run companies*. New York, NY: Warner Books, Inc.

USDA Forest Service. (n.d. a). *Shaping a new culture*. Milwaukee, WI: Eastern Region. (n.p.)

USDA Forest Service. (n.d. b). *New thinking for managing in government*. Washington, DC.

Making it Pay

In our view, it is a 'cop-out' for any site to rationalize not establishing an interpretive program because 'we don't have Williamsburg's budget.' It can be done; . . . many sites may not have the resources to do it all now, but . . . knowing what constitutes good interpretation will give them goals for future improvement."
—Alderson and Low (1985)

Much ingenuity with a little money is vastly more profitable and amusing than much money without ingenuity.
—Arnold Bennett

This chapter discusses ways to make ends meet. A fast growing interpretive business sector must make money to keep operating. Nonprofit interpretive centers and museums have long lived with the necessity of marketing their programs directly to clients and indirectly to donors. Increasingly, the public sector faces the convenience and stability of relying partly on supplemental funding from private sources and user fees.

The worth of interpretation may or may not be best expressed in the open market. Many argue that the public should support interpretation because of its social values as well as individual benefits to clients. Commercial interpreters and museums often feel they must compete with agencies that are giving away the service; therefore, they must provide different and/or more complete services that satisfy clients. Yet, this competition is nothing new. It has been going on since the first private and public museums opened. Commercial, not-for-profit organizations, and public agencies will continue to work side-by-side, offering services that sometimes seem indistinguishable yet at other times seem clearly differentiated.

Commercial Interpretation

Private interpretation for profit has been going on for centuries. Enos Mills (1917) stated that "Scenery is the most profitable resource that we have." Modern ecotourism—peripatetic cultural and natural history seminars—show that people will pay for interpretation.

Guides to the Amazon, the Panda forests of China, and many other exotic places now take in thousands of dollars per visitor for quality interpretation added to the physical travel arrangements for getting there. Ecotourism is the name. Intelligent travel for profit is the game. It is supposed to bring great benefits to the host countries as well as to the guides. The guides earn their fees; it is a lot of work and arrangements for a modest net income.

African safaris were once guided and outfitted hunting expeditions. Lately, the guides have turned safaris into interpretive animal observation and photography trips with large doses of natural history and ecology lessons.

Guides to the old western Canada and U.S. took Europeans on long hunting and fishing expeditions 150 to 200 years ago. Jim Bridger, Kit Carson, and a dozen other frontier guides earned their livings from knowing more than just the route and signs of danger. They could lead scientists and cartographers to the major natural and cultural features. They could anticipate and explain something about the Native American attitudes, ways of life, and economy.

Railroads took the early visitors to national parks, describing their wonders and providing guided tours of the parks until the federal government got its interpretive act together (Figure 17.1). Railroad interpretation continues in Alaska with the efforts of Don Follows (1988). Likewise, cruise ships into Alaskan and Canadian waters feature interpretation of the glaciers, mountains, culture, and ocean life as a prime attraction of their tour packages.

Enos Mills was a commercial guide—a guide who made a difference. He earned his income from the tourist trade—via hotel and cabins, a restaurant, and guided walks, hikes, and climbs into what is now Rocky Mountain National Park. He lectured nationwide, partly for income, partly to promote the scenic Rockies, and partly as an advocate for conservation principles. His fame throughout the nation in the early 1900s arose from his profound knowledge of natural history and his ability to communicate it attractively. He served as a naturalist to the nation, and was received in the halls of Congress as well as in the homes of Presidents, Governors, and many citizens.

FIGURE 17.1
Business heritage in National Parks includes railroads as key promoters of the parks that provide transportation to and hospitality within them.
(AT&SF Railroad)

A mile deep, miles wide, & painted like a sunset

That's the Grand Canyon of Arizona

For art booklets of the train and trip address
W. J. Black, Pass. Traffic Mgr.
A. T. & S. F. Ry. System,
1051 Railway Exchange, Chicago

You can go there in a Pullman to the rim at El Tovar, en route to Sunny California on the train of luxury

The California Limited

Santa Fe
All the way

John Muir interpreted Yosemite and Alaska to the nation in the early 1900s. In addition to serving as guide for the rich, famous, and the members of his own Sierra Club, he wrote to the nation through the mass media of magazines, newspapers, and books. His "word pictures" stirred the imaginations of many readers to support the preservation of natural resources. His commercial interest was less than his crusading spirit. Nevertheless, Muir eventually earned his living from writing about natural phenomena and the urgency of appreciating them.

INTERPRETING FOR INCOME

FIGURE 17.2
An impressive stone barn welcomes visitors to the private, not-for-profit Farmers Museum in Cooperstown, NY.

A large but unknown proportion of the interpretive services offered in the U.S., Canada, and UK operates in the private sector. Some interpreters operate private business that serve the public indirectly or serve other interpreters with supplies, consulting, museum/display services, or in other ways. Some offer interpretation as part of another service, such as sea kayaking, bus tours, travel, camps, book publishing, and entertainment. Still others operate through nonprofit organizations that maintain museums, nature centers, living history farms (Figure 17.2), wildlife parks, and private zoos. Much of this work goes unrecognized by the profession but earns its financial rewards by the paying public. A few specific examples have wide recognition: Gray Line Tours, Camp Tecumseh YMCA, Busch Gardens, Walt Disney World, San Diego Wild Animal Park, Colonial Williamsburg, Baseball Hall of Fame, Iowa's Living History Farms, Amana Colonies, Audubon Center of the North Woods, Catoctin Mountain Zoo, Terragon North, Sanibel-Captiva Conservation Foundation, Mystic Seaport and Marine Museum, and the Polynesian Cultural Center (Figure 17.3).

Increasingly, interpreters have begun to sell their services to individual clients. Several were discussed in Chapter 2. Resorts, bus lines, private

FIGURE 17.3
The Polynesian Cultural Center in Hawaii provides a huge interpretive complex. Visitors pay an entry fee to see architecture and demonstrations of various cultures, while Polynesian students earn and learn at the Brigham Young University branch campus.

museums, private guides, outfitter-guides, dude ranch guides, private nature centers, private camps, contract interpreters, and dozens of other businesses offer interpretation for a price—hopefully enough to make a living.

Some of these form rather large businesses, even if they are nonprofit in nature. One impressive nonprofit interpreter operates on the bluff above Blue Mountain Lake under the name of the Adirondack Museum. Founded by a wealthy hobbyist, it has gradually become a semiautonomous organization, supported by many types of income, including gifts, grants, donations of artifacts and equipment, as well as three major revenue sources. The operating budget for 1992 appears in summary form in Table 17.1. With revenues from its 101,000 visitors amounting to 41 percent of the expenditures, this museum—as most others—relies heavily on gifts, memberships, development events and outside means of support.

TABLE 17.1 THE ADIRONDACK MUSEUM REVENUES AND EXPENDITURES

	REVENUES	
Sources	1992	1991
Admissions	$686,563	$636,091
Gatehouse sales (net)	145,609	7,654
Cafeteria (net)	74,967	73,963
	EXPENDITURES	
Operating	2,001,411	1,887,362
Capital	224,409	380,745

Source: 1992 Highlights, The Adirondack Museum

Over 3,000 annual memberships include categories ranging from $15 to $1,000 plus variable business memberships. This pattern can be found in most private or association museums, except that the Adirondack Museum represents the largest and finest end of the scale in size and services.

Public Interpretation—Mixed Funding

Interpreters must become financial contributors to their agencies to prevent their services from being cut or eliminated by management.
—Paul Romero (1992)

Public sector interpreters have used several strategies to gain revenue from sources other than traditional fiscal appropriations, especially in the past decade. This has arisen from a decrease in financial support from taxes. Taxpayer revolts at local and state levels and increasing budget deficits at the federal level have tightened governmental purse-strings.

In some instances, interpretive programs suffered severe cut-backs or even suspension. In other cases, the use of fees and other mechanisms have saved programs, and even allowed them to thrive. Meeting budget crises with foresight, energy, and imagination has produced better, more stable interpretive services for some agencies. Many public agencies provide interpretive material for sale through nonprofit cooperating associations, thus gaining financial flexibility and market responsiveness.

The rest of this chapter explores various funding mechanisms from user fees to fundraising events. Although the chapter focuses on the public and private nonprofit sectors from here on, many of the ideas dealing with promotion and customer sensitivity apply as well to the private businesses offering interpretation.

User Fees—Generating Revenue with Interpretation

The pricing of interpretive services can be a volatile issue. Philosophical opposition arises from a tradition of interpretation as an important free service for the visitor's education, enrichment, and enjoyment of public natural and cultural sites. Interpretation also serves the agency, protects the resource, and encourages the citizenry to be more sensitive toward society's cultural and natural legacy. Thus, it serves as a public utility, not just a consumer service to be bought for a fee. However, fiscal reality dictates that revenues must come in, one way or another, or programs and services will disappear.

The implementation of user fees at public sites provides perhaps the most straightforward solution to budget woes. Certainly, drawbacks exist for this approach. Fees may deny access to programs for some who cannot or will not afford to pay. Fees will discourage some other people from attending programs. A real and bureaucratic cost arises from collecting the fees in most public agencies. Yet, the precedent of people paying for interpretation exists in many private enterprises, who collect fees with few problems. In fact, many public interpreters frequently turn down offers of pay or tips for their good work.

Even those who believe that interpretation should be offered for free cannot deny the trend toward increased fees at all levels of government. Only when services get cut do many interpreters recognize "that there are diminishing resources and our services are not critical" (Romero, 1992). According to Massey (1988), interpreters must produce top-quality presentations that compete with their commercial counterparts and that meet public needs rather than interpreters' desires.

Fees can provide a minimum base of revenue which assures continuity in services. This produces a psychological investment on the part of the consumers to want to get more out of a service for which they pay. Finally, interpreters may push to new levels of excellence if they see the direct connection between their efforts and the willingness or unwillingness of visitors to pay.

Pricing Strategy

Successful pricing entails the development of a fee that both the agency and patrons find acceptable. The agency can facilitate public acceptance of fees in several ways. First, the agency can seek to learn, through first-hand interaction with the clients, what level of fees they would accept. This requires the agency to immerse itself "in the customer's habits, lifestyle, idiosyncracies and acceptance level of fees" (Jamieson, 1992).

A fee survey can help determine how much to charge without incurring considerable resistance. The traditional approach to assessing users' willingness to pay presents a range of price alternatives along a continuum (e.g., $1, $2, $3, $4, $5). Potential consumers select the price they would be most willing to pay. Often, they select options in the lower price range, artificially depressing the actual price tolerance of users (Howard and Cable, 1988).

A different pricing survey approach may produce more accurate data on acceptance of fees. This first estimates the costs of various services. Next, three separate price levels are calculated for each major program: (1) a low price that represents a cost to the participant that recovers 50 percent of the direct costs of the program, (2) a medium price that reflects the "break-even" point where the fee equals the cost of the program, and (3) a high price consistent with charges in the private sector for a similar program (Howard and Cable, 1988). Questionnaires reflecting the different prices are distributed randomly to visitors or sampled residents. Then, to determine the levels of price tolerance, tabulate and compare the responses for each of the price levels. Use of such a consumer-based pricing method can furnish a realistic predictive device for the agency to formulate pricing decisions (Howard and Cable, 1988).

McCarville (1992) suggested three principles for ensuring that pricing policies are acceptable. First, participants probably want fairness in a price. The idea that participants directly pay part of the cost of services that they use may persuade questioning visitors. Information on the costs of commercial alternatives may also help. Finally, the consumers can be made aware of the costs to present the programs that they attend.

Second, participants seek values or benefits from interpretive services. Attractive program names should convey what the program offers. Make explicit the benefits and values of participation in written and verbal descriptions of the programs. Describe the quality of the staff delivering the service. If the staff interpreters are among the best—winning professional awards—let the public know.

Third, participants seek choices. Offer a variety of services with a range of prices— from free to more expensive. A program that gets heavy use during certain days or hours might be offered for reduced fees at less popular times. This offers price alternatives and may help distribute demand. McCarville (1992) concluded that the success of a price comes not only from the revenue generated or how little outcry it creates, but "the test for a 'good' price must be measured in terms of the perceptions of those involved in the exchange." The agency may expect increased visitor return rates, greater participant satisfaction, more extensive word-of-mouth promotion, and increased revenue from paying customers.

INTERPRETIVE ASSOCIATIONS

Cooperating associations help with interpretation in many public agencies. They include:
- National Park Service associations, such as the Eastern National Parks and Monuments Association.
- National Forest interpretive associations
- County historical associations, often working with county park agencies.
- Appalachian Mountain Club
- Contract interpretation companies, independent firms that have contractual arrangements to perform certain services for a public agency or private recreation firm.

FIGURE 17.4
*The Southwest Parks and Monuments
Association, Inc., helps the National Park
Service avoid red tape by selling interpre-
tive books related to park themes. (TTC)*

Today, virtually all national
parks, many national forests and some
national wildlife refuges maintain
agreements with cooperating associations. These private groups allow
flexibility in fund-raising, book sales,
and other services that governmental
procedures make clumsy or impos-
sible. Cooperating associations facilitate production and sales of materials (Figure 17.4).
The association acts as a nonprofit organization, providing income for its employees. Most
of the money goes into producing or purchasing newly written or gift materials that help interpret the area. The public agency need not hire personnel to handle sales nor keep books
on all the financial transactions. The public agency would normally have to turn the money
into the general fund of the county, state, or federal government; this prevents the ready use
of funds to keep the sales shop stocked. The principle followed is that business is best run as
and by a business—not the government.

One of the oldest interpretive organizations works in several New Hampshire parks and
forests. The Society for the Protection of New Hampshire Forests organized itself in 1901 to
promote more responsible forest management and park establishment. Getting that message
across involved considerable interpretation in a time when there were few foresters in the nation and the frontiers seemed full of boundless forests waiting to be used up. This organization took responsibility, leadership and action when few others did so. Today, it provides
interpretation at several state properties. It hires well-trained naturalists to describe forests,
soils, human impacts, and environmental education, as well as the unique values of the areas.
It maintains a nature center at the foot of Mt. Monadnock and provides a variety of programs.
It cooperates with New Hampshire's Division of Parks & Recreation, State Forests and other
organizations.

The first cooperating association set up with the National Park Service apparently started
as a Friends group in 1920. Ansel F. Hall, a park service employee, spearheaded organization of the Yosemite Museum Association. This private group raised $9,000 to start the
museum. That was a key to later contributions for a more complete museum. The park
naturalist was designated director of the association and editor of its publication. In 1924,
this group became the Yosemite Natural History Association (Burns, 1941).

Other early U.S. associations included the following, most of which still exist: 1931—
Zion & Bryce Natural History Association, Rocky Mountain Nature Assoc.; 1932—Grand
Canyon Natural History Assoc.; 1933—Yellowstone Library and Museum Assoc.; 1934—
Mesa Verde Museum Assoc.; 1936—Shenandoah Nature Society, Hot Springs Natural His-
tory Assoc., and Jackson Hole Museum and Historical Association (Burns, 1941).

The Eastern National Forests Interpretive Association (ENFIA) promotes the historical,
scientific, and educational activities of the Forest Service by selling interpretive material.

ENFIA operates in one historic landmark and eleven of the national forests, from Virginia to Vermont and west to Wisconsin and Missouri. On three of those forests, the association operates through incorporated *Affiliates* such as the Huron-Manistee Interpretive Association. They have their own boards of directors. On national forests not covered by *Affiliates*, ENFIA operates through *Branches*, which are sales outlets in the National Forests, often in the district offices.

Under the contract, ENFIA supplies books, publications and related material for retailing to the visitors. ENFIA handles the finances and returns a minimum of ten percent of the gross sales to each outlet. These funds are designated for expansion, visitor information and interpretive services.

Each forest chooses its own contractors. Within the Eastern Region, some forests choose to contract with the Great Lakes Interpretive Association, which also serves national parks, national wildlife refuges and several state and local resource organizations.

Marketing a Public Service

An emphasis on marketing was recently identified as the most important trend in interpretation through a modified nominal group process involving practitioners, academicians, government agency representatives, and officers of the National Association for Interpretation (Vander Stoep, 1990). Close behind came a related trend: a decrease in government funding with a subsequent increase in user fees.

Like user fees, the issue of marketing carries with it some resistance. Even in the business world, marketing often is misunderstood and accepted grudgingly (Marcus, 1992). A marketing approach, however, does not mean abandoning the principles and philosophy of interpretation or offering only programs that have mass audience appeal. It does mean that interpreters seek first to understand their potential customers better in terms of needs and desires, then design the programs to best fit the market's demands. In other words, study the demand side of the equation (i.e., what the customers seek or can use) rather than starting with the supply side (i.e., what you want to offer).

Thoughtful marketing can contribute to the identity and mission of a site. It can allow management to develop and fit the programs and facilities to the wants and visitation patterns of the public. In terms of drawing participants, for example, marketing research showed that when interpreters go out and inform the visitors about the program schedule and invite them to come, attendance increases by almost 50 percent (Reyburn and Knudson, 1975).

Marketing also searches for new ways to adapt interpretive services to fit the ever-changing needs, wants, and expectations of patrons (Chiat, 1987). It seeks to bring in more diverse audiences (Lawhon, 1992) and can help in protection of the resource (Knopf, 1990).

Most marketing schemes seek to determine what satisfies customers (Box 17.1). Continuous client surveys provide the agency with critical information to keep in contact with customers' needs, requirements, preferences, attitudes, and ideas. These surveys seek to determine what pleases clients, why some are content and others are indifferent, why some feel dissatisfied, and why others have been lost as customers (Rosander, 1991).

A concept known as "aftermarketing" (Vavra, 1992) suggests that interpreters can develop a long-term strategy designed to build lasting relationships with all customers. It differs from "conquest" marketing in that it focuses on retaining current customers, rather than seeking new ones. This approach obviously fits community nature centers and museums, state-wide facilities, and federal areas that could have considerable repeat business from the local area. It probably does not apply to remote, "once-in-a-lifetime" attractions. A study of current visitors may reveal how many make repeat visits to the facility and where they reside.

BOX 17.1: Service Business Characteristics

Ross and Ross (1990) summarized the most important characteristics of service businesses as follows:
1. Reliability. The number one concern of customers—your ability to perform dependably, accurately, and consistently.
2. Responsibleness. Prompt service and a helpful attitude.
3. Assurance. Knowledgeable and courteous employees who convey confidence.
4. Empathy. Individualized attention and a sympathetic ear.
5. Tangibles. Attractive physical facilities and equipment and professional-looking employees.

Two useful marketing approaches from the business world have been effectively applied in the interpretive arena: the marketing audit and market segmentation.

MARKETING AUDIT

An effective marketing strategy begins with an assessment of the agency's current status, an evaluation of the agency's future direction, and the development of service standards, objectives, and actions (Tschohl and Franzmeier, 1991). The marketing audit determines both problem areas to be corrected and opportunities to be maximized. It also determines key trends in the marketplace.

The marketing audit consists of analysis of consumer factors, internal factors, and environmental factors. The marketing audit matrix includes a diagnosis which reviews the current status of the agency, a prognosis which evaluates the direction the agency is moving along, with various options it faces, and recommendations which set a course of action based upon the best options (Figure 17.4).

FIGURE 17.4 MARKETING AUDIT MATRIX (ADAPTED FROM MOKWA, 1986)

MARKETING POLICY	DIAGNOSIS • Where are we now? • Where have we been?	PROGNOSIS • Where are we going? • Where can we go?	RECOMMENDATIONS • Where should we go? • How can we get there?
Consumer Factors			
Internal Factors			
Environmental Factors			

The Look About Lodge Audit

Gober, Hinkle and Mullins (1992) applied the marketing audit technique to determine the potential of reinstituting an interpretive program in the Look About Lodge area of the Cleveland Metroparks. Data came from focus group interviews, a public meeting, and demographic statistics. Three stages of analysis organized the data through sets of questions.

1. Consumer analysis determined the desires of park users. The questions addressed included:
   - Is there a market for this type of service?
   - Is the market substantial and reachable?
   - What are the demographics and characteristics of the target group?
   - What are the service utilization and buying patterns of the target groups?
   - How do current customers and prospects rate the organization, particularly with respect to reputation, quality and service?

   This information helped define the market, determine demand for interpretive services, design the programs, and develop a promotional strategy for Look About Lodge.

2. An internal analysis determined the strengths and weaknesses of the agency through the following questions:
   - What are the organization's management capabilities?
   - What are the organization's strengths that can be maximized?
   - What current problems should be corrected?
   - What can be done to prevent possible future problems?
   - What are the organization's abilities in providing services and reaching consumers?
   - Are the organization's objectives clearly stated?
   - Are these objectives appropriate?
   - What is the strategy for achieving these objectives?

   Data collected in focus group interviews and open forum format identified appropriate uses of the Look About Lodge and surrounding area for interpretive programming.

3. The environmental analysis studied the local social and economic environment (the marketplace), then identified opportunities and threats for instituting an interpretive program in the Look About Lodge area. The following questions were addressed:
   - What effect will forecasted trends in the size and age distribution of the population have on the organization's service?
   - What substitutes might replace this service?
   - What attitude is the public taking toward similar organizations and toward services such as those offered by the organization?
   - What changes are occurring in consumer lifestyles and values that may affect the organization's markets and marketing methods?
   - What changes in the economy may affect the organization?

This complete marketing audit indicated that a market for interpretive programs existed in the Look About Lodge area. The consumer analysis showed the most potential among schools and young families. The internal analysis indicated that a synergistic relationship between Cleveland Metroparks and the Cleveland Natural Science Club would work well for both organizations to promote conservation goals and attracting program participants and club members. Environmental analysis also revealed a potential for interpretive programs for children and families who already enjoyed services offered by other recreation agencies but were looking for opportunities closer to home. The marketing policy recommendations included: a higher degree of public access to Look About Lodge, the initiation of seasonal interpretive programming, and the establishment of a cooperative relationship between Cleveland Metroparks and the Cleveland Natural Science Club.

As this case indicated, the marketing audit helps an agency understand the variables affecting its operations. By studying its customers, internal operations and the environment in which it functions, it can disclose opportunities and problems for its future operations. Begin with a diagnosis, then a prognosis, and finally make recommendations of the best options.

MARKET SEGMENTATION

Segmentation separates subgroups or market segments from a total population. The people in a segment share some similar characteristics. For example, the clients can be segmented into age and interest groups. Once the market segments are delineated, interpretive services and programs can be tailored to each one. This helps balance the numbers and times of programs so the interpreter's (or one segment's) favorite interest does not dominate the whole programming effort.

At Land Between the Lakes, staff and consultants used market segmentation at the Woodlands Nature Center, to develop more knowledge about the patrons served. This information aimed at increasing visitation, enhancing the public image of the facility, and increasing revenue. Burde and Howatt (1993), using personal interviews, identified three distinct market segments, based upon the distance that the visitors traveled to the center: (a) local day users, (b) overnight regional visitors, and (c) those who traveled long distances to the property. Each of these groups had different demographic characteristics. For example, local day users had lower average incomes, less college background, and fewer of them were in managerial and professional occupations, as compared to overnight regional or long distance users.

This confirmed that visitors to the nature center were not homogeneous but could be considered as distinct segments. This prompted several strategies for attracting and serving each segment. In terms of promotion, visitor origin data revealed not only the "home bases" for each segment but also the geographic areas that produced few visitors, representing untapped potential. Promotion efforts then could be directed at these areas, communicating with potential clients about services available to them. As these potential visitors gain more information about facilities, services, costs, and time, they become better equipped to make decisions about whether to visit or not.

For promotion purposes, Burde and Howatt (1993) recommended placing emphasis specifically on the nature center and its facilities for the local day users. Visitors could be enticed to return by offering special events, reducing fees on certain days, and providing seasonal programming to encourage patrons to return during different times of the year. The promotional information could go out to local newspapers, television and radio spots; printed materials could be sent to local businesses, civic groups, recreation agencies, and schools.

Overnight regional users would learn about Woodlands Nature Center programs as part of a larger promotional effort focusing more generally on Land Between the Lakes (LBL). In this instance, promotion would consist of three parts: (a) advertise LBL at travel shows in the surrounding region, (b) use print and broadcast promotions in the larger urban areas in the region to attract the people to LBL, and (c) distribute LBL and nature center brochures at regional campgrounds and resorts where these people tend to stay. Programming for these overnight regional users can first provide an overview of the area's resources, then encourage participation in any scheduled special events.

Data from this study indicated that 38 percent of the long distance users were retired, more than twice the proportion in the other two segments. Therefore, promote to this segment partly through publications that cater to retired campers especially in Florida and Texas—the most common origins. Programming for this segment can also offer an overview of the resources, while keeping in mind that many retirees have considerable experience and knowledge and may be disinterested in programs that are too basic. Indeed, 75 percent of this user segment have some college background. As with regional users, this segment may wish to attend diverse special events and specific programs.

This study defined segments by the distance traveled to this widely-known and popular resource. At other settings, different parameters may be more relevant to designate segments. However, regardless of the segments identified, the results can help delineate subgroups and help to make specific decisions about promotions, facilities, and programs for each.

Fund-Raising

Fund-raising activities often supplement agency resources at many local and regional museums and nature centers. Traditional fund-raising projects include special activities that raise money on-site via craft sales, unique publications, membership programs, and/or newsletters with advertising. Off-site funding sources include grants, endowments, and corporate contributions. These often highly visible sources often come with a caveat that the funds go to specific purposes, usually for capital expenditures to improve or build new facilities (Romero, 1992).

An agency seeking substantial gifts should conduct research on donors to identify promising individuals and businesses. Raising large amounts of money is both art and science, which requires a continual search for new possibilities. Ideally, an agency cultivates a diversity of funding sources. This creates a safety net if one or more sources becomes undependable. It also insures that the agency need not compromise its mission and independence to receive funding from a source that may try to influence its decision making (Froke and Sharp, 1990).

One successful case study comes from the incentive program developed for the River Bend Nature Center in Faribault, Minnesota (Osterbauer, 1987). The board made a decision to spend $1,200 for a nationally known artist to paint a scene at River Bend. Limited edition reprints of the original went to individuals or corporations who pledged $1,000 or more for an endowment fund. The total cost to the nature center for this incentive program was $7,000; some board members felt it threatened the future of the organization. Nevertheless, the incentive promotion produced a $250,000 endowment within five years. Additionally, the reprints provided the nature center continual publicity with their display both in homes and businesses.

SPOOK TRAILS, FANCY RESTAURANTS, CASINO NIGHTS

The Greenway and Nature Center of Pueblo, Colorado, has gained fame for its ability to survive hard times through various types of income-generating activities. The following discussion indicates diverse ways available to the imaginative interpretive staff, which is summarized by the Pueblo center's former director, Tim Merriman (1983, 1984, 1987, 1992).

Merriman's fund-raising activities date back to the early 1980s. Concern for the survival of his nonprofit, private nature center prompted the decision to offer casino nights, as a legal (Colorado) temporary gambling operation. Without exception, members of the Board of Trustees had moral and social reservations about conducting gambling events. Still, the decision came as a last ditch effort to save the center from bankruptcy, to allow it to continue as a valuable contribution to the community. Hence, the group put on back-to-back Gold Rush Casino Nights over a weekend.

More than 150 volunteers learned to deal blackjack or other gambling games; most sported 1880s costumes for the event. The group rented a building, and obtained a liquor license, and a gambling permit. Approximately 550 people paid $3.00 each to enter the casino and play (Merriman, 1983).

The last funds in the center's operating account ($6,000) went for change in the cashier's cage. After the first evening, a count of the "winnings" showed a loss of $1,000 from the operating account. The event also cost all the money made at the door and at the bar. With bills for the first evening in the $5,000 range, the organization had gambled all of its money and lost.

The next day, the board and director, in a second act of desperation to save their center, decided to play the second night in hopes of recovering their losses. A local attorney advised them that they had failed by employing "Vegas" rules, rather than altered rules that would more greatly favor the house. By the end of play on the second evening, they had a gross of $18,000. After all expenses and the recouping of losses from the first night, the center gained approximately $3,000. A few months later, a second weekend of casino nights produced a profit of nearly $13,000.

Since then, the nature center trustees and staff have taken on strategies more consistent with their philosophy (Merriman, 1984). Two retail shops at the nature center—a plant shop and a gift shop—generate funds. The plant shop, a solar greenhouse, offers various house and flowering plants for sale. The gift shop offers bird feeders, field guides, and other nature items. The shops brought in a $14,000 profit in their second year of operation.

The nature center entices growth in numbers of members who pay an annual fee by providing a monthly newsletter, discounts for program fees, discounts in the retail shops, and free use of bicycles on the local trails system. In just two years, membership grew from 47 to 630.

The most innovative fund-raising involved trailside theatrical events for children, including a Halloween Spook Trail, an Easter Egg Trail, and a Christmas Trail. Each of the trails featured historical or literary characters and included a short hike. Admission fees were nominal—$5.00 for a whole family.

As one example of the approach, the Spook Trail offered visitors interaction with characters such as Merlin the Magician, the scarecrow from Oz, Sherlock Holmes, Captain Hook, the Mummy, and Frankenstein. Candles in real Jack-O-Lanterns lit the trail. During three evenings in 1983, this event attracted thousands of participants and produced a profit of $5,000.

The first Christmas Trail lost $1,000, proving that these ventures can lose money for any number of reasons—a "good failure" that was well-planned and seemed worthy but still fell short. Sometimes, changes in the same activity work for future attempts. Other times, the idea is best allowed to die.

Merriman (1987) offered a ten-point timeline for planning and managing special events (Box 17.2).

BOX 17.2: TIMELINE FOR PLANNING SPECIAL FUND-RAISING EVENTS

1. One year in advance. Set date, establish theme, write objectives, find cosponsors.
2. Four months in advance. Write brochures, determine coordination roles, name coordinators, seek approvals and licenses, request advance payment (50 percent of cosponsorship fee).
3. Three months in advance. Contact specialized volunteers, plan other volunteer activities, prepare task lists for coordinators, prepare graphics, contract for supplies that take time to order or prepare, develop pre-event budget.
4. Two months in advance. Begin weekly meetings, build specialized props, print posters and handbills.
5. One month in advance. Call volunteers, order commodity items, confirm security and sanitation services, plan cash setups, plan media promotion with media cosponsors.
6. Two weeks in advance. Begin radio and television promotion, send out pre-event information to volunteers, bill cosponsors for remaining fees, distribute posters and handbills, start ticket sales, confirm progress with coordinators.
7. Two days in advance. Pick up last minute supplies, erect barricades, prepare support materials such as extension cords, lights and phones, issue day of event time and location schedules for staff and key volunteers.
8. Day of event. Check facilities preparations, be available for calls from the public and volunteers, prepare cash boxes, check supplies, post licenses and permits, conduct final setup activities, locate a volunteer check-in table, meet with security and specialized volunteers, pick up rental equipment, conduct the event.
9. Day after event. Return to the site with staff and committed volunteers for cleanup and storage of materials until next year, return rental equipment.
10. Two or three days after the event. Prepare thank-you letters for volunteers and mail them, evaluate income and expenses and compare to pre-event budget, ask each staff member and key volunteers for event critiques suggesting improvements, write cosponsors thanking them for involvement and complimenting them for specific acts of assistance, start thinking about next year's event.

Adapted from Merriman (1987)

The four "P's" of special event planning are Product (the objectives of the event), Price (survey similar events to determine appropriate pricing), Place (location of event), and Promotion (how customers will be attracted). The most difficult of these is promotion. Media experts suggest that a customer has to read, see, or hear about an event at least five times before being attracted to the event (Merriman, 1987).

As an example, to promote a one-day raft race event, the nature center used 25,000 brochures, 500 posters, 10,000 handbills, 600 radio ad plays, 100 TV ad plays, and three newspaper ads.

This level of promotion was possible through cosponsors such as banks, beverage distributors, auto dealers, food stores, and other businesses. The cosponsorship fee pays for advertising on all promotional materials. This donation comes from the ad budget of the sponsoring business.

Other fund-raising strategies at Pueblo have included art fairs, rummage sales, dances, rafting and hiking activities. Although these events are often marginally interpretive of the center's resources, Merriman (1984) pointed out that special events brought close to 20,000 people to the nature center in 1983, most of whom had never been there. Many of these people return and indicate that they first found out about the facilities through participation in a raft race or trail event (Figure 17.5).

FIGURE 17.5
Many interpretive centers such as Fontenelle Forest help cover expenses by charging admission (below), selling member services, and retailing interpretive materials (left). (TTC)

The most recent innovation at the Greenway and Nature Center is a stylish Mexican restaurant (Merriman, 1992). With no food service on the property the board decided to build a modest snack bar to generate income. The frame building of less than a thousand square feet got funding solicited by direct mail and grant proposals. After a year, only $7,000 had come in for the $75,000 project. Rather than delay the project, the center redesigned the building, but three times larger. The $7,000 went to pour the foundation of the $250,000 Santa Fe-style adobe building. The local newspaper ran a story on the building based on an artist's perspective which produced several donations. Then ten contractors donated $60,000 of in-kind services. Television publicity prompted a call from a woman who asked how much money was needed to help. Merriman suggested that $25,000 would be useful. A check arrived in three days.

The Cafe del Rio offers southwestern fare on pottery with cloth napkins. The outdoor seating areas offer a romantic ambiance under majestic cottonwoods beside the Arkansas River. Merriman (1992) insists that the cafe augments the center's mission; it helps define the architectural character of the modest adobe nature center building nearby. Profits from the restaurant support environmental education.

Tim Merriman, a naturalist turned fund-raiser by necessity, suggested the risk these ventures involve. They can frustrate the staff, take time from other important programs, and still reward those who organize them. Most important, they permitted the Pueblo organization to survive in a difficult economy. This type of approach will not fit every facility. If innovative fund-raising is pursued, Merriman (1992) advised: "Make style, quality, and adherence to theme a focus of your work. Brainstorm the possibilities, choose those with potential, and plan the tactical operation involved very carefully."

Summary

Along with business considerations, marketing and finance play an increasingly important role in effective interpretive agencies. Due to the current economic climate, various strategies have developed, ranging from user fees to fund-raising. The past several years have been difficult for interpretive agencies, especially those within the public sector (Figure 17.6). Hard work, innovative planning, and an eye toward the future has permitted many agencies to thrive. A strong philosophical grounding in the values of cultural and natural history interpretation, along with application of state-of-the-art business and marketing strategies, resulted in some stronger and more autonomous agencies, even in difficult times.

You are never given a wish
without also being given the power to make it true.
You may have to work for it, however.
—Richard Bach, Illusions

FIGURE 17.6
Private historic villages charge a fair entry fee ($6.00 for Wheaton Village) and offer special events to draw new customers.

Literature Cited

Alderson, W. T. and Low, S. P. (1985). *Interpretation of historic sites (2nd ed.)*. Nashville, TN: American Association for State and Local History.

Burde, J. and Howatt, G. (1993). Marketing nature centers: Product, price, and promotion. *Legacy, 4*(4):16-21.

Burns, N. J. (1941). *Field manual for museums*. Washington, DC: National Park Service.

Chiat, W. (1987). Do you wanna buy a duck? Marketing interpretive services. In *Proceedings, National Interpreters Workshop*, AIN. St. Louis, MO.

Follows, D. S. (1988). Resource interpretation: The transfusion into Alaska's tourism industry. In *Proceedings, National Interpreters Workshop*, NAI. San Diego, CA.

Froke, J. B. and Sharp, W. L. (1990). American nature centers: Guidelines for their management. In *Proceedings, National Interpreters Workshop*, NAI. Charleston, SC.

Gober, K. L., Hinkle, R. D., and Mullins, G. W. (1992). Using the marketing audit technique to determine interpretive potential. In *Proceedings, National Interpreters Workshop*, NAI. San Francisco Bay Area, CA.

Howard, D. and Cable, S. (1988). Determining consumers' willingness to pay for park and recreation services. *Trends, 25*(2):42-44.

Knopf, R. (1990). Marketing public lands: Is it the right thing to do? *Parks and Recreation, 25*(3):57-61.

Jamieson, L. (1992). Customer sensitivity: The key to successful marketing. *Parks and Recreation, 27*(12):48-50.

Lawhon, K. (1992). Getting the word out: The how-to's of a marketing program. In *Proceedings, National Interpreters Workshop*, NAI. San Francisco Bay Area, CA.

Marcus, B. (1992). *Competing for clients in the 90s: A dynamic guide to marketing, promoting, and building a professional services practice*. Chicago, IL: Probus Publishing Co.

Massey, J. (1988). The new course: Who hauls the freight? Who pays the way? In *Proceedings, National Interpreters Workshop*, NAI. San Diego, CA.

McCarville, R. (1992). Successful pricing. *Parks and Recreation, 27*(12):36-40.

Merriman, T. (1983). Casino operation to support a nonprofit nature center: A case study. In *Proceedings, National Workshop*, AIN, Purdue University. Purdue, IN.

Merriman, T. (1984). Interpretive fundraising events: Smurfing toward solvency. In *Proceedings, National Workshop*, AIN. Callaway, GA.

Merriman, T. (1987). Special events planning and management. In *Proceedings, National Interpreters Workshop*, AIN. St. Louis, MO.

Merriman, T. (1992). Romantic fundraising. *Legacy, 3*(2):6-7.

Mills, E. (1917). [Comments]. In *Proceedings, National Parks Conference*, Jan. 2-6.

Mokwa, M. (1986). The strategic marketing audit: An adoption/utilization perspective. *Journal of Business Strategy, 6*(4):88-95.

Osterbauer, R. (1987). Using marketing incentives to promote program, volunteerism, and financial support. In *Proceedings, National Interpreters Workshop*, AIN. St. Louis, MO.

Reyburn, J. H. and Knudson, D. M. (1975). The influence of advertising on attendance at park programs. *Journal of Environmental Education*, 7(2):59-64.

Romero, P. (1992). Interpretive programs for fee: A change of philosophy. In *Proceedings, National Interpreters Workshop*, NAI, San Francisco Bay Area, CA.

Rosander, A. (1991). *Deming's 14 points applied to services*. Milwaukee, WI: ASQC Quality Press.

Ross, M. and Ross, T. (1990). *Big marketing ideas for small service businesses*. Homewood, IL: Dow Jones-Irwin.

Tschohl, J. and Franzmeier, S. (1991). *Achieving excellence through customer service*. Englewood Cliffs, NJ: Prentice-Hall, Inc.

Vander Stoep, G. (1990). What direction interpretation? *Journal of Interpretation*, 14(1):R7-R11.

Vavra, T. (1992). *Aftermarketing*. Homewood, IL: Business One Irwin.

Personnel and Training

This chapter discusses some of the professional qualifications desirable for most interpreters. It presents the importance and content of university training, along with professional on-the-job training. Professional growth opportunities and effective methods for the training of seasonal employees also appear. Next, interpretive supervision is covered with discussion of planning, organizing, directing, and controlling the interpretive effort. This chapter then presents information relating to the roles of volunteers who support interpretive efforts—in some cases operating them. It concludes with a discussion of "Friends" groups and cooperating associations, which also play major roles in many interpretive settings.

Training

Effective interpreters must be educated and trained. Natural naturalists and innate historians—those folks with a gift of gab and a knack for giving the right answers—are rare cases (Ham, 1992). Outstanding interpreters usually develop slowly through careful study, much experience, and continued training.

The tradition of scholarly interpreters goes back to the beginnings. The National Park Service hired two Ph.D. professors to start its interpretive work in 1920 (Miller, 1960). Ansel Hall, a young forester with experience and exceptional skill in museum collections, served as the year-round interpretive supervisor and did much of the nonpersonal service interpretation.

The NPS rapidly realized the need for training other interpreters. They set up a seven-week summer school in 1925 (Bryant, 1960). So, well before there was any organized interpretive division in the National Park Service, there was the Yosemite School of Field Natural History. It trained naturalists who studied living things in their natural environment. This early training program, centered in a circle of tents, focused on the natural sciences. The 20 students got intensive field work on the Yosemite trees, shrubs, wild flowers, insects, fishes, amphibians, reptiles, birds, and mammals. The course had university rigor but gave a certificate instead of college credit. To get in, the students had to have two years of college completed (Bryant and Atwood, 1932).

Later on, Tilden (1967) criticized scientists and emphasized communications in interpretation. He had reason for his emphasis, but the point can become distorted, if taken out of context. Tilden thought that the early generations of naturalists "were unduly impressed by the word 'education.'" He generalized, from long experience, that these natural and cultural history specialists abhorred artistic forms of language such as metaphor, simile, and analogy. This and the specialist's supposed obsession with trivia ("pedagogical miscellany") make him boring to "the man on holiday."

Today, interpreters can get a professional education in more than 130 university programs at the undergraduate and graduate levels in North America (Vander Stoep, 1991). Once employed in the field, an interpreter may continue training through in-service workshops, professional conferences, and personal attention to developments in the field. Seasonal employees and volunteers who may not have the benefit of a full university background receive on-site, on-the-job training by their supervisors. Given the expansion of interpretation's roles—from the use of marketing to involvement in global issues—some professionals call for tighter definition of who we are and what we do (Vander Stoep and Capelle, 1992). This relates directly to university preparation and professional training.

UNIVERSITY PREPARATION

The interpretive profession has long debated whether a strong grounding in communication or expertise in specific resource subject matter (e.g., natural science, archæology, history) is more important (Risk, 1982, 1983). Interpreters that are well-trained in communications can convey a message, but if they lack expertise about the resource, they have little to say. Interpreters who have expertise in natural or cultural history have much to say but may transmit the message ineffectively. So, for our purposes, both communications and subject matter should be included in university coursework in the preparation of interpreters. In addition to resource-based and communications courses, interpreters can choose from a wide range of possibilities which range from marketing to environmental sciences.

University training will vary according to student interests in natural history or cultural history. It will vary according to a student's interests in performance interpretation or exhibit preparation and other nonpersonal services. Similarly, emphasis will vary depending on whether the student intends to work for a public agency or the private sector.

Academic programs in interpretation tend to be broad in scope. For example, specific coursework in the natural sciences may include ecology, botany, mammalogy, ornithology, herpetology, ichthyology, and entomology. Coursework in resource management often includes forestry, wildlife conservation, and wildland recreation management. Skills in public speaking, public relations, communications theory, and mass communications courses come from the general area of communications. Supplemental coursework may include areas such as business management, marketing, computers, park operations, recreation resource planning, leisure science, the arts, economics, organizational behavior, psychology, and environmental science.

Undergraduate courses in interpretation tend to cover a broad overview of the philosophy, principles, and methods of interpretation and environmental education. Advanced courses generally focus on research, theory, design, management, or other aspects of interpretation such as specific applications of audiovisuals, exhibits, and computers.

LIFELONG TRAINING

Upon university graduation and entry into the profession, the interpreter embarks upon continual training throughout his or her career. Most agencies, both public and private, offer introductory training to expose the new employee to agency philosophy, policies, and resources. Intake training programs offer customized instruction that is relevant and useful to the agency. California State Parks, for example, offer extensive training over the course of many weeks, maintaining a full-time training center.

The National Park Service likewise has the Mather Employee Development Center at Harpers Ferry, West Virginia, and the Albright Employee Development Center at the Grand Canyon, where interpreters and many other employees receive training. The first step for interpreters involves field training around the country in interpretive skills courses. As the interpreter advances up the career ladder, a variety of training opportunities becomes available (Watson, 1986).

Other excellent agencies bring in experts to lead their in-service training programs. For example, the San Diego County Parks Department contracts workshops with San Diego State University faculty members. Bill Lewis has long provided evaluation and critiquing services to the National Park Service. John Veverka and Associates, Team Interpretation, Douglas/Ryan Communication, and Inside-Outside provide custom-made training programs for public and private agencies, including the Army Corps of Engineers. Some of these consulting firms also provide training sessions open to applicants, even those with no agency affiliation.

Supplemental training offered on an on-going basis keeps employees abreast of current research and developments within the interpretive field. Scientific conferences work well for local training needs; in California, for example, meetings range from tide pool ecology and desert ecology to artifact collection and management (Lustig, 1985).

Exchange programs offer a novel approach to increasing depth of knowledge and skills of interpreters. That is, some agencies accept a limited number of outside participants into their training sessions. These interpreters tend to bring in new perspectives and ideas based upon their experiences elsewhere.

Some agencies sponsor or provide tuition assistance to employees who pursue additional college courses related to their jobs. Coursework that benefits the individual ultimately should reflect well upon the agency. All of these training opportunities promote a more knowledgeable interpretive staff, individual interpreter excellence, higher morale within the agency, and better service to the public.

Actual training should be conducted so it serves as "a call to action, a vision for the future—not an end, but a beginning" (Backlund, Dahlen, and Anibal, 1992). This can be accomplished through careful development of the overall training curriculum so the sequence of activities flows smoothly and logically. Well-written and relevant objectives for each session of the training couple with instructors who use imagination and knowledge. The instructors must embody personal commitment to quality interpretation and show concern with the development of the trainees. Heavy participant involvement will help link the course materials to learning activities. These may include task groups, issue-oriented problem solving, and the development of park-related products. High-quality training programs generate enthusiasm and personal commitment to excellence. The same principles apply to both permanent and seasonal employees.

Professional Growth

Most outstanding agencies provide some level of support for active professional involvement in terms of time off and financial aid for attendance at professional conferences and workshops. This is a wise investment of funds. These opportunities encourage interpreters to expand their professional competencies, to try new programs, and to serve their customers better. Specific outcomes for the individual interpreters and the agency include the following, identified by Hankins (1991), a county parks superintendent:

- Making contacts and discussing ideas with other interpreters.
- Comparing problems and pitfalls of other departments (and finding that everyone has them!).
- Observing techniques of peers and thereby developing new ideas to be incorporated in personal programs.
- Talking with experts and leaders in the interpretive field.
- Finding resources at exhibitor booths.
- Showcasing agency innovations.
- Networking.

In addition, the association with other interpreters enhances pride in the profession, gives confidence and encouragement from a sense of belonging to a larger group, develops a sense of broad purpose and enthusiasm for interpretive work. The participation with other interpreters helps affirm the validity and values of the profession as well as of the individual.

Hankins (1991) suggested that the specific benefits of involvement in professional workshops must be relayed to agency administrators and policy-makers to gain support. Some specific activities and projects of St. Joseph County Parks, Indiana, that originated from staff participation in workshops and conferences over the course of one year included:

- Planned a "Bug Day" for children.
- Improved period clothing techniques based on research data discovered at a workshop.
- Gained access to a free electronic bulletin board program for the computer.
- Acquired a simple paper test for evaluating programs and facilities.
- Learned about volunteers and liability.
- Increased storytelling as an interpretive technique.

Professional conferences and workshops can broaden professional interpreters through introducing new trends in the field, providing active exchange of ideas, and sharing interpretive methods.

Seasonal Training

Just as good programs interpret the site and involve the visitor, good training should offer a dynamic process for learning about the resource. Zimmerman (1988) suggested a number of strategies to make training of seasonal employees more effective, as discussed below.

The use of advance materials organizers can help generate excitement prior to the actual training sessions. For example, many national parks (e.g., Denali, Rocky Mountain) send out information to seasonals on park operations and the cultural and natural history of the park before training begins. This serves many purposes: it shows that the agency commits to each new employee, it fosters enthusiasm on the part of the new interpreters, and the serious study of the material allows seasonals to arrive with the ability to ask penetrating questions about the resource and the operation.

Once a training session begins, seek to develop staff cohesiveness. This comes by allowing sufficient time for individual introductions and conversations so everyone learns about their coworkers. The level of cohesiveness needed cannot be gained through standard mumbled personal introductions at the beginning of training. Rather it should pervade the training to have long-term pay-offs building camaraderie and team spirit.

Share agency objectives with seasonal trainees early in the program. New employees should have read this material through the advance information. Agency history, philosophy, and objectives should get explicit coverage, however, to reinforce and clarify the concepts so everyone works together toward a common vision.

Finally, the agency should provide nuts-and-bolts training in preparing new employees. That is, if the job requires leading walks and delivering talks, then trainees should design and conduct these during training. For example, the group could plan and share presentations throughout the session to enhance individual program preparation and build self-confidence. This level of active participation should also fuel the group's enthusiasm for the coming season. Training, then, is more than providing new employees with "the information they need to know." It includes trusting the trainees to have enough knowledge and life experience to be active contributors in the training process (Henry, 1988).

Overall success of any interpretive agency depends on high quality, on-going training. This may range from intake training of new employees and seasonals, to in-service training as their careers develop, to providing agency support so interpreters can attend workshops and conferences. The success of the interpretive program cannot remain static but rests upon continuing development of expertise among the employees of the agency.

Supervision

*It all comes down to one person, the manager of the interpretive program.
...The quality of the interpretive program, then, depends on the human factor
more than on money, facilities, or spectacular park features.*
—Grant W. Sharpe (*Bevilacqua*, 1993)

Interpreters who supervise interpreters have a special kind of job. The following pages offer a few key concepts about the art and responsibilities of supervising interpreters.

Supervisors have to be more than worn-out field interpreters. Seniority is not a good criterion for giving someone supervisory duty—it is not a gold watch job. It requires people skills plus conscientious concern for the agency's goals and productivity, a good work environment for the interpreters, and superior service to the visitors.*

A supervisor is the agent of those supervised, organizing them, coaching them, protecting them from fallout. A supervisor is also seen as the direct representative of the agency or company to the employees.

---

* Source: Cindy Nielsen, Glacier NP: lectures at Harpers Ferry Training course, 1992, paraphrased.

AIMS AND MISFIRES

The productive role of the supervisor is to achieve work through other people's efforts (OPE). Often, supervisors of interpretation feel loaded down by paperwork and scheduling, evaluating, and reporting at meetings. They wish for more contact with people, more time to be in the real museum or park or refuge environment rather than sitting on chairs. Yet, supposedly, they are coordinating and supervising the work of other interpreters.

Here is where some bad bosses develop their problems. One type takes the OPE concept too literally, seldom doing any interpretive work, never filling in for the sick or overloaded interpreters and, therefore, gets out of touch with the front line. A few of these breeze in and out of the nature center on an irregular basis, announce the new work schedule to whoever is there, or make new arrangements for programs, or give a few other orders, and then go off for a "meeting" to return a day or two later. This person is out of touch with the reality of the center but thinks that the job is one of "making a few key decisions" and then issuing orders. Appraisal and coaching of program performances is ignored or put off because other things seem more important at the moment. Employees feel dictated to, but ignored. The supervisor can come off as arrogant, remote and capricious, as well as incompetent and perhaps insecure as an interpreter. Except in the abstract, this type of boss cares little for program quality control or professional development of the interpretive staff.

The other extreme is the supervisor who has difficulty using OPE, who cannot let go of personal performance of programs, cannot delegate many program jobs. This person often takes the responsibility of the center's performance so seriously that personal involvement in most public contacts seems necessary. The other employees are not trusted to do it right ("my way"). The supervisor shoulders the whole load and eventually burns out. Other employees feel less than valuable.

Misinterpreting the aim of accomplishing work through other people's efforts happens quite frequently. Big staffs need more emphasis on the supervision, while in small parks or centers, the supervisor is a performing colleague. Finding the happy medium involves adjusting to the people and the place and the nature of the interpretive task.

FUNCTIONS

The functions of a supervisor include planning, organizing, directing, and controlling (by reporting and evaluating).

Planning at the operational level involves (1) identifying the goals, deciding where you want the organization to be, and (2) analyzing and developing a strategy for how to get there. The goals may be stated in practical terms, e.g., *we will offer 33 interpretive programs per week. We intend that they will be well-attended, related to our major themes, inspirational, and fun.* The strategy identifies the steps: preparing schedules, training, and preparation for the programs; gathering and organizing supplies and equipment for the programs; announcing and advertising the programs. A key role of the supervisor is communicating what the group wants, intends, and expects to all the people involved, including those noninterpreters upon whom the operations depend, such as janitors, contractors, and agency executives. When communication fails, many good plans fail.

Organizing interpretive work is a key supervisory function. It involves people, spaces, equipment, materials, and times. The concept is easy. The practice is often complex, especially where there are many interpreters, volunteers, and programs. The key idea is to set up interrelationships. One important relationship defines who is responsible to whom. An employee should have one boss and should know who that is. This goes for volunteers, too. A supervisor should be responsible for no more than five to nine employees who interact with each other (Forest Service, 1988). The formal lines of command will usually be crossed informally by staff assistants, people who provide supplementary information, assistance, support and coordination. For example, in many state park agencies, a park interpreter responds directly to the park manager. The state's chief interpreter, however, provides interpretive planning help, seasonal personnel training, technical support, and coaching.

Directing interpretive work involves preparing people, scheduling them, and keeping things moving. The key skill needed is that of delegation. Delegation of interpretive work requires constant, conscious effort. It is more than handing out work; it involves empowerment. The employee gets authority to perform, responsibility for the program, freedom of action, and freedom from unwanted interference. In order to empower the employee, the supervisor must have previously given the interpreter:

- *training* in interpretive skills.
- *resources* such as good location, equipment, materials, and supplies.
- *themes* for interpretation, with information on the resource.
- *time* for preparation, with the freedom and guidance to use it.

Along with delegation comes the job of saying what is enough. When time of the staff and the supervisor becomes overcommitted, say so. Let the agency know what will have to be cut or reallocated. Do not blindly accept new requests when at a saturation point.

Delegation sometimes involves contracting specialized work to others. For example, the National Park Service recently increased its commitment to environmental education. In Glacier National Park, an education specialist was hired to tailor the program to neighboring Blackfeet and Kootenay schools. The specialist formed working groups with tribal elders and cultural leaders. They reviewed drafts and tested the lessons. The supervisor's work here involved (1) defining the product wanted from the selected specialist, (2) facilitating the input from volunteer groups, and (3) communicating the results and progress.

Delegation involves giving both work and responsibility to others. The supervisor retains the final responsibility for producing the results, however. The gracious supervisor therefore spreads the credit around, giving it to the employees, the contractors and the volunteers, never indulging in self-glorification.

Controlling involves evaluation, reporting, analyzing, and revising plans for the future. It involves budget and financial accounting, reporting visitor contact hours, quality control, and personnel development. The most critical control function is constructive evaluation and development of other interpreters, both employees and volunteers. Setting annual goals, getting quarterly progress statements and conducting annual progress reviews for individual interpreters are methods to aid growth. The best approach in these activities is positive, focusing on results and ways to remove performance barriers. A boss should know what employees have been doing and what to do for each employee. Recognize good performance more frequently than criticizing weaknesses. Compliments, thank-you notes, credit, awards, increased responsibility, study trips, parties and ceremonies all provide positive reinforcement.

Annual Appraisal Interviews

Annual appraisals help chart the development of employees over time. This should not threaten the employees but serve as a tool for performance growth. They should see the appraisal interview not as salt to be rubbed in a wound, but as a chance to discuss what resources they can use to increase their satisfaction in the work of interpreting well.

The supervisor should:

1. Inform the person ahead of time to allow for preparation. Set up a formal session for both supervisor and employee to discuss questions and methods to enhance performance.
2. Review the person's records and performance in advance.
3. Concentrate on performance and results, not personality or personal events (the latter can be used as a club by either side).
4. Listen to the employee, actively, to hear facts of successes in the past year, performance she or he wants to improve, feelings about selected issues or programs.
5. Do not focus on negative factors nor treat them as if they were immutable.
6. Face problems, discussing them rationally and openly, not as criticism.
7. Agree on a realistic plan of action that defines improvements to be made and how to go about it.
8. Report in writing on the meeting, decisions and next goals and allow the employee to review the report before filing it.
9. Track growth and development over the years through records.

The topic of evaluation gets further coverage in Chapter 19.

Staffing

The staff needs to consider the consumer as an esteemed client. The agency's services and staffing exist to serve the visitors. Its primary, driving purpose focuses on giving them attentive service by the whole organization.

An interpretive organization needs to have well-trained, experienced staff meeting the public. Pay them well to be out front and ready to meet the clients. Praise them when they perform well. It seems odd that some public agencies send out the youngest, least experienced, least knowledgeable (and poorest paid) staff to meet and inform the "owners of the company" when they visit. The experienced interpreters who know the parks or forests intimately should not emerge only to perform when a Senator or Representative or Governor or agency Director arrives for a visit. Interpretive supervision should not preclude an experienced person from front-line interpretive contacts. The customer cannot rank low in the working priorities. Why not put the best staff forward for the paying customers?

Professionalism

Supervisors, who do not produce much, are *not* the only keys to a program's success. The people who develop and enhance the visitor experiences (the real products) through programs, exhibits, films, signs, and booklets are the real stars. The people qualified enough to be supervisors *may* also be qualified enough to be effective interpreters.

Several National Park Service executives have referred to GS-4 and GS-5 workers as "walk and talk interpreters," suggesting unintentionally that the real production of interpretive programs is grunt work for beginners. In other words, upward mobility in this agency may require getting out of using professional interpretive skills. Instead they "supervise." Dealing with visitors, ecology, and history becomes a sort of abstraction, as memories of the good old days. A reward system that pays the best-qualified people to *not* interpret, to *not* interact with the visitor has something wrong with it.

In some cases, talented people develop their interpretive knowledge and skills until they become pretty competent. Then, they switch to another job that takes them away from their competency. That is similar to bringing up a minor league pitcher to the majors, letting him develop into top winning form for three or four years, then putting him on the bench to keep score and coach young pitchers—at the peak of his pitching skills—and paying him more for switching (except that baseball teams do not pay coaches more than players). Likewise, why take an interpreter, who builds up skills and knowledge, develops empathy for people, finds out what works well, how long to hike, talk, walk, when to pause in the stories to make the point, when to use models and artifacts, how to handle school groups for maximum learning, and then—just as the person gets good—banish them from front-line contact with the public?

Why do the stars sit on the bench? Why don't the visitors see the top professionals in action when they come to the museum or park? Why don't clients get the best the agency has to offer? Why do these skilled, experienced people who know the parks well sit behind the scenes, not readily available to the public? Does this suggest "visitors first?"

If the organization hopes to give its visitors more than second-rate, perfunctory treatment, if it seeks to give its visitors star treatment—it makes sense to use its star performers who are at the peaks of their profession.

Fortunately, some agencies value and pay their interpreters for their skills in meeting and teaching the public—being the up-front stars of the show—not turning them into bean counters and schedule makers just as they get good at their jobs. A federal interpreter with experience and skill may well earn GS-11 pay, sometimes more, for actually interpreting. Likewise, in the private sector, the top performers get top billing, center stage, and sometimes unbelievable pay.

PROFESSIONALS OR VOLUNTEERS?

Most agencies, including the National Park Service and local museums, rely heavily on interpretation for public image and contact. Yet, many of the front-line interpreters are volunteers or seasonal employees who receive little or no pay (Figure 18.1). Citing budget problems, some agencies adopt policies that have gone so far as to include volunteer work as part of the career ladder.

FIGURE 18.1
Desk duty placed this recently arrived volunteer as the prime contact with more visitors than any other interpreter.

Few parks, however, receive "volunteer" vehicles, two-way radios or computers; they pay for them. Why not pay for interpreters? The budget excuse is convenient, but it implies that interpreters have less value than hardware gadgets.

Some agencies use volunteers excellently, training them very carefully (see discussion on the following pages). Others seem to accept any willing soul; the result of the latter may be a spate of fresh-faced, untrained liberal arts majors with no background in ecology, art, geology, archæology, or history. Anyone will do, if they prove to be articulate, alive, and smiling.

Mild exaggeration aside, in a few places unqualified people are interpreting a county's, a state's and a nation's outstanding examples of ecological communities, history, archæological finds and geological phenomena. Namba (1991) likened this to entrusting medical treatment to a volunteer physician. He wrote: "Perhaps, interpretation has reached a crucial point in its evolution in which interpreters must come to grips with the future of their field."

If the profession is to live up to its potential, it requires highly intelligent, well-informed, scholarly, outgoing people, educated in the major subjects related to their work. This should include training in interpretive theory, principles, and methods, as well as other courses in communications and/or education. Fortunately, most agencies prefer to choose people who have strong academic qualifications, along with interpretive skills training.

This in no way suggests that volunteers have no place. It simply means that professional interpreters should serve as the main staff offering public programs. A strong volunteer program requires strong professional interpretive leadership. A strong interpretive program requires strong professional interpretive commitment to performance.

INSTITUTIONAL POLICY

An agency's policy toward its interpretive efforts and personnel says much about its professional commitment to serve the recreating public. The policy is what people see in action more than that written on paper.

Interpreters can be most productive under a few key conditions. They will contribute strongly to an agency when:

1. They are integrated into the management team.
2. Their work is treated professionally and evaluated by managers and supervisors with regularity and fairness.
3. Management permits creative innovation and allows trials that fail; management provides feedback but not prejudgement.

4. Their real work of interaction with visitors and other publics is given significance and support, without distracting interpreters to do other jobs that need to be "tidied up," e.g., speech writing for administraters.
5. A professional career ladder exists within the practice of interpretation, including recognition of and progressive reward for expertise and skill in interpreting the resource, with both personal and nonpersonal services.
6. Participation in professional interpretation societies and related activities gets support and encouragement.

Namba (1991) suggested that the professional society members (e.g., National Association for Interpretation) must help employers develop nine areas to firm up the profession.
1. Control admittance into the interpretive field.
2. Maintain minimum standards for interpretive positions.
3. Determine registration, certification, or licensing criteria.
4. Adopt accreditation standards for university curriculum.
5. Set compensation schedules that are competitive with other professions.
6. Establish interpretive mentor programs.
7. Develop a cooperative education program.
8. Utilize quantitative and qualitative evaluation tools.
9. Maintain fair and equitable hiring practices.
These suggestions merit further discussion within the professional society. These valid concerns do not have easy or quick solutions.

Volunteers—Getting Help from Your Friends

FIGURE 18.2
Volunteers and professionals interpret the Hamilton County Park District, Ohio.

Volunteers, sometimes called docents or guides, have long interpreted in museums and parks (Figure 18.2). Their impact has grown rapidly in recent years. For example, from 1980 to 1993, volunteers with the National Park Service grew approximately tenfold to 77,000 (Newman, 1993). Professional interpretive staff usually works with volunteers who extend or multiply the interpretive effort in most public and private museums and parks.

This did not happen as a result of a shift in professional philosophy, but as a response to decreasing financial support. In the United States, taxpayer revolts at the local and state levels and the increasing budget deficits at the federal level have led to reduced funding for public agencies.

Despite budget constraints, the visitors still expect and demand high quality services. They often expect managers to find creative solutions rather than to increase user fees. One such solution is to encourage the unpaid work of volunteers. Each federal resource management agency now has a vigorous volunteer program, each with specific guidelines and promotional materials.

The proliferation of volunteers is a recent social phenomenon. Citizens have strong interests in environmental matters (Tomsho, 1993). Older individuals increasingly show interest in providing their services to many worthwhile causes, including protection and interpretation of cultural and historic resources. Although retirees seem to have more time available than people still in the work force, surveys show that part-time workers volunteer more than either full-time workers or people who have retired completely (Fischer and Schaffer, 1993). However, retirees who volunteer average the highest number of hours of these groups.

According to Dominguez and Robin (1992), the volunteer follows a noble and worthy tradition:

> Volunteering is the epitome of self-expression—choosing what you do based on an inner prompting. Volunteering is dipping down into your internal resources—your commitment as well as your skills, your love as well as your knowledge—to accomplish something in the world that you determine is worth doing.

When used effectively, volunteers have literally saved many programs and services. They fan out to clean up trash, run campgrounds, staff information desks, give nature walks, and provide museum tours (Figure 18.3).

However, one of the most common myths about volunteers is that their work is free. Volunteer programs never operate without cost. Unless the work is thoroughly planned and wisely managed, it can actually lower total productivity. Before initiating a volunteer program, administrators should carefully evaluate whether they want one enough to invest the necessary personnel, time and money to make it successful. Top management and the paid staff have to support it. If staff members see the volunteer program as a threat to their own jobs, they will seldom provide enough support and acceptance to maximize productivity. The National Park Service figures it gets $32 of work for each dollar it spends recruiting and training volunteers (Newman, 1993).

As several examples illustrate, volunteers can have a tremendous positive impact on interpretive productivity.

- The Louisiana Nature and Science Center has about 320 volunteers, donating 20,000 hours annually. This equals 10 full-time staff members, thereby saving the center tens of thousands of dollars each year (Daly, 1991).
- The Tippecanoe County Historical Association puts on a two-day event every fall that draws 60,000 or more visitors to the Feast of the Hunters' Moon. It involves 2,000 volunteer organizers, presenters, and gofers who contribute 40,000 hours of labor for this one event in a county park (Figure 18.4).

FIGURE 18.3
Where only volunteers interpret for a federal agency, visitors from afar feel ill-served if they want to learn about the trees and geology of a place they've never seen before. This federal visiting center was open only when volunteers could get there.

FIGURE 18.4
The Feast of the Hunters Moon attracts tens of thousands of visitors to a county park under the sponsorship of the Tippecanoe County Historical Association.

- The Laguna Mountain Volunteer Association gave 20,000 hours of time improving trails, campgrounds and visitor services in a national forest in the late 1980s (Forest Service, 1988).
- Students from the University of Mississippi's Recreation Program volunteer at a nearby Corps of Engineers' lake. They saved the Corps $24,000 and won the 1989 "Take Pride in America Award" (Dutton, 1990).

PLANNING FOR A VOLUNTEER PROGRAM

Several tasks arise before the first volunteer shows up to work. First, establish a budget for the volunteer program. Expenditures arise from promoting the program, training, equipping, scheduling and recognizing the volunteers.

Second, allot some official staff time for a volunteer coordinator. Only one person coordinating all the volunteers usually produces the best result. It lessens the confusion for the staff and the volunteers if they get direction from one source. The person acting as coordinator should recognize the task as an important part of his or her job, rather than just an additional responsibility. The wrong coordinator can sour the whole program by causing a reduction in the spirit of cooperation and, eventually, the number of volunteers willing to work. Naturally, with large numbers of volunteers, several staff coordinators will be organized in some hierarchy to coordinate different volunteer efforts (Covel, 1990).

Third, write formal job descriptions for each volunteer position. They should be at least as specific as those for regular employees, including identification of specific work projects and their time commitments.

Fourth, allocate space for the volunteers. Depending on the nature of the position, they may need behind-the-scenes work space. A room for gathering, working, and completing paper work enhances morale. So does an area where they can gather informally, study and rehearse. Some historical operations require dressing rooms, a sewing machine, secure wardrobe storage, and showers.

RECRUITING AND "HIRING" VOLUNTEERS

In one study, almost 70 percent of volunteers said they volunteered because someone personally asked them (American Red Cross, 1988). About 25 percent volunteered spontaneously—on their own. Very few responded to mass media appeals. This study and experience suggest that the way to attract volunteers is through personal invitations. An efficient way of doing this is to develop a professional presentation. Use high quality audiovisuals; describe the park or museum and focus on the role of the volunteers. Testimonials from current volunteers can attest to the rewards of service; they can also respond to questions. This presentation could be slanted toward Scout groups, environmental clubs, and the local chapter of American Association of Retired People.

First impressions are extremely important in attracting volunteers; make the presentation as professional and appealing as possible. If you do not have an excellent, easily accessible meeting place at your facility, take your presentation out to where target groups normally meet or use attractive well-equipped meeting rooms in libraries, banks, utility offices, or schools. Advertise these presentations in newsletters and mass media. At the end of the presentation, have a sign-up sheet near or outside the exit where those interested may offer their names and addresses and telephone numbers. This approach avoids embarrassing those who decide not to serve.

Treat the list of candidates the same as a list of job applicants. Formal interviews can determine the interests, motives, and needs of the candidates. This information is critical to determine the volunteer's niche in the organization. During the interview, clearly explain the organization's goals and values as well as any expectations you have of the volunteers. Include the job descriptions, rules of conduct, time commitments, probation periods, training, and evaluation methods. A thorough interview process can save many future headaches and start out a pleasant, productive relationship with clear understanding. Volunteers get to know the organization and their roles in it; the staff gets to know the volunteers' interests and capabilities.

About 150 volunteers donate 10,000 hours of work annually to the Raptor Center at the University of Minnesota. The screening of potential volunteers falls to a veteran crew, themselves volunteers who can personally describe the commitment of time and energy required to do the work. Careful and deliberate screening of applicants produces high retention rates. For example, as part of the interview process, applicants observe volunteers at work, performing various duties. This permits the opportunity for potential volunteers to ask questions while crew leaders assess their apparent aptitudes for various tasks (Ritter, Osterbauer, and Dahill, 1992).

TRAINING AND RETAINING VOLUNTEERS

Once volunteers come on board, they often need training for a successful operation. Training manuals developed for the different volunteer positions and training sessions should be offered for new groups of volunteers. Experienced volunteers should expect to attend at least one training session annually as a refresher or new information course.

The Arizona Sonoran Desert Museum requires four months of training before volunteers offer tours and station interpretation. Once trained at considerable cost, the museum emphasizes the need to perform on schedule, faithfully and punctually. An organization serves itself and the volunteers well to make clear these expectations early on. One of the biggest headaches of volunteer coordinators comes from volunteers who do not sense the importance of meeting regular schedules.

Just as with staff, an agency retains volunteers by treating them with respect, by allowing them to find fulfillment on the job, and by recognizing and rewarding good work (Morris 1990; Daly 1991). Making volunteers feel that they are important parts of the team is good strategy. While training and recruiting volunteers, let them know that the agency expects and needs a steady, fairly long-term commitment. Provide volunteers with their own adequate work space, identification badges, and uniforms to build morale and camaraderie. Inform volunteers about what is going on in the organization just as one would openly communicate with the paid staff.

Margaret Daly, Volunteer Coordinator at the Louisiana Nature and Science Center, offered 15 tips on keeping volunteers happy and productive (Box 18.1). Volunteers may be the most valuable staff, sometimes even more valuable than those the agency pays. They represent the community. They help raise money, lobby for support, and often provide expertise in administration, finance, construction and science. If they become disenchanted with your staff or your operation, they can serve as a quick indicator that something has gone wrong. In more than one historical association and parks board the defection of long-term volunteers has signalled that the paid employees were not doing their jobs well.

BOX 18.1: FIFTEEN RULES FOR KEEPING VOLUNTEERS HAPPY (DALY, 1991)

1. Volunteers must understand the organization's goals and their own assignment.
2. They must feel that their assignment is meaningful and understand how it fits into the scheme of things.
3. Put some fun into their jobs.
4. They must feel needed and wanted.
5. They like to help plan programs and establish goals and timetables.
6. Encourage them to be public relations people and to feel comfortable when addressing community groups.
7. They are leaders in your organization's goal-reaching and money-raising activities.
8. They must be recognized privately and publicly for their roles, results and contributions.
9. They must remain excited about your organization.
10. Listen to their comments, suggestions, and problems.
11. Do not overload one volunteer. Spread the work around.
12. Do not waste their time—volunteers place a high value on the time they give.
13. Build a sense of camaraderie with volunteers from different areas through recognition events.
14. Most importantly, thank them time and time again.
15. After understanding the mission of your organization, volunteers are invaluable "dreamers," helping to shape the direction of programs.

EVALUATING VOLUNTEERS

Evaluate volunteers regularly, just as with all other employees. Evaluation should help give them a sense of value. A positive, nonthreatening process allows the evaluation to be productive. Evaluations can help determine the following: Are the volunteers comfortable and enjoying themselves? Are they being successful in their work? Are they contributing to the excellence of the agency? If not, what can be done to enhance their performance?

Following through with effective interviews and training, along with regular evaluations and feedback, should make dismissals of volunteers a rare event. When dismissal becomes necessary, the process of frequent contact and comment should keep it from coming as a surprise to the volunteer.

A model evaluation program is described in the case study from the Monterey Bay Aquarium (Box 18.2).

To sum up this section, volunteers differ relatively little from regular employees in the normal management process, except that an agency does not pay them and therefore may have less control over them. Much thought should go into "hiring" them. The agency will invest heavily in their training, scheduling, supervision, evaluation and feedback. They should be treated with respect and appreciation for their willingness to share their time and talents. A well-run volunteer program can provide thousands of hours of inexpensive labor to accomplish tasks that would not be completed otherwise. Equally as important, their involvement can enhance community support for the program.

BOX 18.2: A VOLUNTEER EVALUATION PROCESS

At the Monterey Bay Aquarium, we have over 350 volunteers, called guides, that interpret exhibits to visitors. After trying several evaluation strategies with mixed success, we identified some key elements of a satisfactory program:

1. Evaluations should be nonthreatening. Just the word inspires anxiety in many people, and some volunteers were very intimidated by the thought of being evaluated.
2. Evaluations should be interactive, allowing the volunteer to respond to comments and feedback.
3. Evaluations should consider the individual. While minimum standards apply to all, individuals should be challenged to do their personal best.
4. Evaluations should be consistent. The process must be standardized to a level where it is applied in the same way each time in order to avoid one volunteer receiving mixed messages from various staff members.
5. Documentation must be organized and detailed so that any staff member can follow up on an evaluation performed by other staff.
6. Most importantly, the evaluation should be an opportunity to celebrate the success of the volunteer, and should not be applied or perceived as punitive, judgmental or critical.

In our particular application, we decided that there are two principal areas of need for evaluations. The first is content or factual information. We have observed that there is a certain rate of decay in accuracy that starts shortly after training is completed and accelerates in the absence of feedback.

The second area for evaluation is interpretive technique, the interaction between our guides and visitors to transmit information. Interpretive technique is an area that responds very well to the increased motivation that can result from a good evaluation.

RETENTION

Evaluating the level of retention of factual information and accuracy of that information is relatively simple. To meet both our needs and criteria a comprehensive exam was developed. The exam questions were pulled from tests used in training, from common visitor questions, and from exhibit information. There were also questions that were designed to correct common misinformation. The exam was designed overall as a teaching tool, so that correct knowledge would be reinforced and incorrect information would be identified and modified.

This exam was administered as a self-test with volunteers taking the test at home and correcting it themselves. We provided answer keys that also listed where the information could be found in the training manual issued to each guide. If someone wanted to "cheat" and look up the answers, they still learned the correct answers, which fulfilled the objective of the test. The following week we went over the exam with everyone in a small group format.

Volunteers had a chance to raise questions and staff had a chance to focus on particular problem areas. This did not seem to be threatening, and everyone felt that the process was fair and dignified. A nice benefit was that we were also able to identify weak subject areas and can then target those with follow-up training.

OBSERVING VOLUNTEER GUIDES

The next phase of the evaluation process involved observing volunteer guides interacting with visitors at exhibits to monitor the application of interpretive techniques. A two-page checklist was developed to standardize observations to a degree, but also included many open-ended items as well as specific areas for response from the volunteer.

Volunteers were given a copy of the checklist in advance both for comment and to show them the criteria that would be used in the evaluation process. Exhibits that provide good opportunities for interaction with visitors and for observing these interactions were used consistently during this phase of the process.

Staff tried to be as unobtrusive as possible while making observations. We then asked the volunteer to meet with us during a break or after shift to go over the results. At this point we could sit in a quiet place with the guide, complete the notes as we discussed the observations, and incorporate their ideas as well.

Particular focus was placed on reinforcing good techniques; when areas of need were identified we were careful to ask how we could work with the volunteer to address that need. We finished by asking the volunteer how we as a staff were doing in serving their needs and how we could improve. Again, more good ideas for training and communications came from this process. Overall, volunteers appreciated the time and attention they received from staff and were quite positive and receptive.

The entire cycle takes approximately four months to complete with three staff members evaluating about 350 guides. We have found that winter is a good time to start, as the staff has more time. This evaluation process is also used when a volunteer guide returns to the program after an absence of more than three months.

We will go through several evaluation cycles before we can truly measure the effectiveness of this system, and undoubtedly there will be more improvements made in the process. This program has already proved workable and effective and is worth considering as a model where similar needs and conditions apply.

(Covel, 1990) Courtesy National Association for Interpretation

Friends and Community Support

Many private organizations support and encourage public or private interpretation programs. Some, such as local historical associations and art guilds, serve as the interpreters. In many counties, local historical associations provide the interpretation and the museum within local public parks. In fact, in many of these cases, the historical society led the county or city into the creation of a park and its interpretive function. Many other organizations provide collaborative programming aid by sponsoring and organizing exhibitions, contests, fairs, skill demonstrations, bird inventories, and special project work. Among the examples are Lions clubs, quilting clubs, radio stations, farm organizations, collector clubs, folk dance groups, old time fiddlers, local or state Audubon societies, Boy Scouts working on Eagle badges, university fraternities and sororities.

The following paragraphs emphasize the work of friends groups, cooperating interpretive associations, and professional societies.

FRIENDS ASSOCIATIONS

Volunteer "Friends of . . . " organizations operate throughout the natural resources field. They often precede government organizations in getting areas conserved or preserved. They often operate in the political arena as advocates of new public lands projects. Once a project gets underway, they become support groups in the political and financial aspects. Many of them lead in the interpretive work of a property through their advocacy. They identify and explain the special values of the place to the community or the nation as part of their case for protection.

- *Friends of the Wabash* in Indiana recently bore the main advocacy role for a new state park along the Wabash River, supporting the state legislators who sponsored it by lobbying citizens, local officials and other legislators with interpretive information about the historical and natural values of the area. Friends of the Wabash also supports a corridor of public hiking trails and parks along the Wabash River, in a state where private property occupies 97% of the land area and where there is strong resistance to government acquisition of land, for whatever purpose. The biggest job was persuading citizens that the area now in farmland has interesting potential.
- *Friends of He'eia* on the island of Oahu, Hawaii, interprets in a small state park. The group lobbies to expand the park to its full potential, conserving and interpreting a complete, sustainable community landscape of an historic Hawaiian village. The community included all the land from the top of the nearby mountain to the ocean bay, in one relatively narrow watershed, only a tiny fraction of it in the state park. Friends of He'eia operate the interpretive program of the state park, bringing to school groups, local residents and tourists the message of living lightly on the land to sustain a living landscape. Their depictions of the farming and fishing system of native Hawaiians enrich their boat trips and tidal pool studies. They go into the bay with visitors to monitor the problems imposed on the creatures living in the water.

Friends groups can provide tremendous assistance to interpreters who are hired after a project has moved forward. The new interpreter may wish to call on more than the most vocal and available individuals. They can provide base-line information, photographs, and data, as well as helping develop the story-line. Many of the people in friends groups have strong backgrounds in history and natural sciences. Others have know-how about local and state politics. Most of them may feel somewhat embattled if the development of the facility has taken the normal prolonged debate and campaigning to get started. It may be expected that some members of a friends group will have strong interest in the fate of the project and strong visions of how it should develop. While this may intimidate some young interpreters and managers, they can benefit greatly from information, advice, and assistance these people will offer, even if the original friends organization has disbanded or gone inactive.

Professional Associations

Interpretation Canada, the Society for the Interpretation of Britain's Heritage, and the National Association for Interpretation (NAI) provide professional interpreters opportunities to meet, exchange ideas, sharpen their skills and pick up new information from peers, and gain a sense of affirmation of their professional work. These groups hold annual workshops at the national and regional levels, where the simplest and the most sophisticated topics come under scrutiny. The annual workshop proceedings of the NAI and its two predecessors have gathered valuable practical, theoretical, and research information in volumes that all interpreters can use for guidance and ideas.

All three national organizations issue periodic newsletters and journals which help interpreters maintain contact and exchange ideas. Each NAI region issue a newsletter produced by talented volunteers who add this to their normal work as professional interpreters. The newsletters and journals represent valuable collections of the body of knowledge that identifies interpretation.

The National Association for Interpretation brought together two North American organizations in 1987, the Western Interpreters Association and the Association of Interpretive Naturalists. The new group's first annual meeting occurred in 1988. It produces *Legacy*, a refereed journal that contains essays on techniques and philosophy, technical reports, and research articles, as well as valuable advertising directly related to interpretive practice.

Among museum associations, the largest is the American Association of Museums (AAM). Its counterpart to the north is the Canadian Museums Association (addresses in Appendix). These groups have broad interests that include interpretation and education. In the past five to ten years, many articles in *Museum News*, for example, have urged greater investment in the interpretive function of museums. The AAM sponsors various services, including the federally funded Museum Assessment Program (MAP) and the Technical Information Service. MAP involves review of programs and facilities, identifying areas for improvement, including a review from the public perception. In its first ten years (1981-91) it provided more than 2,600 assessments (Igoe et al., 1991).

Four specialized and professional groups that focus on interpretive museums are the Association for Living History Farms and Agricultural Museums, the North American Indian Museum Association, the Association of Science and Technology Centers, and the American Association for State and Local History. The state and local history group has long emphasized interpretation through its published studies and training programs.

The American Association of Zoological Parks & Aquariums coordinates information and accreditation of all kinds for member institutions that provide considerable interpretive activity. It leads in the current debates over animal rights, public education, endangered species and proper care of captive animals.

The American Camping Association provides guidance, enforces accreditation standards, and published materials about interpretation to private and public youth camps throughout North America. Its *Camping* magazine carries occasional articles on environmental education and nature programming.

Summary

This chapter focused on the importance of quality personnel to achieve overall program excellence. The best interpreters have education and training in cultural and/or natural history plus communications techniques. Interpreter excellence requires expertise in the subjects being presented as well as talent in conveying the message.

In addition to university training, the best interpreters embark upon lifelong learning. Part of this continuing education is in the form of customized in-service training provided by the agency. Interpreters also continue to learn through professional conferences, avid reading related to the field, personal visits to other interpretive settings, and informal discussions with colleagues.

Ideally, a professional agency career ladder has built in recognition and rewards for those who educate, entertain, and inspire the visitors through interpretation. The best interpreters should continue doing what they do best and love most—and they should be paid according to their visibility, knowledge, talent and positive impact on the visitor experience. A few of those with managerial and interpretive skills should administer and supervise the program. Effective supervisors will encourage interpreters to contribute to a team effort and to improve individual performance. Ultimately, this gets translated into better service for the clientele.

Volunteers have multiplied rapidly within the past decade or so; they contribute mightily to many organizations. An effective volunteer program requires funding, planning, promoting, training, equipping, scheduling, evaluating and recognizing the volunteers. The effort serves as a supplement to the paid personnel, with thousands of hours of labor to accomplish important tasks.

Friends associations often advocate natural or historical preservation efforts and may give assistance to interpreters. Cooperating associations also help support interpretive efforts as nonprofit businesses that publish and sell books and other educational materials. Finally, professional associations offer opportunities to learn about the state-of-the-art, exchange ideas, hone skills, and develop a sense of affirmation for professional interpreters. Personnel, groomed through training, supervision, and support from friends groups, are the crux of the successful interpretive effort.

Literature Cited

American Red Cross. (1988). *Volunteer 2000*. Washington, DC.

Backlund, C., Dahlen, D., and Anibal, C. (1992). Sharing the vision through interpretive training. In *Proceedings, National Interpreters Workshop*, NAI. San Francisco Bay Area, CA.

Bevilacqua, S. (1993). Milestones, millstones, and stumbling blocks. *Legacy*, 4(4):24-26.

Bryant, H. C. (1960). The beginning of Yosemite's educational program. *Yosemite*, 39(7):161-165.

Bryant, H. C. and Atwood, W. W. Jr. (1932). *Research and education in the national parks*. Washington, DC: National Park Service.

Covel, J. (1990). Evaluating volunteer interpreters. In *Proceedings, National Interpreters Workshop*, NAI. Charleston, SC.

Daly, M. (1991). How to organize an effective volunteer program. *Directions*, 2(3):1,3.

Dominguez, J. and Robin, V. (1992). *Your money or your life*. New York, NY: The Viking Press.

Dutton, D. A. (1990). A thousand points of light need electricity. In *Proceedings, National Interpreters Workshop*, NAI. Charleston, SC.

Fischer, L. and Schaffer, K. (1993). *Older volunteers: A guide to research and practice*. Newbury Park, CA: Sage Publications, Inc.

Forest Service. (1988). *An analysis of the outdoor recreation and wilderness situation in the United States: 1989-2040 (draft)*. Washington, DC: U.S. Department of Agriculture.

Ham, S. H. (1992). *Environmental interpretation: A practical guide*. Golden, CO: North American Press.

Hankins, B. (1991). Professional growth is an asset to all. *Legacy*, 2(6):8.

Henry, R. (1988). Interpretation training: Quick and effective. In *Proceedings, National Interpreters Workshop*, NAI. San Diego, CA.

Igoe, K., Graziano, S., Ater, R., Beeson, A., and Kinnecome, M. (1991). A decade of service. *Museum News*, 70(3):74-76.

Lustig, L. (1985). In-service training for interpretive excellence. *Trends*, 22(4):8-11.

Miller, L. H. (1960). The nature guide movement in national parks. *Yosemite*, 39(7):159-160.

Morris, R. W. (1990). Managing volunteers in the 1990s. In *Proceedings, National Interpreters Workshop*, NAI. Charleston, SC.

Namba, D. (1991). Professionalizing interpretation: Can anyone be an interpreter? In *Proceedings, National Interpreters Workshop*. Vail, CO.

Newman, A. (1993). Volunteers help parks weather cutbacks. *Wall Street Journal* (May 19):B1,6.

Risk, P. (1982). Conducted activities. In G. W. Sharpe, *Interpreting the Environment (2nd ed.)*. New York, NY: John Wiley & Sons, Inc.

Risk, P. (1983). The incompetent interpreter—a new university product. In *Proceedings, National Workshop Proceedings*, NAI, Purdue University.

Ritter, D., Osterbauer, R., and Dahill, K. (1992). Volunteers managing volunteers. *Legacy*, 3(3):9-11.

Tilden, F. (1967). *Interpreting our heritage (rev. ed.)*. Chapel Hill, NC: University of North Carolina Press.

Tomsho, R. (1993). Volunteers aid environmental agencies. *Wall Street Journal*, (July 27):B1,7.

Vander Stoep, G. A. (Ed.). (1991). *Interpretation*: *A resource and curricula guide for the United States and Canada*. Fort Collins, CO: National Association for Interpretation.

Vander Stoep, G. and Capelle, A. (1992). Who are we interpreters, anyway? Establishing interpretive competencies. In *Proceedings, National Interpreters Workshop*, NAI. San Francisco Bay Area, CA.

Watson, M. (1986). NPS interpretive skills training program. *Trends*, *23*(2):4-8.

Zimmerman, R. (1988). Naturalist training: What the beginning naturalist needs to know. In *Proceedings, National Interpreters Workshop*, NAI. San Diego, CA.

Evaluation

Having developed the art of interpretation to a high degree, [we are] increasingly stepping back and looking at the science of evaluating interpretation.
— William Penn Mott, Jr., 1992

Evaluation refers to the process of collecting and analyzing information about interpretation. Ideally, interpreters use evaluation before and during the development stages of a program or exhibit—*front-end* and *developmental* evaluation—and after the program or throughout the time the exhibit stands—*performance* and *post-occupancy* evaluation.

This approach provides periodic assessments of the program or exhibit's is value as well as a record of baseline data for comparing future evaluations. A systematic, unbiased approach following a defined process will serve the agency most effectively.

"Evaluation of interpretation is a multidimensional process used to determine the qualities of interpretation and is an integral part of all interpretive operations. The process includes input and feedback and considers the interrelationship among people, organizations, environments, and technologies" (National Association for Interpretation, 1990).

This chapter discusses what, when, why and how interpreters evaluate. Considerable attention to this subject provides a rich literature and many trial applications (Wells, 1991). From the plethora of information, a few proven approaches were selected to show how an organization and individual can get involved in evaluation on a consistent, yet simple, basis.

WHAT WE EVALUATE

Evaluation of interpretation falls into at least four major categories of whom or what we, as professional interpreters, assess in an evaluation.

1. We evaluate visitors, their behavior and reactions, to determine whether we've arranged things properly, written and designed exhibits well, and achieved our learning objectives.
2. We evaluate individual or group "performances" by interpreters so the individuals may efficiently find ways to improve their delivery methods, messages, and interpretive approach in future presentations.

FIGURE 19.1
Evaluation of signs for legibility may indicate better ways to hold visitor attention.

3. We evaluate nonpersonal installations such as exhibits and trails to learn whether they have achieved their objectives and to modify them for greater effectiveness or timeliness (Figure 19.1).

4. We evaluate overall productivity of the program mix and facilities, to determine whether we're spending our money and effort efficiently. This evaluation will demonstrate benefits (the "products" of interpretation) that will be useful in presenting a case for funding a program or the agency.

WHY WE EVALUATE

If an interpretive program hopes to survive, it must produce a service that draws, pleases and affects people. Evaluation can help to design and adjust programs and exhibits to best serve a public.

Evaluation puts a value on interpretation. It should indicate not just the faults in the program but its strengths and the satisfactions produced.

At the popular and acclaimed parks and museums, evaluation comes almost automatically. At the Henry Ford Museum and Greenfield Village, the motivation to evaluate is a survival skill: "Our attendance . . . is driven by word-of-mouth referrals . . . " (Hood, Short, and Adams, 1992). In other words, virtually nothing can overcome dissatisfied customers. To get new customers, they rely on friend telling friend of satisfactions. Although this museum uses commercial advertising, its administrators know that they must produce visitor promoters to survive.

That helps focus interest on understanding visitor expectations and satisfactions. It helps justify studying visitor experiences—what they do and what they wish they could do, what they learned and what they'd like to know, how we did as interpreters and how they'd like us to do better. Hood, Short, and Adams (1992) summed up a main reason to evaluate: "Research has shown that it is only when a garden or museum probes the motivations, opinions, values, interests, attitudes, social interaction behavior, expectations, and satisfactions of current and potential audiences that it learns why people do or do not go to the garden or museum, and what types of programs and experiences will attract those who do not attend."

Evaluation asks for answers to many types of questions, the most common ones being:
- What do visitors say about our programs?
- Do visitors attend the presentations?

- What do visitors learn from the presentations?
- What do visitors say about the exhibits?
- Do visitors read labels?
- How long do they study the exhibits?
- What do they get from the exhibits/signs?
- Who are the visitors to the institutions?
- How does the audience change through the year and over the years?
- What do staff members say about the visitors?

These questions may start off the process. Effective evaluation demands a systematic process. It requires regular attention. Evaluations must be brief enough and efficient enough to allow them to be done regularly and with meaning.

To put it a little more systematically, Marsh (1986) gave eight reasons for evaluating:
1. To satisfy an interest in knowing our effectiveness—Am I a good interpreter?
2. To provide agency guidance in relation to its objectives.
3. To determine the educational and recreational impact of interpretation.
4. To assess cost effectiveness of various methods.
5. To provide accountability and public responsibility.
6. To convince others of the value of interpretation, providing proof that interpretation addresses and achieves important public goals.
7. To help make policy and planning decisions.
8. To provide the public a way to indicate their responses to interpretive services, beyond simple attendance data.

In summary, evaluation can stimulate improved interpretive programming to the public. Interpreters can demonstrate the value of their work, revealing its effectiveness in a systematic, convincing manner. They also can improve their craft through evaluation.

How We Evaluate

Evaluation may occur at all phases of the interpretive effort—before, during and after the preparation of exhibits or talks or hikes. Two classes of evaluation are commonly recognized:
- *Formative assessments* allow for change in the project during preparation, preinstallation or while an exhibit goes up (Screven, 1975; 1988).
- *Summative evaluation* focuses on how to do it better next time or how to make adjustments through postperformance or postoccupancy evaluations (POE).

Looked at another way, the nature or strategy of evaluation usually will be either goal-referenced or goal-free. The former evaluates how the exhibit or activity meets goals or behavioral objectives, determining whether specified measurable outcomes actually develop or not. In earlier, creative phases, the evaluation may be goal-free, opening the evaluation to reveal any unexpected effects or additions that may be made.

Finally, evaluation may be qualitative or quantitative. The qualitative evaluation describes what people might say or do; the quantitative summarizes results with numbers, scores, or costs. Both approaches usually prove useful (Bitgood, 1988) and most evaluations contain both, the strengths of one method compensating for the weaknesses of the other (Henderson, 1991).

Evaluation provides a systematic means to judge the worth, the effectiveness, adequacy, and desirability of a subject, based on the comparison of observations and data with criteria or standards (Marsh, 1986).

Evaluation is *not* intuitive assessment, such as those identified by phrases such as "well-used," or "visitors seemed to enjoy it." It does involve measuring results against defined objectives and standards. It does require a clearly stated method with data or guantitative processes that another evaluator or researcher can replicate. This will minimize subjectivity and maximize objectivity.

Too often, administrators get caught with unsystematic casual observations that answer questions only in a vague way. They usually offer no numbers. Some vague, verbal, and virtually uninformative evaluations commonly heard at park and recreation boards and in private businesses include:

- How many come? *Oh, a lot of people! We had a full house on the Fourth of July; overall, about 10 to 15 percent more than last year, I'd say.*
- Who comes? *The general public, especially campers.*
- Are they adults or children? *Both.*
- Do they stop to see the exhibits? *Oh, sure. The guest sign-in book in the nature center proves it; there are several thousand names a year and most visitors do not sign in.*
- How long do they stay in the exhibit area? *Well, some come in for a short time; others for up to an hour; some people from Colorado spent three hours in there a year ago. And many come back for more.*

Similar questions for personal performances get similarly vague answers. More than one interpreter confesses that they have really never been evaluated by their supervisor or park manager. They would at least like the courtesy of a superior in attendance.

Attendance is not enough, however, for quantitative evaluation or careful qualitative comparisons. A systematic, unbiased approach that follows a defined process will serve the agency and the individuals more effectively. The process need not be complicated. It should define three key elements:

1. the objectives, sorted into priorities of information needs,
2. the methods of collecting the data in an unbiased way, and
3. the applications or uses of the data.

Evaluation is an ongoing process (Box 19.1). It can be done in-house or with the collaboration of an outside scientist or observer at relatively low cost.

The rest of this chapter describes various processes and approaches for evaluation. Exhibit evaluation is discussed in Chapter 10, so it is only briefly mentioned here. After mentioning how to set objectives for evaluation, the chapter discusses five types of assessments: individual performance analysis, specific program evaluation, total program analysis, using visitor reactions, and assessments of productivity and quality.

> **BOX 19.1:** QUALITIES THAT SUPPORT EFFECTIVE INTERPRETIVE EVALUATION
>
> 1. Evaluation is an integral part of the management process.
> 2. All interpretive efforts should be evaluated.
> 3. The results of evaluation (both positive and negative) contribute to better achievement of an organization's mission.
> 4. Evaluation should be a continuous process.
> 5. Evaluation techniques are effective when they are appropriate for the environment, organization, and visitors.
> 6. Evaluation requires clear standards or goals.
> 7. Evaluation should occur at all levels and between levels.
> 8. Evaluation itself should be continuously assessed and modified where appropriate.
>   Source: National Association for Interpretation (1990)

SETTING OBJECTIVES OF EVALUATION

First, determine the objectives of interpretation. They may be to increase visitor enjoyment, teach the visitors something, modify visitor behavior, or some combination of these.

Second, determine objectives or criteria of the evaluation. Three general types exist:

- *Interpretive effectiveness* evaluation asks if interpretation produces the desired results.
- *Interpretive efficiency* asks what results came from various inputs of time and effort.
- *Cost effectiveness* asks how many desired results come from the interpretive inputs or how one type of program compares with another on the basis of cost per visitor contact hour.

Third, make sure the evaluation can have an effect. Evaluation usually aims at improving interpretation, so it has little value unless it can result in some modification of the services provided (Marsh, 1986). For example, post occupancy evaluation (POE) of permanent exhibits may be good only for the next exhibit or museum (unless the evaluation focuses on moveable labels or artifact arrangement). Little value arises unless the agency plans to use the POE on another exhibit, visitor center, or museum. Likewise, evaluation of an interpreter giving a hike has little effect on productivity if the results are just filed for some future reference; the interpreter should have the comments and ideas presented soon after the program so improvements and adjustments can be quickly applied.

Individual Performance Evaluation

The most frequent and systematic assessments occur in the area of personal performance evaluation. Critiques and coaching of individual talks and slide shows occur routinely in most large museums, the National Park Service, many interpretive villages and parks, and some major county organizations. The sources of evaluation include supervisor, peers or outside experts, self-evaluation, and audience responses.

SUPERVISORY FEEDBACK

An interpretive supervisor's evaluation provides feedback to the interpreter for the improvement of individual programs. Supervisors also use this type of evaluation to determine the overall performance of the employee for continued employment or advancement. Therefore, the supervisor should plan regular, frequent attendance at programs and regularly provide objective feedback to the interpreters, with some kind of objective notes or rating system. This approach does not work well if the supervisor attends and observes only a few events.

During job orientation or training sessions, the criteria and system for evaluation should be explained. A basic list of supervisory evaluation criteria appears in Box 19.2. These (and other) criteria may be used directly as an evaluation checklist, rating each item on a one-to-five Likert scale and adding written comments or explanations for some or all items.

BOX 19.2: SUPERVISORY EVALUATION CRITERIA FOR A PRESENTATION

Interpreter:
- Professional demeanor and appearance
- Arrived early for program
- Mixed with audience
- Established rapport
- Enthusiasm
- Depth of knowledge
- Poise and confidence
- Communicates with entire audience
- Appropriate use of humor
- Nonverbal communication (e.g., eye contact, body language)
- Appropriate technical level
- Delivery (e.g., volume, pace, pronunciation)
- Reaction to unexpected situations
- Ability to answer questions

Program:
- Interesting introduction
- Clear theme
- Organization (e.g., effective sequence, subtopics)
- Effective use of visuals
- Application of interpretive principles
- Diversity of communications strategies
- Accuracy of information
- Memorable, effective conclusion
- Audience reaction and involvement

The purpose of evaluation is *really* to help the interpreter do a better job, to increase efficiency, to improve performance, and to document how things have developed in terms of public visitation. This comes from (1) understanding what part of the work was of greatest value and (2) which parts or attributes can become more valuable by alterations or further development. If a positive, constructive, and frequent evaluation occurs, there will be little need for subjective and mysterious evaluation by a boss who seldom really sees the interpreter perform.

As either the supervisor or the person being evaluated, concentrate on performance and results. Avoid attacks or doubts about personality, physical attributes, or personal habits (unless they disrupt performance of the unit or disturb visitors). Stick to business and the results of the business—interpretive experiences.

In critiquing, emphasize the positive. Reinforce what was done well, for example: "You did the introduction and preview very well; keep it up. Your identification skills are excellent; both the audience and I sensed your interest in careful research of the plants and birds of this area."

The positive approach can continue even where the performance was weak, but not in a wishy-washy way, e.g., "There is one major thing I'd like to share with you about improvements. When you identify thirty trees on one hike, it produces overload in the visitor's minds. They just cannot remember that much. Perhaps you could make your short talks along the trail more memorable if you came up with a couple of short stories about how early settlers in this area used each of three to five trees. Focus on their human uses so people can see how they are valuable to them. If your objective is to help people identify those trees, then you can help them find the 'tonic tree' or the 'headache tree' by some identification tips and comparisons with a few neighboring trees. You can help them reinforce the idea with a quick 'find one' quiz at the next stop. When you want to use the scientific name, relate it to how the tree is used or its peculiar characteristics so people can grab hold of the word easily. Practice the name with them; have it written on a card so they can see it as well as hear: *Liriodendron tulipifera*. Discuss its beauty and meaning. There is no advantage to doing this for every tree; by emphasizing a few colorful names, you may get them interested enough to carry on for themselves."

When a factual mistake crops up, there must be a constructive but clear correction. For most interpreters, a simple "you should check the facts about sap rising and falling; your language is picturesque but did not seem precise to me. I recommend that you consult … ." Or, "that tree identified as Ponderosa pine is really Jeffrey pine. They're quite similar, but here are the differences … ." A kindly but clear list of factual errors can be handed to the really wayward (or new-to-the-area) interpreter, perhaps better for future reference than a verbal recital of each failure in a prolonged, agonizing session.

Critiquing requires diplomacy simply because one is asking another person to change. The interpreter being critiqued has presumably spent some time and energy preparing the best presentation or exhibit possible. The evaluator is merely representing one response (hopefully an educated and sensitive one) to the message as heard.

Before the supervisor attends the event, an "involving interchange" might occur between the interpreter and the critic (Lewis, 1989). The critic might ask the interpreter "on what aspects of your presentation do you most want feedback? How can I evaluate most usefully for you?" This can create a mood of collaboration that will "drain off some of the dread" and prepare for a calm and constructive postevent meeting.

Interpreters need the emotional stability to react positively or analytically to an evaluation. They need to accept that most supervisors have a level of education or experience that qualifies the supervisor to evaluate the work of subordinates. Even if they are not experts in interpretation, they can present points of view that should be helpful.

Supervisors usually do not relish the role of critic. They do not want to argue with an interpreter about their appraisal of a program. They have little interest in hearing excuses. They seek to help the interpreter improve. Although they may not say so, they will recognize that the interpreter spent considerable time and energy preparing the presentation. A critic will be far more impressed with openness to feedback, and desire to improve than with an individual who contests each suggestion or criticism. Consistently challenging the evaluation could lead to strained relations. If the supervisor's feedback proves insightful and useful, one can politely express appreciation for a high quality evaluation that should help him or her produce more polished, better service to the visitors.

PEER EVALUATION

Another assessment may come by asking one or more peers to evaluate programs. Insist on a straightforward and constructive evaluation, using specific and objective criteria. If a colleague only says how wonderful the program seemed, there is no opportunity for improvement. Request specific recommendations for improvement.

One may also evaluate programs of his or her peers. As discussed above, strive to provide constructive feedback without devastating the person. This requires an honest, tactful response. Critiquing other's programs gives insight regarding one's own. One will learn effective strategies to employ in programs; one may also observe habits and approaches that he or she wishes to avoid.

SELF-EVALUATION

The most efficient and least threatening method of evaluation involves the interpreter checking his or her own performance. Ideally, this level of evaluation occurs after each program. Self-evaluation ranges from an overall assessment (outstanding to awful) to a formal recording of various impressions in a journal or self-improvement notebook. One may list specific questions for self-response, such as in Box 19.3, as well as some of those from Box 19.2.

BOX 19.3: SELF-EVALUATION QUESTIONS

In what ways did I show:
- Friendliness to visitors?
- High regard for resources, artifacts, exhibits?
- Concern for safety and welfare of visitors?
- Enthusiasm about my work and profession?
- A high degree of preparation for the program?
- Application of interpretive principles?
  - Did I stimulate the curiosity of visitors?
  - Did I relate information to visitors' lives?
  - Did I reveal the essence of the theme with a unique perspective?
  - Did I treat the topic within a whole, broad context?

What were my strengths that I will want to continue?
What weaknesses should I work on?
What are two things I can do to improve by tomorrow?

Personal evaluations will supplement supervisory and peer evaluations—in fact, they should be more numerous. Sometimes one will criticize oneself harder than one's supervisor. Ideally people will strive for a higher degree of excellence than expected by others. Nevertheless, the peer or supervisor will have insights and suggestions that may not occur to the individual being evaluated.

AUDIENCE EVALUATION

How the audience responds to an interpretive program provides instant feedback that an interpreter can put to immediate use. Direct observation shows instant attentiveness through smiles, applause, and alert eyes. Both positive and negative actions can be seen, recorded and correlated to a location in an exhibit hall or a portion of a talk (Wagar, 1976). Among these are:

POSITIVE REACTIONS:
- Attentiveness, eye contact, smiles, applause
- Participation and involvement
- Questions, compliments, interest after the program or viewing
- Repeat visits
- Word-of-mouth recommendations to other visitors
- Letters to the agency

NEGATIVE REACTIONS:
- Fidgeting and lack of attention, distracted movement
- Side conversations unrelated to exhibit or presentation
- Lack of eye contact (often)
- Leaving the program or short stay in exhibit hall
- Complaints, in writing or verbal, to agency or other visitors

Techniques of observing audience reactions include time-lapse photography or personal observation by a hidden third party to record audience attentiveness and reactions.

More specific audience evaluation can come from individual responses to written or oral questionnaires. This approach provides valuable feedback to interpreters and administrators. A sample of visitors responds to a set of questions to measure knowledge, attitudes, and/or enjoyment. Specific questions will vary according to the property and the purpose of the study. One example, at Florissant Fossil Beds National Monument, determined the effectiveness of hourly natural history talks in conveying (a) the theme of changing climate and ecosystems, (b) information on high country safety hazards, and (c) the mission and responsibilities of the National Park Service. The questionnaire (adapted from Griswold, 1993) appears in Box 19.4.

This questionnaire required people to write out most of their responses. Although this took more time for respondents and for analysts, it provided more detailed information than a survey requiring only yes/no or circled responses. Griswold (1993) indicated that the addition of administering the surveys "did not seem to interfere with the normal activities of the park." This rather remote, casual mountain site seems conducive to rather prolonged responses. Oral interviews with a sample of audience members, using similar questions, provide an alternative to written questionnaires.

BOX 19.4: Florissant Fossil Beds Visitor Questionnaire

Please answer the following questions based on the talk you heard today. If the ranger did not talk about the question, simply write "not covered." This information will help us serve you better and improve future programs.

1.   When did you attend the natural history talk? (Circle one)

10:00   11:00   12:00   1:00   2:00   3:00   4:00   5:00   6:00

2a. List differences in the climate and ecosystem between the fossils and today:

THEN _____   TODAY _____

2b. Why did many of Florissant's plants and animals from 35 million years ago become extinct? _____

_____

2c. How does the story of Florissant Fossil Beds relate to us today? _____

_____

3.   Were safety concerns mentioned or discussed in the talk? Yes___ No___

• If "Yes," what were they? _____

• Were you aware of these safety factors before you came? _____

4.   According to the talk, what is the mission of the National Park Service and its responsibility for this area? _____

_____

5.   Do you have any suggestions to make the program more informative and enjoyable? If so, please explain. _____

_____

Specific Program Evaluation

The timeliness and effectiveness of facilities or programs within the overall interpretive service requires evaluation. Periodic evaluation should result in updating some events or exhibits by deleting, adding, or altering the content. Current research findings may prompt changing the content of certain programs. In other instances, new or different methods may replace the way programs or exhibits have been presented. For example, in many settings, theater, music, and storytelling have replaced some of the more traditional talking programs.

Changing program attendance over time serves as one criterion for evaluating. As noted earlier, attendance figures jumped dramatically at Kananaskis Country Parks in Alberta when programs became more theatrical; they increased again when music was added (Mair and Landry, 1991).

Agency personnel usually evaluate specific programs. Assessment by staff experts can be supplemented by consulting specialists in some cases.

Most interpretive settings offer a variety of programs for the benefits of their visitors. These programs will change over time, depending on how well they serve their clientele.

COST EFFECTIVENESS FOR PROGRAM EVALUATION

In assessing specific programs, one criterion can be cost per visitor contact hour (Morfoot and Knudson, 1981; Yarde and Knudson, 1989; Veverka, 1992). Cost effectiveness evaluation presents useful information. This calculates the costs per visitor contact hour for all types of programs. For example, a sunrise hike may cost $100 to prepare and conduct (staff time). If 50 people attend for one hour, the cost is $2.00 per visitor contact hour. This can be compared to an evening slide program with 150 participants for 45 minutes that costs $300 to prepare and conduct; this program's cost adds up to $2.67 per visitor contact hour. (Both would be $2.00 per visitor contact, not considering the duration of the program.)

Simple record-keeping allows this method to operate over an entire season at low cost, thus smoothing out the vicissitudes of weather and fluxes in visitor numbers. This system allows the interpreters themselves to evaluate their own effectiveness in the various programs, at least in comparative terms. Cost effectiveness allows them to document whether one type of program is producing up to expectations or not. It allows comparisons among the various personal services, determining whether one or another merits some extra attention or experimentation. For example, if 2:00 p.m. museum tours or nature hikes are drawing only a few visitors, the interpreters can try different times and keep track of the response.

Cost effectiveness data, based on real attendance figures, permit comparisons that go beyond anecdotal memories of one or two programs. They can compare the whole programming effort, including up weeks and down. They reduce the influence of "information" such as "we had a full house at that event last year" or "those tours are always popular—lots of visitors;" these statements say nothing about real or comparative numbers. To one person, accustomed to low attendance, a "full house" can be one or two persons per bench in the shelter. To another, the term does not apply until every seat is full, there is standing room only, and people are sitting on the grass outside the shelter. A more systematic, numerical count, with the hours spent in the program, in preparation, and travel, will give future interpreters much more to go on than a "it was nice and lots of people came" type of report. From the latter, the administrator can only infer that interpretation is nice and some visitors attend some programs.

Cost effectiveness data provide administrators with objective facts that give them one firm base for support of interpretive programs. It allows interpreters a first step in considering the optimal mix of program types. As one of several measures, it helps comprise evaluation at its best.

Total Program Analysis

In budget decisions, benefits of the overall interpretive program often serve as one criterion. The assessment may also include the number and kinds of services offered, the number of visitors contacted, the reactions of visitors to facilities and programs, and some measure of actual impact on the visitors. Cost effectiveness measures also may figure in the evaluation.

A basic step involves gathering the key year-to-year data for the agency or park program. This may already exist in agency annual reports. For example, West Virginia State Parks activities data from each park come together in an annual report (McHenry, 1992). In a recent summer, attendance was 90,388 at 3,519 activities. The system's four nature centers attracted more than any other type of offering, followed by recreational activities, interpretive walks, special events, campfire programs, and crafts. The data showed that in one of these parks, for example, three interpreters offered and gave 629 programs, with an average attendance of 28 (McHenry, 1992). Their offerings included walks, slide programs, nature movies, campfire programs, recreational activities, Junior Naturalist, crafts, car tours, nature center, bug-beetles-butterflies, wild bunch, fitness walk, and special events. Data on attendance at each of these activities provided further information for evaluation and future strategy planning.

Total program analysis can be done from within and/or by outside evaluators. The latter will best provide spot studies of operations throughout a year, as well as a fresh look at the way things operate and the levels of visitor satisfaction. The agency staff can objectively collect the detailed program, attendance, and cost input data.

Discussions in staff meetings can start the process, with some limits and structure to prevent wallowing in self-pity or excuses or self-glorification. Giving the whole process over to a few individuals as a committee leaves many feeling excluded and therefore not particularly ready to accept the results. Some sort of mix of informal and formal (written) discussion and questioning should include all. Then, a few people tackling some of the tough issues, then bringing them back to the whole staff for discussion, with iterations of this procedure several times may provide a fair, inclusive system for all. Respect all opinions, even those from the less assertive people who do not always express themselves in the best boardroom fashion.

If the "organization" amounts to only one to five people who really can do an internal evaluation, they probably can operate as a committee of the whole, developing and responding to a set of questions and then making positive, constructive suggestions. In some cases, small groups may need some outside intervention, perhaps from a neutral party who can help identify and sort out the validity of complaints about individuals who seem to be holding up progress or who are not carrying their load. The outside observer can depersonalize the discussion, breaking through the chain of command somewhat, perceiving whether complaints are personal fault-finding or serious impediments to progress.

MUSEUM ASSESSMENT PROGRAM

Many institutions such as museums and visitor centers get no formal objective evaluation of exhibits or total programs, although visitors and staff often have their own unrecorded reactions. To overcome this problem and to stimulate long-range planning, the American Association of Museums (AAM) developed a structured, yet flexible evaluation procedure for its member museums and their programs. Started in 1981, the Museum Assessment Program (MAP) seeks to help museums cope with forces of change. Self-study and peer review identifies museum strengths and weaknesses and finds areas that need improvement. It encourages long range planning and supports efforts to obtain funding (Igoe et al., 1991). Professional standards guide some of the evaluation. One phase involves a Public

Dimension Assessment. This reviews a museum from the outside in, discovering the public's perception, experience and involvement in the museum. Over the first ten years of the program, 700 mid to senior level professionals helped in the assessments of 2,600 museums. The processes and materials are now part of the Cooperstown (NY) Graduate Program in museum management.

SELF-EVALUATION OF THE ORGANIZATION

As an organization develops, the first flush of success may wear off, then something of a decline in interpretive attendance may occur. The time comes when members of the organization look inward—what went right? what went wrong? what should be done to stimulate customers and programming?

No single format or technique for critiquing internally emerges as superior; every group operates somewhat differently. Statistics offer a basis for systematic evaluation. Trends and comparisons give the numerical basis for determining areas that may need attention. Just having services available does not guarantee that visitors will use them. A study at Yosemite National Park revealed that 79 percent of the auto passengers arriving in the valley were aware of ranger-led programs. Only 14 percent attended one, however. The major reason for not participating was "not enough time" (Mott, 1992). Yet 34 percent of the visitors used interpretive trails and exhibits in visitor centers. Base numbers such as these help in gauging the numerical performance of an individual or group.

SELF-ANALYSIS QUESTIONS

Whatever the organizational structure, one way to proceed systematically involves posing and answering a series of questions objectively and constructively. Such a list might parallel those proposed by Osterbauer (1988) for a nature center concerned about its environmental education program.

Basic facts:
- Is participation by area schools increasing, decreasing, or maintaining itself?
- Do people return regularly to become involved in other programs?
- Is the staff (volunteer or professional) larger or smaller than it was five years ago?
- Does budget control/limit the program or does program control/increase the budget?
- Has the budget grown over the last five years to maintain its buying power or has it decreased in relation to inflation?

Demand and supply:
- Are teachers requesting more programs than the staff can provide?
- Have the programs changed over the year to meet a changing society, or are they the same programs that were offered five years ago?
- Are the programs designed around concepts and principles or around interesting facts of history or nature?
- Are the programs designed to be a quick fix or part of a systematic approach to environmental/cultural learning?

Outreach:

- Does the professional staff support other community projects to increase the visibility in the organization's respective areas?
- Does the professional staff actively promote a program or does the staff wait for the public to come to them?
- Is the local school administration aware of the services provided by the staff and the potential of the services as well as the resources which are offered to complement the school's educational curricula?

Responses to this or a similar set of questions may start with a yes or no, but some should provoke spin-off questions that review programs and efforts. For example, the last three questions on outreach may quickly lead to discussion of how to more effectively market the program. Osterbauer (1988) concluded that "We can no longer afford to sit back and let our users come to us with requests; we need to go to potential users, seek out new markets and promote our organization." He also noted the growing tendency to charge for specific services and programs. This may help provide direct feedback from the clients and a sense of increased responsibility for quality from the interpreters. The adage "you get what you pay for" may affect people's concept of services. In an age when a few dollars to rent a videotape seem readily available, even to the lowest-income American families, a rich learning experience at an interpretive center may be worth a reasonable charge.

Visitor Reactions

The users provide the financial support for interpretation, either directly, through fees and donations, or indirectly through taxes. Their opinions should be part of any evaluation. One quantitative approach involves importance-performance analysis. Another of the many methods gathers qualitative information from focus groups. Both of these approaches have been used for interpretive program analysis.

IMPORTANCE-PERFORMANCE ANALYSIS

This form of evaluation comes from the marketing field. Importance-Performance Analysis allows management to develop action strategies without being versed in complicated statistical procedures. This approach bases evaluation on consumer rankings of facilities and programs (Guadagnolo, 1985). To illustrate the idea, the following four steps led to an analysis of the Sugarlands Visitor Center in the Great Smoky Mountains National Park (Mengak, Dottavio, and O'Leary, 1986).

1. Compile a list of attributes that describe the object of study (e.g., the list from Sugarlands Visitor Center in Box 19.5). At any site, the list will require modification.

BOX 19.5: ATTRIBUTES FOR EVALUATION OF A VISITOR CENTER

Setting of the Visitor Center
1. Conveniently located near park entrance.
2. Appropriate building for the location.
3. Relays a feeling of welcome to the visitor.
4. Parking spaces adequate.
5. Has easy access for handicapped persons.

Restroom Facilities
6. Clean and fresh smelling.
7. Necessary supplies present.
8. Uncrowded.

Information Services
9. Personnel friendly and receptive to visitors.
10. Personnel knowledgeable of park events and activities.
11. Campground locations and vacancies listed.
12. Specific information on places of interest within the park available.
13. Park maps readily available.
14. Computer with visitor information available.
15. Warns of potential dangers or problems within the park.
16. Describes park rules and regulations.

Literature Sales Area
17. Quality items available.
18. Good selection of items.
19. Items reasonably priced.
20. Easy to tell which items are official park publications.

Exhibits Area
21. Captures and holds the interest of the visitor.
22. Follows a theme or logical series of ideas.
23. Describes natural features of the park.
24. Describes historical features of the park.
25. Describes important and unique characteristics of the park.
26. Relays information to children through exhibits.
27. Stimulates family/group discussion.
28. Visually appealing.
29. Easy to figure out how to move through the area.
30. Has a good variety of methods to present information about the park.
31. Exhibits are easy to see and read.

General Features of the Visitor Center
32. Encourages exploration of the park.
33. Creates an awareness of the importance of the park.
34. Helps develop an appreciation of the park.

---

2. Develop and conduct a questionnaire and use it on a sample of visitors. First, ask them to rate the importance of each attribute in an ideal visitor center (or other situation). Second, rate the performance of the same attribute in the actual visitor center. Use a Likert scale with ratings from low (1) to high (5) levels.

3. Calculate the average perceived importance and performance for each attribute from the responses.
4. Present the data in an action grid (Figure 19.2), where each attribute is plotted (Figure 19.3). Divide the array with "cross-hair" lines at some middle-occurring value of the data, so managers can segregate and identify areas where attention should be given.

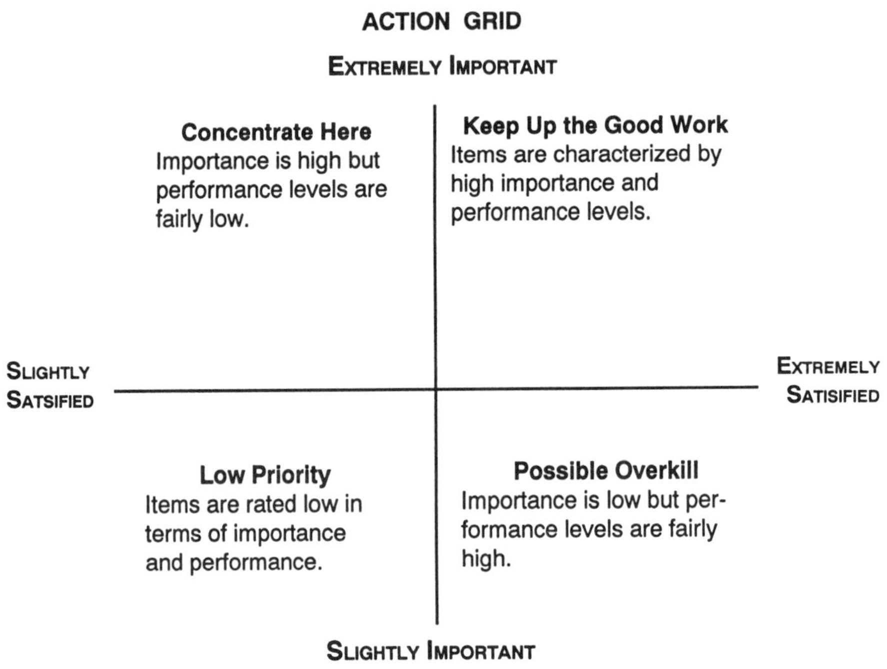

ACTION GRID

EXTREMELY IMPORTANT

Concentrate Here
Importance is high but performance levels are fairly low.

Keep Up the Good Work
Items are characterized by high importance and performance levels.

SLIGHTLY
SATSIFIED

EXTREMELY
SATISFIED

Low Priority
Items are rated low in terms of importance and performance.

Possible Overkill
Importance is low but performance levels are fairly high.

SLIGHTLY IMPORTANT

FIGURE 19.2
Sample Action Grid (Martilla and James, 1977)

The quadrants in the action grid can send the following messages:

"Concentrate Here" quadrant contains features that visitors rate as important, yet received low marks on performance.

"Keep up the Good Work" quadrant contains important attributes that were well met, receiving high marks.

"Low Priority" quadrant features got low importance marks and low performance ratings; there are problems, but they are not serious to the visitors.

"Possible Overkill" quadrant contains attributes rated low in importance but high in performance. Perhaps less attention is necessary for these low priority items.

In Figure 19.3, the Sugarlands Visitor Center got generally high ratings, but three attributes appeared in the "Concentrate Here" quadrant. One concerned interpretation of historical features and two dealt with restrooms. The museum design focuses only on natural

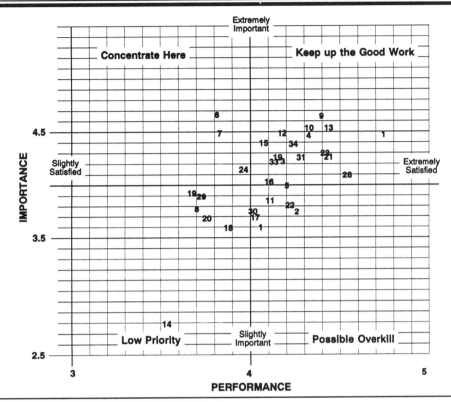

FIGURE 19.3
An Action Grid Showing Results of an Evaluation of Sugarlands Visitor Center in Great Smoky Mountains National Park. Numbers Represent Attributes Listed in Box

features, but visitors wanted something on historical facts—perhaps because this is the park's introductory and orientation center for most visitors. The attribute that received the lowest rating in both importance and performance was the availability of a computer with visitor information (Mengak, Dottavio, and O'Leary, 1986).

This technique could cover the full range of interpretive services offered, from self-guided tours to evening programs. It could provide interpreters and managers with the visitors' viewpoints on how to better serve park visitors.

FOCUS GROUPS

Another tool used to assess reactions of visitors to programs and facilities provides qualitative information through the focus group approach. This amounts to structured group interviews with about ten participants. Discussion focuses on interpretive services (or other subjects) and their effects on the people. Visitors who are willing to participate meet in a group and respond to questions about what they did and did not like about various interpretive services. A moderator guides the discussion with open-ended questions. Focus groups can provide relatively inexpensive, valuable suggestions and impressions, often producing easily-implemented solutions (Medlin, 1992).

Focus group methodology allows an interpreter or museum curator to study visitor attitudes in a qualitative manner. This technique, used by fast food chains and other retailers, helps in understanding visitor expectations (previsit) and immediate reactions after a visit or program. It involves only a cooperative group of people involved in a rather intensive, controlled procedure.

The J. Paul Getty Trust produced a book and video of results of focus group work in eleven art museums around the U.S. (Walsh, 1991). Groups of eight to twelve invited citizens volunteered to be in the focus groups. Each museum had four groups, in addition to a staff group that set the objectives and scope of the trials. Two groups came from museum visitors; two others were people who were not museum-goers. They had a brief group discussion of expectations before the museum visit; some reporting that:

- I never heard of anything important being in a museum.
- It contains things (art) I would not understand or enjoy—it is supposed to mean something, but it does not to me.
- I do not know what to expect.

Then the individuals toured the museum, keeping a diary of their experiences.

Returning after their visit, they discussed their impressions again in the small group. A trained person who used a set of open-ended questions led both discussions. The second group discussion focused on how they felt about the experience, their preferences and responses, as well as difficulties and improvements they might suggest. Meetings were videotaped and watched by museum staff from behind one-way mirrors (with the visitors' consent). Later, the museum staff group met to discuss the comments of visitors. They claimed to gain "an unprecedented understanding of the audience" (Walsh, 1991). A sampling of visitor's comments in the second meetings follows:

- In no way was it boring; exciting, excellent work.
- I enjoyed the still life the most, which is remarkable to me!
- I did see things I did not understand and others I could have done; I wondered why they were selected as great art.
- It was a rat maze—impossible to find your way around!
- Really there was no information, no history behind it.
- The brochure or calendar was too long; I had to read everything to understand.
- The tour guide was marvelous.
- There was no sitting area; I could not sit and absorb the art.
- It was hard to read the labels for some people.
- The new orientation slide show put a frame around the whole exhibition for me.
- It was nice to be where you could wander around quietly and not worry about someone taking your wallet.
- I want "them" to do the work for me—a quick video of what I'll see and then give me clear cues as to where to go and what I'm seeing.

These comments suggested the two major gaps between staff expectations and visitor experiences:

1. orientation and direction gave problems in all eleven museums;
2. information on the works, the museum, and the artists led the list of desired interpretation.

Visitors revealed in this project that they want interpretation, considering it a vital part of the art museum experience. And some of them specified the kind of interpretation they wanted. The visitors to the Denver Art Museum asked for "interpretive materials that articulate how the values and world views of an artist, a user of an object, or its patron affected the aesthetic quality, technical virtuosity, and/or iconography of an artwork." At the Dallas Museum of Art, the focus group asked for more background and explanatory information, including history, geographic and chronological orientation. They asked for signs, text panels, larger labels and videos. Visitors to a test gallery of the Cleveland Museum of Art unanimously sought more information. They found it difficult to read labels (size and location) and noted that the staff had used obscure art historical terms (Walsh, 1991).

A focus group provides diverse and complex information. It takes a while to transcribe it from tapes and understand it, even though the discussion sessions are only ten to forty minutes long. The museum staff, however, can ask visitors questions, both philosophical and practical, ranging widely, without concern for quantification of set responses. The method elicits suggestions for improvements and can give an idea of whether people liked or disliked specific services. The first person testimony, when played back, helps the staff examine goals. It may stimulate communication among museum departments. The free-wheeling nature of the responses allows ideas and observations to crop up that might never appear in a more structured questionnaire or less structured suggestion box approach.

With these advantages, there are some limitations. The method is fairly expensive, although this may vary considerably. A focus group is not a representative sample of visitors. Its small size does not allow generalization or statistical analysis. The method is not particularly useful unless the museum staff intends to use it. It provides little or no direct benefit to the focus group members (Walsh, 1991).

THE SILENT EVALUATIONS—VISITORS' IMPRESSIONS

Evaluations by peers, supervisors, or structured visitor groups offer very useful, focused, constructive ways to improve the presentations. Yet, the ultimate—and usually unmeasurable—evaluation is summed up in the minds and emotions of visitors who walk into a place and walk out without ever being questioned or timed or even signed in. They do not know of all the excuses or awards the agency has. They just know the impressions that they get when they go out somewhere for a bit of interpretation. Sometimes these impressions are unfavorable; usually they are quite favorable.

Often, the only way for interpreters to learn about the real impressions they create comes through anonymous evaluation by critical inspectors who will volunteer information and ideas.

THE INTERPRETER AS VISITOR/EVALUATOR

Interpreters themselves can get a new perspective on their own operations by visiting other places, anonymously, as a client. The change in perspective may produce greater sensitivity to clients and less focus on the bureaucracy.

One interpreter at a state facility now stresses to her staff the need for constant interaction with the visiting public. Recently, she made fifteen unofficial visits to other interpretive facilities. Only once did a staff person greet her. Generally, she saw no one unless she went to the office or arrived when a program was scheduled. This unhappy finding caused her to reinforce her policy of greeting every group that enters her center and inviting them to ask questions. During the summer and off-season weekends, one person of the small (one to three) staff stays visible in the main visitor area as much as possible. This results in much spontaneous interpretation. These interpreters do not simply sit behind a desk, occasionally announce that a film is about to start and wait until a visitor asks the right leading question. They introduce the visitors to the facility, its solar energy features, the property they are visiting, other neighboring agencies, and refer them to publications for more information.

The authors of this book recently visited several hundred visitor centers, museums, historical farms, forests, camps, tour boats, nature centers, and other interpretive activities in seven countries. They went as tourists, wandering around, taking in programs, reading signs, trying to find their way. Fortunately, dozens of fine experiences proved that interpreters work hard to do their jobs well, showing real interest in people.

Three **atypical** cases produced negative reactions and awakened a sensitivity to the importance of accountability from the public's perspective. This type of evaluation may be important to any interpretive agency.

Case 1

In a major public facility during a busy, warm May week, programs were limited to the weekend. The two visitor centers had one cooperating association employee and one seasonal employee at the desks.

Inquiry revealed that the park had fourteen interpreters employed plus others to take care of environmental education. That produced one bewildered and frustrated visitor who had driven 100 miles to observe the interpretive work (*lesson: call ahead if you want interpretation*). Self-guiding efforts were minimal, with one pamphleted trail outside each visitor center, plus some informative wayside exhibits. There were no roving interpreters at key sites, although the park's well-known spring flowers had hit their peak. No interpreter was on the trails.

Perhaps 50 percent of the staff was off during the midweek. But it was not comforting to know that there was no programming except four programs per weekend plus "holding down the centers" by fourteen (or even seven) interpreters.

This operation had seven supervisors and assistant supervisors, most of whom seldom present a program or do actual interpretive work. Who is being bilked? The salaries are low, but the more the person earns, the farther back into the recesses they go, to serve the agency, not the visitors. Rather than multiplying their own work, they subtract their own efforts and explain why there are no programs— "we're really short on people this year." Where is the production for May? The visitor/evaluator was impressed by seeing the operation from the visitor's point of view. Although this park has a fine reputation within its agency, it didn't produce for the clientele, at least in May.

Case 2

This case reinforced the sense that some interpreters are not very productive. During a summertime visit to a somnolent but prominent small park, a rather rumpled woman behind the desk at the visitor center seemed more interested in continuing her discussion with the association clerk than in providing interpretation. During about 30 minutes, this woman interacted perfunctorily with about ten visitors (middle of the week, middle of the day). She made no attempt at interpretation. The level of the conversations was in short answers to directional questions. She invited no one to see the exhibits in the adjacent room. When asked when the programs were, she said there were none except a weekend blacksmithing demonstration and something about a whisky still talk on Sunday(!). When were the hikes, the talks? There were none except one or two on some Saturdays. Were there any interpreters working in the park? "Yes, there are four of us." It took a second look to determine that she was wearing a uniform. Her three full-time colleagues were nowhere to be seen. Evaluation of productivity seemed badly needed.

Case 3

In another case, upon entering Unit Two of a large urban recreation area (the first unit offered fine interpretation) early Friday afternoon in midsummer, the gateman was doubtful that any interpreters could be found—*folks here sort of kick back on Fridays.* He was correct. Except for a few nice exhibits at the small entry building, nothing inside this large historical area suggested that visitors were welcome or provided for. A few old exhibits leaned haphazardly in a messy classroom used for a well-publicized environmental education program—but no one was anywhere near. No signs substituted for absent interpreters. The superintendent's office complex had an official air, not comfortable for visitors. No signs pointed to other facilities where visitors might go; nor were there directions as to what kind of experience might be enjoyed. It seemed like an interpretive desert.

Productivity and Quality

The quality of interpretation is closely allied with interpreters' productivity. One aim of programming is to provide interpretation in an efficient way so as to maximize the number of quality contacts.

> *A fundamental problem with conventional*
> *interpretive planning in land managing agencies*
> *such as the Forest Service has been an*
> *inattentiveness to outputs.*
>   —Pulsipher and Parker (1980)

The real output—the impact of interpretive programs on visitors—has been the subject of considerable debate (e.g., Machlis, 1986). Dustin and McAvoy (1985) suggested that most contributions of interpreters are intangible and beyond the bounds of current measurement practices. For example, Risk (1992) advanced the notion that interpreters should present deep sensitivity for the environment, "a special perception that translates into rich personal experiences" with intellectual and emotional overtones. How can an interpreter know for sure whether audience members respond to intangible, emotional overtones. A few musicians do it with golden platters and big paychecks. Interpreters can best document it through qualitative research, along with attendance figures. Focus groups provide one form of qualitative idea-gathering. Another form comes from qualitative structured interviews (Csikszentmihalyi, 1990) and applications in the interpretive field (Beck, 1993).

Interview questions that have potential for assessing some of the deeper meanings of an interpretive experience may include the following:

- Why did you come to this setting?
- What were the highlights of your visit? Explain.
- Which of the interpretive facilities did you use?
- Explain what you liked most and least about each.
- Which of the interpretive programs did you attend?
- How valuable were the interpretive facilities/services to your enjoyment of the area?
- What does this setting mean to you?
- Was that meaning enriched by interpretive efforts?
- To what extent were you provoked to want to learn or experience more about this area? Explain.
- Describe your reaction if interpretive facilities/services were not available to you at this site.
- Would you classify your experience at this site to be a life enriching one? If so, explain. If not, how could it reach that level, if at all?

Respondents answer open-ended questions in their own words. Results can be transcriptions of the taped narratives or content analysis can condense the data. Enumeration counts the frequency of the appearance of key words or phrases (Howe, 1988), which can be supplemented by representative respondent testimony. The currently popular phenomenological or qualitative evaluation has greatest value in documenting the richness of experience that interpretation can produce. This should help administrators and fund-appropriating bodies who may question the credibility of interpretation.

PRODUCTIVITY AND NUMBERS

Both quality of experiences and numbers of people reached comprise measures of total productivity. Interpreters seek to spread the message of the importance and meaning of their resources to as many as possible. Great interpreters seek to reach all the visitors and those who might visit or have an interest. Great interpreters seek to provide these people with high-quality messages. Less imaginative (but competent) interpreters often react to messages about productivity as if they were threats of some kind—almost as if revealing attendance figures would jeopardize their job or future funding. Others argue that "the numbers game" (as some put it) will automatically dilute quality (Yarde, 1989).

From many personal observations in the field, seldom do numbers of visitors get so large that they cause a sacrifice of quality. In reality, the interpreters who deal with large numbers of visitors adapt their styles of delivery and intensity of program so they may increase quality.

Summary

Interpreters and administrators evaluate interpretation for survival and for better service. They evaluate to assign value to the work. They evaluate to know whom they reach and how well.

Interpreters evaluate to identify and retain what works best for their clients as well as what needs improvement. They measure strengths as well as weaknesses.

Evaluation should measure the interpretive outputs—the visitor experiences—that interpreters plan as an integral part of forest, park, camp, or museum management (Pulsipher and Parker, 1980). It should also measure the processes and performances they use to produce those interpretive products.

Evaluation takes place during design and development as well as after performance or exhibit installations. It can focus on interpretive effectiveness, interpretive efficiency, or cost effectiveness. Interpreters evaluate individuals, specific programs, total program efforts, visitors, and overall productivity and quality.

Interpreters use both qualitative and quantitative criteria and methods of assessment. They include individual critiques, cost effectiveness analysis, organizational self-analysis, importance-performance analysis, focus groups, and systematic observations, among others. Objective, systematic approaches that reduce individual bias offer building blocks for future development, but much evaluation of this art-form requires feedback in the form of subjective reactions. Both the evaluators and the interpreters have to seek the equanimity and emotional stability to permit the process to be helpful and positive.

The expressed and implied attitudes of managers, curators, and administrators can favorably or negatively affect the success and enthusiasm of the interpreters. The investment of time and effort in evaluating these key public contact people called interpreters will do much to encourage them. The administrator often holds the key to providing support and assessment.

The most important message of this chapter urges that every exhibit, every performance, every summer season, every service, and the entire program merits some kind of serious, systematic, open, fair analysis, even if it is by the process of self-evaluation. Without using the various types of evaluation presented here, the interpreters have little basis for asking for new funding, new positions, and continuing support of administrators and funding sources. Likewise, unless they provide for evaluation, the interpreters and curators have only a vague sense of how effectively their programs serve the public—or even what public they serve now and perhaps could serve with minor adjustments. Without evaluation, they can do little to put a value on their work and seek to improve it.

> *Not to alter one's faults is to be faulty indeed.*
> —Confucius

Literature Cited

Beck, L. (1993). Optimal experiences in nature: Implications for interpreters. *Legacy*, *4*(1):27-30.

Bitgood, S. (1988). Visitor evaluation: What is it? *Visitor Behavior*, *3*(3):6-7.

Csikszentmihalyi, M. (1990). *Flow: The psychology of optimal experience.* New York, NY: Harper and Row, Publishers, Inc.

Dustin, D. and McAvoy, L. (1985.) Interpretation as a management tool: A dissenting opinion. *The Interpreter*, 16(Spring):18-20.

Gaudagnolo, F. (1985). The importance-performance analysis: An evaluation and marketing tool. *Journal of Park and Recreation Administration*, *3*(2):13-22.

Griswold, M. (1993). Evaluation tools for personal services interpretation. *Legacy*, *4*(1):12-16.

Henderson, K. (1991). *Dimensions of choice: A qualitative approach to recreation, parks, and leisure research.* State College, PA: Venture Publishing, Inc.

Hood, M. G., Short, E., and Adams, G. D. (1992). Audience research helps informed decisions. In *Visitor Studies: Theory, Research, and Practice*, Vol. 4—Collected Papers, 1991 Visitor Studies Conference, Ottawa. Jacksonville, AL: Center for Social Design.

Howe, C. (1988). Using qualitative structured interviews in leisure research: Illustrations from one case study. *Journal of Leisure Research*, *20*(4):305-324.

Igoe, K., Graziano, S., Ater, R., Beeson, A., and Kinnecome, M. (1991). A decade of service. *Museum News*, *70*(3):74-76.

Lewis, W. J. (1989). Some thoughts on critiquing. *Journal of Interpretation*, *13*(1):19-20.

Machlis, G. (1986). *Interpretive views.* Washington, DC: National Parks and Conservation Association.

Mair, S. and Landry, C. (1991). Musical theater in interpretation: The Kananaskis Country model. In *Proceedings, Third Global Heritage Interpretation Congress.* Honolulu, HI.

Marsh, J. S. (Ed.). (1986). Natural and cultural heritage interpretation evaluation. Ottawa, ON: Interpretation Canada.

Martilla, J. A. and James, J. C. (1977). Importance-performance analysis. *Journal of Marketing*, *41*(1):77-79.

McHenry, K. (1992). *1991 summer nature and recreation program attendance report.* Charleston, WV: West Virginia State Parks, internal report.

Medlin, N. (1992). Tools for evaluating interpretation. In *Proceedings National Interpreters Workshop*, NAI, San Francisco Bay Area, CA.

Mengak, K., Dottavio, F. D., and O'Leary., J. T. (1986). Use of importance-performance analysis to evaluate a visitor center. *Journal of Interpretation*, *11*(2):1-13.

Morfoot, C. F. and Knudson, D. M. (1981). A cost analysis approach for evaluating interpretation. In *Program Papers, National Workshop*, AIN-WIA, Estes Park, CO.

Mott, W. P., Jr. (1992). Changing the interpretation emphasis. *Legacy*, *3*(5):8.

National Association for Interpretation. (1990). *Preparing for the 21st Century: Solving management problems through interpretation.* Ft. Collins, CO.

Osterbauer, R. (1988). Has the mission gone astray—Where does it need to go? *Mini Journal of Interpretation*, *1*(1):5.

Pulsipher, G. L. and Parker, T. C. (1980). Integrating interpretation into land management planning: A Forest Service case study. In *Proceedings, National Interpreters Workshop*, NAI, Cape Cod, CT.

Risk, P (1992). Interpretation and intangibles. *Legacy, 3*(5):6-7.

Screven, C. G. (1975). Exhibit evaluation: A goal referenced approach. *Curator, 19*(4):171-190.

Screven, C. G. (1988). Formative evaluation: Conceptions and misconceptions. In S. Bitgood, J. T. Roper, and A. Benefield, (Eds.), *Visitor Studies—1988: Theory Research, and Practice.* Jacksonville, AL: Center for Social Design.

Veverka, J. (1992). An objective look at interpretation. *Legacy, 3*(6):26-27.

Wagar, J. A. (1976). Evaluating the effectiveness of interpretation. *Journal of Interpretation, 1*(1):1-7.

Walsh, E. (Ed.). (1991). *Insights; museums, visitors, attitudes, expectations: A focus group experiment.* Los Angeles, CA: J. Paul Getty Trust.

Wells, M. (1991). *Evaluating interpretation: An annotated bibliography.* Ft. Collins, CO: College of Forestry and Natural Resources.

Yarde, N. (1989). "Cost effectiveness of interpretive programs, personnel, and agencies." West Lafayette, IN: M.S. thesis, Purdue University.

Yarde, N. and Knudson, D. M. (1989). Cost effectiveness of interpretive programs. In *Proceedings, National Interpreters Workshop*, NAI, St. Paul, MN, pp. 445-454.

Legacy and Growth of a Profession

The interpreter can be a mighty factor in helping people to determine how they will best spend their leisure hours. People are made and nations perpetuated through the right use of leisure time.
—Mills, 1920

Interpretation, an art of transmitting science, history, fine arts, and traditions of diverse people, has a long history as a folk form. As a modern profession, it has diverse origins in North America, ranging from mountain guides to museum educators and teachers.

For the authors purposes, this book traces formal natural history interpreters to Enos Mills in Colorado and his contemporaries in California and Bear Mountain, New York. They started serving clients at mountain resorts and parks. They mixed strong doses of lectures, guided walks, exhibits, and nature trails with the outdoor environment. Mills' book in 1920 defined how nature guiding could best be done; many of his principles appear in this book and most others that describe how to do interpretation (e.g., Tilden, 1967; Grater, 1976; Sharpe, 1976, 1982; Lewis, 1980; Ham, 1992).

The lineage of museum interpretation is not so clear, but it is of about the same age, with much earlier progenitors. Museums, as well as camps, parks and resorts, maintain their long tradition of providing customers with ways to understand their collections or their environment. They provide skills training so the visitors develop ways to enjoy their facilities more expertly.

A View of the Past

Nature interpretation in national parks started long before the National Park Service existed (Table 20.1). Most of it was supplied privately. In Yellowstone's early days, for example, stagecoach drivers described the park to their passengers " . . . in a vein of bold invention. A few voluble guides worked out of the hotels; they cruelly punished the natural sciences. . . . There was little on-the-spot enlightenment" (Shankland, 1954). On the other hand, the private organization called Wylie Camps offered exceptionally good interpretive services for Yellowstone visitors.

The government also got involved well before the 1916 birth of the NPS. Soldiers at Yellowstone and Yosemite, for example, interpreted to many visitors, some of them gaining considerable skill in the natural and geological sciences. Archæologists at Mesa Verde offered tours of the cliff dwellings and started a museum. U.S. Geological Survey writers focused on the natural history of the parks through a series of government pamphlets with photos and drawings on coated paper. These, in 1912, accompanied an article by Laurence F. Schmeckebier, chief of publications for the Department of the Interior, entitled "The National Parks from the Educational and Scientific Side" in *Popular Science Monthly*.

FIGURE 20.1
*C. M. Goethe, adventurer, writer, and philanthropist, had the early vision and drive to bring nature interpretation to American resorts and parks.
(NPS, 1948)*

Charles M. Goethe enjoyed interpretation in Europe, especially Swiss nature guides, and decided to bring the idea to their home state of California (Figure 20.1). They made a trial run in 1918 with Dr. Loye H. Miller (Figure 20.2) and then, in 1919, ran a full-blown resort naturalist program with two professors.

FIGURE 20.2
Dr. Loye Miller, a UCLA professor, pioneered interpretation at Lake Tahoe resorts (1918-19) and at Yosemite National Park (1920), along with Dr. Harold Bryant. (NPS)

TABLE 20.1 CHRONOLOGY OF NATIONAL PARK INTERPRETATION

YEAR	EVENT	PARK	PERSONNEL
1869	*The Yellowstone Guidebook*	(Yellowstone)	J. D. Whitney
1886	*In the Heart of the Sierras*	(Yosemite)	J. M. Hutchings
1888	Soldiers gave visitors "cone talks"	Yellowstone	Lt. Moody
1899	University of Chicago geology summer study	(Glacier)	R. Salisbury
			T. C. Chamberlin, W. W. Atwood
			J. Paul Goode
	Harvard University Classes	(Grand Canyon)	W. M. Davis
	Columbia University Classes	several	D. W. Johnson
	about nine others studied science in future parks		
1901+	Nature guiding, "Trail School"	(Rocky Mountain)	E. Mills
1905	Archæology collection exhibited	Casa Grande	F. Pinkley
1908	Rangers led tours of Cliff dwellings	Mesa Verde	Staff
1908	Smithsonian started archæology digs	Mesa Verde	J. W. Fewkes
1911	Campfire programs well established	Yellowstone	Wylie Camping Co.
1915	Chief ranger exhibited specimens	Yosemite	F. S. Townsley
1916	National Park Service (NPS) established		
1917	Director appointed chief, education division	National Park Service	R. S. Yard
1917	First private woman nature guide licensed	Rocky Mountain	E. Burnell
1918	First NPS area museum opened by Smithsonian,	Mesa Verde	Supertendent T. Rickner,
	75 members—university presidents, representatives		C. D. Walcott
	of conservation organizations—by 1919,		R. S. Yard (executive director)
	committee merged into National Parks Association		
1918	CA Fish and Game Commission (FGC) sent educational		Dr. L. H. Miller
	director to Yosemite to deliver lectures and field		
	trips. Immediate success. Based on worldwide		
	survey by C. M. and Mrs. Goethe		
1919	CA FGC and Goethes sponsored nature programs in six		Dr. H. C. Bryant, Dr. L. H. Miller
	Lake Tahoe resorts with lectures, nature trails, guided walks		
1920	Mather, Goethe's, CA FGC sponsored field trips, lectures	Yosemite	Bryant, Miller, Enid Michael
1920	Infomation ranger/nature guide appointed	Yosemite	A. F. Hall
1920	Park naturalist appointed Yellowstone	Yellowstone	M. P. Skinner
	(1921 two, 1922 five rangers assigned)	Yellowstone	
1921	Cooperative agreement, CA FGC and NPS offered	Yosemite	A. F. Hall
	free nature guide service (government paid)	Yosemite	
	Museum opened/park naturalist appointed		
1922	Educational Department started	Yosemite	A. F. Hall
1923	Montana State University and NPS started guides	Glacier	
1923	Chief Naturalist appointed to extend to all parks	Yosemite	A. F. Hall
1923	New park naturalist appointed	Yosemite	C. P. Russell
1923-24	Beginnings made at four other parks	Grand Canyon, Mt. Rainier	
		Rocky Mountain, Sequia	
1924	Investigate, plan, policy for education	National Park Service	Dr. F. R. Oastler, A. Hall, L. Spelman
	defined duties of naturalists		
1924	American Association of Museums study and support		
	of natural history museums	large parks	L. S. Rockefeller Memorial
1925	Educational Division headquarters in Berkeley	University of CA	Secretary of the Interior
	plans for education in each park written		A. Hall
1925	School of Field Natural History started	Yosemite	H. C. Bryant
1928	L. S. Rockefeller funding for museums	Yellowstone	American Association of Museums
1928	Secretary of the Interior appointed 5 educators to		J. C. Merriam, H. C. Bumpus,
	stimulate growth of educational activities in parks		H. C. Bryant, V. Kellogg, F. R. Oastler
1929	Report of committee (Jan 9)		
1930	Branch of Research and Education	Washington Office	
1931	First park historians hired	Washington Office/	V. E. Chatelain, F. Flickinger, E. Cox
1933	44 historical areas, National Capitol Parks,	Colorado Historical	
	and Forest Service National Monuments added	Society	
	to National Park Service		
1935	Historic Sites Act authorized NPS to interpret		
	historical areas' significance		
1957	NPS interpretive philosophy in new book		F. Tilden
1965	Environmental Education programs introduced	National Park Service	

Sources: Burns (1941); Brockman (1978), other government sources

Six Tahoe resort owners cooperated, along with the California Nature Study League and the California Fish and Game Commission. The Goethe's paid the vacation salaries to Dr. Harold C. Bryant, a University of California professor and Dr. Miller, a UCLA entomologist. These two scientist-interpreters built and marked trails around the resorts. They led nature lovers on hikes, provided evening campfire talks, gave slide talks on wildlife, and showed scientific movies.

At the Goethe's insistence, a doubting NPS Director, Stephen T. Mather, dropped in on a few of the programs. He was impressed with the public response and transferred the whole operation to Yosemite in 1920. He put the two professors under the direction of a young ranger trained in forestry, Ansel Hall. Hall held the title of "Information Ranger" in 1919; in 1920, he became the "Acting Park Naturalist." Mather covered most of the costs out of his own pocket; the Goethe's also contributed. Mather followed the Miller-Bryant programs with "extreme delight" (Shankland, 1954). During the first summer, 1,381 attended field trips; 25,732 went to campfire programs; uncounted children went to "nature-play" sessions. Director (and millionaire) Mather and his friends continued to fund the spreading work in various national parks. Finally, in 1923-24, Congress began to fund interpretation through public tax funds.

Meanwhile, naturalist Hall started a museum. He collected native American artifacts such as baskets, arrowheads, pictures, and conducted oral history interviews with older American Indians still living in the park. He built a scale model of the valley, tying it to rock and soil samples that illustrated glacial action. He collected and mounted flora and fauna, wrote guidebooks, and established the Yosemite Museum Association to raise funds for buildings. The president of the American Association of Museums took over the drive, eliciting a gift of $70,500 from the Laura Spelman Rockefeller Foundation. Hall used it to build a new Yosemite museum building in 1925. He used facts and impressions from his one-year field study of museums in Europe, North Africa, and the Near East in 1923-24, sponsored by the American Association of Museums.

In 1925, Hall became the first chief naturalist of the NPS, with headquarters in Berkeley. (He added the title of first chief forester, in charge of forest fire work, in 1926.) The NPS interpretive/education work continued to expand (Figure 20.3). Parallel development started in 1920 in Yellowstone through the efforts of the Superintendent hiring a naturalist.

By 1930, there was enough activity that a Branch of Research and Education grew out of the chief naturalist office. Dr. Harold Bryant left the University of California to head it as a full-time employee with the title of NPS Assistant Director.

Part of the growth of interpretation came from its quick public acceptance and approval. The visitors came and expressed their delight. Additionally, the Director's support of "education" kept spirits high. Education ranked high among Mather's priorities and he refused to divorce it from fun. Mather, "the eternal freshman," personally organized and conducted campfire entertainment for Yellowstone in 1923 that involved an old mountain man telling yarns, musical selections by a family band, and other talent he recruited from among the visitors (Shankland, 1954).

The history of interpretation stretches far beyond the National Park Service. This agency, however, represents continuity, consistency and dedication to professional interpretation. The NPS provides a model used by many other agencies. The profession grew steadily in state parks from the 1920s to the present. County parks have added many interpreters, often with spectacular results and innovations. Commercial and private-non-profit interpretation has the longest and least-studied history. It deserves greater examination, as the trend toward pay-as-you-go interpretation continues to grow. Museum interpretive tradition came through curatorship domination, educational services, and recently, strong emphasis on interpretation in its broadest sense.

A Vision for the Future

Steve Van Matre, in his critical 1990 book, *Earth Education: A New Beginning*, contended that most interpretive programs and environmental education programs offer "little more than a field trip service that depends heavily upon the natural wonders of their site." In other words, the interpreters merely lead people to the special features and explain them. Van Matre's observation is easy to make and one may wonder why he implied that there is anything wrong with that type of service. He claimed simply that there could be more to it. The experience could change people's way of living. The objective of interpretation and environmental education, he asserted, should promote living with a lighter impact on the earth, with a more harmonious relationship between the individual and the environment—not just mentally and emotionally but also in reality.

Ted Turner, concerned citizen, and owner of the Cable News Network and other properties, asked: "The question is, can five billion people turn it around [change our way of life, our direction] in time? That is all. We're fighting against a deadline for our own survival." (Stutz, 1991). Interpreters can play a role in "getting it turned around." Their tasks are legion. A view of the future of interpretation may look something like what is described and admonished in the next few pages of possibilities. The following aspirations can serve as an agenda for where interpretation might go as a profession.

FIGURE 20.3
The 1926 Yosemite Nature Guides at the Yosemite Museum: E. Rett, R.D. Harwood, G.C. Ruhle, Enid Michael, D.D. McLean, C.P. Russell, and Dr. H.C. Bryant. Mrs. Michael and Dr. Bryant, with Dr. L. Miller and Ansel Hall, formed the first interpretive group at Yosemite in 1920. (NPS)

Interpretation for Every Park, Museum, Camp and Forest

Every park or playground can have some type of interpretation. It may be as simple as a plaque or sign explaining why the place exists or who played there or what used to occupy the site. It may be only a few signs telling the story of the trees. In some neighborhoods, the park manager may shudder at the thought of keeping signs up and fresh-looking, but there are ways.

The stories of Seattle's city parks can be read in a book (Morgan, 1979) that invites, guides, and interprets history and nature of each public open space in the city. It can be as simple as a book or as complex as having visitor centers in the major parks, reaching out with services to the smaller sites.

"Visions of what museums might be" were expressed in a book by Weil (1990). The key emphasis related to letting purpose drive museums (not objects or technical proficiency), making them "socially relevant institutions" that "... enrich our lives and enhance in powerful ways our ability to shape a better future for ourselves, our descendants, and our communities." This requires a visitor-oriented vision and a director and curators with deep content knowledge.

A Park and Interpreter in Every Neighborhood

Enos Mills (1920), one of the founders of the modern interpretive profession, foresaw:

> ... a nature guide in every locality who around his home or in the nearest park could show with fitting stories the wild places, birds, flowers, and animals, would add to the enjoyment of everyone who lives in the region or who visits it.

> Before we realize it, there will be municipal and private nature guides in every city park; official and private nature guides in state parks and in the national parks. ... It is a worthwhile life work and one that will add immeasurably to the general welfare of the nation."

That dream seems close now—certainly much closer than in 1920. Every city with a museum or zoo has some kind of interpreter. Many city and county park systems support interpreters as do private museums, camps, and nature centers. At the state level, the parks, reservoirs, and forest systems that do not offer interpretation are in the minority. Virtually all federal land agencies now offer some form of interpretive service. The goal of an interpreter in every city park has not quite arrived, but the trend remains positive. Perhaps soon the numerous and heavily used private and public interpreters of southwest Connecticut will serve as a model for the rest of the country; there, an interpreter of some kind serves the public in at least every town and city. May they multiply and reach out to all of us.

CITIZEN ACCESS TO INTERPRETERS CREATES READERS OF THE LANDSCAPE

Accessibility to interpretation is far more than providing physical ramps, wide doors and paved trails. Van Tighem (1990) called us to gather audiences in the parks and empower them to see the wholeness of ecosystems: "Our task may…be to show people that neither parks nor ecological principles, in truth, have boundaries."

More than this, the interpreter can seek to reach beyond the property boundaries. Park boundaries and museum walls can serve as the subversive element of our job. Reaching out to every visitor and reaching beyond to all citizens can serve as a goal for all interpreters. One region of the Forest Service saw this as an integral part of its management mission (Box 20.1).

BOX 20.1: WHERE INTERPRETATION CAN GO

The Southern Region of the USDA Forest Service in 1990 looked toward 1994 and wrote a vision statement for its interpretive services (IS) programs. It dealt with several elements—what the visitor gets, how interpretation fares, how the customers see and work with the Forest Service.

THE VISION FOR INTERPRETIVE SERVICES
The year is 1994. Across the Southern Region the Forest Service averages 30,000,000 visitors annually. Everyone leaves the forest having been provided with many opportunities to gain an understanding and appreciation of the natural environment, cultural resources, and the Forest Service and what it does. They have enjoyed their experience. Interpretation is valued as an integral part in communicating how Southern Region forests are managed.

In addition to personal contacts, state-of-the-art communications techniques are used to develop focused interpretive campaigns to explain key issues to forest visitors. The public is actively involved with the Forest Service in resolving common problems. Service to the visitor is recognized as a daily obligation.

Expertise from all staff areas is sought and applied to accommodate visitors and their information needs during land management, project and facilities planning. An inventory of IS facilities and programs is current.

Interpretation serves as a valuable communications tool to present the agency to the public as a leader in efficient, professional natural resource management. This supportive atmosphere generates many partnerships and cooperative ventures.

This scenario is possible because all Forest Service employees are aware of their responsibility to treat everyone as a customer, and those who have the primary job of serving the public have been well trained in interpretive techniques.

LOCAL NATURALISTS/HISTORIANS INTERPRETING THE WHOLE AREA

People need county (and city and private) park and museum interpretive programming to offer lifelong skill development for repeat visitors. The interpreter becomes the facilitator and resource who truly guides lifetime education (Figure 20.4). Interpreters can set the goal of helping all residents of a county to learn the historical and natural features of the area, to sense how it relates to the state and the nation and the rest of the world—its people, their history, its rocks, its vegetation, its rivers and ground water, its birds, mammals, insects, its industry. The interpreter helps make apparently dormant nature and history come to life in the minds of citizens of the community, state, and nation. The interpreter helps everyone think beyond the park, museum, camp, or battlefield.

FIGURE 20.4
Guiding lifetime education can be as simple as providing examples of special plantings for home gardens, as complex as complete curricula for lifetime learning.

INTERPRETERS AS SPOKESPERSONS FOR BETTER LAND USE

The interpreter serves as a key to solving a profound social problem, that of harmonizing humans with the ecosystem. Thus, the interpreter becomes a very important person for the community—an ecologist, economist, and historian, who has broad concerns with and knowledge of the whole ecosystem of the community and county (Wilcox, 1969). One major job provokes people to live so they blend with the environment, walking gently through it so they leave few unpleasant or dangerous traces.

INTERPRETERS AS VOICES OF CONSCIENCE

All the previous aspirations suggest that the interpreter, as community leader, first expresses concerns for environmental quality and the vital role of people in the ecosystem. "As interpreters and educators we can act as messengers of the future by informing people of life in the future if we are not careful in the present" (Bushor-Gardner, 1990). Secondly, the job entails provoking and equipping others to protect clean water, clean air, intact soil, plenty of trees and wildlife.

Natural history interpreters need knowledge and an informed sense of the total environment. This requires competence in botany, zoology, geology, and climatology. Add astronomy, history, archæology, forestry, wildlife, aquatics, and entomology for a complete interpreter. Obviously, few individuals are expert in all these topics, but neither can an individual interpreter remain so narrow as to lack interest or appreciation in history, for example. The field requires a person conversant and sympathetic in most of these areas demanding interpretation if interpreters are to help the public fully appreciate and enjoy their environment.

INTERPRETERS AS SCIENTISTS

In many parks and forests, the interpreter may be the chief monitor, inventory person and scientific authority. Although a science staff seems desirable, it also seems unrealistic in most places. Yet, the state and national parks and forests contain plants and animals that should be monitored. With a proper data base of what is there, managers (who also ought to serve as scientists) can document the effects of disasters such as toxic spills in streams, measure changes in vegetation, guide planning through soils information, and keep records on endangered and other interesting plant and animal species. Likewise, each park or forest can use an inventory of resources that are common and unique to the park.

Every season, the lead interpreter and/or property manager should train seasonal employees on key features and resources of the property. This involves scientific information as well as practical operations and regulations. The interpreters, clerks, and laborers all come in contact with the public frequently and all should have a strong information base about the resources of a place. Too often, this aspect of scientific management gets neglected with the excuse that mowing, cleaning, repairing and fee-collecting have immediate priority. Meanwhile the resources that form the purpose and prime features of the place get scant attention from managers—as if knowing about them and their dynamics had little importance.

If an interpreter would apply the concept of *genius loci*, as suggested earlier in this book, that interpreter must first understand the resources—the characteristics that make the place special, along with the facts and trends in those resources that keep it interesting. Without unique information and data on a particular place, the interpretation may as well all be boilerplate, spouting off the same routines and textbook principles in all parts of the country. To get with the special character of the place, get deeply into the resources that live there, using scientific and historical research at every opportunity to study and document them.

INTERPRETERS AS PROVOCATEURS

> We're all five billion of us on this little earth swimming around in space. And there's too many of us, and most of us are living incorrectly.
> —Ted Turner (quoted by Stutz, 1991)

Ted Turner, as a concerned citizen, provokes people. He proclaims his worries to an audience of millions. One of his major concerns is over-population of a finite Earth.

Turner's concern provokes argument or agreement among most people who hear him. Some spontaneously go out and search for more information. More likely, his worry about the way people live may prompt questions about how people might live differently. Museums and interpretive center personnel can help answer that through study of historical and natural and technological processes. Setting out the facts of what was and is possible and the current real impacts of human existence may be enough provocation for people to make up their minds without getting into insoluble arguments over how many people are too many, technological food supply, and who is at fault.

Care in provocation seems warranted. The rules of evidence have importance. Too often recently, the press and many interpreters seem to have jumped off the deep end of some topics, based upon only a few suggested facts and imagined outcomes. Rather than couching their interpretation in scientific and tentative terms, a few people turn into ideologues, carrying a banner that is showy, but really is nothing but cloth flapping in the breeze. For example, many people have declared firmly that the earth is victim of a human-caused global warming trend, many scientists and naturalists have even devised strategies for "helping" vegetation move North to "save" their favorite plants. While some of the circumstantial evidence suggests that this hypothesis may be true, directly measured facts conflict with the hypothesis. The delayed reaction factor and the masking by volcanic dust clouds, however, may be hiding alarming evidence of trends, just as the hypothesis suggests.

Meanwhile, many climatologists claim that they find no solid evidence of warming. Ignoring the weight of expert opinion seems imprudent. Indeed, the division of opinion about the subject gives one pause about expressing a categorical opinion. It seems more judicious, both scientifically and interpretively, to present the evidence on both sides. Then raise questions. What are people doing that may cause dangers to the planet? Can the atmosphere handle it? What reactions do some expect? Will this result in something catastrophic? Who knows? On the other hand, what evidence suggests no immediate effect? Thinking in the long run, where is the earth geologically? In this interglacial period, is the earth's atmosphere warming up or cooling down, or can scientists even tell in the short span of measurements?

Yet, some interpreters repeat the tentative global warming predictions as if they were the Final Judgment, dogmatically proclaiming them as single-mindedly as if none of the questions above existed. Some have grasped onto whatever causal agent seems current among popular magazine editors and condemn it as loudly and quickly as possible. This unthinking approach may make for fine-sounding speeches and *au courant* political agitation, but it does little to stimulate people to think rationally nor to gain confidence in the scientific acumen of their neighborhood interpreter. On the other hand, the interpreter who ignores all current news or simply discounts it out-of-hand does a similar disservice. More rational interpretation could consist of describing the issue, finding and presenting the information on **both** sides—or at least raising the questions people might ask.

Regardless of the outcome of this global warming discussion, it seems clear that people's stewardship of the environment could use some improvement—right here at home. Instead of worrying only about eventual catastrophes and debating unresolvable outcomes, the interpretive audience can examine actions that are certain to make some difference in the quality of environmental surroundings.

The same idea applies to other topics related to health and welfare. The slogan-of-the month club could become interesting as a collection item, but as a guideline for interpretive themes, it often lacks substance and validity. "Ban Sassafras; Wipe Out Cancer" would make for good bumper stickers, but not sensible science.

INTERPRETERS AS RECREATIONISTS

Interpreters enhance the recreational experience of citizens, making recreation more than games, deeper than entertainment. Interpreters need to project their interpretation objectives into other recreation programs, such as painting, music, photography, crafts (Wilcox, 1969). Interpreters need to see through the leaves and over the rocks and history books, through a refined understanding of people and how they behave. They need understanding in human relations, psychology, sociology, and motivation. They must be skilled in communications and education—e.g., speaking, persuasion, writing, display, audiovisual and technical aids, drama and performing arts. Interpreters will increasingly be looked upon as leading experts in leisure sciences and have a prime responsibility for helping to solve problems in the areas of urban pressure, racial tension, poverty, and cultural privation (Wilcox, 1969).

GADGETS HAVE THEIR PLACE—IN THEIR PLACE

With the rapid development of computer technology and related electronics, many opportunities will arise for expensive investments. Devices with letters for names will entice and plague interpreters in the quest to keep up. D.V.I. (digital video interactive) already has the archæological community of Palenque on videodisk for home and museum use. People can simulate a visit to the Mayan site in southeastern Mexico, can enter the museum, visit the rain forest, learn about hieroglyphics, and even take snapshots off the screen. C.D.I. (compact disk interactive) provides a handier and lower cost way to do similar things. Its recent 28-kiosk installation in the new Muséo Amparo Puebla, in Puebla, Mexico, provides interpretive support to the collections and exhibits in four languages (Mintz, 1991). Similar installations operate at Sea World Florida.

The new Holocaust Museum in Washington, DC, uses electronics to match each visitor with a victim, personalizing the otherwise overwhelming and dehumanizing events of World War II.

Mintz (1991) urged interpreters to consider the constraints as well as the opportunities of new technology. Some technology costs a lot. Therefore, make sure that the gadgets can be used by a wide audience, provide for various learning styles, and can be easily used and quickly learned, turning computer-phobes into technophiles. The devices must provide educational or interpretive value and—if they are truly interactive—respond to the visitor's entries.

ACCOUNTABILITY

Accountability will run responsibly throughout the system. Interpreters will just naturally take care of numbers, visitor surveys, evaluations, and quality control. In the near future, they will have peer evaluation, supervisory critiquing, and self-critiquing with tapes and reflective, self-administered questionnaires. Cost effectiveness of programs will serve as one guideline for determining balance in the programming.

Interagency cooperation in visitor centers offers one way to provide responsible interpretation at a reasonable cost. An example at Florence, Wisconsin, features a building that houses the Forest Service, Soil Conservation Service, County Cooperative Extension Service, and a large visitor contact center. Here, visitors can study a menu of information for the North Woods region. Interpretation by the Forest Service and Florence County Parks is supplemented by information from the National Parks, tourism associations, and the states of Wisconsin and Michigan.

FUNDING

Money for interpretation has seldom flowed abundantly. When it did, it lasted for only a few years in the public agencies and quasi-public organizations such as historic and art museums, YMCAs, and similar groups. Money concerns will continue to challenge interpreters. Fund-raising will occupy the attention of most interpretive organizations. The financial rewards will go to those who provide good service *and* make strong efforts to find funding.

"One thing seems certain: The 1990s promise to be years of economic hardship for many museums. Following on the heels of the relatively flush decades of the 1970s and 1980s, this is a discouraging realization" (Baas, 1990). In the early 1990s, indeed, some museums fell out of favor with the public, while public donor agencies tightened the budget and the criteria of giving. Museums, nature centers, camps, and historical communities need people with integrity, discipline, responsiveness to the public, creativity, and intelligence. They need to draw in new clients. Baas (1990) noted that "the need to attract new audiences has taken on an economic as well as a moral dimension." The positive nature of the work should take priority over time wasted in complaining about difficulties, lack of funding, and "enemies;" focus instead on listening, thinking, and doing the work of interpreting to the public.

MORE PRIVATE, COMMERCIAL INTERPRETIVE SERVICES

With federal and some state interpretive programs vacillating in their budgets and priorities of interpretation, with low pay scales in some agencies and lack of incentive for performing "stars," other alternatives become attractive.

Contract interpretation by private entrepreneurs seems to be growing and have a bright future. Some people contract directly with public park and recreation agencies, forest services, or wildlife agencies. Others contract with camps to conduct their nature education programs. Still others may find fertile ground at resorts and campgrounds. These interpreters add value to the recreational experience of the customers. Where public agencies often offer paltry rewards to those who demonstrate the superior knowledge and sensibility to be good interpreters, there are opportunities to reap the direct reward of the value added.

Some interpreters reap it directly from the customers. In England, private guides in national parks usually charge the clients for the service as the walk begins. In the U.S. and Canada, guides advertise in local tourist information centers, hotels, and resorts, take reservations, then pick up clients and take them on the expedition for a set fee. Many of them interpret the public lands, often more effectively and comprehensively than the "stay-in-the-park" government interpreter. For example, private interpreters in the Harpers Ferry region could easily lead visitors into and out of three to five battlefields in a day, supplementing the federal stops with local, state, and private features that would tie together the stories of John Brown (tracing his route and staging areas), the C&O Canal and the areas it served (including a ride on the railroad that caused its demise), or the War Between the States as it moved back and forth across this countryside.

A plush van, a good meal in an historic building or on a beautiful hillside, connections with special programs, homes, and people, plus a knowledgeable historian and naturalist could add up to $75-150 per person per day and many would call it modest. A two-day tour of key spots in Alaska can run up to $600 or more, including hotel and meals. These private guide services do not replace the public agency interpreters; they can work cooperatively and as complements to each other.

MORE INTERPRETATION BY PRIVATE, NONPROFIT GROUPS

The same rationale as above will stimulate greater efforts by nonprofit interpretive groups. As interpretation's value to people comes to the market place, their willingness to pay will help finance many organizations. Some of these may follow the examples of three groups now offering private interpretation and education.

1. Old Sturbridge Village, MA (OSV) not only takes in hundreds of thousands of tourists every year, it runs a huge summer education program in a fine facility for kids who also get to do some living history activity for the customers. Any visitor to OSV feels the sense of community and pride among the staff; it obscures the fact that these people get paid to do their tasks in the village and its fields.
2. The Wetlands Institute in New Jersey operates like a working research and action organization, holding back the tide of subdivided fill land while visitors pay to study tidewater life and swat mosquitoes. Many of the visitors are local residents, some of whom add financial stability to the endowment.
3. Camp Tecumseh YMCA near Brookston, Indiana, offers a full load of summer camping, spring and fall environmental education for all ages, and winter programming for days, weekends, or week-long challenges, environmental growth, or just plain fun. The staff develops curricular materials and teaches teachers how to use them, then supervises and supports, for a price that keeps the camp afloat financially throughout the year.

PUBLIC SUPPORT OF INTERPRETATION'S ROLES

James Ridenour, in an unpublished address to the 1983 Association of Interpretive Naturalists (AIN) National Workshop, noted the growth in commitment to interpretation in state properties. In the early 1980s, Indiana's economy was not producing the expected government revenues. The governor, instead of reducing services and laying off employees, decided the opposite. Ridenour, then Director of the Indiana Department of Natural Resources, said (from speech text): "His decision resulted in not reducing essential services and no layoffs for full-time personnel, including our interpretive staff. ...Now, that, in itself, is remarkable because we have all heard the old story that interpretation is first to go. Historically speaking, those times are in the past. Here in Indiana, our natural, cultural, and historic interpretive services have proven their worth time and time again, and I am happy to say that they are here to stay as a vital and essential part of our program."

The values of interpretation to communities and the tourism industry were emphasized by the Congress of Heritage Interpretation International, November 3-8, 1991. Its "Honolulu Charter" stated that the signees:

> . . . assert and endorse the indispensable roles of heritage interpretation and preservation in the provision of quality tourism experiences for visiting guests at every community and locality in the world.
>
> We assert and endorse that the unique heritage identity of each community and locality, including its natural and cultural resources, must be perpetuated to maintain the biological and cultural diversity, and thereby the diversity of place identities, of the entire planet. Further, such unique local heritages must be interpreted, not only to visiting guests, but to community residents themselves.
>
> We assert and endorse that heritage interpretation principles and practices, and heritage identity preservation, are at the very core of tourism development approaches such as cultural tourism and ecotourism.
>
> We hereby call upon and encourage both public and private groups to join hands in the perpetuation of global diversity and unique place identities—through the application of heritage interpretation principles and practices in all communities and localities of the world.
>
> We transmit this document to the United Nations Educational, Scientific and Cultural Organization (UNESCO) and to the United Nations Environment Program (UNEP) with a call for governments to take actions that permit and encourage the implementation of the principles of this Charter.

Interpreter Leadership in Community Life

What follows represents one vision of the future—an expansion on and application of some of the ideas presented above. It constitutes an ambitious programming effort for interpretive centers and museums. It could work, with variations, in many museums and interpretive centers.

The prototype used in imagining these ideas was a local historical museum or a county nature center. The concept envisioned such a facility operating and growing as a vital, active, burgeoning community center that develops many regular, repeat customers. They find satisfaction and personal growth in the programs and challenges presented by these centers. This conceptual center/museum seeks to serve all ages and reach the entire community. Therefore, its broad vision requires a can-do attitude and positive enlistment of community collaboration and contributions. Charges for programs and other activities may be needed to financially support the programs. Donations from industry and philanthropists may find their way to such an active program. Where these practices exist, funding is not the principal concern. This could be the interpretive legacy.

PROGRAMMING

In preparing this book, the authors visited several hundred interpretive centers and museums, of all sizes and purposes and categories. The programming variations among the centers surprised and often encouraged them. The imagination and energy and flexibility of many state, community and private facilities inspired anew the old and honored concept that a museum, a nature center, or other type of interpretive facility can become a vigorous community social institution, central to the life of a town, a county, or a state.

To be the most effective interpreter one can be, consider major programming divided into three areas:
- Regular Programming (RP),
- Life Time Learning (LTL), and
- School Support Programs (SSP).

Implementing all of these areas should turn the interpretive center or museum into a busy, popular place, used by the community for developing its personal and social skills.

The programming suggested below would run one interpreter ragged. Other interpreters, volunteers, and instructors must be incorporated. An office manager can coordinate the registrations and perhaps some of the scheduling. The program will grow. These programs, however, are not just the dreams of academicians. Each of these programs operates today in several places. These programs can yield direct and indirect income. The LTL program will move people from beginning stages to eventual stewardship and interpretive expert stages, thus contributing directly to the center's expertise and program support.

REGULAR PROGRAMMING AND SERVICES

Most museums and centers have a regular set of programs including tours or hikes, talks, slides, newsletters, brochures, exhibitions, self-guiding activities and facilities, special events, and festivals. Some of this work, including keeping the nature center or museum open and clean, can be done by volunteer teams. As suggested throughout this book, however, the visiting public deserves to see the real pro in action. The staff interpreter should lead many of the programs, contact the public directly, and prepare the brochures, signs and trail guides. That is the most prestigious job for an interpreter.

Regular programming need not be routine. A diversity of programs and topics will keep visitors coming back for more and will keep the interpreters fresh. Likewise, travel tour programs and interpretive expeditions overseas can supplement income, enrich participants immensely, promote the work of the museum or nature center in the community, and also serve as one component of the Life Time Learning program.

Life Time Learning (LTL) Programs

Art museums have led in adult skill education. Their approach offers three or four levels of art lessons, from beginning to advanced in each of the different media. Those taking the classes pay a reasonable fee to provide for the instructor and the materials.

Just as with art, people readily accept that most life sports involve lessons early on, then practice and play, with occasional checkups by the pro. Nature centers or history museums seldom apply this approach. It is almost as if everything stays at the beginner or first-time visitor level. Perhaps more could be offered to improve and hone skills and knowledge, so visitors become clients who keep practicing and developing their expertise in nature study and history. It might work well; some ideas follow.

Putting together lifetime learning curricula that help residents develop and sharpen their skills in several areas will help make interpretive centers repeat destinations—places identified as valuable in personal life. This could include the following, among others:

- Preschool and school programs, both summer and winter.
- Scout badge and 4-H project areas and facilities, with the interpreter and volunteers to help with advising and certifying accomplishments. Junior Naturalist or Historian projects can work for other young visitors.
- Summer and vacation day camps for 10- to 12-year-olds may suit the facilities and personnel of the nature center or museum. Three to five one-week sessions may accomplish all that the interpreter wishes to do, even with expert help from interns, seasonal employees and volunteers.
- High school physical skills activities and science experiment research center, along with an active High School Environmental Club that helps in school programs and research.
- College resource center, tied in with student volunteer groups, work projects with fraternities and sororities, and interpreter training and seasonal employment. Amphitheater performances by high school and college talent may increase town-and-gown interactions.
- Career starters and early nesters advice and programs on home repairs, historic paint and design, history of neighborhoods, edible plants, gardening, landscaping for birds, and environmental awareness.
- Young parents (and grandparents) sessions on how to teach children about nature and cultural traditions.
- Outdoor/cultural adult skills development in 5- to 10-year series of activities, talks, projects, and lessons on a single topic. Start with two areas. Build the variety of programs with time and experience and with the help of friends of the facility. Sample topics susceptible to development of learning curricula and requirements might include: *birds, French traders, trees and forests, "lower" higher plants, lower plants, Victorian living, medicine and pharmacy, interpretive art, photographing the historic community,* or *insects.* These projects can progress from fairly simple identification, with reading programs, and activities, increasing complexity to preparation of a document, exhibit, trail, or brochure that enriches the interpretive program. Collaboration with other museums or interpreters can help enrich the programs. Box 20.2 sketches some basic sets of activities.

- "Empty nest" nature and history can offer many sociable means for individuals and couples to enjoy the center with others. Special programming for vigorous, interested people can enhance their stewardship, use their expertise and community contacts, and encourage their sustained support of the facility. Get some of these people working on their own properties to better conserve natural and cultural resources. Get them leading the organization's major festivals, publication efforts, public information work and funddrives.
- Elderhostel programs can bring in people over 60 for a week of classes and field trips. This exposes the community and facility to people from other parts of the country. Utilize local experts as faculty. Develop a theme or central concept and allow the teachers two to seven hours each, partly in lecture-discussion and partly in field observations and measurements. The rest of the day goes for eating, attending local functions, and a little personal exploring.

BOX 20.2: Two Skill Training Program Activities

The lists below are only incomplete suggestions for a ten-year skill program. These two broad topics may include a variety of "requirements" to complete some type of certification of expertise. The goal is not a badge as much as a program of systematic, enjoyable study, encouraging a client toward developing high levels of knowledge and skill. Giving them somewhere to go, someone to encourage them, and some dignified social recognition should help develop a community involved with the interpretive facility.

Birds share the community with people:
  A graded program of identification, developing a life list. (Years 1-10)
  Conduct site census counts.
  Observations and notes on feeding, mating, nesting. (Years 2-5)
  Reading program. (Years 1-10)
  Study of behavior and ecology research and field observation. (Years 5-10)
  Community surveys of habitat and distribution. (Years 4-8)
  Preparation of interpretive documents or displays. (Years 9-10)
  Bird habitat stewardship activities. (Years 2, 4, 6, 8)

Victorian living:
  Architecture: read, identify elements of, and find examples in the community.
  Commerce and Industry of the period in this community.
  Medicine and pharmacy—reconstruct a partial pharmacopiæ for the area.
  Education systems and financing in this county.
  Transportation.
  Clothing and home amenities.

SCHOOL SUPPORT PROGRAMS

Many interpretive centers and museums serve schools very effectively. Some have made up educational kits that schools rent for a week. Lutz Children's Museum in Manchester, CT, offers 200 lesson kits, let out for a week at $7.00 each. When returned, they get cleaned, repaired, and resupplied with artifacts, charts, lesson plans, and other activity materials.

In addition, Lutz's staff will make visits to classes, offer class tours of the museum, plus give teacher workshops and tours, lead gifted programs, and arrange for and accompany extended field trips to Boston and New York museums and botanical gardens. The same kinds of programs, the normal hosting of school visits for well-structured tours, and the training of teachers in Project Learning Tree, Project Wild, or other programs, often falls to the interpretive center and its collaborators.

In some nature centers and museums, serving children occupies much time and effort during at least three months of the year. School visits often coordinate with the educational objectives of the classroom.

Interpreters Can Become Proactive and Integral

A visitor to many poorly interpreted museums and parks may become somewhat jaded. One can see all sorts of relics from the past. They strike one's fancy for a moment or jog a memory—"Yup, that's just like a butter churn I saw in granny's kitchen once." Old growth timber and lots of named ferns and flowers please the sensibilities—"Wow, that's sure pretty, isn't it?" Sooner or later, however, one has to ask, "So what?" Why is all that old stuff kept in cabinets or on shelves or in the woods? Why should people go see it except for nostalgia? Too many museums and parks fail to tell visitors why.

One Canadian wrote that parks which fail in this way may give the wrong impression if their interpretation does not relate their beauty to the rest of the world (Van Tighem, 1990):

> A park, in short, is an illusion foisted upon masses by well-meaning idealists who believe that the world is composed of parcels. Some parcels, according to this logic, must be protected, so that when all the other parcels have been ravaged, future generations will still be able to smell the flowers. The earth is not a spaceship; it is a jigsaw puzzle.

Similarly, if interpreters only display the past and the preserved parcels, without encouraging their clients to see the present, future, and the whole landscape, they miss their professional calling and duty. If historians cannot help people avoid repetition of the mistakes of the past, of what use is history other than as a curiosity?

Interpreters can make themselves vital social implements if they relate the information from the site or the collection to what is going on in the world and what the consequences may be and how society can improve things or prevent problems. Be proactive by looking ahead and applying information positively and simply. Be integral by seeing the whole and suggesting how the economy relates to ecology and history and human quality of life.

Gloom and doom hardly sells—except to those already convinced. Concentrating on the possible, the positive and the practical solutions, focusing on facts, seeing through the myths, the interpreter can help clients quietly build a better future, a wiser society, and a healthier, more enjoyable environment.

Interpreters Can Pick Their Audiences

With cool, dispassionate consideration interpreters can select the most effective use of their own time. Premium values will be placed on skills that multiply the effectiveness of the individual interpreter. In other words, reach for large but quality audiences, use media that multiply your effort, think cost effectiveness.

EDUCATING FOR INTERPRETERS

In regard to university programs for interpreters, Grant Sharpe claimed that "the lack of a standard core curriculum and a professional degree are the most grievous problems, in my view" (Bevilacqua, 1993). Yet, the professional society that includes so many different people of diverse expertise cannot agree on a standard core. People who interpret zoo animals, historical homes, living history farms, Civil War battlefields, swamps, mountains, oceans, deserts, forests, factories and flying machines all have different subject matter specialties. A minimum set of courses in communications, education, and interpretive principles hardly constitute a university level core. The quandary continues; a core curriculum and a single professional degree seem almost unattainable, unless the profession narrows itself to one or two specialized areas—not a likely development.

Someone once said that part of the problem is that some interpreters do not know much—they are not deep in any subject. A useful strategy to combat this problem while in college involves in-depth study of some specialty in science or history with strong training in communications in addition. By becoming expert in a substantial subject, as well as solid training in other related topics, the interpreter can contribute to the depth of any staff. The key to a university education should be learning how to learn and think and perform professionally. A strong knowledge base will then continue to develop throughout a career with studious habits and smart application.

A Profession's Self-Identification

All professions are conspiracies against the laity.
—George Bernard Shaw

Professional training can often corrupt,
warp and discourage potentially good people.
—Hudson (1989)

Maybe interpreters over-intellectualize the business of running and maintaining museums, camps, nature centers, and interpretive programs. Real professionalism—not the sterile, virtuous, technical, academic kind—looks after the soul, the heart, the fun, as well as the mind of the client. Hudson (1989) noted that he likes, enjoys, and returns with pleasure to 20 of the 2,000 museums on the British Isles. Those twenty have charm; they offer warmth; some are slightly quirky. He said they leave him alone: "They make no attempt to programme me and discipline me. They never say 'you're here to learn'." Experts are there, not snootily nor ostentatiously, but available and in the same world.

For decades, interpreters have grappled with the question of how to be recognized as a profession. At nearly every national workshop of the major U.S. professional society (The National Association for Interpretation), at least one or two sessions muddle through another discussion of "professionalization." In Britain, "With one hundred years behind it [museum education] is still misunderstood" (Hudson, 1989).

Some suggest that just by declaring it, interpretation could become a profession. Many others seem to think that interpreters are already professionals; let them just get on with practicing the profession as they assert their position quietly, positively and without affectation. Yet, where do interpreters draw the lines to define "this wretched word 'professional'?" (Hudson, 1989)

This book may contribute to the difficulty of professional definition by its inclusiveness. Hopefully, the effect will be the contrary—bringing interpreters from diverse employers and businesses into greater unity. The authors consider interpreters from all types of facilities as united in purpose, philosophy, and—to some extent—in techniques. Interpretation is not performed only by naturalists in the public forests and parks. In fact, it is encouraging to see that more interpreters from zoos, museums, historical associations, camps, industries, and private enterprise strengthen the already diverse membership of the National Association for Interpretation and Interpretation Canada. It seems high time that Corps of Engineers, Bureau of Land Management, and the Fish & Wildlife Service interpreters insisted on clear identification of their professional status, rather than using vague designations that mask what they really do.

Some of the criteria or descriptors of professionalism—just one list among many—suggest characteristics that a profession should have (Sontag and Haraden, 1988) which is followed by the author's evaluation of the current status (in italics):

1. Articulated philosophy: *interpretation has it.*
2. Common terminology or vernacular: *despite confusion, yes.*
3. Standards of acceptable practice: *plenty of support in NAI and American Association of Museums.*
4. Evaluating and monitoring to ensure quality: *considerable, but more needed.*
5. Statements of ethics and acceptable conduct: *implicit, sometimes written.*
6. Skills improvement opportunities/requirements: *many exist.*
7. Research and development: *active and continuous.*
8. Intellectual/emotional contributions from practitioners: *many, in one of the most open, sharing professions known.*
9. Shaping of external influences: *yes.*
10. Peer recognition and respect: *yes.*
11. Recognition and respect by other disciplines: *variable.*

Interpreters must master many talents and much information and offer persuasive, pleasing programs to the public. This work requires considerable intelligence, constant preparation, and many skills. Interpreters seek evaluation, or else they serve as their own worst critics and doubters. They band together periodically for discussions of improvements in their practice or craft. Many would like some kind of official recognition as a profession (from whom?), presumably in hopes of improved status, income, and respectability. In the vernacular, *profession* may be an overused, abused term. Yet, it helps our sense of worth, it flatters, and it seems dignified. Rather than waiting until all interpreters become perfect at their tasks by eliciting some official document of recognition, it seems time that the profession asserts and accepts the fact of its missions in society and then proceeds to comport itself as the fine and noble profession that it already is, always seeking to further develop and refine its principles and productivity. This is well on its way.

Summary

Interpretation aims to enrich leisure experiences. But it does even more. It is not just a "nice" activity to entertain people on vacation. Interpretation adds to everyday perceptions of life and traditions around us. It inspires people to live more fully and more intelligently.

It offers an important way to acquaint our society with its life support system—the environment. It acquaints the people with their heritage—often on the exact sites where notable historical and cultural events happened. Participating in interpretive programs is often the only history and environmental study that many people do.

Three goals for the mission of interpretation follow:

- The interpreter accomplishes a key goal when a visitor/customer gains understanding of the reasons that an historic or cultural or natural site has importance to the community, the state, the nation, the world, and especially to that person (Alderson and Low, 1985). Beyond this, the professional interpreter seeks to build the enthusiasm and skills within that person to enable his or her conversion from a consumer of interpretation into an independent, self-motivated investigator-searcher-interpreter.

- Another key goal involves fun and satisfaction; the new visitor-amateur interpreter may enjoy the satisfaction of self-realization—the highest level of human needs. The visitor-interpreter sees the natural and cultural world with greater perception, understanding, and wisdom. Connections and relationships among things become more evident and intriguing as they are discovered. The skillful, well-prepared "amateur interpreter" visits a park, museum, swamp, or city with an excited, perceptive, and curious mind, with a truly re-creational attitude. That person's attitude, preparation and interest—carefully cultivated by professional interpreters—permit greater satisfaction from the recreational visit and experience.

- The first-time, well-prepared, turned-on visitor should get a high from a discovery visit; the repeat visitor, or the frequent visitor should have even more intense recreational experiences. This challenges the professional interpreter to keep offering new opportunities for repeat visitors—not the same old talk repeated all summer once a week in the expectation that the audience will comprise only one-time visitors or will have forgotten the interpreters lines between visits. The interpreter that helps the repeat visitor grow must be a constant explorer, researcher and collaborator. As a visitor gains skill and knowledge of a site, the interpreter can build a framework for progress, guideposts for development, and paths for personal research. The interpreter may find the advanced amateur passing the professionals in some areas of information—a wonderful consequence of good interpretation. This growth potential suggests a strong reason to have experienced interpreters on site; it suggests the potential that might be lost if only seasonals or volunteers come in regular contact with the visitors. Even though many visitors may come but once and seem to seek only the basic facts, the potential for repeat and deeper recreation requires the offering of more and richer interpretation by true professionals.

Most interpretation done during leisure time should be pleasurable and recreational in nature. After all, our leisure time is about one-third of our life and an integral part of all societies from the most primitive to the most technologically advanced.

Set goals for the agency or organization to reflect the importance of interpretation. Define its roles. Recognize the investments and efforts for interpretive services. Then proceed to serve the clientele with excellent, innovative, effective interpretation in several media, including personal and nonpersonal approaches. The effort should benefit the visitors, the rest of the public, the organization, and civilization in general. A richer nation with richer people will result.

This new occupation is likely to be far-reaching in its influences;
it is inspirational and educational.
—Enos Mills (1920)

Literature Cited

Alderson, W. T. and Low, S. P. (1985). *Interpretation of historic sites (2nd ed.)*. Nashville, TN: American Association for State and Local History.

Baas, J. (1990). Let's spend less time whining and more time listening. *Museum News, 69*(6):67-68.

Bevilacqua, S. (1993). Milestones, millstones, and stumbling blocks. *Legacy, 4*(4):24:26.

Brockman, C. F. (1978). Park naturalists and the evolution of National Park Service interpretation through World War II. *Journal of Forest History, 22*(1):24-43.

Burns, N. J. (1941). *Field manual for museums*. Washington, DC: National Park Service.

Bushor-Gardner, S. 1990. Back to the future for interpretation. In *Proceedings, National Interpreters Workshop*, NAI, Charleston, SC.

Grater, R. K. (1976). *The interpreter's handbook: Methods, skills, and techniques*. Globe, AZ: Southwest Parks and Monuments Association.

Ham, S. H. (1992). *Environmental interpretation: A practical guide*. Golden, CO: North American Press.

Hudson, K. (1989). The flipside of professionalism. *Museums Journal, 88*(4):188-190.

Lewis, William J. (1980). *Interpreting for park visitors*. Philadelphia, PA: Eastern Acorn Press.

Mills, E. A. (1920). *The adventures of a nature guide*. Garden City, NY: Doubleday, Page & Co.

Mintz, A. (1991). Moving target. *Museum News, 70*(3):64-68.

Morgan, B. (1979). *Enjoying Seattle's parks*. Seattle, WA: Greenwood Publications.

Shankland, R. (1954). *Steve Mather of the national parks (2nd ed.)*. New York, NY: Alfred A. Knopf, Inc.

Sharpe, G. W. (1976). *Interpreting the environment*. New York, NY: John Wiley & Sons, Inc.

Sharpe, G. W. (1982). *Interpreting the environment (2nd ed.)*. New York, NY: John Wiley & Sons, Inc.

Sontag, W. H. and Haraden, T. (1988). Gotta move! We've outgrown the house. In *Proceedings, National Interpreters Workshop*, NAI, San Diego, CA.

Stutz, B. (1991). Ted Turner turns it on. *Audubon, 93*(6):110-116.

Tilden, F. (1967). *Interpreting our heritage (rev. ed.)*. Chapel Hill, NC: University North Carolina Press.

Van Matre, S. (1990). *Earth education: A new beginning*. Greenville, WI: Institute for Earth Education.

Van Tighem, K. (1990). Words, perception and subversion. *InterpScan, 18*(1):8-9.

Weil, S. E. (1990). *Rethinking the museum and other meditations*. Washington, DC: Smithsonian Institution Press.

Wilcox, A. T. (1969) Professional preparation for interpretive services. *Rocky Mountain-High Plains Parks and Recreation Journal, 4*(1):11-14.

North American Associations
Specializing in Interpretation

Interpretation Canada
Box 2667, Station D
Ottawa, ON K1P 5W7
Canada
    Quarterly: *InterpScan*

National Association for Interpretation (NAI) ....(303) 491-2255
P.O. Box 1892
Ft. Collins, CO 80522
    Bimonthly: *Legacy* (formerly *Journal of Interpretation*
                and *The Interpreter)*
A 1988 merger of the Association of Interpretive Naturalists (AIN)
and the Western Interpreters Association (WIA)

American Camping Association ....(317) 342-8456
Bradford Woods
5040 State Road 67
Martinsville, IN 46151
    Monthly: *Camping*

American Association for State and Local History ....(615) 255-2971
172 Second Avenue N-202
Nashville, TN 37201
    Periodical: *History News*

American Association of Botanical Gardens and Arboreta ....(215) 688-1120
786 Church Road
Wayne, PA 19087

American Association of Museums ....(202) 289-1818
1225 I Street—Suite 200
Washington, DC 20005
    Bimonthly: *Museum News*

American Association of Zookeepers, Inc. .... (913) 272-5821
SW Gage Boulevard
Topeka, KS 66606

American Nature Study Society .... (607) 749-3655
5881 Cold Brook Road
Homer, NY 13077

American Living History Association
Box 7355
Austin, TX 78296

American Zoo and Aquarium Association .... (304) 242-2160
Oglebay Park
Wheeling, WV 26003-1698

Association for Living History Farms and Agricultural Museums
c/o National Museum of American History—S. 5035
(Smithsonian Institution)
Washington, DC 20560

Association of Science-Technology Centers .... (202) 371-1171
1413 K Street, NW—10th floor
Washington, DC 20005-3405

Canadian Museums Association .... (613) 233-5653
280 Rue Metcalfe—St. 202
Ottawa, Ontario K2P 1R7
Canada

Conservation Education Association .... (414) 465-2000
c/o Robert Darula/Visitor Studies Association
University of Wisconsin—Green Bay
Green Bay, WI 54302

Council for American Indian Interpretation (A unit of NAI)
4735 Unser NW
Albuquerque, NM 87120

North American Indian Museum Association .... (716) 945-1738
c/o Seneca Iroquois National Museum
P.O. Box 442, Broad Street Extension
Salamanca, NY 14779

North American Association for Environmental Education .... (513) 698-6493
P.O. Box 400
Troy, OH 45373

International Council for Outdoor Education .... (412) 372-5992
P.O. Box 17255
Pittsburgh, PA 15235

National Arbor Day Foundation .... (402) 474-5655
100 Arbor Avenue
Nebraska City, NE 68410

National Gardening Association .... (802) 863-1308
180 Flynn Avenue
Burlington, VT 05401

National Wildlife Federation .... (202) 797-6800
1400 Sixteenth Street NW
Washington, DC 20036
    Periodicals: *National/International Wildlife, Ranger Rick,*
        and *Naturescope*

Outdoor Writers Association of America, Inc. .... (814) 234-1011
2017 Cato Avenue, Suite 101
State College, PA 16801
    Quarterly: *Outdoors Unlimited*

Visitor Studies Association .... (414) 238-1916
10336 N. Stanford Drive 97W
Mequon, WI 53097
    Periodical: *Visitor Behavior*

Study Centers

Centre for Environmental Interpretation
University of Surrey
England

Center for Social Design
P.O. Box 1111
Jacksonville, AL 36265
ATTN: Stephen Bitgood, Jacksonville State University

National Register of Historic Places ....(202) 343-9536
c/o National Park Service
Department of the Interior
Washington, DC 20005

Appendix B

Selected Periodicals for Interpretive Information and Materials

NOTE: For more complete current information, ask your local librarian.

American History Illustrated ....(800) 435-9610

Civil War Times Illustrated ....(800) 435-9610

The Picture Professional
   c/o Comstock
   30 Irving Place
   New York, NY 10003

American Visions (Magazine of African-American Culture)..................(202) 462-1779

Material Culture (Pioneer America Society, Inc.)

Chronicle of Early American Industries Association (tool collectors)

Natural History (American Museum of Natural History, NY)

Natural Areas Journal (Natural Areas Association, Rockford, IL)

Science News

Legacy (National Association for Interpretation)

Journal of Environmental Education

Museum News (American Association of Museums)

Curator

Interpretation (National Park Service)

American Forests ....(202) 667-3300

*Nature Study: A Journal of Environmental Education
   and Interpretation* ....(607) 749-3655

National Wildlife

International Wildlife

Visitor Behavior

Appendix C

Acknowledgments

The authors list here only a few of the hundreds of interpreters who gave them examples, advice and information. These are the folks who went out of their way to give the authors major chunks of time and entree. Many of those featured in photographs and the text also contributed time as the authors visited several hundred interpretive sites.

Alejandra Aldred
Peter Allen
John V. Alviti
Mary Anderson
Charles Anibal
Connie Backlund
James Basala
Cem Basman
Michelle Baumer
Chris Calkins
Angela Cannon
Brad Case
Philip Cook
Joseph Cornell
Gerald Coutant
Mary Cutler
David Dahlen
David Dame
Lorna Domke
Thomas DuRant
Michael J. Ellis
Debra Erickson
White Fawn
Richard and Sharon Fedorchak
Lorenza Fong
Dr. Regina Glover
Magaly Green
Dr. Michael Gross
Neil Hagadorn
Gayle L. Hazelwood
Marilyn Hof
Wilson Hunter

Bob Jennings
Dr. Andrew Kardos
Jane Kemble
Tom Kleiman
Cynthia J. Knudson
Michael Laws
Ralph H. Lewis
Nancy Marx
Jay McConnell
D. Bruce McHenry
Carole McLean
Judith McMillen
Greg Miller
David Nathanson
Rev. Nancy Richmond-Herrett
James M. Ridenour
Janet Schmidt
Clifford Soubier
Sandy Staples
Mike Storey
Kip Stowell
Carl Strang
Susan Strauss
Mike Watson
Thomas White
Ralph White
Robin White
David G. Wright
Douglas Wright, Jr.
Sam Vaughn
Ron Zimmerman

Index

OTHER BOOKS FROM VENTURE PUBLISHING

A Leisure of One's Own: A Feminist Perspective on Women's Leisure
    by Karla Henderson, M. Deborah Bialeschki, Susan M. Shaw and Valeria J. Freysinger
Leisure Services in Canada: An Introduction
    by Mark S. Searle and Russell E. Brayley
Marketing for Parks, Recreation, and Leisure
    by Ellen L. O'Sullivan
Outdoor Recreation Management: Theory and Application, Third Edition
    by Alan Jubenville and Ben Twight
Planning Parks for People
    by John Hultsman, Richard L. Cottrell and Wendy Zales Hultsman
Private and Commercial Recreation
    edited by Arlin Epperson
The Process of Recreation Programming Theory and Technique, Third Edition
    by Patricia Farrell and Herberta M. Lundegren
Quality Management: Applications for Therapeutic Recreation
    edited by Bob Riley
Recreation and Leisure: Issues in an Era of Change, Third Edition
    edited by Thomas Goodale and Peter A. Witt
Recreation Economic Decisions: Comparing Benefits and Costs
    by Richard G. Walsh
Recreation Programming and Activities for Older Adults
    by Jerold E. Elliott and Judith A. Sorg-Elliott
Reference Manual for Writing Rehabilitation Therapy Treatment Plans
    by Penny Hogberg and Mary Johnson
Research in Therapeutic Recreation: Concepts and Methods
    edited by Marjorie J. Malkin and Christine Z. Howe
Risk Management in Therapeutic Recreation: A Component of Quality Assurance
    by Judith Voelkl
A Social History of Leisure Since 1600
    by Gary Cross
The Sociology of Leisure
    by John R. Kelly and Geoffrey Godbey
A Study Guide for National Certification in Therapeutic Recreation
    by Gerald O'Morrow and Ron Reynolds
Therapeutic Recreation: Cases and Exercises
    by Barbara C. Wilhite and M. Jean Keller
Therapeutic Recreation Protocol for Treatment of Substance Addictions
    by Rozanne W. Faulkner
A Training Manual for Americans With Disabilities Act Compliance in Parks and Recreation Settings
    by Carol Stensrud
Understanding Leisure and Recreation: Mapping the Past, Charting the Future
    edited by Edgar L. Jackson and Thomas L. Burton

Venture Publishing, Inc.
1999 Cato Avenue
State College, PA 16801